Death Work

Vincent E. Henry

Police,

Trauma,

and the

Psychology

of Survival

Death Work

OXFORD
UNIVERSITY PRESS

2004

OXFORD
UNIVERSITY PRESS

Oxford   New York
Auckland   Bangkok   Buenos Aires   Cape Town   Chennai
Dar es Salaam   Delhi   Hong Kong   Istanbul   Karachi   Kolkata
Kuala Lumpur   Madrid   Melbourne   Mexico City   Mumbai   Nairobi
São Paulo   Shanghai   Taipei   Tokyo   Toronto

Copyright © 2004 by Oxford University Press, Inc.

Published by Oxford University Press, Inc.
198 Madison Avenue, New York, New York 10016

www.oup.com

Oxford is a registered trademark of Oxford University Press

Library of Congress Cataloging-in-Publication Data
Henry, Vincent E., 1957–
Death work : police, trauma, and the psychology of survival / Vincent E. Henry.
    p. cm.
ISBN 0-19-515765-6
1. Police psychology.   2. Death   I. Title.
HV7936.P75H46 2004
363.2'2'019—dc21   2003012097

Lyrics to "Kaatskill Serenade" by David Bromberg. Published by Sweet Jelly Roll Music.
Reprinted with permission.

9 8 7 6 5 4 3 2 1

Printed in the United States of America
on acid-free paper

For Lydia, my best secret weapon,

who was there

with a push or a pull every step of the way

and taught me to believe in myself.

For my late father, Lieutenant James P. Henry,

and my brother-in-law, Sergeant Tom Callahan

—we three share a shield, and more—

and my partner, Detective Mike Dziuk,

who each taught me what it means to be a good cop.

And for the collaborators,

who taught me about heroism, sacrifice, and honor.

Foreword

Robert Jay Lifton

Truly innovative work causes one to ask: why didn't someone think of that before? The response has to do both with the illumination the work provides and its stark appropriateness—its necessity—for the world we live in. With Vincent Henry's *Death Work*, that appropriateness and necessity became painfully evident with the attacks of 9/11. From that moment, Henry's work took on an eerie practicality, as he movingly describes in the last chapter of this book.

Death Work is about the police officer (or in the more affectionate intra-departmental usage, "cop") as survivor—as one for whom death is a presence in everyday work. The special value of Henry's study derives from his interview method. Rather than make abstract assumptions or simply summarize others' findings, Henry went out and talked to his fellow cops—not simply as a friendly insider (though he was surely that) but as a trained psychological interviewer who could find order and meaning in the riveting words of those he talked to.

Henry's work sustains an exquisite balance between the highly specific and the universal. Nothing could be more specific, more concrete, than the death-haunted experiences of police officers—whether taking the form of disturbing corpses, fallen partners, or their own near demise. But the significance of his findings extends to all who work in what historian Michael Lesy has called the "forbidden zone" or "zone of death"—a zone that envelops not only police officers but firefighters and rescue workers of all kinds, military personnel, doctors and health workers (especially in hospices), undertakers, prison staff on "death row," and those working in meatpacking or "slaughterhouse" industries.

Ultimately—and most important—Henry is exploring nothing less than the larger struggle with dying and killing. One can view the police officers he interviewed as "point men"—a kind of advance guard—in that struggle. Their encounters with especially grotesque forms of death challenge anyone's claim to mastery of this insoluble human dilemma.

Yet Henry's research, as much as any I have come upon, demonstrates impressive forms of survivor resilience and illumination. With support of various kinds, men and women can not only weather that extreme trauma but become "better cops." Henry is scrupulous when invoking my own work in some of these areas and has extended and transformed that work by means of his original findings and observations.

This is especially true of his exploration of the rookie's *rite de passage* in becoming a police officer, his need to in some way confront death and make use of a form of selective professional numbing. Henry vividly conveys the inner division that enables the police officer to suppress his emotions in the service of demanding professional tasks. The various elements that enable him to do that—mentorship from experienced professionals, gradual routinization, gallows humor—reminded me of parallel experiences I'd had many years ago as a medical student and young doctor confronted with a corpse to dissect and the task of assisting surgeons who were cutting up live human beings. In this process one evolves one's professional identity and initiates a lifelong struggle to balance numbing and feeling, to both limit intrusive emotions and hold onto one's humanity. We are both moved and enlightened by Henry's depiction of his own experience of this struggle in connection with his herculean actions following 9/11.

Indeed, with 9/11 this overall study took on a terrible immediacy. Meant originally as a probing of psychological reactions of police officers under ordinary conditions—that is, ordinary conditions of a "forbidden zone"—it was suddenly converted by 9/11 into a psychological and ethical baseline for the work of all service professions in that disaster. The psychology of the survivor was painfully at issue for victims and potential victims, and for all who offered help of any kind.

When Henry reflected on his own survivor psychology and his capacity to make constructive use of it in his personal and professional plunge into the disaster, he was calling forth all he had learned from his fellow cops over the course of his study. One wishes that Americans in general, and especially our leaders, were able to experience similar survivor wisdom in relation to 9/11.

This book should become a classic, for its contribution to the most humane form of police work and to all work in the "forbidden zone," and for what it tells us more broadly about the hard-earned psychological possibilities of survivors.

Acknowledgments

One of the subtle themes that emerges in this book, and one that I hope to take up in subsequent research, is the tremendously important role mentors play in a cop's personal and professional development. Certainly the same can be said of the importance of mentors in a scholar's academic development. In line with the formative-symbolic paradigm that is the theoretical underpinning of this study, we can see that in conveying their own hard-earned life experiences and in guiding us toward a more complete understanding of ourselves and the world around us, mentors provide the important images that shape our sense of self and ultimately our understanding of the world. Because they influence our lives so profoundly, and because they so generously permit us to share in their experience, a special sense of connection exists between mentors and protégés. This section represents my opportunity to acknowledge and say thanks to those who mentored me professionally and academically throughout the course of my dual careers.

No project as involved and complex as this could be undertaken without the guidance and assistance of a great many people, all of whom are, in one way or another, my mentors. It is not possible to list the names and describe the contributions made by every individual who participated in this project in one way or another—the identities of the collaborators who so generously shared their time and their experiences to make this book possible, for example, must remain confidential. The collaborators know who they are, and hopefully they know how much I admire and respect them and how much I appreciate the opportunity to bear witness to their struggles. If this research has an impact, it will be more to their credit than mine.

Certain people's contributions deserve special mention, and among them are Police Commissioner William J. Bratton and Deputy Commissioner Mike Farrell, who encouraged this project from the beginning and did a great deal to support my research. Importantly, they recognized the difficult psychological struggles cops have around death and were committed to helping them. Inspector Joe Lovelock made a tremendous impact on my understanding of police history, management, and culture over the seven years I was privileged to work with him, and he spent many hours listening to my ruminations and offering insights as I struggled with this project. He also kept pushing me to complete the project during those too-frequent periods when my formative process seemed to crawl to a halt. Director James O'Keefe and Chief Demosthenes Long of the Police Academy were also instrumental in helping to keep me on track to bring this project to fruition.

A great many cops—too many to mention—also share in the credit for this book. They include the great cops who taught me the Job when I was a rookie, my partners throughout the years, and the many cops who served as a sounding board for the issues that are the subject of this research. The insights they shared helped me to refine my thoughts and to appreciate the many situational variables that shape cops' experience of police work and especially of death events. I must also thank those who read portions of the dissertation and offered cogent comments that contributed to its objectivity and validity.

On the academic side, I must also thank Professors James Levine and Dorothy Bracey of John Jay College of Criminal Justice, who offered important suggestions and encouraged me to pursue these explorations. Their time, effort, patience, generosity, and thoughtfulness mean a great deal to me, and their contribution was considerable.

Any student is truly fortunate if at least once in his academic career he encounters a teacher who exposes him to a set of ideas and principles that affect him deeply and change the way he looks at the world. The student is doubly fortunate when that teacher takes him under his wing to further guide the development of his thought and his understanding. I was that fortunate when I was exposed to Robert Jay Lifton, his formative-symbolic paradigm, and especially his ideas about the psychology of survival. Although some of the nebulous ideas and many of the elementary observations that ultimately led to this research had been with me for some time, it was when I took a course with Dr. Lifton—a course entitled "Victims, Survivors, and Perpetrators: The Lessons of Hiroshima, the Holocaust, and Vietnam"—that they really began to coalesce in a meaningful way. The formative-symbolic paradigm and the psychology of survival provided the necessary framework for me to understand some of my own police experiences and feelings around death and to understand some of the attitudes and behaviors I had observed in other cops. Being the kind of teacher he is, Dr. Lifton encouraged me to further develop these ideas, suggesting they could make an important contribution to the understanding of police as well as to the psychology of survival.

With the support, motivation, guidance, and direction Dr. Lifton continually provided over the years, and with a great deal of additional observation and research, my indistinct concepts took on greater sophistication and meaning and ultimately became the basis for this research. Notwithstanding the demands of his own tremendously busy schedule and his own academic explorations, Dr. Lifton always found the time to discuss issues of theory and method, to share his knowledge and insight, and to continually encourage my development as a scholar. He did so with great kindness, great patience, and a great deal of tolerance for a student whose own busy professional life often presented obstacles to the timely completion of research objectives.

One of the things Dr. Lifton taught me about is the nature of the relationship between a mentor and student. He often speaks of his relationship with his own mentor, Erik Erikson, and of the important ways Erikson shaped his thought and his theoretical perspective, and one of the things Dr. Lifton impressed upon me is the responsibilities the mentor and the protégé have toward each other. It is the responsibility of the mentor to provide intellectual guidance, support, and structure and to honestly impart his wisdom and knowledge so that the student grows and develops as a scholar in his own right. It is the protégé's responsibility, though, to challenge the bounds of the mentor's paradigm and his body of work, and in doing so to expand upon it.

A great many others deserve special mention for their contributions. Professor Albert R. Roberts of Rutgers University has been a tremendous friend, supporter, and mentor through the years, and I have valued the opportunity to work with him on other projects as much as I value his ongoing scholarly and practical advice. An outstanding and very insightful scholar, he recognized the potential value this research might hold for clinicians, for police, and for those interested in understanding a rarely glimpsed but important area of police psychology. He championed the research, bringing it to the attention of Joan Bossert at Oxford University Press. Working with Joan Bossert and her enthusiastic and committed staff, especially my editor Maura Roessner and production editor Stacey Hamilton, has truly been a pleasure. I was made to feel very much a part of the editing and production processes, and Joan, Maura, and Stacey were exceptionally tolerant of delays as I fiddled with the manuscript.

Lucy Silva of the Center on Violence and Human Survival was always affable and obliging as she juggled schedules to maintain the lines of communication with Robert Jay Lifton. Valuable insights provided by John Kleinig, Barbara Price, and Debbie Baskin helped prepare me to undertake this project, and others who helped mold my intellectual and professional development include Pat Weller, Harvey Kushner, Pat Ryan, Aaron H. Rosenthal, Arch Harrison, and Keith Bryett. I owe a special thanks to David Bromberg, a sensitive and caring man who generously gave permission to quote his song "Kaatskill Serenade." Over the years I've also benefited greatly from the kindness and generosity of Elaine Niederhoffer and Victor Niederhoffer. For their gestures of support and interest during a very difficult time I will be eternally grateful.

My spouse and life partner Lydia Staiano did so much more than just put up with me over the years this research took shape: as in every other area of my life, she provided the unremitting love, support, and encouragement that facilitated my intellectual growth. She watched this research take shape from the very beginning, unselfishly putting aside her own needs for the sake of the project, and in more ways than I can relate she nurtured its development as much as she nurtures my evolving sense of self. Lydia is the kindest, gentlest, and wisest person I've ever known, and she believed in this project almost as much as she believes in me. Her love sustains me and defines me, and without her this book would never have happened.

Finally, I have to thank Police Officer James Whittington, who was murdered in the line of duty on October 30, 1982. We only met once, and too briefly, but a part of me was buried with him and I am the better for it. His sacrifice and that of his family became a large part of my own survivor mission. Thanks, Panama.

Contents

Foreword: Robert Jay Lifton vii

Introduction: The Death and Policing Nexus 3

1. Death Work: The General Context 13

2. Police Survivors of Death Encounters: Theoretical Perspective and Strategy of Inquiry 45

3. "Becoming a Cop": Basic Social and Psychological Processes 85

4. The Rookie's Experience: Introduction to Death 108

5. Patrol Sergeants: Routinization of the Death Encounter 148

6. Crime Scene Detectives: "Technicizing" the Death Encounter 178

7. Homicide Detectives: Emotional Reactions to Violent Death 202

8. Police Survivors: Genuine Threats to the Sense of Immortality 239

9. Reflections and Observations 302

Epilogue: September 11, 2001 322

Notes 357

Bibliography 379

Index 391

Death Work

Introduction

The Death and Policing Nexus

This book is about the psychological struggles and transformations urban police officers experience as the result of their routine work-related exposures to the deaths of others, as well as from more profound and personally consequential encounters with their own mortality. Psychological struggles and transformations around encounters with death are significant concerns in all human psychology, but they are particularly salient in the context of contemporary urban policing. Urban police officers can have frequent encounters with the deaths of others, and their death confrontations can take place across a broad range of circumstances and situations. Additionally, some police officers experience death encounters of an entirely different and infinitely more consequential kind: they face mortal combat situations that pose an objectively credible threat to their survival, they participate in the taking of a human life in the line of duty, or they witness the line-of-duty death of a fellow officer but manage to remain alive.

Every human encounter with the death of another person is to some extent a painful reminder of one's own mortality, and every death encounter entails some degree of psychological trauma that results in subtle or profound psychological transformation. Police death encounters, though, differ from more "ordinary" human encounters with death because police work is permeated with an overarching perception of danger—to a far greater extent than in other occupations, contemporary urban police officers perceive in their work the realistic and continual potential for meeting their own demise in the course of their professional duties. In conjunction with the frequency of their death encounters, the wide range of circumstances and situations in which the death encounters can occur, and a variety of other factors intrinsic to police work, this perceived potential for a highly personalized death encounter sets the police officer's experience of death events apart from "ordinary" death experiences, and it sets the experience apart from exposures in other death-work occupations as well. Exposure to death is a highly relevant and influential, if infrequently recognized, variable in police psychology.

This book is based on research that draws its underlying theoretical assumptions and principles primarily from Robert Jay Lifton's psychoformative paradigm and the "psychology of survival" perspective the paradigm subsumes. This paradigm is organized around psychological principles of death and the continuity of life, and it stresses the importance of images in man's vitalizing quest for ongoing symbolization.[1] The psychology of survival deals with the lasting intra-psychic impact or imprint of an encounter with death (either the death of another person or a confrontation with one's own mortality), and with the universal psychological tendencies that inevitably result from that encounter. A survivor is one who has come in close contact with death in some bodily or psychic fashion and has remained alive (Lifton, 1967a, p. 479). This fundamental framework is supplemented and complemented by insights and data drawn from a fairly broad body of empirical and qualitative research on the psychology and sociology of death encounters and on the psychology and sociology of police officers. A fairly eclectic mix of theory, research, and data was employed in this research study in order to adapt the psychology of survival and locate it within a conceptual framework reflecting the practical realities of contemporary urban policing. The specific interview and field observation techniques used to collect the data and the theoretical assumptions used to analyze them are described in greater depth in subsequent chapters. Both the method of data collection and the analytical framework generally conform to the method Lifton used in his studies of death-related psychic trauma and the adaptive processes that accompany death encounters.

To explore the contemporary urban police officer's exposures to death and the kind of psychological transformations that result from them, we will examine the psychological and social processes that shape the way officers experience and make meaning of their world, including its death encounters. We will explore the psychological sequelae of police death encounters, distinguishing the effect of relatively routine job-related death encounters with the deaths of others from the more profound and personally consequential transformations that result from actually surviving or witnessing firsthand a life-or-death mortal combat situation. More specifically, we will examine how four different task environments or types of assignment in policing—those of the rookie police officer, patrol sergeant, homicide detective, and crime scene technician—determine the conditions of death exposure and shape officers' individual and collective responses to them. We will also examine how these fairly routine exposures to the deaths of others differ from the extraordinary experiences of a fifth group: those who survived mortal combat, witnessed the death of a fellow officer, or violently took a life in the performance of duty. We will see how these routine and extraordinary death encounters have a powerful impact not only on the officers who personally experience them, but also on the police culture as a whole.

This book utilizes a "shared themes" approach to illuminate how different types of exposures in different task environments shape officers and their subculture. Because so many individual and situational variables can be present or absent in a given death encounter, and because each of these variables can have different levels of meaning to different officers, every officer experiences a death encounter somewhat differently. Rather than focusing entirely upon a single individual's unique and subjective reaction to particular death events—an approach typically used in case study research—the shared themes approach looks for commonalities in the experience of numerous similarly situated individuals who have gone through comparable or analogous events. The shared themes approach, which is often used in psychohistorical research, allows us to delve into a particular task environment and the kinds of death exposures it typically presents and to observe and analyze the common themes of experience among officers operating in that environment. Although it is firmly rooted in subjective experience, the shared themes approach imparts an important element of objectivity to the research.

Psychology has long recognized that virtually all human encounters with death are potent reminders of our own mortality that entail important psychological consequences. Whether death encounters involve casual exposures to the deaths of others or are more extreme and more personally meaningful encounters involving the realistic potential for one's own extinction, they are emotionally difficult events from which some degree of emotional or psychological trauma is almost certain to accrue. Moreover, the individual's subjective experience of the death encounter may be magnified or diminished by the presence or absence of myriad individual, social, cultural, and contextual factors and variables. Given the multiplicity of forms, situations, causes, and circumstances of death that may occur in a cosmopolitan urban environment, and in light of the fact that urban police officers attend virtually every death scene occurring outside a medical facility, police encounters with death can be conceptualized as occurring along a continuum of psychological significance. This continuum of significance ranges from brief and relatively impersonal encounters with the deaths of strangers through the most profound encounters that involve the realistic prospect of the officer's own demise. By dint of their overlapping and at times conflicting social roles as social service providers, first responders to violent crimes and medical emergencies, law enforcers, and criminal investigators, urban police officers encounter death in virtually all its myriad forms. Each of these roles and situations entails a specific array of prescribed tasks and duties that further influence the type and quality of exposure. The seasoned patrol officer who responds to a death scene at which an elderly person died in his sleep from natural causes, for example, is likely to have a very different subjective experience of the event and will perform entirely different tasks than a novice officer who responds to his first fatal traffic accident or a veteran detective who is called to investigate a particularly gory multiple homicide in which one or more victims is a child.

To explore this continuum of death-related experience and its psychological impact on officers, I carried out field observations and conducted structured interviews with New York City Police Department officers in the four nominal categories or task environments mentioned above. For the most part, officers in these four task environments attend the deaths of strangers, and so their death encounters are somewhat routine and fairly impersonal. I also interviewed a number of officers whose experiences with death have been extreme and extraordinary—those who participated in a mortal combat situation that involved the realistic potential for the officer's own death, and/or who witnessed the violent death of a partner, and/or who took a human life in line-of-duty combat. The goal of these interviews and observations was to explore each officer's subjective experiences in relation to death events, and to discern in them common patterns or "shared themes" of psychological response. The interviews and observations sought to elicit, define, and distinguish the range and types of routine and extraordinary police exposures to death as well as the patterns of psychological transformations and social consequences resulting from them. By illuminating and describing these shared themes and common threads of experience, this research seeks to add color, context, and dimension to the academic landscape of contemporary policing and to provide additional insight into the police officer's social and psychological worlds.

The research this book is based upon was essentially completed several months before the social and psychological worlds of NYPD officers were so dramatically changed by the terrorist attacks of September 11, 2001. Those attacks introduced an entirely new and unprecedented quantity and quality of death trauma to the experience of police in New York City. Never before had NYPD officers dealt, individually or collectively, with death and death imagery on so massive a scale, and never before had their death encounters been so prolonged. The events of September 11 and their aftermath—including the rescue and recovery efforts and the security operations that went on for several months—represent a profound departure from even the most extraordinary and extreme kinds of death encounters NYPD officers had previously faced. The trauma-producing phenomena and images of September 11 were literally unimaginable to many NYPD officers, and their psychological repercussions and manifestations are still emerging. It is altogether safe to say that on September 11, 2001, the social and psychological worlds of NYPD police officers changed forever.

It is important to include those experiences and events in this book, and it is important to distinguish them from the kind of ordinary and extraordinary exposures that characterized contemporary police death encounters before September 11. As this book goes to press, a little over 2 years have elapsed since the terrorist attacks in New York City changed the lives of NYPD officers, and it is still too early to determine with any degree of accuracy what the specific long-term psychological consequences of those events will be for police in New York City. Police officers in New York are still struggling to make sense of their experience, and any particular behavioral alterations they exhibit may still be transitory and impermanent. Quite simply, it is still too early to know what the psychological and social consequences of the September 11 attacks will be, much less to distinguish their impact on different categories of officers.

Because these issues are so germane to the issues explored in this book, I have included a final chapter—an epilogue of sorts—recounting some of my own experiences around the September 11 attacks. For reasons that will become clearer as the reader progresses through this book, it was not possible for me to conduct the kind of in-depth interviews that would have permitted a more objective analysis. Such a project was simply too large and too complex to complete in a compressed time frame. The epilogue differs from the rest of the book insofar as it is almost entirely subjective—it is a highly personalized narrative, but it is an honest narrative and it is told from the perspective of one who, by virtue of having studied and written about police death encounters for several years, had an uncommon degree of insight into the phenomena. Throughout the events of September 11 and its immediate aftermath, as well as in the months that followed, I witnessed the psychology of survival taking place all around me, and I witnessed it in my own psychological and social worlds as well.

As in virtually all qualitative studies in the ethnographic tradition, the researcher's own experiences, perspectives, insights, and biases are critical elements in the research and analysis process. In this instance, my own experience in various patrol, investigative, and supervisory assignments during more than twenty years of service in the NYPD were an integral part of the research process. The research is informed by my own experiences as a police officer, particularly as they relate to comprehending and analyzing the subtleties and nuances of police culture and its powerful influence upon the behavior of its members. To some extent, my experience as a police officer and membership in the police culture comprise a double-edged sword: at the same time they afford me a special capacity to access and make sense of raw data, they also complicate the issue of objectivity. Issues related to my role as police officer cum researcher are discussed throughout this book, but particularly in chapter 3's methodology section.

The issues involved in this research project are both profound and complex, yet they have received relatively little scholarly attention—the body of research and theory relating directly to the meaning of death in the police context is sparse. Collectively, these factors militated for an exploratory study that would incorporate data, theory, insights, and methods derived from several disciplines.

The Poverty of Relevant Research

Significant intellectual inquiry into death-related issues has taken place within the past several decades, and this emerging willingness within the social and physical sciences to deal conceptually with these issues signals a turning point in the history of Western attitudes toward death (Aries, 1974, 1975a, 1975b). As Ernest Becker (1973, 1975) has so cogently noted, a predominant and fundamental theme throughout Western civilization has been an unwillingness to deal emotionally or conceptually with death, and as recently as 1955 Gorer characterized death as the "new pornography"—a topic that contains simultaneous elements of perverse attraction and aversion and is patently unsuited for discussion in polite company.

Despite the recent interest, many factors still obscure and constrain intellectual inquiry into the psychological and philosophical issues surrounding death. As Freud (1961), Feifel (1959, 1969), Aries (1974, 1975a), Brown (1959), Becker (1973), and a host of other psychological theorists have emphasized throughout their work, fear of death is a primary and fundamental source of human anxiety, and we cannot ignore the impact fear, denial, and psychic defense have had (and continue to have) upon the overall research process. Because this is a difficult and complex area of research, scholars who wish to penetrate the complex web of fear, denial, and defense surrounding death issues must be particularly attuned to these processes and especially mindful of their impact (Bolkosky, 1987).

Various social and psychological theories seek to explain man's aversion to dealing with death, and although they differ substantially in the approaches they take, each embraces the essential notion that the fear of death is a universal element of human psychology. Without minimizing the many substantive differences between these perspectives, particularly those differences relating to the etiology of death fear, each concurs in asserting that humans engage in various behaviors that function to deny, diminish, or attenuate the fear of death. In a general sense, each perspective also embraces the notion that dealing with death results in emotional trauma and in psychological transformations that in turn lead to the evolution of new modes of adaptation, thought, and feeling within the individual who encounters death.

Many social and psychological studies have examined how members of various occupations deal with death, and these studies certainly provide some useful insights that may be broadly applicable to police officers' encounters with death. We must be careful in selecting and applying observations drawn from other occupations to police work, though, because none of these occupations is quite like policing and because none of their members deal with death in exactly the same way as police. Every death-work occupation differs from others in important ways, including the way its members are trained and socialized, the tasks and duties its members undertake, the social role its members fulfill, the way work is organized and distributed among its members, and the social, psychological, and environmental settings in which its members encounter death. Each of these factors shapes the ways an occupation's members experience the death event, so there is potentially a great danger in making sweeping generalizations from one occupation to another. Some excellent research has been conducted among members of the medical and medico-legal professions, for example, and observations about the ways in which doctors, nurses, and other medical personnel routinely deal with the deaths of patients can shed some light on the ways police officers experience some types of routine work-related encounters with the deaths of others.

Another useful and pertinent body of literature deals with the death encounters of rescue workers and military combat personnel, since (as is the case with policing) death encounters within these occupations can entail a significant and credible threat to one's own life. To some extent these occupations encounter death in situations and environments that are similar to some types of police experiences with death. Like some police officers, for example, combat soldiers often encounter death in the context of a real and significant threat to their own life, and they frequently face a "kill or be killed" situation under highly personalized though morally ambiguous circumstances. As discussed more fully in subsequent chapters, police officers may never actually encounter these profound mortal combat situations, and certainly few officers actually encounter them on a regular or recurring basis, but the potential for taking a life or losing one's own life certainly exists in policing and certainly influences the police officer's cognitive and emotional processes. While studies of the way other occupations deal with death may not be entirely germane to the police experience with death and may not deal directly with the central issues explored in this book, they can nevertheless shed an oblique light upon the way police officers respond when they operate in analogous situations.

The general theoretical literature on death has also explored or touched upon ways in which physical or social settings, occupational cultures, prior experiences and exposures to death, the frequency and duration of exposures, and other specific circumstances mediate or influence the human experience of death events. Extensive or systematic explorations specifically relating to the impact of death encounters upon contemporary urban police officers, though, are made conspicuous by their absence.

By virtue of the frequency, range, and types of death encounters to which they are exposed and the tremendous number of subjective and objective variables police death encounters may entail, contemporary urban police officers are remarkably appropriate candidates for a study of the psychological impact of repeated routine exposure to the deaths of others. In addition, some officers' profound work-related encounters with their own mortality or the mortality of fellow officers make them appropriate candidates for a study of extreme and highly personalized confrontations with death. The unique range of circumstances under which police death encounters may occur and the unique features of the police occupational culture clearly distinguish police death experiences from those in other occupations.

Unlike most other occupations and professions that entail death work, police officers inevitably become involved in dangerous and life-threatening situations, and circumstances may demand that they employ physical or even deadly force to preserve their own lives or the lives of others. Similarly, circumstances may arise when deadly physical force is used against the officer, and on occasion these struggles may result in the officer's demise. In his insightful and comprehensive analysis of the function of police in modern society, Egon Bittner (1980) asserts that the legitimate capacity to exercise nonnegotiable coercive force—including deadly force—is the central and defining characteristic of the police role, one that sets it apart from all other social and occupational groups. As a practical matter, the contemporary urban police officer whose duties and job-related experiences have not placed him in objectively dangerous situations at one time or another is rare indeed (van Maanen, 1980). Danger and the potential for a violent line-of-duty death are defining variables of the police personality, and police differ from all other occupational groups in that they are the only contemporary peacetime occupational group other than the military with a systematic record of death and serious injury from instrumental violence (Skolnick, 1994, p. 46) and the only nonmilitary occupational group legally empowered to employ deadly physical force (Wenz, 1979). An enduring and overshadowing consciousness of the potential for involvement in a deadly encounter of the most extreme and perhaps most intimate type is thus an intrinsic and ineluctable feature of the contemporary urban police experience.

The available academic literature yields surprisingly few descriptions or substantive conclusions regarding the psychological impact of death exposure on police, although theory, intuition, and anecdotal evidence would suggest that the impact is potentially great. Indeed, evidence of this impact is more readily discernible in the popular nonacademic literature of policing, including police novels, memoirs, and *bildungsromaner*. Niederhoffer and Niederhoffer (1978) and Klockars (1983), for example, have argued that this popular literature often provides an appropriate window through which to access police experience and glimpse many of its subtler and more nuanced features. Because popular literature can serve as a useful adjunct to supplement rigorous academic research, I have referred to appropriate literary sources on several occasions in order to bolster or depict a particular concept or dynamic.

Systematic descriptions or qualitative explorations of the processes, defenses, and dynamics involved in the police officer's struggle to maintain psychic equilibrium in response to death exposures are also notably absent within the academic literature of policing. Indeed, a diligent search of the academic literature reveals that while some sources may reference death-related themes in a tangential fashion, no extensive, systematic, and comprehensive descriptive studies of the social and psychological effects of police death encounters have been conducted to date within any academic discipline.

Only one brief article in the academic sphere (Henry, 1995), in fact, has sought to explore the psychological and social dimensions and repercussions of police officers' exposure to death in this way. In that article, I attempted to integrate strands of psychological and sociological theory along with general observations of police behavior within a theoretical and analytic model based upon Lifton's psychology of survival perspective. My article on the police officer as survivor was intended to generate debate and dialogue, and perhaps to shed some initial light upon the meaning of death within the police occupational culture, rather than to reach substantive and unequivocal conclusions (Henry, 1995). In terms of its direction and goals, this study is in many respects a continuation of that article's initial explorations. This study elaborated on that earlier initial article by exploring in greater depth and in a more systematic fashion some of the psychological dynamics, responses, and behaviors evidenced by contemporary urban police officers in relation to their death encounters, as well as the ways these transformations are mediated by and expressed in the attitudes and behaviors that prevail in the police occupational culture.

The Importance of Police Culture

Occupational cultures are potent mediators of subjective experience (Deal and Kennedy, 1982), and the police occupational culture is certainly no exception. As a whole, the literature of policing supports the notion that officers are socialized into a distinct occupational culture (Bennett, 1984), that the norms, beliefs, and value systems of that culture differ significantly from other occupational cultures and from the larger overall culture in important ways, and that the police occupational culture plays a powerful role in shaping officers' individual and collective experience of reality. The experiences, belief systems, and values that officers bring with them at the time they enter into police work are to some extent imported into the occupational culture (Bahn, 1984), and the events and situations they encounter in their work further shape the contours of their culture (Black, 1980; Brown, 1981; Burbeck and Furnham, 1985; Crank, 1998; Manning, 1978, 1997; Niederhoffer, 1967; Reuss-Ianni, 1983; Skolnick, 1994; van Maanen, 1985; Westley, 1953, 1956, 1970; van Maanen and Manning, 1978).

Particularly during the early stages of their careers, the formal and informal training given to officers tends to increase in-group solidarity and homogeneity, differentiate officers from the public, and reinforce elements of the existing police culture rather than inculcating them with the attitudes, values, and belief systems of the general public (Kappeler, Sluder, and Alpert, 1994, pp. 100–101). Social isolation and anomie (Niederhoffer, 1967; Swanton, 1980), objective and perceived danger (Skolnick, 1994), and the conflicting or ambiguous demands of the police role are frequently cited as fundamental operant bases for the sense of social estrangement that pervades the police subculture, especially at the initial stages of a police career. Because occupational cultures play such a formidable role in shaping behavior and interpreting work-related experience, we can easily infer that the police occupational culture shapes the officer's experience of the death encounter as well. At the same time, I have argued elsewhere (Henry, 1995) that police encounters with death are a formative experience or rite of passage that plays an important functional role in the socialization process through which police norms and values are communicated and learned.

Numerous observers have described and analyzed police behavior and police culture, and they have operated from a variety of disciplines and perspectives; there are a host of sociological, psychological, and even anthropological interpretations available to inform our explorations of policing, and I made liberal use of them throughout the book. In seeking to understand the complex phenomena that are the subject of our inquiry, it became entirely appropriate to eclectically draw upon the data, observations, and insights other disciplines provide. At the same time, one seeks to maintain an ordered perspective—to explain the phenomena using a consistent paradigm or analytic framework. To this end, I am often so presumptuous as to incorporate an observation or insight derived from, say, a dramaturgical analysis of policing, but to recast or explain that observation in terms of Lifton's paradigm.

Since this research is exploratory in nature, it makes no pretense to being a comprehensive and exhaustive final treatment of these issues and makes no claim to absolute generalizability. Rather, it is an attempt to amplify the landscape of contemporary urban policing by describing a psychologically and sociologically important aspect of the police experience. As discussed later in this book, many of the issues we touch upon require further exploration, inquiry, and verification. Beyond the admittedly limited light it sheds, the primary value of this research may lie in its heuristic value—in the questions it raises rather than answers.

In undertaking this systematic exploration of the psychological and social consequences of police encounters with death, my goals were to illuminate some arcane aspects of the police culture and some features of police behavior, to inform and broaden the various theories and perspectives on human reactions to the phenomena of death by providing insight into some conspicuous aspects of the police experience, and to complement the literature of individual and occupation group responses to death. This book seeks to address a current void in the literature of policing by exploring an important sphere of police activity and to point out processes and experiences that have thus far escaped academic attention and inquiry. In writing this book, I also hope to influence police agencies' policies, particularly those related to the psychological health of officers and to the processes by which police agencies manage the training and socialization of their officers. Similarly, it is my hope that the research proves valuable to clinicians by sensitizing them to the needs and experiences of officers who have survived mortal combat situations as well as less traumatic death exposures.

It should also be noted that with the exception of a few occasions where I refer specifically to female officers, the masculine case is used throughout the book. This grammatical device is used primarily to avoid the kind of clutter that often results from continually reminding the reader that police officers can be men or women, and it should not be construed as ignorance or a failure to recognize that fact. With a few important exceptions, this exploratory research does not attempt to distinguish differences in the behaviors or experiences of male and female officers relative to their death encounters. If such differences exist, they are more appropriately the subject of future research.

1.

Death Work

The General Context

The central premise of this book is that unique psychological and social transformations result from the police officer's encounters with death, and that the extent and dimension of these transformations are shaped by a number of variables. In itself, this premise is neither remarkable nor surprising: police officers are human beings, and they are susceptible to the same universal human tendencies and transformations that would affect anyone who witnesses death. Even the fact that police officers encounter the deaths of others frequently and intimately is not all that unique, since members of other occupations also deal frequently and intimately with death. The police officer's response to witnessing death is not "ordinary," however, because the specific array of variables and factors that may be present to shape these universal human tendencies in the policing context are so unique and, often, so powerful. Moreover, the psychological and social worlds in which the police officer functions—what may be referred to as the police officer's "working personality" and the "police culture" or "police subculture"—are potent mediators of experience, and they differ in significant ways from the milieus in which members of other occupations operate.

These variables interact and intersect in a complex fashion, and they include the values, attitudes, and belief systems prevailing within the police subculture, the officer's prior experience in dealing with death and his own attitudes and belief systems about death, the specific facts and circumstances of the particular death encounter, the physical and social settings in which the encounter occurs, and the tasks and procedural responsibilities the officer is required to perform in relation to the particular death encounter. To a significant extent, the officer's task environment and duty assignment determine the number and types of death he encounters, just as the physician's choice of specialty "dictates, to a large degree, what his experiences with death will be" (Hendin, 1973, p. 126). Collectively, these individual and environmental variables conspire to make the police officer's death encounters quite different from those of other death work occupations.

The thrust of the research lies at the virtually unexplored nexus of two disparate bodies of theory and research: policing and the psychology of human responses to death. The fact that this nexus has not been well amplified by direct research poses several distinct impediments to systematic inquiry, not the least of which is a distinct lack of substantive data and clear theoretical foundations with which to draw summary conclusions about police death encounters. Just as the complexity of the issues, concepts, and behaviors involved in this project required a comprehensive method of inquiry that was simultaneously flexible and rigorous, the absence of previous research in this area demanded that special attention be paid to supporting observations with verifiable facts and empirical evidence. Because this study necessarily implicates many practical realities of the police officer's task environment that are not well described or analyzed in the academic literature, quite a few assertions and observations made throughout the book are derived from my own preliminary research (Henry, 1995) and from more than twenty years of experience as a New York Police Department police officer and supervisor.

Paradoxically perhaps, the lack of research, data, and firm theoretical foundations also provided me with a singular opportunity to conduct basic exploratory social science research unencumbered by the limitations and structures that rigid paradigms and highly developed theoretical bases tend to impose.

In this chapter I will set out some basic principles and concepts about human responses to death that have been discerned in other death work occupations and that seem particularly applicable in the police context. Because the principles and assumptions of Lifton's formative-symbolic paradigm and psychology of survival perspective are integral features of the overall research project, they are given expanded coverage and delineation in chapter 2. The literature cited here derives from many diverse sources, and I've organized this chapter according to general areas of research that are intended to serve as a prelude or introduction to the psychology of survival as it pertains to contemporary urban policing. In this chapter, I first present a general overview of the psychological and sociological literature of several analogous death work occupations in the medical and medico-legal fields, where death is often routine and where its psychological impact is often relatively benign. I then discuss the literature as it concerns more dangerous and personally consequential exposures to death in the military context as well as exposure to grotesque death among rescue workers. The chapter then turns its attention to some highlights of the limited body of knowledge relating to police death encounters, leading to a discussion of some dynamics involved in extraordinary encounters with one's own mortality—the type of mortal combat situations experienced by officers who have taken a life, who have witnessed the death of a fellow officer, or who have been severely injured through instrumental violence in the line of duty. Finally, I present a series of general research expectations that distill and integrate appropriate inferences from the literature of other occupations but nevertheless seem applicable in policing.

A great deal of the literature on death work occupations concerns the social mechanisms and psychological processes that contribute to the routinization of death work, and some of these mechanisms and processes appear to be operant in policing. Charmaz (1975, 1980) makes the general but quite salient point that death workers typically make death routine by erecting protective barriers between their work and their self-image, constructing a social reality that implicitly distances and separates them from death's reality and permits them to manage the complex emotional and intellectual issues death raises. This constructed reality, Charmaz says, typically involves the interaction of four major stances toward death: minimizing, hiding, flaunting, and acknowledging death (1980, p. 175). These four stances appear to operate in policing as well. For example, police officers often minimize the psychological impact of death, either through explicit behaviors that deny its impact or through the use of language or linguistic forms that disparage or depersonalize it. Officers hide death by exercising their discretion to limit public access to the death scene, and by avoiding discussions and situations that might reveal to others their intimacy with death events. At other times, officers engage in "backstage" behavior that ostentatiously or comically flaunts death, by making macabre jokes about it, or by otherwise forcing others to confront it (Henry, 1995). As we will see in subsequent chapters, some officers (tenured officers in particular) come to acknowledge death as an inevitable part of human existence, and they tend to deal with it in a more mature, rational, and somewhat intellectualized fashion. Each stance, though, functions to insulate or distance the self from the psychological trauma accompanying death encounters.

Medicine: The Professional Approach to Death

These four stances also exist within the medical professions, although the educational and socialization processes of medicine differ quite significantly from the police occupation's training and socialization in the ways they acquaint practitioners with death's realities. Physicians' training involves an extended period of gradually increasing responsibilities for patient care and gradually increasing accountability for patients' lives, and student physicians' technical and ethical performance is continually monitored by peers as well as by superordinates specifically charged with that responsibility (Bosk, 1979). Medical education trains physicians to think in an objectively dispassionate, scientific, and analytic manner in which death is intrinsically depersonalized (Cassell, 1973), and Coombs and Powers (1976) make the general assertion that medical training and socialization processes as a whole tend to minimize or mitigate death's psychological repercussions.

In contrast to the police, medical professionals typically deal with death in a clinical, "medicalized" setting in which a socially prescribed clinician-patient relationship has been established and in which the clinician has a high degree of referent and expert power. Because medical personnel often operate in teams within a hierarchical system that divides labor according to expertise and area of specialization, such psychologically difficult tasks as notifying the patient he has an incurable disease or notifying family members that a patient has died are easily delegated, and any sense of personal responsibility or guilt the physician feels for a patient's death is easily diffused. Police encounters with death, on the other hand, often occur under volatile, objectively dangerous, emotionally charged, and highly ambiguous circumstances in which immediate social and psychological supports are absent, and they frequently involve death in its most grotesque and trauma-provoking forms. Periods of formal police recruit training are significantly briefer than those in medicine and the allied medical occupations, and police training tends not to emphasize death issues or deal with them in a particularly compassionate way. Rachlin (1991) tracked several New York City police recruits through their police academy training and into the early stages of their career socialization, and he observed both that many police recruits are not aware of the extent to which their work involves death exposure and that the scant training they received did not adequately prepare them for their first death encounter. Hall (1982) espoused a similar view, leading her to conclude that much of the death-related training that does take place is simply not relevant to the day-to-day realities of policing.

Medical doctors are certainly aware from the earliest stages of their training that medicine entails contact with death (Kasper, 1959), and according to Herbert Hendin their career choice may even represent a counterphobic reaction to death fear (1973, p. 135). Feifel (1969) set forth a similar hypothesis, arguing that physicians hope to engage and conquer their above-average fear of death by entering a profession where death encounters occur with some frequency. Hendin also observes that the medical student's first professional contact with death occurs in the anatomy lab, where the mechanical process of dissection and the fact that the cadaver is anonymous in name and background implicitly depersonalizes death (1973, p. 125). He further asserts that although students resolve many of their ambiguities about death by the time they complete their medical education, few physicians ever really adjust to losing a patient (127).

Dickinson, Lancaster, Winfield, Reece, and Colthorpe (1997) conducted an empirical study of "detached concern" and death anxiety among medical students before and after taking the gross anatomy course, and they make the point that the first-semester gross anatomy course is a stressful but highly functional rite of passage for physicians in training. As students grapple with the stress of committing a tremendous amount of cognitive information to memory, they also deal with the social and psychological aspects of cutting and touching a dead body and with the questions this experience inevitably raises about their own and others' mortality. In the short term, these difficulties are compounded when classmates and advanced students subject them to horror stories about cadavers, but the horror stories also serve, in a positive and functional way, to help create a social and psychological world comprised of medical insiders and outsiders and emotionally tough or weak medical students. Emotionally toughened medical insiders are those who deal effectively with death (i.e., they perform their required duties with rather little overt dissonance or emotional distress), while the weaker medical outsiders remain emotionally unsettled or intimidated by it. Although Bosk

(1979) was more concerned with the latter stages of medical socialization—specifically the training of surgical interns and residents—he also describes how young medical practitioners are exposed to horror stories about patients' deaths, highlighting the importance of cautionary tales that increase stress at the same time they informally communicate medicine's norms. It is in gross anatomy class, however, that medical students begin to learn how to deal with the mental stress involved in the practice of medicine (Dickinson et al., 1997, p. 202).

Dickinson and his colleagues (1997) point out that the culture of medicine presents the physician with a host of conflicting roles and expectations, among them the problem of how to provide compassionate and humane care without becoming too intimate with or emotionally attached to the patient. This identity conflict, which can become particularly acute when dealing with a terminally ill patient, is partially resolved as physicians are socialized throughout the course of their medical training to embrace a disposition of "detached concern"—students become possessed of the idea that in order to provide the best possible medical treatment the physician should remain somewhat detached or emotionally uninvolved with the patient. This stance of affective neutrality permits the physician to understand a patient's social and psychological needs and to treat him in an objective and clinical way, all the while avoiding some of the costs of emotional attachment. Detached concern permits the physician to retain enough objectivity to exercise sound medical judgment and allows him sufficient latitude to practice his technical skills and scientific expertise unhindered by the conflicts of emotional involvement. As we shall see, similar attitudes of detached concern are involved in police work and are a part of what Lifton calls "partial professional numbing."

Using survey instruments administered before and after the first-semester gross anatomy course, Dickinson and his associates (1997) measured new medical students' levels of death anxiety as well as the strength of their belief in the need for detached concern. The research revealed that slightly more than half the students showed less death anxiety after the introductory course, less than 30 percent showed increased death anxiety, and less than 20 percent showed no measurable change. With regard to their commitment to medical norms of detached concern, the researchers found no measurable change in half the students, an increase in support for detached concern in 23 percent, and less commitment to detached concern in 27 percent of the medical students. Although these researchers intended to conduct a longitudinal study to determine medical students' desensitization to death and the development of a detached attitude over the entire course of their medical education, the study was terminated before additional information could be collected (Dickinson, personal communication, April 27, 1999). However, even this limited data clearly points to the fact that the experience of intimately dealing with dead bodies during the gross anatomy course brings about important changes in the dimensions of medical students' death anxiety and the strength of their commitment to the norm of detached concern.

Death anxiety has multiple dimensions, of course, and anxiety related specifically to the handling of human remains is only one of these dimensions. Nevertheless, anxiety over handling remains is a potent dimension, as evidenced by the universal tendency—on individual and cultural levels—to avoid physical contact with corpses. While it is unfortunate Dickinson et al.'s (1997) research was prematurely concluded, and while it is unfortunate the survey instrument was not precise enough to measure this dimension more completely, the preliminary data certainly lends empirical support to what we might intuitively expect: the experience of intimate physical contact with a corpse generally contributes in some way to reducing subsequent death anxiety. We might infer that the first-year medical student—or the rookie police officer for that matter—who forces himself to overcome his natural revulsion at the prospect of handling a dead human body learns that he can at least partially defeat or deflect this fear and do what his social role and task environment demand of him. When subsequently faced with this unpleasant task, the medical student or rookie officer is likely to find his fear has lost at least some of its potency. What is less well understood, though—and what the data, conclusions, and insights provided by Dickinson et al. (1997), Hendin (1973), and Bosk (1979) cannot reveal—is the specific subjective psychological processes operating to alleviate one's aversion to intimate contact with dead bodies. As discussed later in this chapter, some research has described the psychological outcomes of dealing intimately with grotesque forms of death at disasters, but it also reveals little about the subjective experiences and psychological processes involved.

Like others in the medical and medico-legal fields, coroners and medical examiners develop self-protective strategies to maintain the routine character of their work and to limit strained interactions with bereaved individuals, and their claims to professional status are an effort to legitimize their emotional distance (Charmaz, 1975). Coroners and medical examiners—here the distinction is purposely blurred[1]—encounter the deaths of others with great frequency, and Charmaz observes they demonstrate both an avoidance of death and discomfort at expressions of grief. Death is explicitly externalized and almost completely separate from the coroner's everyday emotional world, and coroners interpret personal involvement as an interference that prevents them from properly fulfilling their duties and professional responsibilities (Charmaz, 1975). In a general sense, the coroner's job seems fairly analogous to that of the police crime scene technician, who also encounters a tremendous number of deaths and performs specialized technical or scientific tasks that do not implicitly require a great deal of interaction with bereaved parties.

The Literature of Military Psychology and Psychiatry

Research in military psychology and psychiatry, particularly as it relates to the psychological consequences of extreme combat experiences, also bears upon police officers' routine and profound encounters with their own mortality and illuminates some of the basic dynamics and psychological dimensions of death encounters within policing. Due perhaps to a preference for empirical research, psychiatric technicism or psychological reductionism, most of the research in this area is concerned with the extent, prevalence, correlates, and experiential precursors of either combat stress reactions or the diagnostic category of posttraumatic stress disorder (PTSD); qualitative or descriptive research into the phenomenology of soldiers' reactions and adaptive mechanisms is fairly sparse. Bartone, Ursano, Wright, and Ingraham (1989) comment that in general there is little understanding of the phenomenology and specificity of human responses to disasters and other traumatic exposures to death, and they note that many researchers have operationalized their research primarily in PTSD terms since the diagnostic category was introduced in the *Diagnostic and Statistical Manual of Mental Disorders (DSM) III* in 1980. They point out that although the PTSD diagnostic category has an obvious utility for researchers, it is premature to restrict attention solely to that category because a host of psychological phenomena other than PTSD can follow exposure to traumatic stress. Such restriction, they argue, constrains clinical and research activities into trauma-related reactions (Bartone, Ursano, Wright, and Ingraham, 1989). By focusing almost entirely upon the clinical and pathological aspects of PTSD, this body of literature also tends to obscure the fact—central to Lifton's paradigm—that death encounters may have functional and in some cases quite positive adaptive consequences for the survivor.[2]

Our focus is on the area of human psychology that Bartone and his colleagues (1989) have properly identified as lacking in most PTSD research: the phenomenology and specific psychological processes that take place in relation to a traumatic death encounter. Unlike the vast majority of research in PTSD, Lifton's psychology of survival is specifically concerned with intrapsychic matters and with subjective experience. Also in regard to the specific similarities and differences between PTSD and the psychology of survival, it was clearly not the goal of this research project to explore the clinical aspects or dimensions of psychopathological disorder among police officers, nor is it within my capacity as a researcher to attempt a credible diagnosis of psychiatric symptoms. Instead, this research is closely and narrowly focused upon the psychology of survival among officers and the immediate and long-term nonpathological adaptations and transformations that accompany the vast majority of police exposures to various kinds of death-related psychological trauma. Despite these caveats, we can apply some general principles gleaned from PTSD and combat stress reaction research to the kind of death encounters that occur in policing.

Solomon (1989), speculating that the high rate of acute and chronic distress among some combat veterans may indicate a greater initial vulnerability to traumatic stress reactions, points out that some individuals in combat do not appear to manifest overt symptoms of distress while others who participated in the identical combat actions display or seek treatment for acute combat stress reactions. Some individuals subsequently adjust well and regain their emotional balance after time and after the immediate stressors of combat are alleviated, but others continue to display chronic symptoms, and a number of these ultimately suffer profound pathological consequences and/or psychiatric disorders. From these observations, Solomon infers that the individual soldier's inherent psychological resilience may determine whether or not he will break down under the pressure of battle or subsequently suffer from elevated stress or psychopathology.

Solomon's inferences also highlight (without directly articulating) the importance of prior experience, attentiveness to potentially traumatic stimuli, relationships with others involved in the traumatic event, and levels of emotional arousal in the subjective interpretation of traumatic incidents. Solomon's observations do not detract from the conceptual viability of the psychology of survival as a universal *adaptive* human response. We can scarcely argue against the notion that relatively permanent psychological transformations occur in response to death-related psychic trauma, but while others may cast these transformations in pathological terms, Lifton's psychology of survival more optimistically asserts they are for the most part essentially beneficial and result in some kind of illumination or personal growth. To a large extent, these positive adaptations permit the individual to continue operating psychologically (and ultimately, physically) in a relatively healthy way after exposure to a trauma that might otherwise prove immobilizing. Indeed, the lack of overt clinical symptoms in the majority of cases Solomon studied may well reflect the soldiers' adaptive and nonpathological responses to their death encounter. Moreover, Lifton concurs with the observation about individuals' predisposing vulnerability to intrusive death imagery, but he cautions that "predisposition is only a matter of degree: if the threat or trauma is sufficiently great, it can produce a traumatic syndrome in everyone" (1980, p. 169).

Because the roles of the combat soldier and the contemporary urban police officer share some common features, the literature of military psychology and psychiatry allows us to draw some analogies and make some general inferences about the psychology of police exposures to death. Solomon's (1989) research into the psychological sequelae of the combat experience among Israeli combat veterans is again a case in point. Solomon measured the long-term psychological outcomes of war among a group of soldiers who suffered acute stress reactions, comparing them to a socio-demographically matched control sample of soldiers who served in the same frontline combat units but displayed no overt symptoms. Solomon examined these psychological outcomes with a particular reference to two major intrapsychic manifestations of distress: intrusion and avoidance. As a constellation of symptoms, intrusion

> refers to the penetration into consciousness of thoughts, images, feelings, and nightmares about the war, and to a variety of repetitive behaviors. Avoidance reflects the tendencies of psychic numbing, conscious denial of meaning and consequences, behavioral inhibition, and counterphobic activities related to the stressful event. Intrusion is generally the initial phase, followed by avoidance. Intrusion and avoidance may then alternate in the course of the posttrauma period, according to the individual's idiosyncratic pattern, until working through occurs. (p. 342)

Solomon determined that subjects who displayed combat stress symptoms evinced significantly higher levels of chronic distress one, two, and three years after the combat experience, that measurable levels of distress in both groups declined over time, and that indicia of PTSD symptoms were present in both groups. He concluded, based upon interviews that strongly suggested that subjects' ongoing psychological difficulties were closely related to a sense of failure as soldiers, that the elevated levels of distress represent a continuing artifact of the soldier's diminution of self-image. In Israel (as in the police occupational culture), the masculine identity is closely linked to the capacity to perform competently and effectively in a combat situation, and those who break down in the face of battle are viewed as having failed in a major role (p. 345).

Solomon found that intrusive thoughts, images, and feelings are more intense shortly after the traumatic event, and he asserts that as time passes and adaptation occurs, the process of psychic numbing and the struggle to internalize and make meaning of the experience takes on an increased prominence. The successful outcome of the struggle to integrate and make meaning of the traumatic experience becomes manifest in reduced distress. He concludes that the elevated levels of avoidance and numbing found within the control group may also be attributable to a residual resistance to recalling and dealing with the war, or alternatively to the functional effects of an idiosyncratic pattern of response to trauma (Solomon, 1989). These conclusions point up the importance of psychic numbing, showing that its extent and quality, both proximate to and after the exposure, fosters adaptive change by preserving the psychological integrity of the self and by impeding the onset of intrusive or pathological symptoms that might otherwise lead to immobilization and breakdown. The significance of these and other conclusions, and the degree to which they complement the psychology of survival, will become more apparent in chapter 3's explication of the formative-symbolic paradigm.

Solomon does not support his conjectural process of alternating intrusive and avoidance symptoms with any empirical evidence, and at first glance this pattern appears to challenge Lifton's assertion that the five themes of survivorship occur simultaneously and contemporaneous with the death exposure and that all five themes remain viable afterward. It is quite possible, however, that particular themes or responses are more readily apparent to the individual or are closer to consciousness at particular times, and therefore more likely to be detected by a clinical instrument or interview process.

While concurring that a complex set of predisposing individual personality factors and recovery environment factors (i.e., social supports, subsequent events, and social attitudes toward the event) influence adaptation to a catastrophic event, Green, Lindy, Grace, and Gleser (1989) combined empirical and qualitative research methods in an attempt to discern the predictive effect of specific types of assignments, combat duties, and war stressors on the development of PTSD and other related clinical diagnoses among Vietnam War veterans. The wartime experiences most closely associated with a PTSD diagnosis were particularly dangerous combat assignments (such as long-range reconnaissance patrol, being a medical corpsman, "tunnel rat" duties, and demolition work) in which soldiers worked alone or without the close physical and social supports offered by larger units. The life-threatening aspects of infantry patrol (including perimeter guard duties, receiving sniper fire, and being in a firefight) and exposure to grotesque and mutilating death either in the course of other assignments or as the result of "graves registration"[3] duties were also closely associated with a PTSD diagnosis. Of these, the most potent predictive experiences were dangerous special assignment activities that involved exposure to grotesque death—this combination was highly predictive of PTSD with allied panic and phobic disorders, and exposure to grotesque death was in itself highly predictive of subsequent alcoholism.

The association between exposure to grotesque death and subsequent alcohol abuse among Vietnam veterans mirrors the findings of Laufer, Gallops, and Frey-Wouters (1984), and an analogy might be drawn to the police culture's endorsement of after-work drinking parties ("choir practice" or a "four-to-four") often organized in response to death encounters (Henry, 1995; Wambaugh, 1975). Machell's (1993) clinical treatise also discusses connections between death encounters (specifically, combat-related PTSD), excessive role immersion, and alcoholism among police officers. Notable among the effects of alcohol consumption, of course, is a general numbing of emotional experience and a concomitant relaxation of inhibitions. This artificial relaxation of inhibitions, in turn, often leads to feelings of vitality or exhilaration.[4]

Serving in an artillery unit or in offensive helicopter operations, on the other hand, predicted a decreased risk for PTSD. Green and her colleagues (1990) submit that being in offensive helicopter operations "contributed to decreased levels of disorder, suggesting a protective function of distance from ground combat activities, or feelings of increased control over one's destiny or that of other individuals" (p. 333). By virtue of their assignment and task environment, artillerymen and helicopter crews were effectively distanced from many of the dangers and other personalized aspects of combat, both in terms of their physical proximity and by the technical nature of their work.

In reviewing the literature, Green and her colleagues (1990) observed that the intensity of the combat experience as well as the experience of killing civilians or participating in or witnessing abusive violence increases the risk of traumatic stress. Grady, Woolfolk, and Budney (1989) similarly determined that participation in or exposure to abusive violence was significantly related to postwar adjustment problems and was the single most powerful predictor of combat-related posttraumatic stress disorder among members of their sample group. This result was also obtained in several previous studies by different researchers (Laufer, Frey-Wouters, and Gallops, 1984, 1985; Breslau and Davis, 1987; Gallers, Foy, and Donohue, 1988; Woolfolk and Grady, 1988; Yehuda, Southwick, and Giller, 1992). Veterans who reported witnessing or participating in brutal acts of dubious morality demonstrated the highest levels of maladjustment, a result that challenges unidimensional models of war zone stress that focus primarily on the threat posed by physical danger. Lifton (1973) also deals extensively with the psychic repercussions of having observed or participated in atrocities, identifying in Vietnam veterans a protracted and conflicted cycle of self-condemnation and further desensitization, leading ultimately to individual and shared forms of guilt.

Perhaps the most salient conclusions to be drawn from this cluster of research—at least in terms of this book's focus on policing—are that empirical research confirms that different types of assignments implicitly involve different dimensions or conditions of exposure to death, and that the potential magnitude of resulting trauma varies as a function of these assignments. By cautiously generalizing these findings to contemporary urban policing, we can begin to glimpse how certain task environments entail different levels and depths of exposure to death, and consequently, somewhat different traumatic experiences and outcomes.

More specifically, this cluster of research shows that the factors mediating the subjective response to death exposure include the dangerousness of the encounter (i.e., the real or perceived level of threat to the individual), the availability or absence of social and psychological support systems, the physical presence or absence of other persons, the amount of situational control the individual exercises over the event's outcome, his physical proximity to the death event, the degree of attention paid to technical tasks during the encounter, the objective gruesomeness of the death scene, and the perceived morality of the actions undertaken by oneself and others. The research also shows that the performance or dereliction of culturally prescribed role expectations has a profound impact on the subsequent preservation or loss of self-identity, as well as on the extent and intensity of an event's psychic consequences.

Rescue Workers and Grotesque Death

Both the literature of military combat psychology and the psychology of disaster rescue workers strongly support the notion that exposure to massive or grotesque death as well as to individual dead bodies is a disturbing and often frightening experience that produces significant psychological consequences. Victims, onlookers, and rescue workers in disaster situations are often traumatized by either the experience or the expectation of confronting death (Jones, 1985; Tucker, Pfefforbaum, Doughty, Jones, Jordan, and Nixon, 2002; Ursano and McCarroll, 1990; Ursano, Fullerton, Oates, Ventis, Friedman, Shean, Wright, and McCarroll, 1995), but relatively little is known about the specific psychological effects of exposure to dead bodies and body parts (Hershiser and Quarantelli, 1976; Jones, 1985). Ursano and his colleagues (1995) point out that the anticipation or expectation of handling bodies, like the actual handling of human remains, engenders significant distress. They conclude that individuals who have not handled remains but whose job is likely to require it at some point in the future are made more anxious by the prospect than those who have already participated in body recovery activities. Similarly, rookie police officers often experience anxiety prior to handling corpses (Rachlin, 1991), but experienced officers often handle remains with little apparent anxiety (Henry, 1995). In conjunction with Dickinson et al.'s observations about first-year medical students' reduced death anxiety after completing the gross anatomy course, these observations lend additional support to the desensitization hypothesis outlined above: actually performing the psychologically difficult task of handling corpses tends to decrease one's anxiety in subsequent situations.

Especially within the context of grotesque death, exposure to a child's remains is particularly traumatic because the child's innocence, untimely death, and appearance of complete victimization typically stimulates emotional involvement and a sense of familiarity, often to the extent that the sight of a dead child will conjure intrusive images and recollections of the rescue worker's own children (Ursano and McCarroll, 1990; Ursano, Fullerton, Oates, Ventis, Friedman, Shean, Wright, and McCarroll, 1995; Fullerton, McCarroll, Ursano, and Wright, 1992). Pathologists articulate a distinct aversion to performing autopsies on children, and rescue workers report high levels of distress in working with victims' personal effects, since that task tends to enhance identification with the victim (Ursano and McCarroll, 1990). Similar observations were made by Fullerton and her colleagues (1992). Clearly, factors that enhance emotional attachment or identification with victims tend to exacerbate the anxiety and psychic trauma engendered by physical proximity to human remains (see, generally, Thompson and Solomon, 1991).

It should not be surprising, then, that those who are experienced in dealing with grotesque death employ a variety of strategies to insulate or distance themselves from psychic trauma (Ursano and Fullerton, 1984). Some individuals may reify their identification with the dead in a magical way, believing that as a person cares for a body on the battlefield or in a disaster, someone would one day take care of him should it become necessary. Experienced rescue personnel often caution new workers not to look at victims' faces, not to get emotionally involved, and not to think of remains as a person (Ursano and McCarroll, 1990), and, as we will see later, comparable depersonalization strategies can be noted among police officers.

An extremely bothersome aspect of body handling is profound sensory stimulation. This usually involves the smell of decaying bodies, although visual and tactile sensitivity is also frequently reported (Ursano, Fullerton, Oates, Ventis, Friedman, Shean, Wright, and McCarroll, 1995; Fullerton et al., 1992). Body handlers who worked at the Jonestown, Guyana, mass suicide and the Beirut Marine barracks bombing developed behaviors and strategies to mask the overwhelming odors, including burning coffee grounds, smoking cigars, working in the cold, and using fragrances (Cervantes, 1984). Police use virtually identical strategies at death scenes (Henry, 1995). Ursano and McCarroll (1990) observe that the body handler

> is traumatized through the senses: through viewing, smelling and touching the grotesque, the unusual, the novel, and the untimely dead. The extent and intensity of the sensory properties of the body such as visual grotesqueness, smell and tactile qualities are important aspects of the stressor. Exposure to a child's mutilated body appears to be extremely toxic, regardless of the body handler's age or whether she/he has children. Although all sensory modalities are involved in contact with a body, odor may have the highest potential to recreate significant past episodes in a person's life. (pp. 397–398)

Police officers may have occasion to observe images of grotesque death while performing rescue work at the scenes of disasters, automobile accidents, fires, homicides, suicides, and other scenes where multiple or particularly bizarre casualties occur. Raphael, Singh, Bradbury, and Lambert (1983) studied police officers, firefighters, emergency medical personnel, and other rescue workers after a rail disaster in Australia and found that the helper's role and sense of agency in the rescue effort are critical in determining psychological outcomes, since occupational and organizational roles provide guidelines for action at the time of the disaster. When the actions undertaken by officers conform to organizational and personal role expectations, the individual is less likely to experience feelings of helplessness and frustration and less likely to experience subsequent depression or emotional disturbance. When occupational roles are less well defined, though, or when the individual is in some way prevented from fully participating in the rescue activities, feelings of frustration, helplessness, distress, and depression become more prominent (Raphael et al., 1984). These findings seem to complement Solomon's (1989) observations about role expectations among Israeli combat soldiers and their impact on the development of pathological symptoms.

Almost half of the police officers in Raphael et al.'s study identified feelings of helplessness—which they variously described as feeling inadequate, unprepared, or frustrated at the inability to act more vigorously to aid victims—as the single most distressing aspect of their involvement in rescue activities. Another prominent and related pattern of responses among police officers involved distress at being powerless to alleviate the emotional anguish of relatives and the suffering of the injured, as well as identifying with these victims or relatives. Interestingly, demands to work under pressure to release the injured and to prevent the realistic possibility of their own deaths were the least frequently identified distress factors among rescue workers (Raphael et al., 1984). It is apparent that the performance of physically dangerous work, which is central to the police officer's role and identity (Skolnick, 1994), did not produce a sense of role incongruence in the same way a lack of agency or sense of helplessness did.

We can better understand this sense of helplessness at being unable to provide solace to victims by recognizing that the social role of police is, like the police self-identity, complex and multifaceted. There are several implicit dualities in the police role, and their etiology and dimensions are spelled out in subsequent chapters. At this point, though, it should suffice to point out that police are expected to have the capacity to act with toughness and courage in the face of danger or when enforcing the law, as well as to behave compassionately and humanely with regard to those in need. One difficulty in resolving this basic duality is made apparent in the fact that a single situation may present multiple and seemingly contradictory demands for both kinds of action. This constellation of potentially conflicting expectations results in part from public demands, in part from subcultural demands, and in part from the officer's own police identity—his subjective sense of self-as-police-officer. When an officer is unable to fulfill or adequately respond to one of the demands, expectations, or images that comprise the constellation, a kind of failed enactment occurs and a host of psychological consequences can be triggered.

Fullerton and her colleagues (1992) conducted a study of firefighters' responses to deaths encountered in the line of duty, obtaining results that are generally consistent with other findings about rescue workers. They found four characteristic patterns of psychological response to death trauma: identification with victims, feelings of helplessness and death guilt, fear of the unknown, and physiological reactions. Fullerton and colleagues (1992) also determined that the type and quality of available social supports, the support and sympathy of leaders, the level of training or preparation for rescue work, and the effectiveness of such distancing rituals as gallows humor all tended to mediate the psychological impact of exposure to grotesque death.

Police Death Encounters

New York Police Department procedures and the New York City Administrative Code mandate that police investigate all deaths other than those occurring within medical facilities. Police death encounters may therefore occur in public or private locations and may involve homicides, suicides, accidents, and deaths from chronic or sudden illness. Several relevant variables that elude precise quantification may also be present or absent at a particular death scene, and they can significantly influence the officer's subjective experience of the death event. These variables include the extent to which the corpse is physically mutilated or decomposed, the extent to which the officer interacts with witnesses or the deceased's family members, the quality and duration of that interaction, the officer's subjective preparedness to deal emotionally and cognitively with the range of conditions at the death scene, and his previous experience in dealing with death events.

The fact that patrol officers encounter death frequently and repeatedly is well supported in the literature of policing. Wenz (1979), for example, examined the frequency with which officers in one unnamed agency encountered death, noting also that the exposures took place across a wide range of situations and circumstances. He found that 43.3 percent had their first job-related encounter with death in their first year of service and nearly all encountered death by their third year of service. Lewis (1973) surveyed another agency where officers reported that the average officer encountered a death once every three months. It is unfortunate that neither Wenz (1979) nor Lewis (1973) specified the agency they studied or provided greater detail about its characteristics, including the demographics of the communities they serve. The absence of these data make it difficult to generalize from those agencies to policing in the New York City context, since community and agency demographics as well as violent crime rates certainly influence the number, type, and quality of death exposures an officer may have. Intuitively, the frequency of death exposures Wenz (1979) and Lewis (1973) cite seem fairly low by New York City standards.

Any attempt to assess the frequency with which NYPD officers in particular assignment categories or task environments are exposed to death must be undertaken in light of several important caveats. In 1999, for example, there were approximately 2,000 NYPD sergeants and about 14,000 police officers assigned to 76 Patrol Services Bureau precincts, 225 sergeants and 1,700 police officers assigned to 9 Housing Bureau Police Service Areas, and about 210 Sergeants and 1,350 Police Officers assigned to 11 Transit Bureau Transit Districts.[5] Additionally, approximately 1,500 investigators in the rank of detective or police officer were assigned to precinct detective squads, and about 60 detectives and police officers were assigned to the Crime Scene Unit. In the same year, 671 homicides were investigated, 137 people died in fatal auto accidents, 99 suicides were recorded, and almost 11,000 other DOAs were officially recorded.[6]

It would be incorrect to assume, however, that the various types of death exposures are equally distributed among all the department's 76 patrol precincts, nine Police Service Areas, and eleven Transit Districts, just as it would be incorrect to assume that every officer assigned to a command has an equal probability of responding to one of these deaths. A Transit District officer, for example, would not ordinarily encounter the at-home death by natural causes of an elderly person, any more than a Housing PSA officer would ordinarily encounter a "man under"—a person crushed to death under the wheels of a subway train—or a "space case"—a person crushed between a platform and a train. With the exception of the crime scene unit, staffing levels for these commands vary greatly according to the geographic area covered, the population served, crime rates and a variety of other operational and workload factors. Patrol precincts, for example, might have as few as 150 or as many as 350 police officers assigned to them.

The population demographics and violent crime rates of particular commands are also an important factor in determining the number and type of deaths officers may encounter—officers and detectives working in precincts with high murder rates, for example, would necessarily have a statistically greater likelihood of responding to a death by violent means than officers working in less violent areas. By the same token, officers assigned to precincts characterized by a large number of multigenerational working-class families and a high percentage of elderly residents can be expected to encounter a greater number of deaths in which an elderly person dies at home of natural causes.

It would also be incorrect to assume that death exposures are equally distributed among all the officers working within a particular precinct, since rookie officers tend disproportionately to receive these assignments (Henry, 1995). Finally, it would be incorrect to assume that only one or two officers respond to each death scene—given the abundant variety of factors influencing police response and assignment practices, it is both conceivable and likely that multiple officers will attend the same death scene, although the duration of these exposures can also vary greatly. Notwithstanding these caveats and our inability to precisely estimate the frequency of exposure within each category, we can safely conclude that NYPD officers generally have ample opportunity for frequent encounters with the deaths of others.

Although police procedures governing the initial investigation and processing of any death scene assign specific tasks, roles, and responsibilities to patrol officers, patrol sergeants, and the precinct desk officer, it must be emphasized that it is a conventional, if informal, practice within the NYPD that the least-tenured available officer (i.e., a "rookie") actually performs virtually all the prescribed administrative tasks (Rachlin, 1991; Henry, 1995). These required tasks and duties include the preparation of various official reports and forms, notifying friends or relatives that a death has occurred, performing a physical search of the corpse and the premises, the removal and safeguarding of valuables or evidence, and assisting the medical examiner, detectives, and morgue personnel in various ways (see, generally, New York Police Department, *Patrol Guide,* sec. 106).

The paperwork and administrative duties involved in recording the death and investigating and safeguarding the death scene are not particularly complex or onerous by NYPD standards, but they play an important role in mediating the officer's experience of the death exposure. Charmaz (1980) comments generally that bureaucratic procedures contribute to the process of routinizing death work: bureaucratic procedures tend to attenuate or dilute a death's social consequences by providing the worker with an element of control as he manages and defines the situation and the strained social interactions it may involve. By focusing his attention on requisite tasks and procedures, the death worker can limit or avoid uncomfortable interactions with bereaved family or friends and find protection from anxiety, embarrassment, or personal feelings (pp. 182–183).

On quite another level, the police officer's procedural responsibilities and report-taking duties also serve as an important functional mechanism of police socialization: they provide supervisors and more tenured officers the opportunity to informally evaluate the rookie's technical proficiency, his willingness to share the risks and burdens of policing, and his capacity to deal with unpleasant or emotionally taxing death-related tasks (Henry, 1995). Because it is the informal practice to assign a rookie to the death scene, and in conjunction with the data cited above, we can safely infer that rookie officers are typically exposed to the deaths of others fairly early in their careers. Indeed, my own survey of probationary police officers in a recent police academy class (described in chapter 3) indicates that almost 7 percent of rookie officers had a death encounter—that is, they were assigned to at least one DOA job—during their first month of patrol duties.

Wenz (1979) found that rookie officers experience a higher level of death anxiety than more tenured officers, and that for all officers death anxiety was inversely proportionate to length of service. He suggests that repeated or extended exposures desensitize the officer to the fear of death and, in a functional way, permit him to deal more effectively with the death events he subsequently encounters. Subcultural support for this desensitization hypothesis may also explain why senior officers (like the medical students Bosk [1979] described) sometimes go to great lengths to enhance the rookie's discomfort at the death scene (Henry, 1995). This is not to say that senior officers are motivated to engage in such behavior through a conscious belief that it will ultimately benefit the rookie. A far more plausible explanation, and one that compliments Charmaz's (1980) observations about flaunting death, is that they simply enjoy "showing off" how inured they have become to death, or because they simply enjoy "breaking a rookie's chops." By demonstrating their comfort with death and how inured they have become to it, the tenured officers also subtly draw attention to their own seniority, their "insider" status, their emotional toughness, and the higher levels of experience they bring to bear in police work. Whatever its motivation, if the behavior results in the rookie's desensitization to death it has a functional outcome.

The concept of anticipatory grief, as advanced by Kutscher (1973), would seem to bear on this desensitization dynamic as well. Kutscher argues that the experience of grief and bereavement resulting from superficial exposures to the deaths of others prepare us to cope with greater and more personally significant losses, including the deaths of loved ones, valued others, and ultimately the loss of our own lives. By ensuring the rookie's exposure to the deaths of others at the earliest stages of his career, the subculture may be operating functionally to ensure the development of adaptive processes that will prepare the rookie for the greater and more personally significant losses police work may potentially entail. It may also operate to better prepare young officers to deal psychologically with potential danger and with future threats to their own mortality.

Like other death workers, the police officer's involvement and interaction with coworkers and grief-stricken relatives or friends at a death event exerts a potent influence over his subjective experience of it. While the tasks and responsibilities of patrol sergeants and crime scene technicians implicitly require little interaction with bereaved individuals at the scene of a homicide, for example, patrol officers and detectives tend to spend more time at death scenes and have more extensive interaction. Observation and intuition also point to the fact that the type of death (e.g., violent homicides versus death by natural or accidental causes) influences the character of the grief experienced by family and friends. In turn, this influences their interactions with officers and shapes the officer's experience of the event. Yarmey (1992, pp. 91–92), for example, describes a two-phased pattern of reactions among close relatives of homicide victims: an immediate period of acute grief followed by a longer period of reorganization.

Immediate post-homicide reactions appear to be more powerful and more difficult to control for family survivors than those that occur in response to other types of death. A profound sense of violation and loss, compounded by the violent nature of the death and mixed with obsessive thoughts and vengeful desires to hurt the killers, is a common reaction.

Over the longer term, grieving friends and relatives attempt to come to terms with their loss by trying to make intellectual sense of the death, a quest that is often complicated when the facts and circumstances of the murder seem objectively "senseless" and absurd. Survivors often struggle with the philosophical question of what issue or set of circumstances could be so important as to merit the taking of a human life. This quest for emotional reintegration and cognitive meaning is in pursuit of closure—of going beyond the acute grief phase to "get on with life." Police officers, especially homicide detectives, can and do play an important role in this struggle to find or make meaning of death, both by providing information (i.e., supporting the cognitive process of integrating factual data about the circumstances of the death to facilitate cognitive comprehension) and in the emotional support and comfort they provide. Homicide detectives often struggle with conflicting internal and external demands: the need to solve the case quickly and efficiently competes with the humanistic urge to render comfort and support to these secondary victims.

The need to resolve the basic conflict between the professional responsibility to be an impartial finder of fact and a personal tendency toward empathetic feeling for grieving family and friends constrains the police officer to handle death scene interactions with tact and compassion—concern for the well being of bereaved family and friends "must be coordinated with the officer's need for professional detachment in order to carry out basic police tasks" (Yarmey, 1992, p. 92). The inherent incongruence between a personal and benevolent concern for the survivor and a professional mandate to impartially investigate the facts and circumstances of the death can easily be exacerbated when the case is a death by homicide.

The academic literature of policing, psychology, and death work occupations provides rather little direct information about the psychological impact of death encounters on police officers, and this seems especially true of police officers' extreme encounters with their own mortality. Psychological theory, intuition, and anecdotal evidence, however, suggest that the impact is formidable. The research literature also provides little insight into the psychological and social effects of surviving mortal combat, primarily because none of these other occupations (excepting that of combat soldier in time of war) typically involves the credible potential for encountering one's own demise as the result of fulfilling the demands of the occupational role. Because the experiences and emotions conjured by extraordinary personal confrontations like mortal combat are of an entirely different order than routine exposures to the deaths of others, we might also expect that the psychological transformations they engender are also amplified.

Officers are keenly aware that the potential for violence and for meeting a violent death in the line of duty exists, and it is widely acknowledged that this knowledge plays an important role in the police officer's day-to-day activities as well as in the police socialization process (Cullen, Link, Travis, and Lemming, 1983; Bayley and Garofalo, 1989; van Maanen, 1980). This awareness of the potential for violence and death also operates in the formation of subcultural belief systems and norms (Westley, 1951, 1953, 1956, 1970) and the forging of the police officer's "working personality" (Skolnick, 1994). Research on police perceptions of danger is particularly relevant to police attitudes toward death, insofar as both danger and death are ultimately potent reminders of one's own mortality and are primarily distinguishable in terms of their degree and intensity. Nevertheless, little research has been specifically directed toward illuminating the subjective psychological and social impact this knowledge has on officers and their behavior.

Jerome Skolnick offers some important insights into the ways the perception of danger shapes the officer's worldview, particularly in what he terms the "symbolic assailant"—the construct of an unspecified other who represents the potential for danger, serious injury, or death. According to Skolnick (1994), the occupation's inherent potential for danger permeates and sustains the police subculture: the element of danger "requires the police officer, like the combat soldier, the European Jew, the South African (black or white), to live in a world straining toward duality, and suggesting danger when 'they' are around" (p. 46). Practically everyone the officer meets, with the exception of other officers, represents a potential symbolic assailant.

The literature of policing is replete with references to the use of deadly physical force by and against officers, but despite the extensive compilations and analyses of empirical data about deadly force encounters (Fyfe, 1980, 1981, 1982, 1988; Skolnick and Fyfe, 1993; Binder and Scharf, 1980; Scharf and Binder, 1983; Geller and Scott, 1992; Alpert and Fridell, 1992; Fridell and Pate, 1992, 1993; Pate and Fridell, 1993), these quantitative studies generally fail to elaborate upon the quality or personal significance of mortal combat situations. Scholarly depictions of police violence and the impact of shootings on police officers tend to minimize "the immediacy of threat and danger, reduce to quantitative measures matters of qualitative concern to police officers, and brush aside the world within which the police live as if it were merely a source of mystification and confusion rather than a source of value and meaning" (van Maanen, 1980, p. 147). Given the tremendous variety of circumstances these "messy matters" may encompass, police mortal combat situations are much less amenable to typification than routine encounters with death. They are typically "hot, frantic, hair-raising, lurid and insane" events that "are inchoate, highly variable, and shaped by contextual, historical and technological background features" that conspire to defy attempts at precise cognitive classification (p. 146). Police mortal combat situations, in other words, have all the requisite elements of absurdity.

Van Maanen describes generally how mortal combat events are felt and acted upon throughout the police organization, and he found that three distinct versions of the event—an official, a collegial, and an individual subjective interpretation—are likely to be constructed. Official versions are impersonal recitations of factual circumstances that are generated by police administrators and are reflective of organizational interests. For example, the official NYPD reports prepared whenever an officer is involved in a shooting or killed in the line of duty are dispassionate narratives that explicitly avoid any reference to the incident's emotional content. If, after investigation, the incident is found to be a so-called clean or good shooting, the officer may be nominated to receive one of several grades of combat medals, and here a somewhat different official version emerges. The official post hoc citations are crafted for the department's annual Medal Day ceremony and they relate the basic facts of the case, but their primary focus is on the officer's heroism and the way his actions symbolize the public image the agency seeks to project; invariably, they omit any reference to the horror the officer may have experienced and they emphasize his selfless actions on behalf of others.

Collegial versions or "war stories" are a type of "introverted or hermeneutic organizational history within which key characters, events, places and relations can be located and understood" (van Maanen, 1980, p. 152). These symbolic depictions take the form of cautionary tales that illuminate the culture's shared meanings and interpretations of shooting events, affirm the occupational culture's "cynical, hardened, violent, and involuted" belief systems and values, and serve as an important medium of police socialization (p. 153). Rookie officers eager to "learn the ropes" from an admired seasoned veteran are particularly attentive to these cautionary tales, and tenured officers who relate war stories—their own or others'—not only provide important tactical information, but they raise the rookie's overall level of anxiety and subtly reinforce ideas about policing's inherent dangerousness and the absurd unpredictability of situations the rookie may one day face. In this way, the deadly force war stories that proliferate in police culture serve much the same function as the cautionary tales imparted to medical students: they emotionally toughen the rookie, provide practical information on how to avoid critical missteps and errors, and help create a world of policing insiders (those who are privy to policing's absurdity and danger) and outsiders (those who are not). Internalizing the complicated lessons of these vicarious experiences also provides the officer with a kind of tentative plan for action should he ever face an analogous situation: in a very practical way, the stories tell him how to behave (or not behave) in the face of imminent threat, as well as how the subculture expects him to behave and feel after the event.

Individual subjective interpretations of the deadly force encounter, van Maanen (1980) says, are significantly less scrutable. He emphasizes that the subjective meaning-making process involves an attempt to protect the officer's sense of self, and notes that this process is shaped by the particular circumstances of the shooting as well as by the relationships the officer maintains with his colleagues and organization. These "personalized responses are deeply penetrated by the immediate reactions of the various valued members of the audience the officer must confront on a day-to-day basis" (p. 155). The officer who survives a deadly force encounter, then, may find his initial subjective interpretation of the event and his subsequent behavior significantly at odds with what others expect.

Danger: The Perception and the Reality

Although police work is undeniably a physically dangerous occupation, particularly for officers in certain assignments and locales, objectivity demands that we recognize several important caveats. Police officers tend, for example, to overestimate and overstate the actual quotient of violence they encounter and the degree of danger that violence poses to them (Bayley and Garofalo, 1989; Cullen et al., 1983; Garner and Clemmer, 1986). Research by Cullen and his colleagues (1983) found that although officers believe their work is dangerous and in fact perceive it as a lot more dangerous than most other occupations, their view is shaped by a consciousness and sensitivity toward the *potential* for physical injury that is inherent in police work and to the types of situations and settings they enter, rather than to the actuarial *probability* of being hurt. Cullen et al.'s (1983) study determined that despite officers' deeply held conviction that theirs is an implicitly dangerous job, less than ten percent of those surveyed responded affirmatively when asked if many of their workmates were physically injured in the line of duty. While every officer will ultimately experience situations that are dangerous or that threaten to become dangerous, they need not actually experience an objectively hazardous situation in order for the overshadowing and perhaps overblown perception of danger to take on its psychological and behavioral significance. Rather, the perception of danger results from officers' close identification with other officers who have been injured or killed (Skolnick, 1994, p. 47).

Cullen and his colleagues (1983) also argued that the officer's overblown perception of danger is concomitantly functional and dysfunctional—the perception of danger encourages officers to remain cognizant and vigilant, but this sensitivity "is not without its negative personal effects" (p. 461). Indeed, they determined that the perception of danger was positively and significantly associated with work stress as well as with depressive symptomatology (pp. 459–460).

Other empirical data (Federal Bureau of Investigation, 1970–2001, 2001) support the view that policing is a far safer occupation than many would imagine. Southwick's (1998) economic analysis of the murder and accident risk for police officers nationwide shows that police are significantly less likely to be murdered than members of the public in a comparable age and sex cohort, although police do run a moderately higher risk of accidental death than other workers.[7] After controlling for annual increases in the number of American police officers employed, Southwick's aggregate data also reveal the police officer's actuarial risk of being murdered—either on or off duty—has steadily declined since 1960, with a total decrease of more than 60 percent since that time. Since about 1980, the police officer's overall risk of being killed by a felon has actually been lower than the corresponding risk faced by members of the public. The police officer's risk of accidental death (in automobile accidents, for example) has remained fairly constant since 1960, while the accidental death rate for all other workers shows a steady downward trend. The police officer's risk of accidental death has consistently exceeded that of other workers since about 1979. Southwick's data show the police are about ten times more likely to be assaulted than members of the public, with about 15 percent of all officers likely to be assaulted in a given year, but he cautions this data may in part result from a higher tendency among police to report these crimes.

The actuarial decline in the murder rate for police officers may be attributable to various factors, including better tactical training and the increased use of bullet-resistant soft body armor, but the *perception* of danger and of an increased likelihood for meeting one's demise through instrumental violence remains rife in policing. Indeed, we can see how increased use of body armor and increased or improved tactical training supports this perception of danger: psychologically, the daily ritual of strapping on body armor and the discomfort it causes throughout the workday is in itself a subtle reminder of the potential for deadly violence, and one goal of an effective tactical training program is precisely that of raising and maintaining officers' awareness of the dangers they face. The psychological dynamic is similar to one described by Fyfe (1980) in his study of policies requiring officers to carry their weapons while off duty: on or off duty, the highly symbolized accouterments of policing subtly but continually remind the officer he must be prepared to deal with danger and violence at a moment's notice. In terms of subjective psychological importance, symbols, images, and experiences that reinforce the officer's firm (if erroneous) conviction that his work is particularly dangerous are more salient than almost any amount of empirical data to the contrary.

The salient points emerging from this constellation of research—that police tend to overestimate the potential for danger in their work and that this perception infiltrates their worldview, subcultural belief systems, and work-related behaviors—are complemented by empirical research conducted by Garner and Clemmer (1986). That research exploded the police subculture's staunchly held conventional wisdom that domestic dispute calls account for more police officer injuries and deaths than any other type of enforcement action—mortality and assault statistics simply do not bear out this notion. Instead, Garner and Clemmer point out that the ambiguity, volatility, uncertainty, and high levels of confusion and emotional discord typically present during many police-citizen encounters (specifically family disputes) magnify the officer's perception of the combatants' hostility toward each other and toward the officer. In these emotionally charged and chaotic environments, officers tend to overestimate the danger they face, equating *potential* danger with objectively *real* danger. In a broader sense, this body of research suggests that officers' perceptions of danger are magnified when their degree of control over the outcome of an encounter is diminished.

Training and the Potential for Violent Death

Evidence that mortal combat situations have significant social, psychological, and behavioral consequences for all officers (and not merely those who are personally involved in them) can also be readily discerned in a variety of police behaviors and agency practices. Officers often discuss the mortal combat experiences other officers have had, and the important tactical lessons the encounters may convey are also reinforced through various training modalities. For example, it is the NYPD's policy to base a significant portion of its preservice and in-service firearms and tactics training and role-play scenarios upon actual combat events.[8] This training, along with policies and subcultural systems that encourage or permit officers to carry their weapon while off duty, underscores the potential for becoming involved in a combat situation and encourages officers to remain in a state of perpetual preparedness and hypervigilance (see, for example, Fyfe, 1980). This training also emphasizes (within the bounds of culturally prescribed conventions) the tactical lapses and errors other officers have committed.

This emphasis on correcting tactical lapses is carefully placed, insofar as the subculture is tacitly reluctant to associate tactical errors or omissions with a personalized notion of blame or fault. Criticizing or ascribing blame to an officer in such cases is taboo, since it might subtly mitigate the culpability of his assailant and erode the threat of the "symbolic assailant" construct that helps to sustain the culture. Rather, the scenarios are presented in a manner congruent with the subculture's characteristic belief in a dangerous generalized other or "symbolic assailant" as described by Skolnick (1994): the training scenarios explicitly externalize the source of threat, relieve the officer of any complicity or responsibility for his injury or death, and generally impart a conviction that the officer's death was due to a series of inexorable factors and circumstances that conspired against him. As a rule, officers staunchly resist ascribing blame to injured or deceased officers through "Monday-morning quarterbacking."

An important goal of this training is to encourage dialogue and discussion about officer safety and proper tactical responses, in line with the view that the more officers know about and talk about tactics and potential combat situations, the more likely they are to respond effectively should they ever encounter such a situation. In contrast to many other elements of the NYPD's in-service training programs (whose curricula are often maligned and dismissed by officers as irrelevant to the practical realities of street policing), very few officers demonstrate any resistance to attending the department's semiannual firearms and tactics qualification training and very few display inattentiveness during this course of instruction. This is true not only of officers assigned to operational and enforcement duties that entail a realistic potential for combat, but of officers in administrative and support assignments as well.

Tactical lessons and combat considerations also resonate in police war stories—the type of cautionary tales described by van Maanen (1980) that comprise and communicate a sort of organizational memory or subcultural mythology. These dramatic and often emotionally compelling tales delineate the contours of the subcultural value system, and the lessons they convey are often clearly discernible through symbolic or dramaturgical analysis.

Police Funerals: Reminders of Death

Further evidence that a consciousness of the potential for meeting one's demise in mortal combat resonates in urban policing can be found in police line-of-duty funerals. Line-of-duty funerals are a unique study in the sociology of policing because they involve distinctive police behaviors, ceremonies, and symbolism and because, like all funeral practices in all cultures, they bring members of the subculture together to affirm subcultural values and beliefs (Roberts, 1994; Rachlin, 1994a, 1994b).

To an extent that is simply not found among members of other occupational groups (with the possible exception of firefighters), police officers individually and collectively feel tremendous empathy for fellow officers who are killed or seriously injured in the line of duty as well as for those officers' families. The empathy, affinity, and solidarity felt within the police organization and within the police culture as a whole are evidenced by the number of officers motivated to travel great distances at their own expense to attend the funerals of officers from other jurisdictions. The fact that some NYPD line-of-duty funerals draw well in excess of 10,000 officers (Firestone, 1994; Alvarez, 1996; McAllester and Plevin, 1994; Lyall, 1988b) also speaks to the sense of commitment and sense of connectedness officers feel for their fallen comrades. Clearly, because officers are so keenly aware of their own potential for being killed in the line of duty, the death or serious injury of another officer holds significance beyond the mere loss of a friend, colleague, or member of the same occupation.

Both the specific circumstances under which a line-of-duty death occurs and the officer's actions during the incident also appear to influence how meaningful the death is to members of the subculture. When the circumstances and actions reflect some elements of the subculture's mythology or value system, or when they effectively dramatize or convey a cherished value or subcultural belief system, officers can more readily identify with the officer and the circumstances of his death. The subcultural constructs serve as a kind of cognitive template that helps officers more easily integrate and understand the death.

Concomitantly, officers seem to invest certain deaths with greater esteem and honor than they do others. The honor and esteem in which officers hold a particular death seems to vary proportionately to the extent that the death upholds or illustrates a subcultural value, and the differential esteem is evident in the number of officers who attend the funeral. The funeral of an officer who died a "hero's death" (as defined by the subculture) with which other officers can readily identify by virtue of their own experiences in similar situations or through their identification with the particular police role the officer was fulfilling is likely to draw a significantly larger crowd of police mourners than a less "heroic" death. The death of an officer as the result of instrumental violence directed against him by a criminal who is committing or fleeing a serious felony crime, for example, complements subcultural notions of the inherent danger and unpredictability of enforcement situations. Such a death would likely be afforded greater status and would have greater personal significance for officers than an officer who died, for example, of a heart attack while directing traffic. It is quite likely that significantly more officers would attend the funeral of a "hero" cop than the funeral of an officer who died a more prosaic line-of-duty death.

Police wakes and funerals serve several integrative purposes, including bringing members of the agency together at a particular time and place to celebrate and reaffirm their shared identity and shared values. The shared identity and values are manifested in a number of subtle yet telling behaviors, including the fact that detectives and other plainclothes officers will frequently attend in their dress uniforms, a potent and visible universal symbol of the police identity. The salience of this behavior as a mode of expressing common identity is made all the more apparent by the fact that a plainclothes assignment generally entails greater status than a uniformed assignment. Niederhoffer (1967), for one, has linked status in the police organization to attaining an assignment that does not require wearing a uniform. By attending the wake or funeral in uniform, these officers put aside their own earned status in favor of expressing their connection through a more universal and more unifying symbol.

Further, while attending wakes for police officers killed in the line of duty, I have noted that virtually all the off-duty civilian-clothed officers present wear their police shields pinned to their outermost garment. There is no instrumental reason or functional purpose to this spontaneous and highly symbolic display of credentials other than to signify, perhaps unconsciously, their solidarity and the singularity of their identity. Certainly, no one would challenge their identity, status, rank, or right to attend the wake. In the NYPD and many other agencies, tradition also dictates that officers affix black mourning bands to cover the crest of the city on their shields upon the death of an officer, and while regulations stipulate the period of time officers may wear the mourning bands, these limitations are frequently exceeded; some officers wear the mourning bands for protracted periods without reproof from supervisors. The NYPD's regulations also require uniformed officers to wear breast bars denoting their commendations and medals above their shields, and insofar as these service ribbons convey the type and quality of the heroic acts for which the officer has been recognized and are decipherable only to other officers, they are important in-group symbols of status and experience. Officers who knew or worked closely with a fallen officer often attach unauthorized "in memory of . . ." plaques above these symbolic representations of their own heroism, tangibly commemorating their affinity for a fallen officer. These commemorative bars also symbolically convey the prestige they ascribe to their own loss, their sense of connection to the fallen officer, and a vicarious participation in that officer's heroism. Although superiors have often instructed police officers to remove unauthorized American flag breast bars and other unofficial emblems, I have never heard of a case in which an officer was admonished to remove this particular non-uniform item. Indeed, I have observed ranking officials—including those with a reputation for strictly enforcing uniform regulations—wearing these items.

Real and objective physical danger, as well as the magnified potential for physical danger, is thus part and parcel of the police occupation and its culture. Potent symbols and images of real and perceived danger permeate policing and the police occupational culture, to an extent simply not found in any other death work occupation. Police work is unique and emotionally hazardous, in part because it is "one of the few occupations in which one is feared, sometimes hated, occasionally reviled or even assaulted in the ordinary performance of one's duties" (Symonds, 1970, p. 155). The core role of the police—the exercise of nonnegotiable coercive force upon citizens (Bittner, 1980)—inevitably engenders some degree of public resentment, hostility, and the potential for violence against the officer. However overblown or exaggerated this perception of danger may be, the officer's psychological reality is that he continually faces the prospect of violent death, and that reality is more important than almost any amount of data to the contrary. No other nonmilitary occupation is defined by its capacity to use force, and in no other death work occupation is the potential for meeting one's own demise through instrumental violence encountered in the line of duty so intrinsic an element of the member's subjective or objective reality. The realistic prospect of meeting one's own demise through instrumental violence in the performance of duty is simply not as viable for other death workers as it is for police officers.

Summary of Research Findings

In summary, the academic literature of policing rarely deals with the psychology or sociology of police encounters with death—especially qualitative issues related to profound mortal combat experiences—but intuition, observation, and a host of anecdotal and theoretical data alludes to the fact that these encounters have profound psychological consequences for officers. In the absence of a firm grounding in the research literature at this point, we can draw few substantive conclusions about the extent and dimension of these consequences, or the specific processes by which they become manifest in the police occupational culture, in enduring individual images, or in individual and collective experience. Moreover, many of the inferences we can draw are by analogy from observations we make about other occupations.

The literature does permit us to conclude with some certainty, though, that police encounter death frequently and under tremendously varied physical and social circumstances, and that a number of variables potentially influence the officer's experience of the death event. These variables include (but are not limited to) the extent to which interactions with grieving others take place, the officer's previous experiences in dealing with death, the grotesqueness and physical condition of the remains, and the extent to which the officer identifies with the victim and the victim's circumstances. The different roles, tasks, and responsibilities prescribed by various police assignments mediate both the subjectively experienced quality of death exposures and the number of deaths an officer is likely to confront, and within each task environment the relative strength and coherence of an officer's role conceptions and professional identity may also account for differences in subjective experience during and after a death encounter.

A variety of psychological and social processes can operate to depersonalize or routinize death work, to erect psychological barriers that suppress emotions and protect the self from death anxiety, and to facilitate the officer's capacity to perform effectively in the face of death. Police officers' interpretations of their death encounters are also affected by the value and belief systems operating within their occupational culture, and their awareness that police work entails the potential for meeting a violent death or serious injury plays an important role in shaping their day-to-day behaviors and worldview. The potential for encountering death or violence at the most profound level of personal significance is an overshadowing feature of the police experience, and this potential resonates through the contemporary urban police experience regardless of whether an officer is ever called upon to participate in a mortal combat situation. Perhaps the most salient observation to be drawn from this review of the research literature, though, is how very little substantive information exists about the qualitative and subjective psychic impact death encounters have upon police officers.

Nominal Categories of Research Collaborators

In sketching some of the background issues and research that bears upon this project, I have alluded to the fact that the forces and factors operating within a death work occupation, like the circumstances that typically surround the deaths members of the occupation encounter, have substantial impact on the way the events are subjectively and objectively experienced. The social, cultural, and psychological factors that shape the experience of death among members of one death work occupation may operate very differently—if at all—in another, and the same can be said for the behavioral manifestations of those experiences.

Since the focus of this research is upon police as death workers—an area we know relatively little about except by intuition and inference from other death work occupations—it is important that we carefully define the nature of police work, the contours of the occupational culture, and the various roles, tasks, and duties its members perform in relation to death events. If we are to appreciate and understand the formidable impact death encounters can have on police officers, we must appreciate and understand the variety of forces and factors that surround police death encounters.

At first glance this may seem a practical impossibility, since policing is certainly among the most complex of social institutions (and arguably one of the least transparent), because police work is often highly specialized, and because it may involve such a broad range of death encounters. Fortunately, though, the very complexity of contemporary urban policing and the specialization of the functions, roles, and responsibilities it entails can work in our favor in terms of conceptualization and analysis. We can examine the broad array of police death encounters and the social, cultural, psychological, and organizational variables that surround them in much narrower and more precise terms if we consider them in terms of the specialized task environments in which the encounters take place. At this point, it is appropriate to specify and operationally define the four task environments and five nominal categories of officer we will consider in this study.

This study examines the death-related experiences, imagery, and psychological transformations common to contemporary urban police officers, but more specifically it seeks to further illuminate these psychological features by comparing and contrasting the ways that different task environments—different sets of officially prescribed duties and responsibilities officers perform in relation to a death event—shape the individual and collective psychohistorical experience. Notwithstanding the tremendous number of variables that can shape the subjective impact of a death event, it is possible to identify and operationally define at least four task environments in which police officers are exposed to death and to describe some of the variables typically present in each environment. The operational definitions and brief task environment descriptions listed below are based upon an examination of the duties and responsibilities required of officers under the NYPD's *Patrol Guide* (NYPD, 2003) as well as upon my own experience and observation of officers within each nominal category.

Rookie Police Officers

By virtue of his limited tenure and limited experience as a police officer, the rookie patrol officer has usually attended few death scenes, but these exposures may encompass a range of causes and circumstances of death, since patrol officers and patrol sergeants are required to respond to all deaths occurring outside medical facilities. The instrumental duties rookies perform are fairly complex, though, and may be emotionally taxing. The *Patrol Guide* allocates some administrative tasks and notifications to the first officer arriving at the death scene and allocates others to the patrol supervisor, but in practice they are usually performed by an available rookie officer whether or not he or she was actually the first officer at the scene (Henry, 1997). Various items of paperwork must be completed, and regulations require that a chain of custody over the human remains and its effects must be maintained and documented. They also require that a preliminary investigation into the cause and circumstances of death be conducted pending a determination (by Medical Examiner's Office personnel) that the remains can be released from police custody. The entire process can be quite protracted, and the rookie is often required to remain in close proximity to the corpse for a prolonged period. The corpse and the death scene must be searched, and personal effects must often be removed from the body and vouchered. Official notification of the death must be made to next of kin (except in the case of a homicide, where this responsibility is sometimes assumed by detectives). All these duties are typically relegated to a rookie officer, and their traumatic impact may be exacerbated or mediated by factors that include the presence or absence of the deceased's friends or relatives as well as other police officers and the extent and quality of personal interaction the officer has with them, as well as the circumstances of death and the state of decomposition in which the corpse is found.

For the purposes of this research, "rookie officers" are operationally defined as New York City Police Department officers in the rank of probationary police officer who have been assigned to patrol duties for a period of not more than one year, and who have been assigned on at least one occasion to an aided case involving a dead human body.

Patrol Sergeants

Patrol officers and patrol sergeants are required to attend the same types of death events, although they differ in terms of the frequency and duration of their respective death exposures. Patrol Sergeants are mandated to attend all death scenes occurring within their precinct during their tour of duty, but their duties are not extensive and they generally remain at the scene for a relatively short period of time. The patrol sergeant's interactions at the scene are primarily with other police personnel and revolve primarily around his supervisory duties—interaction with witnesses or the deceased's friends or relatives is infrequent and may be largely superficial. The sergeant's role and duties at the death scene are brief and highly routinized, and typically limited to witnessing the patrol officer's search of the corpse and the premises and endorsing the requisite forms and reports prepared by the officer.

For the purposes of this research, "patrol sergeants" are operationally defined as New York City Police Department officers in the rank of sergeant who have been assigned to patrol duties and the supervision of patrol officers for at least one year, and who have been assigned on at least one occasion to an aided case involving a dead human body.

Homicide Detectives

Detectives attend significantly fewer death scenes than either rookies or patrol sergeants, since they are not typically summoned to deaths that are clearly the result of natural causes. The deaths they attend are generally of the more grotesque and macabre type—homicides, suicides, and deaths by other violent (if accidental) means. Once summoned to these death events, homicide detectives may remain in close proximity to the corpse for a significant period of time while they conduct their preliminary investigation at the scene. Although homicide detectives are required to perform certain administrative tasks and prepare various reports that might contribute to the process of routinizing death, these chores are typically completed at the office at some later point in time.

Detectives at a death scene often have fairly extensive physical contact with the dead body, and they have substantial interaction with witnesses and with the deceased's friends or relatives in order to gather information necessary to solve the case. This interaction often continues over the course of their investigation and well into any criminal proceedings that result. Detectives usually conduct an extensive investigation into the victim's background, lifestyle, and relationships and often come to possess a great deal of intimate knowledge about the victim. In this sense, homicide detectives may develop a kind of relationship with the victim, and the potential exists that they will come to identify with the victim in various ways. The relationship between homicide investigators and the victim's family or friends can be distinguished from the relationships developed by other officers involved in the case by its depth, intensity, and duration.

It is also worth noting that homicides in New York City are jointly investigated by precinct detectives and homicide specialists—the precinct detective who "catches" the case and has the responsibility to bring it to closure is often teamed with a detective assigned solely to assist in homicide investigations. Both precinct detectives and homicide specialists were interviewed in this research.

For the purposes of this research, "homicide detectives" are operationally defined as New York City Police Department officers in the rank of detective or higher rank who have been assigned to perform or supervise general investigative duties or specialized homicide investigations for a period of at least one year, and who have conducted or supervised at least one homicide investigation.

Crime Scene Unit Technicians

The duties of Crime Scene Unit technicians are predominantly technical in nature, in that these specialists are tasked with the identification, collection, documentation, and processing of forensic evidence at the death scene. Crime scene personnel do not ordinarily attend death scenes other than those a preliminary investigation has determined to involve homicidal, suicidal, or suspicious means. The deaths they attend are therefore often extraordinary, macabre, and grotesque deaths resulting from instrumental violence. The particular tasks and responsibilities they undertake are specific to the case itself but generally include photographing the scene and examining the corpse, dusting for fingerprints, creating a precise crime scene sketch, and the collection and preliminary processing of various items of forensic evidence. Because none of the scientific or technical tasks performed by crime scene personnel implicitly require interaction with witnesses or with the victim's family and friends, they are unlikely to develop meaningful relationships with them.

While the number of homicide cases a precinct detective or homicide specialist handles may be comparatively small, NYPD statistics indicate that the average crime scene specialist responds to several dozen homicides, suicides or suspicious deaths annually.

For the purposes of this research, "crime scene technicians" are operationally defined as New York City Police Department officers in the rank of police officer or detective who have been assigned to the department's crime scene unit for a period of at least one year and who have collected forensic evidence from at least one homicide scene.

Police Survivors

At some point in their career, officers in any enforcement capacity or task environment may encounter a situation in which deadly physical force is directed against them or another officer present, or where they use deadly physical force against another person. Some of these encounters result in death. The ambiguous nature of these situations and the multiplicity of factors and variables that may define it conspire to defy attempts to neatly or simply classify them. Police officers may encounter a deadly force situation at almost any time, in almost any place, and without regard to their assignment or their task environment.

For the purposes of this research, "police survivors" are operationally defined as New York City Police Department officers who have had a profound encounter with their own mortality as the result of actively participating in or witnessing a mortal combat situation in which another person died, but who themselves remained alive.

Research Expectations

Up to this point our review of the literature of death work in various occupations has led to some preliminary insights and conclusions about those occupations and what we might expect to find in policing once we gather and examine some relevant data. In terms of structuring the research process, one often follows the literature review with a series of carefully defined research hypotheses—a set of specific assumptions or statements the researcher will attempt to prove or disprove. Due to the exploratory nature of this project and the lack of prior research findings specifically related to policing, there is danger in specifying our assumptions too precisely or in characterizing them as "hypotheses," even though they have hypothetical elements. Because we are taking a natural history approach to explore some important features of police experience, it seems inappropriate to set forth a detailed slate of specific statements, much less to "prove" or "disprove" them. Instead, the following general statements describe, in a summary way, what we might expect to discover once we have explored the issues more extensively and once we have collected and analyzed more data.

- Because different types of police assignments involve different types of exposure to death, we should expect that officers who operate in different task environments also differ in terms of their subjective experiences and the degree of trauma they accrue. Despite the tremendous range of circumstances, mediating factors, and situational variables presented across the broad spectrum of police death encounters, and notwithstanding individual differences in susceptibility or vulnerability to death-related trauma, we should also expect to discern similarities or shared themes of experience among officers within specific assignment categories. Since the experiences common to members of an occupational group or subgroup shape the development of group values, belief systems and occupational cultures, we should also expect to find that each assignment category produces somewhat different death-related attitudes, beliefs and behaviors among its members.

- We can also infer that officers who have a poorly defined role identity or whose sense of efficacy and agency is in some way diminished will experience greater distress when they confront death.
- While the concept of identification is a complex and multifaceted variable mediated by a host of other subjective and objective factors, we can expect that the extent to which an officer identifies with the victim or the circumstances of death will also affect the psychological outcome of his experience.
- The availability or absence of social support systems, including the presence or absence of other officers and the roles they play at the death scene, will have immediate and long-term impact on the officer's experiences as well as on psychic outcomes.
- An officer's previous exposures to death (in either a personal or professional context) can be expected to affect his experience at a particular death scene. Generally, officers with greater experience in dealing with the deaths of others (the result of either earlier police experiences, prior deaths of friends and family members, or participation in another death work occupation) are likely to manifest somewhat less distress and somewhat less powerful transformations than officers with fewer death-related experiences.
- The extent of interaction an officer has with others at the death scene, including interaction with officers, with civilian witnesses, and with grieving persons, will also affect his experience. Many types of interaction are possible at death scenes, and each functions to enhance or diminish the officer's distress.
- The extent of subjectively perceived or objectively real danger present in a given death encounter will affect the officer's experience of it. Officers in more dangerous situations will have greater distress and will experience more powerful psychological transformations than officers in less dangerous situations.

Conclusion

This chapter broadly sketched some generic observations about the human response to death encounters, and about how these responses are shaped by the tasks and experiences common to members of various death work occupations. From these broad observations and from some of the limited research on police death encounters, we then distilled some more specific observations about the social and psychological impact of exposure to death in contemporary urban policing. These observations, in turn, led us to identify several research expectations about the psychological and social phenomena we might find in policing and the impact they can be expected to have upon officers who have had one or more death encounters. But because we seek a more precise and thorough knowledge of death's impact in policing, we must explore the police officer's death encounters within a coherent and comprehensive theoretical framework.

Our goal, then, is to achieve a perspective or understanding that is at the same time more precise and more global—to understand the breadth *and* the depth of the phenomena at issue—and for this reason the following chapter sets forth the basic contours of Lifton's formative-symbolic theory and the psychology of survival perspective it subsumes. After examining that theory and the methods used to collect data, we will be better prepared to turn our attention to the phenomena involved in police encounters with death, to explore and analyze them, and to reach substantive conclusions.

2.

Police Survivors

of Death Encounters

Theoretical Perspective

and Strategy of Inquiry

This chapter provides a basic overview of Robert Jay Lifton's formative symbolic paradigm and his psychology of survival perspective—the basic theoretical frameworks we will use to structure, guide, and inform our exploration of police encounters with death. Lifton developed this paradigm and perspective in his studies of survivors—individuals and groups that have had profound encounters with death in some physical or psychological way but nevertheless managed to remain alive (Lifton, 1967, p. 479). The holocausts and events experienced by these survivors vary tremendously in terms of their intensity, personal and collective impact, and historical significance,[1] but the survivors nevertheless share certain universal psychological tendencies. These universal psychological responses to profound death exposures, of which a great deal more will be said, take the form of five characteristic themes of survivor psychology:

1. psychic numbing;
2. the death imprint;
3. death guilt;
4. suspicion of counterfeit nurturance; and
5. the struggle for meaning.

The constancy and consistency of these psychological themes among survivors of vastly different types of traumatic death encounters points up the psychology of survival's strength and coherence as well as its overall explanatory power. The themes may find different forms of expression even among survivors of the same event, but their universality and the extent to which they transform and inhabit the survivor's sense of self are compelling evidence that they are natural and universal adaptive human responses to death encounters. Because the psychology of survival has such strength, coherence, and explanatory power for profound death encounters, it is also a viable model for exploring the impact of less extreme encounters.

The psychology of survival is an appropriate model to inform our explorations, since its basic principles have already been successfully applied to members of other death work occupations (Lesy, 1987) including police officers (Henry, 1995). The psychology of survival is also appropriate because it is part of Lifton's larger formative-symbolic paradigm, in which the human sense of immortality and the continuity of life are central ideas or "controlling images." Because this larger paradigm is rooted in some of the most compelling issues and concerns of our time, it permits us to examine features of the contemporary urban police officer's experiences beyond those narrowly related to the death encounter.

Because the formative-symbolic paradigm and the psychology of survival are so central to our subject and to the psychological and social dynamics we will explore, it is necessary to explicate or outline some of their main points. This chapter therefore seeks to set out Lifton's overall perspective and the psychology of survival it subsumes in a fairly broad framework, pointing out some of the ways they apply to police and police death exposures. In subsequent chapters we will deal with police officers' death experiences in greater depth, expanding upon these basic principles and fleshing them out within the specific context of policing.

Paradigms are fundamental cognitive models or schemes that shape our understanding of something, and as Lifton points out (1976b, p. 22), they are important in psychological and social research because they determine what he calls the "controlling image" or the central idea around which we organize our understanding of some phenomenon. To a large extent, a paradigm's controlling image determines the type of problems and issues we examine, the methods we use to explore them, where we look for information, and the kind of information we consider most relevant in our search for answers. Thomas Kuhn (1962), often credited with bringing the term *paradigm* into the common vernacular (Horwich, 1993), used the term to describe how a specific set of organizing principles, concepts, definitions, ideas, and assumptions about physical phenomena shape the way scientists make sense of the world. Paradigms, Kuhn said, not only shape the way the physical sciences understand the world, but they also propel or inhibit scientists' progress toward learning more: knowledge tends to increase incrementally within the paradigm's conceptual bounds. In this sense, the rigid adherence to a particular paradigm tends to promote orthodoxy and stifle exploratory "outside-the-box" thinking. Paradigms also influence thinking in the social sciences, providing a sort of general point of view about human nature and the factors that shape human behavior. Paradigms also provide the conceptual and operational tools social scientists use to excavate and make sense of knowledge.

As they can in the physical sciences, social science paradigms may also operate to promote orthodoxy and stifle exploration. In psychology, for example, the tendency toward psychological reductionism limits the scope and the impact of behavioral research by insisting that complex human behaviors be explained solely in psychological terms. A less restrictive search for explanation would incorporate data and insights from other disciplines and would make better use of the methods other disciplines use to excavate and explain data. A number of paradigms operating in the social sciences provide useful insights into human responses to death, but only Lifton's is organized around principles of death and the continuity of life.

As chapter 1 made clear, what little we know about death's impact in policing derives from work done in several disparate disciplines using different paradigms and, often, different research methods. This fact, and the fact that studies of human responses to death exposures have historically been stifled by a kind of orthodoxy of denial, practically demands that we break free of these paradigmatic bonds to take a fresh look at the meaning of death in policing. Lifton's continuity-of-life model and the psychology of survival provide this fresh look; moreover, they accommodate and encourage the use of methods and data from other disciplines.

Freud's psychoanalytic paradigm, which has had a profound influence on twentieth-century thought, is organized around controlling images of sexuality and moralism, issues of compelling significance during the late Victorian age in which Freud's work emerged. The Freudian paradigm also emphasizes duality and the clash between instinctual drives and restraining forces whose resolution (largely through the defensive and compensatory mechanisms Freud proposed, especially repression) shapes human behavior in generally predicable ways. Now that "unlimited technological violence and absurd death have become more pressing themes for contemporary man," Lifton (1976, p. 26) argues, a paradigm organized around controlling images of death, the innate human sense of immortality, and the continuity of life is more appropriate and meaningful. Because concerns with death and expressions of man's sense of immortality are so much a part of contemporary human experience, we need to develop new ideas and new theories that will include them and lead us to a more comprehensive understanding of the behaviors and psychology of our times. Because death encounters are also so much a part of contemporary urban police experience, it seems appropriate and necessary to seek understanding of police behavior and police psychology (or at least police behavior and psychology involving death encounters) within a paradigm organized around these same issues, ideas, and theories.

One of the most important concepts in both the formative-symbolic paradigm (or continuity-of-life model) and the psychology of survival is the human "sense of immortality." It is important to clarify that man's sense of immortality does not equate with a complete denial of death's reality or a firm belief in literal afterlife. Many cultures and theologies certainly embrace concepts of spiritual or corporeal afterlife, but man's sense of immortality "reflects a compelling and universal inner quest for a continuous symbolic relationship to what has gone before and what will continue after our finite individual lives. That quest is central to the human project, to man as a cultural animal and to his creation of culture and history" (Lifton, 1983, p. 17).

The traditional Freudian psychoanalytic paradigm deals inadequately and tangentially with issues of death, and especially with man's sense of immortality as a life-affirming expression of continuity and connectedness. Freud, ever the realist, outright rejected the idea of immortality as a literal afterlife, insisting instead that man confront and acknowledge the reality and finality of biological death. By rejecting the idea of a literal afterlife, Freud also summarily cut off the psychoanalytic school's deeper exploration of the psychological importance of immortality as a symbol and the role it plays in human psychology. Man's flirtations with ideas of immortality and denials of death's reality, he said, occur as a function of repression. Due to his insistence that death has no representation in the unconscious, Freud explained death anxiety as a derivative of the fear of castration—placing the fear of death within the ambit of psychosexual conflict his paradigm stressed.[2] By dogmatically and prematurely closing discussions of the role of death and the sense of immortality within his system of human psychology, Freud preempted their further discussion and relegated them to an area of study better suited to philosophers and theologians than to psychological theorists.

Although Freud and his system had no tolerance for expressions of immortality, Jung recognized the pervasiveness or universality of immortality themes in the constitutive mythology of all cultures and saw fit to include them in his system of psychology. Also in contrast to Freud, Jung demonstrated less regard for the rational demands of scientific knowledge in the way he addressed psychological issues, including questions of death and immortality. He recognized that there are a host of opinions about immortality and no scientific proofs of life beyond biological death, concluding that questions of man's literal immortality are simply beyond knowing. At the same time, his system of psychology emphasized that the human psyche is comprised, in part, of ingrained primordial images and symbols that are older than historical man, and that a full life is one lived in harmony with these images and symbols. In terms of psychological health, Jung said, intellectual or scientific certainty is less important than a harmonious concordance between our thinking and the primordial images of the unconscious. Man cannot ignore these primordial images because they exist and fulfill important functions whether or not we understand their source or purpose, and whether or not they are objectively real or scientifically knowable. One of the fundamental images and symbols that has transcended time and is present in every culture, Jung observed, is the idea of immortality: from time immemorial, a large majority of people have felt the need to believe in the continuation of life (Jung, 1933, pp. 111–114).

Jung believed the idea of immortality and religious teachings about some type of life after death were psychologically important and relevant. As a physician, he was convinced that it is psychologically beneficial

> to discover in death something towards which one can strive; and that the shrinking away from it is something unhealthy and abnormal. . . . When I live in a house which I know will fall on my head within the next two weeks, all my vital functions will be impaired by this thought; but if on the contrary I feel myself to be safe, I can dwell there in a normal and comfortable way. From the standpoint of psychotherapy it would therefore be desirable to think of death only as a transition—one part of a life-process whose extent and duration escape our knowledge. (Jung, 1933, p. 112)

The psychologist Otto Rank (1950, 1958) also observed that man shows a universal need for reassurance of the self's eternal survival and a related tendency to create and embrace "immortality ideologies." For Rank, as for Freud, the sense of immortality was irrational. Where Freud dismissed such ideas *because* they are irrational, though, Rank saw them as irrational but nevertheless recognized their importance in human psychology.

Lifton's formative-symbolic paradigm draws upon many general Freudian and Jungian concepts and incorporates observations drawn from Rank's work, but it places much greater emphasis upon the importance of symbol formation as the fundamental process in man's psychic life. Rather than focusing on particular symbols as representations or equivalents for some other thing (a flag as symbolic of a nation, for example, or a pencil for a penis), Lifton's emphasis is on the continual psychic process of creating and re-creating experiences as viable inner images, forms, and meanings. Although the term *image* is typically used to describe visualized "pictures" in our inner world, it can be extended to include any kind of psychic representation of experience. We can therefore speak of auditory, tactile, olfactory, or taste images as well as visual images. The formative-symbolic paradigm is based on the principle that

> in human mentation we receive no perceptions or stimuli nakedly, but inwardly re-create each exposure or encounter in our on-going struggle toward form. That re-creation is always retrospective as well as prospective . . . but must be understood in terms of its own timing, in terms of the present. The *image* is the more immediate link between nervous system and environment. It suggests a picture, though the word can be extended to imply an anticipatory interpretation of the environment (or "schema for enactment," in Olsen's term). "Form" (or constellation) in this sense . . . contains many images, and tends to be more enduring than most images. Being more highly symbolized, it possesses greater structure and contour evolved from more elaborate psychic re-creation. Thus employed, the term "form" has the philosophical meaning of "the essence of something as opposed to its matter" (*Oxford English Dictionary*), rather than the seemingly opposite popular meaning of appearance as opposed to content or reality. (Lifton, 1976, pp. 74–75; italics in original)

Lifton says, in other words, that the sensory stimuli we take in from the surrounding environment are perceived as mental images. The immediate images we experience at a given moment connect with and activate similar preexisting images from past experience, and both the immediate and preexisting images combine or integrate in some way. As the two connect and integrate, both are to some extent changed: the preexisting image becomes more highly symbolized and more complex as it integrates new information from the immediate image, and the immediate image is interpreted or given meaning (i.e., it is perceived and understood) in light of the images from earlier experience. Thus the immediate images or experiences take on cognitive and emotional qualities from environmental cues as well as from past experience. This ongoing and continual psychic process of symbolization leads to the development of increasingly complex and sophisticated inner images that allow us to cognitively and emotionally interpret our experiences, and as inner images connect with each other they become even more sophisticated forms or constellations of images. Because our inner images, forms, and constellations are highly complex and because they give meaning to immediate images, they provide a kind of plan or schema for action that gives us some ability to anticipate future experiences.[3]

In Lifton's view, the image is integral to human life, and images are the source of all human motivation. The individual images we accrue from the interaction of environment and our central nervous system (that is, our sensory experience) combine with other preexisting images during the symbolizing process to create increasingly complex forms or constellations, so each image and form must be understood in terms of a configuration in itself as well as part of a larger configuration (Lifton, 1976, p. 70). All our experiences, then, are interpreted and given more complex meaning in light of our earlier experiences, and any individual experience can be understood only in terms of earlier experiences. This process of creating and re-creating images and forms is the basis of symbolization and a source of vitality. The self is the most inclusive of all individual forms: it is the symbol of one's own organism and the sum of all one's earlier images and experiences. Because every new experience results in some subtle or overt alteration in our inner images and forms, our sense of self is constantly evolving and changing.

Maintaining the life of the self, then, essentially involves the process of continually creating and re-creating viable inner images, forms, and constellations. When new images or experiences are absent or when the symbolization process becomes impaired, the viability and vitality of the self are threatened (Lifton, 1983, pp. 38–39). As Lifton points out, all of "human existence can be seen as a quest for vitalizing images and image-constellations" (Lifton, 1983, p. 39).

Lifton's model also places great emphasis on man's sense of immortality as an expression of continuity and connectedness, asserting that we have an ambivalent kind of "middle knowledge" of the idea of death: we know intellectually that we will die but also resist and fail to act upon this knowledge. No matter how profound our resistance to the idea of our own death may be, we can never completely obscure or evade the fact that we will someday die, and man requires symbolizations of continuity and other imaginative forms of transcending death in order to continue functioning psychologically and to avoid becoming completely overwhelmed and immobilized by the prospect of death. For Lifton, the need to transcend death by clinging to ideas and symbols of immortality and continuity "represents a compelling universal urge to maintain an inner sense of continuous symbolic relationships, over time and space, with the various aspects of life. In other words . . . a sense of immortality is in itself neither compensatory nor pathological, but is man's symbolization of his ties with both his biological fellows and his history, past and future" (Lifton, 1974b, p. 275). From the continuity-of-life model's point of view, man's sense of immortality is neither rational nor irrational: it is an appropriate and psychologically necessary symbolization of our biological and historical connectedness (Lifton, 1974a, 1974b). The sense of immortality reflects man's inner quest for a continuing symbolic relationship between the self and that which existed before and will continue to exist beyond the biological death of the individual. The sense of immortality finds expression in five general modes of symbolic immortality (Lifton, 1987, p. 14).

The *biological* mode is the most fundamental and universal mode of symbolic immortality, and in its most basic form involves the sense of living on in one's sons and daughters and their progeny, as well as ties to one's biological forebears. At some level of consciousness we can envision an endless succession of biological attachments to others, and the attachments stretch into the future as well as into the historical past. Because man is a cultural animal, though, the biological mode never remains entirely biological. Rather, it extends outward to encompass cultural and biosocial connections that include kinship groups, tribes, subcultures, people, races, and nations. In the broadest sense, the biological mode of symbolic immortality provides the individual with an image or idea that he can transcend death because "I live on in mankind" (Lifton, 1976, p. 32; 1983, pp. 18–20).

Within policing, the biological mode can find expression at an immediate level in what we might call the "family tradition" of policing: perhaps especially in the NYPD, many officers have parents, children, or other blood relatives who are or were members of the department, and they feel a special kind of connection to them. At a more universal and ultimate level the biosocial mode can find expression in the shared sense that all officers belong to a unique and special group that is tied together by common experiences, traditions, attitudes, and belief systems. This sense of belonging is one basis for the strong bonds and affinities within the police subculture, and it is a particularly powerful form of connection because it affords the sense that one is tied to the past and to the future through the enduring subculture.

We can see the *theological* mode in the pervasive theme, throughout world religions, of transcending the burdens of a profane or earthly existence to some sort of existence on a higher plane, usually achieved through some sort of spiritual attainment. The theological and philosophical notion of an "immortal soul" is associated with this mode of symbolic immortality. Although the belief systems of many religions involve belief in a literal afterlife of either corporeal or spiritual dimension, a more important and more universal idea is that of transcending death by achieving unity or harmony with a spiritual state: one becomes connected in some way with an eternal principle that extends beyond the self and beyond the individual biological life span. Lifton (1983, p. 20) points out that a common thread in all great world religions is the hero-founder's spiritual quest that leads to the realization of ultimate principles. These ultimate principles permit the hero-founder to confront and transcend death, providing generations of followers with a model for living one's life in a way that promises to divest death of some or all of its "sting." In many theological systems, the spiritual power that permits one to symbolically or actually transcend death comes from an affinity for some philosophical doctrine or set of ethical principles, or by living one's life according to the precepts of a faith. In the Christian tradition, Lifton (1974b, p. 276) points out, the symbolic state of possessing a spiritual power over death equates with the term *grace;* in the Japanese Shinto tradition, the idea of transcendence is linked to connectedness with others and with nature and is conveyed in the term *kami,* a complex concept that literally translates as "divinity" and refers to particular mythological creator-gods but also connotes the life force or sacredness that is implicit in all things. At the heart of all theological systems, though, there is the image or idea of an attainable spiritual energy or knowledge that in some way affords the individual a mystical or actual power over death (Lifton, 1976, p. 33; 1983, pp. 20–21; 1987, p. 14).

Another mode of symbolic immortality is achieved through *creative works* that have enduring impact or significance. This mode involves the idea that we live on or are remembered because we have had a profound or meaningful influence upon the lives or thoughts of others, or because we somehow "made a difference" in the world. One can also symbolically extend one's life and influence by undertaking or contributing to some lasting project that continues to have influence beyond one's biological death: scientists, physicians, and members of the professions, for example, experience this sense of continuity and connection by participating in a tradition or an enterprise that is larger, more enduring, and more important than the individual. While the creative mode can certainly find expression in great works of art, literature, or scientific achievement, it can also be seen in the more commonplace influences we have on people around us. The works or achievements with which we symbolically extend our life and influence need not be of enormous consequence and need not be publicly recognized for their importance, but rather they can include simple everyday acts of kindness or altruistic service that in some way carry forward in the lives of others. The urge toward philanthropic activities as well as ideas about "leaving a legacy" or making important lasting contributions to society are certainly tied up with this mode of symbolic immortality, but any form of acting upon others in a way that alters the course of another person's life span or the contours of another's self contains elements of timeless consequences (Lifton, 1974b, p. 277; 1976, p. 33; 1983, pp. 21–22; 1987, p. 15).

Police officers certainly have ample opportunity to influence (positively or negatively) the lives of others, and their participation in the ongoing enterprise of policing and the police culture includes them in a tradition that is larger, more important, and more enduring than the individual. Although some officers may be initially reticent to proclaim the value they place on altruism and unselfish public service, many or most were to some extent motivated to enter policing by a sense of idealism—the idea they could make a significant contribution to society by working to "do justice." To the extent that altruistic acts positively influence the lives of others and contribute to the betterment of society as a whole, "doing justice" offers access to this mode of symbolic immortality.

The sense of immortality can also be expressed in the theme of connectedness with eternal *nature*—embracing imagery that links the self to the enduring and limitless aspects of nature. Lifton (1974, p. 277) points out that this expression of symbolic immortality is especially pronounced and vivid in Japanese Shinto beliefs and can be glimpsed in European Romanticism, but it appears in one form or another in every culture. This mode involves the perception that the natural environment is timeless and eternal, and the idea that by our symbolic connection to it we share in these enduring elements. Because the natural environment continually renews itself through seasonal change that is representative of the cycle of life, death, and rebirth, connectedness with nature provides images of continuity and of things that are greater and more enduring than the self (Lifton, 1976, p. 33–34; 1983, pp. 22–23; 1987, p. 15).

The fifth mode of expression for symbolic immortality is the attainment of a state of *experiential transcendence*—an ecstasy or rapture so intense that one's sense of the material world, of time and place, of past and present, and of death and disintegration disappear. This euphoric state of "losing oneself" can be achieved through an intense focus on a creative process (such as creating or appreciating art, writing, or music), through athletic exertion or sexual activity, through the ecstasy of battle, through religious or secular mysticism or meditation, through drug experiences, or through any other activity that brings us to a transcendent state of extraordinary psychic unity and perceptual intensity. In many cases, achieving this transcendent state is accompanied by a process of symbolic reordering of one's life—we feel somehow different and changed and liberated after returning from such a state, and this sense of renewal may be likened to a symbolic death-and-rebirth experience. In these ecstatic states, the self feels uniquely alive and vital and centered in the moment. Importantly, the transcendent state often involves cultural or religious images of communion with others, producing an inner sense of unity and connectedness as the boundaries of the self are diminished. Once these temporal and psychological boundaries are diminished, the self is free to experience a sense of greater participation in the larger human process (Lifton, 1987, p. 15; 1976, p. 33–34; 1983, pp. 25–35).

Once again, the contemporary urban police experience provides various types of access to this mode of symbolic immortality. Many officers who find themselves engaged in mortal combat experience a kind of ecstasy, and many or most officers will at some point experience the exhilaration and the unique perceptual intensity that often accompanies other forms of physical combat. The "thrill of the chase" that typically accompanies the hot pursuit of a criminal can be a transcendent experience, as is the "adrenaline rush" of responding to an emergency or crime in progress. There can be an invigorating sense of elation or euphoria in witnessing a birth or saving a life by administering first aid, and many officers experience a sense of transcendent elation in the simple acts of integrity and decency they perform each day. Indeed, any act that provides connection to a mode of symbolic immortality can lead to an ecstatic sense of vitality.

Each of these five modes of symbolic immortality, it should be well noted, involves images of vitality, continuity, and connection to some tangible or intangible thing that is greater or more permanent than the individual self, and each mode is threatened or challenged by images of death, discontinuity, or disconnection.

The Sense of Mortality

A theory that places such great emphasis on man's sense of immortality and involves images and symbolizations of immortality, though, must also account for man's sense of *mortality:* the idea or image of death as the extinction of the biological self. Lifton accounts for the sense of mortality by describing a process in which the psychic representation of death evolves from rudimentary and relatively unformed articulation in the young organism's *inchoate imagery* and moves toward more sophisticated symbolizations in maturity.

The *inchoate image* is an innate tendency, direction, or physiological "push" that is present in the young human organism, and the undeveloped "wired-in" inchoate image involves an "interpretive anticipation of interaction with the environment." From the time of birth, the infant has innate inclinations for certain behaviors that cannot be explained by learning or by instinct. The infant "expects" to be fed, and it "knows" something about the breast and how to make use of it to enhance its own life process: it has an inchoate biological inclination to receive nourishment and is equipped with the basic images—the suckling response—necessary to act upon it (Lifton, 1983, p. 39). This unlearned knowledge and expectation of nurturance exemplifies the inchoate image: "an inborn psychobiological plan or scenario" that "determines the direction of an organism's activity and calls forth the energy necessary for that activity." As physiological and psychological development occurs through growth and maturation, sensory impressions and images add to the inchoate image, leading to increasingly complex and increasingly symbolized constellations of feeling that eventually include ideation (p. 40).

The Struggle for Vitality

Just as man struggles from the time of birth to maintain the integrity and viability of his physical organism and to avoid biological extinction through physical death, so too does man struggle psychologically to create form and to preserve a sense of the self as alive (i.e., to achieve and maintain a sense of vitality) while struggling against formlessness and a sense of the self as dead. This motivation toward the life-affirming creation of images and forms is the basis of the paradigm's emphasis on the importance of imagery and symbolizations of human continuity. This continual struggle to achieve a sense of vitality and continuity takes place simultaneously at proximate and ultimate levels. At the proximate level, the struggle involves immediate feelings and images, and at the ultimate level it has to do with symbolizing our connection to the continuity of history and biology. The two levels combine not only in the struggle to remain alive, but also in the struggle to *feel* alive.

At a proximate level, the struggle for vitality involves three polarities or subparadigms: *connection versus separation; integrity versus disintegration;* and *movement versus stasis.* Each polarity or subparadigm represents, psychologically as well as physically, a fundamental lifelong struggle to achieve vitality and wholeness while avoiding death and disintegration. When, in any or all of these polarities, the struggle to achieve images of vitality and wholeness fails or when these images are somehow unavailable, alternative images of death and disintegration arise.

Lifton calls these images of separation, disintegration, and stasis *death equivalents,* and they serve as psychic precursors and anticipatory models for the more highly symbolized images and feelings about death that will develop with maturity. These rudimentary images and death equivalents continue to develop through the formative-symbolic process and they shape death imagery throughout our life cycle. As we mature and develop the cognitive skills that give us an increased capacity for complex symbolization, images that evolve from death equivalents lead us to a more complex understanding of death (Lifton, 1983, pp. 53–72).

Each of the subparadigms, Lifton notes, progresses from

physiological inclination to enactment to inner imagery to symbolization (or psychoformation). Each takes shape initially in relation to bodily impulses and physical relationships to sources of nurturance and protection; each issues ultimately in complex adult capacities mediated by symbolization: capacities for participation in love and communal relationships, for moral and ethical commitment, and for maintaining a sense of self that includes symbolic development, growth and change. (1976, pp. 70–71)

Connection versus Separation

The struggle for connectedness and against separation first becomes evident in the infant's simple movements toward the mother and her nurturance of physical needs, but it eventually comes to involve connection with other people, attachment to groups, and affinity for ideas and historical forces: the struggle becomes a lifelong quest with emotional and psychological components. As a social animal, man seeks meaningful and satisfying human connections with others, and these connections and commitments are the basis for all sorts of affinities and social arrangements. The quest to achieve connectedness is inseparable from social and cultural life, and in many respects it underlies the sense of connectedness and comradeship felt by members of the police subculture. Similarly, the quest for connectedness ultimately extends to commitments and affinities for philosophical principles, ethical convictions, and belief systems. These affinities, too, are a source of connection and meaning that bind police officers together, and many of the convictions and belief systems are subsumed by the idea of a police personality (see, generally, Balch, 1972; Murrell et al., 1978; Smith, Locke, and Fenster, 1970; and Skolnick, 1966, 1994). Where the psychic struggle for connectedness fails or when images of connectedness are unavailable, alternative images of separation arise. These images of separation are a kind of psychological precursor for the idea of death, and they develop through the same kind of process that leads to images of connection. In the police context, images of separation also figure prominently in officers' struggles around retirement (see, generally, Raub, 1988; and Gaska, 1980).

Integrity versus Disintegration

The struggle between integrity and disintegration is, again, first manifested in physical terms in the infant and his innate fear of physiological threat. Perhaps especially in the infant, the sense of disintegration is often associated with separation and isolation, and these two subparadigms often have an extensive overlap. In early life the struggle for integrity is primarily associated with maintaining the physical integrity of the biological organism—with maintaining wholeness and avoiding physical deterioration. Although the image of physiological disintegration never loses its potency, integrity eventually takes on ethical or psychological dimensions, and we see the development of larger principles about morality and ethical integrity. Especially toward the end of the life cycle, when awareness or anticipation of actual death activates all kinds of death imagery, we see the emergence of compelling ideas and images related to the integrity of one's death—the idea, for example, that the manner and circumstances of death, as well as one's relationship with the prospect of death, should equate with the way one lived his life. We develop concerns around the image or idea of death without integrity or dignity—a death that is disintegrative because it involves elements of humiliation, incoherence, absurdity, physical deterioration, or prematurity. To the extent that one's death illuminates one's life, to imagine a death without integrity, dignity, or meaning is to see one's life in the same terms (Lifton, 1983, pp. 100–101).

Movement versus Stasis

In terms of movement and stasis, Lifton points out that an infant held so tightly that it is unable to move becomes extremely anxious and uncomfortable, and it struggles to move freely: the infant's thrashing of arms and legs are its first expressions of individuality and vitality. In early life the meaning of movement is most often the literal idea of movement from one place to another, but with maturation and development the image later takes on symbolic qualities tied to physical, emotional and intellectual development, and to progress, growth, and change. The absence of movement in either a literal or figurative sense is a form of stasis, a deathlike experience closely related to psychic numbing.

Centering, Decentering, and Grounding

In discussing the formative-symbolic process we have touched upon the idea that the self undergoes changes as new images and experiences are incorporated. This capacity for change ensures the psychic and biological survival of the self since it imparts a vitalizing sense of personal movement and growth and because it permits us to respond to new environmental conditions that could otherwise threaten our survival. This idea raises the important question of how the individual maintains the fundamental images that form the core self while avoiding too much change, too quickly. Absent the capacity for change, the self would become static and incapable of anticipating or responding to future events, but too much change could erode the fundamental contours of the self. Here the related capacities for centering, decentering, and grounding come into play.

Centering and decentering work in conjunction with each other to essentially filter and assess new images and experiences and selectively incorporate them. Centering ensures the integrity and continuity of the core self by distinguishing between images that lie at the core of the self and those that are less important, and decentering is a kind of detachment that permits the limited incorporation of images that do not serve exclusively to maintain the status quo of the core self. Decentering thus permits the individual to change, innovate, and adapt in response to a changing environment and to alter the boundaries of the self in a less permanent or less fundamental way. If we fail to maintain an appropriate flexible balance between centering and decentering, the self becomes incapable of incorporating new images and becomes static. Either radical centering or radical decentering can prevent the self from symbolizing, from moving forward in adaptation to the environment, and from feeling alive (Lifton, 1983, pp. 26–27).

Centering and decentering both depend on grounding, or the relationship of the self to its individual and collective history as well as to its physical organism, to maintain their flexible equilibrium. When grounding becomes impaired or overwhelmed—when one loses connections to his history or biology—the centering and decentering processes are disrupted. The self becomes estranged from the environment and it cannot adequately respond to it, a situation that leads to a loss of the capacity to symbolize. Lifton calls this state of impaired symbolization "psychic numbing." Psychic numbing "is characterized by various degrees of inability to feel and by gaps between knowledge and feeling. Its subjective experience need not be only that of apathy or "deadening," but can take the form of anger and rage (at those seen as responsible for the "killing" of feeling or meaning) or even guilt and shame (where one takes on the responsibility for the "murder"). Psychic numbing, as the central impairment within the formative process, can occur in association with the entire gamut of survivor experience, including that of everyday life" (Lifton, 1976, p. 79).

Psychic Numbing

Although psychic numbing involves diminished feeling and impaired symbolization, it can also result from overinclusion of stimuli when the individual is seemingly bombarded or overwhelmed by unmanageable images and emotions, as well as from real or perceived threats to the physical organism. Further, Lifton (1976, p. 79–80) points out, psychic numbing can be understood to exist along a kind of continuum: at one pole exists a debilitating and profoundly immobilizing loss of the capacity for symbolization that Lifton calls *psychic closing-off,* while at the other pole there exists a constructive kind of selective perception that Lifton calls *partial professional numbing.* When psychic closing-off occurs, the individual loses the capacity to symbolize, and images cannot adequately anticipate future events. Depending upon the circumstances surrounding the event and the potency of the threats it presents, psychic closing-off may result in complete physical and psychic immobility. The far more frequently encountered in-between forms of psychic numbing include the sort of everyday numbing that accompanies the technological distancing and bureaucratizing of human relations that are so much a part of contemporary existence.

The constructive dimension of psychic numbing—partial professional numbing—can be glimpsed in "the surgeon who operates the more skillfully for not permitting himself to feel the potential consequences of failure, the pilot who lands his plane more safely by focusing on the technical details rather than on the beauties of the sunset, or the artist who avoids certain kinds of imagery and feeling in order to give fuller expression to those he has chosen to re-create" (Lifton, 1976,

p. 80). Partial professional numbing enhances our capacity for function and symbolization by selectively blocking, managing, or failing to immediately integrate images of internal or external threats that would otherwise impair the formative process. Insofar as psychic numbing protects the self and permits the organism to continue functioning in the face of potentially immobilizing physical or psychic threat, it is not always a bad thing (Lifton, 1976, pp. 78–80).

The psychological responses and experiences of the survivor—the individual who has had a close physical or psychic confrontation with death but remained alive—can scarcely be understood without a discussion of psychic numbing and especially of its more extreme form, psychic closing-off. Contemporaneous with a profoundly threatening event or image, the survivor experiences a debilitating loss of the capacity to symbolize, and often the simultaneous loss of the capacity to fully experience emotion. In the face of profound threat, the survivor experiences a kind of temporary separation of the affective and cognitive components of the self—the affective or emotional components become suppressed or extremely diminished, but to a large extent the cognitive or intellectual components continue to operate. This temporary suppression of affective elements is quite functional, insofar as it permits the individual to react and to deal cognitively with the threat-inducing situation that might otherwise result in his injury or demise, without the interference of potentially overwhelming emotions. At some point after the threat subsides, the affective and cognitive components reintegrate, often resulting in a flood of images and emotional energy. The more debilitating forms of psychic numbing are invariably tied to trauma and threat, and in this regard numbing is the desymbolizing center of the survivor's experience.

Psychic numbing, then, is bound up in desensitization, the breakdown or impairment of the symbolizing function, and a reduced capacity to experience a sense of vitality. When these connections to vitalizing images and forms are lost or impaired, alternative images of stasis, disintegration, and separation arise. Because psychic numbing involves so many aspects of breakdown in the symbolization process as well as the rudimentary images that are the psychic precursors of death imagery, the more extreme states of psychic numbing are in themselves "death equivalents."[4]

Numbing and Dissociation

Psychology has long recognized that dissociation or psychic numbing is a complex neuropsychological process in which a disturbance or alteration occurs in the normally integrative functions of identity, memory, or awareness. Theorists of various schools and systems have also recognized that the extent or depth of the dissociative response runs along a continuum ranging from the normal everyday experience of intently focusing on an event or activity to the exclusion of other stimuli (getting "lost" in a book, for example, or being so caught up in an activity that time seems to "fly away") to the most profound and permanent kind of dissociative disorders.

Pierre Janet was the first psychological theorist to systematically study dissociation, and in 1989 he asserted that it is a crucial defensive process with which the organism protects itself from potentially overwhelming trauma (Putnam, 1989). When frightening or novel experiences do not fit into the existing cognitive schemes or frameworks, Janet theorized, memories of the experience are split off from conscious awareness and voluntary control. Fragments of these unintegrated events, Janet said, may later show up as involuntary pathological "automatisms"—actions, behaviors, or psychological events that are triggered by ideas and accompanied by emotions (van der Kolk and van der Hart, 1989; van der Kolk and Fisher, 1995).

Janet articulated some important and enduring observations about the nature of dissociation and its links to trauma, noting that "traumas produce their disintegrating effects in proportion to their intensity, duration and repetition," and that a significant period of time may elapse between the traumatic event and its full-blown psychopathological expression (van der Kolk and van der Hart, 1989, p. 1532).[5] Janet also pointed out that the relative severity of a traumatic event's immediate and lasting impact depends in part on one's capacity to cognitively integrate the events, which in turn depends upon temperament and prior experience, the novelty of the situation, the speed of events, and the individual's physical state at the time the traumatic event is experienced. Arousal, intoxication, fatigue, depression, and other physiological or emotional states thus influence the cognitive appraisal of the situation, its integration in the memory system, and its lasting impact (van der Kolk and van der Hart, 1989, p. 1533).

Janet's contributions continue to inform contemporary perspectives on the nature and treatment of dissociative disorders (Putnam, 1989), and they bear upon Lifton's concept of psychic numbing. Both Lifton and Janet agree, in substance, that an adaptive psychological process involving the separation of cognition and emotion takes place in the face of overwhelming psychic threat, and both agree that this diminution of feeling can give rise to subsequent patterns of withdrawal, depression, apathy, and despair.

Trauma, Numbing, and Perception

In summarizing a broad body of research on trauma and dissociation, Charles Marmar (1997) notes the clear relationship between previous traumatic life experiences and a general propensity for dissociative response: those who have had especially traumatic life experiences continue to demonstrate a propensity for dissociative responses even in situations that might not otherwise induce dissociation. In line with Lifton's model, one might say that prior experiences with death trauma (and the constellations of death imagery they provide) make psychic numbing (and death-equivalent states) more readily available to the survivor. Marmar also notes that trauma victims often report alterations in their experience of time, place, and person, conferring a sense of unreality to the event as it is occurring. He terms these acute dissociative responses to trauma as the event is taking place "peritraumatic dissociation," noting that they may "take the form of altered time sense, with time being experienced as slowing down or rapidly accelerated; profound feelings of unreality that the event is occurring, or that the individual is the victim of the event; experiences of depersonalization; out-of-body experiences; bewilderment, confusion, and disorientation; altered pain perception; altered body images or feelings of disconnection from one's body; tunnel vision; and other experiences reflecting dissociative responses to trauma" (p. 1).

It should be well noted that each of these dissociative phenomena can be seen in terms of impaired symbolization. Marmar goes on to note that "emergency services personnel with less work experience, more vulnerable personality structures, higher subjective levels of perceived threat and anxiety at the time of incidence occurrence, greater reliance on the external world for an internal sense of safety and security, and greater use of maladaptive coping strategies are more vulnerable to peritraumatic dissociation" (1997, p. 2). Marmar's (1997) observations echo those of Reiser and Geiger (1984), who applied this concept more specifically to police. Recognizing the functional nature of the dissociative process among police officers involved in highly traumatic situations, Reiser and Geiger note that officers often experience a powerful traumatic reality as if they were dreaming or watching a movie. They assert that during deadly force encounters and other traumatic incidents, police officers "often experience perceptual changes that are a function of shifting into an altered state of consciousness. This shift can affect all five senses, especially sight, hearing, and touch. It can also affect one's perception of time. Moving into an altered state of consciousness affords the officer a protective mechanism that enables him or her to react and perform in ways not possible in the normal state of perceiving and reacting" (p. 318). Among the perceptual effects Reiser and Geiger described as typical are the development of "tunnel vision" or the narrowing of the visual perceptive field, distortions in hearing, and a "slow-motion effect" they assert occurs to about 50 to 60% of officers involved in shooting incidents. This perceived slowing of time is functional insofar as it makes more reaction time available to the officer, allowing greater concentration and a heightened capacity to focus cognitive attention in an objectively narrow time frame.

Reiser and Geiger do not speculate about the specific psychological processes underlying these perceptual distortions, but the formative-symbolic model suggests they result from impaired symbolization and the related functional suppression of the affective components of the self in the face of trauma. In each of these perceptual phenomena, the distractions of emotion are absent or severely diminished, permitting the individual to cognitively focus his attention on the business of ensuring survival. In terms of surviving these and other real or perceived threats to the viability of the organism, the functional nature of psychic numbing and affective dissociation is quite clear. But as we will see, less extensive numbing and partial distancing can accompany many other kinds of less threatening situations police officers face and can be quite beneficial.

Regardless of his assignment or role, the police officer's capacity to perform his required duties with minimal emotional distraction and minimal psychic cost is quite functional on both a personal and professional plane. As I have argued elsewhere (Henry, 1995), partial professional numbing permits the officer to maintain his composure in the face of adversity and chaos—a quality thought to inspire public confidence—and the distancing of emotion endows the officer with a certain "edge" or degree of situational control in dangerous or threatening situations. As importantly, partial professional numbing permits the officer to maintain the *appearance* of composure—the kind of impassive and depersonalized professional demeanor that, in the extreme, is perhaps best illustrated by the stereotypic "just the facts, ma'am" attitude of the *Dragnet* television series' fictional Sergeant Joe Friday. On a personal level, the distancing of emotion can help prevent burnout from the cumulative effects of the emotions the officer encounters on a daily basis.

Numbing and the Psychology of Survival

The processes of psychic numbing, dissociation, and desensitization are essential to our understanding of the formative-symbolic paradigm and our understanding of the impact of death encounters in policing. This is so not merely because psychic numbing, dissociation, and desensitization impair the formative-symbolic process of symbolization, but also because that impairment lies at the very core of survivor psychology. Psychic numbing is one of the five themes of survivor psychology, and the other themes are closely associated with the numbing, dissociation, and desensitization the survivor inevitably experiences in the face of a traumatic death event. When faced with such potentially overwhelming death-related trauma, the numbed survivor "initially undergoes a radical but temporary diminution in his sense of actuality in order to avoid losing that sense completely and permanently; he undergoes a reversible form of symbolic death in order to avoid a permanent physical or psychic death," and this diminution of the capacity to process viable new images is neither voluntary nor conscious (Lifton, 1967, p. 500). Although the extreme form of psychic closing-off that takes place in the face of profound threat may be temporary, less acute forms of psychic numbing eventually become chronic and take on more permanent features of depersonalization, insensitivity, and an impaired capacity to think and feel.

The survivor is never quite free of residual numbing, since each of the other themes of survivor psychology continues to evoke and reinforce a numbed response. Psychic numbing may begin as a defense against the psychic trauma presented by threats in the immediate environment, but it is not so selective that the survivor is numbed only to those immediate threats: if the threats are sufficiently compelling, numbing spills over into other areas of the survivor's life. Numbing inundates the survivor, characterizes his entire lifestyle, and overshadows virtually every aspect of his existence to the extent that he may no longer feel fully connected to the social world around him (Lifton, 1967, p. 500). Among survivors of extreme death encounters, Lifton finds a "pervasive tendency toward sluggish despair—a more or less permanent form of psychic numbing that includes diminished vitality, chronic depression, and constricted life space, and which covers the rage and mistrust that are just below the surface" (1967, p. 504).

There can also be circumstances in which the survivor confronts an immediate image of such extraordinary horror, destruction, grotesqueness, and devastation that there are no existing psychic forms and images with which it might connect. These images are, literally, unimaginable and incomprehensible. While events of this dimension (that is to say, events presenting images for which absolutely no images or forms are available for connection) invoke the same kind of psychic paralysis and inaction as relatively less extraordinary events (i.e., events in which psychic images and forms are available but connection with them is radically impaired), they are not typically part of the police officer's everyday world. Generally speaking, in fact, the contemporary urban police officer is equipped with a range of images, forms, constellations, and anticipatory models for many of the "ordinary" death events he may encounter. Because of his training, experience, and general understanding of the nature of police work—especially an acute awareness that he may face the threat of assault and/or be called upon to use deadly physical force—the police officer can easily conceive of these death encounters and usually has at least rudimentary anticipatory plans for dealing with them. This is not to say that the police officer's forms and images of potential death encounters are realistic, accurate or fully formed or that his anticipatory models are entirely viable and appropriate to all situations he may encounter. The fundamental problem for the police officer lies not so much in the absence of adequate forms and models, but in the more universal human difficulty of connecting with and adequately enacting them.

The police officer who witnesses the death or severe injury of a partner during a gunfight, for example, is confronted with an immediate traumatic image combining horror at the situation, profound fear for his own personal safety, and compassion for his partner, as well as an immediate plan for action. The plan for action contained within the immediate image might consist of an urge to render aid to his partner, to neutralize the threat to his own personal safety, or to undertake some other action or combination of actions the anticipatory model prescribes, but the circumstances and perhaps the overriding demand to ensure his own physical survival may preclude full actualization of the anticipatory plan. The officer can ill afford emotional feelings of compassion or rage that might distract him or increase his vulnerability to the threat, and because of numbing he does not in fact experience those emotions. Nor, because of numbing, can the officer fully connect the immediate image to preexisting images and forms, and he is therefore unable to fully actualize the emotional and cognitive components of the anticipatory models they might otherwise provide. Instead, attention and cognition are narrowly focused on the event and on surviving it. Although the officer may deal cognitively with the situation and therefore remain alive, at that time he feels nothing and perhaps does nothing for his partner. Neither the emotional elements of the immediate image nor the emotional elements of its anticipatory plan for action are fully enacted.

At some point after physically surviving the encounter, once the traumatic imagery and the threat have subsided, psychic numbing abates and the individual once again connects to his historical self, to preexisting images and forms, and to the anticipatory models they contain. The affective and cognitive components of the self reintegrate, and the vitalizing process of creating and integrating images and forms resumes, albeit in an impaired fashion. With the resumption of the symbolizing process comes a renewed quest for vitality, connection, movement, and integrity, and that quest may take on special urgency or salience. At that point, although the survivor has physically lived through the encounter, he inevitably recognizes the disjuncture between the actions he has taken or not taken and the anticipatory model's ultimate demands for action. More important, perhaps, the survivor recognizes the ethical and moral disjuncture between what he *should have* felt and was actually felt. One inevitably comes to feel "responsible for what one has not done, for what one has not felt, and above all for the gap between the physical and psychic inactivation and what one felt called upon . . . to do and feel" (Lifton, 1983, p. 171). This sense of responsibility is the source of an enduring death guilt.

The survivor also retains an extraordinarily powerful and indelible image or death imprint of the encounter—an image that keeps resurfacing in dreams and in waking life precisely because it has never been adequately integrated or completely enacted. The survivor continues to replay the image of the death encounter, perhaps attempting to reexamine the situation or scenario and find a more acceptable and less blameworthy enactment in an attempt to expiate his sense of guilt and responsibility.

The Death Imprint

This indelible and enduring death imprint is another of the five themes of survivor psychology, and it is closely associated with guilt at having survived while others died. The death imprint is an intrusive and durable image that continues to evoke and reactivate other images and feelings associated with the death encounter as the survivor struggles to master and integrate it. The struggle for mastery of the death imprint is further complicated by the fact that it also conjures and reactivates images and feelings associated with prior death encounters and with earlier death equivalent states. When the death imprint results from a traumatic death encounter involving an extreme or protracted exposure or a particularly absurd or grotesque death, it can be practically impossible to master and integrate. Lifton also stresses the subjective impact of personal vulnerability to death imagery due to previous death encounters and preexisting images of separation, stasis, and disintegration, but says that this relative vulnerability is simply a matter of degree: if the threat or trauma is sufficiently great, it can produce an enduring death imprint in anyone (Lifton, 1983, p. 169–170).

The death imprint is closely tied to death guilt, but it also involves continuing struggles to resolve the important questions and integrate the ultimate meanings raised through the death encounter. The survivor's extreme death immersion reactivates prior images and constellations of separation, stasis and disintegration, shatters his magical sense of invulnerability, and challenges his sense of immortality at a profound level. The survivor's connection to any or all of the five modes of symbolic immortality may be challenged, and part of his ongoing struggle involves reconnecting to these modes in order to recapture and reinforce the damaged sense of immortality. The survivor is therefore confronted with a compelling need to reconstruct all these forms and constellations in a way that reasserts vitality and integrity and restores some sense of immortality, but that need can never be entirely or adequately fulfilled. The survivor has a sense that the death imprint has forever changed him, and at some level of awareness feels irrevocably tainted by death.

This "death taint" derives not only from the survivor's perception of himself as permanently imbued with or possessed by death, but from others' irrational anxiety that death's corruption is somehow contagious. Although the survivor of a profound death immersion poses no actual threat of "infecting" others with death, the notion of death's contagion takes on its symbolic qualities simply because others associate him with the same raft of fears and anxieties that possess the survivor: "fear of death, particularly of violent and premature death, of symbolic world breakdown, and of the loss of human connection and the sense of immortality. The essence of contagion anxiety is 'If I touch him, or come too close, I will experience his death and his annihilation'" (Lifton, 1967, p. 518).

The death imprint imparts a lifelong sense of vulnerability to death and to death imagery, but that vulnerability can take one of two separate paths or polarities. On the one hand, the survivor experience can heighten and intensify one's sense of vulnerability to death and death imagery, since the survivor's profound encounter with his own mortality shatters important protective illusions of personal invulnerability and replaces them with a penetrating awareness of death's reality and inevitability. This sense of heightened vulnerability often permeates the survivor's entire worldview, and it may include an acute sensitivity to death-equivalent states of stasis, separation, and disintegration. It may also include an acute sensitivity to images, experiences, and feelings associated with death.

At the other pole is a sense of reinforced invulnerability derived from a sense of having conquered death—a sense that the survivor, like the classic hero of myth, has encountered, been immersed in, and overcome death, returning with a special knowledge or mastery of death that is not available within the realm of "ordinary" human experience. The survivor is set apart from "ordinary" society by dint of his intimate knowledge and supposed mastery of death's mysteries. This sense of reinforced invulnerability, though, can be quite fragile and because it does not involve true mastery can easily revert to the state of heightened vulnerability it tends to mask (Lifton, 1970, pp. 481–482).

Because mastery of the death imprint can never be achieved through full and appropriate enactment, the survivor remains in its thrall and becomes subject to subsequent symbolic reactivations. Exposure to death equivalents or to images and experiences that are specifically reminiscent of either the profound death encounter or of earlier death-related experiences can easily trigger intrusive imagery and feelings related to the survivor experience—what some have called "flashbacks."

The indelible image can take the form of a single horrible image that encapsulates the totality of the death event and evokes intense guilt feelings, and because the survivor may not be able to move beyond the image (i.e., achieve some form of appropriate enactment), he may become "stuck" in a static pattern of guilt and psychological incapacity that eventually leads to traumatic neurosis. The indelible image may also encapsulate the trauma of the event in the form of a relatively benign image that is related to or part of the event, but at the same time seems collateral to its horror. These "screen images" or "screen memories" are nonetheless indelible, but they function to shield the survivor from even more painful images and feeling-states. Some survivors, though, find some sort of alternative enactment for the haunting image, and the pursuit of alternative enactment may become a vehicle for personal transformation and moral growth.

Death Guilt

Death guilt is an inevitable consequence of every survival experience in which one person dies before another, since this sequence implicates the unconscious notion of survival priority—that one's own life was somehow purchased at the cost of another's. The survivor's question—"Why did I survive while another died?"—has an ethical corollary: "What right have I to live while another is dead?" In a larger sense, death guilt involves the feeling that the survivor is somehow responsible for the death of another because of his own inaction, and his feelings of self-condemnation can be exacerbated by the moral conflict of feeling relief or joy at having himself survived. Death guilt can be compounded and reinforced when the circumstances of the death encounter provide the survivor with rational or factual reasons to believe his inaction may have led to the death of another, or at least with well-founded doubts that he may have contributed to it in some way. Perhaps the single most carefully documented case study of this dynamic can be found in Wambaugh's (1973) *The Onion Field*, a nonfiction work that relates the experience of a Los Angeles police officer whose sense of responsibility for his partner's murder was exacerbated by his department's response.

Whether or not he is plagued by rational doubts about his complicity in the death, the survivor feels he has no right to be alive and no right to experience vitality until some adequate and appropriate sort of enactment is achieved, and he may avoid vitalizing mental or physical activities (Lifton, 1983, p. 171). At the same time, the survivor feels the need to overcome his impairment and devitalization by reestablishing life-affirming connections, and he may experience an ambivalent lifelong struggle between the alternative polarities of embracing or rejecting vitalizing activities and relationships.

The process of identification with the dead—of putting oneself in the dead person's situation and imagining what he did or what he might think, feel, and act—can also compound death guilt. Guilt and shame are always bound up in issues of connection to others and in what one ethically should or should not do and feel as a result of that connection, so identification seems a natural consequence of the need to reestablish viable forms of human connection. In identifying with the dead, the survivor feels himself to be dead, condemns himself for not being dead, and condemns himself even more for being relieved that he is not dead (Lifton, 1970, p. 496).

Psychic numbing, death guilt, and impaired symbolization are also at the core of two other themes of survivor psychology: *suspicion of counterfeit nurturance* and the survivor's *quest to make meaning* of the death encounter. Both these themes are tied up in the survivor's struggle to reexperience himself as a vital human being (Lifton, 1983, p. 176).

Suspicion of Counterfeit Nurturance

Because numbing, guilt, and a sense of overall devitalization infiltrate every aspect of the survivor's life, he develops special needs and special vulnerabilities. The specific needs and special vulnerabilities take different forms depending upon the individual and the circumstances under which the death encounter took place, but they invariably involve the need for emotional comfort and support and may include the need for some sort of physical assistance as well. Numbing and devitalization, though, also impair the survivor's capacity to develop and maintain the kind of satisfying relationships that might otherwise provide emotional comfort and restore a needed sense of vitality, and this is especially true of the important human relationships that involve a great deal of emotional intimacy and trust. Moreover, the survivor's sense of victimization and the feeling that he is tainted by death create severe conflicts over autonomy and dependency and make him particularly sensitive to actions or events that remind him of his weakness.

The survivor, possessed of a strong sense of guilt and an acute awareness of his own vulnerabilities, becomes noticeably "touchy." This "touchiness," which may become manifest in a host of behaviors ranging from extreme withdrawal to explosive anger, presents yet another obstacle to establishing satisfying human relationships since those around the survivor must tread carefully in order not to provoke him. In the case of a profound or severe death immersion, the survivor's impairments, dependencies, and weaknesses become a permanent feature of his life and his lifestyle. The survivor ultimately comes to feel abandoned and misunderstood when those with whom he seeks satisfying and vitalizing relationships either cannot or do not provide adequate comfort and sustenance. Depending upon the extent of the survivor's impairment and the scope of his special needs, it may be practically impossible for others to ever completely fulfill these needs.

Lifton calls this theme of sensitivity to one's own vulnerabilities and the concomitant resentment of offers of help that remind him of his weakness *suspicion of counterfeit nurturance*. The survivor, tainted by death and haunted by the indelible image and the feelings of guilt it repeatedly conjures, resents and comes to suspect the legitimacy of offers of help because they confirm his tainted self-image, his weakness and lack of autonomy, and his overall devitalization.

The survivor struggles with a set of seemingly contradictory attitudes that comprise an unmanageable catch-22 situation: on the one hand, he seeks affirmation and acknowledgment of his status as one transformed by the death encounter, while at the same time he resents overtures that reactivate his sense of guilt, dependency, and continued devitalization. If offers of help and assistance are not forthcoming or if requests for help are not fulfilled, he feels the rejection is due to his survivor status and the death taint it conveys. He feels abandoned, devalued, and misunderstood. If others *do* respond to his special needs, though, he sees the offer of nurturance as inauthentic and ultimately unfulfilling because it again confirms his weakness, dependency, and death taint: he feels abandoned to the manifestations of a narrow victim identity. By confirming his survivor status and survivor identity, these offers of nurturance magnify his dependency, reaffirming his separateness and fundamental devitalization. The basic conflict, Lifton observes, is intrinsic to any form of victimization: "the victim inevitably feels himself in need of special sustenance, which, when received, intensifies his 'victim consciousness' and thereby perpetuates a vicious circle of counterfeit nurturance and abandonment. Nurturing offered threatens to isolate the victim and further undermines his self-esteem, but the humiliating temptation to accept it is always there" (Lifton, 1969, p. 194).

Closely related to the survivor's predisposition toward viewing others suspiciously are his identification with death and his tendency to form an identity around death and victimization. Lifton calls the more extreme forms of victim consciousness "survivor paranoia," noting that images and feelings of victimization can become entwined with feelings of profound rage at having been rendered helpless. By projecting this rage and sense of complete victimization onto the "enemies" surrounding him (for example, those who do not or cannot provide authentic nurturance) the survivor can at once express vitality as well as an acceptable sense of himself as victim. This does not, of course, resolve the survivor's struggle, since projected rage presents yet another obstacle in his quest for authentic, satisfying, and vitalizing human relationships.

Suspicion of counterfeit nurturance also explains the survivor's intolerance for evasiveness, equivocation, and broken promises. This intolerance can easily translate into a sense that the survivor has been betrayed by those around him, especially when offered nurturance fails to materialize or is insufficient, or when others refuse to recognize the survivor's special status. This theme is quite pronounced in the narratives of Vietnam veterans, and it was evident among the police officers I interviewed. Many officers who experienced a profound death encounter came to resent the medals conferred upon them and the unfulfilled promises made to them by ranking department officials.

Another significant impediment to the development and maintenance of satisfying relationships that comfort and sustain the survivor's special needs is his death taint and the fear of contagion it conveys to others. Throughout history, survivors who have been seen as contagious "carriers" of death's supernatural evil have often been subject to outright hostility, although subtler forms of real or perceived resentment are more common. Lifton notes (1967, p. 520), for example, that while Jewish survivors of Nazi persecution are frequently asked the question, "Why didn't you fight?" the question is often unconsciously interpreted as "Why didn't you die?" Beyond the fact that such specific questions about the death encounter are likely to reactivate the survivor's sense of death guilt and his entire constellation of death imagery, it is clear that the fear of death's contagion (as well as, admittedly, a naive or prurient interest in the death event) often causes others to raise issues that reinforce the survivor's doubts about his right to be alive, undermine his fragile self-esteem, or otherwise exacerbate his struggles. In terms of the latent hostility they subsume and the extent to which they illuminate the survivor's devitalization and special needs, these issues clearly impede the development of nurturing relationships.

The struggle around death taint and contagion anxiety may lead to what Lifton calls *survivor hubris:* a tendency to embrace and reify his "special knowledge" of death to the point of rendering it sacred. The survivor's efforts to reinforce this potent and vitalizing sense of power over death can result in a fascination for death or a passionate craving for the process of survival (Lifton, 1967, p. 521). In a quest to restore and hold on to a sense of symbolic immortality, the survivor may draw upon images of death and destruction and his sense of power over them to create a compelling fantasy of eternal survival—the survivor may imagine himself indestructible and engage in recurring close flirtations with various forms of death. Survivor hubris and the fantasy of eternal survival may become manifest in the survivor's pursuit of dangerous or potentially life-threatening activities that evince a preoccupation with death and destruction, leading to repeated engagement in extremely risky or dangerous activities—what one might term, in the common parlance, a "death wish."

The survivor's tendency to embrace and reify death is also related to the pattern of *survivor exclusiveness,* or an absolute distinction on the part of survivors between those elites who have touched and been touched by death and those who have not. The survivor's sense of exclusiveness emanates from his conviction that in possessing a unique knowledge of death, he and other survivors possess the highest and purest form of experiential knowledge. There is a certain power and vitality in this costly and hard-earned possession of knowledge, as well as in the perception that in the eyes of others this special knowledge renders survivors the untouchable bearers of death and death taint. Survivor exclusiveness binds the survivor to others who possess the same knowledge and who have had a similar set of experiences at the same time it underscores the survivor's distinctiveness and isolation from those who have not. The survivor's own sense of contagion and death taint therefore reinforces his exclusiveness (Lifton, 1967, p. 524).

The Quest to Make Meaning

The fifth and final psychological theme of survival is the survivor's lifelong struggle to restore some sense of coherence and order to the world his death encounter has rendered absurd. The survivor's *quest to make meaning* of his death encounter and its aftermath seeks an equilibrium or mastery of death that will in some way permit him to return to the familiar world of the living—to the kind of ordered symbolic universe he experienced before the death encounter. Once again, impaired formulation, death guilt, and the quest for renewed vitality are involved in the struggle, as is the survivor's acute sensitivity to the counterfeit and to matters of hypocrisy. In his quest for formulation and meaning, the survivor seeks redress for the wrongs committed against him through recognition that he and others have suffered, through the identification and proper punishment of those responsible for it, and through some sort of reparative action that will at least partially restore his sense of vitality and help make his tainted victim identity more acceptable. In formulating a new identity that incorporates the death encounter and at the same time permits him to experience a sense of vitality, the survivor must first understand and attribute causality to the absurd event that has so devitalized him. The survivor may, for example, dwell or focus upon the death event in a seemingly obsessive way, struggling all the while to reconstruct and understand its absurdity in a coherent way. At least part of the survivor's sense of victimization stems from the fact that numbing, at the time of the death encounter and afterward, deprives him of the capacity for understanding *why* he was victimized through traumatic exposure to death. In the kind of ordered universe the survivor seeks, everything has a reason or cause, and the survivor's attempt to understand why he has lived and why others have died compels him to seek a rational explanation for the circumstances leading up to the encounter.

In this quest to make meaning of the death encounter, survivors may be consumed with a compelling urge for justice. The kind of justice the survivor seeks, though, extends beyond simple acknowledgment of the wrongs committed against him and punishment for those who perpetrated them to include the restoration of a morally ordered world in which his suffering can be made comprehensible to himself and to others. In their quest for justice and meaning, survivors demand that others appreciate both their victimization and the moral absurdity of their experience.

Two manifestations of the quest to make meaning are the survivor's tendency to scapegoat or focus blame exclusively on the person or groups perceived as responsible for his victimization, and the will to bear witness about the death event and the moral wrongs committed against them. Both manifestations give meaning to the survivor's experience, both tend to expunge residual death guilt, and both are a source of vitality.

The survivor's conflicts can easily lead to scapegoating, in which he seeks to relieve or externalize his own guilt by focusing it exclusively on a particular person, group, or symbol. In some cases the circumstances of the death encounter lend themselves to the legitimate placement of blame on the person or persons factually responsible for the survivor's sense of victimization, while in other instances resentment is irrationally focused on targets that are entirely symbolic or at least somewhat removed from legitimate factual responsibility. In either case, the tendency toward scapegoating emerges from the survivor's struggle between internal and external blaming, giving him the opportunity to express his guilty outrage and become less of a victim by victimizing or vilifying others. Scapegoating also permits the survivor to confer an element of order and causality to his understanding of the death event. In this regard, the tendency toward scapegoating and fixing blame is functional and adaptive. Lifton observes that "the more closely these scapegoating tendencies attach themselves to the actuality of events, the better the survivor's chance to transcend them, or at least combine them with more inclusive approaches. What the survivor seeks from his scapegoating formulation is the reassuring unconscious message that 'You, and not I, are responsible for the others' death and my suffering, so that I have a right to be alive after all.' It is a message that he can neither fully believe nor entirely cease to reassert" (1967, p. 531).

Because scapegoating never completely expurgates the survivor's death guilt and because its guilty anger can be difficult to sustain, it can readily disintegrate into an amorphous bitterness that once again impedes the development of vitalizing relationships. The survivor, angry with everyone and everything, can become mired in an existence characterized by absurdity, guilt, and rage. This static rage can prevent his reconnection with the kinds of connection, movement, and integrity that are necessary to recapture the feeling of vitality and the sense of immortality. By channeling his indignation and rage into a constructive project, though, the survivor can find meaning, purpose, and significance for his existence, reestablish some moral order to his world, and achieve some sense of vitality. Hence the survivor's universal and compelling quest to bear witness to the traumatic event and to the wrongs committed against him and others.

The impulse to bear witness, which often begins with a sense of responsibility to the dead and may involve elements of scapegoating, "can easily translate into a *'survivor mission'*—a lasting commitment to a project that extracts significance from absurdity, vitality from massive death" (Lifton, 1980, p. 123). In contrast to static rage, involvement in the survivor mission is vitalizing precisely because it permits access to forms of connection, movement, and integrity: the mission creatively joins the individual with others in an common cause or ongoing crusade in which ethical and moral issues are a primary focus. When the survivor mission takes on the characteristics of a moral crusade—an ongoing endeavor that is larger and more important than the individual—the mission also provides some access to the creative mode of symbolic immortality. Moreover, the survivor mission permits the survivor to recapture some self-esteem by reformulating a self-identity in which death taint, death guilt, and the traumatic death experience are meaningful and significant.

The survivor mission may include such common practices as establishing memorial foundations or endowing charitable trusts, the involvement of crime victims in political campaigns to rectify perceived inadequacies in the law, or a host of other activities that seek to carry on the victim's life work or complete some worthwhile endeavor in which the victim was involved. The survivor mission can involve any activities that operate psychologically both to honor the life of the victim and to concretely reify a tragic death into a vehicle that reclaims or sustains some noble, humane, and life-affirming purpose. Whatever form their survivor mission takes, though, survivors seek to achieve a kind of personal transformation by restoring a lost sense of order and meaning to their world. In time, the quest to find meaning through the survivor mission may seem to lose some of its urgency as the self-identity is reformulated and the sense of order and meaning is restored, or as the specific goals they set out to achieve come to fruition. Although survivors may eventually devote less time and effort to the mission, they remain forever sensitive to the moral and ethical issues involved.[6]

The survivor mission can take many forms in the context of policing, and we will explore them in subsequent chapters. The scope and direction of police survivor missions are shaped by many factors, but once again they tend to reflect the unique concerns of the police subculture and the social demands of the police role. We can see some aspects of the survivor mission in the profound commitment some officers have to finding a kind of justice for certain victims, and especially in the tendency among some homicide detectives to develop a kind of fixation with a particularly meaningful case and to continue pursuing the investigation long after other cases have taken precedence (see, for example, Sudetic, 1995; Gourevitch, 2000; James, 1992; Hampson, 1994).

Up to this point, this chapter has presented a basic overview of the formative-symbolic paradigm and the psychology of survival, pointing out some general examples of how these principles apply in contemporary urban policing. Despite my best attempts to introduce them in a simplified way, the theoretical principles set forth here may initially appear to be fairly intricate or complex. In truth, they *are* intricate and complex because they deal with very complicated and fundamental issues of human psychology. The cognitive models we use to organize our understanding of any phenomena can appear, at first glance, to be complex and unwieldy, but much of our inability to fully grasp them derives from our lack of familiarity with them and from our inability to immediately apply or evaluate them in the context of real-world experience. When we do, in fact, apply theories or paradigms to real-world phenomena we often find that both the cognitive models and the phenomena make much more sense. As I have noted, my strategy in presenting the formative-symbolic paradigm and psychology of survival in this way is to give the reader a basic acquaintance with them; they will be amplified and made more comprehensible as we begin to explore police officers' death-related experiences.

Before we begin to explore or analyze those experiences, though, it is necessary to understand how the data were obtained. The remainder of this chapter therefore briefly sets out the methodological strategies I used to access and collect data about officers' death-related experiences.

The Strategy of Inquiry

The exploration of any set of issues and phenomena as complex and multifaceted as those considered here—the individual and collective psychological features and transformations resulting from police officers' death encounters—demands a rigorous and multifaceted approach or method of inquiry. The nature of this study, as well as the broad range of intertwined social, cultural, and psychological issues it encompasses, requires a data collection strategy or method that is simultaneously rigorous and flexible. The strategy I used to excavate and explore the data combined an eclectic review of the research literature of survivor psychology and the literature of police and other death work occupations with a series of structured and unstructured interviews with police officers, as well as with unobtrusive participant observation activities and some analysis of quantitative data obtained from NYPD records and sources. The range of social, cultural, and psychological issues involved, along with the fact that this study seeks to illuminate death's impact on police at the individual, group, cultural, and organizational levels, collectively defy any attempt to locate the research within a single academic discipline.

This study is primarily psychological in its orientation, but the psychological features involved are influenced and mediated by many social and cultural factors, and they must therefore be considered in light of principles derived from sociology and cultural anthropology. The death encounters that are the focus of this research take place within a criminal justice setting, specifically that of a major metropolitan police organization, so organizational demands also play a role in mediating officers' experiences. The psychological transformations and adaptive themes explored here certainly affect the officer's sense of self and his worldview, and to a significant extent they also affect the officer's social interactions with others inside and outside the police culture. These interactions include relations with other officers, with family and friends, and with members of the public. The academic literature supporting the theoretical and practical research issues is therefore drawn from several disciplines, including psychology, psychiatry, sociology, anthropology, criminal justice, and organizational behavior. The complexity of the issues involved and the constellation of psychological, social, cultural, organizational, environmental, and individual variables they implicate therefore require a comprehensive and flexible method of inquiry.

Multiple Methods, Reliability, and Validity

One strength of a multifaceted method of inquiry in qualitative research is that it lends itself to triangulation of data sources and methods of inquiry, a process that enhances the reliability and validity of the data as well as the research findings proceeding from them (Brinberg and McGrath, 1985; Kirk and Miller, 1986). Triangulation, in this sense, refers not to the use of three methods, per se, but to the practice of approaching the same fact or data from multiple angles or points of view. As Webb, Campbell, Schwartz, and Sechrest (1966, p. 173) have pointed out, the problem with using a single research method or approach is that "no research method is without bias. Interviews and questionnaires must be supplemented by methods testing the same social science variables but having *different* methodological weaknesses" (p. 1; italics in original). They also observe that the "most fertile search for validity comes from a combined series of different measures, each with its idiosyncratic weaknesses, each pointed to a single hypothesis. When a hypothesis can survive the confrontation of a series of complimentary methods of testing, it contains a degree of validity unattainable by one tested within the more constricted framework of a single method" (Webb et al., 1966, p. 174).

In triangulating, the researcher focuses on the same phenomena from a variety of perspectives and in doing so exploits the best and most productive elements of each method. Triangulation of sources and methods permits researchers to develop especially rich, robust, and conceptually dense data. Conceptual density, in turn, often points up relationships between variables in a way that single-method analysis simply cannot, concurrently giving essential context to the phenomena. The relative complexities of integrating several methods and the quest for objectivity, though, make it incumbent upon the researcher to provide an especially comprehensive discussion of the overall research process and of the way each method was used to generate and assess data.

Interviews were the primary means of data collection in this study, and the specific interview format and method of administration was based on the interview style Lifton used in his explorations of similar death-related issues. No matter the method of collection, though, all the data were analyzed using Lifton's continuity-of-life and psychology of survival models, and Lifton's "shared themes" approach was taken. This incorporation of Lifton's interview style, approach, and perspective is entirely appropriate given the fact that they derive from the same set of interrelated theoretical bases and assumptions (Strozier and Flynn, 1992) and have been successfully utilized in other studies of death-related matters, including a study of police death encounters (Henry, 1995).

The interview data were supplemented by participant observation activities. These included spending five extended tours of duty (a total of fifty hours) with crime scene unit technicians to observe the types of tasks and duties they perform as well as to observe their interactions with other squad members and with homicide detectives and uniformed officers at death scenes. I accompanied crime scene unit (CSU) technicians, rather than homicide detectives or uniformed patrol officers, for several very pragmatic reasons. First, despite my overall familiarity with police procedures and policies, I knew rather little about the specific technical aspects of their work and about how they organize their activities to fulfill their responsibilities. The organization of work—for example the division of labor within teams—can reveal a great deal about those who do it. Second, I was interested in observing various types of interactions that occur at homicide scenes, and the tremendous number of death scenes CSU technicians visit, as compared to homicide detectives and patrol officers, seemed a likely way to make the most efficient use of my time. Finally, this strategy gave me the opportunity to observe and discuss their work and their emotional responses as the CSU technicians were actually doing the work.

Other forms of direct observation included attending parts of the criminal trial of an individual charged with the murder of a police officer. This activity permitted me to observe the testimony of practically every police officer testifying in the case and, at the conclusion of their testimony, to informally discuss the death event with them as well as their reactions to it. I also attended the wakes and funerals of several officers killed in the line of duty. Although I have attended many of these in the past, while collecting data for this study I approached these events in somewhat different way: I paid particular attention to the police occupational culture's rites and rituals with a view toward understanding them in formative-symbolic terms.

Investigator as Instrument

My personal experiences and insights as a police officer—particularly those relating to my own death encounters and my observations of police behavior through the years—also informed the research. This was both inevitable and desirable. As McCracken (1988, p. 18) points out, the interviewer "cannot fulfill qualitative research objectives without using a broad range of his or her own experiences, imagination and intellect." The notion of self as instrument does not imply that the researcher substitutes, projects, or impresses his own experience upon that of the individual observed, but rather is analogous to a "bundle of possibilities, pointers and suggestions that can be used to plumb the remarks of a respondent." Elements of one's own experience and the practical insights derived from them are a tool the researcher uses to seek points of correspondence and divergence between his own experience and that of the respondent (p. 19). Particularly when a researcher is working within his own subculture, as I did, these practical reality-based experiences and insights facilitate conceptualization and analysis because they help illuminate, interpret, and organize interview data into similar conceptual models. This seems especially true when the research issues are complex and nuanced. By drawing upon my own practical experiences during the interviews and field observations and by using them as a rough template with which to assess the officers' behavior and experience, I gained important insights into their feelings and personalities as well as my own.

The interviewer who works within his own subculture "can make the interview do powerful work. It is by drawing upon their understanding of how they themselves see and experience the world that they can supplement and interpret the data they generate" (McCracken, 1988, pp. 11–12). At the same time, my familiarity with the police subculture might have a deleterious impact on the research if I permitted it to blind me to cultural assumptions and practices (p. 12). This treacherous potential was at least partially allayed by my sensitivity to and critical awareness of the limitations cultural familiarity can impose on research. Throughout the research process, I was quite cognizant of, in McCracken's terms, the need to "manufacture distance" between myself and the culture and the need to remain sensitive to the underlying taken-for-granted beliefs and assumptions submerged within it (pp. 22–23). Manufacturing distance refers not only to the limitations imposed by the researcher's interpretation of submerged meanings, but to the respondent's expression of them as well. Taken-for-granted meanings are often expressed in aphorisms or code phrases that make little sense outside the culture or that can have subtly different meanings depending upon the context in which they are used. They can also be easily misconstrued by researchers who are not part of the subculture.[7]

As suggested by McCracken (1988, p. 24), I frequently used conversational cues and direct questions in an effort to have officers using such aphorisms articulate their embedded meanings more precisely. I was also scrupulous in ensuring that my own beliefs and assumptions did not obscure or constrain my objectivity, and I used my experience solely as an analytic tool: unless explicitly noted, my own experiences were never used as a source of data in this study.

The notion that the researcher must bring his own experiences, advocacies, and convictions to bear in qualitative interview research is also central to Lifton's method, which demands that the researcher openly and honestly discuss the moral, intellectual, and psychological struggles encountered in conducting the research. Claims to moral neutrality in exploring profound issues are disingenuous, and they detract from the candor as well as the intellectual and personal integrity of the research (Lifton, 1983, 1986). Moral concerns are always implicated in explorations of profound issues, Lifton says, and integrity demands that the researcher strike an appropriate balance between "advocacy" and "detachment" in approaching them (Lifton, 1986, p. 14).

Advocacy and Detachment

These demands for personal and intellectual integrity require that I briefly digress to candidly address my own advocacies and convictions. My advocacy takes the form of a sincere concern for the welfare of fellow officers and a generally optimistic view of police officers' behaviors and motivations. Notwithstanding my admitted areas of cynicism, my familiarity with police officers over the course of a twenty-one-year career and my associations with them while growing up in a police family have confirmed rather than eroded my belief that the overwhelming majority of officers are men and women of good impulse who are often placed in psychologically, socially, and morally untenable positions. I am a cop, and I like cops.

Having experienced the deaths of others—as a rookie patrol officer, as a plainclothes anticrime officer operating at the edges of homicide and suicide investigations, and as a patrol sergeant supervising activities at death scenes—and having reflected deeply on these matters over the past several years, I am perhaps particularly attuned to the emotions of other officers in relation to their death encounters. Over the course of my police career, I also encountered many objectively dangerous situations that threatened my own survival and raised concerns about my own mortality. While I am an admitted advocate for police officers and am sensitive to their emotions, my view is not encumbered or obscured by simplistic romanticized concepts of cops or of the subculture we share. The cynicism and skepticism accrued over twenty-one years of police work have served me well in the academic sphere, as has my training in the investigative aspects of building a factually strong and legally viable criminal case. Like many other cops, I've learned to accept little at face value, but rather to always probe beneath the surface for deeper meaning or an ulterior motive. Scrupulous skepticism and rigor encourage objectivity, and they were very much a part of this study.

In terms of detachment, the position I held for a number of years on the staffs of several police commissioners made me a de facto member of management, and in conjunction with my academic studies of public policy, my knowledge of police operations is informed by a somewhat broader and more holistic view than that of many other members of the agency. Elizabeth Reuss-Ianni (1983) has argued persuasively that the notion of a police culture actually subsumes a "street cop culture" and a "management cop culture" whose subtle differences are distinguishable in terms of an incongruence in their value systems, expectations, loyalties, status systems, and mobilizing principles. Her conclusions and observations are important, well founded, and relevant to this research and I reference them at other points in this book. In this interpretation, my rank and my assignments cast me as a member of the management culture, although my heart is most assuredly in the street cop culture. The personal and career struggles I've encountered in trying to resolve the two bears upon the research methodology insofar as my position in this middle ground adds a distinct layer of detachment from both.[8]

Lifton insists that objective interpretations of complex phenomena must not only proceed from an understanding of one's own and others' subjective experiences, but that the interpretations must include the voices and perspectives of the individuals studied (Strozier and Flynn, 1992). Fontana and Frey (1994, p. 373) point out that including these voices and perspectives conveys our respect for the humanity of those we are interviewing and portrays them in a more realistic light:

> The "other" is no longer a distant, aseptic, quantified, sterilized, measured, categorized, and catalogued faceless respondent, but has become a living

human being, usually a forgotten or an oppressed one . . . up to now sociologically invisible, finally blossoming to full living color and coming into focus as real persons, as the interviewer recognized them as such. Also, in learning about the other we learn about the self. That is, as we treat the other as a human being, we can no longer remain objective, faceless interviewers, but become human beings and must disclose ourselves, learning about ourselves as we try to learn about the other.

Throughout the research process I sought to incorporate the voices and experiences of the officers I interviewed, to appreciate and convey their humanity, and to bear witness to the way their lives and worldviews were shaped by death encounters. This was, once again, pragmatic in terms of the research goals: to interpret how these events influence shared images and symbolic relationships and reveal the motivations and values of the police subculture, it is essential that we grasp the officer's subjective definition of the situations he encounters.

My status as a serving member of the NYPD helped me to grasp officers' subjective meanings and definitions, just as it helped me gain their trust and get honest answers from them. The men and women I interviewed knew that I encountered situations and events similar to their own, and this gave me a certain credibility another purely academic researcher might not receive. Our common membership in the department and the subculture also impacted the trust they placed in my assurances that the information they provided would be held in the strictest confidence, since I stood to suffer a loss of credibility and professional standing if I divulged sensitive information or engaged in any deception. While I am not aware that any officer "checked me out" or assessed my reputation for honesty and integrity with other officers prior to our discussions, I was aware that my credentials as a cop—in which operational units and precincts I had worked, for example, as well as the levels of arrest and enforcement activity I maintained and my overall reputation as a "stand-up" cop—were of more than passing interest to some participants. Because several officers discreetly inquired as to my operational experience and bona fides as a street cop prior to our discussions, I made it part of my repertoire to indirectly reference my cultural credentials as part of the preinterview trust-building process.

The Interview Approach: Mutual Exploration

McCracken (1988) observed that the interview is one of the most powerful methods in the qualitative researcher's tool kit precisely because it permits us to enter and explore the individual's cognitive and emotional world and to glimpse the subjective images, processes, categories, and logic by which he or she organizes and makes sense of experience (p. 9). No other method, according to Webb et al. (1966, pp. 172–173), permits the investigator to "swing his attention into so many different areas of substantive content, often simultaneously, and also gather intelligence on the extent to which his findings are hampered by population restrictions." In Lifton's view, the interview is the "fundamental approach to psychological knowledge" (Strozier and Flynn, 1992, p. 135) and the "pragmatic core" of his method (Lifton, 1986, p. 6). Although Lifton's interview style is adapted from the conventional psychoanalytic interview, it differs insofar as it rejects the classic psychoanalytic distinction between patient and therapist. Rather, this interview style seeks to establish a relationship of mutuality in which experiences, images, feelings, and formative processes can be jointly explored in something resembling an open dialogue.

Lifton (1974, pp. 31–32) describes the relationship as "neither that of doctor and patient nor of ordinary friends, though at moments it can seem to resemble either. It is more one of shared exploration—mostly of the world of the person sought out but including a great deal of give and take, and more than a little discussion of my own attitudes and interests. It requires, in other words, a combination of humane spontaneity and professional discipline." While research of this type may be undertaken in a therapeutic spirit, the interviewer must never cast himself primarily in a therapeutic role. That is, while the interview encourages the subject to discuss and express his feelings, and in elaborating them perhaps gain insight into his personal experiences, these potential benefits must be separate and distinct from the goals of research. The researcher's goals—to collect qualitative and perhaps some empirical data—can easily be obscured by the obligations and commitments entailed in a therapeutic relationship. Illumination and personal growth may result from the interview, but the interviewer's primary interest and emphasis must be on collecting useful data.

Indeed, quite a few officers commented favorably and without prompting that the interviews had therapeutic value for them, asserting that they gained insights into their own feelings and behaviors as well as those of other officers. "I never thought about it much" and "I never thought about it in this way before" were frequent refrains during the interviews. This was not simply a manifestation of the human tendency toward a denial of death, since their images and feelings were rather easily accessed and expressed. The fact is that the police officers' world is full of complexities, ambiguities, and profound ethical and moral issues that do not promote a great deal of introspection and self-analysis. The fast pace and, often, the rapid flow of novel images in policing permits little time or motivation for reflection or contemplation. Police officers are not ordinarily given the opportunity to explore profound experiences and highly personal feelings with another officer in a confidential and supportive environment, but I became quite used to seeing moments of self-discovery during the interviews. The only officer who requested copies of the interview tapes, for example, spoke directly to the interviews' therapeutic benefit—he joked that a psychiatrist would charge $100 an hour for what I had done for free, but then stated in a more serious way that he wanted to listen to the tapes again in order to give the issues more thought. Another officer likened the interviews to a good session with his Alcoholics Anonymous sponsor.

It is all to the good if some or even all the participants in this research project benefited by gaining insight and perspective on their feelings and behaviors, but it must again be emphasized that this was not one of the project's goals or objectives. Stating that I did not pursue a therapeutic goal and did not conceive of the participants as beneficiaries of therapeutic intervention, though, begs the question of precisely how I did perceive our relationship.

Throughout the project, I conceived of and referred to the officers as my collaborators in a research endeavor, openly addressing this position from the earliest stages of contact with them. A sense of mutuality and collaboration provides the basis for a fuller and ultimately more humane exploration of issues, while at the same time it cements the bonds of trust and expectations of confidentiality that are so essential to honest self-disclosure. While the term *research subject* suggests a relationship in which one individual is subordinated to the power and authority of another in order to be dispassionately scrutinized or examined, collaboration implies a degree of reciprocity, empathy, and partnership for a joint intellectual effort. I therefore never conceived of or referred to the research collaborators as "subjects."

I also eschewed the role of expert or therapist, making it clear that I sought access to their experience in order to serve as a conduit for its expression—to honestly and humanely explore the officers' subjective worlds and bear witness to them in an honest and humane way. I candidly discussed my philosophy of collaboration with each officer, acknowledging that although I stood to benefit from the project's completion I was also deeply concerned that police officers as a group benefit from it as well. I emphasized that to the extent their witnessing sensitized others—academicians, clinicians, and police officers—to the psychological realities and struggles of police work, the collaborators would be performing a service to all officers. This appeal to the greater good of police officers was well taken, as evidenced by the number of officers—those whom I solicited to participate as well as those with whom I casually discussed the overall project—who spontaneously volunteered to assist me in the research.

The sense of mutuality and ethos of joint exploration I sought to achieve is also an integral part of Lifton's shared themes approach—the same approach I took. This approach is partly empirical, insofar as it gathers data; partly phenomenological or formative, insofar as it emphasizes gathering and interpreting images that are simultaneously individual and collective; and partly speculative or conceptual, insofar as it combines interview material with other modes of observation and analysis (Lifton, 1974, p. 32; Strozier and Flynn, 1992). The shared themes approach is based in the classical psychoanalytic notion that what goes on inside of people is most important, but its focus is less upon the individual than upon the collective historical experience (Lifton, 1974, p. 31). The shared themes approach examines the "role of metaphors and images in the construction of narrative and the sense of self and world" and elicits from them the "psychohistorical images held in common by a group of people"—the commonalties that "shape personal and collective experience" (Strozier and Flynn, 1992, p. 134). The approach thus emphasizes the recurring images and meanings shared by members of groups who have had similar historical experiences.

The Interview Technique

To explore the themes of survivor psychology and officers' death-related transformations, I conducted structured and unstructured interviews with officers in each of the five categories described earlier. The number of interviews necessary to explore each officer's police-related death encounters varied as a function of his experience and tenure. The rookie police officers I spoke to, for example, had generally experienced only one death encounter during their limited careers, and the single encounter could easily be explored in one interview of approximately an hour's duration. More experienced officers necessarily required two or more interview sessions, and I spent as many as nine hours interviewing a single officer. As a general rule with tenured officers, the interviews were typically conducted in three stages, each session lasting an hour or more. The initial round of tape-recorded interviews was structured by a formal interview protocol and directed primarily toward the collection of basic empirical and descriptive data about the facts and circumstances of the officers' exposures to death. The protocol's open-ended questions were crafted to encourage a wide range of associations and images, but were not so rigid as to preclude the pursuit of other potentially illuminating avenues that opened spontaneously during our discussions. The open-ended format and flexibility of the protocol facilitated the exploratory and conversational tone I tried to foster throughout the interviews. While the initial interview sought to collect basic data, the second and subsequent interviews examined and conceptually refined the shared themes and images that emerged from the first, focusing upon and clarifying ambiguous or nebulous responses to the initial protocol's questions. I often revisited topics discussed in the earlier interview and probed them in greater depth. The follow-up interviews narrowed in on the shared themes and explored in much greater depth the extent and dimension of collaborators' death encounters, the constellation of individual and shared images, and their individual and collective meanings.

This technique combined the best and most productive features of structured and unstructured interviewing: although I used the formal interview protocol to ensure that every issue was raised and discussed with every collaborator, my overall tendency was toward a more unstructured and relaxed interview style.

Thus the sequence in this research project moved from the collection of basic empirical and personal history information toward accessing the emotions, feeling-states, and transformations resulting from specific death events, and ultimately toward more encompassing transformations of self and of worldview. It progressed, in other words, from "what happened" to "how did it feel" to "what does it mean" to the collaborator, both as a police officer and as an individual.

The Interview Protocol

The interview protocol was conceptually developed through a process of careful reflection on the issues that emerged from the literature review, from my own experience, and from my observations of police officers. This subjective conceptualization process identified a range of experiences common to the police experience that I believed could help discern and illuminate the shared themes and psychological transformations. In order to make these subjective interpretations more objective—and therefore more valid and reliable—I conducted a series of informal and relatively unstructured trial interviews with police officers with whom I am acquainted. These officers were effectively precluded from participating in the actual research project by virtue of an existing personal friendship or professional relationship with me, and because my goal at that point was to operationalize a viable protocol rather than to collect data for the study their interviews were not recorded and I did not include their observations and experiences in the research study per se. These informal discussions were geared toward developing, expanding, and refining my preliminary subjective sense of the range of issues and variables typically involved in police officers' death encounters, and toward developing suitable objective open-ended questions for inclusion in the interview protocol. This process of trial interviews also allowed me to craft the specific language of the interview protocol and to predict or evaluate the actual research participants' interpretations of those questions.

It should also be noted that a slightly modified version of the protocol was prepared for each category of officer. Each version was crafted to address the same research issues, albeit with slightly different language to reflect the realities of the participants' tenures, assignments, and task environments. In keeping with the collaborative spirit and conversational character of the interviews and in order to avoid setting a mechanical and perfunctory tone, I used the protocol as a springboard into the collaborators' subjective experience and as a sort of checklist to ensure that all issues were addressed in each interview. Therefore I typically did not read the questions verbatim from the protocol. While I may have rephrased a question and tailored it to the flow of conversation and the specific experience of the collaborator, every issue and question contained in the protocol was addressed.

The Sample Frame

The officers who collaborated in this study were all currently serving or recently retired sworn personnel in the New York City Police Department whose assignment and duties qualified them as members of one of the five nominal categories. The decision to confine this exploratory study to members of the New York City Police Department was shaped by a number of practical, methodological, and theoretical constraints, including my familiarity with and access to members of the agency as well as the potential difficulty of gaining access to other agencies and of achieving sufficient familiarity with the subtleties and nuances of their occupational cultures and task environments. The New York City Police Department gave its approval to this research project, and the police commissioner agreed to permit me to conduct confidential interviews with on-duty officers. As a general rule, I tried to schedule the tenured collaborators for three interviews about one week apart. However, due to many collaborators' rotating work schedules and such "exigencies of the service" as tour changes due to arrests and court appearances, I frequently encountered logistical and scheduling problems requiring that more than one week elapse between interviews. In a few instances several weeks elapsed between interview sessions.

Because this project involved in-depth explorations and descriptions of subjective psychological processes and does not aspire to the goal of absolute generalizability, it did not require an extremely large sample. Indeed, the important issue was not generalizability but sample bias, which I addressed in my sampling technique. Strozier and Flynn (1992, pp. 137–38) observe that the depth and rigor of Lifton's method have permitted him to interview a small number of survivors but nevertheless obtain robust data, and they comment that Lifton always takes pains to clarify for readers the number of individuals interviewed.

In all, a total of nearly 100 hours of tape-recorded interviews took place. These were supplemented with innumerable brief and less formally structured discussions with collaborators and with other experienced cops in a variety of assignments and task environments. The formal interviews included more than 20 hours of interviews with 13 rookies, 28 hours of interviews with 8 sergeants, 16 hours of interviews with 5 homicide detectives, about 8 hours of interviews with 4 crime scene technicians, and more than 26 hours of interviews with 7 police survivor collaborators. It should be noted that while all the collaborators had the rookie's experience of a first DOA, and were therefore interviewed about those experiences, several collaborators had other unique professional experiences that shed light on task environments other than the one in which they currently operated. Thus one highly experienced sergeant, a former homicide detective and former field training officer for rookies, provided personal insights into three task environments. Several collaborators in different categories had worked in a precinct where an officer was murdered in the line of duty, had investigated an officer's suicide and/ or a line-of-duty death, or had a close personal relationship with a murdered officer. They were able to describe the kind of events, feelings, and emotions that take place around these events.

In addition, I spent over 50 hours observing and working with crime scene technicians as they performed their duties, as well as observing their interactions with homicide detectives and other officers at various kinds of violent death scenes, including one in which an officer killed an adversary in a gunfight. I also attended the trial of an individual charged and ultimately convicted of a police officer's line-of-duty murder and was able to examine the evidence and hear virtually all the police testimony in that case.

Sampling Technique

An important question in any research project is how the researcher obtained an unbiased sample that reflects the overall population he is studying. To avoid sample bias, I identified potential collaborators using a purposive or judgmental sampling technique. Purposive or judgmental sampling is a kind of nonprobability sampling in which the researcher selects individuals from an array of candidates based on his own judgments about which ones will provide the most comprehensive understanding of the subject and are representative of the population (Babbie, 1992, pp. G5, 292–293). These judgments, in turn, are based upon an intuitive feel for the subject that comes from extended observation and reflection. As an additional safeguard against sample bias, I incorporated a "snowball sampling" technique: collaborators identified through judgmental sampling were asked to nominate additional people for interviewing.

In each category of officer other than rookie, I contacted officers who fit the category definition, explained the study's goals and methods, assured them of confidentiality, and solicited their participation as collaborators. Every collaborator was also asked to nominate other officers in his own or other categories whose experiences would be valuable and informative, and I solicited those nominees to participate. This snowball sampling process was repeated with each successive collaborator.

A slightly different (though equally nonbiased) sampling technique was used to identify rookie officers who might consent to be interviewed. The police academy's recruit training program includes a field training component in which recruit officers who have successfully completed the majority of their training are assigned to supervised patrol duties in precincts for a one-month period prior to graduation. They return to the police academy at the conclusion of the field training component to assess their street experience, to finish the remaining academic curriculum, and to take their final examinations. Because they perform a range of patrol duties, some of the rookie officers are exposed to deaths during field training.

The police academy's field training component provided a unique opportunity to interview rookie officers who had a recent death exposure, and to select officers in a completely nonbiased fashion. I contacted the academy and requested that they survey the entire class of almost 1,600 recruits to identify those who had an assignment that entailed the death of another person. The academy provided me with a list of 109 recruit officers fitting these criteria, along with the recruit companies to which they were assigned. This rudimentary survey revealed that almost 7% of the recruit officers had a job-related death encounter during their first month of operational police work.

I arbitrarily chose to conduct interviews on 3 successive weekdays and determined which recruit companies were working day tours on the 3 days and were assigned to physical education class at selected times.[9] The officers who fit the criteria and who were assigned to those companies—about 25 in all—were brought together in the academy's library on the first weekday morning, and I explained the research project to them as a group. All but 3 of the recruit officers volunteered to discuss their first police-related exposure to the death of another person, and 12 of the volunteers were given scheduled interview appointments. The 12 were selected in an arbitrary manner, on the basis of their company number.

Ethical Considerations

Virtually all research projects involving human beings raise ethical issues and concerns, and this project was certainly not an exception. The research implicated a raft of privacy issues including the manner in which sensitive personal data would be acquired and discretely managed, as well as the exploration of experiences and emotions that were potentially anxiety-provoking. The fact that both the researcher and the collaborator-participants were members of the same police organization and police subculture added another ethical dimension to the research. To ensure that my own substantial concerns for the protection of participants' dignity and privacy as well as the academic norms of ethical research are satisfied, I incorporated a variety of measures into the research design to ensure that it was conducted in an entirely ethical and principled manner.

Academic norms of ethical research impose several burdens and constraints on the researcher, including the demand that participants are volunteers who are fully apprised of the purpose and intended uses of the research project before any data are collected from them, and that no harm come to the participants (APA, 1982; Babbie, 1992; Punch, 1993, 1994). The canons of ethical research also impose strict limitations on the use of deception and demand the project be approved by an impartial human subjects research committee. No deception was involved in this research, and the project was approved by the City University of New York's Human Subjects Research Committee. In the interests of informed consent, a research ethics protocol modeled after one suggested by McCracken (1988) for use in interviews was prepared and signed copies were obtained from all collaborators prior to their first interviews. In line with Punch's (1994) suggestion, the protocol also informed collaborators their comments might be quoted in publications derived from it, but in no case would they be identified. As noted, all collaborators were volunteers, and they received no tangible benefit or reward as an inducement to participate.

The canons of ethical research also require researchers to consider the potential costs and benefits to participants (APA, 1982, p. 27) and impose a responsibility for the researcher to protect participants' welfare during and in some cases after the research process. Although the study's subject might at first glance appear likely to engender some minor anxiety or distress, the issues were explored in a supportive and sensitive manner. Moreover, since the collaborators were police officers who exist in a high-stress environment, the potential anxiety or discomfort their recollections might conjure pales in comparison to many of the day-to-day activities they routinely undertake. The research ethics protocol cautioned collaborators that they might experience some anxiety or recall unpleasant memories, and it assured them they could discontinue the interview at any time. It also assured them that, if necessary, arrangements would be made for them to access professional counseling services at no cost. Although the situation never arose, I would have unilaterally discontinued an interview if I observed signs of excessive anxiety or distress.

I also used a number of tactics to ensure that the norm of confidentiality was not compromised, and I apprised the participants of the steps I took to ensure confidentiality. A single master list cross-referencing the collaborator's name with an identification number was created, and it remained under my sole and secure control. The collaborator's name did not appear on any document other than the master list and the ethics protocol, and only identification numbers appeared on the audiotape cassettes and written interview notes. No descriptors or unique data that might tend to identify a particular individual appear in the book, and individuals are identified only by their identification numbers.

Participants were assured that the interview data—the audiotapes, research notes, and other documentation—would be protected from scrutiny by the police department or by any individual. The tapes, notes, master list, and signed ethics protocols were stored in a locked file cabinet in my home for the duration of the research and were available only to me.

Conclusion

Up to this point in our explorations, we have conducted a basic review of the academic literature as it relates to various death work occupations, examined some basic dimensions of police officers' exposures to death and their duties in relation to death events, outlined the fundamental principles of the formative-symbolic or continuity-of-life paradigm and the psychology of survival, and described the methodological strategies used to collect data. These efforts were necessary to explain the purposes of the research and the direction and approach it takes as well as to give context to the data and the police experiences we will examine and analyze. It is now time to turn our attention to those data and to begin exploring the substantive issues that are the central concern of this research: how various kinds of death encounters shape the contemporary urban police officer's experience and his self-identity. We begin our exploration in the following chapter with a formative-symbolic interpretation of police socialization and the initial formation of the police self-identity.

3.

"Becoming a Cop"

Basic Social and Psychological Processes

The social and psychological worlds of the rookie police officer are in large measure shaped by the officer's involvement in a fundamental transformative process in which he struggles with a raft of potentially conflicting social roles, each with its own set of unique rules, norms, and prescribed or proscribed behaviors. The transformative process is a central feature of the new officer's quest to develop viable personal and occupational identities and to integrate them in a cohesive sense of self, and this process of transforming identity involves incorporating the images provided by police experience. The psychological struggle to incorporate new images and forms in order to resolve and make sense of the conflicts and ambiguities that characterize police work may begin even before entry into the police academy, but it typically endures through the initial training and socialization process and well into or even beyond the police career. The effort to resolve conflicting social roles, to decipher police work's ambiguities, to cope with its physical, emotional, social, and ethical demands, and to define a personal identity as a police officer may, in fact, become a lifelong undertaking for those who choose police work as a career.

This array of struggles and conflicts shapes and affects the rookie's everyday activities, experiences, and feelings, and they infiltrate the rookie's thoughts and behaviors both on- and off-duty. The struggle to resolve and integrate these diverse images becomes an impetus for adopting police-like behaviors and attitudes, and the rookie is motivated to emulate the attitudes and behaviors he perceives in police role models in order to project the appearance or illusion of comfort with his new social role. The process of radically redefining the self thus begins with emulation and conformance of the outwardly presented self, but is not complete until new elements of the police self are incorporated and incompatible elements of the civilian self are restructured in a way that diminishes their relative importance to the overall identity. These more immanent elements of the police identity are acquired primarily through the images acquired in job-related experience, including death encounters.

This gradual process of becoming a police officer—of altering the contours of the existing "civilian self" through the integration of new images, forms, and constellations—is essentially a formative-symbolic process, albeit a process that is greatly influenced by the social context in which it takes place. Police work and police socialization experiences present the individual with a host of new and unique images that combine with existing forms and constellations, ultimately altering them in profound ways. Eventually, this continual symbolizing process transforms the individual's core identity: a somewhat different symbolization of self emerges as the sum of all the individual's images, old and new. Because the new self-identity develops through ongoing symbolization, the rookie officer experiences the same sense of vitality that accompanies any process of creating and re-creating viable new images, forms, and constellations. This vitalizing process is implicitly rewarding, but it can be made all the more meaningful when the images connect with one or more of the symbolic modes of immortality or with the elements of connection, integrity, and movement that are involved in the overall struggle toward vitality and against formlessness.

Further, the new officer's transformation of self can help alleviate many of the social, role, and identity conflicts he faces at the beginning of the police socialization process. As the new sense of self emerges, the officer forges new and meaningful connections and relationships, he experiences a satisfying sense of movement toward achieving his career aspirations, and he begins to find a kind of integrity or consonance between the idealized self (i.e., the self-as-police-officer he desires to become) and his actual self. Like the police socialization process that integrates and moves the young officer toward a vitalizing membership in the police culture, the psychological process of growing toward the police self-identity is in large measure a struggle against the formlessness and anomie that confront the newly appointed officer.

Because the images and experiences a rookie officer encounters during the socialization process take place in a personal context of great social conflict, it is important to understand how these conflicts play out and how the rookie officer seeks to resolve them in his work. This is important not only because the social conflicts shape the overall contours of the officer's persona but also because they are clearly manifested in the first death encounter. In interviewing my collaborators, I found that the same pervasive themes of conflict, ambiguity, and struggle to create identity—in both the psychological and social dimensions—that characterize the overall rookie experience also resonated within their narratives of the first death encounter. Because the first death encounter is in itself a profound socializing experience and a psychologically important point of passage along the rookie's path to acquiring a professional identity, it constitutes a microcosm in which many of the larger conflicts can be viewed.

Clearly, the process of "becoming" a police officer—of both acquiring a police self-identity and being recognized and accepted by others as a police officer—involves the interplay of social and psychological factors, and the social context should not be ignored. The social conflicts and pressures the rookie faces have multiple dimensions: they involve the rookie's relationships with his family and friends as well as his relationships with other officers and the civilian clientele encountered in his work. The conflicts and pressures alter his social relationships with all these people, and in terms of his internal psychological life they shape and influence his evolving sense of a professional or occupational self. In this chapter, my goal is to delineate the social settings and contexts that shape the images and experiences involved in the rookie's overall identity change. In chapter 4, we will more closely examine how the images specifically provided in death encounters take the process a step further in forging the police self.

Conflict and Ambiguity in the Police Officer's Social Relationships

The processes of police socialization and of recasting personal identity may actually begin long before the recruit enters the police department's employ: the transformations often begin with the conscious decision to consider a career in policing, since the very act of publicly announcing one's intended or hoped-for career is an often risky articulation of one's commitment to a set of beliefs and to a lifestyle that inevitably sets the candidate apart from the body politic. Publicly articulating a desire to become a cop is often the first step toward redefining the social relationship between self and other, and depending on how others respond to his decision the articulation may be the police aspirant's first experience with the social conflicts he will face throughout his police career.

The rookie's conflicts are firmly rooted in ambiguity—both in terms of personal ambivalence or lingering uncertainty about the career choice and in terms of society's inconsistent attitudes toward police work and police officers. Bonifacio (1991, p. 23) maintains that "virtually from the day he enters the police academy, the police officer is the target of ambivalence from just about everyone. He is confronted by ambivalent messages from the public, from the police department itself, from his family and friends, and from fellow officers." This ambivalence may "take the form of 'mixed' or 'double' messages" and the officer may even endure countervailing "feelings of admiration and contempt, affection and hostility, love and hate from the same individual at almost the same time." Public ambivalence is an important psychological factor in shaping the officer's world, Bonifacio (p. 24) says, and it stems from the tremendous power and authority police officers wield as well as from the element of perceived or real danger that pervades their world.

As Egon Bittner (1980, pp. 6–7) points out, police work is a tainted occupation in the public's view, and the historic origins of the stigma are buried in the distant past. While contemporary police may no longer "represent the underground aspects of tyranny and political oppression" (p. 6), they nevertheless continue to maintain a monopoly on the legitimate use of nonnegotiable coercive force in society, and the vestiges of old attitudes endure: "The mythology of the democratic polity avidly recounts the heroic combat against the police agents of the old order. But even if the police officer of today did not evoke the images of the past at all, he would still be viewed with mixed feelings, to say the least. For in modern folklore, too, he is a character who is ambivalently feared and admired, and no amount of public relations can entirely abolish the sense that there is somewhat of the dragon in the dragon-slayer" (p. 7).

Indeed, Bittner's (1980) entire analysis and perspective on the social role of the police rests in their monopoly on the legitimate exercise of nonnegotiable coercive force. In an earlier article that has become a classic in the literature of policing, Bittner (1974) points out that the police mandate to impose or coerce a solution upon emergent problems they encounter is extremely broad, and in fact "extends to every kind of emergency, without any exceptions whatsoever" (p. 17): "I am saying more than merely that patrolmen, like everyone else, will suspend the performance of assigned tasks to turn to some extraordinary exigency. While everyone might respond to the call of an emergency, the policeman's vocational ear is *permanently and specifically attuned* to such calls, and his work attitude throughout is permeated by preparedness to respond to it, whatever he might be doing" (p. 25, emphasis in original).

Bittner (1974) summarizes a long and quite diverse list of potential police involvements, noting they have in common the fact of "*something-that-ought-not-to-be-happening-and-about-which-someone-had-better-do-something-now!*" (p. 26, emphasis in original). The police officer is, in formative-symbolic terms, expected to respond immediately and forcefully with appropriate enactment to the images he encounters in a wide range of exigent and emergent situations, many of which involve the potential for great personal danger or significant emotional costs. Regardless of the physical danger or the emotional costs involved, the officer's role, his mandate, and his professional identity demand appropriate enactment under very difficult conditions: "A policeman is always poised to move on any contingency whatever, not knowing what it might be, but knowing that far more often than not he will be expected to do something. The expectation to do something is projected on the scene, the patrolman's diagnostic instinct is heavily colored by it, and he literally sees things in the light of the expectation that he somehow *has* to handle the situation" (p. 29, emphasis in original).

Skolnick (1994) argues persuasively in a similar vein that danger, authority and the potential for violence are defining features of the officer's "working personality," and Westley's (1953, 1956, 1970) seminal work also illuminates the centrality of violence and secrecy in policing as well as the isolating impact violence and secrecy have upon the police culture. In fleshing out the police officer's "working personality," Skolnick (1994) alludes to the simultaneous sense of attraction and aversion that danger, violence, and authority hold for the public as well as for the police. Because police specialize in dealing with the type of dangerous situations the public fears, Skolnick (1994) argues, danger and the potential for violence set police apart from society, intensify public estrangement and resentment, and galvanize the police culture's solidarity and insularity. Police must cope not only with public ambivalence rooted in danger and authority, but with internal ambiguities as well. Skolnick (1994) comments that the "police officer, as a personality, may well enjoy the possibility of danger, especially its associated excitement, while fearing it at the same time" (p. 46). Officers experience a kind of ambiguity or internal conflict in relation to danger, he says, but they do not "necessarily emphasize the peril associated with their work when questioned directly and may even have well developed strategies of denial. The element of danger is so integral to an officer's work that explicit recognition might induce emotional barriers to work performance."

Arthur Niederhoffer (1967), a noted police sociologist and retired NYPD lieutenant, also wrote extensively about the experience of ambiguity and anomie at various stages of the police career and about the social and psychological conflicts officers encounter while interacting with the public and the department. He observed that the young officer's initial sense of idealism is rather quickly eroded and replaced with a protective mantle of cynicism as he struggles to harmonize the seemingly insuperable ambiguities presented by police work. The images of optimistic idealism that may have impelled the officer toward a police career are never completely lost or extinguished, however; they remain with the officer but become a less prominent feature of his identity and his outwardly presented self. While these latent images and constellations, along with the idealistic impulses their schemas for enactment contain, may be masked by a cynical veneer, they can be reanimated and given expression then they connect with appropriate images from the environment. The seeming paradox of the hard-edged officer who is nevertheless capable (at times) of performing acts of great kindness and altruism can be explained in terms of the durability of idealistic images and constellations: these images and constellations remain below the surface of the outwardly presented police self and they can easily be reanimated by vitalizing experiences, especially those tied to connection with others and matters of personal integrity. Interviews with collaborators as well as my own observations point to the fact that these acts of kindness often take place in nonpublic settings, and that some officers—perhaps especially younger officers who have not yet developed a more expansive, flexible, and inclusive role identity—are somewhat embarrassed when they are "caught" performing an altruistic good deed. Their embarrassment can be attributed to informal role demands prescribing that cops present a stoic aura of strength and detachment in public settings. This paradox or duality—the perceived need to balance stoic professional detachment with compassionate and humane behavior—resonated throughout my collaborators' narratives.

The literature of police cynicism, which is primarily based in sociological analysis, reveals both that measurable levels of cynicism vary at different stages of the police career and that cynicism tends to correlate with the degree of ambiguity and role conflict present in the officer's occupational life. Niederhoffer (1967) and other investigators (Lotz and Regoli, 1977; Wilt and Bannon, 1976; Chandler and Jones, 1979; Regoli, 1976; Singer, Singer, and Burns, 1984; Regoli, Poole, and Hewitt, 1978; Regoli, Crank, and Rivera, 1990) consistently found that measurable cynicism increases rapidly during police academy training, continues on a more gradual upward cline for the first several years of service, and then levels off before declining in the later stages of the career as the officer comes to find greater comfort with social conflict, ambiguity, and anomie. More specifically, Niederhoffer's (1967) work[1] showed that over the course of a typical twenty-year career, the tendency to maintain a cynical outlook eventually reverses and officers move toward increased idealism in their last four or five years of service. Police cynicism is certainly a sociologically complex dynamic, but it has psychological components as well. In terms of the formative-symbolic paradigm, we might say that in conjunction with increased social comfort, police experience eventually provides images that broaden the officer's concept of his role to permit altruistic acts as well as images that reanimate his dormant idealistic constellations.

Niederhoffer (1967) encapsulated the public's ambivalence toward the police officer and its rootedness in the officer's power in this way:

> The policeman is a "Rorschach" in uniform as he patrols his beat. His occupational accouterments—shield, nightstick, gun, and summons book—clothe him in a mantle of symbolism that stimulates fantasy and projection. Children identify with him in the perennial game of "cops and robbers." Teen-agers in autos stiffen with compulsive rage or anxiety at the sight of the patrol car. To people in trouble the police officer is a savior. In another metamorphosis the patrolman becomes a fierce ogre that mothers conjure up to frighten their disobedient youngsters. At one moment the policeman is a hero, the next, monster. (p. 1)

The rookie police officer has certainly chosen an occupation and a social role imbued with inherent and unavoidable conflict, but these conflicts extend well beyond the public's potential antagonism or appreciation. On a more personally meaningful level, the recruit, the rookie, and the tenured officer may continually encounter a similar constellation of conflicting attitudes—ranging from respect and admiration to ambivalence or outright hostility—from friends and family members.

Conflict and Ambiguity in Personal Relationships

Skolnick (1994) agrees that the conflicts of the police role, especially those involving danger and authority, affect personal relationships by promoting social isolation and police solidarity. The dangerous aspects of police work make the officer suspicious and distrustful of others and "especially attentive to signs indicating a potential for violence and lawbreaking," even when off-duty in social settings. This attentiveness to images of violence and lawbreaking—which may become manifest in hypervigilance[2]—is the basis for what Skolnick (1994) calls the "symbolic assailant"—a constellation that also serves as an anticipatory model for action. In formative-symbolic terms, these individuals present an image or set of images that animate the constellation, raising the officer's suspicions and mobilizing his senses to prepare for some kind of action. Skolnick goes on to point out that the danger inherent in the "character of police work makes an officer less desirable than others as a friend, because norms of friendship implicate others in the officer's work. Accordingly, the element of danger isolates the police socially from that segment of the citizenry that they regard as symbolically dangerous and also from the conventional citizenry with whom they identify. The element of authority reinforces the element of danger in isolating the police" (p. 42).

Bonifacio (1991) alludes to the young officer's sense of estrangement when friends begin to regard him differently:

> One of the most frequently reported occupational hazards of police work is that the officer's friends treat him differently once he joins the department. Even as a recruit he finds some friends are reassessing their relationship with him because he is no longer the friend they knew—he has become a cop. Once sworn in, he may be told that he cannot be invited to parties because some guests may do drugs there and the host does not want them to risk being arrested by the police officer. Another common experience is having friends refer to the cop in the past tense: "You were a nice guy, but now that you're a cop I don't know how I feel about you." Those friends who continue to maintain their relationship with the police officer also express ambivalent feelings toward him. (pp. 36–37)

As evidenced by the tremendous number and variety of television shows and films reputedly depicting the realities of police work, there exists a great public appetite for "inside" information about the world of the police officer, which is often seen as mysterious and exciting. This appetite does not always translate into an appreciation for police officers, nor does it seem to be based in a true intellectual quest for understanding the complexities of police work. Instead, public interest in police work tends to be voyeuristic, vicarious, and laden with overtones of cautious misgivings and latent or overt resentment: "Because they are posted on the perimeters of order and justice in the hope that their presence will deter the forces of darkness and chaos, because they are meant to spare the rest of the people direct confrontations with the dreadful, perverse, lurid, and dangerous, police officers are perceived to have powers and secrets no one else shares. Their interest in and competence to deal with the untoward surrounds their activities with mystery and distrust" (Bittner, 1980, p. 7).[3]

Every police officer has at one time or another been present at a social gathering where other guests display great interest, tinged with elements of fascination and revulsion, for the type of work police do and the darker side of human existence they often witness. Police are frequently pressed to describe their work or to relate "war stories" about their experiences, and questions often revolve around how realistically a particular television series portrays police work. Paradoxically, the same kind of simultaneous fascination and revulsion that underlies a great deal of the public's interest in police—an interest experienced officers often deride as "buff stuff"[4]—may also have initially attracted the police aspirant toward his own career choice. The opportunity to vicariously or actually experience images from the darker side of human existence has a powerfully seductive draw, and this attraction was evinced in many of the interviews I conducted. In particular, several detectives commented on the status afforded them when people at parties or informal social gatherings learn they are homicide detectives. As one opined, most people are far less interested in meeting a chief or even the police commissioner than they are in meeting a real homicide detective. Doctors, lawyers, and others in high-status professions, he said, are inevitably in awe of the homicide detective. The same basic conferral of status seems to apply, albeit with less potency than for the detective, to other police ranks as well. As we will see in subsequent chapters, the intrusive nature of the police role gives legitimacy to many officers' excursions into the macabre.

In pressing their demands for "inside" information on the mysteries of police work, civilians subtly confer some measure of expert status upon the officer, and this attention can have quite an impact on young officers whose police identity has not yet solidified. This seems especially true of rookie officers who have not yet earned respect and status from their peers but are clearly seen as full-fledged police officers by naive civilians who fail to appreciate or distinguish their relatively low status in the police world. Civilians will often draw an officer out for his "expert" opinions on crime and criminal justice matters, but the tone and tenor of such conversations often change direction quickly. The officer may have to vigorously defend his opinions or the actions of other officers to a civilian who cannot or will not understand the reality the officer knows. In time, the officer may learn the hard way that in order to avoid this kind of conflict it is often simpler not to reveal his occupation or even to lie about it in casual social interactions. At the same time a young officer is solidifying and coming to terms with his role and his occupational identity, he learns not to proffer that self in casual off-duty encounters.

Given the public's fascination for the sordid side of policing and the potentially macabre aspects of the police experience, it should not be surprising that many of the questions posed at social gatherings concern images of violence, death, and mayhem. It is not at all uncommon for a civilian to initiate conversation by inquiring whether an officer has ever killed someone or been shot at, and to betray some vague disappointment upon learning that he has not. Between police officers, on the other hand, it is considered taboo (or at least very poor form) to casually pose such a question. This is not to say that such information is secret or concealed, merely that it is recognized as a potentially sensitive topic and is not casually discussed. Indeed, an officer can "read" or decipher the breast bars worn on a uniform, surmising with some degree of accuracy the extent to which another cop has been involved with danger and whether he has survived a mortal combat situation. The breast bars and medals for heroic actions in the face of danger are, of course, to some extent emblematic of one's status and overall police experience.[5] The particular hidden meaning of breast bars are not, however, generally decipherable by civilians, and a civilian's casual inquiries about the acts they represent may lead the officer to respond with some embarrassment or to demur. Rather than responding "Oh, that one's for killing the guy who shot my partner," a far more socially acceptable response is "I got that one for good police work."

Conflict and Ambiguity: Family and Friends

Quite apart from his social interactions with members of the public and with casual acquaintances, it is clear that the police aspirant sets in motion an assortment of conflicts with family and close friends when he announces and acts upon the desire to enter policing. Virtually all the officers I interviewed noted the ambivalence or outright antipathy of family, friends, and significant others toward the career choice. Mothers and spouses, in particular, seem especially likely to oppose this career choice, and most collaborators described the opposition as centering around the notion that police work is physically dangerous, with somewhat less initial recognition or emphasis on the emotional hazards involved. This is certainly understandable, since few mothers or spouses would be expected to look favorably upon the prospect of their loved one taking up an occupation in which the possibility of physical injury or death is a salient, if often somewhat exaggerated, feature. There is also, generally speaking, less public knowledge of or appreciation for the emotional hazards of police work than for its physical dangers. These observations, corroborated through my interviews with rookies and serving officers, raise the interesting empirical question of how the potential for serious physical injury or death contributes to the officer's later strategies for the minimization of danger and denial of the possibility of death in the line of duty. We will touch upon this issue at other points in the book as we explore police experiences with death.

The ambivalence of family members may take an interesting turn when the aspirant's parent, relative, or close family friend is a police officer. Family members may be simultaneously proud and dismayed at the career choice, once again reflecting the theme of ambivalence: the sense of pride emerges from the police candidate's embrace of a career and a belief system they personally cherish, while the dismay often arises out of an intimate knowledge of policing's hazards and an impulse to protect the aspirant from them.

Despite the fact that in many police agencies, including the NYPD, there exists a strong tradition of sons (and more recently, daughters) following their fathers (or mothers) into police work, officers who proclaim that they would be pleased to see a son or daughter enter police work appear to be the exception. Their failure to actively encourage, or perhaps more accurately, to *admit* actively encouraging a son or daughter to enter the field is itself indicative of the lifelong personal ambivalence with which officers regard their work. My discussions, observations, and personal experience as a member of a family with a police tradition points to the fact that despite lingering concerns about safety, many officers are pleased and proud when their child makes that career choice.

Crank (1998) comments upon the transmission of police culture through family generations, noting that officers' children generally develop strong esteem for police officers as a group and strong loyalties toward the culture and its values, regardless of the career they ultimately pursue. These children possess an absolute belief in the good that police can do for society, and they staunchly believe that the police are a powerful moral force acting in the best interests of society. At the same time, officers are also concerned that exposure to the darker side of human existence will erode their children's idealized view of police and police work (p. 192). This concern partially explains the reluctance many officers feel for frankly discussing some aspects of their work with family members, including their general tendency to avoid discussing issues of death, danger, and emotional hazards.[6]

Many officers go to great extremes to protect and insulate their families from the realities of police work. They not only withhold or make light of the details of

dangerous or disturbing situations they encounter, but they also justify their silence on grounds of protecting the family from undue worry. Some collaborators went so far as to offer the view or rationalization that a spouse's concrete
knowledge of the specific dangers and difficulties faced would increase family
tensions and possibly inhibit the officer while performing his duties: if the
spouse's concerns about safety began to intrude upon the professional sphere,
the officer might hesitate or be distracted during a dangerous confrontation,
thereby increasing the possibility of injury or death. In a larger sense, though,
actions taken to protect the family from worry serve to separate and compartmentalize the personal self from the professional self. Officers struggle with
competing urges to shield family members from the dangerous or disturbing
aspects of their work and, at the same time, to find a kind of solace in frankly
sharing their occupational burdens with a loved one. Some officers are fortunate to have a partner at work with whom they can speak frankly about the images
and experiences bothering them, but to some extent the burdens always infiltrate the officer's family life.

The realities and difficulties of police work inevitably impact the family despite cops' efforts to separate their two worlds in protection of the family. In many
police families, there exists a kind of informal "don't ask, don't tell" policy: officers try to present a sanitized version of their work environment, and family members do not press them for sordid details even if they suspect the presented version
is somewhat less than complete. It is this sanitized and idealized image of police
work that gives rise to the loyalties, idealized images, and romanticized belief systems Crank (1998) observes in cops' children. By withholding information and by
minimizing the emotional and physical dangers of police work, police officers are
to some extent misleading their loved ones, and this can become especially problematic if a cop's child decides to pursue a police career.

A great many cops I know from police families related that their father, uncle,
or brother sat them down for a cautionary talk to elaborate upon the difficulties
of police work, ostensibly so that the career decision would be an informed one.
The same behavior, though, can also be seen as an attempt to come to terms with
lingering personal dissonance or ambivalence about the police aspirant's career
choice. While part of the ambivalence is surely rooted in the continued urge to
protect a loved one from the emotional and physical hazards of police work, the
officer's sense of personal integrity may also demand he make clear the realities
he may have previously hidden from his children.

The same urge to protect and shelter may, however, also compete with the
powerful draw of mutual participation in a kind of immortality system. Although
to some extent the entire process of police socialization and integration into the
police subculture involves gaining access to an immortality system, the urge may
be especially powerful when a family tradition of policing is involved. Whether or
not a family tradition is involved, though, immortality systems are important in
policing because they bind generations together in a continuing allegiance to a set
of animating belief systems as well as to the special traditions, lore, and experiences of the police culture.

In itself, a police career can offer access to a kind of immortality system, but that system can be especially powerful when a family tradition connects with the sense of biological immortality. Images of the child following in the parent's occupational footsteps can add meaning and dimension to one's innate sense of biological immortality: not only do parent and child share common genetic material as "blood relatives," but they share an occupation and the unique ethos, values, struggles, and worldview the occupational culture entails. Participants in the family tradition may experience a sense of legacy in the idea that the lifework that played such a powerful role in creating and shaping the parent's sense of self is being carried forward by his biological offspring. At some level all the participants are aware that the occupation will shape the child's sense of self in a unique way, making it more like the parent's, and in taking up a career that will shape his sense of self in this way the child affirms his esteem and admiration for all that the parent is: he willingly accepts the challenge of policing with the knowledge it will make him even more like the parent.

One need not come from a family tradition, however, to experience policing's immortality system or to access a sense of biological immortality: we recall from our earlier discussion of the formative-symbolic paradigm and the sense of immortality that the sense of biological immortality reaches outward to take on biosocial elements that in this case include the larger "family" of policing and the police culture. These biosocial or cultural ties play a part in the police culture's solidarity and its tendency to dichotomize the world in terms of "us versus them," and the sense of kinship and connection is reflected in the culture's jargon—cops often speak of their culture in terms of a family and they often refer to other cops as "brother" or "sister" officers.[7]

Policing's immortality system can offer other forms of connectedness in terms of the theological mode, as well as the mode of achieving immortality through creative works, insofar as the tradition's participants share a common philosophical doctrine or even a set of seemingly eternal ethical principles. Like many members of the legal and medical professions, for example, members of the police occupation may share the notion or image of involvement in a highly principled historic tradition that is altruistically concerned with justice, integrity, "healing," and the overall betterment of the human condition. A great deal of the vaunted police solidarity that cuts across ethnic, racial, cultural, national, and agency lines can be attributed in part to a shared (if somewhat simplistic and romanticized) sense that all police officers everywhere are engaged in a common struggle to achieve a noble goal. Once again, this sense of struggle on behalf of a noble goal underlies the images of crusading knights battling metaphorical dragons.

That struggle is more than just a battle of good against evil—although that polarity is important[8]—it is a struggle against individual and social stasis, disintegration, and separation. Because this struggle involves personal sacrifice and a potential for danger, and because it is undertaken on behalf of others, police see their work as a noble and selfless endeavor. Commitment to this eternal struggle is yet another basis for the sense of connectedness cops share, and the struggle's universality across the spectrum of policing makes it much larger and far more important than the individual. The sense of connection to other cops and the knowledge that one's work will be carried on by others beyond the individual lifespan gives the officer a certain power over death.

The mode of symbolic immortality through experiential transcendence can be accessed in many police activities, especially the risky or dangerous activities that demand an intense focus on the here and now. Notwithstanding the fact that police work actually provides many opportunities to engage in dangerous transcendent activities—racing through streets in a speeding police car, engaging in physical struggles to apprehend criminals, and perhaps even involvement in mortal combat—it is important to recognize that these images are, to a large extent, the public face of policing. The objective likelihood of regularly engaging in these dangerous activities and experiencing the transcendent "adrenaline rush" they involve may be somewhat exaggerated, but to the police aspirant they *seem* an important and frequently experienced part of the job. Other potential transcendent images may come from the less risky altruistic adventures of delivering a baby, rendering first aid to an injured person, or performing a rescue; these and other "heroic" activities, like the experience of being recognized and honored for a heroic act, can involve transcendent images of ecstasy, psychic unity, and perceptual intensity that diminish temporal and psychological boundaries and bring the individual to a sense he is part of a larger and more important endeavor. He further achieves a sense of immortality in recognizing that he has in some way affected the course of history and had a powerful impact on the lives of others.

One way the sense of biological immortality is expressed in the family tradition is through the ritual passage of shields or other tangible police symbols (such as nightsticks, handcuffs, or other cherished "tools of the trade") through generations of officers in a family. Because this ritual of continuity illuminates the immortality system, it merits some elaboration.

Biological Immortality and the Shield

The officer's shield is the property of the NYPD, and it must be surrendered upon promotion to another rank, retirement, or separation from the police service. It connotes, in both a symbolic and an actual way, one's rank and formal status within the agency and the culture. Because each rank's shield is identical in every respect but its number, the shield number takes on special significance as the clearest stamp of individuality in a symbol-laden world of uniforms and surface uniformity.[9] Many officers request that the shield worn by a father, uncle, or other family member be issued to them, and it is not uncommon for a shield to remain within a single family for several generations. Such a request is more than a mere honorific to the person who wore it before: the ritual passing of the shield through generations binds the officer psychologically to its previous bearers as well as to their occupational and personal experiences, tying him historically to the past as well as to the future. The shield is a tangible symbol and image of continuity in a world and an occupation marked by fluidity, uncertainty, and flux, and it has a power-ful symbolic content. When that symbol of continuity connects with the biologi-cal continuity of the family, it becomes particularly powerful.

Just as the biological mode of symbolic immortality eventually comes to encompass the biosocial sphere, the symbolism of the shield can take on impor-tant overtones outside the immediate family. This became quite apparent in at least one documented case involving a police officer's profound death encoun-ter. Shortly after investigating a police officer's homicide and bringing the case to successful conclusion, a veteran detective retired and his shield was assigned to a newly appointed detective. The veteran homicide detective knew the slain of-ficer and his partner very well before the murder, and in the months following the murder the detective and the officer's surviving partner—bound together by their loss and by the death immersion they shared—became even closer. When the surviving officer was eventually promoted to the detective rank, he requested his retired friend's shield be issued to him but learned it had already been reassigned. The detective to whom the shield had been assigned was contacted, and he gladly returned it so that it could be issued to the surviving officer. The point here is not that an officer or detective will easily give up his shield—quite the contrary[10]—but that the detective understood the shield had great significance to the surviv-ing officer, and that giving it to him would honor both the retired homicide detective and the slain officer (Beaming, 1998).

While officers in other police agencies may refer to the emblem of office as a "badge," in the NYPD it is universally called a "shield," and all the heraldic images and meanings associated with that term apply to it. For many or most NYPD offic-ers, the shield is more than a mere insignia of office and rank: it opens the possibil-ity of a shared romanticized vision of themselves and of police work and connects them personally to the vision. For them, the shield is in every sense a heraldic es-cutcheon, a coat of arms denoting membership in a proud band of crusading war-rior knights possessed of a principled mission to battle the dragon. It is a symbol permitting transcendence of the banal realities of everyday police work and access to an even greater and more enduring cultural immortality system.[11]

The primacy of this immortality system to the officer's overall sense of self can be glimpsed in the fact that retired officers typically acquire a "dupe" or "fugazy"—a full-sized replica of the shield they surrendered. Often partners or workmates will present these "dupes" at a retirement party, symbolizing the recipient's continued connection to policing and the police identity. Although department regulations specifically prohibit possessing duplicate shields, many active and retired officers nevertheless acquire them.

Symbols and images of knighthood are pervasive in policing (e.g., Bittner's allusions to slaying dragons and especially Wambaugh's [1972] frequent use of images and metaphors of knighthood and chivalry in his novel *The Blue Knight*),[12] and even the most cynical cops buy into them at one level or another. This imag-ery figures prominently in the names officers choose for their work groups and fraternal or social organizations—there is, for example, a Blue Knights motorcycle club for officers, and many officers purchase precinct T-shirts, hats, or jackets whose logos incorporate terms or images relating to chivalry and knighthood.[13]

Finally, we might extract additional significance from the passing of shields, nightsticks, and other cherished trappings of police work if we consider the fact that with few exceptions, these items are the symbolic or actual representation of offensive and defensive weapons. In line with Bittner's (1980) observations, they symbolize the police monopoly on the legitimate use of coercive force. We should also recognize the ritual and the emphasis so many warrior cultures place upon the ceremonial passing of weapons in their rites of initiation to manhood. From a functionalist anthropological view, we can see that such rituals develop in warrior cultures precisely to reinforce the culture's bellicose orientation and to remind the warrior-initiate of his responsibility to defend the culture's way of life.

Altruism, Idealism, and Early Images of Police Work

Notwithstanding the powerful images entailed in policing's immortality systems and the potent connection officers may have to them, it is a curious truth that many officers resist admitting their pride in seeing a son or daughter enter their occupation. It is also a curious truth that many officers are reticent to initially admit their romanticized feelings about police work or the altruism that often impelled them toward it. These truths, which many officers will admit once sufficient trust is gained to lower their mantle of cynicism, are once again part and parcel of the ambiguity and ambivalence that characterizes their world as well as the hardened personae they present in an emotionally defensive response to it. It is not surprising that so many officers formed their altruistic and idealistic image of police work in childhood or adolescence, a relatively unsophisticated time of idealism, but even most of those who drift into police work come to embrace some romantic notions about it.

Certainly not all officers are initially drawn to police work solely or substantially by pure or romanticized motives—Niederhoffer (1967), for one, observed that most rookies claim to have entered the field for the pay and job security[14]— but for the most part even those who drift into police work are to some extent eventually won over by idealism and by the occupation's potential for performing prosocial or altruistic works. Van Maanen (1973, p. 409), too, comments that

> the security and salary aspects of the police job have probably been overrated. Through interviews and experience with [one agency's] recruits, a rather pervasive meaningful work theme is apparent as a major factor in job choice. Virtually all recruits alluded to the opportunity afforded by a police career to perform in a role which was perceived as consequential or important to society. While such altruistic motives may be subject to social desirability considerations, or other biasing factors, it is my feeling that these high expectations of community service are an important element in the choice process.

As I conducted the interviews, I found that a desire to "make a difference in people's lives" was a prominent factor in the decision to enter police work. Some officers were quite frank and open about this, while some tenured officers adopted a more guarded or even wistful tone of voice connoting their own awareness that their sense of altruism had been somewhat eroded during the course of their careers, but my sense in all cases was that the officers were honest about their innate or acquired sense of commitment to a larger unifying purpose.[15] This sense of "making a difference" is, of course, closely tied to the mode of symbolic immortality through creative works.

The police aspirant thus possesses an initial understanding of police work that is amorphous, unsophisticated, and often highly idealized. In general, he values police work's potential to make a difference in people's lives, and he seeks vitalizing connections with images, experiences, and human interactions that can activate the constellation. At the same time, he may be attracted to the danger, violence, and authority the police role offers and may pursue experiences that connect him with these images as well. He is, in brief, uncertain and conflicted about his chosen career, and he seeks to relieve his sense of ambiguity and estrangement through a transformation of self.

The Police Academy: Transforming Attitudes and Belief Systems

Coupled with these and other ambiguities, paradoxes, and conflicts operating within the rookie's world are tremendous pressures to conform his attitudes and behaviors to standards set officially by the department or unofficially by the occupational culture. John van Maanen (1978a, p. 117) points out that members of all occupations develop ways to negotiate and manage the structural strains, contradictions, and anomalies inherent in their roles and tasks and to cope with the emotional realities of their work, but

> in police work, with danger, drudgery and dogma as prime occupational characteristics, these tensions are extreme. Correspondingly, the pressure on new members to bow to group standards is intense. Few, if any, pass through the socialization cycle without being persuaded—through their own experience and the sage-like wisdom passed from generation to generation of policemen—to accept the occupationally accepted frame-of-reference. This frame-of-reference includes, of course, both broad axioms related to police work in general (role) and the more specific corollaries which provide the ground rules of the workaday world (operations). . . . These perspectives provide the perceptual filter through which a patrolman views his work life. In a sense, they provide him with something akin to an occupational ideology. Such an ideology—rooted in common experience and knowledge—serves to support and maintain the codes, agreements and habits existing in the work place.

From a formative-symbolic perspective, we can see how van Maanen's (1978a) observations emphasize the importance of experiences and images in shaping the officer's sense of self and his response to the environment. As the "occupational frame of reference" develops, it becomes a highly symbolized constellation containing anticipatory plans ("rules of the workaday world") that prescribe actions or responses to specific images the officer may encounter, while at the same time it gives a particular kind of meaning to those images. Because others who have experienced similar images share the constellation, it supports and maintains the informal and unstated "codes, agreements and habits" that are the stuff of the police subculture.

Pressures to conform and to accept the established frame of reference are first brought to bear in the police academy. Like monasteries, prisons, and military boot camps, the police academy is the sort of "total institution" described by Erving Goffman (1961) as a vehicle to resocialize and radically redefine the individual's sense of self and his place in society. While the police academy may not be as rigorous or demanding as some other total institutions, it nevertheless shares many of their characteristics and is certainly a social system operating to alter and remold the professional and personal identity.

The total institution separates the initiate from the larger society, mortifies and strips him of the artifacts and trappings of individuality and civilian life, and imposes a new set of rules for behavior, dress, social interaction with peers and superiors, and overall deportment. Recruits wear a distinctive uniform that resembles but is not identical to the "real" police uniform, and they are not issued a gun or shield until the last few days of training. Male recruits must crop their hair short, and female recruits are defeminized by rules requiring that hair be worn pinned up to fit under the uniform cap. Jewelry, earrings, makeup, and nail polish are also forbidden in the academy, and instructors informally counsel female recruits to avoid injury in a fight by keeping their nails trimmed and by forgoing jewelry and earrings while on patrol. Although recruits are technically sworn police officers with all the legal powers that title implies, they are repeatedly admonished under threat of termination that department policy forbids recruits from exercising their arrest or enforcement powers while on- or off-duty. They are implicitly assumed not to have amassed sufficient knowledge and experience to use their powers wisely, and this assumption is frequently communicated to them. The police recruit exists in an uncomfortable sort of middle ground—he is no longer a civilian but not yet a real cop. He is expected to behave like a police officer, but not to take police action. He is developing a set of forms and constellations that will eventually transform his sense of self, but he is strictly warned against enacting any of the anticipatory plans they may contain.

Within this unfamiliar, artificial, and authoritarian police academy environment of paradox and conflicting roles and identities, and in addition to a rigorous physical fitness program and an academic curriculum designed to equip the recruit with a large and specialized body of cognitive knowledge as well as specific psychomotor skills, the recruit faces an array of direct and indirect pressures to alter or modify his attitudes, appearance, and belief systems. Moreover, the recruit is under pressure to amass this knowledge, develop these skills, and internalize these attitudes quickly and thoroughly. Mere completion of the police academy course of study and assignment to a precinct is not sufficient for the rookie officer's acceptance within the subculture, however. The rookie must also internalize and demonstrate allegiance to the subculture's norms and standards, and must demonstrate his technical proficiency in the real-world tasks and duties of police work. The subculture's norms and standards are initially transmitted through police academy instructors and field training officers, and subsequently refined through interaction with "real cops" in the precinct setting. Under these pressures, the images provided in the attitudes, assumptions, belief systems, and idiosyncratic behaviors of police academy instructors and early partners become important templates that recruits wittingly or unwittingly emulate.

The rookie's socialization process and the quest to define and internalize a viable professional identity continue after his graduation from the police academy and assignment to a patrol precinct. Rather than finding resolution, though, the rookie finds that conflicts, ambiguities, and struggles are intensified and brought into sharper and more realistic focus in the precinct environment. The problem of defining and internalizing an identity is now complicated by the problem of gaining acceptance in the patrol cop culture. Relationships developed with peers during the academy experience may have buffered the recruit's sense of social dislocation, since to some extent all the recruits share the sense of anomic dislocation, but when the rookie is assigned to patrol duties he experiences additional discontinuity and estrangement from the precinct's established work group. Precinct life involves an entirely new set of personalities and informal rules, presents him with novel and genuine images of police work, and entails an entirely new and largely unfamiliar status system. In contrast to the safe and rarefied pseudo-academic environment of the academy, precinct life is "the real thing"— the life the young officer has been looking forward to with anticipation, excitement, and more than likely, some trepidation. Most importantly, precinct life is different because performance really matters. There are no make-up exams or second chances, and some errors can have serious or even deadly consequences. The rookie's task—a daunting one—is to become a "real cop" by applying the mass of arcane knowledge and the range of untested skills acquired in the police academy in a realistic environment (Bayley and Bittner, 1984).

Precinct Life

In the precinct, the physical and emotional dangers of policing are no longer abstractions. The rookie soon encounters threatening images of objective danger, and he is realistically exposed to the public's hostility, fear, awe, and admiration. The social and psychological variables that operate in the young officer's personal life continue, and his estrangement may even intensify in light of the additional disruptions to his ordinary social interaction patterns caused by rotating shifts, mandatory overtime, and other exigencies of police work. These variables, along with the conflicts and ambiguities they engender, certainly become more intense and more salient in his occupational sphere.

As the rookie continues his quest for transformative "real" police experience, senior officers become important role models, and through their example the rookie acquires some of the images needed for his evolving identity. We have alluded to the fact that in order to be an effective officer, one must be capable of flexibly responding to a range of contingent situations. Frequently, these situations—perhaps especially those involving the deaths of others—demand the officer combine a basic competence in the tasks and skills of police work with empathetic and humane interactive skills. As we shall see in the next chapter, rookies seem much more comfortable fulfilling a given situation's administrative tasks than its interpersonal demands. In particular, the recent police academy graduate has a great concern for avoiding any violation of rules and procedures, and this concern may constrain his urge to interact compassionately or blind him to the discretionary options for humane interaction that are available to him.

Because they are, after all, still "learning the ropes" and taking directional cues from more senior officers, rookies are generally reluctant to take the risky step of going beyond what is minimally expected of them. Bayley and Bittner (1984) discuss how police learn the skills of discretionary decision making, and they postulate a continuum of situations ranging from the cut-and-dried to the problematic. Officers have few doubts about what to do at a vehicle accident, for example, because the appropriate responses are easily learned, clearly enumerated in department regulations, and clearly recognized by everyone involved. Other situations are more complex and involve considerable room for choice, but even when inexperienced officers recognize the complexity and the demand to act, they may not perceive that they have a range of discretionary options at their disposal. They may recognize the need to act but simply not know what to do to. The process of recognizing and acting upon the problematic situations with appropriate discretion is highly uncertain, Bayley and Bittner say, because it is shaped by experience and learned through exposure to other officers.

The type of skill acquisition process described by Bayley and Bittner (1984) is analogous to the development of an integrated and multifaceted police identity, and it points out the importance of internalizing new and more flexible modes of response in the process of transforming identity. As the young officer becomes more conversant with and adept at fulfilling basic technical tasks and administrative responsibilities, he also has the opportunity to observe and learn more complex interpersonal skills by observing seasoned officers. As the skills are acquired, he concomitantly faces greater pressure to practice them. Seasoned officers may permit a callow rookie to confine his activities to the simple tasks of preparing paperwork at a death scene, but they would not give a veteran officer the same leeway to avoid interacting with the deceased's family and friends—an important and necessary part of the job.

In a similar way, the transformation of the police identity progresses from a limited and rudimentary conception in which the police self is primarily defined in terms of basic task competence to that of a more complex and flexible police self that is also capable of responding more humanely and with greater sensitivity to the needs and problems of others. Again, the process by which the professional self develops and becomes more complex mirrors the overall process of self-development as described by Lifton: through the accumulation and integration of increasingly sophisticated images, the organism moves from satisfying its most basic needs toward the development of a more highly symbolized sense of self.

The rookie self is a sort of "just the facts, ma'am" self, but a more holistic and integrated sense of the police identity emerges as interactive skills are observed, learned, and practiced. The rookie not only learns that the "real cop"—the cop he aspires to be—is capable of deftly exercising both roles, but that the capacity to deal comfortably with more complex human issues is a desirable police characteristic well worth acquiring. It is a characteristic worth acquiring not only because it facilitates his development and hastens his acceptance within the police culture, but in a functional and very practical way because it makes many public interactions within police work easier and less confrontational. As these additional skills and elements of self adhere and as the more complex and multifaceted police identity continues to form, the rookie also moves toward greater acceptance among peers and greater social and psychological comfort with his police role.

The novel experiences and images required for the transformation of self present themselves readily enough as the new officer explores police work, but some officers actively seek out and immerse themselves in the experiences and images as a means of hastening their transformation. Both in my interviews with collaborators and in less formal discussions with officers over the years, it became apparent that the differential urge to seek out transformative police experiences occurs across a kind of continuum. Certain personality traits and certain motivational, philosophical, and dispositional characteristics seem to correlate with the relative strength of the officer's impulse to seek new images and new experiences that will transform the self and bring him closer to a police identity. At one pole are officers who aggressively seek out the entire range of potential police experiences and images, seemingly with little regard for the personal or emotional costs involved, while at the opposite pole are officers who show a more conservative selectivity in the kind of experiences they seek. To a far greater extent than the passive recipients of police experience, these assertive officers immerse themselves in novel police images and experiences and appear to have a more realistic sense of the moral, social, intellectual, and physical complexities involved in police work. They have a rudimentary understanding that by taking in and being affected by a wide range of images and experiences they will ultimately become better and more effective cops. At some level of awareness, they understand that absorbing different kinds of images and experiences permits them to develop the multiple forms and constellations they need to deal effectively with the complex challenges of policing.

This is not to say that the experience-seeking officers are oblivious to the physical dangers and emotional hazards they face, however. On the contrary, they seem quite attuned to the fact that becoming a competent cop requires some measure of personal sacrifice, but because they have a generally altruistic nature and a high positive regard for the police role and identity, they are more than willing to face danger and to suffer the emotional costs involved in doing a job they see as good and positive and personally ennobling. At some level, these officers seem to understand that the transformation to a role, an identity, and a sense of self they value so highly can only be achieved through the crucible of police experience, and they are more than willing to embrace these experiences. For these officers, police work can best be described as a vocation, and for many of them the quest to attain a police self-identity and to become a competent and experienced cop takes on an almost spiritual quality. As a practical matter, the rookies who most actively seek transformation are probably more likely to volunteer for dangerous or otherwise less desirable assignments, including those they know will involve a death exposure.

At the other extreme of this polarity are the passive rookies who will, for the most part, accept and complete the assignments given them but who are less willing to go the extra yard. Their concept of the police role, at least at this stage of their career, is a narrower and less complex constellation, and they tend to see police work more as a steady and secure job with good benefits than as a vocation. As a result, they are less concerned with achieving the kind of competence and the kind of police identity so cherished by some other rookies. They tend also to be more concerned with avoiding the physical perils of police work than with avoiding its emotional dangers, if only because their somewhat constricted or unidimensional conceptualization of police work does not include a well-developed appreciation for policing's unique emotional hazards. Because these pragmatic rookie officers are far less committed to the kind of high-minded principles rookies at the other extreme might embrace, from the beginning of their careers these officers tend to seek the greatest maximization of reward with the least investment of self. These rookies often take the path of least resistance, and they generally have a more bureaucratic and less humanistic orientation.

All of this is not to say that rookie police officers are immutably locked into a career-long pattern of actively seeking or eschewing transformative images and experiences. On the contrary, some officers progress from passive acceptance of police experiences to a more active embrace of vitalizing images that transform the self, but this process generally occurs when early images and exposures animate in them a more comprehensive and expansive image of policing's complexities as well as the psychological and social rewards that can accrue from mastering them.[16] One of the primary distinctions between the aggressive and passive image seekers, then, is the relative strength of their initial rudimentary image of police work, and hence the relative strength of the images that early police experience awakens in them.

The transformation of self-identity during early socialization has both profound and subtle manifestations that are exhibited both on and off duty. Among the more overt expressions we can glimpse in a young officer's outward behavior are an increased tendency to primarily associate or hang out with other officers while off duty, wearing police-related clothing like baseball caps or T-shirts bearing police logos, and the particular attention or deference young officers pay to more experienced cops who offer them "tips of the trade" or other forms of professional advice. In some young officers, we see an increased (and perhaps affected) swagger in their walk, or perhaps a change in the overall demeanor they present to friends and others outside the work environment. In each of these behaviors, the young officer appears to be "trying on" the attitudes and characteristics he perceives as coplike.

In a more subtle way, one can observe differences in the young officer's language, which he may knowingly or unwittingly pepper with police jargon. Like the use of jargon in any occupation, conversing in police idioms expresses a kind of connection with other in-group members, but using jargon with family and friends also serves both to socialize or familiarize the outsider a bit with the police culture and to underscore the officer's separateness from them. The words we use to express ourselves and communicate information are, of course, merely commonly accepted symbolizations of the images we hold in common. Words alone are often insufficient to fully express our more complex or amorphous images and forms, and in order to adequately communicate or comprehend these symbolizations we often rely on contextual cues that have common meaning to the speaker and the listener. As the young officer is acculturated through police experiences, his images, forms, and constellations become increasingly difficult to communicate to those outside the culture, since they may not fully appreciate the significance of his words or the context in which they are spoken. In communicating with each other and in attempting to convey subtle shades of meaning, officers often rely on context as well as idiomatic expressions that are particular to the subculture.

An example can be found in the terms *police officer* and *cop*. The terms may seem synonymous to members of the public and to the uninitiated rookie; if a distinction is made it is probably that the term *cop* conveys a kind of disparagement or derision, and outsiders usually see *police officer* as a more respectful term. To more fully integrated members of the police subculture, though, these sets of meaning are inverted: to be a "cop" one must have incorporated sufficient experience to have evolved beyond simply being a police officer. Within the police culture, anyone who passes the examination, is hired by the agency, and takes the prescribed oath of office can be a "police officer"—in itself the term contains little or no status, does not implicitly differentiate one member of the agency from another, and can even be used pejoratively. To "be a cop," on the other hand, implicitly expresses that a transformation of self—a process of "becoming"—has taken place. To refer to someone as "a *good* cop" is to bestow a particular kind of honorific, characterizing him as someone who has been transformed by police experience into a different and special kind of person who embodies a set of values and attitudes that are highly esteemed within the group. The term *police officer* thus conveys a somewhat constricted and unidimensional image, while "cop" conveys a more fully structured and richly textured constellation of meaning. In this construction, the term reflects the police culture's staunchly held conviction that the "good cop" must be a person of many parts—his occupational identity and working personality must be multifaceted and capable of dealing effectively with a vast range of contingencies.

How does the rookie make the transition from "police officer" to "good cop"? Gradually, if at all, and entirely through the integration of transforming images police experience provides him. Even the language and idioms of policing thus reflect the importance the subculture places on transformative images and experiences.

Perhaps a more interesting and, from a continuity-of-life model perspective, a more illuminative set of related terms is that of *the Department* and *the Job*. Here again, the terms may seem synonymous to the police initiate or the layman—assuming the layman is even familiar with the term *the Job*—but they have vastly different meanings within the occupational culture. More importantly, the terms reflect the dimensions of another primary immortality system. In discussing the meaning of these terms, it should be made clear that cops may at times use them interchangeably, and at other times use them with great specificity. In their specific meaning, the terms are tied to the polarities of connection versus separation and integrity versus disintegration.

As tenured cops understand and use the term, *the Department* involves images of the structures, policies, procedures and, to some extent, the people that comprise the police agency at any given time. Each of these elements is, by its nature, transitory and ephemeral—policies and procedures can and do change with the stroke of a pen, organizational structures and tables of organization are intangible representations, and people move through and eventually leave the agency at the end of their careers. In the broadest sense, the construct or constellation of "the Department" captures the superficial face of the agency, and even the most cursory examination of police history reveals how much and how quickly these surface elements can change. "The Department" is subject to many social and political influences that shape and influence it. Because "the Department" is so ephemeral and because it is subject to political influence, the term can take on pejorative connotations for cops who see it as fundamentally lacking in integrity.

"The Job," on the other hand, is a more complex constellation representing the philosophy, the humanity, the ethos, and the sense of personal commitment to policing as a vocation that "good cops" share. To draw an analogy, one might say "the Department" is the agency's skeleton and some of its flesh and blood, but "the Job" is the heart and soul that gives it life. "The Department"—the superficial and impermanent dimensions of the policing enterprise—changes on almost a moment-by-moment basis, and in this sense change and impermanence can provide important images of movement and progress. But "the Job" represents continuity and the enduring principles that tie the individual officer and his fellows to the past and future, and it represents connection to those, past and present, who share a commitment to policing's eternal principles.

As a group, cops are not given to philosophical pronouncement, but when they wax philosophical they often express a sentiment along the lines of "the Job never changes—cops do the same thing today they did one hundred years ago. They may wear different uniforms, and today they may drive cars, but the basic Job never changes." In a biosocial sense, this sentiment also extends to cops in other agencies. The officer's sense of connection to "the Job" gives him access to a sense of symbolic immortality because it affords a sense of continuity and participation in an enterprise that is rooted in the historic past but extends into the future. There is also a special sense of integrity and wholeness in sharing or ascribing to the Job's strong group ethos, particularly when that ethos explicitly maintains that its adherents operate in service of good, on the side of morality, and in protection of the social order. At a fundamental personal level, cops believe that they and other members of "the Job" represent integrity and prevent the disintegration of civilization.

Having set forth some of the processes operating to shape the rookie's sense of self, and after emphasizing the importance of images and experiences in the overall formative-symbolic process, we can turn our attention to the more specific psychology of the first death encounter. As noted earlier, the images and experiences provided in the first death encounter serve to further forge the young officer's sense of self and his professional identity, and in many respects the struggle to integrate and assimilate these same images and experiences illuminates the larger struggles the officer faces in becoming a police officer.

4.

The Rookie's Experience

Introduction to Death

The rookie officer's first professional exposure to the death of another person is a fundamental rite of passage and a milestone event in his quest to forge a police identity. As outlined in chapter 3, the early days of a police career involve a process of acquiring new images and forms that combine with existing images in a way that animates and enriches them, ultimately producing a more complex and multifaceted police self-identity. In this chapter we will see how exposures to death are one type of experience that supplies new images and forms to animate and develop the rookie's initial sense of self-as-police-officer. Death encounters and death imagery are, in themselves, very powerful in terms of shaping any individual's sense of self, but the rookie's death encounters have an especially potent impact on the developing professional identity by virtue of their relative recency, their relative novelty, and the fact that the images and forms they will connect with and alter are still amorphous and evolving. For the most part the rookie's initial sense of his professional self, like his understanding or conception of the police role, is comprised of fairly narrow and constricted images and forms that contain limited schemas for enactment. But early professional death encounters supply an abundant quantity of death imagery that ultimately leads to a more complex and inclusive sense of self, concurrently opening him to a broader range of anticipatory possibilities. In other words, the images acquired in early death encounters function to help the rookie develop into a better and more complete cop.

Because the first death encounter almost always takes place at the earliest stages of the police career, it also takes place against a larger backdrop of great social and psychological ambiguity, uncertainty, and pressure to demonstrate competence in the tasks and duties of police work. These factors are reflected in the way the rookie experiences the event and in each of the five themes of survivor psychology, but they are perhaps most readily discerned in the way they facilitate the natural tendency to distance oneself psychologically from death events. To the extent they encourage psychic numbing, they are quite functional because they protect the rookie from potentially overwhelming psychological threats. This is not to say that rookies cannot be overwhelmed or traumatized by the novel death-related images they might possibly encounter, but rather that in the vast majority of cases the rookie is sufficiently detached to avoid permanent or severe traumatic reaction. Although I heard dozens of first-exposure narratives as I conducted this research, none of the collaborators experienced or knew of another officer who experienced acute dissociative reactions along the lines of psychic closing-off. The rookie's first death encounter is therefore more than simply his first professional experience with the death of another, since it is also often his first experience with the constructive dimension of psychic numbing: partial professional numbing. Because the various forms of psychic numbing and the impairment of symbolization they involve are at the core of survivor psychology, this chapter begins by exploring the rookie's experience of psychic numbing and partial professional numbing before examining how the other four themes of survivor psychology also become manifest in the rookie's first death encounter.

Although we will examine these five themes sequentially, we must bear in mind that they cannot be examined discretely. The five themes of survivor psychology arise simultaneous with the death event, and because all the themes are related to or intertwined with each other, they cannot easily be disentangled; a specific experience or image often illuminates more than one theme of survivor psychology and more than one aspect of the rookie's quest to transform his self-identity. After examining each theme as it applies to the rookie police officer's first professional death encounter, we will conclude this chapter with a more in-depth exploration—a case study of sorts—of how each theme was reflected in one young officer's death encounter.

Psychic Numbing

The natural tendency toward psychic numbing in the face of a death encounter can certainly be formidable, but an array of other pressures also operate to enhance distancing and influence the rookie's experience of the first death event. Pressures to demonstrate competence, for example, facilitate distancing by forcing the rookie to focus much of his cognitive attention on the performance of unfamiliar tasks and duties, rather than on the death event's emotional content. The rookie's sense of ambiguity and uncertainty also facilitates distancing insofar as it is rooted in his lack of adequate images and forms that would provide appropriate schemas for enactment and that would give fuller meaning to his experience. Absent these images and forms, the rookie relies primarily on his cognitive abilities to puzzle out what he should do and to understand the novel images he confronts. Each of these factors operates in service of numbing and dissociation, but the pressure to demonstrate competence seems especially powerful.

When the rookies and tenured officers I spoke with reconstructed their first on-the-job exposure to the death of another person, they universally described a great concern for properly and completely preparing the paperwork and performing the other duties required of them, notwithstanding their inclination to give assistance and emotional support to the deceased's family and friends. When faced with the alternatives of demonstrating administrative competence (and avoiding potential trouble or embarrassment) or lending potentially costly emotional support, the urge to manufacture some distance by defaulting to the prescribed tasks of the job at hand can be compelling, and in general that less risky urge wins out.

For the most part, rookies are uncomfortable with their new social role and are generally unpracticed in the kind of behaviors that would allow them to present the appearance of competence to the public and to other officers. Although police academy training to some extent prepares them for the administrative aspects of police work, it less effectively equips them to deal with the raft of complex interpersonal issues various situations present. Every situation rookies encounter prescribes different demands for interaction, and we can scarcely expect 6 months of classroom training to provide the broad social interactive repertoire necessary to deal with every situation. Moreover, by retreating to the realm of paperwork, which is not public behavior, the officer can shield his inadequacies from public view and avoid social embarrassment. If the officer screws up the paperwork, it can be corrected at a later date without damaging his public persona, but an interpersonal gaffe will immediately make him feel like a fool before his peers as well as the public. Paperwork errors are to be expected, and they do not implicate the officer's public role in a potentially negative way.

A sergeant who is also a former field training officer had ample opportunity to observe rookies' behaviors during their initial death encounters, and his comments made it clear that paying attention to procedural details serves to insulate the young officer from the encounter's potential emotional components:

> I think the rookies look at it *only* from the procedural aspect. As in "I got through it and now it's over." In other words, they don't preoccupy themselves with the person that's dead, they preoccupy themselves with "Did I handle the job right? Did I do what I was supposed to do? Did I make the notification, did I identify the body, did I get the proper complaint number, and aided number? Was the medical examiner . . . you know? Is my supervisor or the Job going to say, "All right, you handled this one right?" I think they're preoccupied with that more than with the dead body itself, from my point of view. Because as I see them when they get back in the car, unless it was a tragic death they won't even comment on it. They're thinking, "Did I do the Aided Card right, did I word it right?"

The partial separation between the affective and cognitive elements of self at the time of the death encounter and the preoccupation with administrative details became manifest in several other ways, including the collaborators' tendency during our discussions to initially recall the task-related difficulties they encountered. Generally speaking, when officers were asked to describe their first death encounter they did not begin by elaborating on their own and others' emotional states. Instead, their initial narratives focused on factual recapitulations of events, and with few exceptions it was only with gentle prodding that they shifted toward recounting their emotional experiences. In terms of reducing the degree of emotional trauma they experienced during the first death encounter, this was fortuitous: by focusing cognitively on these novel and unfamiliar tasks, they had less time or capacity to attend to the disturbing emotional aspects of the death encounter.

The separation of affective and cognitive elements of the self at the time of the first death encounter can also be glimpsed in the tremendous amount of factual detail many officers—especially tenured officers—were able to recall from their first death encounter, and the slight difficulty some displayed in recalling their emotional state. Tenured collaborators frequently closed their eyes as they pictured and described death scenes in minute detail, and several volunteered they could still picture the scene "as if it were yesterday." This tendency to initially recall factual details certainly speaks to the durability of the death imprint image, an issue we will take up later in this chapter. I also found that this tendency to recall visual elements of the death scene image occurred with seemingly little regard for the objective grotesqueness of the scene: especially among tenured collaborators, officers were generally as apt to provide meticulous depictions of mundane or "ordinary" death scenes as they were to describe gory or otherwise unusual scenes. The mannerisms collaborators used and the extensive details they provided indicate the potency and durability of the images involved, and the straightforward factual manner in which they were presented as well as the relative importance officers placed on factual events relative to their emotional experiences illustrate the primacy of the cognitive component of the self during the first death encounter.

The tendency to recollect the factual details of the first death encounter and the durability of the visual image can be glimpsed in the way one veteran officer, a detective with 32 years of service, recalled his first exposure to death as a rookie. The precision with which he recalled seemingly inconsequential details is all the more remarkable for the fact that he handled several hundred homicides during his career. The officer was assigned to guard the body of a young man of approximately his own age who had died of a drug overdose in a bathroom "with a needle still in his arm." The deceased was "a skinny kid wearing a blue shirt and dungarees" who had a common Hispanic name the detective could not specifically recall. When I asked if he could recall the scene, this officer closed his eyes and gestured as he visualized it. "Oh, yeah. I can. . . . The door, the bathroom. How he was, where the head was up near the toilet bowl. When you come out, there was a door to your right, you see the railing for the stairs going down. Matter of fact, it was, it was the top floor, there was a ladder going up to the roof to the skylight. . . . It was on 8th Avenue, between 20th and 21st Street. Yeah, between 20th and 21st Street."

In sharp contrast to these and other rich factual details he offered, the detective had a bit more difficulty recalling his emotional state at the time. To some extent his comments also reflect a commonly observed tendency (discussed more thoroughly below) to thwart potential identification with the deceased by attributing the death to personality factors or situational factors he cannot personally identify with. "I think he was about the same age I was, twenty-one years of age. He died with a needle in his arm. He was *dead*. I thought, look at this, what a *waste*. Here's this guy, he's the same age as I am, and this is how he dies. That was really it. There was nothing, really, more than that."

As we will see later in this chapter, some tenured officers come to recognize the beneficial aspects of psychic numbing and they develop elaborate strategies to insulate themselves from potentially traumatic events. But some rookies also become aware of the distancing they experience at their first death event and, recognizing its value, attempt to enhance it in various ways. A rookie who responded to the death of an elderly man became aware he was identifying with the victim, saw the need to create distance, and responded by actively seeking to objectify the event and the deceased. The strategy he used was to focus on completing the paperwork so that he could wrap up the job and leave the scene and the emotions it conjured. He was asked to describe how he felt during the assignment:

[*Pause.*] Two ways. I don't know, I don't want to say I was being cold, but I was just trying to distance myself from it, personally. You know, I thought of when my grandfather died and all that, but this was nothing like it. It was like, "I don't *know* this person. It's just a body in the other room on a bed and I never met them and I never will again or the wife for that matter." And it was like, "Let's make this as easy as possible for everybody and get the heck out of here." I mean that was basically my thoughts.

Pressures to maintain the public illusion of professional competence through task proficiency also create an especially salubrious milieu for temporary partial distancing to take place. A sergeant described such pressures in his first death encounter, which occurred on his very first tour of duty as a uniformed patrol officer. He was writing his first parking ticket on a rainy evening when he discovered an elderly man lying unconscious in the street with his false teeth on the pavement. As was the case in many other narratives, the competing themes of concern for the feelings of the deceased's loved ones and of maintaining the aura of competence and control, especially in the presence of civilian onlookers, took on a special prominence in his account:

I really didn't know what to do. I wanted to be helpful to the person, but I knew he was gone already. I was just glad the ambulance responded because it took a lot of pressure off of me. Because people look—you're the cop, you're supposed to be doing something. We got the gentleman up on the stretcher and put him in the ambulance and his teeth were still laying on the floor and the sergeant said, "Pick up his teeth and put it in a bag." I had an experience there [*laugh*], and we had him in the ambulance. He was an elderly gentleman, maybe in his seventies. We had to do a search of the body for identification and he had nothing. He was totally without papers and there was no way of identifying him. The sergeant instructed me after we conducted the search that I would go with him to the hospital. And I did. It was kind of a weird situation because you want to do so much, and yet there's nothing you can do.

As it turned out, the victim remained unidentified and a few days later the officer saw a notice in the newspaper that the police were trying to identify the man. He saved the clipping and put it in his scrapbook. In this officer's case, the immediate demands of the situation, the novel activities involved in processing the scene, and his need to maintain the appearance of competence effectively created a distance that, temporarily at least, insulated him from emotion. Although he was able to ward off the emotions and did not identify with the victim at the time of his exposure, a subsequent event reanimated these images. He continued:

> I wasn't so much concerned about the death, I just was concerned about what I had to do as a police officer. So there was a little barrier there for me. I wasn't trying to, you know, put myself in his place, or anything else like that at that time. Later on, when I saw the article in the paper and I saw that he was unidentified and now they're trying to identify him, now I started to feel, "Boy this guy's got no family, he's laying somewhere in a morgue." When I read the article in the paper I said, "Wow, look at this here, that's my case." The only thing I felt was that here's a *person*, obviously no identification, his family might be looking for him if he had a family, and nobody knows. So I felt for him in that way because if it was someone in my family, then I would want to know right away, you know, that something happened to him or where he is, or how to find him. Now when I see he was in the newspaper, he's a *person* now. Now I'm being reintroduced back to this person. I kind of like . . . he went to the hospital, I finished the case, and I forgot about it. But now when I read this article, and I said "Oh, that's my case," it's bringing me back to the guy. So now I'm starting to feel some attachment to it because, hey, I had that case. It was my first, it was my guy. So I had the attachment there. But the initial part, there was no attachment. I was just concerned with, like "I gotta do the right thing here. I gotta do the right reports, and I gotta look good."

Perhaps because other novel experiences of police work commanded his attention, or perhaps because other forms of numbing or denial took place, the officer never followed up on the case to determine if the man was ever identified.

Other rookies have less success at separating out from the emotional context of the event, especially when they are alone at the death scene. Without the social support, guidance, and company of another officer, and especially when they have no paperwork or other tasks to perform, there is little to distract these officers from the death event's emotional content. I discerned a distinct difference in the narrations of those officers who had at least one senior officer at the scene to guide or assist them and those who were thrust into a death encounter without such guidance: when another officer was present and that officer directed them to perform certain tasks or duties, the rookie typically had some sense of agency, leading to a kind of enactment. In these cases, the entire experience generally caused less distress, less death guilt, and less overall impairment of his symbolizing process. Senior officers also typically took the lead in interacting with the civilians present, relegating the far simpler administrative tasks to the grateful rookies.

Further, those rookie officers who were merely assigned to "sit on the body"— to safeguard the remains and await their removal by the medical examiner's personnel after all the paperwork had been completed by other officers—generally described a different quality and quantity of emotional costs. Their exposures tended to be of longer duration, and because they had no functional tasks to distract them or give them a sense of agency, they often paid more attention to the corpse and to the deceased's social circumstances and manner of death. For the most part, the images involved in reflecting on these details entailed more profound emotional costs. The experience of "sitting on the body" with nothing to do for a protracted period reflects elements of separation and stasis and if the death involves images of grotesqueness or humiliation it may have disintegrative elements as well. As we might expect, young officers struggle against disintegration, stasis, and separation when they "sit" on a DOA, seeking various forms of integration, movement, and connection.

Numbing: "Sitting on the Body"

Another collaborator, a sergeant, recalled being assigned, alone and on his very first day of patrol duties as a rookie, to safeguard the remains of a woman in her eighties who died alone in her small apartment in a senior citizens' residence complex. While his experience was somewhat unusual in terms of the severity of its psychological impact and while he demonstrated uncommon insight into his own emotional state at the time of the incident, his experience illustrates the type and quality of emotional costs that may accrue to young officers, especially when they become immersed in the death equivalent states of separation, stasis, and disintegration. The young officer was left alone in the shabby apartment with no instructions and no tasks to perform. He recalls the scene and his response to it:

> It seemed she went to the bathroom, defecated, and got up still half naked and collapsed in the living room by the drapes. You could see from the drapes that she started to realize death was coming over her and she *clawed* at the drapes, almost like she was trying to stay alive. And she *shredded* the drapes and you could see the claw marks in the drapes like the grip of death coming over her. An 80–year-old woman laying half naked dead on the floor with feces still in the toilet and on her and I thought, "This is fucked up."
>
> And I remember looking at her and thinking several things. I thought, "This lady is dead; when am I going to die?" And I thought, "What a morbid thought that was. Why am I thinking about my own mortality?" But I couldn't help it and I remember getting very depressed, despondent. I remember kicking myself for wanting to be a cop. I was a college graduate and I just didn't plan my life right. I remember getting very annoyed at myself for becoming a cop because I'm sitting there guarding an 80-year-old dead woman and I saw absolutely no value to that. The whole scene was morbid. The apartment was dirty because she lived alone and was old and weak. The kitchen had dirty dishes and a sparse amount of food and I thought, "Is this going to happen to me when I get old? If I die before my wife is she going to live like this the remaining years of her life? And just keel over and die this way?" And it was sad, and I was sad. And I have to say it affected me. It affected me emotionally.

This officer, an unusually bright and well-educated man who also had several profound death-related experiences before joining the police department, actively articulated an acute awareness that both his discomfort and the distance he actively sought (for example, after a while he left the apartment and sat in the hallway to physically remove himself from the images at the scene) were rooted in a confrontation with his own mortality. In this respect he was somewhat unique, since few officers articulated any insight into this important connection. He was also somewhat unique insofar as he articulated a keen awareness of the event's immediate and long-term psychic impact on him.

I remember going over there, it was my first dead body, so not knowing what to expect but being nervous, maybe even shaking a little. And then blocking out that it was a dead body. I've seen them before as a Marine, dead bodies. I said, "Fuck it, it means nothing." But obviously it did mean something if I was trying to convince myself that it didn't.

vh: *Was any one feeling or combination of feelings more powerful than others?*

I guess a feeling of despair. I guess the feeling of my mortality was the most prevalent. "This person is dead; when am I going to die? Am I going to die the same way?" I have to say, any DOA I came across as a cop, that same feeling came through. "This guy is dead; when am I going to die?" It never came to me as a Marine, it never came to me when my brother got killed. It came to me on every DOA as a cop. Every one. Maybe because none of these deaths had any meaning for me. There was no social value to their death, and I had no connection to them. But the recurring theme in all my DOAs was, "This person is dead; when am I going to die?" When you start getting one or two DOAs a week, as a rookie, it starts bothering you. You start saying . . . it starts having an impact on your psyche, on your mental health. You get depressed and despondent and it changes your outlook on the world. You get cynical.

Being alone at a death scene with no functional or distracting tasks to perform can certainly cause one to reflect upon death and one's own mortality, and, as evidenced by the narration above, these reflections can have a potent emotional impact on a young officer. Some rookies physically distanced themselves from the remains, but their concern for following rules and procedures was also evident when several articulated a concern that they might somehow be violating some arcane rule by failing to keep the body in view. Many described taking a chair to a hallway outside the apartment, and several even spoke of sitting on the floor or on stairways outside the residence when a chair was not available. In a similar vein, others spoke of their amazement or awe of officers who seemed not at all upset by the body, to the extent that some of the senior officers they met were so adept at partial professional numbing they could nap comfortably in close proximity to the corpse. But just as the absence of others shapes the death experience, the presence of others can also change the psychological dimensions of the death encounter.

Numbing: The Presence of Others

Most of the officers I interviewed described first encounters where other officers were present, and for the most part that presence helped reduce the rookie's distress. Senior officers typically (but not universally) took the time and effort to guide the young officer in performing the necessary tasks and responsibilities, and the rookies were grateful for this and for relieving them of the uncomfortable responsibility to interact with the family and friends. This was apparent in the narration provided by a rookie who responded to a "difficulty breathing" job[1] on his foot post:

> So I walked down about two blocks. There was already [a patrol car], there was an ambulance there, and the fire department. The fire department came out and, uh, I walked up and they were shaking their heads. They said "No, it's a DOA." I said OK and they said there were two officers in there already, you know, you don't have to go in. I said, "Well, I'm out of the academy less than a month and I'd like to go in and talk to them and see what's going on. I can learn from this." They said, "Come on in, we'll go in with you." There were two officers there. [Someone, the rookie could not recall who, asked if he had ever seen a dead body.] I said, "Well, yes. We went to the morgue." It wasn't too long ago, maybe about three weeks before I was at the morgue. They said, "Oh, but you never saw one in its natural state." He says, "Why don't you come up with me and I'll show you so you know what you're going to see."
>
> We went up the stairs and, you know, she was covered, so we pulled the sheet off of her. I think she was 74 or 75. She had just passed away in her sleep and, uh, he just showed me, you know, he was explaining to me how a body begins to decompose. We went downstairs and I was just with the officers and, um, they were basically just showing me. We went through the whole thing together, you know, uh, fill out the '61, the Aided Card. And then he called the ME, then he called the TS.[2]

The rookie, who clearly sought out the exposure because he viewed it as a potential learning experience, went on to explain how the senior officers interacted with the relatives and to expedite the body's removal: they called the deceased's doctor to ensure he would sign the death certificate, notified the medical examiner's office of that fact, and told the family they could notify a funeral home to remove the body.[3] The rookie was gratified they took the time and effort to show him the paperwork, to review the slightly different procedures they would follow if the deceased had lived alone, and to provide him with various telephone numbers he would use in making his own notifications in the future.

Numbing and Humane Interaction

Recalling feelings of uncertainty in their own capacity to interact effectively with the deceased's family and friends, rookies nevertheless expressed a will to provide solace and relief, even if they lacked the skills and experience to do so successfully. They saw this capacity to synthesize affective and cognitive competence—

to integrate effective crisis intervention with administrative sophistication—as central to the police officer's role, and they saw it as a desirable professional attribute worth acquiring. Most rookies placed a great value on the capacity to practice both roles, to the extent that some were offended when senior officers did not display what they believed was the appropriate degree of concern and compassion toward grieving relatives or friends. Although rookies saw the need for this synthesis, in many cases they lacked the experience to do it effectively themselves: they just didn't know how.

One rookie, for example, described how he and another rookie became upset at the cavalier attitude displayed by one particular veteran at the scene, at the same time alluding to his own attempt to gain distance through immersion in paperwork. Their dismay revolved around this idea of blending empathy and concern for others with professional competence:

> One officer we met that we, we didn't like very much—he was just, he wasn't nasty or anything, he was just, to the point. Like the sergeant walked in and said, "What have you got?" and he said [matter-of-factly] "DOA" right in front of the wife and we didn't think that was very nice. Instead of quietly over to the side. It was loud and just no emotions. [*quietly*] "We have a DOA, sir." And the wife was in there. I mean the wife was an older woman and she really wasn't, she probably didn't even pick up on it, but someone else could have. So we didn't think that was very nice.

Notwithstanding the offense he took at the officer's nonchalance, the rookie appreciated the connection between a cognitive focus on procedures, partial professional numbing, and the fulfillment of role expectations. He continued, offering an opinion as to the source of their numbing:

> They've done it so many times. You could tell. They've done it a lot and like, going right through the steps. That's the first thing that popped into *my* mind—as soon as [we learned it was a] DOA I started thinking procedure. "What did I learn in Police Science? Who do I have to call and whatever." I'm glad they showed up because I would have been in there forever, lost. Because I knew I had to call the Patrol Supervisor, and I had to do a '61 and an Aided Card but after that I don't know who to call. I don't have the phone numbers for the ME, I don't have, I don't even think we even had the phone numbers for the Desk. So we were like, "We're lost." Just wait for someone to get here. I think that's how I handled it. I mean mentally, emotionally. I just kicked right into procedure. [My partner, a female officer] talked to the wife and was being very nice with her, and I just started with the procedure.

Another tenured officer recalled how a senior officer's inconsiderate attitude shocked and appalled him at a death scene early in his career. He described feeling outraged and deeply embarrassed at a senior officer's behavior and comments in the presence of grieving family members when the senior cop, who was apparently quite numb to compassionate emotion, made a lewd comment and sexual gesture in relation to a naked female body:[4]

In essence, the lady was lying in the bed, totally nude, a young girl, and her husband—as you walked into the apartment, the door swung like this [*gestures to illustrate*]—he was behind the door. So if you were entering the apartment you would see the body but you wouldn't see who was behind the door. I'm next to the body, and the sergeant—he became a lieutenant—comes in and goes [*gestures with hand*] and says [*sexual comment*], not knowing that the husband's behind the door. The comment was . . . sadistically comical. That's all I can say. And I look up and the man was weeping, and you know when you're startled but you say, "No, it couldn't have been what I heard?" And he went back to weeping.

Perhaps as a reflection of our cultural emphasis on women as nurturers and caregivers, female rookies seemed somewhat more comfortable with family interactions than their male counterparts, and when female officers were present these duties were typically delegated to them. The female officers' relative comfort level may also indicate an evolving police role identity that is less concerned with displaying masculine qualities. A former field training officer who often witnessed rookies struggling with the tension between compassion and control commented on the struggle's connection to a stoic masculine identity, which he in turn linked to demands for a professional appearance of imperturbability:

Cops supposedly have this macho thing, like, you know, we're supposed to be beyond all emotions, these feelings, or whatever. But we're not. We have feelings like everybody else. We shield a lot of times because people look up to us. If we go to a scene and we act like the people that are on the scene, then who takes charge of the scene? So you have to have this, ah, this strength, the ability to show people that you know how to deal with it. But yet be compassionate and understand that this isn't a job, it's still a human being who's died or whatever it is and still have compassion for the people who lost this person. And try to guide them and assist them. That's the way I've always . . . I've always, I do for people what I would expect someone to do for me or my family. I always told the rookies when I had them, "Remember, it's because of them you have a job. Without their problems, you wouldn't have a job." So you have to, I think the word is *empathize, empathy,* have empathy? And understanding and yet be strong enough to take charge and do your job and guide the people on through this crisis.

All of this speaks to the fact that at some level rookies have a rudimentary understanding that police work requires complex interpersonal skills as well as administrative proficiency. They also know that in order to become proficient police officers, to acquire the police self-identity they so avidly desire, and to gain satisfying acceptance in the police culture, they must develop a complex, multi-faceted, and flexible repertoire of attitudes, behaviors, and cognitive and emotional skills. In the specific context of death scene interactions, young officers perceive the demand to blend compassionate crisis intervention with administrative competence, although they typically lack the kind of images and experiences that will permit them to do so effectively and comfortably. Many officers sought or felt compelled to perform both roles during their first death encounter, although many also expressed experiencing a tension between a personal urge to act compassionately toward family members present at a death scene and a reluctance to engage in behaviors that might potentially violate police procedures. This tension was often exacerbated by their fundamental lack of familiarity with procedures and their responsibilities under those procedures.

A sergeant, for example, explained that in his first job-related death encounter as a rookie he was assigned alone to safeguard remains in a private residence when the family arrived. The deceased, an elderly woman, was lying in bed and had been covered with a sheet by other officers. Because no determination of the cause of death had yet been made, the room was considered a potential crime scene, and he knew he should not permit anyone access to it. The family asked if they could view the remains to "be alone with Grandma" and "say goodbye for the last time," and the officer was torn between his humane urge to provide whatever solace the visit might offer and an acute awareness of his professional responsibility to maintain the integrity of a crime scene. The humane urge ultimately won out and he permitted the family access, but the officer was quite aware that he faced a range of sanctions if the scene was disturbed and the death was ruled a homicide.

The presence of the deceased's family often adds to a rookie's distress, especially when family members are openly grieving or visibly agitated. When civilians and relatives are present, the rookie is more likely to have to interact with them and he can less easily hide behind paperwork as a means to facilitate numbing. When others are visibly agitated, the officer may feel especially compelled to offer the kind of compassionate response he is not experienced or comfortable in delivering. Rookie collaborators frequently expressed the tension they felt between the humanistic urge to provide assistance and relief to distressed family and friends versus professional and personal pressures to create a comfortable distance from the event.

Numbing and Identification

Many young officers are made uncomfortable as they try to resolve administrative and procedural requirements with personal demands for compassionate response, but quite a few nevertheless endeavor to perform both during their first death encounter. A female rookie, for example, described her concern for the adult son and daughter-in-law of an elderly woman who died suddenly at home, noting that she was particularly drawn to the daughter-in-law because her own husband's mother had recently passed away. Importantly, the daughter-in-law and the officer shared several other points of identification: they were of the same race, both had two young children, and the daughter-in-law was scheduled to enter the next police academy class. The young officer drew upon her recent experiences with the deaths of her own family members to help the woman, and her overall receptivity to the situation's emotional components was also shaped by the fact that her own husband had recently been diagnosed with a potentially terminal disease. The officer also demonstrated substantial insight into the similarities between her own situation and that of the daughter-in-law.

When we got there the son was in the bedroom, um, holding his mother. We basically tried to get him out of the bedroom so he can, you know, well, gain his composure, you know. We tried to get him away so he wouldn't be traumatized that much but we really couldn't get him and he just was grieving for his mother. And it, it was, you know, understandable. You know that he would be grieving. It would be the last time he was really able to hold his mother so basically we said just leave him alone. Just leave him in the room with his mother. So that's what we did.

But she [the wife], she basically had to tell everybody that the mother had died and, you know, answer all the phone calls. And we were trying to comfort her, you know. We asked her if we could get her something to drink and if she had to go and check on her kids—she had two sons and they were at a friend's house. We told her to sit down for a while, and that she was going to have to be strong for her husband and stuff, there were a lot of plans they would have to make . . . you know, they were crying. I basically dealt with the wife. She's supposed to be coming into the next [police academy] class and she said she was due to come in to the next class and I was comforting her and I told her, you know, I basically had to go through somewhat the same thing when I had to comfort my husband when his mother and his brothers had passed away. Just be strong and everything because he needs you right now.

That's what basically what's going on now, you know. My husband, I know he needs me to be strong and everything, and that's what I'm doing. I have two children so I have to basically be strong to help my family out. I can't, I can't be weak right now. With him being in the hospital I have to make sure that I let him know that I'll handle everything. Just take care of yourself and be strong. Just that you want to live and don't give up, and everything, you know. That's it. That's basically that.

Forced Numbing

Several officers I interviewed described what we might characterize as attempts to force partial professional numbing and to preclude excessive empathy for the deceased by focusing their attention on practical, even banal, personal matters. These attempts mirror the strategies adopted by the rescue personnel described by Ursano and McCarroll (1990), which included efforts to avoid looking at a victim's face and to consciously avoid thinking of the victim as a person. Rookies showed a particular aversion to looking at the deceased's face, which might enhance their identification, reinforce the notion that this was a person and not an object, and increase the overall potency of the death imprint image. Empathy and identification with the deceased draws one closer to a confrontation with one's own mortality—to the fearful recognition that one day we too will die—and in making a connection with the deceased, one opens the possibility of commitment and the related possibility that unpleasant elements of the professional world will carry over into one's personal life.

In one first-exposure account, a rookie described concentrating his thoughts on the logistical arrangements he would have to make to pick his child up from school that afternoon in order to actively exclude the unpleasant thoughts, images, and emotions conjured by his proximity to the corpse. Note also the rookie's linguistic depersonalization and objectification of the deceased by referring to him as "it":[5]

> I was thinking of other things besides the actual body laying there. . . . I thought about it [arranging to have his child picked up from school] while I was there. "Oh, I've got to sit in the same room with this body . . . " But it wasn't even . . . At that point I didn't—I blocked out that it *was* a body. "I'm going to sit here and I'll make overtime and my wife will have to pick up my son." And that's what I was thinking. I looked at the body a few times and then I just started to avoid it because after they did CPR, the face, it just kind of didn't look right. Someone told me that happens after CPR, that sometimes the face gets distorted looking and stuff. "That's in *that* room and I'll stay in *this* room and that's it."

VH: *You looked at it a few times, but . . .*

> I watched while they were doing the CPR until it started making some strange noises and then I stopped watching. Supposedly the lungs had filled up with liquid and it was kind of gurgling a little bit, and I said "That's enough of that."

This somewhat disjointed bit of narrative reflects the confusion and distress rookies experience when confronted with so many unfamiliar images, particularly when grotesque or disintegrative death images are involved. Time and repeated exposures to the deaths of others afford veteran officers the means to integrate and make more coherent meaning of the images they encounter and to reconstruct them in a less fragmentary way. This was reflected in their narratives, which were far more coherent and more highly elaborated than those of rookies. In the absence of more highly developed forms, though, the young officer struggles to make sense of his recent experience. This tendency was generally observed throughout the interviews: tenured officers' accounts were generally presented in a more systematic, more complete, and more logical way than rookies' narratives. Tenured officers also evinced generally greater insight into the feelings and emotions operating during their first death encounter than rookie cops. Time and experience, in other words, gave tenured cops the capacity to make greater sense of the difficult visual and other sensory images they encountered—to understand them for what they are and, by comprehending them in a more cohesive and meaningful way, to impart meaning to them.

Numbing: Controlling the Environment

Just as the rookie officer cited above attempted to force partial professional numbing by actively excluding troubling images from his consciousness, other (generally more tenured) officers achieve a kind of distance by controlling the environment in ways that limit the emotional content of the situations they encounter. That is to say, at some level they are aware the kind of partial professional numbing they experience at death encounters is functional, and they actively seek to find or create it in all sorts of other emotionally difficult situations. A young officer who had about 18 months of patrol experience, for example, described how he and his partner developed tactics of distraction and deception to curtail emotional outbursts and achieve control in highly emotional situations, including those involving deaths. In one of his early death encounters, the officer answered an "unconscious aided" call in which a man died in a small apartment. The man's wife, mother, and five children were present, and upon arrival the officers found a highly agitated and chaotic scene. The wife was particularly hysterical, and in order to control the frenetic situation the officer told the woman that he felt a pulse, and that she would have to leave the room while he administered CPR. The woman complied. The young officer stated that he knew the man was definitely dead, that he had no intention of administering CPR, and that he felt no residual guilt in lying to the woman—it was simply pragmatic to lie in order to curtail her emotional outburst and gain necessary control over a chaotic situation.

The officer, who was assigned to a very busy precinct that has one of New York City's highest rates of violent crime, said he used similarly deceptive or distracting tactics in many other tumultuous situations. People who are under great stress, he noted, will often shift their attention from the immediate problem to some other unimportant issue if a question is asked sincerely or a direction is given authoritatively. He described applying these tactics in the case of a hysterical stabbing victim whom he asked what recipe she used for the chicken cooking on the stove. She stopped wailing and described the recipe in detail, and after calming her in this way the officer was able to obtain and broadcast a detailed description of her assailant. The tactic served a useful police function to the extent that it helped him to quickly obtain a description that might aid in the apprehension of a criminal, but the officer also volunteered that he uses these tactics purposefully in order to soften or moderate the emotional impact such events might have on him. It should be pointed out that these tactics work because they give both the victim and the officer some degree of distance from the immediate traumatic images that are so upsetting to them.

The Death Imprint Image

As we have thus far explored the context and dimensions of numbing among rookie police officers during their first professional death encounter, we have glimpsed numbing's close relationship with the death imprint image. We saw this, for example, in the case of the officer who recalled the disintegrative image of the woman clawing at her drapes as she died, and in the case of the officer who avoided watching as paramedics applied CPR to the gurgling corpse. The death imprint—the intrusive and enduring image that continues to evoke and reactivate images and feelings associated with the death encounter as the survivor struggles to master and integrate it—lies at the very core of his impaired symbolization. The death imprint is so durable and has such capacity to continually conjure images and feelings associated with the death encounter precisely because it is so difficult to integrate and master: the threat or trauma associated with the image is so powerful it practically defies full or complete incorporation with existing images and forms and can scarcely lead to full and complete enactment. The death imprint resulting from an extreme or protracted exposure to a particularly grotesque death can be practically impossible to master.

Almost without exception, the officers I interviewed were able to recall and articulate vividly detailed images of the deceased as well as other images associated with the event. These recollections ranged from such seemingly insignificant details as apartment numbers and specific addresses (in some cases these details may have served the function of "screen images"), to highly specific sensory images of the sights, sounds, and smells of the corpse or the surroundings in which the exposure occurred. As a rule, they tended to provide more richly detailed descriptions of the more objectively unpleasant and distressing exposures. At the same time, not one of the officers I interviewed could recall the name of the deceased, and this was indicative of the tendency to depersonalize the event and limit identification.

When we examine rookies' experiences as they pertain to the death imprint image, we can discern how it can enhance feelings of disintegration, stasis, and separation. We can also see how these feeling-states become an impetus to seek and achieve a sense of connection, movement, and integrity. This was perhaps best illustrated in the detailed account offered by one rookie for whom the death imprint image was the most salient and memorable feature of his first death encounter. This rookie's narration also makes clear that the death imprint image need not be an entirely visual image; while most death imprints somehow involve visual images of grotesqueness, humiliation, or mutilation—these elements can certainly contribute to the imprint's potency and the survivor's inability to fully assimilate or enact it—death imprint images can and often do involve tactile or olfactory images as well.

The Death Imprint and Gruesomeness

Although at age 35 this officer was older than the typical rookie,[6] he had few prior experiences with death. Perhaps as a function of his maturity, the officer also displayed an uncommon degree of insight into his own feelings during and after the death encounter. He said he understood police work involves exposure to death and was aware of his own anxiety around the idea of dealing with death, but prior to joining the agency he managed to avoid this cognitive awareness through a kind of magical rationalization: "Maybe I'll be lucky and not have to deal with gruesome stuff. Maybe I can avoid it and let other people do it." His trepidation was in no way eased by his police academy training, where he heard "war stories" of the hours he might have to remain at death scenes and the sights and smells he might confront.

The officer's first exposure took place a few days before Christmas and began when a sergeant picked him up from his foot post and told him he had an assignment. The sergeant did not tell him it involved a DOA until he arrived at the building, at which point the rookie's stomach dropped. His discomfort increased when he learned the DOA had been dead about a week, and it became extreme when the odor of putrefaction hit him outside the apartment door. He had "never smelled anything that bad before," noting that the apartment's excessive warmth intensified the odor. He observed a bloodstain on the carpet where, he was told, the deceased apparently vomited blood before making his way to bed to die, and a detective showed him a Polaroid photo of the decomposing corpse that further added to his anxiety and physical distress. Other officers at the scene observed his discomfort and although one tried to coax him into entering the bedroom to view the deceased, he resisted greater exposure to the death image.

> One cop offered to show me the body, but I said, "No thanks." He tried to coax me in but I was resisting, getting scared. My stomach started to bubble and the smell started to irritate me. I said "I'm just going to try and suck it up, do what I have to do, and sit here if I have to." At that point I'm thinking, "Why did I ever take this job?"[7] . . . I think at first when I walked through the door it was like they could see it on my face from the smell. But after a while I tried to act like one of the boys. Like, "Hey, I'm going to do this too." But I didn't feel like that. All the funk started going out of me.

The senior officers were somewhat solicitous, but they also tried to desensitize him through greater immersion in death imagery. The rookie's cognizance of the other officers' possible ulterior motives also subtly alludes to an emergent suspicion of counterfeit nurturance.

> I just couldn't take the smell. So he said, "Did you get a cigar?" He said, "You should keep a couple of cigars on you because they help you deal with the smell." So I ran to the store real quick and got two or three cigars and put them in my pocket. So I'm lighting the cigar and smoking it, but it really didn't help.[8] . . . One officer was very professional, you know. He did what he had to do with notifications and whatever. Like I said, he tried to get me to go in the room. But I don't think he was maliciously trying to get me in the room. He just wanted me to be exposed to what was going on, to be exposed to what a DOA is all about and this is what I'm going to see, you know. Like "This guy is bad but he's not that bad." He said, "If it was summertime, you really don't want to come in this place." So in a way I think he tried to help me, but at the same time they got a little kick out of doing it.

The Imprint Image and Identification

The rookie was at the scene for about five hours in total, and most of this time was spent alone in the apartment. During this period he avoided going into the deceased's bedroom to view the corpse but was nevertheless sickened by the pervasive stench of decomposing flesh. At one point the telephone rang and, because the rookie thought it might be the sergeant or desk officer, he answered it. It was the deceased's brother calling from another state with questions about the death. The officer's description of the conversation illustrates the somatic impact of the overwhelming stench associated with the death imprint image, and it points up rookies' overall sense of personal and professional inadequacy when they fail to provide appropriate emotional comfort to bereaved people. Here the rookie was also coping with demands for a detached professional demeanor and his own physical nausea. The narration further reflects his struggle to make coherent meaning of the death, to convey that meaning to another person in a caring and humane way, and to find some sort of appropriate enactment that is consonant with his incomplete understanding of and limited practice in the police role.

He's asking me how did I think he died and I said I didn't know. I never talked to anybody about this before. I was, you know, explaining to him about his brother's death and trying to comfort him at the same time. I never had to do that before. So I'm on the phone with the guy, I'm trying to be caring but I'm getting ready to throw up. He's asking me questions they already told his mother, who was probably distraught and didn't tell him. So he wants to find out from me and I'm just the guy sitting on the body. I didn't see the body, I wasn't the first one on the scene. I'm explaining to him what happened, how we found his brother, what we think happened. Apparently, you know, he threw up some blood and went into bed and died. The ME said he probably died from internal bleeding. And choked on his blood. I said to him the last newspaper in the house was last Sunday's so he died between Sunday and Sunday, and he had a few messages on his machine. From that previous Sunday.[9] He's looking for information, asking if he can come stay in his brother's house. I said, "I don't think you want to stay here right now."

And I talked to him about 20 minutes. He gave me his name, I took his telephone number and put it in my memo book. I gave him my phone number[10] and the precinct's phone number. After that I ran out the door. And I left the toe tag behind and just locked the door and left and went downstairs. It was just before Christmas, and the fact that he died alone, I just felt that everybody needs somebody by their side. You know, I'm pretty sure before he died he had to have a headache or nausea and he would call somebody and say, "Hey I'm not feeling so good. Why don't you come over and bring an aspirin or something." And it seems like he didn't call anybody because nobody knew he was that sick. It was just the fact that he died alone. That he died alone like that.

When he left the apartment, the rookie asked the building's doorman for a bathroom, where he got sick: "I was feeling really sick, and my stomach started to bubble. And everything I ate for the past week just came out. It was a relief." The doorman "asked if I was OK and I said, 'Yeah, I'm fine. I just have to wait for the morgue guys.'"

Shortly thereafter, the solicitous officer he dealt with earlier returned with another rookie to relieve him for his meal period. The rookie was in no mood to eat, and notwithstanding his own discomfort and anxiety he sympathized with the other rookie's plight and decided to return with him to the apartment. The other rookie was also affected by the odor. "Just from the smell, he turned pale, really pale. I said are you all right? And I gave him a cigar. He didn't want to see the body either. It was like, 'I was *the man*. I've been through this.'" The morgue attendants came about 15 minutes later and both officers were asked to help carry the deceased from the apartment. At that point, the rookie took his first direct look at the corpse, and the numbed impairment of his symbolization process was evident in the way he incompletely assimilated the image of the man's face. The rookie's ability to recall the deceased's license picture but not his face also seems to constitute a protective "screen image."

> I remember the guy, on his side, black and blue looking nothing like his driver's license picture. He was swollen, and I didn't know if he was black or white but I just remember his pose when I walked into the room and saw him lying there. It wasn't a natural pose, he was laying on his side with one leg cocked up. I remember the ME saying earlier when he went in there, "You may want to open a window because when I move him he may fall apart. It's going to get really wretched in there." I said OK and opened the living room window. And when I went in he was laying on his side with his leg up. That's what I remember. I can't remember his face, but I remember his driver's license picture. He didn't look nothing like his picture on his license.

The Imprint Image and Guilt

The morgue attendants asked the officers to help move the corpse, which was about 6 feet 9 inches tall and weighed over three hundred pounds, and help carry it from the apartment,[11] but at that point the rookie demurred: "Hey, I'm on meal. I'm gone." He called the desk officer, who said he could leave, and he did. Although the rookie left the scene, the feelings and emotions associated with the death imprint stayed with him. As he continued the narrative, elements of death guilt began to emerge but did not concretize as a conscious awareness of guilt, per se. His amorphous sense of death guilt was animated by the inadequacy of his response to the brother's need for compassionate connection, and therefore his failure to fulfill his perceived role as a competent police officer. Still immersed in a milieu of separation, stasis, and disintegration, he struggled with competing impulses to once again reach out and connect with the brother in hopes of achieving enactment and to default to a more distant professionalized police persona. He also struggled with the problem of an inability, by dint of his limited experience, to make meaning of the death and to understand its proximate and ultimate causes. These struggles combined with a sense of personal and professional inadequacy and resulted in anger. He described his feelings as he left the scene to return to the station house:

> I still felt the tension, I still felt the sadness. I was still thinking about this guy's brother, calling me and talking to me. And I've got his telephone

number in my memo book. And I'm saying, "Maybe when I get home, maybe I could talk to him again." Then I said, "Well, I'm not going back to [that precinct], so let them handle it." But I did want to call the brother because I couldn't really talk to him while I was in the house because of how I was feeling. Maybe he needed comforting and maybe I could tell him something that, you know . . . I don't know what, but maybe I could have helped him out.

VH: *So you felt a connection, over the telephone, to this guy you never met?*

Yeah, and I felt maybe I should have done more. He called and there was nothing I could do because, for one, I didn't know how he died, I didn't know when he died, I just know he was dead. And I didn't know him, but when he called he felt that I'm a police officer, I should have known his brother. The way he was talking, maybe I should have known things I didn't know. I told him I was just a recruit so he wouldn't think he was talking to someone who should know. I remember getting home and being upset with my wife because it was like somebody did me wrong by doing that to me. I was just a recruit. I was upset with her, I don't know for what reason, but I was upset with her. I told her about the situation, but I didn't tell her the whole thing. I was mad because I didn't think they should have put me on it that day. Two, it kind of upset me. It was just eerie, and I just said, "Why did I take this job?" I was making more money at the bank.

Death Imprint Image: Subjective Differences

In the course of interviewing my collaborators, I was able to interview two rookies who attended the same death event but experienced it in very different ways. By juxtaposing their experiences and their narratives, we can readily discern the durability of the death imprint image and we can see how two young officers of different backgrounds were differently affected by it.

Rookie 9, a married African-American male in his early twenties, had relatively few prior exposures to death and no prior exposures in a professional or occupational context. He became a police officer, he said, because he was deeply concerned with the level of crime and violence in New York City's communities, especially in the tough Brooklyn neighborhood where he grew up. Referring to his young daughter, this earnest young man said he wanted to make a difference in the community and to make the city a safer place for children. Rookie 8, a single white male in his late twenties, had quite a few previous exposures to death: he witnessed a fatal vehicle accident and also worked at a renowned cancer hospital. Although his hospital position did not include responsibility for patient care, he saw dead and actively dying patients on a daily basis and commented that some of the patients he saw looked worse than any DOA he expected to encounter in police work.

Both officers were assigned to "sit" on the body of a male who died of AIDS in a rooming house a day or so earlier, and the situation was objectively revolting: the body was decomposed to the extent the first officers to arrive required a Scott air pack and protective clothing to enter the third-floor room and examine the body. Both rookies stated they could smell the odor of death from the street. They were both also taken aback by the nonchalance of officers at the scene. As Rookie 9 said, "It was like nothing to them. In fact they had a snowball fight with the fire department when we came. Apparently they're used to it. I found it strange."

The rookies had quite different reactions when a detective at the scene showed them photographs of the deceased. Rookie 8 mentioned the photographs in passing, but the images were far more memorable to Rookie 9:

> It shook me up. I didn't particularly care for it. I know he's a homicide detective and it meant nothing to him. I mean he's walking out the door all nonchalant. And, um, I saw the picture and um, I didn't even want to see the body. I didn't even go inside to see the body. After the photograph I couldn't even look at it. It bothered me. It was a young guy. They showed me a picture from his license and a picture of him dead and it didn't look like the same person. [Rookie 8] didn't have a problem with it. I can picture it now. His head was so swelled up it almost exploded, and his trousers were halfway down, part way down.

The officers were at the scene for about 5 hours in all, and because of the overpowering stench the sergeant instructed that they could remain outside the apartment. The rookies remained together on the stairwell, but experienced the event very differently. During our conversation, Rookie 9 presented a much stiffer demeanor, his narrative was more fragmented, and he admitted the death encounter was much more uncomfortable for him than for Rookie 8. He was, in essence, immobilized by the death and his symbolization process was much more impaired. In contrast, Rookie 8 presented a very relaxed and affable demeanor during the interview. He studied a traffic regulations book as he sat on the stairs and noted that in the future he will prepare himself for DOA assignments by carrying a more interesting paperback novel on patrol. He joked about discovering that there is a statute prohibiting the use of a white-tipped cane by anyone other than a blind person, and in a bit of self-mockery he joked that he could not wait to issue a summons for that particular infraction.

> We stayed on the landing and got comfortable. We opened the window and stayed on the landing one floor below. I checked out the apartment quickly but didn't go in. But I went in with the ME. I thought it was interesting the way the whole body blew up and it was only 24 hours old. The ME said to stay outside so I stayed at the door.
>
> My partner, he wasn't used to death. He was almost frozen in place. He wouldn't come upstairs. The only time he saw it was when they showed us the pictures, the only time he saw the body. The victim was on parole, I don't know what for, but they had pictures from parole. He was in his midthirties, a male dark Hispanic. You really couldn't tell from the photos, but from the pictures and the name. It bothered [Rookie 9] a lot more than it bothered me. I basically sat on the stairs by the window with the window open, and he basically stood in the corner and didn't move too much. It

took him about 2 hours to get his hat off. [*Laughs.*] The smell was getting to him. I asked if he wanted me to get something for him to eat and he almost turned green. I was trying to crack jokes and get him to loosen up a bit. I actually got him to move from one spot to another spot, to move around a bit.

Rookie 9 recognized his partner found it funny the death bothered him so, and he recognized his partner's joking manner was intended to help him. He could not really recall what he did for the 5 hours he spent at the scene, other than the fact that the stench of death and the visual image of the death scene photograph sickened and revolted him. His numbing and residual closing-off can also be observed in the fact that he did not discuss the event with anyone.

When asked what images stayed with them from the scene, Rookie 9 referred simply to the death scene photograph and to the odor of death, while Rookie 8 offered more expansive and more insightful comments:

His tongue and his lips. They swelled up to the size of a baseball. That was the main thing. And you'll never forget the smell. The body actually swollen up like that. It was the first time I'd seen a body that's, not fresh, let's say. It was sitting there for 15 or 20 hours or something. It was a little disgusting. I mean, I didn't know a body did that. I just distanced myself from it. I said, "It's dead, it's over, I can't do anything about that."

Other than mentioning to his wife that he had a DOA assignment and that the images bothered him, Rookie 9 did not mention the event to anyone. Rookie 8, on the other hand, joked about it with friends and his peers at the police academy.

The Death Imprint Image and Lasting Impact

Few collaborators indicated the death imprint image from their first exposure had a lasting and deleterious psychic impact on them, and indeed many tended to downplay or minimize the degree of trauma they experienced. Only one collaborator reported having nightmares or other sleep disturbances involving residual images from their first death encounters, and none claimed to have needed or even considered the need for counseling of any type as a result of the first exposure. This minimal degree of manifest psychic trauma seems more than mere macho posturing to minimize the need for help, since some of the tenured officers described troubling death encounters at other points in their careers that *did* cause them to seek or consider counseling. These distressing incidents will be discussed later, but several points should be clearly made at this juncture.

Although collaborators may have downplayed or minimized the first exposure's lasting psychic impact, virtually all of them—regardless of rank, experience, or the amount of time elapsed since the first exposure—gave accounts that nevertheless evinced a powerful and lasting death imprint image. Almost all could recall in great detail images associated with the first death encounter, but fewer were able to recall the factual and emotional components of subsequent death encounters with the same clarity. To test our hypothesis that the first DOA is a defining professional experience and a career milestone, I asked each of the tenured officers if they could recall their first arrest or the first ticket they wrote—experiences that are also central to the police role and which, importantly, are more closely associated with public and police conceptions of the police role—and very few could. None could recall emotions associated with writing their first ticket, and with the exception of a few who recalled strong fear, objective danger, or other compelling emotions, few could recall any emotions surrounding their first arrest. This again points up the importance and durability of images associated with the first DOA and their lasting psychic impact.

Suspicion of Counterfeit Nurturance

While outlining the psychology of survival in chapter 2, we noted that because of numbing, guilt, and devitalization the survivor has special needs and vulnerabilities that typically include the need for emotional comfort. The same numbing, guilt, and devitalization, though, hinder his capacity to develop and maintain the kind of relationships that will give him comfort and restore some sense of vitality. To the extent the survivor is aware of his dependency and his special needs, he may also be especially sensitive to or resentful of actions or events that remind him of his weakness. Lifton refers to the survivor's acute sensitivity to his vulnerabilities and resentment of efforts to comfort him as "suspicion of counterfeit nurturance."

In listening to rookie collaborators' narratives, I was struck by the apparent absence of this theme of survivor psychology. Rookies certainly feel a numbed and guilty devitalization and may have need of emotional nurturance, but none actively sought comfort from coworkers, peers, or family members. In the case of the senior officer who advised the rookie to get some cigars to help deal with the odor of death, as in other instances where senior cops tried to coax rookies into viewing the corpse, the assistance offered was not so much directed toward easing the rookie's emotional burden as it was toward helping him deal with the immediate situation—it was offered in the interest of overcoming the rookie's immediate immobilization and in the interest of administrative efficiency.

The relative absence of suspicion of counterfeit nurturance (or at least of conspicuous manifestations of it) among rookies can be attributed to several factors. First, most rookies did not experience the kind of profound death encounter that we would expect to engender a profound kind of numbing, guilt, and devitalization. This is not to say the rookies did not experience these things at all, but that few were so overwhelmed or overpowered by them that they appeared in need of nurturing. All the rookies I interviewed had relatively benign first exposures, and all of those who experienced substantial devitalization tried to maintain the culturally prescribed aura of stoic professional detachment. Because they did not seek any out forms of emotional assistance from peers or coworkers, there was little actual nurturance of which the rookie might be suspicious.

Tenured cops do not, as a rule, pay much attention to rookies' emotional needs at a death encounter or at any other emotionally difficult event. Because at some level they recognize the first death encounter is an important rite of passage, they do not perceive the rookies' upset as a particularly bad thing. If an awareness of the rookie's plight does penetrate their own indifference and their numbed attitudes toward the event, there are no subcultural demands to provide assistance or nurturing, and in fact the opposite may apply: having experienced similar emotions themselves and having grown professionally from them, the attitude of tenured cops is along the lines of "That's the way the Job is. Live with it. I got through it, and it made me stronger. You'll get through it, too."

Also underlying this indifference is the fact that rookies, who are not fully integrated into the culture, lack the close working relationships that might induce or compel another officer to minister to their emotional needs. A tenured cop who is close to his steady partner could privately confide his troubles, and the trusted partner could also safely inquire whether a particular incident was troublesome, but the unintegrated rookie cannot seek or accept such nurturance without unacceptably betraying his own weakness. In the following section we will glimpse how subcultural beliefs and constructs operate to limit the provision of nurturance even when the need for it is recognized, and especially in chapter 8, on police survivors, we will see the types of situations where nurturance and comfort can and cannot be safely offered.

Death Guilt

As discussed in chapter 2, Lifton points out that the theme of death guilt has several sources or dimensions, including the notion of survival priority and the related survivor's question, "Why did I survive while he did not?" To some extent, every death encounter raises this question and results in some measure of death guilt, since at some level of consciousness every encounter with the death of another is an encounter with our own mortality leading to a recognition of the fact that we remain alive while another has died. The sense of death guilt has a complex etiology, but it is always tied to the failed enactment that results from some combination of numbing, the implicitly inadequate schemas for enactment contained within one's limited images and forms, and circumstances that in some way prevent one from acting out those schemas. Failed enactment also inevitably generates a kind of ethical struggle between recognition of what one *should* do and *should* feel and the inadequacy of our actualized behaviors and feelings. We feel guilty, in other words, because we recognize that we have not behaved or felt as we know or think we should behave or feel. That basic ethical struggle can in itself be quite complex, as when one experiences simultaneous countervailing feelings of responsibility for the death of another as well as a sense of elation or relief that one has survived even though another died. The ethical struggle is also important because it animates the quest to make meaning of the death event and under some circumstances may become the basis for a survivor mission.

For the most part, we can say that issues of survival priority are more likely to be raised to conscious awareness when one is present and somehow involved (either through action or inaction) in the actual death of another person. The problem of survival priority and death guilt can also become particularly acute when one identifies closely with the deceased and/or the manner and circumstances of his death, since identification amplifies the moral imperative to do something on his behalf. This level of involvement or identification simply does not occur for most rookie officers, and none of the rookie collaborators consciously recognized that part of what they felt was death guilt. The rookie death encounters we are considering here generally involved strangers, a fact that implicitly limits how closely they identify with the deceased. Rookies are also not typically involved in efforts to resuscitate or to kill the victim, and a host of other factors operate to distance them from the event and from any rational or conscious sense of responsibility that might accrue.

For rookies, the sense of death guilt is a much more amorphous, irrational and sub rosa feeling-state that does not typically infiltrate consciousness as an awareness of guilt, per se. None of the rookies felt responsible for the death, articulated an awareness of guilt, or in any way consciously extracted a sense of guilt from the jumble of feelings they experienced. Indeed, when pressed for detail, most rookies had great difficulty excavating and articulating their specific emotions. Anyone might find it difficult to disentangle a complex web of emotions and precisely identify and articulate those feelings, but the problem is all the more challenging when the situations and emotions involved are novel and unfamiliar. The difficulty also speaks to a more general tendency to avoid taking conscious guilty responsibility for our acts or omissions when that guilt is irrational.

As a corollary to the idea that death guilt arises because the death imprint image can never find full or complete enactment, we can expect that the degree of death guilt experienced by a rookie officer varies according to the quantity and quality of the enactment he *can* achieve. Those rookies who experienced some sense of agency by performing various administrative tasks and/or who were able to provide comfort to family members were generally able to achieve more enactment, concomitantly experiencing a less formidable death imprint image, less death guilt, and less overall emotional trauma than officers assigned to idly "sit on the body."

We can see traces or elements of death guilt in the uncomfortable feeling-state of the rookie who felt compelled by virtue of his professional role and public expectations to *do something* for the unidentified dead man and his family ("Because people look—you're the cop, you're supposed to be doing something. . . . It was kind of a weird situation because you want to do so much, and yet there's nothing you can do"). He experienced a moral urge to act on the man's behalf, but his still-developing professional repertoire did not provide viable strategies or schemas with which to properly enact that urge. We can also see traces of death guilt in the rookie who, due to his nausea and lack of suitable forms and images with which to enact his urge to provide effective solace, could not adequately comfort the deceased's brother from Ohio ("I said I didn't know. I never talked to anybody about this before. I was, you know, explaining to him about his brother's death and trying to comfort him at the same time. I never had to do that before"). In both instances, the amorphous sense of death guilt was associated with failed enactment and the inability to fulfill their own professional and personal expectations. Later in this chapter, we will examine the case of a young officer whose experience provided sufficient images to substantively act upon his urge to do something for the benefit of a victim. His death guilt may not have been entirely expiated, but he did identify and carry out a dedicated course of action aimed at finding justice for a victim.

Death Guilt: Limiting Identification

Another factor mediating the quantity and quality of death guilt is the extent to which the rookie identified with the victim, and we recall how some officers actively sought to avoid identification as a means of severing connection with the deceased and allaying the sense of moral responsibility to feel for him and/or act on his behalf. ("I thought of when my grandfather died and all that, but this was nothing like it. It was like, 'I don't *know* this person. It's just a body in the other room on a bed and I never met them and I never will again or the wife for that matter'"). Where identification with the deceased or with grieving family members is unavoidable, as in the case of the female rookie who identified so closely with the young woman who was about to enter the police academy, we can see how the capacity to fulfill personal and professional demands for appropriate action serves to counterbalance the experience of death guilt. Notwithstanding the similarity of their circumstances and the degree to which she identified with the young woman, the rookie officer was able to enact her personal and professional impulse to render aid and comfort, felt no overt guilt, and overall was quite comfortable with her emotions. The factual circumstances of the event permit us only to surmise what that rookie's experience might have been if she did not achieve such an admirable degree of compassionate and appropriate enactment, but it is quite likely her residual death guilt would have been much greater.

For the most part, collaborators in each of the categories were less affected by the deaths of those whose actions or deviant lifestyles somehow contributed to their demise, and rookies were no exception. Clearly, these actions or lifestyles provide a reasonable basis for the rookie to consciously reject or dismiss any potential points of identification, to numb himself to the reality of the death, and to deny or escape any sense of moral obligation to the victim. The idea that someone somehow contributed to his own death through criminal activity, a deviant lifestyle, or simple stupidity seems to help cops depersonalize the death and, at the same time, to more easily make meaning of the death through a logically simplistic attribution of cause and responsibility. That responsibility, of course, is implicitly externalized: "I am not responsible; he is." These deaths also seem less tragic because the victims are not truly innocent or because they are perceived as less entitled to the quality of respect afforded other human beings. The officer is able to partially block identification by consciously asserting that the victim is *not* like him—"He is not like me," the officer reminds himself, "because I am a *good* person—a cop—who would never do the bad things this person has done to bring about his own death." As we have seen, this tendency toward what we might call "identification denial" was reflected in the seasoned detective's narration about the young man who died of a drug overdose "with a needle in his arm," as well as in other narratives.

A young officer who attended the death of a "skell"[12] who died of a drug over-dose in the common room of a halfway house for ex-convicts reported feeling absolutely no sense of guilt, sorrow, or affinity for the man. This officer briefly visited the death scene out of interest rather than as a matter of assignment to it—he was one of those rookies who actively pursued transformative experiences and the identity change they facilitate—and he noted that the other residents who were watching television in the same room seemed oblivious to the corpse in their midst. The officer also surmised that the other residents may have robbed the corpse prior to the officers' arrival, and although he saw this as ironic he was not offended by the theft—after all, he said, in his view the dead man had probably deserved it. The death was not a suicide, but because the individual caused his own demise through his own actions the officer saw him as having less worth as a human being. The officer said he experienced no compelling emotion, much less guilt, in rela-tion to this death event.

The officer's depersonalization of the skell's death was not simply a matter of an insensitive disposition on his part, since he also described another case that deeply affected him and which motivated a course of committed actions resem-bling a survivor mission. We will examine that particular encounter in greater depth at the end of this chapter, but at this point it should be noted that identifi-cation denial attenuates or diminishes an officer's sense of death guilt and substi-tutes a sense of indifference for any feeling of connection the rookie might have for the deceased.

Because death guilt is always tied up with issues of connection to others and with moral ideas about what one should or should not do or feel as a result of that connection, numbing and any kind of psychological strategy that limits iden-tification also diminish the moral demand for reciprocity and ultimately reduce death guilt: "I don't know him, I am not like him, and I owe him nothing." Denial of identification also obviates the survivor's question, "Why did I survive while another died?" The answer, of course, is that "I survived because I didn't (and wouldn't) take a drug overdose, or shoot myself, or engage in any other behav-ior a person like this would engage in. I am not in any way responsible for his death; I am absolved because he is responsible for it through his own actions." By deper-sonalizing the death, externally fixing responsibility, and limiting their identifi-cation with the deceased, officers avoid emotionally taxing ethical commitments.

Death Guilt and Attachment

This is not to say, however, that efforts to limit identification are always under-taken or always successful. A sense of commitment or attachment to a particular victim was fairly common among the more tenured collaborators, and a similar set of predisposing factors was almost always present. The most prominent and prevalent feature is the victim's perceived innocence or goodness, which appeals to the cop's identity as protector. These victims are almost always perceived as innocent, at least in terms of having no complicity in the cause and circumstances of their death, and often the circumstances do not adequately permit the officer to denigrate the individual. Because they are perceived as "good" people, rather than skells, these deaths are interpreted as more unfortunate. Generally speaking, victims whose deaths have the greatest immediate and lasting impact on officers also tend to be of the same race and socioeconomic background as the officer, or in some way they remind the officer of another person they knew and cared about. That is to say, the death encounter conjures and animates preexisting images and forms and these associations make the present death encounter more personally meaningful. I am thinking here of the rookie who associated the death of an elderly man with his grandfather's death. Another rookie noted that other than the permeating odor of death, the most distressing thing about his police academy visit to the morgue was viewing the body of a child: "But what hurt me most was that I saw a little girl about my daughter's age, and apparently she had overdosed on some pills. I saw the little girl and I almost cried. And I wanted to walk back out of there." While death of a child under any circumstances has a powerful impact, the death of a child by violent means or by misadventure seems particularly difficult.

The particularly toxic psychological impact of dealing with the death of a child was best illustrated by the narrative of a sergeant I interviewed.[13] Although his experience was not that of a rookie, his detailed articulation of the images involved and of his emotions illustrates how several themes of survivor psychology intertwine and his narration encapsulates the range of conflicts and emotions an officer can experience when a child dies. Despite the officer's active resistance to identification with the deceased and with a surviving family member, the account shows how attempts to deny or limit identification can ultimately be futile. The account also conveys the frenzied and disintegrative nature of so many police death encounters. Although the narrative presented here is interspersed with some of my analysis and commentary, it was actually rendered in a continuous and emotionally infused monologue.

I was a sergeant in Brooklyn. About 5 o'clock in the morning, we get a call, a 3-week-old baby just stopped breathing. So we rush to the scene and we pulled up, and I said to my driver, "We're the first on the scene[14] and we're going direct to the hospital." I remember yelling it because the adrenaline starts pumping. I remember being really tired because it was 5 o'clock in the morning. We pull up in front of the address and we're the first on the scene. I could see from a distance that the other cops didn't go that fast, and my feeling was they were afraid to see what was really there. They wanted somebody else to be first to break the ice. Being a sergeant, I had the dirty task. And standing in the doorway is this woman, she had a big glass door, holding a baby in her hands. About 3 weeks old. I remember jumping out of the car, running to the front steps and taking the baby from her. She jumped in the back seat and I jumped in the front seat and off we went to [a local hospital]. With a 3–week-old baby not breathing and I started doing mouth-to-mouth. I couldn't get any movement out of the chest. It just was not moving. I remember puffing and it wasn't moving and I'm saying "Oh shit I'm fucking this up. I don't know how to do mouth-to-mouth." And I'm trying to give CPR and blow air into it and it ain't fucking working. So I stick my finger in the mouth and tried to do a sweep, thinking something was blocking it, and I can't move the jaw.

Here we see the first expression of failed enactment and the first emergence of what will ultimately become death guilt. The officer recognizes the compelling demand to fulfill his professional responsibility—to *do something*—and although training has provided him with images that contain a very specific and detailed schema for action as well as the specific skills necessary to enact the demands (he was trained in CPR and first aid), circumstances inexplicably thwart his attempt. The rapidity with which the events unfolded, his excited somatic state, and the barrage of fairly novel but very potent death imagery—this was certainly not a typical job—combined to create a chaotic situation.

We're flying through the streets like a hundred miles an hour whipping around corners. I'm on the radio screaming, "Central, we're 2 minutes out, Central, we're 30 seconds out." Pulling up in front of the emergency room in [the hospital] and kicking the door open on the car and barely being able to step out and I remember having a hard time even standing up. And running over to the emergency room door where the doctor was waiting and handing him the baby. He continued CPR and continued to rush inside. I saw him running into the emergency room and he stopped and he looked at the kid and he just started walking. Being a doctor, he realized the kid was dead, and the kid was dead for many hours. Rigor mortis had set in. That's why I couldn't get the lungs to expand and the jaw to move. I didn't know that, I thought I was doing something wrong. I thought I could help it, I thought I could save it.

In the doctor's sudden stop and the realization of finality and failure it brought to the officer, we see a powerful death imprint image as well as the image's connection with failed enactment leading to a contemporaneous manifestation of death guilt ("I thought I could help, but I failed"). The officer's failure is all the more telling because it relates to a primary professional responsibility and because the victim of his failure is an innocent.

Anyway, that was really traumatic, that was probably the most traumatic DOA I ever had. And several things went through my mind as soon as it was over. How did the baby die, was it criminal? I've got to send a car to the house to investigate. Maybe the baby died from some virus, and I did mouth-to-mouth on it: "Oh shit, am I going to get sick?" I had to call the [police department's] sick desk and get a control number. I'm calling around, how do I find out how the baby died? How do I know what the baby died of? I called the morgue and the morgue says we've got to wait for the toxicology report. Like what the fuck is that, a toxicology report? At that time AIDS was just kicking in so I thought about AIDS. So I've got all these things going through my head. Holy shit.

Professional and personal concerns like these are part and parcel of the police death encounter; the officer is, after all, a participant in the transaction and in an emotionally compelling situation like this his personal interests and issues are likely to come to his conscious attention, but personal concerns can conflict with the professional responsibility to represent the agency's interests and follow its procedures and to put those interests before his own. He cannot forego or set aside these responsibilities, either in favor of the victim or for his own benefit. To the extent these responsibilities conflict with his own needs or his sense of commitment to the victim, they are a potential source of guilt.

So we get back to the precinct and I'm wiped out. Hurting, emotionally hurting. Maybe the only time I was really emotionally hurting like that as a cop. I remember getting back to the precinct and thinking I couldn't do anything for the kid. It was like 7:30 now, and the tour was changing and everyone at the precinct knew that I had to rush the dead baby to the hospital and do mouth-to-mouth. And everyone was staring at me and feeling sorry for me. There's about 40 to 50 cops standing around. The commander was looking at me and everybody knew what was going on and they all felt bad and there was a hush in the whole precinct. I had to write the '49. I remember sitting down and saying, "I'm not going to rush this," and I started worrying did I do anything wrong that I could get in trouble? . . . I spoke to the two cops who went to the house, and so I finally write the '49 and I remember I had to call home and tell my wife I'm going to be late. "I had a dead baby," I told her, "and I'm going to be late."

Plagued by death guilt and cognizant of his own need for comfort, the officer was particularly sensitive to others' attitudes and behavior toward him. Importantly, none of the 40 to 50 cops took steps to comfort him, but this was probably not a simple matter of insensitivity. Perhaps they knew nothing they could say would truly alleviate his pain, and we might imagine they were also reluctant to deviate from a subcultural ethos of stoic detachment: although it is quite acceptable within the culture to offer solace to civilians, officers are often reluctant or embarrassed to offer comforting words to fellow cops. Indeed, to some extent the acknowledgement or articulation of his distress might in some way shatter their own magical sense of invulnerability to death-related trauma. Public acknowledgement of his pain would illuminate his dependency, and public displays of dependency are anathema to the stoic "tough cop" stereotype ("Cops supposedly have this macho thing, like you know, we're supposed to be beyond all emotions, these feelings, or whatever"). Although this personal narrative offers little in the way of direct evidence of their reasons, we might also guess they resisted taking on his death taint and wished to avoid the ethical responsibilities that further identification with him and his situation might entail. Had some form of emotional comfort been offered, though, we might see elements of suspicion of counterfeit nurturance emerge.

And so at that time I had a 3-month-old daughter. The baby was 3 weeks and my daughter was 3 months. And as I was going to the hospital and coming back from the hospital and sitting in the precinct all I could think about was that it could have been her. It could have been my 3-month-old daughter. I remember being really upset over that. When I was done—I was up all night on a late tour—driving home and the baby's face kept flashing in my mind. It kept flashing in. And I was really upset and I had to pull over on the side of the highway. I tried to shake it off. I remember saying, "Shake it off, shake it off." I had to talk myself into putting the car in gear and driving home. When I finally got home, I remember going in the house and going upstairs and going into my bedroom and falling down on the bed and I think I just cried for a while. And probably because I was tired, and the trauma and because I myself had a 3-month-old kid, and also just the horror of a 3-week-old child in my arms dead. And I couldn't revive it. I can remember the thoughts I had—they were, I'd heard in the academy and from other cops that the worst thing you could come up against was an injured or dead child, and it was true. It was true, it was really so true. And I also thought about my younger brother dying, being hit by the car that time, it came flooding back. And so I fell asleep and I woke up 3 or 4 hours later and for the next 3 or 4 days the child kept coming back. The child came haunting back into my memory and into my life. There are times when I'll be shooting through that part of Brooklyn, and I'll remember that DOA. I'll remember that child. And that was 6 years ago.

That was the worst, the most traumatic DOA I had. And that did come back and I had trouble sleeping for the next couple of days. And every so often I'll still have a dream about it. Over the past 6 years, 2 or 3 times I had a dream about that job. And I remember it hurting, I just remember hurting emotionally. The other thing I remember, too, was I really didn't know where to put it. I didn't know where to file it. I didn't know who to tell, how to tell them, but I knew I had to close it out. So it sits there, it remains there like in limbo.[15]

Once again we see guilt over failed enactment ("And I couldn't revive it") and we see how the death imprint image triggers associations with a series of intrusive and recurring images, including images from a previous death encounter (the childhood death of his brother). The fact that the images continue to resurface in the officer's dream life and continue to be conjured by other images that are only tenuously associated with the death exposure (while driving through a neighborhood, for example) is evidence of the death imprint's potency and the fact that it can never be truly mastered or integrated.[16] The officer expressed this, as well as the absence of coherent meaning in the death, by noting that he did not know where to "put" or "file" the experience: it did not fit with his existing images and forms in a way that would neatly categorize or impart meaning to the experience.

One other thing I remember. I remember the mother, the mother was a young woman . . . I remember when I finally walked out of the emergency room the mother looking at me. She had a look on her like I thought my mother might have had when she found out that *her* 5-year-old son died. I remember looking at her and feeling sorry for the lady and saying to myself, "I wish I could help you but it's not my job to help you," and I should be saying to myself, "Fuck it, nothing matters."

The officer's thoughts ("it's not my job to help you") are an immediate protective attribution belied by his compassionate feelings and actions. The fact is that the officer did try to help, and one suspects he would try again—even more vigorously—if he ever faced a similar situation. Similarly, the pessimism of his derisive dismissal ("Fuck it, nothing matters") is seen as an attempt to limit identification, but it also reflects his immersion in the death-equivalent state of disintegration and stasis. There is no meaning to be found in such a death, he is saying, but despite his reflexive protestations we cannot say the experience meant nothing to him.

The Quest to Make Meaning

The rookie's quest to integrate the experience of his first death encounter and make immediate and ultimate meaning of it is a complicated struggle. Due to numbing and failed enactment, his immediate images are to some extent fragmented and incomplete, and his difficulty in connecting them with earlier experiences is compounded by their novelty and the absence of similar images and forms. In terms of immediate meanings, the rookie struggles to attribute causality in order to understand how and why the death occurred, and at a more ultimate level he looks for universal meanings or lessons he can take away from the experience.

The rookies' struggle to incorporate fragmentary images was evident in their narratives, which were much more disjointed and incomplete than those of tenured cops. Without exception, rookies' narratives flowed less smoothly than those of veterans, who had more time and experience to make sense of their death encounters and were therefore better able to render them in a coherent, comprehensive, and logically ordered way. Experienced cops were better able to separate emotional components from factual events and were better able to "track" or sequentially order events as they actually occurred. Experienced cops showed greater insight into the immediate and ultimate meanings that could be extracted from the experience, while rookies almost always said they learned nothing—other than some procedural information—from the encounters. In point of fact, the rookies probably had learned a great deal from the encounter, but they would not recognize how much they learned until additional experience fleshed out the constellations that would allow them to make sense of it all.

To determine how much and what kind of meaning rookies extracted from their initial experience, all the collaborators were asked whether the experience had changed them in any way. Not a single rookie said the death encounter changed him or his outlook, notwithstanding evidence to the contrary several provided in their narratives. They did not consciously recognize any immediate or ultimate meanings. Once again, this contrasted sharply with tenured cops, in whose retrospective view the first death encounter often led to some alteration of their understanding of themselves and their outlook on life and death.

Particularly when the death encounter involves extensive numbing, failed enactment, and elements of disintegration, stasis, and separation, the destabilized survivor seeks to master the death imprint image and other related images as a way of recommencing "normal" symbolization processes that will allow him to return to the ordered and coherent symbolic world he knew before. Before he can do so he must understand and attribute causality to the death event. He seeks, in other words, to rationally explain the event in a way that fits with his previous cognitive and emotional experiences and images.

Notwithstanding their numbing, all of the rookies sought to clarify and understand how and why the death took place—to extract a cognitive understanding of the factual circumstances of the death and to attribute causality to it. Regardless of rank or tenure, every officer I spoke with, in fact, sought a cognitive knowledge of the cause of death. This is not surprising, since the issue of cause is a matter of professional concern in the initial death investigation, because they must determine and record the cause of death in their paperwork, and because there are a finite number of rather easily understood causes of death. Unlike the multiform complex of emotions they might experience, these are simple and rather straightforward cognitive concepts that any adult can readily identify and understand. By understanding the death in this way, they satisfy the need for rational explanation and, at the same time, deprive death of some of its mystery, awe, and power. By identifying and attributing cause to a set of external factors rather than his own actions or inactions, the officer also achieves a kind of moral distance from the event, assuages his sense of death guilt, and avoids the moral and ethical commitments that might otherwise accrue.

At yet another level, we saw that several rookies actively sought out the death encounter with the idea that by experiencing and understanding it they would become better and more competent police officers ("Well, I'm out of the academy less than a month and I'd like to go in and talk to them and see what's going on. I can learn from this"). These rookies certainly sought out the experience in part to achieve a better cognitive understanding of the technical and administrative tasks involved, but also to integrate this administrative competence with the emotional components of the event as a means of forcing the development of the complex police identity they recognize as desirable. The rookies who sought out the death encounter also tended to articulate and to demonstrate a more comprehensive awareness that policing is a complex business requiring a complex and multifaceted working personality. For example, the female rookie who identified so closely with the deceased's daughter-in-law and who brought her own experience to bear in providing emotional comfort to the woman had this to say about her visit to the morgue, which took place several weeks before the encounter described above:

> At first I was scared. I was kind of hesitant about, you know, going in and seeing the dead bodies. But just like I said, I knew we would encounter it, so I said, "Let me go and get a feel of it now to see how it would be out there on patrol." Instead of going out there on patrol where I'd definitely have to be dealing with it by myself, I might as well get the reaction now on how I would feel.

She recognized the experience would be difficult, but nevertheless sought it out to become a more effective cop. We also see the pursuit of death encounters as a means of identity transformation in the words of an eager young officer who also makes clear that the transformation is vitalizing:

> I like to strive and push myself to be the best. And if I said, "How can I be a better cop?" I know I have to work in a bad neighborhood and learn. Because that's the only way you're going to be able to do it. So when I hear that [a radio call assignment involves a death], I think you kind of look forward to it. "Yeah, all right, I *want* to go to this scene, I want to see somebody shot, I *want* to do this, I *want* to do it. You look forward to it. You're young, you *want* to do it. It sounds . . . you kind of look forward to it. . . . I thought it would be exciting."

Also affecting the quest to make meaning of the death encounter is the fact that at some level the survivor feels personally victimized by the death of another, if only to the extent that the experience devitalized him by impairing his symbolization process. For reasons we have discussed, the rookie officer does not generally experience profound impairment leading to an overwhelming sense of victimization. No matter the degree of his impairment and victimization, though, the survivor needs to make sense of the experience, to attribute causality, and to expurgate his guilt and sense of devitalization that can become manifest in a propensity to focus blame externally. This found expression in officers' tendency to blame the victim or the police department for their devitalization and emotional distress. The tendency was expressed by the officer whose dehumanization of the "skell" implicitly placed responsibility and blame on the deceased. In terms of blaming the police department, we need only look as far as the officers who took umbrage at the emotionally difficult position the agency placed them in, but there is also a tendency for a more diffuse and irrational placement of blame ("I remember getting home and being upset with my wife because it was like, somebody did me wrong by doing that to me. . . . I was upset with her, I don't know for what reason, but I was upset with her"). In each case, the young officers found some way to make sense of the situation, to externalize responsibility for their sense of victimization, and to avoid some measure of death guilt.

The Quest for Meaning and the Urge to Do Justice

The survivor's personal sense of victimization can also be reified and transformed into a compelling urge for justice—not only for himself but for the actual victim or his family members. The survivor's urge to find justice is especially compelling among police officers since images, ideas, and concerns about justice are so central to the constellations that make up his personal and professional identities. When the factual circumstances of a death clearly point to an injustice, the officer who is equipped with adequate professional constellations can easily find a very appropriate kind of personal and professional enactment that restores justice to the victim or, by proxy, to the victim's family and friends. The officer may seek justice for the victim or other survivors as a subculturally acceptable way of expurgating his own sense of devitalized victimization and of reestablishing viable forms of humane and compassionate connection. Since it is not always possible to find perfect justice, the desire may be subsumed within the urge to provide comfort and solace.

The quest to seek meaning or find significance in death is also rooted in a belief that the manner and circumstances of death should illuminate the manner and circumstances of life: a death that lacks meaning or significance reflects a life that lacked meaning or significance. There is a universal fear of death without integrity—of death that is disintegrative in its humiliation, incoherence, absurdity, or prematurity. To imagine one's own death or to witness the death of another in this way is to perceive that life as lacking completeness or authenticity. In discussing the quest to extract meaning from death, Lifton (1983, p. 100) cites Octavio Paz:

> Tell me how you die and I will tell you who you are. . . . Our deaths illuminate our lives. If our deaths have no meaning our lives also lacked it. Therefore we are apt to say, when someone has died a violent death, "He got what he was looking for." Each of us dies the death he is looking for, the death he has made for himself. A Christian death and a dog's death are ways of dying that reflect ways of living. If death betrays us and we die badly, everyone laments the fact because we should die as we have lived.

One way for the officer to find enactment and a kind of justice is through actions that bring real or symbolic closure to the victim or that involve some simple acts of kindness. Cops may find ways to perform more extraordinary acts on behalf of the victim, but because these actions involve the use of discretion and are somewhat risky they are not typically in the rookie's repertoire.

The phenomenon of going above and beyond the call of duty on behalf of the deceased resembles a survivor mission in many respects, but it would be improper to characterize these compassionate acts as a survivor mission because they do not typically become a permanent or lasting feature of the officer's personality. An officer might feel a sense of attachment and act compassionately, but his emotions are relatively ephemeral and they do not typically galvanize the officer or impel him to undertake a lifelong crusade on behalf of the victim. Rather, the officer usually seeks a more immediate way to find justice for the victim—to achieve some form of suitable enactment—and in doing so to fulfill public and personal role expectations. Once that task is completed the officer, having fulfilled his role expectations, can usually bring the matter to closure and move on. Except in atypical cases involving an extreme exposure or extreme identification with the victim coupled with a sense of outrage at the circumstances of death, finding justice for the victim is for the most part an impermanent quest that can be satisfied through relatively simple professional actions. A true survivor mission is rooted in a transformative death encounter so profound that closure can scarcely be attained.

Several of the rookies I spoke with had a fairly strong identification with the deceased, although most did not go above and beyond what was required of them for the benefit of the deceased. That their commitment did not spur them to action, though, does not diminish the fact that they felt the commitment and the need for some sort of enactment. Indeed, many of the rookies who saw the need or opportunity to act for the benefit of the deceased also stated or alluded to the fact that they did not have appropriate resources within their repertoire, and as a result they felt conflict over their inability to perform effectively. For the most part, when they failed to act the failure was the result of a conscious decision not to pursue the risks involved in taking an uncertain course of action.

A sergeant who trained many rookies in the police academy as well as in the field operations setting spoke about rookies' discomfort with their new role and with the difficulty they have in integrating elements of their own backgrounds and experiences into the police self-identity. In particular, he observed that rookies are often reluctant to use their personal experiences to comfort family members at death scenes, simply because they are uncomfortable in the police role and have not yet integrated their personal and professional identities. In his experience, rookies typically feel a deep sense of compassion for victims and for family members but lack the experience to enact their feelings through appropriate words and behaviors that will bring solace and comfort *and* be "acceptable" police behavior. Rookies, he said, try to emulate the attitudes and behaviors they observe in senior cops but because they have such little experience and relatively little opportunity to observe officers closely in a variety of situations, they wind up emulating a narrow and constricted set of stereotypic behaviors. He described one rookie, a female officer with a fairly strong religious background, who was nevertheless very uncomfortable when family members expressed religious sentiments or engaged in prayers at a death scene. Although she told him she felt a personal impulse to join with them in prayer, she did not know if that behavior was compatible with her role as a professional police officer.[17] In time, though, she found that joining or even leading bereaved people in informal prayer often had a positive impact on them and on her; in time and with experience, she was able to integrate elements of her personal self and her professional self. According to the sergeant,

> She was initially reluctant to do that because it simply didn't fit with the stereotype of what a cop does. As she got more comfortable with what she was all about as a cop, she was able to share that part of herself with people. And she found it had a very positive reaction with people. Before she became comfortable with herself as a cop, she tried to live up to the stereotype of what a cop does and doesn't do. . . . After a while, you're able to incorporate your personal emotions, your personal feelings, with police procedure. But initially it's a period of big confusion.

The sergeant went on to comment that many rookies operating within the stereotype find it difficult to express their compassionate feelings and especially to express the sorrow they feel for someone's loss.

> They don't know how to say to people, "I'm sorry for your loss. I'm sorry for what you're going through." That particular word, for many cops, is

taboo. In other words, in the stereotype, being a police officer is never having to say you're sorry. They carry it forward in dealing with other people's tragedies. They just don't know how to say it and still be a police officer.

We should also recognize that humane and compassionate behaviors help both the officer and family members break away from the feelings of stasis, separation, and disintegration that are a part of so many death encounters. The officer's benevolent expressions of compassion provide all involved with a sense of connection—they convey the idea that family members are not alone in their sorrow, that even this stranger shares in their sense of loss—and they help the family and the officer move forward in their lives. The young officer's conception of the police role may still be fairly undeveloped, but it contains at least a rudimentary schema for enactment that calls for humane expression; by following through on the schema he experiences an important sense of vitalizing connection to others, he finds a kind of integrity or consonance between self-expectations and actual behavior, and he experiences a sense of movement or growth toward a fuller and more authentic police identity.

The Quest to Make Meaning: Integrating Competence and Compassion

Officers who are comfortable in their roles and in exercising their discretion are more likely to take affirmative steps to act upon their commitment to certain victims. With time and experience, officers develop a multifaceted professional identity; in general, the first elements of professional identity to develop are the simpler ones related to professional task competence, with the far more complicated and intricate interpersonal elements accruing later. The officer is thus likely to first acquire elements of what we might call the self-as-law-enforcer-and-competent-practitioner, a self that subsequently comes to take on elements of the self-as-caring-and-compassionate-human-being. Both in the interviews and in my informal talks with police officers, I heard numerous stories of officers who acted with great compassion or sensitivity toward the deceased or their families, and who did so comfortably. In virtually every case, the officers were experienced veterans who had fully formed their police identity as one that simultaneously permitted both compassion for the good and enmity for the bad, and in virtually every case the victims were "innocent" or infirm. One seasoned officer, for example, summed up his admiration for his partner by relating how effectively his partner practiced both roles. His veteran partner has a crusty disposition and is generally perceived as a "tough" cop who tolerates no nonsense from peers or the public, but is also prone to acts of kindness. He related a case in which an elderly woman who lived with her infirm husband died. His "tough" partner returned to the man's home after work and, on his off-duty time, helped him make funeral and burial arrangements and thereafter stopped in on the old man from time to time to comfort him in his bereavement. The officer's admiration for the "best cop he ever knew" was rooted in precisely that capacity to embrace and effectively practice both roles.

Throughout this chapter we have delineated and expanded upon the five themes of survivor psychology as they apply to the rookie's first death encounter. For very practical reasons, most notably to illustrate how a variety of circumstances and situations affect the rookie's experience and shape the evolution and transformation of his personal and professional self, we considered each theme separately. Nevertheless, there was significant overlap among the themes and experiences: we saw how closely intertwined the themes are, and we saw that a single image or experience can illuminate and apply to more than one theme of survivor psychology. By way of analogy, one might say that up to this point the chapter's structure presented a series of fragmented images that comprise an incomplete form or constellation. As part of our quest for immediate and ultimate meanings, the chapter concludes with a more holistic rendering of one officer's overall experience in relation to a kind of death event.

The officer in this vignette had been assigned to a high-crime precinct for about 1 year, his professional self was rather well-formed and complex, and he was competent in the administrative and interpersonal spheres. Despite his still-limited tenure, his attitudes, skills, and knowledge of policing were far more highly developed than those of the rookies we have discussed, and his experience permits us to sharpen our understanding of rookies through comparison and contrast. The fact that the victim in this case did not actually die is basically beside the point: her injuries were extreme and rather grotesque and her condition was grave, and the officer did not expect her to survive. These almost-deaths can have traumatic impact as formidable as an actual death, since they evoke the same kinds of imagery and, in illuminating the fragility and ephemeral nature of life, evoke a similar confrontation with one's own mortality. Moreover, the officer himself articulated that he equated the experience with a death encounter, volunteering that of all the deaths and violent crimes he attended, this "death" affected him the most.

The young cop responded to a crime scene in which a young woman was brutally beaten and sexually assaulted, and his description of her injuries and his reconstruction of the sequence of events leading up to the attack was detailed and graphic. It was quite clear that the imprint images remained vivid in his memory. Although his narration reflects elements of numbing, identification, and an awareness of his own unsuccessful attempt to achieve distance, the factual situation did not adequately permit him to depersonalize the experience by limiting identification or by attributing responsibility for the event to the victim herself. His tone of voice during our dialogue evinced his reanimated shock and horror at the extent of her injuries, and although the woman did not die he was profoundly affected by the image of her in seizure as the result of the extensive head injuries she suffered. After visiting the scene and canvassing the neighborhood for witnesses—a professional activity that gave him an important sense of agency—he was directed to respond to the hospital's emergency room to check on the victim's condition.

I said to the doctor, "Oh, she's conscious?" He said, "No." She was shaking, she was moving like a chicken when you cut their head off. She had been through so much trauma, unconscious, her body was shaking and she was moving. And when I saw that, I was getting nauseous, I guess because I was thinking, "Here's a girl, she's going to a good university, she's *trying*, you know? She went out drinking, but there's no crime in that, she's trying. And here some guy does this to her. She's probably someone trying to do the right thing with their life, a good student." And this is happening all so quickly, they're trying to find out who she is, now it turns out she's a great student, she grew up in [*names town*], a [*nationality*] girl, she wants to be a teacher, and now she's. . . . Like you start thinking, "Wow, this could be somebody I know." It could be. And it made me nauseous right there. That made me nauseous. Just because I guess, knowing that she's still alive she might die, that she was raped and just the whole fact that it was so *brutal*. He banged her head, he raped her, had sex with her. And I was very nauseous. It was rough. I felt bad for her. Like I said, because I knew that in my mind she was a student trying to do the right thing and this happened. She was no dummy. I think maybe when you try to figure out, when you're on the scene, in your mind in half a second you've got to figure out how this death came about. And if, maybe if the person, not that they deserved it but this is the type of life they were leading that led to this . . . . If the person looks bad and they're dead, at least they're dead. But if the person's looking horrible but they're still alive, or they're going to die any second or are they going to make it, it's kind of worse. You're thinking, this person may look dead, but they're not.

Clearly, the cop identified with the young woman, an attractive college student of the same race, approximate age, and level of education, whose positive and altruistic career goals were not unlike his own. He volunteered that this was the kind of girl he would date, and in contrast to every other rookie I interviewed he could recall her name and a host of other personal data about her. The young cop was deeply affected but not overwhelmed by the incident: he was able to compartmentalize his feelings and play a customary game of basketball with some other cops at the end of his tour, and he had no thoughts of her during the game.[18] He recalled the young woman's plight when he arrived home and was upset enough to call his mother to talk about the case. He felt some emotional release and received a kind of authentic nurturance simply by speaking to someone in whom he could safely confide his emotional upset, and by putting his thoughts and feelings in perspective he achieved a kind of mastery over them. He also subsequently discussed bothersome aspects of the case with his partner. He reported no sleep disturbance or bad dreams, though, and was not preoccupied with the graphic images he had witnessed.

Although the officer never actually met the woman and has never actually spoken to her, his connection with her and his commitment to finding justice for her was quite evident. He followed her case in the news media, repeatedly spoke with detectives handling the case, and questioned informants and street people for leads in the case. On a number of occasions he and his partner left their assigned patrol area—fully aware that they risked disciplinary sanction for doing so—and drove several miles across town to check out leads in the case. In doing so, he found an appropriate and meaningful kind of professional and personal enactment—he actively engaged in a course of committed action aimed at finding justice for an innocent victim with whom he identified closely. His more complex and inclusive police identity opened a host of professional possibilities, making it possible for him to fulfill a well-developed and professionally appropriate plan of action. To the extent some parts of the plan lay outside the scope of his professional duties or were constrained by rules and regulations, he was willing to knowingly bend or break the rules to achieve a greater good.

The officer's affinity for the victim and the many points of identification with her engendered a deep sense of commitment, which he acted upon by giving special attention and special effort to her case. His depth of commitment is all the more notable because he freely assumed it and had no official responsibility for bringing the case to conclusion. Nevertheless, he followed the case intently: he was aware of the type of medical treatment and rehabilitation she underwent, the extent of her residual impairment, and he knew that she ultimately returned to her college studies. He expressed satisfaction and relief that someone was arrested for the assault, and felt he contributed to the case even though the information he provided detectives played a minimal role in their investigation. In terms of limiting his death guilt and dealing with his numbing and devitalization, it was more important that he engaged in the actions—that he *did something* in a professional way—than that those actions led to actual results.

Although she ultimately survived her injuries, at the time of the incident the young woman seemed severely deprived of her future, which the young officer perceived as bright and virtuous and worthwhile. If the young woman had actually died, her death would have been all the more tragic for its lack of dignity and integrity—a dignity and integrity, the young officer felt, she deserved. That her innocence was violated through sexual assault added to the young cop's outrage, and the humiliation she suffered and the lack of coherence or meaning to be found in this "senseless" act made it difficult to extract any real or life-affirming meaning from it. All of these factors contributed to his quest to pursue justice for an innocent victim he never actually met, and they also served as the impetus for a committed course of action resembling a survivor mission. That committed course of action, in turn, satisfied his personal and professional schemas for enactment, limited his residual devitalization and death guilt, allowed him to participate more fully in policing's vitalizing immortality system, and permitted him to experience movement, connection, and a sense of personal and professional integrity. Had he not recognized or engaged in that course of action, the event might have had a significantly more traumatic impact and he might have remained "stuck" in the encounter, most likely resulting in significantly greater and more deleterious psychic impact.

5.

Patrol Sergeants

Routinization of the Death Encounter

Several salient psychological and environmental variables operate to distinguish the quality and psychological impact of the patrol sergeant's experience of job-related death events from the experience of rookies and the other categories of officers we consider. Because sergeants have fairly frequent contact with death, and because the death scenes they visit run the gamut in terms of the type of death and the quality of death images involved, we might initially expect their exposures to result in significant trauma and we might expect that they would manifest the characteristics of survivor psychology in a profound way. In general, though, sergeants seem much less affected by the deaths of others than do officers in other categories. Sergeants experience much less trauma and exhibit fewer characteristics of survivor psychology in part because they have had many previous experiences with death in the occupational context, but also because conditions within their task environment limit the death scene's traumatic potential: their death-scene duties are essentially administrative in nature, their exposure is usually of relatively brief duration, and their interactions are primarily with other police personnel.

The sergeant's task environment also prescribes a fundamentally different role than the roles played by other officers: he is, first and foremost, a supervisor who is not so much responsible for performing tasks or doing work at a death scene as for ensuring that the officers he commands do things properly. This primary focus upon procedural and administrative detail, with a secondary focus on the interpersonal factors that may be present in a given situation, helps the sergeant to maintain a psychological distance from the event and its emotional content. The supervisory role also gives the sergeant greater discretion than that enjoyed by the patrol officer, and this discretion permits him a variety of means to negotiate and manage the kind of images to which he is exposed. Individually and collectively, these factors operate to make the sergeant's subjective experience of a death event significantly less traumatic.

An important subjective factor in mediating the sergeant's experience of the death event is his own previous experience as a police officer handling DOA jobs. Since New York City Police sergeants must have at least five years' tenure prior to promotion, they are likely to have had a significant number of previous death encounters and to have already witnessed many types of deaths and death scenes. As a result, the sergeant is likely to have developed the protective capacity to invoke selective professional numbing in the face of new death encounters, and he is likely to be somewhat inured to death anxiety and traumatic death imagery— professional experiences with death generally hold little novelty for the sergeant. Tenure and police experience also give the sergeant a more fully developed sense of his police self, he has less anxiety about practicing its procedural and humane dimensions, and he has a greater sense of agency in terms of fulfilling schemas for enactment in professionally and subculturally appropriate ways. The sergeant knows what he and others are expected to do when called to a DOA scene—both in terms of the tasks and duties the department requires and the interactions he will have with others—and he is far less concerned than a rookie might be about his overall performance there. Sergeants also benefit from a more fully developed repertoire of interactive skills they can bring to bear in dealing with officers and civilians. Finally, we can see that tenure and experience equip the sergeant with a host of images, forms, and constellations that help him to integrate his immediate experience in a way that imparts some immediate and perhaps ultimate meaning to the death event. Each of these factors makes the sergeant less psychologically vulnerable to the disintegrative impact of death imagery than the inexperienced rookie.

The narratives provided by sergeants made it clear that they felt less vulnerable and less affected by death imagery than rookies: they described their recent death encounters in very general, almost businesslike terms, and with few exceptions their narratives were remarkably devoid of emotional content. In many cases, the impassive descriptions they gave of their death exposures as sergeants contrasted sharply with the emotional narratives they had provided about their rookie experiences only a few minutes earlier. Sergeants' narratives were far less detailed but much more coherent and logically ordered than those provided by rookies, and sergeants focused almost exclusively on the administrative and procedural issues their role entails. While rookies also tended to initially focus on the procedural difficulties they encountered, with gentle prodding they could easily shift to a description of the event's emotional content and its impact upon them. Sergeants, on the other hand, had greater difficulty recalling and describing any specific emotion they felt at a typical DOA job, or even at a specific death event. Several remarked upon the difficulty they had in recalling emotions, commenting that with the exception of a vague sense of sorrow for the victim and his or her family they really do not feel much at a typical DOA. This relative difficulty is further evidence that most job-related death encounters have far less emotional impact on sergeants than on rookies.

Unlike rookies, homicide detectives, and crime scene unit technicians, sergeants had great difficulty recalling specific images and details of their first DOA assignment as sergeants, and some had difficulty distinguishing between particular deaths they subsequently encountered. Several sergeants paused while providing an account to interject that they were uncertain if a particular detail or image belonged to the experience they were describing or if they were confusing it with another event. This was not a feature of the accounts provided by rookies or homicide detectives, and the tendency to confuse the details of particular cases was far more pronounced for sergeants than for crime scene unit technicians. As we will see in subsequent chapters, the roles homicide detectives and crime scene unit technicians play and the duties they perform impose significant demands that important details of one case not be confused with the details of another. These demands are not as compelling in the sergeant's task environment.

On the basis of this tendency, though, we can say that the images experienced by a sergeant at his many death encounters are likely to combine or merge in a kind of vague generic constellation that is conspicuously lacking in specificity and detail. The fact that sergeants have some difficulty recalling their first DOA job as sergeants and distinguishing the details of subsequent death encounters also illuminates the extent of their numbing and shows that they have relatively few struggles around the death images they experience and minimal difficulty interacting with family members and police personnel. It further illustrates that, unlike the rookie, the sergeant does not experience his first DOA in his new task environment as a rite of passage.

In light of the factors we've briefly described, we can understand why the sergeant's "typical" DOA job does not engender an unusually high degree of psychic trauma and is not especially troubling to him. The sergeant's duties at a typical DOA job are highly routinized, his exposure to death imagery is fairly brief, and the police experience resulting from his tenure gives him a high level of comfort with his job as well as the capacity to numb himself to the event's emotional content. This is not to say that sergeants never experience death events in a traumatic or emotionally costly way, but rather that such deaths are, in terms of the totality of the death scenes they visit, fairly infrequent. Like any other operational police officer, sergeants can respond to deaths whose circumstances, untimeliness, or grotesqueness are so objectively horrific that virtually no amount of psychological preparation, numbing, or procedural routinization can adequately insulate them from the death's traumatic potential. These deaths are of somewhat greater concern to our exploration of death in contemporary police experience since they have far greater potential to produce features characteristic of survivor psychology, and we will examine some of these unusual encounters and their specific impact on sergeants later in this chapter. We should also note that these objectively horrific deaths would be likely to produce extensive numbing and some impairment of the symbolizing process in practically anyone who experienced them.

Before turning our attention to them, though, and in line with the emphasis the shared themes approach places upon the similarities and differences in individual experience resulting from shared historical experience, we will first examine the "typical" or "ordinary" DOAs that comprise the vast majority of deaths in the sergeant's task environment. The goal of our examination is to elaborate how variables in the sergeant's task environment typically interact with subjective psychological variables, and to provide a basis for comparison with the other task environments and collective experiences we consider elsewhere in this book.

The Sergeant's Task Environment: The "Typical" DOA

Except in fairly unusual cases (i.e., when the death is a homicide or suicide or it requires some additional investigation), the sergeant's duties at a death scene have a relatively limited scope. The department's *Patrol Guide* (NYPD, 2003) regulations require that he be present to supervise an initial investigation into the cause of death and notify detectives if the death is of a suspicious nature, that he supervise the assigned officers' preparation of required paperwork, and that he supervise the physical search of the remains and inventory of the deceased's property. The search becomes more comprehensive when a person who lived alone dies in his residence, since the officers must inventory and remove all valuables, and this may require the sergeant to spend some additional time at the scene.[1] After completing these fairly straightforward supervisory duties (or ensuring they are completed) and directing the assigned officer to safeguard the scene pending the arrival of the detectives (if the death is suspicious, an apparent homicide or suicide, or the result of some other misadventure requiring investigation) or the removal of the remains (if the death is apparently from natural causes), the sergeant has no operational reason to remain there.

Because in many or most cases the sergeant responds to the scene simply to witness the search and perhaps the inventory and removal of property, delegating the other duties to the officers who remain to "sit on the body," he can often return to his supervisory patrol duties and endorse the paperwork at a later time. It is very possible, in fact, for a sergeant to comfortably complete all his required duties in less than 15 minutes. Death scenes are only one of the many assignments to which sergeants must respond, and especially in busier precincts the sergeant is likely to be called away to an emergency, a crime in progress, or to another assignment requiring his attention. The patrol sergeant is often the only field supervisor working in the precinct, and he is responsible and accountable for all police activities taking place in the field during his tour of duty. Especially in busier precincts, the patrol sergeant is simply too busy to remain at a death scene for a protracted period, and in busy precincts there can be considerable pressure to complete the assignment and return to other patrol supervisory duties. The same pressures operate to create a functional distance from the event by forcing the sergeant to focus on quickly completing his administrative and supervisory duties in order to free himself for the next assignment. A sergeant working in a busy precinct noted these pressures.

> The longest DOA I ever stayed on as a sergeant, other than a crime scene where you have a murder or something, was just a few minutes. It's just, "OK, did you get this done?" As a sergeant, my attitude is more business-like because I have the responsibility to make sure things are done right.

Certain integrity issues have to be maintained.[2] So I'm like, "OK, did you get this done? Did you get that number? Did you do this report? Blah, blah, blah." I'm not so much concerned with "Is everyone emotionally OK?" I have other business to take care of . . . The radio is always calling you so you just get it done.

Another sergeant commented:

As a sergeant what you want to hear when you arrive is, "It's natural causes, the family is present so there's no search of the premises, and the family doctor will sign off on it." All I have to do then is give the cops a scratch[3] and go off to the next job. You also offer condolences to the family and say "I'm sorry for your loss," but it's almost cold. You just go on to the next job.

The sergeant's very routine and relatively simple supervisory duties do not explicitly require interaction with grieving family members or nonpolice personnel. Although some sergeants take it upon themselves to interact with the deceased's grieving family or friends, and in doing so put into practice the humane schemas for enactment called forth from the compassionate dimension of the police self, they are cautious not to do so in a way that might substantially increase their own vulnerability. They are, in other words, motivated by a genuine concern for those in grief, and are comfortable enough to extend themselves emotionally, but only to a degree. When sergeants interact with grieving family or friends they tend to do so in a limited and fairly superficial way that precludes excessive identification and limits the potential emotional costs. Most of the sergeant's interactions, though, are with other officers with whom he is familiar and comfortable.

As in other death work occupations, routinization and the division of labor within the sergeant's task environment (like his role as a supervisor directing the work actually undertaken by others) provide him with a psychological and often a physical distance from potentially traumatic images and interactions. For example, several sergeants noted that they are not required to physically handle the remains and can delegate this task to others. As one noted, "I had a great aversion to touching the body and one good thing about being a sergeant is you don't have to do the search. It's 'OK, Officer, search the body.'" In conjunction with partial professional numbing, routinization and the delegation of tasks and responsibilities insulate the sergeant from a great deal of the event's potential emotional impact.

In summarizing the kind of exposures sergeants most frequently encounter and their subjective psychological impact, we can say that their most remarkable feature is that they are so unremarkable. Despite their greater frequency vis-à-vis the patrol officer and especially the rookie, these everyday death encounters do not have an especially powerful traumatic impact on sergeants and they do not substantially transform the sergeant's well-formed sense of personal or professional self. Notwithstanding the exceptional situations we will discuss below, they are for the most part brief, impersonal, and easily managed events that do not present a significant challenge to the sergeant's sense of immortality in the personal or professional sphere. The images involved are not particularly unusual or unfamiliar to the experienced cop or sergeant, and a host of situational and subjective psychological variables often function to further mediate their impact. For patrol sergeants, the demands of the task environment operate to make most death encounters conventional, prosaic, and routinized almost to the point of being pedestrian.

The Sergeant's Task Environment: Subcultural Dimensions

The sergeant's death exposures are certainly shaped by formal procedural demands, but his experience is also mediated by various subcultural factors. We recall, for example, that rookies responding to their first DOA often did not recognize that the "10–54 Unconscious Aided" call they answered was likely to involve a death, and they were therefore psychologically unprepared for the situation, the tasks and interactions involved, and the images they encountered. In the belief that the call actually involves an unconscious person in need of medical assistance or first aid, the rookie may in fact prepare himself by mobilizing and reviewing an entirely different set of interactions, skills, and cognitive knowledge than those he will actually use at the DOA scene. Experienced cops and sergeants, though, recognize the call's implicit possibilities and while responding they can mobilize an appropriate array of preparatory psychological defenses, including the invocation of partial professional numbing. Further, as a practical matter many or most sergeants do not usually respond immediately when a sector car team of experienced cops is assigned to an "Unconscious Aided" call; instead they monitor the radio and wait until the patrol officers summon them after determining that a death has, in fact, occurred. This delay provides sergeants with additional time for any psychological preparation that may be necessary.

Sergeants delay their response not necessarily with the conscious goal of avoiding a death scene and its images—although some may—but because they have arguably more important work to do in supervising other patrol activities. Because it ties them up in this way, responding to an ordinary DOA job for the formality of witnessing the search and "giving a scratch" may, in fact, be viewed as a nuisance. Even before the radio car team calls him, though, the sergeant has a pretty good idea whether the "10–54 Unconscious" involves a DOA—he picks up subtle hints about the on-scene condition by monitoring police radio traffic, the radio call dispositions, and especially the arrival and departure of emergency medical service (EMS) paramedics: if EMS departs the scene without removing the victim, a DOA is almost certainly involved.

There are also strong (if informal) subcultural expectations that experienced responding officers will undertake various activities to further reduce the time the sergeant must spend at the scene as well as the difficulty of his tasks and duties. This expectation generally holds true for all types of assignments requiring a sergeant's response, and not just those involving death. In practice, an experienced team of "heads-up" patrol officers who are well integrated into the police culture will typically respond to the scene, ascertain the condition, make any required notifications, and initiate the necessary paperwork before calling the boss. They undertake these actions in accord with a set of subcultural reciprocity norms that informally structure relationships between officers and supervisors. One such norm is encapsulated in the aphorism "don't give up the boss": it prescribes that if a ranking superior officer—especially a "shoofly"[4] or captain from an overhead supervisory command—catches a cop "off base," the cop will take responsibility for his actions in a way that does not implicate his immediate supervisor. In return, the cop expects his allegiance and loyalty will result in some softening of the disciplinary sanction his immediate supervisor will be responsible for imposing. In addition to the very practical expectation of reciprocity, this norm ties in to the high value the subculture places on loyalty and on being a "stand-up guy"— one who stoically takes responsibility for his own actions without betraying others. By demonstrating allegiance to these subcultural norms, the officer gains some access to the subculture's immortality system, since his reputation as a "good cop" is enhanced.

In a similar way, experienced street cops expect that if they make the boss's job easier by taking the brunt of a difficult assignment, the sergeant will reciprocate by taking care of them in some way—the sergeant may, for example, pick up a rookie from a foot post and assign him to "sit on the body," allowing the radio car team to return to other patrol duties. On the other hand, if the DOA is "fresh," the scene is relatively benign, and the weather is particularly cold or inclement, he may permit the officers to remain at the scene until the end of their tour and perhaps even earn some overtime if they desire it. Like many other subculturally prescribed behaviors, the expectation that patrol cops will begin to undertake the tasks and duties required of the sergeant has a secondary or collateral impact: by reducing the amount of time the sergeant must remain at the scene, it also limits his interactions with civilians and his exposure to death imagery.

The foregoing analysis assumes that a conscientious and experienced team of officers picks up the DOA job and performs according to the sergeant's expectations; the sequence does not apply in all cases, though.[5] The sergeant may respond sooner if a rookie picks up the job, for example, and he may respond sooner if the officers are inexperienced or otherwise troublesome. If the officers do not perform according to the sergeant's expectations (either in regard to the DOA assignment or in some other sphere), he may also use his discretion to require that one or both officers remain at the scene to "sit on the DOA" as a form of "attitude adjustment" or informal discipline.

In order to fully comprehend the apparent contradiction of using the DOA assignment as a type of reward or a type of punishment, it is necessary to understand that to a large extent the police culture views the DOA assignment as "rookie work." Beyond the fact that DOA jobs serve as an important socializing event or rite of passage for young officers, in a very practical sense the rookie's lack of experience makes him the most expendable of the sergeant's personnel resources: rookies require more field supervision than experienced officers, they are more likely to make errors on patrol that ultimately cause trouble for the supervisor, and they are generally less productive in terms of generating arrests, summonses, and reports. Inexperienced rookies are also devalued because they are generally the least proficient officers in terms of safe tactical response to crimes in progress and other dangerous calls that are the substance of "real" police work. Since the sergeant must assign someone to "sit on the DOA," it is usually the most expedient and practical alternative to assign the least valuable officer—the rookie—so that more valuable experienced personnel remain available to respond to crimes in progress and other more important assignments.

Further, partly as a function of its civil service orientation, the police culture places a great deal of emphasis on the notion that rank (or more accurately, experience and seniority) should have its privileges, and these privileges extend to the type of assignments one is given. Generally speaking, tenured officers expect to be given the most desirable assignments. All things being equal, then, the sergeant who makes the point of taking a tenured officer off patrol—away from "real" police work—and assigns him to an unimportant or tedious job when a rookie is available is almost certainly sending that officer a message. The sergeant is saying, in essence, that the rookie is more valuable (and has greater status and importance in the sergeant's estimation) than the tenured cop. As is the case in any other successful cultural form of degradation ceremony, the interpretation of the message depends not only on the circumstances surrounding it but also on the way it is publicly communicated and acknowledged (Garfinkel, 1956).

Every sergeant and officer I interviewed was familiar with the practice of using a DOA assignment as punishment, and there were two schools of thought about its effectiveness as a disciplinary or motivational tool. As one sergeant put it:

> I've used it. I had two guys who I felt just didn't work hard enough, and they were my two main customers when it came to DOAs. And I'm not the only one to do that. I've also threatened to do it to shake people up. "Straighten up your act or you'll have to deal with these unpleasant situations all the time." I even told other sergeants, "If I'm not here and you need a cop for a DOA, take one of these two."

Others were aware that "sitting on a DOA" is often used as punishment, but did not choose to use it as a corrective strategy.

> I wouldn't do that, and not just in DOAs. It's something I learned in the military: never assign someone to a duty that's normally done by other people. An example is KP—it's often used as a punishment, but sometimes it comes up in the normal rotation. When it comes up in normal rotation, people think, "What did I do wrong?" If you use it as punishment, people are going to see it as punishment. So everyone takes a turn.

Yet another sergeant saw the possibility of punishment but rejected it for practical as well as humane reasons.

> I always tried to be attentive to who is best for the job, but often it's like, "The guy over there doesn't have much to do, give it to him." Basically, it's

just a matter of job priority. In terms of punishment, I wouldn't do that. If you did that, he may act inappropriate because he's mad he's assigned to this DOA. I just find it's not a professional way to supervise, and there are other ways to discipline. You're punishing someone but you may be punishing the family, too, because you put a knucklehead on the job.

The highly structured formal demands of his death-scene task environment, along with his practiced capacity for partial professional numbing and the informal mediating practices of the police subculture, tend to limit and minimize the psychological impact of the death imagery to which the sergeant is frequently exposed. The sergeant's death encounters are so frequent, his duties are so routinized, and the images presented are so familiar that he does not generally experience these "ordinary" deaths as particularly novel, unusual, or traumatic events. "Ordinary" deaths are, on the contrary, one of many routine assignments to which the sergeant must respond, and they present him with relatively few challenges— in terms of challenges to either his sense of professional competence, his personal or professional identity, or his sense of immortality.

As we've pointed out, though, some death events transcend the ordinary, and because they involve exacerbating features of grotesqueness, personal identification, or other factors that challenge the sergeant's sense of immortality in a powerful way, they are more likely to illuminate the themes of survivor psychology. When sergeant collaborators were asked to describe a particularly memorable death event, in every case they described situations presenting powerful images that challenged one or more of the subparadigms comprising the personal or professional sense of immortality—they involved potent images of disintegration, stasis, and separation. In the remainder of this chapter we will examine more specifically how the five themes of survivor psychology play out in sergeants' typical and atypical death encounters, emphasizing how the more unusual events, while relatively infrequent, especially challenge his sense of immortality.

Psychic Numbing

Psychic numbing certainly plays a part in the sergeant's death encounters, but its effect is subtler and in many ways more constructive than the numbing rookies experience. While the rookie tends to experience a fairly profound degree of numbing during and after the death encounter, insulating him from the event's emotional content and moderately impairing his symbolizing process, the sergeant's numbing tends more toward the constructive pole of partial professional numbing. The sergeant is to some extent insulated from his own and others' emotions and his symbolization process is slightly impaired, but he isn't nearly as immobilized as the rookie. Because his capacity for partial professional numbing was acquired in earlier death encounters and because he has probably become adept at conjuring it to help deal with many other chaotic, dangerous, or emotion-laden situations, the sergeant can use distancing in a selective way. That is, he can partially numb himself to the more disintegrative or immobilizing images and emotions he confronts while remaining open to others.

The capacity to selectively filter out some aspects of the encounter is quite functional, since it permits him to remain receptive to images and experiences that connect with his core police-self and, because his symbolization process is minimally impaired, to find appropriate enactment for those images. All of this is to say that partial professional numbing permits the sergeant to more easily fulfill the role demands placed on him by the department (i.e., demands for administrative competence) as well as those closer to his sense of self-as-police-officer (i.e., demands for humane response) if he chooses to do so. The fact that in practice some sergeants emphasize one role more fully than the other has more to do with their conception of the police supervisory role than with an inability to perform the role.

As John van Maanen (1985) points out, police sergeants undergo a resocialization process—albeit a less powerful process than that experienced by the rookie—when transitioning to their new rank, and the process of integrating new and old images, forms, and constellations ultimately alters their sense of self and their conception of their own and others' roles. For some sergeants, the new sense of self-as-police-supervisor can be dramatically different from his old self-as-police-officer—every cop can name one or more supervisors who "used to be a regular guy before the stripes went to his head"—but for the most part the contours of the professional self, developed through time and police experience, remain basically the same: a caring and compassionate cop who acts charitably toward other cops and toward his civilian clientele will be a caring and sympathetic boss, and a more detached cop whose orientation tends more toward administrative efficiency will be a "by-the-book" boss who places less emphasis on the humane dimension of policing. The difference in a sergeant's role conception and sense of self will be reflected in the way he directs and manages the behavior of the cops he commands, including their behavior at death events. Because partial professional numbing does not radically impair their capacity to recognize the range of available discretionary behaviors and to select those most appropriate and most consonant with their role conception, sergeants can enter into situations and act in a way that is consistent with their professional selves. They can, in a sense, more easily flow between or put into practice the administrative and humanistic schemas for enactment prescribed by the complex professional self. By facilitating or permitting this congruity between self-concept and actual behavior, to some extent partial professional numbing preserves the sergeant's sense of integrity and authenticity at the same time it prevents the disintegrative effects of failed enactment.

We can glimpse these different professional orientations by referring to the narratives of two particular sergeant collaborators whose outlooks differed along these lines. One sergeant put it this way: "The primary thing I was concerned about as a supervisor was to get to the scene, that the cop was there, the family was present, the property secured. And that the death was natural and not suspicious. Most of the time the people are elderly, and the family is present. So I'm mostly concerned with procedures and compliance." In contrast, a sergeant with a somewhat more benevolent professional orientation expressed his role in a different way: "My struggle as a sergeant is not to be caring and compassionate—I can do that easily enough—but to get my people to be caring and compassionate." While both points of view reflect the idea that the sergeant's role is to supervise and direct officers' work rather than to do it himself, they also reflect very different perspectives on the nature and quality of appropriate police work.

Sometimes, due to the cumulative effect of frequent death exposures or because a specific death event is objectively horrific, partial professional numbing insufficiently protects the sergeant from death imagery and a more powerful form of numbing takes place. The inadequacy of partial professional numbing in the face of multiple death exposures was illustrated in an account provided by a sergeant who worked steady late tours—the midnight to 8:00 A.M. shift—in a precinct with a fairly high violent crime rate and a large elderly population.

> I hated, I hated to hear on the radio "[names precinct] Sergeant, we have an unconscious male, an unconscious female." Because you knew that that was a dead body and you had to go. You had to face death, you had to see death, and you had to see it in a very unnatural way. In a very natural way, but not antiseptic. I used to hate that. I used to cringe. I remember always feeling sick, always getting a nauseous feeling in my stomach when I heard an "unconscious" job. I worked late tours for 6 months, and a lot of people died in the early morning—they didn't wake up. I would say I went to 20 or 25 DOAs in a 6-month period. I felt a little jealous because as a cop, you didn't go to so many DOAs. Being a cop wasn't so bad. After a while you start getting cynical, like, hard. "Let me block this out. I don't give a shit. Fuck it."

The need to remain aloof and to limit interactions that might lead to excessive identification can be compelling, and it can easily conflict with the professional self's urge toward caring and compassionate response. One of the prominent themes to emerge from interviews with sergeants was this basic struggle between the protective tendency to maintain a dispassionate and austere professional persona—to remain physically distant and emotionally detached from the death images—and the tendency to humanely empathize with the plight of the deceased or his family and friends and engage in behaviors that might prove emotionally costly. Here again, the sergeant struggles with an issue of integrity—of achieving consonance between the philosophy of benevolent regard for those in need and actual behaviors that may entail great personal costs. The struggle, rooted as it is in the basic duality of the police role, is never easily resolved but it can be made all the more difficult when administrative rules and regulations limit the sergeant's discretion and his ability to manage the situation. We can see this additional complication arise when bereaved family members ask for help or advice with some sensitive personal issues, or when requests conflict directly with police department policy. An appropriate example can be found in a sergeant's comments about family members seeking advice on the selection of a funeral home, since department policy generally proscribes recommending any business or service. One sergeant commented on this struggle and the benefits of partial professional numbing as a means of resolving it.

Relatives would ask you for help with arranging for the funeral home. "Can you tell me a funeral parlor?" "I don't know." That's not a good thing.[6] After a while, there's so many dead bodies, hey, give me a break. Most people, you try to put up a front, you try to become callous in a way but the result is you wind up turning off citizens. The citizen gets 1 DOA, maybe 2 DOAs in their entire life, and here I was on my 25th DOA in 6 months. After a while you have to build a wall.

It is quite common for bereaved family members to ask an officer for advice or assistance in making funeral arrangements, selecting a funeral home, etc. Quite apart from the psychological barriers they erect to this kind of intimacy, most officers are, justifiably, quite reluctant to offer such advice because the department considers it a corruption hazard—allegations might be made that the officer is "steering" for a particular funeral home.[7] Another sergeant commented on this conflict, noting that in his predominantly Jewish and Italian American precinct many residents had affiliations with religious institutions. There were only two funeral homes in the neighborhood, one catering to Italian Americans and one catering to Jews, and when asked for guidance he would say that perhaps a clergyman would be in a better position to advise about funeral arrangements. He would also volunteer to call a clergyman on their behalf and request that the clergyman visit the family, noting that this strategy served the needs of the family at the same time it limited his own sense of attachment or commitment to them. What is most important here is that official demands to avoid the reality or appearance of impropriety foster a detached and businesslike demeanor, and the same demands may implicate the delivery of compassionate police service.

Partial professional numbing and, in some cases, more profound kinds of numbing play an important role in preventing excessive empathy and identification, in managing the conflicts that occur when sergeants attempt to balance the requirements of their official role with more personal tendencies toward compassionate response, and in protecting sergeants from some of the traumatic death imagery they encounter. Were it not for this capacity to selectively invoke partial professional numbing, it is likely that patrol sergeants would experience significantly more death-related psychic trauma from their numerous death encounters and that they would be far more reluctant to engage in humane interaction.

The Death Imprint Image

Along with the partial professional numbing they selectively use, the brevity of their exposures and the highly routinized nature of their task environment usually minimizes the emotional costs involved in the majority of sergeants' death encounters. Not every death is routine, however, and sergeants may attend events so objectively horrific that partial professional numbing inadequately shields them from the death imprint image. In these cases sergeants experience a more profound kind of numbing and some deterioration or impairment of their symbolizing process, although their numbing is still not as powerful as a vulnerable rookie might experience under the same set of circumstances. When these unusual death events occur, the death imprint image is more potent and more durable.

A collaborator who served as a patrol officer and as a sergeant in the transit division described two particularly gruesome types of subway assignments known colloquially as a "man under" job and a "space case";[8] both assignments involve grotesque death, literally in its most disintegrative form. A "man under" involves someone who falls or is pushed into the path of an oncoming subway train and is crushed beneath it. The body is typically "all chewed up" and usually dismembered—"you see body parts scattered around on the tracks and under the car"—and although death is usually instantaneous some individuals remain alive for a short time. It is not uncommon for an officer to arrive at the scene while the victim is still alive and conscious (Haberman, 2000).

> A space case, that's where someone gets caught in the space between the train and the platform. There's only about 4 to 6 inches there, and someone would get a foot caught in there and the train will drag them and they'll actually get spiraled in between the train and the platform. The train will stop but by then it's too late. They're still alive but when you move the train they'll die.

The grotesque images presented in a "space case" can be difficult enough to deal with, but the difficulties are compounded because an experienced officer knows the victim will die in a matter of minutes: the police and rescue workers will almost certainly kill him when they lift the train. Physiologically, the sudden release of pressure sealing the victim's massive wounds will cause a tremendous drop in blood pressure and a huge gush of blood. Death is virtually simultaneous with the release of pressure.

The trauma is further intensified when the officer's efforts lead to an empathetic connection to the victim. The certainty of impending death adds a unique ethical dimension to the "space case," as does the fact that because a halted subway train strands thousands of passengers in remote tunnels and can lead to other medical emergencies, officers are under tremendous official pressure from the agency to get the trains moving again quickly. As the sergeant put it, "If you've ever seen people coming out of a packed train that's been stuck in a tunnel 2 hours, you know it [getting the trains moving] is worth it." Again, department regulations stipulate that officers expeditiously remove the victim from the scene and restore subway service. Cops who attend a "space case" or a "man under" are in a morally invidious and emotionally difficult position—the dialectic between the tendency toward compassionate response and the exigent demands of police procedures is magnified tremendously, but there can be only one outcome.

The traumatic potential of the "space case" is partially managed through numbing, but cops also limit their death guilt by clinging to the belief that because the victim cannot be saved under any circumstances they are not really killing him. The actual lifting of the train is managed in much the same way as death row prison guards manage executions (Lesy, 1987; Johnson, 1989), soldiers manage massive killing on crew-fired weapons systems (Bourke, 1999; Grossman, 1996; Pierson, 1999), and medical personnel manage the deaths of patients (Bosk, 1979):

a division of labor with carefully defined and limited roles facilitates the diffusion of personal responsibility. Patrol officers on the scene shut down power to the third rail and close off the area to public view, call for EMS paramedics, and notify the emergency services unit to respond and perform the actual extrication. A team of emergency service unit officers places an airbag under the train and inflates it "like an accordion" with an air compressor, lifting the train off the victim. The entire process takes a matter of minutes, and the airbag inflation takes just seconds. The victim is immediately rushed to a hospital by EMS ambulance, but the attempt to save his life is invariably futile.

The sergeant described his first "space case" as a patrol officer, and in his narration we again see the police officer's fundamental conflict between demands for detachment and the will toward humane connection:

> The guy was talking to us. We got down there [beneath the train] and the guy's talking to us. I was kind of naive. A couple of old-timers were there and the guy says, "Hey, I want a cigarette. Anybody got a cigarette?" Somebody was giving him a cigarette and I said, "I don't think that's wise," and they said, "It doesn't matter anyway." "Why?" "Because they're going to lift the train off him and he's going to fall apart." Holy shit. So they were talking to this guy and they're going to lift the train. On the side they're saying, "Kiss your ass goodbye" and "Better make your peace with the Lord" and whatever. People are praying and everything, but nobody told the guy. Maybe they should have waited for a priest or something, but nobody called a priest. But you've got to take care of business. They lifted the train and that was it. The guy went "Aaah" and that was it. Dead. They picked him up, put him on a backboard, and gone. That was an eye-opener. Holy shit.

When the officer became a sergeant, his new task environment afforded him greater discretion, which he used to manage space cases differently: he maintained a greater physical distance from the victim by directing police activities from the platform rather than the track bed, a strategy that limited his visual image of the victim and precluded conversation that might lead to identification. He supervised the scene and directed the activities of the officers under his command, but did so with an emphasis on procedural compliance. He purposely did not interact with the victim.

Sergeants can attend other kinds of deaths whose factual circumstances make it difficult not to identify with the victim, and these deaths also have a lasting psychic impact. These encounters are not altogether rare: every sergeant collaborator described one or more death encounters that upset him greatly, and identification with the deceased was a factor in every case. As compared with the vague and general descriptions they gave and the slight difficulty they had in recalling the facts of routine encounters, these exceptional encounters resulted in unusually detailed accounts and powerful descriptions of the death imprint images involved. It is important to note, though, that the majority of these exceptionally powerful encounters had little to do with the sergeant's supervisory role or task environment per se: the impact resulted from factors, such as the death of a child or another kind of objectively horrific death, that would likely impact any officer who happened to attend the event.

One type of situation involving significant identification with the deceased is a police officer's suicide or a police-involved shooting, and one sergeant collaborator noted he had supervised the initial investigation in at least six such incidents. Police suicides and shootings are particularly difficult, and not merely because the sergeant identifies to some degree with a fellow officer's plight—he has a specific role and must perform specific duties that the ordinary cop does not, and these roles and duties mediate his exposure in a unique way. Because they do identify closely with their fellow officer, though, sergeants may be a bit reluctant to treat the preliminary investigation as "business as usual" and may feel the urge to selectively "turn off" partial professional numbing so as to be more empathetic to the officer and his situation. This tendency to identify with the plight and circumstances of another officer operates to enhance empathy, making the sergeant more receptive to the death imprint image, and at the same time it again sets up the conflict between his humane inclinations and his professional responsibility as an impartial fact finder.

While trying to remain open to the experience in order to make immediate and ultimate sense of it, this particular sergeant recognized that his professional responsibility was to conduct a preliminary investigation, not to determine the underlying reasons for the suicide. "It's very businesslike," he said, "I'm as upset as anyone would be to see a suicide or a cop shot or a cop shooting someone, but you deal with it the best you can. You have to carry on and be professional, businesslike. Maybe it's experience, but I'm able to do that."

Some amount of identification is inevitable, though, and that identification is inevitably manifested in anger, guilt, and conflict. Investigating a police suicide

> can be distressing because you identify with the cop and with his family. You also feel angry. You look at the wife and kids and you say, "Look at what you did to them." The most traumatizing thing is when you see the family, you see the kids, and you picture your own kids. You get an emotional attachment in the fact you could almost picture yourself there. Not that I could picture myself doing suicide, but I can picture my own family, how upset they would be at my demise however it came about. It just sucks. That's where you feel emotionally upset.[9]

The suicide of someone we know or identify with personally is always a particularly powerful confrontation with our own mortality, and it is perhaps even more so in the policing context. This is partly due to the high rate of suicide among cops (Nelson and Smith, 1970; Heiman, 1975; Friedman, 1967; Wagner and Brzeczek, 1983; Lester, 1992, 1993; Violanti, Vena, and Marshall, 1996; Quinnett, 1998) and retired cops (Gaska, 1980), but other factors are also at play. As members of the tight-knit police subculture, almost every tenured cop I interviewed knew or was at least acquainted with an officer who committed suicide, and even the publicized suicides of cops one doesn't know are likely to be the subject of hushed conversation and locker room speculation. One of the sergeants who collaborated in this project, in fact, personally knew 3 officers who committed suicide in a span of 8 years. A police suicide does not generate quite the same attention or emotion that a line-of-duty death might, but many of the same factors of identification and connection that make a line-of-duty death so personally meaningful apply equally to suicides.

Like anyone who loses a friend or colleague to suicide, part of the cop's struggle involves the need to make meaning and to find some reassurance in understanding why the death occurred. This need to attribute causality can never be fully satisfied, of course, since we can never really know why someone has taken his own life, but when identification or friendship is a factor the cop invariably questions his own complicity in terms of a failure to recognize and act upon any telltale behaviors or hints the dead officer might have given. Perhaps because the limited information available also makes these deaths so difficult to comprehend, cops (as well as the department, in its "official version" of the event) often seize upon the simplest viable answer. The very simplicity of the answer or attribution, however, can easily escalate the cop's sense of identification: the "typical" police suicide is usually attributed to some combination of alcohol abuse, marital difficulties, the recent breakup of a relationship, job stress, or disciplinary problems—problems that are far too common among far too many cops. This sergeant noted he felt empathy for many innocent victims,

> but with a cop I identify a bit more. There are certain things that just bring it closer. Certain things you hear, and you say "Yeah, I've been under some stress at the precinct, I remember having those kinds of feelings, I know guys with marital problems who are running around with a wife *and* a girlfriend. I know people who have drinking problems." Hell, until a few years ago, running around, lots of girlfriends, drinking and lots of stress were part of *my* lifestyle. You can see how it might eventually catch up with you, so in that sense I can identify more.

Another officer's suicide resonates with other cops on a variety of levels and has the potential to raise conflicts around a number of personal and professional issues.[10] Due to the heightened identification and sensitivity that accompany the death of a fellow cop under any circumstances, the suicide represents a more powerful and highly personalized encounter with one's own mortality than, say, the death of an unknown civilian. In itself, heightened identification is likely to magnify all the other themes and dimensions of survivor psychology, but identification also makes the confrontation more powerful because it shatters the magical sense of invulnerability that supports the police identity and is so important to officers who deal with death on a daily basis. Police can (and do) conceive of the possibility of their own death through instrumental violence or even through line-of-duty accidents, and as much as they compartmentalize them, these images provide a kind of schema for enactment: a cop's own death by violence or accident is rendered somewhat less absurd and less incomprehensible simply because it can be (or has been) imagined. While there is always some psychic resistance to imagining our own deaths, imagining our own death by suicide is especially difficult because the social and cultural proscriptions surrounding it can raise particular kinds of guilt.

The sting of imagining one's line-of-duty death is also lessened because such a death provides access to an immortality system: the officer would be heralded as a hero in the culture, his name would be immortalized and enshrined in the Hall of Heroes in the police headquarters lobby and at the police memorial walls in Washington, D.C., and Battery Park City in lower Manhattan, he would be awarded (albeit posthumously) a medal, and the death would be the subject of much discussion among other cops. The line-of-duty death, in other words, is a glorious and heroic death. The cop will be remembered, and his death will have meaning for others. The officer who commits suicide, on the other hand, will not have the benefit of this immortalizing system; his death may perhaps be seen as unfortunate and it may engender some sympathy, but he will not be regarded as a hero. On the contrary, he may be remembered as one who "took the coward's way out."

Another task or professional responsibility that often causes the sergeant some distress is the search for valuables that must take place if the deceased lived alone. The sergeant's official responsibility is merely to supervise and witness the patrol officer's search and the removal of property for safeguarding pending surrogate's court review and distribution to lawful heirs, but as a practical matter the sergeant often participates in the search to expedite the process and hasten his return to patrol supervision. We can learn a great deal about someone by examining his belongings and personal papers, and the intimacy of exploring the artifacts of someone's life easily facilitates identification.[11] Thus professional demands for expediency can impede the sergeant's struggle to avoid excessive attachment and identification through professional numbing. The struggle around identification, which is not unlike the struggle homicide detectives experience when they investigate a victim's background and relationships, can lead to a sense of commitment to the victim and his family. Rifling through the deceased's closets and drawers is a necessary part of the officer's duties, but it also violates social and cultural norms about showing "proper respect" for the dead. The natural tendency to experience amorphous guilt around the death of another person can be exacerbated or concretized when we identify with him, and when we have a factual or rational reason—such as the violation of these social and cultural norms—to feel guilty. Most frequently, the sergeant's sense of guilt crystallizes around the idea that the search is an invasion of the deceased's privacy.

> With the searches, it's really like an invasion of this person's life, his property. You're doing it to secure it, to make sure that no one steals it and it goes to the proper people, but it is kind of an invasion in this person's life. You're going through their drawers, you're looking at personal things, wills, bankbooks. It's a necessity to do these things, but its still an invasion of the person's private life. Because you didn't know them but now you're going through their stuff and you're beginning to know more about them. Their wealth, what they were sick from, their medical history, even their family. Here's a person that maybe all his life kept how much money he

had to himself, and here you are, Johnny-come-lately, and you're going right through his bankbook. You're looking for wills, who he's leaving his money to or whatever he has. . . . If he was alive you definitely wouldn't have a right to know these things.

Searches become all the more uncomfortable if family members arrive at the scene. Although the officers' activities are legitimate, necessary, and prescribed by law, to some extent they still violate social and cultural norms about respect for the dead. The cops' guilt can be more easily managed when these violations take place in a private environment among trusted cops who feel the same sense of amorphous guilt, and privacy also permits some opportunity for levity or humor to expurgate their immediate discomfort. When family members are present the search is no longer a "backstage" behavior, but rather the cops' "guilty" behavior takes place in a very public way before an audience that is particularly sensitive to the norm violations they are committing. The cops cannot engage in any levity or jokes to mediate their discomfort while family members are around, and they feel constrained to comport themselves differently and handle the property with a bit more respect than they might if no audience was present. While sergeants and cops are generally sensitive to family members, the search must be performed and the property must be removed, and they cannot permit the urge for compassionate action to completely override their professional responsibility. At the same time, it is not unheard of for sergeants to authorize the stretching of rules or even to turn a blind eye when family members wish to remove small personal items, such as photographs, that have limited value.

Several sergeants noted they always try to explain to the family members the reasons for the search, but they never feel entirely successful at explaining it to the family's complete satisfaction. A collaborator related that despite his explanation of the legalities and assurances that the property would be returned once the proper heirs were identified, one family became so upset they called a lawyer to the scene. Tensions between cops and family can at times escalate to the point of violence, and one sergeant related an incident that, although fairly humorous in retrospect, required a call for backup to prevent a possible assault of officers.

In this incident, a young woman of about 30 years of age died naked in bed. She was wearing some rings that had to be removed, and because partial rigor mortis set in the rookie assigned to remove them was having some difficulty. The sergeant directed the rookie to get up on the bed in order to get more leverage, and as the rookie straddled the body while pulling at the jewelry the sound of the squeaking bedsprings caused a family member to open the bedroom door and look in at the scene of a uniformed police officer perched atop the naked corpse of his relative while three other officers stood around watching and offering encouragement. The family's understandable outrage precipitated a call for back-up officers while the sergeant tried to explain the reason for this highly unusual scene and avoid an assault.

Certainly not every search the sergeant supervises leads to this level of tension, but there is always some tension with family members who may arrive on the scene.

If there's family present, you feel a little more uncomfortable because here you are coming into the house and you have to explain to them why you're there. In a lot of cases I've gone on, they don't understand why we have to be there. So if it's necessary I take a few minutes to explain to them why we're there. People don't understand why we have to do searches. And I tell them, because we have to make sure that the person who's entitled to the property gets it. Otherwise there are family members who would come in and raid the apartment, and they're not rightfully entitled to it. They just lost a loved one, and now we explain to them that since the person lived alone I have to go through the closets and take jewelry, money. And they're not still quite sure why you're taking this. I have to tell them, we're taking it so that the right person who's entitled to it gets it. Now whether they buy that or not, I don't know. So it's an awkward situation where you have a job to do and you don't want to hurt people's feelings so you try to explain to them why, even though sometimes they don't understand.

Another collaborator described a case that was particularly difficult due to its grotesqueness, the fact it was a suicide, the presence of family members at the scene, and his own bond of identification with the deceased. A young man of about 30 committed suicide with a shotgun, blowing off "the entire left side of his head." The body was discovered 4 days after death, and the "unbearable stench" of putrefaction, the blood and gore and the grotesque swelling of the body made the premises search and the preliminary investigation all the more difficult. The young man's age, occupation, social situation, physical size, and body type were strikingly similar to the sergeant's own brother. "It was traumatizing to see him. He could have been my brother's twin. I felt traumatized by the similarities. My brother even had the same brand of shotgun at home." These similarities were the basis for a particularly close identification with the deceased.

As difficult as it was to supervise a search in this physical and emotional setting, the situation worsened when the deceased's mother and brother arrived on the scene. Although they were not permitted entry to the apartment—it would be considered a crime scene until the investigation was completed—they remained on the street outside. The sergeant felt quite awkward in dealing with them, and as we might expect he also identified with the woman and imagined how his own mother would feel under similar circumstances. He became quite angry at the suicide victim for causing her such distress. Because he felt so awkward, the sergeant struggled to "remain professional" (i.e., detached) while dealing with the mother and brother. He explained they could not enter the apartment or have access to the young man's property for an indeterminate period of time, but also tried to offer some solace by retrieving some photographs from the apartment and giving them to the mother. The sergeant retains the image of her sobbing with her hands covering her face, calling her dead son's name and holding his photograph. That image conjured an image of his own mother, and he reflected on how she would feel if her son committed suicide. He also retains the grotesque image of the dead man, although he consciously avoided looking directly at the man's wounds.

These images haunted the sergeant for several days. He was "very sad" and emotionally debilitated, and although he had actively avoided looking directly at the dead man's wounds had intrusive thoughts of the grotesque injuries for days. He worried he would have bad dreams about the event, to the extent that for several nights he actively tried to convince himself not to dream about it.

The Struggle for Meaning and the Survivor Mission

Since sergeants' death encounters do not typically involve extreme impairment, the images they experience are rather easily integrated into existing forms and constellations, and their meaning-making process is not unduly impaired. Given their enhanced discretion and the degree of situational control they exercise at death scenes, sergeants usually have an adequate sense of agency and their schemas for enactment are more easily and more fully implemented than are rookies', or even for experienced patrol officers'. As a result of this appropriate enactment and the availability of previous images, forms, and constellations that can connect with the immediate images in a meaningful way, the survivor mission was not a particularly prominent theme among sergeants. We can nevertheless discern some elements of survivor mission among sergeants, especially after atypical exposures that challenged their integration of images and meaning making. We can also see the vestiges of earlier unresolved death encounters where full and appropriate enactment was not achieved, and we can see how a limited survivor mission can tie in to a kind of immortality system.

Some of the more conscientious sergeants are quite cognizant that the supervisory role involves a responsibility to continually train and develop the patrol officers they command, and they consciously use death encounters as a vehicle to shape officers' attitudes, skills, and knowledge. This day-to-day process of informal on-the-job training typically involves passing along practical tips and lessons learned through one's own police experience, and the relationship between an experienced sergeant (or an experienced street cop, for that matter) and a young officer often resembles that of a mentor and protégé. Quite aside from the practical benefits that accrue to the trainee, and aside from the less tangible but nevertheless important ego boost the sergeant receives from conveying the wisdom of his years, these relationships constitute a kind of immortality system. They permit both parties to share in the arcane experiential knowledge that is so esteemed in the police culture and that separates "real" or authentic cops from rookies and civilians, they connect the trainee to the historic past, and they give the mentor a sense that his knowledge and expertise will shape the development of a successive generation of officers. The mentor's knowledge and experience, in other words, will continue to benefit the enterprise of policing beyond his own limited career; he will be remembered and valued. Such relationships are cherished in the police subculture: police war stories are replete with references to "legendary" cops who passed along a particularly useful piece or information or taught a young cop an important lesson. Many or most experienced cops credit a particular mentor with developing their skills, refining their tactical approach, shaping their professional worldview, and molding their police personality by taking them under a protective wing.

Two sergeants noted their affinity for informal mentoring and the training of cops under their command, and both consciously used death encounters as a vehicle to shape officers' attitudes, skills, and knowledge. Moreover, they pointed out that they recognized the need for such training in death-related matters precisely because, as rookies, they felt so inadequate and ill prepared to deal effectively with a death event. The two sergeants had very different rookie experiences and derived very different kinds of meaning from their first death encounter, but the meanings they took away from the experience continued to inform and shape the way they dealt with death throughout their respective careers. Because their initial (and some subsequent) death encounters entailed elements of failed enactment, and because the immortalizing effect of the training they provided was an attempt to repair the failed enactment and achieve some mastery over it, their training efforts have all the hallmarks of a survivor mission. The important distinction here is that the mission is not to find justice for oneself or for a particular victim but to help other cops deal effectively with their death encounters.

Notwithstanding that both sergeants recognized the importance of training cops to deal effectively with death events, they differed greatly in the way they used the events for training purposes. Their two different approaches to training also illustrate two basic ideological or philosophical positions I discerned among collaborators throughout the interviews: one sergeant saw the first death encounter as a necessary and functional rite of passage that toughened and made the rookie less vulnerable to emotions, while the other embraced the less prevalent notion that the rookie's confusion and lack of expertise are the unintended consequences of inadequate training and preparation, resulting in unnecessary trauma that eventually leads to poor public service.

When he was a rookie, the first sergeant's struggle revolved primarily around task-related duties and paperwork, and because the corpse was removed quickly from a public place[12] and no family or friends were present, he was somewhat less affected by the event's emotional content. Since he managed to deal with the administrative issues, fulfill his own and others' expectations, and bring his first encounter to a successful conclusion without help, he reasoned that other rookies would also emerge from the struggle as better and more effective cops. As a "by-the-book" boss, he was particularly attentive in instructing young officers about procedures and paperwork but otherwise adopted a kind of "hands-off" approach, permitting rookies to experience and make meaning of the event in their own way and intervening only when he saw a definite problem emerging. He believed his own confusion had been functional since it forced him to focus on and learn procedures and because it toughened him. He received little help from other officers but was not unaware that help might be beneficial to other rookies. As a result, he saw his role in training rookies and young cops as "part Father Flanagan and part Knute Rockne"—he sought to combine guidance with tough supervision, never letting the balance tip too far in either direction:

At a DOA . . . I let them work just as hard as I worked, but I also work with them and give them some of the guidance a rookie needs—or any officer needs. I make sure everything is done right, and then I leave the scene. But I definitely find out, "Do you need coffee or anything?" As a boss you have to take responsibility for your people, but you also have to take the personality out of it so it's all business. Nothing is personal, it's all business. You have a role to do, and you do it. I guess I could be more supportive but it doesn't bother me when I'm not.

The second sergeant, a former police academy instructor, was much more concerned with developing cops' social skills to make them more aware of and responsive to the needs of bereaved family members—issues that were of great concern to him at his first DOA. In his view, procedural and administrative responsibilities are important, but far less important than humane interaction. His rookie DOA experience left him feeling frustrated and incomplete, but his struggle was very different: while the paperwork posed little problem, he felt ill equipped to adequately minister to the needs of bereaved family members. He subsequently recognized and felt frustrated by the agency's overriding concern for administrative efficiency and procedures, cogently articulating his view that these concerns were often pursued at the expense of compassionate interaction. There is no reason, he said, that with effective training and ongoing reinforcement a police officer could not easily achieve both objectives, but when a conflict arises between the two goals the cop's superseding moral duty is to act humanely. Although the agency's impersonal bureaucracy officially allows the officer little discretion to violate procedures in service of compassionate action, he saw his role of supervisor as that of a facilitator and supporter of appropriate rule breaking. Rookies, in particular, are reluctant to use their discretion to violate rules, he said, and they must be trained to do so appropriately. This officer clearly recognized that death events often implicate the implicit duality of administrative efficiency versus compassionate response, and he spoke at length to the fact that rookies have to develop and integrate both in order to become effective cops.

Unlike the first sergeant, he specifically rejected the idea that the first death encounter should be a rite of passage; he said some sergeants and cops "*try* to make it a rite of passage, when they *should* make it a learning experience" that leads to a "more fully actualized" police officer. He would, for example, regularly inquire about an officer's experience in handling DOA jobs and if necessary review the tasks and duties they would have to perform, emphasizing and suggesting ways they could make the ordeal less difficult for the family. He also took it upon himself to interact with family members, to introduce the assigned officer to them, and to explain what he and other officers would be doing, in the belief that this cognitive knowledge and role clarification would make the event more tolerable for all involved and especially because it would "take some of the heat off" the officer assigned to remain at the scene. "Taking the heat off"—reducing the cop's anxiety—would in turn make the officer more receptive to the needs of others as well as his own feelings.

In all respects, this sergeant's combination of experiential training strategies, emphasis on developing the compassionate elements of the police self, mature acknowledgment of the difficulties and potentials involved in a death encounter, and overall outlook on death experiences was quite unique. Indeed, these are precisely the kind of humane, compassionate, and effective behaviors police should practice in making death notifications (Death Notifications Guidelines Committee, 1992; Helm and Mazur, 1989; Hendricks, 1984; Leash, 1994; Clark and Labeff, 1999). As we might suspect, his sensitivity toward these issues and his survivor mission of educating officers about the need for compassionate response were in part the product of earlier formative death-related experiences. His first death encounters as a police officer certainly raised concerns about his inability to fully enact what he perceived to be an important set of professional role expectations, but those concerns were predated and magnified by earlier death encounters: during his military service as an army officer in the Vietnam War era, he was assigned as a survivor's assistance officer—the liaison to families of soldiers killed in the line of duty—and was at that time keenly aware of the difficulties involved in adequately fulfilling the role.

This sergeant was particularly attuned to the problems police officers face in making death notifications because they had been a substantial part of his job in the military. He described several notifications he made in police work and the military in terms of his fear[13] and sense of inadequacy, affirmatively stating that his military experiences were a significant source of his commitment and concern[14] for ensuring police death notifications were made as compassionately as possible.

The sergeant's police experience in making death notifications was easily integrated into a larger and considerably more meaningful constellation rooted in his military experience, and his descriptions of police notifications were salted with military references and images. To his way of thinking, the two were practically the same. As revealed in his orderly and insightful analysis, it was also obvious he had given these matters some thought over the years.

> The hardest part was always just before, standing at the door. Knowing that when I knock on that door someone's life is going to change forever, and not knowing what the reaction will be. . . . There are really three things going on. First is making the notification, telling someone their loved one is dead. Next is the counseling, whether and how much you're going to do. Third is providing information. People want to know why this person is dead and they look to you for information. They want you to provide a reason. . . . Those experiences were the starting point for my sensitivity to death notifications and to dealing compassionately with people whose loved ones have died.

Unlike any of the other sergeants I interviewed, he freely assumed the responsibility to accompany officers when they made death notifications. Because death notifications should properly be made in person rather than by telephone, other police agencies often request that local officers make the notification on their behalf. Problems can—and, not infrequently, do—arise when the local officers are given incomplete information about the victim and the circumstances of his death. This sergeant's method of training cops to make compassionate notifications was also uniquely powerful because it was based in a hypothetical but very personal death encounter. Rather than simply equipping them with words they could use—a depersonalizing script designed to make the experience easier on themselves but no less difficult for the family member—he would have each partner tell the other about someone close to him—a family member, friend, or spouse—and each would in turn role-play the delivery of a notification that the loved one had died. He would then discuss with them how this hypothetical but very personal encounter made each one feel and how they could use their insights and feelings to craft a compassionate notification. The goal of this and all the other death-related training he provided was not to give officers an effective patter or a set of procedural protocols, but to push them toward a more genuine expression of their always-evolving police self. Young officers in particular, he said, have the urge to act humanely and are almost always motivated by the will toward compassionate public service, but police procedures too often inhibit humane self-expression by permitting them an easy retreat from the humanity of police work. Although administrative procedures are important and necessary, he said, when they become paramount they can inhibit the development of an integrated and actualized police self.

With the exception of these two individuals, survivor missions were not prominently reflected in sergeants' experiences, and this was due in large measure to the fact that the duties and responsibilities that are specifically part of the sergeant's task environment generally provide an adequate and sufficient opportunity for meaning making. All sergeants related instances where they went "above and beyond" on behalf of a particular victim or they articulated a particular kind of affinity for certain types of victims, but their attitudes and behaviors were not unlike those of any experienced police officer: their commitments were rooted in the kind of unusual or atypical death encounter that any officer might experience, they were generally transitory and of relatively brief duration, and they generally occurred when the sergeant had an unusually high degree of empathy with the victim, his family and friends, or the specific conditions at the scene. Sergeants' overall lack of compelling survivor missions, which so resemble those of experienced cops, is attributable to the same set of factors: partial professional numbing effectively limits the impact of most potentially traumatic death imagery, sergeants can readily integrate and make meaning of the images they encounter, and they experience rather little death guilt. From a pragmatic view, this lack of a survivor mission or of excessive empathy is quite fortuitous for sergeants: given the sheer number of deaths they typically encounter, the commitments would certainly prove emotionally exhausting.

Death Guilt

For many of the reasons we have reviewed thus far—perhaps most important, the effectiveness of partial professional numbing—sergeants do not suffer from an inordinate amount of death guilt. Some amount of death guilt is incurred in every death encounter, though, if only from the notion of survivor priority: regardless of his real or imagined culpability for the death of another, at some level the sergeant, like any other human being who confronts death, recognizes and feels a guilty responsibility for the fact that he has survived while another has died. Since sergeants are not typically present at the moment of death—we recall that they usually respond only after other officers have determined that a death has occurred—their actions or inactions rarely contributed to the death and they do not typically bear the burden of this more potent form of death guilt. If the circumstances surrounding a particular death led to an individual sergeant feeling this more reasonable type of guilt, the guilt would be the result of the circumstances and not the sergeant's task environment per se.

In fact, certain elements of the sergeant's task environment, most notably his role as an objective initial investigator of the cause and circumstances of the death, operate to insulate or further distance him from death guilt. The fact that sergeants are responsible for conducting a preliminary (if, in practice, a cursory) investigation to determine the circumstances of the death requires them to gather facts and make an objective determination. The factual circumstances of a given death are often quite clear, and if there is some doubt the actual responsibility for further investigation is passed along to detectives and the medical examiner, but the sergeant must nevertheless gather information and reach a conclusion. In routine deaths where the cause is readily apparent, the sergeant will usually obtain these facts from the patrol officers and base his conclusions on those facts. For example, if the police learn the deceased had a heart condition, the physical conditions at the scene are consistent with a coronary, and no physical evidence at the scene points to foul play, they will likely conclude the death was by natural causes. The paperwork and reports they prepare will reflect these conclusions. By determining and attributing causality in this way, sergeants are—at least at a conscious level—absolved from complicity or blame: the victim's medical condition, rather than any factors over which the sergeant had control, led to the demise. Similar dynamics play out in most violent and accidental deaths as well. In some of these violent or accidental deaths, the sergeant may have to prepare a supplementary Unusual Occurrence Report (in the agency's parlance, a U.F. 49 or simply a '49)—a narrative report detailing the facts and circumstances of the event—and this process of marshalling facts and rendering them in a comprehensible written narrative format may assist him to make meaning of the death in a way that further attenuates any rational sense of death guilt. These official narratives are invariably composed in the somewhat stilted and dispassionate summary style that is characteristic of most police reporting: the reports typically contain an abundance of factual data but few (if any) allusions to an event's emotional content.[15]

As we've noted, though, some deaths are objectively more tragic and difficult than others, and because these deaths may be felt at a deeper and more personal level more death guilt may accrue. One factor that may make a death seem particularly tragic and difficult is the perceived innocence of the victim, but several distancing mechanisms help sergeants (and other cops as well) attenuate their sense of guilt. One such distancing mechanism is the objectification or denigration of the victim in some way, and we can see this subtle denigration in the trivializing, comical, or ironic linguistic forms cops use to describe victims as well as the tendency to recall and describe death events by their circumstances rather than by the victim's name (Henry, 1995).[16] For example, the Chicago police officers interviewed by Fletcher (1990, p. 70) referred to the double homicide of an amputee and an obese person as the "Stubs and Tubs" case, and the murder of a homeless man found in a barrel was recalled as the "Bum in a Drum" case; Rachlin (1991) quotes an NYPD crime scene unit detective who refers to the discovery of a single human buttock as "a half-assed case." New York City police have an informal typology for DOAs: a "fresh DOA" is a relatively recent death, a "ripe DOA" is a noticeably decomposing corpse, and a "floater" is a body in an advanced state of decomposition which may or may not have been recovered from the water. While these terms are used most frequently, there are also other more colorful terms used to describe various stages of morbidity, and many of the terms tend to mock the victim, his condition or the circumstances of death. These terms, which include "jelly belly" (an extremely swollen corpse), "road pizza" (a corpse mangled in an auto accident), and "two canner" (a reference to the practice of burning coffee grounds—in this case, two cans—to dispel the odor of putrefaction), also flaunt the officer's affected indifference to the victim and to death itself (Henry, 1995, p. 99).

Ironic humor and trivialization certainly distance the officer from dwelling upon the objective horror of the death, but the tendency also subtly connotes that the officer is unaffected by death trauma and death imagery to the extent that he is capable of laughing at it. Taken a step further, this affected nonchalance implies the officer is superior to, or at least different from, those people who would be immobilized or made uncomfortable by the death (i.e., civilians). Since this tendency toward affected nonchalance is seen as a coplike behavior shared by so many members of the police subculture, and because the use of in-group lingo expresses one's ties to other members, it also serves as an important form of cultural connection to other officers in the face of death imagery. Perhaps the greatest irony in the use of these colorful terms, though, lies in the paradoxical fact that cops immerse and express themselves through an exaggerated kind of grotesque imagery to protect themselves from that very imagery.

The gallows humor or derisive comments cops use to denigrate the victim (and in a larger sense to denigrate death itself) illuminate the fact that the linguistic forms are at least partially motivated by death guilt. This verbal denigration of the victim takes place in even the most tragic kinds of deaths—indeed, some form of verbal denigration is perhaps most likely to occur when the death is especially tragic.[17] Cops may not blatantly make light of such deaths and they may not clown around at these kinds of scenes—at least not in the public view—but even the tendency to refer to the deceased as "the victim" rather than by his or her name suggests a subtle attempt to depersonalize the death and to attenuate its impact.

The notion of a victim's innocence plays out in the sergeant's death encounters, and their response was not unlike that of the crime scene unit technicians and homicide detectives discussed in the following chapters. The victim's real or perceived innocence can aggravate the situation and result in greater emotional costs, but sergeants—like other cops—were quick to seize upon a victim's perceived complicity in his own death as a means of denigrating the victim, limiting identification and creating distance from the event.

Most of the DOAs in the [*names precinct*] were not innocent—their actions caused their own deaths. A lot of times they'd be drug dealers who got in a shoot-out and lost. With those deaths I'd say, it's hard to say but you're almost gleeful. It's like, "Good. You died and you deserved it. You're walking around with a gun, you probably shot or killed a lot of people yourself, so now you're dead." So that part of it didn't bother me.

The same sergeant described the details of a death scene in which a drug dealer was slowly tortured to death, apparently by other drug dealers, expressing his feelings for the victim in this way: "The sight was hard to take, but I had no feelings for him. It was just like, 'Good, another dead drug dealer. They should all kill each other.'"

The sergeants' task environment and their supervisory role and responsibilities also shape the dimensions of the humor they witness and express at death scenes. As supervisors, and in light of their generally businesslike demeanor as well as the constraints they face to quickly wrap up a DOA job and return to other duties, sergeants are not likely to witness a great deal of cop humor at a death scene. Patrol cops may joke around in the presence of peers but they do not generally misbehave or engage in horseplay in front of a supervisor, and the sergeant is also unlikely to engage in "undignified" behavior that would erode his stature and status in the eyes of subordinates. In conformity with his role and responsibilities, the sergeant's brief presence at a scene imposes a certain seriousness to the event. We have noted that other cops will often tease or provoke rookies as a kind of initiation or hazing, but sergeants are unlikely to directly engage in relaxed comic behavior that typically takes place among peers. Indeed, when I've seen sergeants perpetrate pranks at death scenes it is typically with tenured officers they consider peers. Only one sergeant I interviewed admitted to clowning around with a rookie at a death scene, and he attributed the behavior to a kind of performance appraisal.

Sometimes you joke around with them [rookies] to make it more uncomfortable. It's almost like an initiation rite—you say "Hey, he's moving," or something like that to enhance their discomfort. You egg them on or create a little fear. We've all gone through it and we're all OK with it, and you want to see this guy's reaction to it.

Another sergeant described the humorous "razzing" of a rookie subsequent to a death event, but the teasing had less to do with enhancing the rookie's discomfort at the scene than with his overall level of anxiety and his precipitous reaction at what should have been a relatively easy assignment. In this instance, a very anxious rookie was assigned alone to "sit on a body" when a cat knocked over a garbage can in the alley outside. The startled officer panicked at the noise and called a 10–13—the absolute highest priority "officer needs assistance" emergency call one can make—over the radio. Because cultural loyalty norms require that cops drop everything and respond instantly to a 10–13—even at the risk of endangering their own safety—the call is transmitted only in extreme cases where the need for immediate help is truly compelling. The sergeant and other cops teased him about his overreaction for days, but his description made it clear that the ribbing was in service of a normative subcultural goal: the rookie, who was apprehensive and "shaky" about police work in general, had potentially endangered the safety of other officers and the ribbing would cease when the young cop became calmer and more reliable.

Suspicion of Counterfeit Nurturance

The least prominent theme of survivor psychology among the sergeants I interviewed was suspicion of counterfeit nurturance, and this lack of prominence can be explained in terms of the sergeant's capacity for partial professional numbing and his consequent lack of devitalization and death guilt. We recall that suspicion of counterfeit nurturance is a sensitivity based in the survivor's recognition that, as a product of the numbing, guilt, and overall sense of devitalization that results from his victimization, he has special needs and special vulnerabilities. The survivor is painfully aware of these needs and vulnerabilities and of the death taint he bears, and is resentful of behaviors or offers of assistance that reinforce his vulnerability. The devitalized survivor struggles to achieve affirmation of his status as a survivor and to reclaim vitalizing relationships, while at the same time he resents and rejects offers of assistance that reactivate his sense of dependency.

Due to the various environmental and subcultural factors we have discussed in this section, though, the sergeant experiences minimal impairment as the result of his death exposures. He is, for the most part, not significantly devitalized from his death encounters; his integration into the police culture provides some means for vitalizing relationships that diminish his sense of disintegration, stasis, and separation, and he experiences little residual guilt. He does not bear a particularly strong death taint, and his immersion in death and death imagery is not typically so profound that it brings about a special dependency or a particularly strong need for sustenance. In essence, the sergeant has minimal or no struggle around the suspicion of counterfeit nurturance because the factors that give rise to it are largely absent from his experience.

In addition, we should recognize that with the possible exception of extreme cases, policing's macho ethic generally precludes even genuine offers of nurturance: cops are expected to be able to handle, on their own, whatever emotional tribulation comes their way. There is a certain paradox here, insofar as cops will literally drop everything to respond to a 10–13 and will often rise to the occasion when another cop needs some minor help or assistance in the personal sphere (even in terms of such simple acts as volunteering to help paint one's house), but they are reluctant to cross the boundary into another cop's personal emotional affairs. To do so would be a tacit acknowledgement of the cop's emotional weakness, a characteristic that is anathema to the police identity. As a supervisor, the sergeant also confronts the additional problem of a reluctance to violate the artificial barriers imposed by his rank and responsibilities: in theory (if not always in practice) the sergeant is supposed to minister to the professional and perhaps the personal problems his subordinates face, but there is no demand that subordinates reciprocate. By way of illustration, we recall the account of the sergeant (described in chapter 4) traumatized by the death of a baby; cops stood around the station house watching him and knowing that he was in pain, but none felt comfortable enough to step forward with an offer of assistance.

Indeed, if sergeants manifest any feature of the struggle around death taint, it is in the way they subtly express the notion of their own survivor exclusiveness—the tendency to embrace and reify their special knowledge of death in a way that gives them a power over it and to distinguish between those elites who have been touched by death and those who have not. While none of the sergeants I interviewed spoke directly to this perceived power, their descriptions of their own professional detachment and, at the same time, their ability to easily connect with bereaved family members in a humane way were tinged with a certain pride and expressed a kind of integrity. That hint of pride betrayed their sense of superiority and specialness: unlike many other people (including, in their view, most civilians), they possessed the ability to transcend potentially immobilizing death imagery and act compassionately toward others. They were, in other words, proud of their ability to integrate and put into practice the professional and humane dimensions of the police role. Here again, the sense of a certain power over death is not unique to sergeants and it does not solely result from the unique characteristics of their task environment: we have seen how, with time and experience in dealing with death, many other seasoned officers come to possess this ability to flow easily from one dimension to the other or to practice both at the same time. Because this ability and sense of exclusiveness is shared with other experienced cops, and because it is highly esteemed within the police culture, it provides yet another form of connection to the culture.

Conclusion

In reviewing and summarizing the features of survivor psychology as they exist among patrol sergeants, we can see how the fairly simple and straightforward formal demands of his task environment, his role as a supervisor and the enhanced discretion and situational control it affords him, various subcultural norms and practices, and his previous occupational exposures to death combine to mediate and minimize his vulnerability to potentially traumatic death imagery. These factors combine in a highly functional way to effectively distance the sergeant from the numerous deaths scenes he witnesses, to protect the contours of his professional self, and to limit overt manifestation of survivor psychology. At the same time, elements of these factors provide some opportunities to experience an immortalizing sense of integrity, movement, and connection.

To a large extent, the relative absence of survivor psychology's other themes and features can be attributed to the beneficial effects of partial professional numbing: the sergeant's numbing is not so profound as to be immobilizing or disintegrative, but rather it permits him to function effectively in the face of death trauma and to selectively open himself to some images while closing off others. In sharp contrast to the rookie, whose sense of self-as-police-officer is still evolving and who generally lacks the capacity to selectively choose the transformative images to which he is exposed, the experienced sergeant has a well-formed and relatively resilient professional identity, so death confrontations do not challenge his sense of self or his sense of symbolic immortality in quite the same way. The sergeant also has greater discretion and can control his environment, as well as the images presented to him, in ways the rookie cannot.

6.

Crime Scene Detectives

"Technicizing" the Death Encounter

In light of the tremendous number of death scenes they visit as well as the objective grotesqueness of the images they often confront at those scenes, one might reasonably expect to find that the members of the NYPD's Crime Scene Unit manifest many overt or pronounced features of survivor psychology. In an empirical sense, members of the Crime Scene Unit (CSU) witness death far more frequently than any other category of officer we consider in this research, and the images they confront are often of the most graphic, violent, and disintegrative kind imaginable. Virtually every death scene they attend, in fact, involves some bodily trauma as the result of violence or tragic misadventure. Moreover, these officers deal with death in a somewhat more intimate way than any other category of officer: they not only confront extraordinarily disintegrative visual and olfactory images of death, but they experience tactile images as well. Their duties often require them to closely examine and handle corpses, body parts, and bodily fluids in ways that would be repulsive and under conditions that would be revolting to the vast majority of people, and they are often exposed to these images for protracted periods of time. Many CSU members perform these duties and witness these images repeatedly over the course of years of assignment to the unit, and one might expect the cumulative impact of these images and experiences to have powerful and long-term deleterious psychic consequences.

Given these presuppositions or expectations of what CSU members and their task environment are all about—a kind of presumed or projected death taint—one could also easily assume the unit is populated by strangely behaving ghouls who are entirely immersed in death. The themes and features of survivor psychology are certainly present and observable among individual CSU members and within the group's ethos or culture, but they are reflected and expressed far more subtly than one might at first imagine. Indeed, at first glance CSU members seem to be a bright but otherwise fairly ordinary collection of cops, and it is only with a fair amount of exposure to them that features of survivor psychology become apparent. Only when one probes beneath the surface of their work and of the self they present does it become apparent that their task environment and their professional selves are structured to offer an array of protective psychological devices and processes that attenuate and limit the impact of the traumatic images they experience.

In terms of the quantity and quality of death imagery they encounter, we should note that despite the precipitous decline in violent crime within New York City between 1994 and the present, the 60 or so men and women of the Crime Scene Unit still witness an unparalleled level of death, mayhem, and other results of violence.[1] In calendar year 2000, for example, one or more crime scene teams of two or more detectives attended the scenes of each of New York City's 671 murders; just 7 years earlier, approximately the same number of CSU officers attended the scenes of 1,927 murders, and in 1990 they attended the scenes of 2,245 murders, including the infamous and particularly grotesque "Happy Land" nightclub arson-murder in which 83 people perished.

During calendar year 2000, crime scene personnel processed the scenes of more than 3,100 serious crimes. These included 536 deaths known to be homicides at the time the scenes were processed, 187 other suspicious deaths subsequently deemed to be homicides, suicides, CUPPIs,[2] or deaths by accidental or natural causes, and 431 serious assaults in which the victim was likely to die or subsequently did die, as well as 5 attempted murders of police officers. They also processed 275 rape scenes, 527 robbery scenes, 175 burglary scenes, 21 explosions, and 11 kidnappings in which one or more victims may have been injured.[3] In considering the overall psychological impact of witnessing these deaths and acts of violence on a daily basis, we should bear in mind that these statistics reflect a single year's workload and that some CSU members have tenure of more than 15 years in which violent crime rates were substantially higher. By any statistical measure, though, it is clear that attending this many murders and violent crime scenes is extreme and beyond the scope of "ordinary" human experience.

These statistics, while informative, cannot adequately convey the quality or quantity of graphic images of human carnage to which CSU officers are exposed, nor do they describe the quality and quantity of potential psychological trauma involved. Indeed, one would be hard pressed to convey—in statistical measures or in words—adequate details of the shocking, obscene, morbid, and gory images these officers confront on a daily basis. Certainly every violent crime scene presents officers with disturbing images, but it would be wrong to imply that every scene is equally shocking: some murders present objectively less traumatic images, while others present objectively more traumatic images.

One issue that makes the Crime Scene Unit officer's job so psychologically difficult is that the scenes he attends run the gamut from the most innocuous homicides (if such a thing is possible) to the most extremely disturbing, violent, and grotesque homicides imaginable, and these exposures do not take place in an orderly or predictable fashion. Teams are dispatched to scenes on a rotating basis— when a call comes in the "next-up" team responds. Because homicides and other violent crimes occur in a somewhat random temporal fashion, a series of homicides that present relatively few technical or psychic challenges may be followed by an intensive flurry of intensive, difficult, and particularly grotesque events. Their workload, determined by forces beyond their control, can thus vary greatly in terms of its manageability and intensity from day to day.

We must bear in mind that the average (i.e., nonpolice) person's image or conception of a murder scene is typically not based on firsthand experience; most people are rarely, if ever, exposed to violent death scenes and most have no accurate idea of the kind of images involved. To the extent that the average person has a preconceived image of a murder scene, that image is typically based upon the brief visual or aural images, staged by television or movie actors and directors, that appear in the popular media after being "sanitized" by network or ratings board censors. The media images do not convey the odors of death or the tactile sensations that may be experienced at a crime scene. The viewer knows the scenes are not real, that he is not actually present, and that he can always avert his eyes for the few seconds the scene will last.

This is clearly not the case with Crime Scene Unit personnel. The scenes they witness often assault the senses with objectively revolting and offensive images, to an extent literally not imaginable to the average person. The corpses they deal with are often terribly mangled or actively decomposing, and the images can be, in every sense of the word, extreme. It is not entirely uncommon, for example, for CSU technicians to attend a crime scene where they need masks or artificial breathing apparatus, and because the odors of putrefaction easily permeate clothing they may put on protective jumpsuits.

Some of the horrific visual images CSU members confront can be glimpsed in the crime scene photographs they take, and in addition to accompanying teams to several homicides and shootings I had ample opportunity to examine crime scene photographs retained in files at their office. The CSU also maintains several large binders containing well over 100 8-inch by 10-inch full color photographs of various crime scenes, and they present these binders so that visitors can get an idea of the work they do. The images contained in the books are quite graphic and shocking, and when they presented the books to me my first thought was that they intended to "get a rise" out of me in the way tenured patrol cops manipulate a rookie's exposure to enhance his discomfort. The officer left the room and could not have gauged my reaction, though, and I subsequently learned the books have another far more utilitarian purpose: the images, including close-ups of various unusual wounds, are a kind of reference book or atlas of death the CSU uses for formal and informal training. I also learned CSU members refer to the books, with some irony, as "the family albums."

The "family album" photos depict tremendous brutality and some of the most depraved aspects of human behavior imaginable, and one's first inclination is to recoil from them. Indeed, as a result of my own prior exposures to similar (yet, objectively speaking, not quite as shocking) images of death, I literally felt a sense of partial professional numbing coming upon me as I leafed through the binders. The photos conjured associations and images of homicide scenes I had experienced long ago, but I would hesitate to characterize them as intrusive or disturbing flashbacks. Within a few minutes, though, any residual aversion to looking at the images abated, replaced by a kind of professional interest. This experience also brought home the fact that there is a certain paradox about witnessing death and death images: the photos I examined were graphic and in a visceral way somewhat repulsive, but at the same time and at an intellectual and professional level, they were curiously fascinating. This experience of partial professional numbing and the concomitant insight into my own powerful sense of fascination with them gave me a clue to the CSU technician's psychology: because partial professional numbing selectively screens out the most traumatic and repelling elements of the images they encounter, they are free to experience elements that are intellectually stimulating. We will say more about this later in the chapter, but at this point we might do well to recognize the latent potential of death imagery to stimulate professional scientific curiosity as well as the fact that this intellectual vitalization gives the CSU member a kind of subtle power over death. That power is all the more important when we recognize it is not a kind of power possessed by the average person.

The Crime Scene Task Environment

As we have with the other categories of officers we consider in this study, we commence our exploration of how the five themes of survivor psychology are manifested among members of the CSU by examining this unique occupational group's task environment. As we have also seen in the task environments we've previously examined, the CSU technician's environment operates to shape the number, type, and quality of death images these men and women confront. At the same time, the task environment imposes a set of formal and informal demands and provides the basis for a number of functional processes that, in conjunction with individual and informal subcultural factors, permit the CSU technician to manage these images in a way that averts an entirely immobilizing death immersion. That is, the demands of the environment and the group ethos or culture generally provide the CSU technician with the means to prevent the images of disintegration, stasis, and separation that pervade the work from completely infiltrating his identity and worldview.

In considering the CSU technician's task environment, we can see that at least four factors operate to create a functional distance from death images by facilitating the development of a substantial capacity for partial professional numbing: the process of becoming a member of CSU screens out officers who are particularly vulnerable to death imagery; CSU applicants are tenured cops already experienced in dealing with death; they are highly trained technicians who view their work with scientific detachment; and their work environment is structured in a highly organized way that narrowly defines duties and delegates specific tasks to specific individuals. Because this partial professional numbing is so readily achieved and so easily maintained, it prevents or precludes an immobilizing impairment of symbolization, and many of the same factors also operate to maintain a sense of integrity, movement, and connection in the face of potentially overwhelming death imagery.

Selection and Experience of CSU Members

First, it should be emphasized that CSU members volunteer for the unit, and this self-selection process culls out those officers with an unusually high degree of death anxiety—those who might be the most psychologically vulnerable to death images and those who have special difficulty dealing with death simply do not apply for the assignment. Even within the police culture, the CSU is associated with death, but in this case the death taint works to the unit's advantage. Every cop knows or imagines the kind of exposures involved, and those with a particular sensitivity to death or to taking on the death taint would probably pursue some other avenue of career advancement. If anything, we would expect those with a fascination or affinity for death images to apply.[4]

The CSU's status as part of the elite forensic investigations division of the detective bureau also allows it to maintain high selection standards for those who do apply, and these selection criteria also tend to assure that applicants who are especially vulnerable to death imagery and death trauma are not assigned. An officer who is "shaky," tentative, or reluctant to deal with corpses would not last long in the unit. In addition to the unit's formal requirements that members have specific kinds of skills and knowledge (gained primarily through earlier police experience in assignments related to evidence collection and crime scene techniques), we recall that the police culture and the police organization place a high value upon experience and tenure. As a practical matter, an officer who lacks tenure (and the death-related experiences that go along with it) would probably not be a successful candidate for the CSU even if he had the requisite technical skills and/or an academic forensic credential. The unit's elite status and the fact that police officers assigned to the unit are promoted to detective in 18 months ensures that the pool of qualified applicants is larger than the number of available positions, and every member earns his position in part by accumulating police experience.[5] This is not to say that a relatively untenured or inexperienced officer with an influential "hook" or "rabbi" could not conceivably be assigned to the Crime Scene Unit before a more objectively qualified and psychologically prepared officer, but an officer with such powerful allies would probably negotiate a "contract" for an assignment to a less psychologically challenging but equally elite unit.[6]

Based upon the career narratives of the CSU members I spoke with, it is possible to sketch out the typical current career path to assignment in the unit. After several years of patrol experience, officers who demonstrate an interest and affinity for forensic work (and accumulate sufficient seniority) can apply for assignment to a precinct- or borough-level fingerprint detail in which they respond to reports of past burglaries and other crimes to dust for latent fingerprints.[7] After several years, officers who perform well in this evidence collection team apprenticeship can apply for an interview to join the Crime Scene Unit, and the most experienced and technically proficient are chosen as vacancies occur. Others join the unit in a lateral transfer after earning their detective shield in the police laboratory, the ballistics squad, or another unit requiring specialized forensic skills and training. Because the unit is considered elite, because its standards are high, and because the work generally permits members to participate in activities they find personally and professionally stimulating, vacancies are fairly rare: once assigned, CSU technicians tend to remain in the unit.

The distinction between the Crime Scene Unit and the evidence collection team is analogous to the "farm team" system in professional sports: the detective bureau's CSU has higher status because it handles the "real" or "serious" crimes like homicide and rape, and it draws its members from the patrol bureau's evidence collection teams who handle past burglaries and other "minor" crimes. In addition to ensuring that CSU applicants have street experience as well as the technical and psychomotor skills necessary to retrieve fingerprints and other forensic evidence, this apprenticeship system also serves to develop a certain mindset or focus: by focusing his attention on the immediate task of lifting a latent print, for example, the evidence collection team officer learns to screen out distracting images. While the images presented at the scene of a past residential burglary are likely to be fairly innocuous in terms of their traumatic potential, the system nevertheless facilitates the development of partial professional numbing. Similarly, lateral transfers from other forensic units have generally developed a scientific focus and an objective distance from their work, and this capacity, once developed, is easily transferred and applied in the CSU context.

Scientific Training and Orientation

Crime scene unit members are also highly skilled technicians who have an expertise in various forensic techniques and, generally speaking, a background in the physical sciences. In this very specialized area of police work, CSU members find an environment in which they can experience the vitalizing rewards that derive from integrating and practicing their personal interests in the professional sphere and from bringing their specialized knowledge to bear in major criminal investigations of "serious" high-profile crimes. Several CSU technicians I spoke with have academic degrees or some sort of advanced training in the forensic science area, and this education equips them with some degree of scientific detachment. This scientific orientation is subtly expressed in the systematic and factually logical way they respond to questions about their work. One can also discern their scientific and technical orientation in the kind of books and journals they read and the off-duty courses they undertake at their own expense: while members of other detective squads might peruse magazines or read popular novels during their down time, CSU members can be seen reading books and scientific journals on such topics as forensic entomology and forensic taphonomy, firearms and terminal ballistics, gunshot wounds, forensic pathology, criminalistics, forensic anthropology, DNA analysis, and other related topics.[8] Crime scene unit members tend to belong to various professional associations in the forensics field, and many attend forensic science conferences and courses on their own time and at their own expense to further develop their knowledge and expertise. Their great interest in these fields also becomes apparent when an interviewer asks a technical question about some seemingly arcane forensic technique: a question about the use of a gunshot residue (GSR) test in a specific case resulted in a lengthy, thorough, and quite interesting explication of the test, the techniques used to conduct it, and its inherent fallibilities and strengths. The CSU technician I asked this question not only demonstrated a great fascination with and (to my relatively untutored view) a great knowledge about the scientific technique, but also seemed quite pleased with my curiosity about a subject of such professional interest to him. I witnessed this fascination with various bodies of scientific and technical knowledge on several occasions, and it was clear that CSU members tend to be enthralled with the nuances of the forensic sciences.

I also noted the collegial approach they take and the ease with which they will consult with another technician who is objectively more knowledgeable or experienced in a particular forensic area; there are few apparent professional jealousies among CSU members, and I saw this as indicative of their own well-formed sense of confidence and competence. As individuals and as a group, CSU members place great value upon technical sophistication and expertise, and the strength of their professional identities can be seen in the way they are keenly aware of their individual limitations without being hypersensitive to them.

The CSU technician's scientific orientation and logical approach helps him to maintain a dispassionate and objective view of his work and the images it presents, and it helps him make a particular kind of meaning from his death encounters. To the Crime Scene Unit technician, each crime scene is a puzzle to be solved using a variety of technical skills and an acquired body of scientific knowledge. Properly interpreted, every piece of physical evidence at a death scene provides a piece of the puzzle leading him to an understanding of the totality of the facts surrounding the death, including its proximate and ultimate causes. Indeed, while the proximate and ultimate cause of death is formally determined through a medical examiner's autopsy, it is incumbent upon the CSU technician to provide the homicide detective with a preliminary working hypothesis of the cause. Properly interpreted, each piece of evidence can also provide potential clues to the behaviors and motivations of the victim and the killer. Part of the technician's expertise thus lies in the ability to sift through the mass of evidence, to "read" or decipher evidence using his special knowledge to uncover and interpret its manifest and latent meanings, and to integrate or combine these images in a way that gives insight into a larger and more holistic picture of the crime. The process is, essentially, a formative process in which individual images combine to create forms and, ultimately, constellations of meaning. As a formative process, it is inherently vitalizing and to some extent serves to counter images and feelings of disintegration, stasis, and separation that may be presented at the scene.

The psychological importance of this special kind of meaning in maintaining a functional distance from disturbing death images was brought home to me by one veteran technician. I asked how he managed to view grotesquely mutilated corpses on a daily basis without becoming overwhelmed, and as he struggled to verbalize his response he suddenly grabbed one of the "family albums" and opened it to the nude photo of a woman who had apparently been raped and slashed to death. "What do you see?" he demanded. I replied, "A female Hispanic, about 30 years old, probably a rape victim. She has numerous knife wounds . . . " "That's not what I see. You see a person, I see a *very interesting piece of evidence.*" He went on to point out that a skin discoloration on her shoulder that appeared to me to be a bruise or abrasion looked to him like a heel print. Based on the size and configuration of the print, and based on his technical proficiency in photographing or otherwise memorializing the evidence, the killer's shoe size might be deduced and a particular shoe might even be linked to the crime. That forensic work, which could clinch a prosecution and result in justice for the victim, would be performed by another expert in the police laboratory; it was his ability to recognize the potential value of the evidence, though, that mattered at the crime scene. Moreover, the fact that the killer stepped on the victim is a potentially valuable motivational or behavioral clue that might give the investigating detective insight into their relationship or the events that transpired at the scene. "If I look at this as a person," the technician concluded, "I'll never see the evidence and I'll never do my job."

Another CSU technician expressed the same sentiment in this way:

VH: *Basically, as you said, you're not looking at a body . . .*

Right. When people say, "How can you do that work?" they are referring to looking at a bloody, mutilated body. But that's not what you're looking at. You're looking at an overall scene. At that scene you already know what you have, you know what you're walking into. It's not like you're happening on a homicide while you're strolling down the street. Cops are there, bosses are there, detectives are there, Homicide is there. When you get there you look at the body, what type of wounds, bullet wounds, what type of evidence do we have here, do we have bullets? Do we have a knife, do we have semen or hair? Is there anything under her fingernails? Was there a struggle? How long ago was the death? You know, you're looking at everything. We're somewhat medically minded, you know. You're not looking at a bloody body like, "Oh my God, it's a dead body." You're looking at the whole scene.

VH: *I would think that in looking at the whole scene, the skin underneath the fingernails, et cetera, it takes your mind off the fact that this used to be a human being.*

I imagine it would. I mean, you're not there as a spectator dwelling on the fact that it's a dead body. You're there to do a crime scene run and part of your job is looking at the body and looking for forensic evidence. You don't really dwell upon that this was a living, breathing human being. You *know* it was, but you don't dwell on it and you want to do whatever you can to help find out what happened.

We can see that these larger experiential constellations of meaning are what permit the technician to read the scene and make holistic sense of it—the immediate images fit easily into a larger preexisting constellation (based in part on previous experience) that in turn imparts special meaning to them. At the same time the constellations are a sort of cognitive template that offers a kind of schema for enactment: they tell him, in essence, what additional clues will complete the picture and perhaps where to look for them. On the several occasions I observed CSU technicians decipher the subtleties of evidence to construct a more meaningful and comprehensive picture of the scene, I was struck by the parallel to the fictional Sherlock Holmes's extraordinary ability to observe an array of subtle and seemingly disparate clues and immediately infer a more complex meaning from them. Like Holmes, the CSU technicians did not generally need to engage in a protracted or tortuous logical process, but rather the conclusions were almost immediately apparent to them. To expropriate a term from a different school of psychology, the CSU technicians open themselves to all the available images and quickly grasp a gestalt that is larger than the sum of the individual images.

The ability to infer motives and hypothesize behaviors based on post hoc examination of physical evidence is an esteemed attribute among CSU technicians, but it is also an imprecise art that requires them to venture outside the more comfortable realm of the empirical physical sciences. This imprecision and related dependence upon inductive logic engenders some internal conflict, and many CSU technicians are therefore reluctant to take excursions into the behavioral realm, or at least to commit themselves to behavioral conclusions. Some of the more tenured and experienced CSU detectives I spoke with were very comfortable offering behavioral insights and opinions, while less tenured members tended to be more guarded. This makes a great deal of sense in light of the importance they place on their attributed status as experts: if they offer an opinion in an area outside their area of demonstrated competence and that opinion ultimately proves to be erroneous, their own sense of expertise as well as the expertise others perceive in them will be diminished.[9]

In all cases, though, technicians were careful to distinguish between the kind of objective and verifiable empirical facts they found in the physical evidence and the behavioral inferences and opinions they drew from it. This primary focus on factual scientific evidence illuminates and is related to another important element of the CSU technician's task environment: at some point he may have to testify in court about his observations at the scene and the evidence he collected. To withstand a vigorous cross-examination, the technician must be particularly precise in making and recording his observations and in justifying his evidence collection decisions and practices with practical logic and scientific reasoning. The fact that a defense attorney may someday attempt to undermine his credibility and attack his expertise—the technician's stock in trade and a significant component of his core professional identity—causes him to be rather wary about offering any opinions or presumptive conclusions that are not empirically based. Technicians take care to ensure that their notes accurately record the facts and circumstances of the scene, and they avoid recording superfluous details or opinions.

> I had a case last month, a homicide in Manhattan from 2 years ago. Every time you testify, you learn. When you go to a scene you get the victim's name, date of birth, address, who's catching the case, who's the safeguarding officer. In my notes from the scene I had the perp's name and address. I was asked [in court], "Where did you get that information?" Well, it was given to me by someone at the scene. I don't recall who. Now, at the trial, all the cops at the scene—the patrol supervisor, the detectives, every-

body—said they didn't have that information but it turned up in my notes somewhere along the line. Somebody had it because somebody gave it to me, but I don't know who. So now, when I take down anyone's name or ask anyone what happened, I write "advised by so-and-so."

Especially at the outset of an investigation, the ability to provide the homicide detective who is ultimately responsible for solving the case with behavioral and motivational inferences can be quite important because it often sets the direction of the investigation and can affect its outcome.[10] For example, the CSU technician's examination of the wounds inflicted on a corpse may lead to a preliminary opinion (subject to verification by a qualified medical examiner's autopsy) about the quality and duration of the struggle that preceded a stabbing death: particular kinds of defensive wounds on the victim's hands and arms, for example, may indicate whether the victim put up a vigorous struggle. In conjunction with other evidence, this information may indicate whether the victim was surprised by his killer and, in turn, whether he was likely killed by a stranger or a trusted acquaintance. The technician may be able to venture a tentative opinion (again, subject to verification at autopsy) as to the size and configuration of a knife (i.e., the approximate size of the blade and whether it has a single, double, or serrated edge) used in a stabbing by examining the configuration and apparent depth of a wound.[11] Based upon the appearance of a gunshot wound and the presence or absence of stippling from unburned gunpowder, CSU technicians can often infer with some degree of accuracy the distance from which a shot was fired. If some gunshot wounds were inflicted from a distance while others were fired close-up, technicians may be able to hypothesize the order in which they were fired: did the killer first shoot and immobilize the victim and then administer a fatal coup de grâce? Such evidence and opinion may help lead the homicide detective to reach important preliminary conclusions about the killer's motive as well as his specific behavior, or perhaps even his identity.

The point here is that the CSU technician often relies upon factual scientific evidence to reach behavioral and motivational conclusions, carefully and logically selecting from an array of images to create a particular kind of meaning that is valuable to other investigators using a process that is intellectually stimulating. They are, however, extremely cautious about indulging in formal behavioral profiling or crime scene reconstruction, since these areas generally lie outside the scope of their legitimate expertise, and they are always careful to couch their conclusions in terms of an opinion rather than a fact. The CSU technician might inform a detective that a particular wound *appears to be* a gunshot entry wound and another *appears to be* an exit wound, but because these observations are subject to verification by the more qualified expertise of the medical examiner, he will record the location of the wounds on his body diagram worksheet with the abbreviation *BW*—bullet wound. They do *not* record conjectural opinions in their notes or their official paperwork, all of which are potential evidence at trial. If asked about their opinions at trial, the CSU technician may offer his conjectural conclusions but will always be careful to emphasize that they are opinions based on experience rather than on scientific fact, and he will probably emphasize that he is not specifically trained or qualified as an expert in the particular field.[12] One CSU technician was asked if catching detectives ever ask him to make forensic determinations and conclusions about physical evidence:

> Sometimes they ask you. Basically, you know, it's just common sense, a little bit of off-the-cuff intelligent reasoning. They'll ask you, "Are the bullet wounds entries or exits?" They will ask you, "Where do you think the guy was standing when he fired?" Sometimes they get crazy with themselves—they want to know the trajectory of the bullet or something—you know, I wasn't here, pal. When you have a running gun battle down the street that kind of stuff is impossible. But yeah, you run down the scene for them, you kind of run down what you think might have happened, you try to figure out a scene you think might have happened, but it's all basically commonsense reasoning. You look at the evidence, you look at what you've got, you get as much information as you can. What do we know? We know how many shots were fired, but do we know for sure where the guy was standing? There's two reasons we're out there. One reason is to get the bad guy, the second one is to get a good case to court. So I never give my opinion. I'll say, "You can't quote me on this. I'll give you a package and you walk around with it and figure out what happened."

vh: *Do they expect you in court to give an opinion that someone in the lab, for instance, should be giving?*

> Yeah, some of them do. I'm not a ballistics expert, and I'm not going to answer those questions. I'm just going to tell you what I did at the scene. I'm like the middleman: I go there, I gather evidence, and now it's up to you to decide what to do with that evidence. That's all I'm going to say—what I did. I'm not going to fabricate anything, I'm not going to give you any deductions, I'm not going to make anything up, I'm not going to tell you a story. I'm going to tell you what I did. That's it. When they try to get your opinion, that's all it is—*your* opinion.

In informally reconstructing a series of events at a crime scene, CSU detectives draw heavily upon their prior experience as well as physical evidence; given the depth of their experience and expertise, many can effectively "read" the arcana of a scene using clues that are simply not apparent to the untutored eye or not sensible to the unschooled mind. To illustrate this, one technician handed me a sheaf of photos from a crime scene and asked me to tell him what transpired. After I studied the images and formulated or hypothesized a series of events, he pointed out clues and features whose meaning had eluded me. I had seen and noted the same clues, but either overlooked them or derived a very different and very superficial kind of meaning from them. His analysis was more logical, more cogent and, in light of his experience and expertise, far more sensible and complete than mine.

As we've noted, the "family album" binders comprise an encyclopedic depiction of death by shooting, stabbing, burning, evisceration, fall, electrocution, torture, beheading, and a host of other unusual causes, and each photo illustrates some unique wound or evidentiary issue the technician may someday encounter. It is worthwhile to briefly digress a bit here and discuss some of these photos, because they illustrate the CSU technician's ability to decipher or "read" physical evidence and behavioral clues that are not readily apparent to the uninitiated.

One photo is of a rape-homicide victim tied spread-eagle on the floor of an apartment's entry foyer. A large knife protrudes from her left chest and ropes are attached to her wrists and ankles. Upon inquiry, a technician explains how the photo reveals the victim was bound, tortured, and raped in another room before her death, and how the murderer, a sexual sadist, moved and positioned her body to shock and offend the person discovering it. He pointed out bits of evidence showing how the corpse had been moved to stage the scene and noted how the scene had all the hallmarks of a sexual sadistic murder. Another photo shows the parts of a dismembered body arrayed on a morgue gurney like an unassembled jigsaw puzzle. The clean cuts at joints showed the victim was systematically butchered, indicating the murderer probably had some knowledge of human anatomy or some butchering skills. One photo shows a man's head with a small bullet hole and one eyeball popped from the socket. It was explained that the sudden increase in intracranial pressure from a gunshot, rather than the projectile itself, can cause eyeballs to literally blow out of the head. Another shows a male corpse dressed in pajamas with numerous stab wounds and minimal bleeding, his severed genitals stuffed in his mouth. A technician explained that multiple stab wounds, especially postmortem stab wounds that produce relatively little bleeding, often indicate the killer was in a frenzied rage and angry with the victim. The symbolic severing of genitals often indicates a sexual motive, and in conjunction with other evidence found at the scene the picture indicates the man was murdered by his homosexual lover. Another photo depicting a female corpse seated in a freezer shows the physical effects of death by freezing. Other photos provide exemplars of different kinds of stabbing, slashing, and puncture wounds from knives, bullet wounds inflicted at various distances, bodies in various stages of decomposition, postmortem lividity, and rigor mortis.

Organization of Work in the Task Environment

Homicide scenes can be chaotic affairs, and part of the CSU technician's struggle involves the imposition or restoration of order. The need for order in the face of disintegrative images is compelling not only because the scene can be easily disturbed and contaminated, making the technician's job more difficult, but also because distractions interfere with his protective focus and impede his professional numbing. Crime scene technicians approach their work in a logical and orderly way and have rather little tolerance for any factors that undermine their concentration and focus. This intolerance is evident in the highly methodical way they approach their work even before they arrive at a scene.

When the CSU's services are required at a scene, procedures mandate that a detective bureau supervisor make the telephone notification to the dispatcher at the CSU office. The CSU member designated as the dispatcher takes the call and uses a standard run sheet to gather and record an extensive list of preliminary information about the crime, the time and location it occurred, the number of victims, whether a suspect is already in custody, and other items of information particular to the case. The dispatcher's task is to gather as much information about the crime and convey it to the team designated to respond. In repeatedly observing dispatchers going about these tasks, I noted a certain rigidity or touchiness in some of their interactions. On one occasion, for example, a dispatcher refused to take a notification from a patrol bureau supervisor, demanding strict compliance with procedures; dispatchers also refused to send a team when the notifying detective supervisor provided sketchy or incomplete details of the crime and could not specify the number of victims or whether one or more had been removed to a hospital. When I inquired about the need for such detailed information, the explanation was deceptively simple: a complete rundown of all the available facts ensures a sufficient number of teams will be dispatched and that they will bring the equipment necessary to process the scene. Subsequent observations confirmed there was more to this attribution than the simple explanation revealed: CSU technicians use this information to begin planning and organizing their on-scene activities even before they leave the office and as they travel to the scene. The plans they formulate are based in standard operating procedures, but from a psychological view it is important to recognize that the superficial process of mentally reviewing procedures helps to focus attention and invoke partial professional numbing. To make the most effective use of numbing, CSU technicians rely on established procedures and protocols, and they want no surprises.

When they arrive at the scene, technicians will briefly confer with detectives to gather additional information about the crime before setting about their technical work. The expectation is that the detectives will have adequately secured the scene, removing any witnesses or police personnel who might contaminate the scene or distract the technicians, and technicians can be rather sensitive about any individuals or events that interfere with their focus. With the exception of the investigating detectives and perhaps the first patrol officers to arrive at the scene, they have few interactions with others.

VH: *Your job really doesn't have you interacting much with living people.*

No. Other than with cops, not at all. When I get to a scene I first want to know what happened. What do we know, what happened here? When did this occur, did someone call 911, did it come in as a robbery, was it a pickup job? You do not really deal with other people. We do not interview witnesses, we're there as a support unit for the Squad.[13] The Squad does all the interacting. They canvass the area, they do the interviews, they deal with the family. . . . Sometimes you have scenes where the family gets there when you're halfway through with the job and family members come in and start screaming and crying. You might be at the hospital and all of a sudden the family comes in all hysterical and crying. . . . You hope there's a supervisor at the scene who's on the ball and will move the crowd. I had a job in Brooklyn where a gunshot victim died on the street and you had to examine the body in front of a big crowd. His face was covered with blood and I wiped his face and the mother came up to me and said, "I want to thank you for being gentle with my son." But that's basically the only way we interact with people.

Technicians are intently focused as they go about their business at a scene, but their professional numbing is not so extreme that they go about as if in a trance or that they completely exclude all other images and stimuli. Rather, they seem to operate simultaneously at two levels: at the same time they intellectually focus on the work, they may engage in conversation or superficial small talk about an entirely unrelated subject. In this sense their behavior and somewhat disjointed conversation resembles that of a team of surgeons working at an operating table, or a pilot and copilot discussing weekend plans in the midst of a takeoff or landing. Their attention is primarily focused on the task at hand and on the psychomotor skills they are practicing, but their conversation flows easily between giving instructions or commenting on the evidence and whatever other subject they are discussing. The remarkable ease with which they shifted attention from professional to personal concerns also illuminates the extent of their professional numbing and how easily they negotiate the boundaries of their personal and professional identities.

I observed this dynamic taking place as two technicians examined and photographed the corpse of a male murder victim who died shortly after arriving at a hospital emergency room. In their division of labor, one took photos and described each shot aloud in clinical terms (e.g., "Number 1, full-length frontal view, feet to head," or "Number 6, close-up of thoracic area, waist to neck") while the other recorded the dictated notes, rolled the corpse to obtain a specific view, and held a ruler alongside each bullet wound as it was photographed. A few minutes later they switched, with the first technician taking notes while the second examined the clothing doctors had removed from the victim, counting and matching holes to wounds.[14] They performed these tasks and carried on their own intermittent technical conversation in the midst of a conversation with me about the risk of HIV transmission through bodily fluids, at the same time interjecting explanatory comments about the meaning they found in particular wounds. These multitasking capabilities illustrate how easily they divide their labors, work together as a system or team, and easily shift attention between technical chores and other matters. They seemed entirely unaffected by the image of a naked bullet-riddled corpse, and their professional detachment was infectious: I found myself engrossed in the technical aspects of their work and was easily enlisted to perform some tasks to assist them, experiencing little or no queasiness in handling the still-warm corpse or in peering into its mouth to observe the effects of a penetrating facial wound. Even as an observer with no special training or extensive knowledge, for a few minutes I also felt a sense of agency from being a useful part of the team.

In summary, the CSU technician's task environment implicitly creates a salubrious environment for partial professional numbing to take place. More specifically, the technician's scientific orientation imparts a distinct objectivity in his approach to work and a definite detachment from the reality and humanity of his experience. Science and technology provide them with a "disconnect" or, in Lesy's

(1987) term, a "cut-out" that effectively removes a great deal of the human element from their work. They witness objectively horrific images of death not as the remains of a human life, but as "very interesting pieces of evidence." This preliminary outline of the forces and factors shaping the CSU technician's task environment gives us a basic feeling for their work as well as some of the important background information we need to explore how these technicians manifest the themes and features of survivor psychology.

Psychic Numbing

We've seen how the CSU technician's task environment, with its demands for objectivity and a scientific/technical orientation, facilitates partial professional numbing. In conjunction with the natural inclination toward diminution of feeling and emotion in the face of traumatic death imagery, these factors operate to effectively shield the technician from a great deal of the potentially immobilizing trauma he encounters and to reduce the images' latent capacities to impair his process of ongoing symbolization. The technician is not entirely numbed, but rather partial professional numbing acts as a kind of selective filter that screens out the more disintegrative and emotionally difficult elements of the images while permitting him to experience and make more coherent sense of other elements. We've also noted how environmental and individual subjective factors concomitantly create avenues for creative expression, meaning making, and the continuation of the formative process.

The upshot of all this is that the CSU technician experiences fairly minimal impairment and, in turn, few patently obvious manifestations of survivor psychology's other themes. The extent and the effectiveness of partial professional numbing to limit the psychic impact of traumatic images permit the CSU technician to continue functioning in the face of the violent images he encounters each day. This is not to say that the technician's exposures have no cumulative impact: partial professional numbing cannot entirely screen out the most emotionally traumatic elements of these images, and some impairment of the formative process inevitably occurs. Cumulatively, repeated exposures to these traumas over an extended period of time can lead to a profound kind of numbing that can easily come to permeate the technician's professional and personal identity, and this potential leads to an ongoing struggle to maintain connections to vitalizing experience in both spheres. In essence, we can say that the greater the quality and quantity of traumatic imagery the CSU technician experiences at work, the greater his need for images of connection, integrity, and movement in his personal and professional life.

The technicians I interviewed and observed managed the professional struggle for a sense of movement in part by continuing to educate themselves by developing additional forensic skills and scientific/technical knowledge. This professional development is a means for additional creative expression, while at the same time it enhances the technician's sense of connection to the tradition of scientific inquiry and solidifies or reinforces his professional identity. Professional development also opens additional avenues for connection to the important notion—central to the overall police identity—that the technician is participating in the pursuit of justice. We can also see how the unit's overall mission of seeking objective truth through science, along with individual members' overarching awareness that they may some day be called upon to explain their activities and judgments at a trial, provides the basis for a sense of integrity. The CSU technician's sense of professional connection is reflected in the unit's generally high morale, its strong group identity and the overall lack of professional jealousies among members. Technicians work closely with one another under often difficult conditions but nevertheless show little friction: they like and respect each other. To some extent this sense of connection and community is reinforced by the death taint they bear, by the elite status of the group within the subculture of police, and by the sense that they are different from other people and other cops—they can witness images and can do specialized work that few other people could manage. The technicians' connection to the larger police culture was also evident among those I interviewed and observed, insofar as they appeared to be well integrated into the police culture and, more specifically, the detective culture: they frequently participate in fishing trips, family picnics, and other social events sponsored by various detective bureau units or by the police department's fraternal organizations.

The CSU technicians I interviewed and observed found various modes of actualizing their need for a sense of vitalizing connection, movement, and integrity in the personal sphere, and the modes varied according to their particular circumstances, relationships, and lifestyles. Notwithstanding individual differences, all the technicians I spoke with described their off-duty lives in ways that made clear their connections with others. At the same time, it was evident that technicians (like many cops) erect a kind of psychic firewall to keep their work from infiltrating their personal lives—they do not take their work home with them.

> When I get off work at 8 o'clock in the morning, I couldn't tell you what job I went on that night. I'd have to think, "Now, wait a second, let me think." Maybe because when you're in it, crime scenes just run into each other. We've been busy lately. Last week we went for days and days. You came here and you went right out on a run. Last week my partner and I had at least two jobs every day. We were out in Queens, and then the Bronx and back in Brooklyn, and they all run into each other. I don't know if it's any kind of, you know, subconscious thing to try and close it away but there's definitely something to what you say. I don't know what it has to do with anything, but if I look at my photos 2 years later, then it's like, "Oh yeah, I remember that one." I get off work and that's it, but I can pull the report out when I'm going to court two years later and it's, "Yeah, I know this one. You know you were standing over here, and you know who you were talking to. This is what happened." It all comes back.

There is, of course, no easy way to measure or assess the viability of individual technicians' sense of connectedness, movement, and integrity in their personal lives, but I did notice that several became much more animated when discussing their families and children and it was clear that many technicians are markedly devoted to their families and especially to their children. One technician, for example, said that he never thinks about his work while off-duty in part because he is so completely focused on the goal of spending quality time with his son. He described, in animated and quite touching terms, a caring and nurturing relationship that involved helping his son with homework and participating in sports activities. He seemed to genuinely enjoy the time spent with his wife and son, who are clearly a source of vitality in his life. Other technicians avidly pursue off-duty hobbies and avocations or participate in sports, especially group sports activities. Without exception, every technician I spoke with seemed to have a full and viable personal life that included participation in vitalizing activities and relationships.

Quite apart from the CSU technician's pursuit of vitalizing connections in the personal and professional spheres, his environment facilitates psychic numbing in many of the same ways we saw among patrol sergeants, both in an immediate sense at the death scene and especially in terms of limiting other subsequent manifestations and characteristics of survivor psychology. The CSU technician's exposure to traumatic death imagery is of longer duration than the sergeant's and his exposures entail a far more intimate and multisensory experience of those images, but both are to some extent concerned with making cognitive meaning of the images presented at a scene. While the patrol sergeant's meaning-making task is far more limited than the CSU technician's—the sergeant simply assesses the patent images and conducts a cursory and preliminary investigation to determine whether the death is of apparent natural, accidental, or homicidal cause and whether specialized investigative personnel are therefore necessary—the technician delves much more deeply into the images to derive a far more complex set of meanings. The technician's ability to make comprehensive meaning of the evidence is largely predicated on his capacity for screening out various elements through partial professional numbing, but the comprehensive meaning he makes also functions to limit his sense of death guilt.

Death Guilt

Throughout this book, and in line with the precepts of survivor psychology, we've seen that to some extent every death encounter engenders some form of death guilt. As Lifton points out, we can conceptualize death guilt as a continuum, with an amorphous and irrational type of death guilt arising solely from the notion of survival priority at one pole and a more rational and genuine sense of actual responsibility for the death at the other. Guilt feelings can be magnified when one has a legitimate reason to believe he is responsible for the death of another through his actions or inactions, and that sense of responsibility depends largely on the meaning one derives from the event. The meaning-making process therefore bears upon the type and quantity of death guilt one experiences: one inevitably seeks to make proximate and ultimate meaning of a death encounter in part to mediate death guilt and to reassure oneself that one lacks actual culpability.

Death guilt plays an important part in the psychology of the Crime Scene Unit and its members, but like other features of survivor psychology it is effectively minimized through substantial professional numbing and its expressions are subtle. Due, once again, to the demands of the task environment, the more profound kinds of death guilt—those involving a rational belief that one is actually complicit in or responsible for the death—do not seem to affect CSU members. One of the demands of the technician's job is to use science and forensic techniques to determine the proximate cause of death—to dispassionately and logically examine an array of physical and perhaps some behavioral evidence and infer causality from it. The fact that many technicians are reluctant to publicly espouse an expert opinion about the cause and circumstances of the death is almost beside the point: whether or not they articulate an opinion, they reach a firm personal conclusion based on factual evidence as well as their extensive knowledge and expertise. That is, they make logical sense of the death in a way that implicitly removes any lingering doubts about their own actual or moral responsibility for it.

We are left, then, to consider the technician's potential for experiencing the less acute forms of death guilt conjured by the notion of survival priority. This less formidable kind of guilt is almost impossible to avoid, and its cumulative impact on technicians is reflected in their individual psychology and the group ethos.

One way death guilt becomes manifest among CSU technicians is in humor, and especially gallows humor. We have seen gallows humor among rookies, who are typically the target of gallows humor and the butt of stunts perpetrated by tenured cops, and to a lesser extent among sergeants. In both groups, we once again see that the task environment and individual subjective factors shape the dimensions of humor: rookies are generally too numbed, too rule-bound, too self-conscious, and too lacking in a sense of agency to actually generate any humor, and in their numbed state many inherently humorous elements of the death scene may elude their comprehension. These characteristics concomitantly make them the perfect foils for tenured cops. As supervisors, sergeants are rarely the butt of any kind of practical joke and tenured cops may be reticent to joke or play around in their presence, but they often perceive the humor or irony in a given death situation. Likewise, the task environment and group ethos shapes the dimensions and expressions of humor among CSU technicians: their humor, reflecting their own nature and the seriousness of their work, is of a more cerebral kind. Technicians tended toward puns and other verbal asides quietly shared among technicians and detectives, and I saw no overt flamboyance or grandstanding behavior. They did not ostentatiously flaunt or trivialize death, but rather treated it with a kind of mature respect befitting their detached identity and scientific/technical orientation.

The understated and somewhat self-effacing gallows humor in which CSU technicians indulge is psychologically linked to death guilt, but in many ways it also reflects their struggles to master the death imprint and their awareness of the death taint they bear as individuals and as a group. This psychological link is important because, as we discussed in the chapter outlining the basic tenets and processes of survivor psychology, the theme of death guilt is closely linked to the indelible and enduring death imprint.

The Death Imprint

The death imprint's potential to reactivate prior images and constellations of separation, stasis, and disintegration—to fundamentally challenge the sense of symbolic immortality—leads to an ongoing struggle to master death images. The survivor experiences the need to reconstruct these images in a way that will assert his sense of vitality and will connect him with vitalizing images of connection, movement, and integrity, and this need is at least partially satisfied among Crime Scene Unit technicians through the particular kind of humor in which they engage. An analysis of CSU technicians' humor in the face of death imagery is an appropriate window through which to view the struggle to master death images by reformulating them in a comical and less threatening way. At the same time, such an analysis permits us to glimpse how particular expressions of humor communicate and reinforce the group ethos, convey a sense of connection to other group members, and reinforce the core sense of integrity and objectivity that is so important to the CSU technician's professional identity. We can also see that humorous expression, especially when it takes the form of witty repartee, provides a sense of intellectually stimulating movement.

Police humor is a complex behavior that often involves, in Pobregin and Poole's (1988) term, the use of "jocular aggression" that permits officers to deflect the petty annoyances of their work, to promote group solidarity (especially through a kind of in-group, "you had to be there" humor), and to allay tensions. Aggressive humor and "ball breaking" are an accepted part of police culture in which officers individually or as a group expose and magnify another cop's peculiarities and foibles. Paradoxically, aggressive "ball breaking" can be used to express one's esteem and admiration for another cop: since direct and forthright expressions of positive regard run somewhat counter to the culture's macho ethic, the culture accommodates by inverting these expressions and presenting them in a seemingly callous way. At the same time, depending upon the conditions and situations in which it takes place, "ball breaking" can be used to illuminate and punish another cop's transgressions. Because this punishment is meted out in the guise of well-intentioned camaraderie, some of its overt sting is minimized and it becomes incumbent upon the recipient to accept the social construction of camaraderie and to present the appearance of taking the ribbing good-naturedly.

As we noted in chapter 2, Charmaz (1975, 1980) points out that death workers often construct a social reality that erects a protective barrier between their work life and their self-image. In terms of humor, this constructed reality is implicated not only to the extent that members of the police culture must accept the cultural definition of aggression as humor, but also in the way humor is reflected in the four stances toward death (minimizing, hiding, flaunting, and acknowledging death) Charmaz identifies. Within the CSU technicians' culture, it is inauthentic to minimize, hide, or flaunt death—death is too much a part of their work and their identity to be hidden or minimized, and flaunting death trivializes it in an unprofessional way—so their sense of integrity demands that they acknowledge and deal with it as a reality. In turn, the realistic acknowledgment of death that is part and parcel of their professional identity shapes the dimensions and expressions of their humor.

Crime scene technicians did not, during my observations, ostentatiously flaunt death to demonstrate or imply their mastery of it. To do so, in fact, might at some level undermine their sense of professional competence, their dispassionate scientific/technical orientation, and the objective detachment that lies at the core of their professional identity. If death is not a serious business, and if death is not treated as a serious matter, how can the technicians be taken seriously? The humorous expressions I observed tended to be ironic humor and gentle self-mockery, and this again illuminates the well-formed character of their professional selves: the technician's sense of self is sufficiently resilient to withstand the threat of mockery. Indeed, at some level this self-mockery reassures the technician that he is psychologically healthy because he can still see the humor in life's difficult situations. At the same time, CSU work is serious business and it is important that CSU technicians not lose sight of its seriousness, so their humorous expressions are finely balanced.

Perhaps the most outrageous expression of humor I saw occurred in the unit's lunchroom when one technician related a news article he had seen: the personal possessions of the infamous cannibal and mass murderer Jeffrey Dahmer were scheduled for auction. The technicians constructed a fairly elaborate tongue-in-cheek scheme to purchase Dahmer's kitchen appliances to refurnish their own kitchen. To possess and use Dahmer's refrigerator was particularly important, since Dahmer used it to keep the heads and various body parts of his victims prior to cooking and consuming them. In their humorous analysis, the CSU's kitchen would be the perfect place to put these historic artifacts to good use. They joked about stocking the refrigerator with "spare parts" from crime scenes, noting that such a strategy might be just the thing to deter a particular technician's penchant for eating other people's lunches. The implicit self-mockery and overstated comparison of CSU members to a notorious cannibal reflects an awareness of the death taint they carry as a part of their own identity as well as the group's perception in the eyes of others, at the same time it conveys that they are fairly comfortable with bearing that taint.

As many other cops do, CSU members also used humor (albeit not gallows humor per se) and gently mocking irony to maintain group norms. In one instance I observed, the victim of their humor was a relatively untenured technician who, it was subsequently explained, was "a bit too full of himself"—in the eyes of his peers, he had a somewhat overblown perception of his own knowledge and skills, and his manner at crime scenes was seen as a bit too cavalier. His behavior, in their collective view, bordered on an unacceptable and immature flaunting of death. Their good-natured ribbing took the form of a patently overstated and highly laudatory group discussion of his superior abilities and considerable accomplishments, conducted as if he were not actually present in the room with them. All the participants spoke of their admiration for him and all voiced aspirations to someday be just as good as he was. Their "ball breaking" was not scathing or mean-spirited, though, and it was not personalized in a way that implied a lack of respect for his actual talents and technical proficiency. Rather, it was intended to send a message that would bring him into line with group norms and to help him maintain a proper perspective on the serious nature of CSU work. Their ribbing was certainly intended to deflate his ego a bit, but its subtext also conveyed the idea that if a CSU technician achieves some authentic mastery over death he earns it through tenure and experience. To the extent that a hard-won mastery over death is ever achieved, it is something to be cherished and respected, and any illegitimate pretense of having achieved mastery (including the pretense of mastery by flamboyantly flaunting death) shows a lack of integrity that is unacceptable to the group ethos and demeaning to the hard-earned experience of others.

The Quest to Make Meaning

The survivor's quest to make meaning of death at a proximate and ultimate level is certainly a feature of the CSU technician's experience. As we've discussed, the CSU task environment demands that the technician bring his knowledge, skills, and expertise to bear to integrate and synthesize images in a way that imparts meaning to the individual images as well as a to a larger picture of the crime scene. The technician must make immediate sense of the images and convey at least part of their overall meaning to detectives at the scene and perhaps subsequently to a judge and jury. Earlier in this chapter we saw some of the ways this demand for immediate meaning-making serves to solidify the technician's sense of his professional self, provide him with a sense of agency and vitality, and diminish some of the images' traumatic potential.

In chapter 2's description of the basic processes of survivor psychology, we noted that the quest to make meaning can translate into a compelling urge to bear witness about the death event the survivor has experienced and the moral wrongs he has seen committed. Bearing witness can help impart meaning and restore a sense of purpose to the survivor's experience, but in the extreme it can also lead to a tendency toward scapegoating and eventually disintegrate into a sense of amorphous bitterness that further reduces the capacity for vitalizing relationships. Because the technician witnesses so many violent deaths and so many moral wrongs, if the urge to bear witness became fully actualized it could easily consume his personal and professional life. Crime scene unit technicians are certainly afforded ample opportunity to bear witness in the professional sphere, but their ethos also demands that they remain *impartial* witnesses; they cannot permit themselves to indulge in scapegoating or to permit other personal feelings about a case to infiltrate their lives or their courtroom testimony.

Once again, we see that the ability to remain impartial rests upon technicians' capacity to focus on objective fact and to screen out the moral or ethical components of the images they experience, and so these components barely enter their awareness. I observed several instances where technicians maintained a moral neutrality and avoided implicating the moral dimension of an event, even though

I personally experienced a sense of outrage or sadness and an impulse to comprehend how one human being could perpetrate so heinous an act on another. On one occasion, a technician returned from court after testifying in the case of a woman accused of neglectfully starving one of her children to death, and he discussed the case and the evidence in very factual and unemotional terms. He showed me photographs of the scene and of the child's emaciated body, and to me the images were shocking and compelling; I tried to grasp some reason or set of factors that might explain why a mother would commit such a moral outrage on one of her own children. When I wondered aloud about what could possess a mother to do such a thing, the technician's noncommittal response—along the lines of "Yeah, it really is a shame. You see it from time to time"—illuminated how easily he separated out the moral and psychological issues involved and remained focused on empirical fact. The moral and psychological dimensions were, quite simply, not part of his job. Because technicians' task environments do not require potentially taxing excursions into deep ethical, psychological, and philosophical issues, they do not actively seek to raise and explore them.

It would be inaccurate and unfair, though, to suggest that CSU technicians entirely lack a moral compass. They may not immerse themselves in the ethical questions others might find in their work, but they do have strong intertwined senses of personal and professional integrity, and we can see how a personal philosophical involvement in the moral issues of violent death could easily compromise their professional integrity at a trial. By relying on all the forces and factors that support objectivity, a factual focus, and ethical neutrality, they avoid this dissonance and maintain the essential sense of ethical integrity. The pride CSU technicians find in their objective stance was revealed in an anecdote one related. He processed the scene of a highly publicized incident in which a police officer was tragically wounded by a fellow officer who was subsequently brought up on criminal charges. Notwithstanding a personal belief that the incident was nothing more than a tragic accident, and notwithstanding the potential impact of powerful cultural proscriptions against testifying to the detriment of another cop, the technician testified honestly as to the evidence he obtained and processed as well as the conditions he observed at the scene. The jury inferred reckless negligence on the part of the second officer and convicted him. By virtue of the random "next-up" assignment scheme, about a year later the same technician was called upon to process the scene of a crime allegedly committed by the first officer, who had recovered from his wounds, and his testimony played a part in that officer's conviction as well. The point the technician was making in relating the anecdote was that CSU members testify honestly, objectively, and factually and do not allow personal feelings, subjective ethical beliefs, or other pressures to color their testimony; he was proud of his integrity even though it led to outcomes he personally saw as unjust or unfortunate. If the facts to which they testify lead to the conviction of a fellow officer, so be it. By the same token, if their testimony led to the acquittal of an accused cop-killer, they would probably experience as little dissonance or sense of responsibility. To do their job effectively and to maintain the sense of integrity that is so functional and so important a part of their professional identity, they cannot psychologically afford to be swayed by the moral components of an event or by any other external pressures. They cannot afford to become consumed by the tendency to scapegoat or to indulge in moralizing.

In a larger sense, though, technicians also grapple with the need to make ultimate sense of their world—to grasp larger unifying principles and concepts that will give meaning to their immediate experience and at the same time lead them to a more fundamental and ordered understanding of human existence. This is a continuous and Sisyphean endeavor for the CSU technician, since it is apparently never fully resolved. The search for an ultimate understanding of death can be difficult under any circumstances, but it is doubly troublesome because the tremendous number and range of death encounters and death images CSU technicians experience collectively tend to defy rational explanation and render the overall quest absurd. One highly tenured technician, who had also investigated many murders and violent crimes as a squad detective prior to his CSU assignment, summarized this ongoing struggle to find ultimate meaning in death. His words and his tone of resignation conveyed the ultimate futility of that struggle, while at the same time they illuminate that he has not yet abandoned the quest.

At one time I thought I understood homicides, but the more I see the more I know I'll never understand them. You think, "Okay, I can understand how this thing made someone so angry they could kill," but I don't see that anymore. The more I see the less sense it all makes. I just don't see any sense in it at all, and I don't think I ever will.

Conclusion

The members of the CSU are a unique group of dedicated professionals who do a psychologically difficult job. They experience the deaths of others more frequently and in some ways more intimately than any other group of officers but nevertheless manage to avoid the complete and immobilizing immersion in disintegrative death imagery one might expect to result from these encounters. While they are not entirely unaffected by these death images, their task environment and the unit's unique culture or ethos permit them to manage their experiences with minimal psychic cost and few overt manifestations of survivor psychology.

As we have discussed throughout this chapter, features of the technician's task environment combine with individual subjective factors to create a remarkably salubrious environment for partial professional numbing to take place. Technicians can easily invoke partial professional numbing to screen out the more toxic and psychologically harmful elements of the death images they confront, reducing the potential impact of the images and permitting them to focus cognitive attention on matters of empirical fact. The highly technical nature of their work involves the application of specific psychomotor skills and a body of scientific knowledge, providing additional psychic distance from the distractions of their own and others' emotions. The overall viability of this capacity for partial professional numbing effectively prevents a more profound kind of numbing as well as the other themes of survivor psychology from taking hold.

Other environmental, cultural, and subjective factors operate to counter the possible intrusion of significant threats to CSU technicians' sense of immortality. They are possessed of a strong professional identity and a sense of connection to other unit members, a powerful sense of personal and professional integrity, and they continually seek the means to experience a sense of professional growth and movement. They also counter threats to their sense of immortality through their philosophical commitment and practical contribution to the impartial pursuit of justice—a vitalizing enterprise that is greater and more important than the individual, and one that has important social consequences. Importantly, their work prescribes that they make meaning of their death encounters at a variety of levels: they creatively combine and integrate images to "read" the arcana of a scene in a way that few individuals can (imparting a subtle kind of power over death), and in doing so they reach preliminary conclusions about the cause and circumstances of a death in a way that limits their rational death guilt.

7.

Homicide Detectives

Emotional Reactions to Violent Death

There is a certain mystique about detectives, especially detectives whose job it is to solve murders. This mystique molds our conceptions of homicide investigations and homicide detectives, it structures our relationships and interactions with them and theirs with us, and it has a formidable impact on their worldview and their sense of personal and professional identity. The powerful mythology surrounding homicide detectives is in large measure shaped by their depiction in literature and the media, which often take great dramatic license in emphasizing their heroic involvement in solving violent and mysterious crimes, but there are nevertheless many elements of objective truth in the popular image of the homicide detective: they do specialize in dealing with deaths that occur through instrumental violence, they may encounter violent and disintegrative death imagery on a fairly frequent basis, and they often deal with the most depraved and savage kinds of human behavior. All of these factors—the mystique and the reality of homicide investigation—influence the way homicide detectives experience and make sense of the deaths they encounter.

The detective mystique, rooted in part in a fascination for the special knowledge detectives seem to possess about matters of life and death and the secrets of human nature they seem to hold, often leads members of the public toward simultaneous and countervailing feelings of attraction and aversion to them. To the extent that detectives actually do possess a special experiential knowledge of life and death that is not part of ordinary human experience, they also possess a kind of power over death. That power—which is, in a literal sense, an "awesome" sacral power—also contributes to what many perceive as detectives' aura of aloof conceit.[1] This special knowledge and power exerts another potent influence over the detective's experience of death events, at the same time as it compels our ambivalent attention. The detective's real or perceived power over death and his intimate knowledge of its secrets also confers a kind of death taint, albeit not the kind of death taint that merely causes one to recoil. If anything, their power and knowledge often draws one toward them in order that we might safely glimpse or participate in their awe-producing experience in a fascinated and vicarious way.

From our discussion of public ambivalence toward police in chapter 3, we recall that Bittner (1980) characterized police work in general as a "tainted profession in the public's view," observing that although this stigma has its origins in the distant past, the police officer is still a character to be viewed with mixed feelings. Because police are "posted on the perimeters of order and justice" and are intended to spare the rest of society from "direct confrontations with the dreadful, perverse, lurid and dangerous," they are ambivalently feared and admired. The police "are perceived to have powers and secrets no one else shares," their activities are surrounded by "mystery and distrust," and one is always left with "the sense that there is somewhat of the dragon in the dragon-slayer" (pp. 6–7). This characterization seems particularly pertinent to homicide detectives, since their roles and mandates place them squarely in the midst of things dreadful, perverse, lurid, and dangerous.

We cannot adequately comprehend homicide detectives' experiences of the deaths they encounter, nor can we understand how these encounters shape the contours of their identities and the dimensions of survivor psychology they manifest, unless we explore and partially deconstruct the mystique to identify and describe the actuality of the homicide detective's task environment. At the same time, we must recognize the importance of the mythology and the misconceptions it involves since it shapes their world and since, as we will see, detectives often use elements of their mystique in a functional way to help them solve murders.

The detective mystique has multiple sources, not the least of which is the notion of detective work as more glamorous, more exciting, and more dangerous than ordinary police work. In the media and in popular literature, detectives are typically portrayed as the elite of the elite—they are the smartest and the most physically courageous cops, who may wear disguises and use specialized investigative techniques to solve baffling mysteries, and they are almost always seen as relying upon their wits and their senses to bring the most dangerous criminals to justice. This public conception of detectives is to some extent shared by members of the police culture, and both inside and outside the police culture detectives enjoy a special status that sets them apart from the ordinary cop.

Niederhoffer's (1967, pp. 82–83) observations about detectives' position and status in policing still seem rather accurate today:

> A detective's clothes, mannerisms, easy familiarity with superior officers, and snobbish aloofness from uniformed patrolmen are all part of his impressive front, helping him to dramatize his status and work performance. Within the police hierarchy the detective also enjoys an exalted status. Almost every cop dreams of the day he will one day "make the bureau." . . . All members of the force know the benefits of detective work. Most imagine more than exist, but there are three immediately apparent advantages: higher salary, more interesting work, and "getting out of the

bag."[2] ... Detectives are the upper class of police society and they haughtily guard their special status and privileges. Their quarters are separate from those of the uniformed force. Within this private domain democratic camaraderie eliminates the social distance that ordinarily divides the various ranks of a bureaucratic hierarchy. A lower-ranking detective may call a detective captain by his first name without causing any surprise; he may walk arm-in-arm with a detective inspector (a very high superior officer) while discussing an important case.

We can see that being a homicide detective is a rewarding job that affords high social status. Homicide detectives are admired within the agency and among members of the public, but being an NYPD homicide detective has a special cachet. One collaborator, a homicide squad supervisor for many years, related how an investigation took him to another jurisdiction and how deferential that agency's senior homicide investigators were toward him and his detectives. At that time he was the NYPD's youngest homicide squad supervisor—a distinction of which he was, quite properly, very proud—and his relative youth doubly impressed the other agency's detectives and enhanced his estimation in their eyes. He described the rewards in this way:

It was a lot of status. Wherever you went it was "squad, *homicide* squad." You are the elite. I felt, and I mean this to today, it was absolutely the best job. For a sergeant, I had the most rewarding job in the city and I wouldn't have changed it one bit. If you ask me what I want to do as a sergeant, I want to be in the homicide squad. And I want to *catch* the cases. There was a lot of status assigned to it, especially when you catch the cases.[3] And to tell you the truth, my people didn't want to give up that responsibility. They didn't want to schlep it off. They were all seasoned people, all professionals.

As is the case with so many perspectives on policing, reality and perception do not always perfectly align. Baker (1985, pp. 96–97), in an oral history of urban police, points out the disparity between the media-cultivated myth and the reality of detective work:

The world of the detective does not glitter. Drug busts are rarely made in million-dollar penthouses. There are very few diplomats operating houses of prostitution and slave trading posts from the back doors of exquisitely decorated embassies. Heiresses who bump off their favorite designer for a one-of-a-kind party dress are scarce these days.

The aftermath of crime is sordid, tragic, ugly. There may be bodies and coagulated blood, the smells of death and decomposition. There are bound to be pain and terror. The sounds are the sobs of the violated and the frenzied cries for justice from families of the victims. To one side are frightened children with hollow eyes. This is where a detective works.

In a more scholarly deconstruction of the mythology surrounding detectives, Herman Goldstein (1977, pp. 55–56) points out that part of the mystique of detective operations is the impression that a detective has difficult-to-come-by qualifications and skills, that investigating crime is a real science, that a detective does much more important work than other police officers, that all detective work is exciting and that a good detective can solve any crime. It borders on heresy to point out that, in fact, much of what detectives do consists of very routine and rather elementary chores, including much paper processing; that a good deal of their work is not only not exciting, it is downright boring; that the situations they confront are often less challenging and less demanding than those handled by patrolling police officers; that it is arguable whether special skills and knowledge are required for police work; that a considerable amount of detective work is actually undertaken on a hit-or-miss basis; and that the capacity of detectives to solve crimes is greatly exaggerated.

Goldstein goes on to argue that empirical data does not support the common perception of detectives as the smartest, most effective, and most productive of police officers. The empirical data he cites may be accurate and the conclusions he draws may have great validity, but it is almost beside the point in our analysis: what matters here is that this mystique is accepted as an accurate depiction by detectives, by many members of the police subculture, and (even more so, perhaps) by the public. This depiction or mystique shapes our view of detectives' work and our interactions with detectives (and theirs with us) in a powerful way precisely because it is the accepted perception.

This cursory review and partial deconstruction of the detective mystique permits us to begin distinguishing reality from perception, setting the stage for a deeper exploration of the homicide detective's world. Following the model we have used with other groups of officers we have considered, we begin our inquiries by examining homicide detectives' task environment and the way it structures their exposure to death events before going on to explore how they individually and collectively manifest the five themes of survivor psychology.

The Homicide Detective's Task Environment

In examining the reality of the homicide detective's professional world, we can see how at least four primary factors operating in the task environment influence his immediate and ultimate experience of a given death event. First, we can see that homicide detectives are among the most elite and experienced detectives within the elite detective bureau, and have perhaps the highest individual and group status in the subculture of police. Second, in terms of the specific kind of images to which he is exposed, we should recognize that the homicide detective sees death in its most violent and disintegrative forms and that he sees these deaths with some frequency. Third, we must understand that the most important attribute a homicide detective can possess and put to practice is the ability to interact effectively with others in order to obtain information that will lead to solving the case, and that he must integrate this information with other images to achieve a particular kind of meaning. Finally, there are specific practical and organizational factors that influence the mechanics of homicide investigation and specific tasks and required duties detectives undertake to solve a murder. Collectively, these factors make the homicide detective's experience of death very different from the experience of the other categories of officers. Moreover, not only does the detective mystique resonate in each of these factors in one way or another, but to some extent his personal and professional identities are bound up in each of them as well (see, generally, Simon, 1991; Sewell, 1994).

Experience and Status

The tremendous status homicide detectives enjoy within the police subculture is partially based in the fact that they investigate what is often viewed as the most serious of crimes, but it is also based in the fact that they are, almost universally, highly experienced and highly tenured cops. All of the homicide detectives who collaborated in this research had a significant amount—up to 14 years—of patrol experience prior to their first investigative assignment, and all developed their skills in some other investigative sphere before gaining a valued opportunity for an assignment to homicide investigation.[4] While the collaborators had very different career histories, the current formal career path for detectives illustrates the importance placed upon acquiring police experience.

The NYPD's current formal career path has been operating since the late 1980s, and it stipulates specific criteria for advancement. Patrol officers earn career points based upon their tenure, annual evaluations, medals, and the overall level of crime and disorder within their precincts—in other words, by acquiring "real" police experience. After accruing a certain number of points, the patrol officer can request an interview for assignment to an investigative unit or another specialized detail. Those accepted for an investigative unit—typically the organized crime control bureau's (OCCB) narcotics or vice divisions, a robbery investigation program (RIP) team or the internal affairs bureau (IAB)—serve as "white shield investigators" for 18 months before an automatic, legally mandated promotion to the "gold shield" rank of detective investigator. Career path assignments directly to precinct detective squads in the Detective Bureau are rare; instead, detectives usually win the coveted transfer to "the Squad" or "the Bureau" as vacancies occur after they have completed several more years of investigative duties in OCCB, RIP, or IAB.[5]

As a matter of civil service law, and notwithstanding the mandatory promotion after 18 months of investigative work, detectives are technically police officers designated to serve as detectives (at a higher salary and with a distinctive gold shield) at the discretion of the police commissioner. They do not enjoy the same civil service protections as police officers and can, in theory if not often in practice, be demoted or "flopped" back to police officer for poor performance. They have no official supervisory role over police officers, and they are outranked by sergeants and all other supervisors. With the exception of activities at a crime scene—where the *Patrol Guide* gives them a vague authority to direct certain activities—they cannot legitimately order anyone around. In practice, their status allows them a great deal of discretion to direct activities at a scene, and many or most supervisors will defer to their "suggestions" as to how other officers' activities should be directed.

This is a delicate dance—some patrol bureau supervisors resent detectives' status and prestige, and will do their best to interfere and let the detective know who's the boss. Detectives generally rely upon their interactive skills and prestige to negotiate and coax others to do what they deem necessary, but conflicts between patrol bureau supervisors and detectives (as well as between patrol and detective bureau supervisors) at the scene of a crime are not uncommon (Gelb, 1975; Count, 1995; McKenna and Harrington, 1996).[6]

Despite their street and investigative experience, squad detectives may not immediately begin investigating homicides (Rachlin, 1995). Ordinarily cases are assigned on a strict rotation basis: as crime reports of robberies, assaults, and other less serious crimes come in to the squad, they are "caught" by the "next-up" detective who becomes ultimately responsible for bringing the case to closure. This system is intended to equally allocate the workload among all the squad detectives, but it does not apply in homicides. Instead, there is a separate "next-up" system in place for most homicides, although the squad supervisor will often deviate from the rotation to assign particular cases to particular detectives, based on their experience and expertise and the objective difficulty of the investigation. A simple "ground ball" homicide (say, a domestic violence homicide in which the facts immediately and convincingly point to the spouse) will probably be assigned to a relatively junior detective, who may be partnered with a more experienced detective to assist and guide him. On the other hand, a more complex "mystery" homicide, or a murder that is likely to take on a high media profile and therefore greater official pressures for a "good case" and a quick resolution, will usually be assigned out of rotation to a seasoned detective with considerable homicide experience. For example, a homicide squad supervisor pointed out that when a cop is shot or killed all the ordinary case assignment conventions are thrown out and the case is assigned to the best and most experienced detective; these cases are simply too important to risk entrusting them to anyone but the best. As we'll see, the demands of investigating a police officer's murder place tremendous formal and informal burdens on the detective who catches it.

When a homicide occurs, the entire precinct squad is mobilized to assist and the catching detective and his partner are usually "taken off the chart" to work on it around the clock. The detective who catches a lot of homicides can thus earn considerable overtime, making homicide investigation an even more desirable assignment. Other squad members drop their other cases to assume a support role and take informal direction from the lead detective, conducting canvasses of the area and performing other investigative duties at his behest. We will consider this and other mechanical aspects of homicide investigation below, but the main point here is that the junior detective operating at the fringes of the investigation has ample opportunity to observe seasoned investigators before he ever officially catches a murder case. This system also comprises a kind of apprenticeship program, since there is a clear assumption that the neophyte will learn his craft under the tutelage of an experienced mentor. Every one of the homicide detectives I interviewed or spoke with evinced a strongly held conviction that his role encompassed the training of younger detectives, and all credited their own mentors—street cops and detectives—for guiding their personal and professional development.

> To be *chosen,* it was to be part of a team. They [the mentors on patrol] chose me to be a fill-in partner when one of them was off or on vacation. These guys were seasoned—they'd seen it all, I mean shoot-outs, the whole thing. These are the guys you learn from. They're going to teach you to survive, and they're going to teach you to communicate with people. I learned how to communicate with people from them.

This avuncular 38-year veteran went on to describe a sense of responsibility to pass on his experience to young cops and detectives, and in doing so to also transmit and preserve the detective culture's core values:

> Not to blow my own horn, but there are guys in this office who are seasoned, qualified, excellent detectives who I broke in here. And it gives me a tremendous amount of satisfaction because I have been able to pass on some of my knowledge and expertise to those guys. They still come to me with a question or whatever, but they can *do the job.* When I'm not here they can do the job. A lot of that's getting lost because every squad doesn't have a [*says own name*], a senior man with X number of years who can pass on this stuff. There's a lot of jaded cops out there—you hear them saying "20 and out"[7]—and young cops are learning from them and that's too bad. If a guy gets broken in by a guy who's bitter or has an axe to grind, he'll adopt these attitudes and he's not going to be a good cop. He's not going to be understanding, he's not going to be able to communicate with people. And you can't learn this stuff out of a book. You've got to go out there and say, "Look, guys, I'm not Professor So-and-So, but you can take what I say or you can discount it." So when I hear young detectives express a negative attitude I sit them down and say, "Hey, you're not going to make it. You're going to be a miserable SOB."

The role of trainer and mentor to junior detectives confers a sense of symbolic immortality, while at the same time it implicitly recognizes the detective's expertise and his superior status even among those who are technically peers.

After a squad detective acquires substantial experience and a good reputation as a homicide investigator, he may be tapped as the squad's homicide specialist or receive an assignment with the borough homicide squad. Homicide specialists are usually the best and most experienced detectives in a precinct squad, and they are usually relieved of other investigative responsibilities to concentrate on homicides. They may catch the most challenging homicides or simply partner with the detectives who catch the cases in the normal rotation, but in either case their expertise and specialization cast them in the role of mentor or coach for less experienced detectives. When homicide specialists are not actively engaged in a current investigation, they reinvestigate old unsolved murders. Their duties also generally involve the perquisite of flexible tours of duty and steady days off—a very unusual and highly valued benefit for squad detectives—making the assignment even more elite and desirable.

Homicide squad detectives fulfill a similar role. They are also expert homicide investigators, and they respond to every murder occurring within their geographic area of responsibility. They provide additional manpower and expert assistance to the catching detective and to other precinct squad members involved in the investigation. The homicide squad's level of involvement in a particular case is determined by several factors that include the difficulty of the case itself, formal organizational or media pressures to quickly bring the case to closure, the experience and expertise of the catching detective with whom they partner, and the availability of a homicide specialist within the precinct squad. Thus an "ordinary" homicide caught by an experienced detective in a squad with capable homicide specialists will require and receive less ongoing assistance from the homicide squad than a difficult case in a precinct where murders are few and no homicide specialist is assigned. Absent such extenuating circumstances as a pattern murder[8] or a case with an extremely high media profile, homicide squad detectives never catch the case, per se. They may be involved in every step and every aspect of the investigation, and to some extent they will be judged on the crime's successful solution, but the catching detective is primarily responsible for bringing it to closure (see, generally, Gelb, 1975; McKenna and Harrington, 1995).

In wrapping up this brief discussion of detective promotion and deployment policies and their related status systems, it is worth mentioning that there is an experience- and expertise-based advancement system within the detective rank, with a concurrent status structure. In this system, the best and most productive Detective Investigators (or "Third-Graders") can be recognized through promotion to the rank of Second-Grade Detective, and the best and most effective of these can be recognized through promotion to the coveted rank of First-Grade Detective. Beyond the salary increase involved (about 300 of the agency's cadre of 3,000 detectives are designated Second Grade and earn a sergeant's salary, and about 100 First Graders earn a salary equal to that of a lieutenant), "having grade" entails tremendous prestige.

VH: *There's a lot of status that goes with being a homicide investigator.*

> I was very proud. I was very proud of my accomplishments in the police department, and that I was a First-Grade Detective. And there were only 104 First-Grade Detectives in the entire city. It felt good, really good. I'm not blowing my own horn, but I worked very hard for it. In all the cases I ever did, I gave it 100 percent. I always did my best, and I was rewarded for it.

In the informal code of the police culture, and especially among members of "the Bureau," it is practically taboo for any supervisor to "pull rank" on a First-Grade Detective or to otherwise give him a hard time, just as it is practically taboo for a detective "with grade" to immodestly flaunt his status. One First-Grade collaborator, a 32-year veteran of the agency and a 25-year veteran of the bureau, described a conflict he had with a young "snot-nosed" lieutenant recently assigned to his squad from a patrol command; the somewhat insecure lieutenant challenged his position as the squad's de facto leader, characterizing him as a "dinosaur"[9] likely to cause the new boss trouble. Beyond the fact of the altercation, which was in itself a minor thing, the squabble crystallized for the First Grader the erosion of essential cultural values he held precious, signaling to him that it was finally time to retire. It was a matter of personal and professional integrity that he would not engage the young lieutenant and become a boss-fighter, so he simply "put in his papers" and retired.

In summary, this brief analysis allows us to once again glimpse the cultural theme of a linkage between "real" police experience, advancement, and status systems. We can also see a kind of synergy operating: the quantity and quality of a detective's experience in homicide investigation affects his status, but it also shapes the quantity and quality of his death exposures. That is, the more experience a homicide detective has in handling difficult cases, the more likely he is to be assigned additional murders and to gain more experience and, ultimately, more status. In light of this synergy and the other factors discussed above, we should not be surprised at the preponderance of First- and Second-Grade Detectives among precinct squad homicide specialists and homicide squad members. Finally, we can see that homicide squad members and precinct squad homicide specialists are distinguished from most other detectives by their almost-exclusive monopoly over murder investigations.

Number and Type of Images

It is difficult to categorize or describe the quantity and quality of death imagery homicide detectives encounter in their work because murder rates vary greatly between and among different geographic areas and because murders can take place in so many types of locations and under so many divergent conditions. The number of murders occurring in New York City has fallen precipitously in recent years—from a record high of 2,245 murders in 1990 to just 584 murders in 2002—but we should bear in mind that these crimes were never evenly distributed among the NYPD's 76 precincts. A few precincts once averaged well over 100 murders per year, while homicides were relatively infrequent in some other geographic areas. Detectives informally rate their own and other detectives' performance on the basis of their homicide solution rate.

In part because murder is seen as a bellwether of the overall level of violence in a precinct—and is therefore indicative of the amount of "real" police work done by its officers—there has evolved a kind of informal murder rate rivalry between certain high-crime precincts and squads. In a somewhat perverse way, being assigned to the squad or (for patrol cops) the precinct with the greatest number of annual murders became a source of status and pride, and when murders were more frequent cops would often brag that their precinct led the city in murders. The recent crime reductions have altered the patterns of status a bit—cops may now be as likely to brag that their work led to the greatest decline in murders and other violent crimes—but these informal bragging rights were passed among a small group of high-crime precincts from year to year. An example of the pride and status can be seen in a sign that hung in the 75th Precinct squad in Brooklyn's East

New York section: mimicking the advertising slogan of a local news radio station, the sign read, "You give us twenty-two minutes, we'll give you a murder."

In my opinion, homicides are the ultimate investigation you can do in police work. If you went into a squad room, I don't care what squad room it is, you would say, "Hey, how many homicides do you have here?" Homicide is always the topic of conversation because they're like a score— how many did you catch, how many did you solve? Yes, homicides are the ultimate case to catch.

Notwithstanding the workload variance among precinct squads, the homicide detective's specialized role gives him ample opportunity to observe violent death taking place under conditions readily capable of intensifying its objective traumatic potential. These conditions can include the on-scene presence or absence of traumatized relatives and witnesses, the location and weather conditions, and the physical state of the corpse. While these features are practically impossible to fully enumerate, they directly or indirectly contribute to the difficulty of solving the case as well as the difficulty of managing it psychologically. Rather than attempting to explicate all these images and exacerbating factors, it should suffice to simply say that the homicide detective may be called to a scene involving any of the grotesque and violent images witnessed by crime scene unit technicians, described in our discussion of the crime scene unit's "family albums," or mentioned elsewhere in this book. They do not, however, generally respond to the scenes of death by natural causes or the other types of deaths we characterized as relatively benign: almost every death they encounter involves death by instrumental violence.

We will deal with the specific impact these factors have on the homicide detective's experience of the death event later in this chapter, but they certainly include the age and perceived innocence of the victim, the degree to which his lifestyle and actions contributed to the death, and myriad other factors that can enhance identification or compound the images' traumatic potential. As important as these objective factors are, it is also important to recognize the less tangible features that shape the homicide detective's experience. As we will see, the homicide detective's greatest vulnerability generally lies not in the visual, auditory, or olfactory images to which he is rather briefly exposed, but to the subjective images and experiences involved in his interactions with others.

Especially in relation to the crime scene unit technician's experience and the experience of the rookie officer, the homicide detective's temporal exposure to death imagery may in some instances be fairly brief. Homicide detectives certainly need to view a crime scene and make mental note of the images presented in order to conduct a thorough investigation and make adequate sense of the crime, but the particular facts and circumstances of the case may permit or require them to quickly leave the scene and pursue leads elsewhere. In describing his investigation of a police officer's murder, for example, one homicide detective noted that he did not view the indoor crime scene per se until almost two days after the crime. He responded to the location and took custody of the suspects other officers had apprehended, but at that time emergency services unit officers were still searching the building for additional suspects and it was unsafe to enter until they finished. After conducting show-ups[10] with witnesses and taking some other basic investigative steps at the scene, he removed the suspects and witnesses to the precinct where he immediately began what proved to be a protracted series of interviews and interrogations,[11] eventually obtaining valid confessions and verifying the details of their stories. These more pressing and potentially fruitful investigative issues made it impossible for him to physically visit the crime scene at that time, so assisting detectives assumed responsibility for that part of the investigation and kept him apprised.

While this two-day delay may represent an extreme case, it points up the fact that every homicide has its own unique set of exigent circumstances that make it unlike any other. To some extent the crime scene unit technician, the patrol sergeant, and the rookie fall back upon routines and rote behaviors as a means of distancing themselves emotionally from the deaths they witness, but the dynamic and emergent character of homicide investigation dictates that there are relatively few routine or standard procedures operating in the homicide detective's task environment. Part of the challenge of homicide investigations, then, lies in the detective's ability to quickly assess the available facts and make decisions about the most productive use of his time and the resources at his disposal. He must remain open to the images presented, rapidly integrate and make meaning of them, and flexibly pursue a course of action geared toward quickly obtaining additional information that will lead to a more comprehensive constellation of meaning and, ultimately, to a successful prosecution. The formative nature of the homicide detective's work is implicitly vitalizing, and all collaborators agreed that this is one reason homicide investigation is the most rewarding work a detective can do. One homicide detective, asked why these investigations were so rewarding, said,

> I guess I enjoyed doing investigations, and even more so homicide investigations. I guess it was taking an investigation all the way through to the conclusion. And apprehending the person who committed the crime, you know, to finish it all up. I think that was one of the reasons I really liked homicides. The digging, the delving, the tracking, and whatever. I enjoyed that. The mystery and trying to solve it. To take this jigsaw puzzle and put it together and finally get the whole picture and come to the final realization of the whole thing.

Detective work, especially homicide investigation, can also be very satisfying work in terms of the subparadigms and modes of symbolic immortality. It permits detectives to participate in the pursuit of justice, to experience connection with others, and to integrate images in a meaningful way that has important social consequences. The detective's pursuit of justice is not only part of a larger ultimate philosophical purpose connecting him to other cops and permitting him to feel a sense of movement, but at a more immediate level it also permits him to restore something to the victims—to find a kind of integrity in what he does to counter the disintegrated lives he encounters. As important, each of these activities is highly esteemed within the police culture, and that esteem reinforces the professional identity.

Another homicide detective's comments illuminate the formative nature of the investigative process and hint at the immortalizing sense of power over death experienced when cases are successfully resolved and justice is achieved. We can also see elements of transcendence in these comments:

They're challenging. I'd say it's two-fold. The challenge and the rewards. The challenge of the investigation and the rewards of solving the case. And giving a sense of closure to the family when you solve the case. So I'm going to give a lot there. The challenge and solving it and giving a sense of closure to the family. They lost someone but at least we got the person who did it. And obviously those times when we didn't get the killer, you would feel, maybe not upset but you wouldn't feel as happy. . . . The more challenging it was, the better I liked it. I had gotten to a point—and I'm not bragging about this—there could be any homicide, I don't care what the circumstances were, I could handle it. I felt I could handle anything. With homicides, building up as you get more expertise in it, I felt that I could . . . I don't care who was murdered, I felt very comfortable handling the case. All aspects of it.

In line with this need to remain open to images and the lack of routine procedures, we can also see how the task environment prescribes a different quality of partial professional numbing for homicide detectives. The crime scene unit technician, for example, can invoke substantial professional numbing to screen out the emotional content of an event and yet do an adequate job of processing the scene. He does not interact with witnesses and his specialized task environment does not implicitly require any sensitivity to their emotions and behaviors. The rookie is generally so numbed by the novelty of the images and so drawn to the safe refuge of procedure that his interactions are minimal and largely superficial. By virtue of his experience as a street cop and investigator, the detective is able to invoke the constructive dimension of partial professional numbing and approach difficult or grotesque death images with some detachment, but he cannot afford to entirely close off the images he confronts. It is important for him to take in and comprehend visual images since they are important evidentiary matters and because he may be asked to describe and review them at trial, but the more important images are those experienced during his interactions with others. The homicide detective's job is all about interacting with people and paying attention to subtle behavioral clues and images that may be laden with emotional content.

Interactive Skills

One of the most important things to bear in mind about homicide detectives is the extent to which they rely upon their interpersonal skills. The tasks and responsibilities of homicide investigation certainly require the detective to possess a body of cognitive knowledge and perhaps some psychomotor skills, but successful homicide detectives are first and foremost good communicators and good listeners. A homicide detective must have some knowledge of anatomy, for example, in order to understand the cause of a particular death, and he must also understand the basics of forensics in order to make meaning of the physical evidence presented at a crime scene (Geberth, 1993; DiMaio, 1993; DiMaio and DiMaio, 1993). He should certainly know the law, especially as it applies to the legally permissible search and seizure of evidence and to interrogations and confessions, and he must be able to quickly integrate and apply this knowledge according to the exigencies of the moment. The homicide detective may also apply tactical knowledge and perhaps some physical prowess while apprehending a dangerous murderer, but to a large extent the physical demands of homicide investigation have been exaggerated in literature and in media depictions of the job. What the popular conception of homicide investigation seems to lack, though, is a more comprehensive representation of the logical capacities and artful "people skills" possessed by good and effective detectives.

The homicide detective's stock in trade is information, and in a very practical sense his ability to obtain information rests upon his ability to interact with witnesses, family members, and others—any of whom may be or may become a suspect—in a way that elicits timely and accurate information. The inherent difficulty of this task is often complicated by the fact that the individuals with whom he interacts may legitimately be in distress or may have a vested interest in concealing the truth, as well as by the fact that the homicide detective often needs to obtain and integrate information quickly. As we mentioned briefly in the preceding chapter, the unwritten "24-hour rule" (as well as a host of other pressures that may include official demands for a quick resolution of the case or substantial media attention) compels the homicide detective to quickly amass and assess evidence in order to formulate viable tentative working hypotheses. Once formulated, these preliminary hypotheses guide the scope and direction of the case, and although they are constantly revised in light of newly obtained information their initial accuracy ultimately impacts the case's solvability.[12] More abstractly, but importantly to the detective, their accuracy ultimately impacts his credibility and standing within the detective culture.

These essential interactive skills are first developed in street experience and eventually refined through investigative experience, and seasoned detectives justifiably take great pride in their ability to elicit information. They take particular pride in the ability to develop an easy rapport and put someone at such ease that he reveals much more than he intended, but this is by no means the only tool in their extensive repertoire of interviewing tactics and strategies. Depending upon the situation and the individual they are interviewing, they draw upon an array of tactics that can range from the classic "good cop/bad cop" scenario to making a connection based on an apparently sincere concern for the individual's overall well-being, with an entire spectrum of techniques and variations in between. Homicide detectives must be good listeners and good communicators, but they must also be adept at quickly switching interview tactics and strategies according to the potentialities of the moment and the subtle clues they pick up (Inbau, Reid, and Buckley, 1985; Fisher and McCauley, 1995). All of this requires them to remain open and receptive to the images and emotions presented, but a receptivity that involves empathy also opens the possibility of meaningful connection and a host of related emotional costs. Whether they are dealing with a casual witness, a traumatized relative, or a suspect, many detectives avoid this trap by skillfully feigning empathy to mask their suspicions (Hess and Gladis, 1987; Hess, 1997; Skolnick and Leo, 1992).

We will revisit the compelling need to obtain information through interaction when we examine the dimensions of psychic numbing below, but we should conclude this section by pointing out that demands for rapid denouement and the complex cognitive processes involved in detective-subject interactions interpose significant barriers to real empathetic connection.

Organizational Factors

We can identify and describe some of the mechanics and processes typically involved in a homicide investigation, but only in a general way. As we saw when we examined the task environments of the rookie and the patrol sergeant, those officers are mandated to perform certain specified routine tasks and duties that provide an element of distance from the images and individuals they may encounter. The crime scene unit's task environment had fewer formally prescribed responsibilities, but its technical nature nevertheless gave technicians a degree of distance from the traumatic images they witness. These elements do not operate as potently in the homicide detective's environment, which is less bound up in formal agency directives and is not of a strictly technical character. To be sure, there are certain technical tasks involved and there are certain items of paperwork the homicide detective must complete, but they comprise a very small (and many would say, relatively unimportant) part of his job.

The lion's share of paperwork in homicide investigation consists of the narrative case reports (or DD-5s) he must type up, but other than their number and the fact that they concern murder they are not substantially different from the reports involved in any other type of investigation. Each investigative step is memorialized on a separate DD-5 along with the information obtained, but most homicide detectives use some kind of formal or informal checklist to ensure their paperwork is complete. There is little pressure to prepare reports contemporaneous with the completion of each step, and most prepare the DD-5s when the investigative pace has slowed. Paperwork, then, does not operate as an immediately available mechanism for retreating from death images or for achieving distance from an event as it might for rookies or patrol sergeants.

Regulations do require that certain notifications be made to specified department entities, but they do not specify that the catching detective make them himself—they can easily be delegated to another detective, freeing the catching detective to pursue the case without administrative delay. In all, the homicide detective's task environment involves few official directives or formal regulations that limit his discretion or impede his involvement in the important matters at hand. While the duties and responsibilities of rookies and patrol sergeants are prescribed and circumscribed by formal policy directives, the homicide detective enjoys tremendous discretion to pursue his investigation as he sees fit and as his experience guides him.

The homicide detective also typically has substantial resources at his disposal, at least during the initial phase of the investigation. Homicides are an all-hands affair, so all detectives in the squad drop their other cases to respond and pitch in; they may even be called in early or held over (on overtime) to work on the case. The detective supervisor is in titular command of the investigative team, but in practice he and all the other detective bureau personnel marshaled for a homicide investigation willingly perform what are essentially support roles: after assigning a lead detective to catch the case, the supervisor typically (and unofficially) steps back to organize the work of other detectives in a way that allows the catching detective sufficient discretion to manage his own investigation without distraction. The supervisor will coordinate the assignment of detectives to systematically canvass the area for witnesses, to conduct background and criminal records checks on the victim and suspects or witnesses, and to generally manage the development and flow of information. Depending upon the facts presented in a given case, he may for example direct that the license plates of all automobiles parked in the vicinity be recorded and run through the Department of Motor Vehicles database to identify their owners; it is possible the killer's car may be parked nearby. Similarly, depending upon the circumstances and the personnel available, he may have parking tickets and moving violation summonses issued in the area pulled and reviewed, or he may direct that bus drivers, subway token booth attendants, or postal workers in the vicinity at the time of the murder be located and interviewed. Mug shots of potential suspects (and/or the victim) may be retrieved from files in the squad or at headquarters, incoming and outgoing local, toll, and long-distance telephone records may be subpoenaed and reviewed, search warrant applications may be drawn up and presented to a judge—in short, many important but time-consuming tasks may be necessary (Geberth, 1993). The goal is to support the lead detective by assigning these potentially important but tangential pieces of legwork to others so that he can be fully involved and focused on the most essential parts of the investigation. The extent of the supervisor's involvement and the amount of guidance he gives depends not only on the facts of the case but also on the expertise and experience of the catching homicide detective. In practice, all the squad's detectives and supervisors work together in a collegial way during an active homicide investigation, suspending the traditional chain of command and the formal lines of authority and discretion. One homicide detective described how consensus decisions are reached and tasks are allotted. After spending a few hours at the scene to collect information and evidence, detectives will

> go back to the office to collate the material we've got and see where we're going to go. We'll get coffee and rolls and sit with the boss to talk the case through. Everyone throws their 2 cents in, and we discuss the crime and figure out where we're going from here, what everyone's going to do . . . More than anything else on the Job, it really is a team effort.

In a rule-bound semimilitary organization, this suspension of traditional lines of authority and discretion is significant: it highlights the homicide detective's exalted status and recognizes his superior expertise in an implicitly rewarding way.

The spirit of collegiality is a source of vitality and connection for all involved. Squad members and supervisors put aside the kind of petty differences that occur in any work group, and they put aside the distinctions of rank and position to unite in a common activity that is in itself vitalizing. The collegiality is also in service of a larger unifying principle embraced by the police and detective cultures: the pursuit of justice. All play a part in the enterprise, and whether one is running license plates through a computer or interrogating the prime suspect, all parties are important to the ultimate outcome. All feel the rewarding sense of connection and all participate in the rewarding pursuit of justice, but the rewards of collegiality are especially powerful for the lead investigator—he sets the essential direction of the investigation, and he accrues the greatest share of the accolades, the recognition, and the status that result from a successful case. This is yet another reason homicide work is so attractive and, often, so heady an assignment.

The homicide detective, thus generally unencumbered by the formal demands of paperwork and sundry other petty tasks, is free to begin exploring the facts of the case and organizing his own work accordingly. Like crime scene unit technicians, homicide detectives said they actually begin organizing and planning the investigation as soon as they learn a homicide has occurred. They are less rigid than CSU technicians in terms of insisting that all available facts are provided them prior to departing the office, but they do review the available facts, monitor the police radio, and discuss a preliminary case management strategy as they travel to the scene so that they can commence gathering information upon arrival. One collaborator, a former homicide detective, put it this way:

> On the way I'm starting to prepare myself for the case. So that when I get to the scene I can start putting that part into action, getting the facts. What do we have? Do we have a male, female, how old, what's the circumstances? Do we know how the person died yet? Even though there's a puncture wound, we don't know if they're stabbed or shot. All these things go through your mind as you're going to the scene.

The practice of preparing for an investigation en route to the scene, like many other things they will do upon arrival, is a matter of discretion shaped by experience. Nowhere in department regulations does it specify that detectives must or should do these things.

The main points to be culled from this admittedly cursory review of the homicide detective's tasks and duties are that there are few formal requirements or mandated activities to shape his experience of the death event, that the homicide detective's work is supported by a division of labor and a related collegial spirit of cooperation from peers and supervisors, and that he has far more discretion than any other category of officer whose experiences we explore. Each of these environmental factors makes homicide investigation a particularly rewarding specialty. Each limits the traumatic potential of the encounter in some way at the same time it opens the possibility of a different kind of traumatic exposure.

Our brief exploration of the detective culture and of the primary organizational issues and task environment factors involved in homicide investigation gives us a rudimentary understanding of the way homicide investigators go about their work and experience their professional world. More specifically, this basic understanding gives us some clues about the way their task environment shapes their exposure to death and their experience of violent death images. Many of these clues will take on additional meaning and lead us to a more comprehensive understanding of the homicide detective's world in the remainder of this chapter, where we explore how the themes of survivor psychology play out in his experience.

Psychic Numbing

Given the number and quality of objectively traumatic images the homicide detective encounters, the capacity to screen out the more visually grotesque elements of death imagery through partial professional numbing takes on special salience. Absent this capacity, the visual images could have a powerful and detrimental impact, effectively immobilizing him and radically impairing his overall formative process. The essential formative process of integrating images, making sense of them, drawing cognitive and affective judgments from them, and fulfilling the schemas for enactment they create must remain viable if the homicide detective is to perform his job effectively.

Homicide detectives develop the basic psychological capacity for partial professional numbing in much the same way other tenured cops do—through the accumulation of police experience. The attenuated process of gaining police experience that leads to the detective designation virtually ensures that he has had numerous prior death encounters and witnessed numerous violent and grotesque deaths. The homicide detective has experienced the difficulties encountered by the rookie officer and transcended them to achieve the kind of relative comfort around death that other tenured cops enjoy. He is likely to have had many DOA assignments and to have seen many kinds of death as a police officer—all the homicide detective collaborators described numerous exposures in their patrol career, and all related that they eventually became quite comfortable dealing with violent and disintegrative deaths—and many also witnessed violence and death as "white-shield investigators."[13] Once assigned to the squad, neophyte detectives assist at the scenes of murders, suicides, and other violent death investigations before they ever assume the responsibility of catching a homicide. By the time the detective catches his first homicide he is well inured to the impact of violent and grotesque visual death images, and, not unlike the crime scene unit technician, he can easily view disturbing images of violent death with some degree of professional interest and detachment.

As we've noted on several occasions, the capacity for partial professional numbing operates to reduce the traumatic potential of visual images, but it also entails a reduced capacity to feel or experience the emotional elements of the death images he encounters. Experienced cops can easily become cynical and hardened to the kind of emotions others display and they might not experience the same quality of emotion the ordinary civilian might. This presents a problem for homicide detectives, since their job requires they remain somewhat open to the full range of images and emotions without becoming overwhelmed or impaired by them. It also presents a problem in that a cynical retraction from emotion and feeling runs counter to the humane inclination toward genuine compassionate response. Insofar as the ability to render compassionate assistance to those in distress is a valued attribute among members of the detective culture and likely a personal inclination as well, obstacles to its enactment can challenge the detective's sense of integrity at two levels.

Homicide detectives master this dilemma and retain their sense of integrity in part through the skillful application of their interactive skills and perhaps some acting skills, without sacrificing their investigative goals. Regardless of their true estimation of a witness, his character, and his potential involvement in the crime, seasoned detectives almost always open their interviews in a friendly yet professional way. They initially treat witnesses cordially and, if the situation demands it, can easily "ratchet up" to adopt a tougher demeanor. They may be solicitous and may articulate a compassionate concern for the witness's needs—especially if they believe it will facilitate the flow of information—but they always remain surreptitiously and scrupulously suspicious of him until the investigation proves his innocence and legitimacy. Given the broad palette of interactive skills and information gathering techniques they've acquired and refined over years of police experience, for the most part this delicate balance is easily achieved.

Throughout the interview process homicide detectives continually size-up the witness, make contemporaneous judgments about his personality and about the veracity and completeness of the information he provides, and flexibly adapt their technique to elicit more information that, in turn, informs their subsequent judgments and tactics. Invariably, investigative interviewing also involves some deception, if only to the extent that detectives collect rather than share information, but deceptive tactics often play a much larger role: homicide detectives cannot initially betray their suspicions lest the witness recognize his jeopardy and stop talking. A witness's inconsistencies may subsequently be raised to essentially coerce a more truthful or complete statement, but at the early stages of an interview the witness is generally encouraged to talk without interruption (Geiselman and Fisher, 1988).[14] As we use the term here, *deception* can extend to the practice of actively manipulating a witness's emotions by playing up his submerged guilt or fears, by implying that his secrets will be revealed through further investigation, or by subtly or overtly intimating he will face some other sanction if he fails to fully cooperate. Deceptive tactics are legitimate and legally accepted investigative tools, and detectives may generally mislead, lie, or feed false information to a witness or suspect as part of a broader strategy to uncover the truth (Skolnick and Leo, 1992).[15]

Deception is thus an integral and frequently used part of the homicide detective's repertoire, and because it is viewed as a viable, productive, and necessary tactic that achieves the desired results and takes place in service of the worthwhile pursuit of justice, detectives experience little dissonance or guilt. The use of deception scarcely implicates the homicide detective's sense of personal or professional integrity. It does not implicate his personal integrity because it takes place in the professional sphere and is essentially perpetrated by his professional persona while playing a particular role like an actor on stage. Detectives have no personal motive for engaging in deception, and they accrue no tangible personal benefit other than the collateral benefits of professional status and peer approbation if it leads to the successful solution of a murder. Indeed, a detective's ability to skillfully manipulate a witness or suspect through deception or other lawful psychological suasion is an esteemed attribute within the detective culture, and the status and recognition he gains can ameliorate any dissonance he might feel. Detective lore and individual "war stories" resonate with the theme of the crafty detective who adeptly manipulates or deceives a suspect into revealing key evidence that cracks a difficult case or leads to a valid confession.

In a more practical sense, maintaining a balanced and cordial professional relationship with witnesses (and especially with family members) despite the detective's suspicions or estimation of their character is important because the investigator may need their continued cooperation and can ill afford to alienate them. Genuine compassion and concern for the witness's well-being, though, can easily translate into internal or external demands for action and lead to a personal involvement that opens the possibility of a costly emotional connection. Detectives must exercise caution so as not to become so involved with a witness that a true bond forms; one collaborator, for example, said he knew of more than one detective who became romantically involved with a murder victim's spouse and wound up leaving his own spouse for her. The key to avoiding the emotional trap of excessive personal involvement is to maintain a completely professional and detached relationship without appearing to lack empathy (Vessel, 1998; Hess and Gladis, 1987; Hess, 1987).

We will discuss the occurrence and outcome of these costly emotional connections in greater depth below, but we can easily see how a failure of partial professional numbing and the sense of objective detachment it supports can lead to extreme identification and how such connections can complicate or compromise an investigation. One former homicide detective summarized how interaction can lead to identification and how an objective detachment born of suspicion operates to allay it:

> In homicide cases, you get to know a lot about people. You know their family, you get to meet their friends, their habits. You learn all the good things and all the bad things. You have to build a rapport because the family's got to be open to you, especially in a case where there are no leads. And as a detective, *everybody* is suspicious. You trust *nobody*. The way I looked at it is everybody's guilty, everybody's the perp except me because I know I didn't do it. And then you start the process of elimination. If it's a woman I eliminate the husband or the father or whatever. It becomes a process of elimination.[16] So you can't occupy yourself with the person, you're occupying yourself with the case.

VH: *In some cases you may develop a relationship with the family?*

> Yes ... you become attached. Not to the person who's dead, but to the survivors. You feel you owe them something. I want to try and find out why this happened and who did it and get them. You get to know everything because you're constantly interviewing them ... You have to know

who your good people are, who your bad people are, who your suspicious people are. But other than that there's no real bond between you and the dead person because it's a job you have to do. I think you have a transference from the victim to the family because the victim, he's at peace. He's gone, and there's nothing I can do to bring him back but I can give the family peace of mind by bringing the responsible person to justice. So if I bond, it's with the family, not the victim. I know I can't help him anymore but I can help the family through the crisis by making an arrest, and try to give them peace of mind. So you really transfer from the victim to the family with homicides. At least I did.

Absent other factors or information to the contrary, at the initial phase of their investigation detectives typically focus upon the victim's family and friends as potential suspects. The homicide detective is therefore placed in a difficult and divisive position: in order to fulfill his mandated role and solve the case, the detective must display tact and compassion in order to develop and sustain an ongoing relationship with the victim's family and friends, each of whom is almost certain to become a focus of the investigation at some point and any one of whom is likely to be eventually arrested and charged in the murder (Sourcebook of Criminal Justice Statistics Online, 2001; Geberth, 1993).

Several collaborators described how their initial interviews with family members involved communicating what are essentially the ground rules of the relationship. Homicide detectives generally communicate the fact that they will work diligently and impartially to solve the case and find the murderer so as to bring closure to the family and they say they will need the family's help and cooperation throughout the investigation, but they almost always avoid articulating a personal commitment to the case or to the murder victim.[17] Sometimes homicide detectives wittingly or unwittingly violate this convention and make a pledge to the secondary victim, and we will see how verbally solidifying the commitment erodes his professional detachment, complicates the investigation, and can implicate a constellation of issues related to the quest to make meaning and find appropriate enactment.

These ground rules set the stage for subsequent interactions at the same time they demonstrate the detective's professionalism and affirm his role and position as the person controlling the investigation and its progress. Setting up ground rules and prescribing relationships has a secondary benefit as well: it tacitly negates any expectations that the detective will be entirely candid and forthcoming in revealing investigative details (limiting any guilt he might otherwise feel as the result of deceiving an innocent) or that family members will have a substantive role in setting investigative priorities and objectives. These expectations can undermine the investigative process through distraction, and repeated unnecessary contact can enhance the possibility of additional connection. Several collaborators described cases where family members continued to call the detective for new information on almost a daily basis, long after the investigation went cold and after the detective's time and attention were required by newer and more promising cases. One collaborator's narrative illustrates how a demeanor of professional detachment frames the relationship in a way that protects against personal involvement at the same time as it permits the detective to experience some of the personal and professional rewards of helping people with their problems.[18] He was asked if he had much personal interaction with family members during the investigation.

> Not too much. The initial talking with them, it all depended on the circumstances. Where you would have to find out background on the victim, and go in depth, you would sit there and talk with the person and find out where he worked, and all the background. Who were his friends and did he have any enemies, that type of thing. As far as conversing with them, you'd let them know that you'd made an arrest, or periodically while you were doing the investigation you would [contact them and] say "I'm still working on it, its not forgotten. We didn't forget about it, anything like that. We're still working on it." Just to give them a little more encouragement that it's not in a drawer and that we didn't forget about it. That was it, there was not really much more. [He describes making an arrest in an old homicide and notifying the spouse.] I found out where she was and went down to the house and she threw her arms around me.

The kind of attachment this detective describes is primarily a professional commitment—he reassures family members he has not forgotten the case not so much because he has a personal commitment to them as individuals but because a good detective—as defined by their culture—is a tenacious detective. His contacts keep the relationship alive and tend to ensure continued cooperation, and to the extent any personal commitment is involved it is subsumed and obscured by the professional quest to pursue justice. Similarly, the rewards he receives from solving the case, making an arrest, and experiencing the family's gratitude primarily animate elements of his professional persona. Notwithstanding these professional rewards, knowing that one has successfully achieved justice and provided some closure to secondary victims can bring personally rewarding feelings as well. There is always a fine balance between the two, and because detectives never know at the beginning of an investigation what the outcome will be, they strive to keep relationships and the commitments they entail within the bounds of the professional self. When asked if he ever developed a lasting relationship or personal commitment to a family, one homicide detective replied:

> No, I wouldn't. I guess I wouldn't get involved with the families as much. I'd keep it at a very low-key type of level, you know, and keep a professional manner. You know, it's bad enough that the people have lost a loved one. If you really get close to them you would say, "Gee, I've got to do something more." Of course you always did the most you could do on a case, but maybe then you'd feel worse from the fact that you couldn't do more. Maybe that was one of the reasons I didn't, I didn't get so involved with people. I mean, there were people who'd call me afterwards, you know, "Hi, Detective." "Oh, hi, how are you doing? How have you been?" "Oh, good." "How's your mom doing, is everything okay there?" "I need some professional advice." And they would call me for professional advice,

that type of thing. They would feel free enough that they would call me. I always left people with a good taste in their mouth, you know, on good terms. That was the way I worked. I always conducted myself as a *professional*. Nobody can say anything else [about my style], and that's all they can ask of you.

Detectives also invariably withhold certain details from family members so that they may later be used to manipulate a suspect or to validate a confession. Information management, especially the management of information known only to the killer and the detective, is an essential practical aspect of the investigative process and detectives lose some control of the investigation when details of the crime become public (Geberth, 1993). Indeed, one theme resonating in the cautionary tales detectives tell concerns the victim's friend or family member who calls the investigator several times a week to stay abreast of developments. Only after several months of discussing the case does the friend emerge as the prime suspect—a suspect who now knows almost as much about the case as the detective who must interrogate him. Withholding information also feeds and supports that part of the detective mystique that portrays the detective as knowing much more than he lets on—what one detective called "the Columbo factor."

Another way homicide detectives manage the dilemmas posed by the tendency toward excessive connection is by managing information to maintain a clear separation between their personal and professional lives. They do not share their personal feelings about the case or any personal details of their own lives with witnesses, since doing so would complicate the relationship, diminish their power by creating an expectation of reciprocity, and breach the important protective barriers between their personal and professional personas.

By the same token, homicide detectives (like other cops) are careful not to let the disturbing images and experiences they encounter in the professional sphere spill over into their private lives. Much like crime scene unit technicians, homicide detectives easily compartmentalize their two spheres and rarely share disturbing images encountered at work with their own family. This clear separation of personas certainly operates to minimize the psychic costs of homicide investigation and permits them to experience greater vitality in their private relationships, but it also takes place in service of a prevalent theme I saw operating among all the collaborators, but perhaps especially among homicide detectives: they have a compelling and highly altruistic urge to protect others—their loved ones in particular—from the depravities, horrors, and dangers they willingly engage at work.

In describing a homicide—the brutal murder of a child by a parent—that particularly distressed and consumed him (in part because he had a child of about the same age), one homicide detective digressed to explain how he always tried to prevent work experiences from intruding on his family relationships.

VH: *What did you do at the time? When you say it bothered you . . .*

I have a very understanding wife.

VH: *Did you talk a lot to her about your cases? Some people don't bring anything home.*

That thing, that trial, I think I mentioned it to [name]. As far as any other cases, no, I really didn't bring anything home. Everything, you know, it stayed at work. I think that cops, they can't talk to their wives about certain of these things that happen at work. So instead they go and talk to a girlfriend. [Laughs.] Maybe that's why there are so many divorces. Or the guys in the office, or whatever the case may be. But you don't bring it home.

VH: *Some people make it a point never, under any circumstances, never to bring anything home.*

It was just, especially with my daughter, I wouldn't say things in front of her, because you know . . . . I wouldn't even tell my wife things I was doing because, why worry her? Why have her worrying about you? If she thought I was doing crazy stupid things then she'd start harping at me and aggravating me. "Don't do that . . . " So the best thing is to leave things unsaid.

In the vast majority of cases these mechanisms of partial professional numbing and related compartmentalization of personal and professional selves are sufficient to forestall the tendency toward immoderate identification, emotional involvement, and compassionate response, but the homicide detective can also encounter situations in which partial professional numbing fails to fully protect him emotionally and he develops a deep sense of commitment. Some homicide cases present images so objectively compelling that they simply overwhelm the detective's partial professional numbing, but some detectives also knowingly permit themselves to experience emotions and images that forge connections and commitments. In either case, when partial professional numbing fails, some degree of formative impairment occurs and the detective personalizes the emotional and visual elements of death imprint images in an especially powerful way. In a few cases, the murder investigation takes on all the trappings of an obsession as the detective struggles to make meaning of it (James, 1992; Gourevitch, 2000; Sudetic, 1995).

Death Imprint Image

When we first discussed the death imprint image in chapter 2, we noted that this theme of survivor psychology is closely tied to death guilt and that it often complicates the struggle to make immediate and ultimate meaning of the death encounter. We also noted that to some extent the various types of numbing experienced in relation to a death event could mediate the subjective potency of the death imprint image and we pointed out that the imprint image's subjective impact can also be affected by residual images of separation, stasis, and disintegration experienced in previous death encounters. Although to some degree these and other subjective factors define one's vulnerability to the death imprint image, a sufficiently threatening or powerful image can produce an enduring death imprint image in anyone.

Each of the homicide detectives collaborating in this study experienced one or more extreme death immersions that led to an unusually powerful and lasting sense of commitment to the victim (and to a lesser extent to the victim's family), and several common threads ran through their narratives. In every instance, the facts and circumstances of the case resonated so profoundly at a personal level that the detectives either permitted the images to penetrate or were unable to prevent the images from penetrating the protective psychic firewall between the personal and professional self. Images and emotions that would ordinarily not infiltrate the personal sphere in a meaningful way did so, and they became inextricably tied up with core elements of the personal self. These immersions galvanized and profoundly altered the contours of the detective's personal self to the extent that they recognized that the experience had changed and debilitated them. Each death involved gruesome and objectively traumatic imagery that was remarkable in terms of the victim's perceived innocence, the degree of disintegration, and the lack of integrity or the amount of humiliation involved. The power of these images to overwhelm the detective's psychic firewall is all the more remarkable when we consider that these detectives had previously investigated up to 400 homicides without significant attachment to a victim or significant impairment of their formative process. Indeed, as we noted above, if a detective forged any type of commitment it was typically to family members rather than to the victim himself.

In some of these cases the detective's vulnerability can be attributed to remarkable similarities between his personal experiences and the manner and circumstances of death—identification was intensified by the death imagery's connection to powerful and unresolved preexisting death-related images of separation, stasis, and disintegration in the detective's personal sphere. In every case, the detective's commitment to the victim also represented an opportunity to master, resolve, and make meaning of their own personal death experience and to experience a sense of vitality by engaging in a principled quest to find justice or, more simply, to just *do something* for the victim. In sharp contrast to the transitory and fairly superficial quests we saw among sergeants and rookies, these quests were durable and lasting. As we will see, the failure to fully actualize that quest's demands can also frustrate the detective's attempt to master and reformulate the imagery.

One homicide detective who participated in more than 400 murder investigations described two experiences that were, more than 10 years after their occurrence, still capable of reducing him to tears. In the first instance, the objective horror of the situation was exacerbated by the remarkable similarities between the victim's circumstances and the detective's own experience as well as by his inability to *do something*—to fulfill personal and professional expectations—on behalf of the victim.

> Okay, we're talking 10 years ago. I'm driving home with a department car. [*He describes a highway location.*] And all of a sudden, traffic abruptly stops and I see a commotion. What had happened was, a young boy, who lived in [neighborhood], was trying to go across to get to his house. My, my thought was he's trying to get home to dinner. He had a bike. I pull over, I

pull over and the boy is lying down, okay. The boy was black. There was a white businessman there who was screaming, "Somebody, help"— screaming, he was frantic, *screaming* about what happened to this poor boy. And I, I identify myself as a police officer and I call for an ambulance to immediately get someone over here. And the boy was lying down and he looked up at me like this [*illustrates looking up over shoulder*]. I had been on the Job—I was in the homicide squad—there was no blood but you *knew* this boy was in terrible, terrible shape. You couldn't move him. He looked up like, "Can you help me?" but you knew that his internal injuries were massive. . . . I tried to do the best I can. . . . We've got a 9– or 10–year-old boy, and what upset me about this particular incident was I felt helpless that I could not put him in the radio car. I probably would have killed him. I remembered when the ambulance came, one man saying to the other, "He's in extremis." They brought the flat board and they put him on the flat board and I didn't have that in the radio car. I knew you had to do that, I knew from my experience you had to do that. And I called for Highway, and Highway came. I went home that night and spoke to my wife. I said, "I had a bad one."

The detective's somewhat jumpy and fragmented narrative, like his interjected expressions of an irrational guilt born of helplessness and incomplete enactment, are emblematic of the immediate and lasting impairment he suffered. The ability to make coherent meaning of a situation and describe images in coherent temporal order is an important part of being a homicide detective, but these powerful images overwhelmed his ability to do so.

I was really upset; I said, "I wonder if that boy died. What happened to that boy?" But I left when Highway came. I called the next morning, I called Highway and said, "Listen, just out of curiosity," I remember exactly where I was sitting. I was sitting in the den of my house in [town]. And I said, "How did that boy do?" and he said, "The boy died." I sobbed. I sobbed. [*Pause of 3 seconds, whispers.*] Bothers me now. Bothers me now. [*Pause of 5 seconds.*] Bothers me now. [*He begins crying.*]

Approximately 2 years earlier, the detective's own 10–year-old son fell off his bicycle, fractured his skull and lapsed into a deep coma for several days. It was, he said, the worst time of his life—the doctor told him his son's condition was "as critical as any human being can be"—but his son emerged from the coma and survived. This incident reactivated those powerful personal images of disintegration, stasis, and separation, but the child's grave condition precluded any real opportunity to repair or master them through immediate and appropriate enactment. His ongoing struggle to master, integrate, and impart coherent meaning to these images emerges from his narrative, which also hints at an amorphous guilt and sense of commitment.

I think the problem was that my son had an accident on a bike and he went into a coma and he almost died. And I had flashes of that going through my mind. [*Pause of 8 seconds.*] That was 10 years ago; I still can't talk about it without crying. [*He is crying, wiping his eyes with paper towel.*] The boy died. I was even thinking of going to his wake. I didn't know who the kid is. Didn't know who he was. But he died. I knew I couldn't do a thing for him but, ah. . . . And at that time I had been to how many homicide scenes? Hundreds. I had seen *hundreds* and I never, I never had a problem. I had a problem with that. It was the worst—that was the only time I cried in my career. The only time I cried in my career. And as you can see I'm still emotional about it, the tears and that.

The only time that I got upset in terms of breaking down was when that boy. . . . And that could have been triggered my son's near-death experience. That was part of it, I think. The second part was I'll never forget him looking at me. Lying down flat, he couldn't talk. Maybe it was the frustration that I couldn't, that I couldn't help. I knew I couldn't move that boy. Or else I would have thrown him in the radio car. But I knew I couldn't. You know, I'm not a doctor, I'm not an EMS technician, I'm not qualified. But I could see he had massive internal injuries and very little bleeding. It was just the circumstance of the boy getting hit by a car and I felt helpless, and I was thinking of my son, and everything else.

Beyond the objective horror of the image and its inherent readiness to seamlessly unite with and reactivate personally consequential preexisting imagery, situational variables compounded his trauma and infused the immediate experience with death-equivalent elements of disintegration, separation, and stasis. Although the detective had literally hundreds of prior violent death encounters involving disintegrative images not altogether unlike those presented here, this exposure took place without the kind of supports provided in his usual task environment. Unlike the other exposures, he had no time to prepare himself cognitively or emotionally for the images, there was no diffusion of responsibility through a division of labor or the delegation of tasks, and there were no collegial supports available at the scene. He was alone and separated from other officers, and although he experienced potent personal and professional demands to *do something,* he was effectively deprived of almost any sense of agency. The child's youth and perceived innocence certainly contributed to the trauma, as did the fact that he forged a connection while the child still lived: detectives almost always see the results of violent death after the fact, and the victims are invariably strangers. Occasions where detectives actually witness the death or interact with the victim in life (even so much as briefly looking into the victim's sentient eyes) are few, and these exposures are particularly toxic.

The same detective described another experience involving an especially powerful and objectively grotesque visual death imprint image that continued to haunt him and evoke deep emotions years later. He responded to an incident in which a young boy was killed and partially devoured by polar bears after entering their enclosure at the Prospect Park Zoo in Brooklyn. He described what he saw:

An angelic face, about a 9- or 10-year-old boy with a just paw mark here [*indicates left side of face*]. Everything was intact above the neck. His chest was like a surgeon ripped it open [*illustrates*] this way, and part of his internal organs had been eaten. And this leg [*indicates right leg*] was just bones. They had eaten all the flesh. No leg here [*indicates left leg*], this was pulled off and they [the bears] were in the den, they had eaten that [*indicates left leg*]. So you saw a boy, who from the head up was an angelic 9 or 10, maybe 11. [*Points to face.*] Paw mark. The chest opened like a surgeon. As if a surgeon had [*illustrates*]—instead of crossways, downward. No leg. Eaten away. I *had* to talk, I had to talk about that for 2 days. At that time I had 20 years on the job, and I'd been to a lot of scenes. It affected me and I wasn't, I hadn't been, I'd never seen *that.* [The commanding officer of the crime scene unit] said it was the worst he'd ever seen. But I *was* upset and I probably should have gone for counseling on that one. And in fact, I couldn't sleep for 2 nights.

He went on to relate that despite the bright lights illuminating the area and the intrusive presence of police, rats appeared and began eating the scattered pieces of flesh, an indignity that compounded the disintegrative nature of the imprint image and continued to disgust and torment him. Notwithstanding its capacity to generate compelling emotions after almost 15 years, what was perhaps most illustrative of the death imprint image's power and durability was the remarkable accuracy with which the detective recalled it: I'd seen photographs of the child's body in the crime scene unit's "family albums" about 2 weeks earlier, and the detective's description of the wounds' locations and the position of the boy's body was perfectly accurate. The wounds were precisely as he described them.

The death imprint images that had the most profound effect on collaborators and resulted in the strongest sense of commitment had in common the fact of immoderate identification with the deceased, who were further distinguished from run-of-the-mill homicide victims by their complete innocence. We've seen how easily cops denigrate and avoid identification with victims who bear some culpability in their own demise—sergeant, crime scene unit technician, and homicide detective collaborators all specifically mentioned how unperturbed they were when a drug dealer is murdered—but in each of the cases that affected a homicide detective deeply the victim was truly innocent. In keeping with another theme to emerge in our explorations, in many cases the victims were children or infants murdered under particularly brutal circumstances, including babies left abandoned to die.

Death Guilt

Death guilt is not a particularly prominent feature of the homicide detective's survivor experience, and this is largely attributable to the fact that in the vast majority of instances detectives effectively maintain a professional outlook and screen out especially toxic elements of the images they witness through partial professional numbing and adherence to cultural conventions of professional behavior. They can generally prevent disturbing images that might conjure profound forms of guilt from becoming even more powerful by infiltrating the personal sphere, and because they experience images through the objective lens of professional detachment their resulting impairment is minimal and largely confined to the professional sphere. Since they experience rather little impairment, homicide detectives can more easily make meaning of their work-related death encounters in a way that identifies the objectively guilty party.

The homicide detective's formative process of integrating and making sense of images is supported by various inductive and deductive logical processes and a body of physical and especially testimonial evidence that ultimately leads to firm cognitive judgments of guilt and innocence. The deliberate and methodical process of developing objective facts that clearly and convincingly establish the guilt of the responsible party and the innocence of others is the homicide detective's raison d'être, and we've seen how the process is fortified by formal and informal organizational and cultural practices. The investigative process of amassing and assessing objective facts leading to firm conclusions about guilt or innocence effectively precludes any lingering rational doubts the homicide detective may have about his own complicity in the crime. As reflected in the words of the homicide detective quoted above, from the beginning of the investigation they know they are not to blame and every investigative step they take from that point on is aimed at determining who *is* responsible. As is the case with crime scene unit technicians called to a scene after the victim has died, there is simply no rational reason for the homicide detectives to suppose his actions or inactions contributed to the death. The rational pole of the death guilt continuum thus has little bearing on our analysis of the homicide detective's survivor experience.

Homicide detectives may struggle a bit with the less rational but universal notion of survivor priority—traces of amorphous guilt accompanying the recognition that the survivor remains alive while another has died—but for the most part he becomes so immediately and deeply focused on the tasks and intellectual processes of investigation that he has little time to reflect or dwell on such issues. To whatever extent they do occupy him, the moral and ethical issues they raise are easily subsumed within the highly ethical professional quest to achieve justice. These thoughts do not inordinately impair him, and any sense of reciprocity this irrational form of death guilt conjures also finds appropriate enactment through the investigative process, the urge to make meaning, and the quest for justice. Death guilt does not substantially impair the homicide detective.

As we discussed in chapter 2's outline of survivor psychology, Lifton points out that regardless of the relative strength of one's sense of guilt, those who confront death universally feel the need to experience vitality through some form of appropriate enactment and to overcome devitalization through life-affirming connections. In the case of the homicide detective, the need for vitalizing connection with others is largely satisfied by the spirit of collegiality and teamwork that accompanies a homicide investigation, and the culture also provides other means of experiencing connection, movement, and integrity. Here again, we see how the informal norms and mores of the detective culture operate in a functional way to provide necessary support and nurturance in the face of stasis, separation, and disintegrative death encounters.

A basic tenet of survivor psychology is that the survivor inevitably experiences guilt, impairment, and a sense of devitalization leading to a struggle to reexperience himself as a vital and authentic human being. Depending upon the degree of impairment involved, the circumstances of the encounter, and a host of other subjective factors, the survivor may develop specific needs for emotional comfort and support. These needs can affect his relationships with others and can result in conflicts over autonomy and dependence. The survivor's need for emotional support and his sensitivity to issues of autonomy and dependence make him particularly sensitive to the motives and behaviors of those offering emotional sustenance: he becomes suspicious of counterfeit nurturance.

This theme was not particularly pronounced among homicide detectives. They experience little suspicion of counterfeit nurturance largely because they experience so little of the impairment and guilt that might result in substantial devitalization and emotional need, but also because relatively little nurturance is offered them. They may not expect and do not receive much nurturance, so they cannot experience it as counterfeit. Moreover, when other members of the detective culture do offer support, it is for the most part genuine and effective. This is not to say that other detectives will, on an individual basis, actively seek opportunities or means to identify his issues of devitalization or his vulnerabilities and seek to ease them through caring and compassionate response, but that other detectives may recognize and tacitly acknowledge his emotional difficulties in a manner that is consonant with the subculture's stoic ethos. It would be very unusual for one detective to illuminate another's emotional vulnerability through overtly compassionate public gestures or expressions. A far more common response would be a quiet and understated expression that implicitly recognizes the need without stating it and conveys support without requiring an acknowledgement of dependence. In a private setting, another detective (especially a partner) might, for example, put a hand on another's arm and ask, in a tone laden with significance, "Are you doing OK?" "Yeah, I'm fine." "If you need anything . . . " "I know. Thanks."

Due to the factors that minimize homicide detectives' impairment and guilt, a powerful sense of dependence or vulnerability rarely emerges. Detectives are aware that it can occur, though, and when they perceive it in another detective they have even greater respect for him. They know he has grappled with profound and personally consequential issues, they know the same issues might one day affect them ("There but for the grace of God go I . . . "), and they have the deepest respect for his struggle and his stoicism.

By participating in the collegial effort to solve the case and by upholding cultural values in various ways, the homicide detective experiences various authentic connections and relationships that mediate another feature related to the suspicion of counterfeit nurturance: the death taint. The universal tendency to perceive oneself (and be perceived) as tainted by death can be reinforced when others treat the survivor differently, especially when their behavior highlights his dependency and undermines his self-esteem. While the death taint often translates into hostility and resentment toward others, in the case of the homicide detective it paradoxically becomes a source of status. The homicide detective is certainly perceived as one tainted by death—both within and outside the police culture—but because he has achieved substantial mastery of death he is perceived as having some power over it. Many homicide detectives reify their special knowledge and power over death, transforming it in a positive way into a kind of survivor hubris or survivor exclusiveness that is vitalizing and immortalizing. We recall the words of the homicide detective cited above:

> I had gotten to a point—and I'm not bragging about this—there could be any homicide, I don't care what the circumstances were, I could handle it. I felt I could handle anything. With homicides, building up as you get more expertise in it, I felt that I could . . . I don't care who was murdered, I felt very comfortable handling the case. All aspects of it.

Just as we saw in chapter 2 that survivor hubris can lead to a fascination with death and to repeated flirtations with it to reinforce the magical sense of invulnerability, we find a variation on this theme among homicide detectives. Every collaborator articulated that he felt a palpable excitement or even joy upon learning that a homicide had occurred—not a perverted joy that someone had died, but an exhilaration at the prospect of once again becoming involved in a challenging formative effort. Part of the attraction is the opportunity to once again test his own mettle.

The attraction others have for the homicide detective's special knowledge and power over death can also be seen in the respectful and deferential way others treat him in social settings outside the police culture. Almost every homicide detective collaborator related that he is often the center of attention at parties or social events; most civilians are fascinated by the work homicide detectives do, and as one put it, "There can be chiefs, doctors, captains of industry. Everyone wants to talk to you."

We can easily comprehend how this immortalizing sense of power over death and this easy familiarity with death's mysteries shapes the homicide detective's sense of professional self, and we can see how his confidence can help maintain the viability of his formative process. It also serves as a special source of connection with other homicide detectives who share the power and as a source of professional status.

The Quest to Make Meaning

Throughout this chapter we've seen how homicide detectives make meaning of a death encounter through a complex formative process of integrating images to achieve forms and eventually constellations of meaning. The homicide detective's job, in essence, is to take in or experience various images, to cognitively order and logically analyze them, and to extract a more complete and comprehensive understanding of the event—it involves a quest to make cognitive meaning of the death. We've seen the complexity and difficulty that may be entailed, and we've seen how factors operating in the task environment and the detective culture influence the cognitive process as well as the event's impact on the homicide detective's sense of professional and personal self. We can thus explore this theme of survivor psychology on two levels: we can examine some of the specific cognitive processes involved (and in doing so flesh out the formative principles to which we've alluded), and we can explore how the quest to make meaning resonates at a deeper level to transform his professional and personal identity. We begin this section by examining in greater depth how homicide detectives make cognitive meaning from the array of complex images they experience while interacting with others before concluding with an example of how the struggle to make meaning operates in terms of the larger formative-symbolic paradigm. Specifically, we will conclude by looking at how difficult the struggle can become when especially powerful images infiltrate the personal sphere, impair formulation and devitalize the survivor, and lead to a compelling need—a survivor mission—that seeks to reconstruct the images in a way that reasserts a sense of vitality. The experience of the homicide detective whose survivor mission we will explore ties together many of the themes of survivor psychology and many of the principles of the formative-symbolic paradigm.

When detectives undertake a homicide investigation they are generally more concerned with the information they receive through interaction with others than with physical evidence. The recovery and interpretation of physical evidence can be an important part of the investigation, but physical evidence also falls within the province of the crime scene unit technician, the laboratory analyst, or the medical examiner. Homicide detectives' reputations are not built on their skillful handling of physical clues, and physical evidence alone is often insufficient to obtain a confession. To develop a prosecutable case and build or maintain their reputations and status, homicide detectives typically want to obtain a valid and voluntary confession, so interviewing and interrogation skills take on a special importance. In terms of survivor psychology, valid and voluntary confessions are also important because they give the detective a kind of closure by entirely eliminating any residual guilty feelings of responsibility for the death.

Effective interviewing and interrogation typically involves some degree of strategic manipulation and tactical deception (Skolnick and Leo, 1992)—if only to the extent that detectives take in much more information than they reveal and must be careful not to betray surprise or other reactions—and it helps to be a good actor. The detective's ultimate goal of eliciting information may also require that he operate, almost simultaneously, on multiple cognitive levels. He must follow the interviewee's narrative while proficiently directing its uninterrupted flow, sort objective facts from opinions and surmise, and assess these pieces of information in light of the physical evidence and other objectively verified facts. He must listen carefully for implied or overt contradictions and factual inconsistencies at the same time he remains open to the subtle cues of body language and verbal intonation that may indicate deception. He must do all this while appearing focused on the individual and without betraying the suspicions, deeper analytic thoughts, or doubts that might impede the narrative flow. The overall idea is often to lull the subject into a sense of comfort so that he commits to a particular factual pattern that the detective will subsequently dismantle by identifying inconsistencies (Hess, 1997; Inbau, Reid, and Buckley, 1985).

Interviewing and interrogation are complex arts, and although numerous books, manuals, and articles have been written about investigative interview methods and strategies, they provide a general kind of guidance at best. The arts of interviewing and interrogation are best learned through the application of experience gained by observing other skilled detectives. With time and experience, proficient detectives develop the Zen-like capacity to "read" a subject in much the same way as crime scene unit technicians "read" a scene: immediate images fit (or don't fit) within a larger constellation that provides meaning at the same time it presents various schemas for enactment. They are totally focused in the moment yet completely attentive to all the details—an experience that can be transcendent. The complex cognitive processes involved in an effective and successful investigative interview—processes that include the ability to continually shift attention while remaining open to subtle images and other bits of information—provide the detective with a degree of distance from his interlocutor. He may appear to be fully engaged in the conversation and may seem quite solicitous and sympathetic, but especially at the early stages of an investigation he is always mindful of the fact that the subject may become a suspect, and this and other thoughts are always operating in the background.

A good example of one complex cognitive process—essentially, a meaning-making process—is illustrated in the practice of forensic psycholinguistics (Smith and Shuy, 2002). This is, in essence, what one homicide squad supervisor described as "listening for distortions in individual linguistic patterns" to identify deception, inconsistency, and "hot buttons" that may later be exploited to obtain additional information or gain a confession. Each of us, he pointed out, has particular speech patterns or mannerisms that characterize our communication with others, and anomalies in the patterns are often indicative of some deception or psychological stress. By way of illustration, he produced the typed transcript of an actual interview and pointed out some odd phrases and responses.

The subject of the transcribed interview, the mother of a child found murdered several days earlier, responded to several questions in a way that, upon reflection, seemed unusual but not patently evasive or untrue. Throughout the course of the interview, for example, she never referred to her murdered child by name but did mention the names of other children and repeatedly (but without prompting) gave their ages. After answering a series of fairly innocuous questions with a definitive "yes," she responded to a more sensitive question with an "uh huh" before volunteering information that was not entirely germane to the question. She did not speak of an urge to find out *who* killed her child, but rather of a need to find out *why* such a terrible thing happened so that she could find closure. The detective pointed out that none of these things, in themselves, pointed to evasiveness, guilt, or involvement in the crime, but one might legitimately consider whether they seemed typical of the responses we might expect from the innocent mother of a murdered child. The skilled interviewer must be able to discern these very subtle linguistic anomalies and consider them in light of other more probative facts to create a larger and more comprehensive picture of her and of the crime as a whole. These latent linguistic anomalies were difficult enough to pick up from a typed transcript, but the expert homicide detective has to be able to pick them up almost contemporaneous with their utterance during a highly emotional encounter and immediately incorporate them with other more obvious images to fill out a larger constellation of meaning.

The art of interview and interrogation involves what is essentially a very complex formative process of attending to and integrating an array of images, and the process is further complicated by the legal issues involved. To be admissible as evidence, a confession must be valid and voluntary, and the information a suspect provides should also be objectively verifiable. Detectives apply various legal decisions enshrined in case law to ensure the confession is valid and voluntary, and because case law sets forth broad principles rather than bright-line standards he must assess and apply complex abstractions as part of the formative process.

Good homicide detectives are also acutely aware of the power of images, and so they manipulate these images in various ways. They make the detective mystique, especially those elements that contribute to the perception that they are crafty, all-knowing individuals who "always get their man," work to their advantage. For example, one homicide detective pointed out that he always prefaced an interrogation by confidently telling the suspect that the "interview" the detective was about to conduct (the word *interrogation* has connotations that are to be avoided) would inarguably prove the suspect's innocence or his guilt. Detectives generally "set the stage" in an interrogation room by removing superfluous items and images that might distract the suspect, but they may also prominently display items of physical evidence or photographs (or dramatically produce them at an appropriate moment) if they believe the display will have a desired psychological impact. They also use the science of proxemics to gain a psychological advantage, physically moving in from the suspect's "social zone" (generally, more than 4 feet) to his "personal zone" (between 4 feet and 18 inches) and finally into his "intimate zone" (less than 18 inches) as the interrogation proceeds and intensifies—as one homicide detective put it, "I want to move in so close our knees are touching." Detectives remove symbolic barriers (such as tables and desks) between themselves and the suspect, and effective interrogators insist that the suspect must be seated in a straight-backed chair with no arms—some even prefer to give the suspect a chair that wobbles—while they generally sit in armed chairs that are larger, taller, and more comfortable. Even as they implement these tactics and flexibly respond to new information and changing interpersonal dynamics, homicide detectives must be certain to stay within the boundaries of legally permissible psychological suasion as defined by a continually evolving body of case law. The days of the so-called third degree involving the physical or psychological abuse of suspects are definitely over— indeed, elite homicide detectives pride themselves on their ability to lawfully elicit information without resorting to any sort of physical intimidation or threats—but to some extent the bare interrogation room itself may conjure disconcerting images of detectives with rolled-up shirtsleeves standing over a sweating suspect and shining a bright light in his eyes to compel a confession.

Homicide detectives use these and other techniques to facilitate their own formative process and to impede or diminish the subject's attempts at formulation. They may, for example, ask a suspect to begin his narrative at the middle or end and work backward to gauge his veracity—it is far easier to describe in reverse order images one has actually experienced than to sequentially track and relate fabrications in the same way. The point here is that homicide detectives are highly dependent upon and acutely aware of the formative process as it relates to mentation and cognitive function. They know the power of images and manipulate them with great dexterity.

At quite another level, homicide detectives are also aware—often through their own experiences—of the basic themes of survivor psychology and the dimensions of the formative-symbolic paradigm. They certainly do not approach this knowledge in a systematic fashion but they are keenly aware that the powerful images they encounter in their work have the potential to change them personally and professionally. Although they struggle to maintain firm control over powerful images to prevent their intrusion upon core elements of the personal or professional self, there can be occasions when this struggle fails. One outcome of the transformation can be the emergence of a survivor mission. Like every other theme of survivor psychology among homicide detectives, the survivor mission is mediated and shaped by the immediate circumstances of the death encounter, the task environment, and the detective culture.

Powerful death images can easily debilitate the survivor and substantially impair his formative process, so part of his ongoing struggle involves a compelling need to master and reconstruct them in a way that reasserts the vitalizing sense of immortality. The survivor can become mired in death imagery—both the immediate images of separation, stasis, and disintegration he faces and the unresolved images and death-equivalent states the death encounter reactivates—so he needs to reformulate them, repair the formative process, and experience vitalizing images of connection, movement, and integrity. The survivor who fails to move beyond the death imprint by recapturing his vitality and achieving some appropriate form of enactment remains in a static pattern of guilt and impairment.

One homicide detective collaborator found his way out of this static pattern by devoting himself—personally and professionally—to solving a murder. His obsessive and as-yet-unresolved quest to find justice for the victim and her mother—the case remains unsolved after more than a decade—has prolonged his struggle, but it nevertheless permits him to continually experience a vitalizing sense of personal and professional connection, movement, and integrity. Not long before he caught this particular case, the detective experienced a profound sense of personal renewal when he recognized his alcoholism and began to recover from it. In many respects the alcoholic lifestyle represents the death equivalent states of separation, stasis, and disintegration, and like many recovering alcoholics he also sought the means to experience a new and uplifting sense of vitality that might in some way atone for his past, expiate his guilt, and repair his damaged sense of self. Sobriety, he said, "Was a gift given to me—the best thing I ever did in my life. I got a lot of strength out of it. I was able to meet the demon. My life was changed." Like any consequential gift, sobriety activated a constellation involving feelings of reciprocity and he felt the urge, as he put it, "to give something back." The murder of an innocent young woman presented a signal opportunity to do just that. He wholeheartedly embraced the case and forged both a strong connection with and a commitment to the victim as well as to a secondary victim. He did not know that despite his best efforts the case would remain unsolved, and he didn't know his quest would become what some might characterize as an obsession.

His experience vividly portrays and ties together many of the themes we've explored. The homicide's impact was intensified and personalized by virtue of the victim's innocence, by the fact that the crime took place a few days before the Christmas holiday (generally a happy time of connection with family and friends), by the fact that he made the death notification himself and his consequent connection with the victim's mother, and by the unique intimacy of the relationship he developed with the victim and her mother. He arrived at the scene—in a remote area frequented by drug addicts—and found a dead female in her early twenties with no identification on her person.

> My first reaction was, it's a junkie or prostitute. I wasn't too concerned about solving it at the time. I thought "Well, we're not going to get much on this one." The ME came and took off the ligature and opened up her clothing. We were looking at the body and the ME said, "Detective, we have a well-nourished girl here. She's probably from the neighborhood." I was looking at her and my reaction is changing because as I'm looking at the girl I'm thinking "Wow, this is an innocent victim." As detectives, we look at victims differently. You look at a dead Colombian drug dealer and don't really give a shit but you've got to do what you've got to do. And then you've got the innocent victim where you're going to care about it.

After completing necessary on-scene tasks the detective and his partners went back to the office to try to identify the victim and plan the investigation. Shortly thereafter he was notified that a woman called the precinct to report her daughter missing. The physical description and clothing matched the victim's.

> I knew I had to make the notification and that was the hardest notification of my life because I know, I know this is an innocent victim. I drove out there [to the girl's mother's home] and I said to [my partner], "Man, I don't want to do this." As I'm walking in I didn't know what I was going to say, and I said a prayer. I said a prayer.[19] Unrehearsed, I took her [the mother's] hand and I said, "Do you believe in God?" "Yes." "Sit down." I'm holding her hand and she started to shake and I started to shake and I said, "What I'm about to tell you is the worst thing you can tell a mother." She picked up a glass ashtray and threw it across the room and shattered a mirror. She went crazy. She was hugging me and crying. "Is she dead? Is she dead?" and I said, "Yes." It was a tough notification because it was an innocent victim.

He embraced the case fully, and the opportunity to work on it exclusively for an unusually long period of time allowed his to solidify his relationship with the victim and her mother. The intimacy of that relationship was the basis for a deep sense of commitment, and he knew that by indulging in this closeness he broke all the established rules that help detectives keep their work from invading their personal sphere.

The case took on a life of its own. I was off the chart about 6 weeks on it.[20] I'd visit her mother every day. I spoke with all her friends. I was given her diary, and I was given the opportunity to go through her closet. I learned everything about her life, her education, her boyfriends, her sex life, what she thought about herself, and she became like a partner to me.[21] And her mother would call every day and say, "[His first name], did you follow up on this?" What happened was I made a mistake. I gave her too much but by then it was too late and I couldn't stop giving her information. To this day she calls me at least once a month. . . . It became like the case of my career, where I could give all my energy to this and nothing else. . . . I came to a point after about 2 years where I had to let go of it a bit. I wanted to solve it. I was in a rage that this was done to her.

We've earlier seen how officers going through a deceased person's belongings experience feelings that they are invading the person's privacy, and we've seen how this can engender some guilt and shame. In this case, the homicide detective (a man of deep religious faith) reified the experience, permitting it to infiltrate his core self in a way that further solidified his connection and commitment to her. I asked him how he felt going through her diary and learning all these things about her.

I felt like a priest. Like confession. I was careful with a squad full of guys to keep it to myself. Keep it in a corner where they wouldn't read it. I felt like I was invading her privacy, and I have to keep it private. And I believe she knows I'm working on it. Its weird, but I think she knows I'm here trying to do the right thing by her.

The crusade to solve the case became both a professional quest and a personal one, and it proved deeply liberating in both spheres. It gave him the professional opportunity to pursue justice for an innocent victim, it became an opportunity for exploration of self and a vehicle for movement and growth, and it allowed him the latitude to assert his personal feelings and convictions in a professionally acceptable way. In particular—and largely because he broke the detectives' unwritten rules about allowing emotions to infiltrate one's personal life—he experienced a profound sense of personal and professional integrity.

It was a growing experience for me. It was good for my sobriety. I was able to show—as cops we don't show any emotion and I think I showed a lot of emotion in this. It hurt me but in a positive way. That I was able to mourn for somebody that I didn't know. The whole thing was very good for me. . . . Being honest. Looking at my fears. It was a growing experience to be honest with the victim's family. To say [to the victim's mother], "Look, this is what we have, and I'm working my balls off and I'm not going to give you any excuses." If I ever solve it, it will be the culmination of my career.

VH: *Why is it the most important case of your career?*

[*Pause.*] Because she was an innocent victim, because of my interaction with her family, because it was around the holidays, because I was able to get into her life like I have never gotten into a person's life before, and because it became personal and homicides are not supposed to be personal things for detectives. It certainly became a personal thing.

VH: *Do you regret that?*

No. It will be the only one that will be personal with me, but I don't regret it at all. It was a good thing for me and it still is.

The detective's professional commitment to the case was also made clear by the fairly extreme investigative steps he pursued and the fact that his case file of DD-5s fills 6 bulging folders. Among other things, he traced the lot numbers on snack food wrappers found at the scene back to the neighborhood bodegas where they were sold and interviewed proprietors and customers, he identified and interviewed graffiti artists whose "tags" were left in the vicinity, and he even went so far as to contact NASA to determine whether satellite photographs might have been taken of the area that day. The fact that he pursued the investigation so vigorously was not lost on his fellow detectives, and their respect for him as a detective and as an individual is evident in the backhanded compliments they continually give him.

He continues to work on the case after almost a decade, and although he's stepped back from it a bit he still speaks with the victim's mother at least once each month. His wife and family know all the details of the case, his children have written college papers about it ("this is Daddy's case and he's going to get the guy"), and his wife accompanied him to a memorial service he attended at the victim's high school a few years ago. He speaks of the victim in endearing terms, and says he would have liked her—she was a person who was quiet and thoughtful but had a bit of a wild streak, and he says that is something he can identify with. Although the area where the murder took place has since been fenced off, he returns there all the time. "Every partner I've worked with since then has been to the scene. Looking for what? I don't know. But I keep going back."

8.

Police Survivors

Genuine Threats to the Sense of Immortality

In this chapter we consider the formative-symbolic paradigm and the themes of survivor psychology as they are reflected in the experiences of police survivors—officers who have had the most profound kind of line-of-duty encounter with their own mortality. The officers in each of the nominal categories and corresponding task environments we've thus far considered have all had death encounters that to some extent affected them personally and professionally, and in this regard they all conform to Lifton's definition of a survivor: they've come in close contact with death in some physical or psychic fashion but managed to remain alive (1967, p. 479). We've seen how the themes and features of survivor psychology, mediated by their task environment and the ethos of their occupational culture and subculture, become manifest in their attitudes, belief systems, behaviors, and worldview. We've seen how these death experiences changed their sense of self, often in powerful and lasting ways. To varying extent, and depending greatly upon the specific circumstances involved as well as the demands and constraints of their task environment and a host of subjective factors, each encounter challenged their sense of immortality and reminded them, at some level of consciousness, of their own mortality.

The cops we consider now are also survivors, but their death encounters and the manifestations of survivor psychology that result from those encounters are of an entirely different order than we've previously seen. Officers in the other categories and task environments encountered the deaths of *others*—typically strangers with whom they had no preexisting relationship or implicit sense of connection—and therefore experienced those deaths in a relatively impersonal way. Any death encounter serves to remind us of our own mortality, but a close and highly personalized encounter that entails the realistic prospect of our own demise brings the specter of our own death into considerably sharper focus. The officers whose death encounters we explore in this chapter have had an eminently more profound and personally consequential immersion in death as the result of having witnessed or participated in a mortal combat situation that raised the objectively realistic prospect of *their own* mortality. These cops faced the authentic and genuine possibility of their own death in mortal combat with an armed adversary, they witnessed the death of another officer or partner, or they took a life in the performance of police duties. Their experiences differ from those of the others primarily in terms of the extreme closeness and personal significance of their physical and psychic contact with death. While cops in the other categories and task environments experienced *exposures* to the deaths of others involving images of disintegration, separation, and stasis, these police survivors experienced a more complete and thorough *immersion* in death involving powerful death imagery that radically challenged their sense of biological and symbolic immortality.

Our explorations and our attempts to make sense of police survivors' experiences are much more complex endeavors than we have undertaken in previous chapters. For one thing, these officers' experiences were not shaped by the inherent demands, constraints, and possibilities of a particular task environment: they encountered a profound and objectively life-threatening death immersion while operating in a variety of assignments and while engaged in a broad range of police duties. There is a staunchly held belief in contemporary urban policing that almost any cop working in almost any assignment at almost any time can encounter circumstances leading to a mortal combat situation. This shared reality or conventional wisdom is closely tied to the cop's perception of pervasive danger in the world around him and to the construct of the symbolic assailant, and it is so central to the police identity that it is virtually futile to engage cops in dialogue in hopes of changing it. Knowledge—really a "middle knowledge" that officers fail to fully act upon—of this shared conventional reality resonates deeply throughout the police organization and the police culture, and it resonates deeply at a personal level as well. As we observed in earlier chapters, this dangerous knowledge shapes cops' behaviors and their sense of self in complex ways, and because it is shared by cops it becomes a cohesive source of individual and group identity among members of the police culture. For police survivors of the close and personally meaningful encounters we consider in this chapter, this middle knowledge of death and danger is no longer a transitory abstraction submerged at some lower level of consciousness—their death immersion has transformed it into a fully perceptible reality they have squarely faced and continue to recognize.

The fact that we have no single task environment with which to structure our inquiries poses a bit of a problem, but it is by no means the only difficulty we face. A related difficulty lies in the fact that these potent death immersions can and do take place under so many vastly different situations and circumstances. A cop can be thrust into an objectively life-threatening situation while engaged in the most routine and banal police activities—sitting in a radio car reading a newspaper, for example—or the most extraordinary and electrifying—for example, following a prolonged foot pursuit of a criminal he knows is armed and dangerous—but regardless of his level of physical and emotional arousal the mortal combat encounter almost invariably takes him by surprise, overwhelming his formative capacity to fully integrate the images he experiences. The compelling traumatic power of the images presented in these deadly situations is such that virtually no amount of anticipation or psychological preparation can adequately equip a cop to elude or mediate their immediate and lasting psychic impact.

These life-threatening encounters are precisely the kind of "messy," inchoate, highly variable, and uniquely "hot, frantic, hair-raising, lurid and insane" events to which van Maanen (1980, p. 146) refers, and we recall his observation that although these events confound our efforts to neatly classify them, attempts to make meaning of them are nevertheless undertaken at the individual, collegial, and organizational levels. An array of deadly weapons and instruments of violence may be brought to bear against the cop—guns and knives being the most common—and he may face one or multiple adversaries. The cop may be alone or with a partner, on duty or off, in uniform or plain clothes. The event may take place indoors or outdoors, at night or during the day. The officer can be a tenured and highly experienced veteran or a callow rookie. The cop and his adversary may be yards apart or they may be desperately grappling in a sweaty hand-to-hand struggle to seize control of the same weapon. The officer may be gravely injured, he may witness the death or severe injury of a partner, or he may emerge physically unscathed (Pinnizotto, Davis, and Miller, 1997). He may intentionally or accidentally take a human life (Vasquez, 1985). He may deliberately try to take a human life and fail. The entire incident typically unfolds in just a few seconds, but the particular events that transpire immediately before or after the encounter can easily exacerbate its traumatic potential in highly subjective and unpredictable ways. He may encounter the phenomenon known as "suicide by cop," in which a suicidal or disturbed individual essentially forces or provokes an officer to kill him during a violent encounter (Harruff, Llewellen, Clark, and Hawley, 1994; Hardaway, Russell, Strote, Cantor, and Blum, 1998).

What these encounters *do* have in common is their objective capacity to result in the officer's death—to challenge his sense of immortality in some of the most fundamental ways imaginable—and the fact that the officer managed to physically survive the encounter. Of all the categories of cops we consider, these police survivors of mortal combat are, in terms of the psychology of survival's themes and manifestations, the truest and most authentic survivors. Because their death immersion is so complete, and because their experiences were not mediated through a single task environment, the manifestations of survivor psychology among police survivors can take many different forms. Because their death immersion is so complete and their experiences are so psychologically compelling, the manifestations of survivor psychology are also considerably more pronounced among police survivors than among other categories of cops we have considered. As authentic survivors whose transformative death encounter images and experiences have penetrated to the very core of their identity, the features of survivor psychology are more readily discerned in their behavior and more actively articulated in their narratives. At the same time, the themes and features of survivorship often intertwine in complex ways, making it somewhat difficult to disentangle and explore the expressions of a particular theme without making reference to other themes and their manifestations.

Because the police survivor's death immersions can take place under so many varied circumstances and can involve so many objective and subjective variables, and because we lack a single definable task environment with which to structure our inquiries in hopes of making sense of their experiences, we adopt a slightly different approach to this chapter's explorations. We begin with a brief review of some objective statistical data concerning the actual incidence of mortal combat involving NYPD officers, following it with a substantially abbreviated recapitulation of the factual circumstances surrounding one officer's line-of-duty death. This explanatory vignette hints at some of the ways an officer's murder is experienced by individual survivors, but more importantly it sheds some light on collegial interpretations and cultural meanings as well as formal organizational responses to a line-of-duty death. Every cop in the agency subjectively experiences and interprets the death at an individual level, but by virtue of their preexisting relationship with the murdered officer and their identification with the circumstances surrounding his death, members of his command are particularly affected by it. All the murdered cop's coworkers are in a sense police survivors, but some—most notably his partner and those actually present to witness the death—can be expected to be the most profoundly affected and to most actively manifest the features of survivor psychology. This admittedly cursory outline of the event's impact at the cultural and organizational levels serves as a rough sketch or template that informs our understanding of typical police reactions to an entirely atypical event. By framing our explorations in this way, we can more easily turn our attention to the experiences of police survivor collaborators and see how the themes of survivor psychology affect them and their subsequent lives. We can also better appreciate how cultural and organizational responses shape their experience.

The Incidence of Mortal Combat Situations

In the interests of objectivity it must once again be said that in a purely empirical sense, cops' perceptions of the realistic threats to their own mortality are somewhat exaggerated. Police work is inarguably dangerous, and for many of the reasons we've discussed in previous chapters the deaths of other officers or the serious injuries other officers suffer through instrumental criminal violence certainly register deeply with individual officers and within their culture. The perceived dangers of police work, as Skolnick (1966) and others (Westley, 1956, 1970) have described at length, are a source of cohesion among cops and an article of faith within their cultural ethos, but the actuarial probability that an individual officer will be killed or severely injured in the line of duty or will kill another person in the line of duty is low. Officers in operational enforcement assignments, in particular, may frequently encounter objectively dangerous situations that could easily escalate to the point that they involve the use of deadly physical force, but in reality police officers usually exercise tremendous restraint and these situations only rarely escalate to the level of a true mortal combat situation. Virtually every cop can point to one or more encounters where he "almost" killed someone (i.e., he came very close to using deadly physical force readily capable of causing another person's death), but few have ever actually killed in the line of duty. These highly subjective "almost" situations are psychologically important, especially because some can have a psychic impact almost as formidable as actual mortal combat, but they are less essential to our analysis than the situations in which someone— an officer, an adversary, or an innocent person—actually dies in a deadly force encounter involving a cop.

A rough idea of an NYPD officer's actuarial likelihood of becoming involved in bona fide mortal combat can be gleaned from a brief review of the agency's annual firearms discharge report (the SOP-9 report), which recapitulates statistical trend data specifically for shooting incidents. These data confirm the fact that, notwithstanding some statistical variance from year to year, the level of deadly violence involving NYPD officers has declined substantially and steadily in recent years. For example, in 1971 NYPD officers shot and wounded 221 adversaries, killing 93 of them, but only 32 adversaries were shot and wounded and only 11 were killed in 1999. Fifty NYPD officers were shot by perpetrators in 1973, but only four were shot by perpetrators in 1999. Thirteen NYPD officers were killed by perpetrators in 1971, but only 3 were murdered in 1998 and none were shot and killed in 1999 (although 1 died after being struck by a speeding vehicle as he directed traffic at the scene of an accident).[1] These data should also be viewed in light of the fact that there were approximately 10,000 fewer officers employed by the NYPD in 1971 than in 1999 (NYPD, 1970–2000).

The SOP-9 report for calendar year 2000 reveals that a total of 155 firearms discharges took place in 1999, a 38 percent decrease from 1998, when 249 such incidents occurred. This statistic reflects every instance where an officer discharged his weapon, including 37 accidental discharges, 43 incidents involving dogs attacking an officer or civilian, 4 police suicides, 1 attempted suicide and 8 "other" incidents not involving a criminal event. Clearly, the majority of these discharges (about 60 percent) do not involve mortal combat situations (NYPD, 2000).

Of the more than 40,000 sworn members of the agency in 1999, only 36 were involved in a total of 20 gunfights (defined as "any incident during which both the perpetrator and the member of the service fired their weapons at each other") in 1999. These gunfights resulted in the deaths of 2 adversaries, and 6 adversaries were wounded; fewer than half the actual gunfights, then, resulted in a death or injury. Thirteen of the officers involved in gunfights were assigned to uniformed radio motor patrol, 5 to plainclothes anticrime patrol, 4 were off duty, and the remainder were performing other enforcement duties (NYPD, 1999).

In 1999, a total of 56 officers were involved in 41 incidents where an officer fired a weapon but the perpetrator(s) did not return fire. Again, a preponderance of these cops (26) were performing uniformed radio motor patrol duties; 13 were performing plainclothes anticrime duties, 10 were off duty, 5 were in undercover assignments, and 2 were on foot patrol. Nine of these perpetrators were killed and 26 were shot and injured.

In 1999, a total of 54 officers were involved in 47 incidents in which one or more officers were assaulted by perpetrators armed with a weapon (including a firearm), but the officers did not use their service weapons to subdue the assailant(s). Forty of the officers were injured; 7 were shot, 10 were struck by vehicles, 3 were cut by knives, and the remainder were injured with various other objects (NYPD, 1999).

Clearly, and without minimizing the importance of the collateral psychological impact other less deadly violent encounters have upon officers, these shooting incident data show that NYPD officers engage in far fewer mortal combat situations than one might imagine. While mortal combat situations arise infrequently and line-of-duty deaths are relatively rare nowadays, we cannot ignore their capacity to galvanize cops' attention and the depth to which they infiltrate the agency and culture.

Important methodological and ethical considerations also arise from the fact that line-of-duty mortal combat shootings and deaths of officers are relatively rare. Since the death or severe injury of a police officer commands other cops' attention, NYPD cops are quite likely to be familiar with the facts and circumstances surrounding a particular case. It is thus virtually impossible to describe all the relevant facts of a given encounter without a de facto identification of the officer(s) involved and without implicating the assurance of confidentiality I gave to collaborators. I could not, for example, credibly maintain confidentiality if I referred to an officer who, although paralyzed and confined to a wheelchair as the result of grievous injuries sustained when a young man shot him, took up a survivor mission involving deep religious faith and forgiveness: every cop (and many members of the general public) would immediately know the officer is Steven MacDonald. The dilemma—whether to provide particular factual data that are important to their narratives and ultimately to our understanding of survivor psychology or to uphold the pledge of confidentiality—can only have one ethical outcome: at various points throughout this chapter I've summarized and abridged substantive facts or elided important details that might tend to identify a particular collaborator. Although this may have detracted in some small way from a more comprehensive and nuanced understanding of their survivor narratives, the experiences are sufficiently compelling in their own right to accurately represent the themes of survivor psychology without further elaboration. At no point, though, did I insert deceptive or misleading facts to actively mask a collaborator's identity.

Collegial and Official Reactions to Line-of-Duty Death

As we discussed earlier, every officer identifies to some degree with the cop who is killed in the line of duty, and the extent of identification can be magnified by various features of the death. Recalling van Maanen's (1980) observation that three versions—official, collegial, and individual subjective versions—of the deadly force encounter are constructed and communicated throughout the agency and its occupational culture, we are also reminded that these versions can differ substantially from each other in terms of the amount of objective truth they contain and the extent to which they convey meaningful symbols and images.

Official versions of a line-of-duty death reflect the formal organizational needs and the values it publicly espouses, and they are usually carefully crafted so as not to assign any blame to the deceased officer or suggest any complicity in his own demise. We must understand that the death of a police officer presents the agency with a range of difficult legal, public-relations, and employee-relations issues. Public statements that could be construed as imputing an officer's potential errors or culpability would certainly be interpreted within the police culture as an affront to the officer's sacred memory and a denigration of his sacrifice, and the same statements might later be introduced at a criminal trial or in a civil liability lawsuit against the agency. Although statements released to the media inevitably involve some public-relations spin, internal official versions tend to be dry recitations of fact.[2]

In sharp contrast to the official versions, collegial narratives capture and convey the horrors of the event from a cop's perspective, and they emphasize cultural values and belief systems. Some line-of-duty deaths become the stuff of legend and cautionary tales because their objective horror fundamentally challenges cops' individual and collective sense of immortality, its various modes of expression, and the immortality systems that sustain cops and their culture. Others become part of the enduring cultural narrative because they convey fundamental lessons or represent belief systems in an especially dramatic or culturally meaningful way. By examining a well-documented line-of-duty death we can identify several themes that resonate at the individual, cultural, and organizational levels.

Almost every NYPD cop knows about the February 1988 murder of police officer Edward Byrne, whose death conveys powerful images and symbols of stasis, disintegration, and separation and ultimately became emblematic of a new and especially pernicious form of evil. His death is admittedly an extreme example of the impact a line-of-duty death has on individual cops, their culture, and their agency, but its very extremity captures in an especially revealing way the patterns of response and the organizational dynamics that play out in the aftermath of a cop's murder.

Eddie Byrne, a 22-year-old rookie sitting alone and in uniform in a marked radio car during a midnight tour, was guarding the home of a drug trial witness when he was deliberately and cold-bloodedly assassinated at the behest of a recently jailed drug dealer. Using a jailhouse telephone, the drug dealer ordered that a uniformed officer—any uniformed officer—be randomly murdered as a way of expressing the dealer's contempt for the justice system, to intimidate potential witnesses, and to reassert the dealer's presence on the street (Fried, 1988b; "Witness Says Revenge," 1989; Dunlap 1989). Witnesses later testified the dealer who put out the $8,000 "contract" casually told them, "That's the way it goes. They get one of ours, we get one of theirs" (Fried, 1988b, 1989a, 1989b). The killers drove up behind Byrne, exited their vehicle and shot him five times in the head with a large-caliber handgun (Fried, 1988a). News of his murder, which came at a time of emerging public concern about the lawlessness and violence accompanying the so-called crack epidemic, captured national attention and appeared on the front pages of newspapers of record from coast to coast (Fried, 1988a; "Officer Guarding Witness Slain," 1988).

Beyond the fact of Byrne's youth and perceived innocence, cops identify with him because at one time or another almost all have had the experience of sitting alone and bored on a midnight "fixer" (Lyall, 1988a), and every cop has probably dozed or otherwise dropped his guard on such routine and prosaic assignments. To be caught unawares in this way, of course, violates the cardinal rule that a good cop must always be attentive to his surroundings and alert to the presence of real or symbolic assailants, and so to some extent their identification stimulates an amorphous sense of residual guilt at their own professional lapses and perhaps some defensiveness.[3] The callous brutality, seeming randomness, and lack of coherent reason for his death also reinforce the police officer's perception of the pervasive and unidentifiable danger that is inherent in their work, fitting easily within this constellation. As one officer put it, "It could have happened to anyone out there, any time" (Lyall, 1988a).

The circumstances of Eddie Byrne's death also defy cops' meaning-making processes because they do not easily fit with their preconceived notions or constellations of how and why a line-of-duty death *should* occur: Byrne was not involved in the kind of "real police work" cops readily associate with objective danger, drug dealers are not "supposed" to have uniformed cops assassinated by hired hit men,[4] and the unprecipitated nature of the ambush gave him no warning and therefore no chance to respond by actualizing a schema for enactment. In this sense the death is especially unacceptable and disintegrative because he was deprived of the important opportunity to defend himself and to respond courageously to a recognized threat—one theme that emerges from cops' renditions of his death involves horror at the fact that Byrne never even had the opportunity to draw his weapon. In essence, the cowardly ambush rendered him a more complete and more humiliated victim—anathema to cops and to the professional identity that sets them apart from (and somewhat superior to) victims—and deprived him of the opportunity to recapture some elements of immortality by dying a more legitimate hero's death. It is also important to note that Byrne was the son of a retired NYPD lieutenant (James, 1988), a traumatic element of biological discontinuity that all can recognize but that is perhaps particularly challenging and meaningful to officers participating in policing's "family tradition" immortality system.

We can see how his murder involves potent and obvious images of stasis (sitting for hours in a parked radio car in an assignment that did not develop significant police skills or move him closer to a reputation as a "good cop," as well as being unable to move out of the line of fire), disintegration (multiple gunshots to the head grotesquely mutilated his corpse), and separation (he died alone on a quiet street in the early morning hours, unable to even call for assistance on the radio). Although the specific circumstances implicating these subparadigms are particularly relevant in the police sphere, they also have a more universal appeal: even those members of the public with little knowledge or understanding of police work or police culture can easily grasp the symbolism and identify with the objective horror of Byrne's death. This may partially explain the tremendous public and media attention his death generated at the local and national levels ("Thousands Mourn Slain NY Policeman," 1988; Lyall, 1988), and why his death ultimately became a powerful symbol of the social evils associated with drug abuse ("Murder of Rookie Officer Inspires Anti-Drug Drives," 1992).

As part of his own survivor mission, Byrne's father became politically active on behalf of stronger drug laws and presented President George Bush with a copy of his son's shield, which the president kept on his desk in the Oval Office. Bush often invoked Byrne's name and displayed the shield during "get tough on crime" antidrug speeches (Weintraub, 1989), the Department of Justice named its $3.2 billion law enforcement grant program after him, the house he was guarding was turned into a community center named for him, the street in front of his precinct was renamed in his honor, and a local park was dedicated in his memory (Fried, 1990; *New York Times*, 1992). Byrne's death also became the impetus for the agency's creation of a new drug enforcement initiative—the catchily named "tactical narcotics teams" or TNT—in which several hundred officers were assigned to aggressive street narcotics enforcement. The initiative began in the South Jamaica neighborhood where Byrne was killed and was later expanded to other neighborhoods citywide (Anderson, 1992). Byrne's posthumous medal of honor—the agency's highest decoration for heroism—was presented to his parents at the department's annual Medal Day ceremony, a bronze memorial plaque bearing his likeness and shield was ceremoniously installed at the 103rd Precinct next to similar plaques honoring other members of the precinct killed in the line of duty, and his name was inscribed in the Hall of Heroes in the lobby of police headquarters (Dunlap, 1989; Fried, 1990). Cops throughout the city wore black mourning bands across their shields, and those who knew or worked with him affixed unauthorized blue "In Memory of PO Edward Byrne" breast bars to their rack of medals. More than 10,000 cops from the NYPD and agencies as far away as Texas attended his funeral to demonstrate their connection and esteem, creating a six-man-deep line of blue that stretched for more than eight city blocks (Lyall, 1988b).[5]

We can imagine, in the broadest terms, the kind of personal impact Eddie Byrne's death had upon his family, friends, and coworkers and can glimpse some of the impact's expression in the immortalizing survivor missions they undertook. We can see additional enduring collegial and cultural impact in the way Byrne's name continues to evoke emotion-laden memories or associations even among officers who did not know him personally more than a decade after his death, and we can understand that the admittedly amorphous lessons of his death are still transmitted through cautionary tales related to rookies by veterans. The police culture immortalizes him in its own fashion, reifying his death in a life-affirming way as a means of imparting lessons that potentially save other cops' lives, at the same time rendering him an enduring symbol, martyr, and hero. The potent latent symbolism of Eddie Byrne's tragic death was also appropriated by the agency and by the political establishment, again transforming the event into a narrative form that reflected their own goals and objectives.

To some extent the agency's reformulation of an officer's death always reflects its political and public policy concerns,[6] and this becomes a delicate issue that may engender some resentment among cops. A police line-of-duty death is always highly publicized in the media, and while the official version—coordinated and transmitted largely through the press relations office—serves in some respects to strengthen the culture and magnify some of its values by portraying the officer in the best possible light and by publicly communicating the dangers police willingly face on behalf of society, the official version can also easily subsume or be subsumed by political rhetoric. There is typically some (albeit fleeting) public recognition of the tragedy and the dangers cops face, and the public's expressions of support for cops are rewarding (Roberts, 1994).

Although cops certainly appreciate the articulations of support for them and for their mission when a cop dies in the line of duty, there is also a bit of resentment at the fact that these expressions were purchased at so high a price. They feel some ambivalence and subtle resentment at the fact that a police officer's death essentially becomes a political event.

Cops see that elected and appointed political figures almost always appear and are prominently positioned at the public funeral—New York City's mayor and police commissioner, all the agency's top brass, various federal law enforcement officials, a U.S. senator, and the U.S. attorney were among those attending Byrne's funeral (Lyall, 1988a)—but fewer appear at the officer's wake and even fewer, in their estimation, can seemingly be counted upon to speak out in support of cops in less politically advantageous or "ordinary" times. Indeed, various officials at Byrne's funeral availed themselves of the opportunity to decry the scourge of drugs by calling for a federal crackdown on drug trafficking, stricter penalties for drug dealers, or the imposition of the death penalty for those convicted of murdering a police officer (Lyall, 1988a); another memorial ceremony for Byrne served as a forum for political statements about the abolition of parole and the removal of telephones from prisons (Dunlap, 1989), and his name was invoked in the presidential campaign to generate support for the death penalty for drug kingpins (Boyd, 1988).

While individual cops may or may not support these conservative political positions, they are certainly ambivalent about political figures exploiting the tragic death of a fellow officer—a death they closely equate with their own. Partly as a function of their own cynicism, and partly due to their heightened suspicion of counterfeit nurturance, they see these expressions as a kind of cynical posturing for personal political gain that diminishes the significance of the officer's (and, by extension, their own) commitment, sacrifice, and death.

Part of the agency's press relations efforts serve to shape the department's public image by creating a symbolic hero, but some of the efforts are directed internally as well. Police agencies need symbolic heroes, and in a very practical way police officials—members of the "management culture" Reuss-Ianni (1983) describes—need the rank-and-file to see them supporting the ideals of heroism and self-sacrifice that are so much a part of the "street cop culture" ethos. As Reuss-Ianni points out, management cops are easily dismissed by cynical street cops as being out of touch with the realities of "real police work" and preoccupied by self-serving interests. The line-of-duty death represents an opportunity to demonstrate management's participation in that cultural ethos, but in line with the survivor's tendency to suspect counterfeit nurturance, the rhetoric often falls flat. Where were the chiefs and the politicians, cops ask, when the hero they now lionize was alive?

Eddie Byrne's death continues to resonate in the NYPD and its cultural mythos, but we should recognize that it is the nature of organizations and organizational cultures to continually evolve and embrace more current symbols and images. As new images and symbols are presented and integrated into existing forms and constellations, the older and less compelling images lose some of their power to capture and hold our attention, and as they lose currency their relative importance fades. This is perhaps especially true at the organizational level because images of danger and death are less central and less meaningful to the official organizational identity than to the individuals who comprise its culture. To whatever extent the police organization can be said to have an identity it is considerably more ephemeral, less cohesive, and more responsive to its external political and social environment than the cultural identity. The upshot of all this is that in time the agency tends to move on and essentially forget the survivor and his needs, while individual officers and the culture remain more authentically committed to him. As one officer with a great deal of experience helping and counseling traumatized cops put it, "The hierarchy doesn't really help. From the mayor on down, they'll show up at the hospital and say, 'Whatever you need . . .' But they don't deliver down the road. They talk a good game, but the reality is that later when cops say, 'OK, this is what I need' do they actually get it? Most times, no."

Eddie Byrne's immortalizing legacy, like that of other cops killed in the line of duty, lives on not so much in the official plaques and memorials erected in his honor and certainly not in the eloquent but ultimately hollow-sounding platitudes of officially crafted rhetoric—new names have been added to the Hall of Heroes and new political issues have captured the public discourse—but in the minds and hearts of cops who remember him and the difficult lessons of his death. The ultimate and most important meanings cops extract from the tragedy are communicated and kept alive when veterans pass on his story to the new generation of rookies they mentor, and the impact of his life and death is most powerfully felt when rookies think of a cop they never knew as they struggle to remain alert on a midnight fixer.

Eddie Byrne's murder embodies many exceptional features and qualities that may or may not be present in the other line-of-duty deaths and mortal combat events, and so other police deaths and the mortal combat situations officers survive may not always resonate quite so profoundly at the individual, cultural, and organizational levels. Although our review and analysis of Byrne's death has been admittedly brief, the compelling nature of the event and the depth of its impact are such that we can easily recognize the resulting patterns of individual, cultural, and organizational response with some clarity. We will continue to see these general patterns in one form or another as we turn our attention to the impact a line-of-duty death has upon members of the dead officer's command.

Manifestations among Coworkers

The collegial and cultural manifestations of survivor psychology following the death or serious injury of an officer first become apparent in the overall sense of numbing cops feel and in their numbed behaviors. When news that a cop has been killed or seriously injured is transmitted—either by police radio or through the broadcast news media—cops will typically stop whatever they're doing to devote their full attention to it. Only a limited amount of information about the event and the officer's identity is available at this point, so even in their numbed state, cops want to know more about what happened and who is involved in order to make some coherent meaning of the death. Is the cop someone they know? Whom do they know who works in that precinct? Is he working this tour? Radio cars pull to curbs throughout the city as cops learn of the event and alert others by broadcasting unauthorized messages across neighboring divisions' radio frequencies; cops switch their portable department radios to the citywide frequency used by the emergency service unit to learn more; the AM/FM radios in police cars and police facilities are tuned to all-news stations; telephone calls begin to come in to the precinct of occurrence as cops seek the identity of the officers involved. Off-duty cops learning of the incident through the news media may call their commands to ascertain details and identities. Many cops, sensitive to their own loved ones' reactions to the news that an unidentified cop has been killed, will also call home to casually let a spouse or other family members know that they are safe.

Cops effectively cease performing their assigned duties during this initial period, but their shock is rather quickly transformed into action by the urge to *do something*. The compelling nature of this demand and the extent to which cops identify with the dead or wounded officer is seen in the fact that cops in other precincts will often abandon their assignments and respond to the scene in hopes of assisting in some way. Others may respond to the hospital and volunteer to donate blood if the death has not been confirmed, or they may show up at the cop's precinct to participate in the search for his assailants. Off-duty cops, particularly those assigned to the dead or injured cop's command, may show up at work in the hope that they can be of assistance. Has the family been notified? Have the spouse or parents been located, and has someone been dispatched to bring them to the hospital? Cops who continue their assignments go about their work in a somewhat numbed way: they complete their tasks in a pro forma or rote fashion, remaining rather detached from the emotional content of the jobs they handle. Their attention is divided between the immediate tasks at hand, their concern for the cop and his family, and the penetrating knowledge of their own mortality that the death of another cop raises to full consciousness.

Other and somewhat more lasting collegial manifestations of numbing can be seen among members of a murdered officer's command in the aftermath of the event. They are much more deeply affected than cops in other precincts because they personally knew and perhaps worked with the cop from time to time, and this preexisting relationship magnifies their psychic trauma. Beyond their personal relationship, though, members of the cop's command are also privy to particular details of the incident that cops in other commands are not, including specific images reflecting elements of stasis, disintegration, and separation. This more detailed and accurate knowledge provides a more complete and comprehensive picture of the event, of the cop's actions (and perhaps his tactical errors) prior to and during the event, and of all the facts and circumstances surrounding it. Even if they were off duty at the time and not physically present to witness the scene—most will visit the location at their first opportunity, though—they can accurately picture it and may have even responded to a similar call at the same location themselves. This more complete, more detailed, and more accurate set of images inevitably contains elements that make the death even more traumatic and personally relevant: the inherent tendency to identify with the dead cop and imagine themselves in his place becomes all the more meaningful when these images so easily connect with their own experience. Importantly, the closeness of the death and their identification with the officer shatters their magical protective illusions that such events happen only to other people in other precincts, and they are reminded of their vulnerability in an especially powerful way.

Kardiner and Spiegel (1947, pp. 26–27) wrote of an analogous illusion of invulnerability among soldiers in combat units: "Among the psychological protections is the narcissistic idea of invulnerability—'Nothing can happen to me'—an idea that is readily extended to the team. The death of a 'buddy' shatters this idea of invulnerability because it revives the actual possibility of death that is so strongly contested by the notion of invulnerability. In short, this notion is an illusion that lasts only as long as nothing happens to any member of a fighting team or to the particular instrument which is their fighting weapon." Several tenured collaborators made the point that other members of their command were psychologically unprepared for the death of their coworker because no cop had been murdered or grievously injured in their precinct for many years. The line-of-duty death of a coworker was not part of their experience, allowing them to more easily maintain protective illusions that they worked in a "safe" precinct where such things do not and will not occur. Collaborators who previously experienced a line-of-duty death in their command had no such illusions, and they felt their resulting awareness of the potential for death made them less personally vulnerable when it occurred again. In a similar vein, one police survivor collaborator expressed a belief that he was made more vulnerable by the fact that in all their years of working together he and his murdered partner had never discussed the possibility that one would die in the line of duty. He thought it odd in retrospect, since they had discussed other police deaths and each separately knew a cop killed in the line of duty, and he wished that they had talked about this possibility and what it would mean for the other.

Anecdotes related by collaborators in several precincts where cops have been killed illuminate some common themes of shared survivorship among the command's members. Most notably, members of the murdered cop's command experience a profound and isolating kind of numbing in the immediate aftermath of the event, leading almost immediately to other features and manifestations of survivor psychology. Collaborators universally described the precinct atmosphere in the days following the murder in terms of the morose disconnection cops feel from each other and from their work. Everyone walks around, as one collaborator put it, as if they were in a fog, and there is little interest in doing police work other than that related to finding the killer. Cops from other precincts and from patrol borough task forces are usually mobilized to patrol the precinct and handle jobs while precinct personnel remain at the station house. Counselors from the employee relations section and the psychological services section are called in to minister to the needs of precinct cops. The dead cop's partner and others involved in the incident will be placed on sick report and temporarily assigned to employee relations section for an indeterminate period until they are assessed and deemed ready to return to work.

Handling Personal Effects

The dead officer's personal effects must be removed from his locker, inventoried, and eventually delivered to next-of-kin. The locker, symbolic of the cop himself and of all the important or intimate things he needs to keep secure, is often sealed and left in place as a perpetual memorial.[7] In earlier chapters we saw how emotionally difficult it was for some officers to examine and handle personal effects belonging to a relatively anonymous DOA, but the task is all the more difficult when the effects are those of a murdered officer. A collaborator described in reverential terms the ritual of emptying his murdered partner's locker:

> What comes over your mind is, you know he's gone but you don't want to accept he's gone so you want to protect everything he owns. Like as if he's going to need it. You want to right away protect everything he owns. So my main objective was to get there right away and get and protect his things. You don't want anyone else touching his things. Let me go and get everything he owns and hold it so that nobody can mess with it. Let *me* take care of this, let *me* take care of this. Right away you're not accepting of the fact he's gone so you want to hold everything he owns, thinking that he's going to come back. That's what I thought when I was cleaning out his locker. I wanted to safeguard everything he had.
>
> When I went to clean out his locker everybody was so worried about me cleaning out his locker. And I said, "No. I'm going up to clean out his locker." Everyone was like, "Do you want me to come with you?" "No. I want to do it alone." So I went up there with two bags. I knew his combination. I'm basically taking everything out of his locker and separating everything. I went right to his house and [the officer's spouse] was there and I said, "These are his things. This is his uniform. These are some pictures he had pasted on the inside of the door." The night he died, they took off his watch and gave it to me to hold and I asked [the officer's spouse] would she mind if I kept it. For a couple of days I had it and was afraid to put it on.[8]

Another collaborator—not a police survivor per se but one who worked in a precinct where a cop was murdered—described how some very personal items recovered from the dead officer's body were vouchered at the precinct pending delivery to next-of-kin. Department regulations require that the officer assigned to property duties must examine all vouchered property and compare it to the property invoice once each tour, and the collaborator became aware that the assigned officer was being repeatedly traumatized when he handled these items. The collaborator expedited the removal of these items to another storage facility.

Chaos prevails at the station house in the aftermath of the incident as ranking officers arrive to supervise the official investigation, which necessarily includes interviews of the officers involved. Depending upon the circumstances of the death (i.e., how "clean" the shooting is from the agency's point of view), the tone and direction of the inquiry can readily antagonize the survivor's emerging sense of guilt. In any case the questions revive and reanimate traumatic images. Once the preliminary investigation is completed, the agency's top brass may arrive to address and reassure the members of the command, but here again they run the risk that their message will fall flat and they will alienate the cops. This shooting investigation is quite separate from the criminal investigation conducted by the precinct squad if an officer is murdered or if a police officer shoots and kills a perpetrator in the line of duty. Precinct squad members, perhaps especially the catching detective, feel tremendous pressure to solve the murder, apprehend the suspects, and develop a solid criminal case against them.

The inherent difficulty of their task—both in terms of the technical difficulty of conducting an intricate homicide investigation and the emotional difficulty of investigating a cop's murder—is often exacerbated when top officials (many of whom have no investigative experience) insinuate themselves into the investigation and attempt to influence its direction and scope. A homicide detective collaborator who "caught" the murder of a police officer angrily described such interfering bosses as "idiots" and went on to describe the other kinds of pressures involved:

> I think the biggest pressure is to make sure you don't screw up. The investigation, the thought that some attorney's going to turn around and get these guys to walk because of maybe something you did or didn't do. . . . I caught the homicide, and it was like 5 days later I went sick. I was so run down and wiped out that I couldn't even . . . I couldn't do anything. I went to the doctor and he gave me medication and stuff like that because I was really drained. There are not that many detectives that can handle police homicides and I think, I always thought that afterwards, that someone should just go and sit down with the powers that be and say that, "You know, there's a lot of pressure on the detective who handles a case like this." It's really, it's a lot of weight. And in reality, it's not on the boss in an office, it's on the detective who is assigned to the case. To make sure that everything is done, and done right.

Images and Associations

Police survivors' numbing is reinforced when innumerable images, some only tangentially associated with the dead officer, conjure reminders of him and of the horrors they witnessed. A collaborator who witnessed the death of a fellow officer described an experience that took place a few days after the incident.

> I was going in my front door, and going in my own front door I was scared. I was scared shit to walk into my own living room. It's my own home and

I'm scared to go in. I thought maybe I was losing my mind. I stayed outside to have a smoke and there was a hose and there was water dripping from the hose and it looked like a puddle of blood and I freaked. I thought, I thought I was losing my mind. So later [another cop involved in the incident] called me up and we're talking and he says, "I hate to tell you this, but last night I heard two cats fighting in my yard and it sounded like that woman screaming. Dude, I couldn't get to sleep. I had to sleep with the lights on." It's the trauma. There are things that happen to you that you can't control.

These triggering images can arise at the most unexpected times, adding an additional measure of trauma because the survivor is not psychologically prepared for them. A collaborator related an incident in which, several years after his partner's death, he unexpectedly came across a newspaper clipping with his partner's photo. He had not anticipated the image and because he was psychologically unprepared for it he suffered a particularly devastating emotional reaction along the lines of traumatic flashback. He was immobilized, became physically ill, and could not complete his tour of duty.

Several collaborators spoke of associating specific places or locations they passed in their work—a bagel shop the dead cop frequented, for example, or a street corner where they had a chance off-duty encounter with him—that resurrected memories of the dead cop. These images and associations did not necessarily have any direct connection with the cop's death, but rather with his life. Although the memories these places conjure were for the most part pleasant, the collaborators nevertheless felt some ambivalence about revisiting them because they were invariably tinged with sadness and a sense of loss.

The lively repartee that ordinarily characterizes so many interactions between cops is notably absent in the precinct in the days following a death, replaced with a kind of sullen and irritable self-involvement in which petty conflicts that would ordinarily not cause a ruffle are magnified, sometimes leading to overt hostility. In turn, these disagreements may trigger a guilty cycle: the amorphous survivor guilt they feel connects with and is compounded by a sense of guilt at having squabbled during a time that calls for unity and connectedness, leading to further isolation and additional guilt. Guilt and hostility can also be reinforced as cops try to make sense of the event, asking questions that others, in their own heightened sensitivity, interpret as impugning the dead officer's courage, judgment, or heroism—an affront to his cherished memory and cultural status. These questions or comments can also raise various forms of rational and personalized guilt when an officer entertains thoughts that he may have in some way failed the dead cop or contributed to the death.[9] Partners and cops who were personally involved in the incident are especially sensitive to these rational forms of guilt and to any questions that potentially implicate them in the death. In all, these dynamics can and often do lead to great dissension within the work group. Guilt, numbed hostility, and a tendency to compete for survivor status inevitably lead to the formation of divisive cliques and coalitions within the command.

This tendency to compete for survivor status is related to cops' suspicion of counterfeit nurturance, but more specifically to the need to try and recapture a sense of immortality, to alleviate or transform their death taint, and to restore a sense of mastery over death by embracing and reifying it through patterns of survivor exclusiveness. We recall that in the struggle to overcome devitalization, dependency, and guilt, the survivor seeks some form of legitimate sustenance that will not continually reactivate these constellations and undermine his ideal self-esteem. Some survivors become embroiled in the catch-22 scenario: they need and accept (and perhaps actively seek) expressions of comfort and sustenance, but at the same time these expressions reactivate their feelings of guilt and illuminate their dependence. Moreover, as their emerging victim consciousness takes shape they may struggle with the death taint others seem so willing to confer on them, questioning the sincerity and authenticity of consoling expressions.

Other survivors fully embrace the death and the taint it confers, finding within it the vitalizing means to distinguish themselves as part of an elite and exclusive group that possesses a sacred knowledge of death as well as a special power over it. The police culture's overall tendency to honor heroes and martyrs and to respect those with knowledge and power over death confers some legitimacy to the death taint these officers bear, and these immortalizing status systems have many life-affirming qualities that may in some way help repair the cop's damaged self-image.

The problem that gives rise to resentment and discord, however, is not so much that some officers embrace and reify the death of another officer, but that some of them are perceived as illegitimately claiming and flaunting this hardearned status. Others may resent the fact that officers who merely had a casual passing relationship with the dead cop and were not substantially involved—physically or psychologically—in the death event exaggerate their own survivor status and "wear it on their sleeve." While a partner, a close friend, or a cop who participated in the event might have an authentic claim on survivor exclusiveness, inevitably some cops who were at most peripherally involved in it embrace the death and flaunt their survivor status. More than one collaborator pointed out that a sense of competition emerges for who will be, as one put it, "the mourner-in-chief." This very subtle and paradoxical competition for victim status typically involves a kind of informal pecking order that also tends to fractionalize the command along shift and squad lines: partners and those who worked the same shift or squad—those who ostensibly knew him best—have the greatest claim to the legitimacy of their trauma and survivorship, and other individuals and work groups are less entitled to participate in the immortalizing rites and rituals that ensue.

Those who feel they've earned their elite status by virtue of their relationship with the dead cop or their participation in the fatal event are therefore especially resentful when another officer becomes the dead cop's champion and takes up a survivor mission on his behalf. They feel their own more profound death immersion entitles them to define the collegial meaning of the death and to pursue appropriate survivor missions in which all can participate. They feel it is both their right and their responsibility to represent the dead cop and the entire command at dedication and memorial ceremonies, for example, and they feel deprived of recognition and needed sustenance when others assume this position. Moreover, in line with their survivor's quest for authenticity and integrity, they are especially sensitive to the idea that those who bear witness to the dead cop's life and death must do so honestly and accurately, and they feel this is their responsibility because they knew him best. Collaborators described how emotionally difficult it was for them to attend and participate in memorial activities, but as one put it:

> You want to go there to make sure he's honored. You're going as his partner, and you always watch out for your partner. You want to make sure it's right. When people say, "Well, who was he?" you say, "I'll tell you who he was. He was my partner. He did this and he did that." It's something I just can't explain. You're doing what a partner would do if you're working together. That's why you do it. It hurts like hell but you want to do it. To make sure he's remembered. You're doing what a partner would do. You want to do everything for his wife because you know he'd do it for you. I've got to make sure [his spouse] is okay at the ceremony. You want to carry on the memory.

To the extent their survivor mission and close identification involves the notion that they must take up and complete the dead officer's projects or life work, they also believe they are the appropriate person to bear witness to his life. They, the partners and closest friends of the dead cop, should be entitled to eulogize him and to describe his personal qualities and professional achievements to the media and to gatherings of cops.

Several collaborators—police survivors as well as those in other categories—therefore commented angrily on the deep enmity they and others felt toward particular officers who (in their view, at least) illegitimately took up the dead cop's mission and, in doing so, accrued personal benefits from the public, political, and agency recognition their efforts received. In several cases related to me, these officers (both street cops and ambitious ranking officers) reportedly parlayed the political and department contacts they made in leading the survivor mission to gain career advancement or reap some other personal benefit. They not only usurped the attention and recognition to which others were entitled, but cheapened the dead cop's sacrifice by personally capitalizing on the tragedy.

The point should be made in the strongest terms that these conflicts and the competition for survivor status are not always a matter of selfish conceit or deficiency of character. They may be, on the contrary, a matter of deeply wounded psyches desperately seeking to somehow repair the damage done to them by finding some way to once again experience a vitalizing sense of connection and immortality. The universal features of survivor psychology generated by their profound death encounter result in needs and vulnerabilities that are specific to the individual, but only limited resources are available within the culture and the agency to effectively address them. There is only a finite quantity of attention and authentic consolation to be lavished on the survivor, only so many ceremonies and memorials to attend, and only so much self-involvement to be tolerated before survivors must put aside these powerful needs and return to the hard realities of contemporary urban police work.

At the same time, and notwithstanding the aura of isolation permeating the precinct, cops are also drawn together by shared grief and by a will to experience a healing sense of individual and cultural connection to other cops and to vitalizing cultural symbols. Despite the conflicts that inevitably arise, cops are concomitantly very willing at this time to forgive past transgressions and put aside differences that separate them in service of unity and commitment to the murdered cop. In this paradoxical time of countervailing emotions and behaviors that at once unite and separate, there can be a tremendous feeling of renewed personal and group commitment to the ideals of good police work as well as to the ethos of "the Job" and to its cultural immortality systems.

When this commitment connects with or is subsumed by the survivor mission—as often occurs—it can provide an especially rewarding and important sense of personal and professional connection, integrity, and movement. A number of collaborators—both the police survivors who suffered the most profound and personal immersion and those who were more casual observers of another cop's death—articulated a conviction that their experience transformed them into a better and more caring cop because they consciously resolved, as part of a survivor mission, to always honor their fallen comrade's memory by carrying on his work in an exemplary fashion.

We've seen that cops need not be physically present or actively involved in a deadly encounter to be deeply affected by it, and this is especially true when a partner or a close friend is severely injured or killed in the line of duty. The kind of identification every cop feels when another cop dies or is badly hurt is immensely magnified when a close personal friendship is involved, and their psychological participation in the event is magnified as well. By virtue of their heightened identification and vicarious participation in the event, cops who lose a close friend or especially a steady partner[10] in a line-of-duty incident manifest each of the themes of survivor psychology, including substantial numbing, in especially powerful ways.

Partners

Police partners certainly spend a great deal of time together—they may, in fact, spend more time together at work than either spends with his spouse or with any other individual in the personal sphere[11]—but more important they spend that time in close proximity to one another during periods that alternate between profound boredom and extreme excitement. In order to spend this amount of time together amicably, it is practically a prerequisite that partners first like each other—petty differences and annoying personality traits quickly become a source of conflict and antagonism leading to the dissolution of the partnership.

To comprehend the unique dimensions of identification and the depth of psychological connection often shared between partners, we must recognize that theirs is not the ordinary kind of friendly occupational association we might find among coworkers in most other lines of work, and we should understand how these relationships are developed and forged. Many of the formative-symbolic principles we discussed in relation to the development of the individual's police identity apply as well to the psychological and social relationships between steady partners. In essence, the experiences that comprise and shape the individual's police identity are inextricably bound up with the experiences of his steady partner.

Notwithstanding the importance of earlier subjective experiences and the individual interpretations that partially define the officer's sense of personal and professional self, police partners who regularly work together as a team have parallel and simultaneous exposure to identical work-related images and events. These exposures shape the overall contours of their personal and professional identities in similar ways, and because they share similar formative experiences steady partners grow to be more like each other psychologically. The mutuality of these shared historical experiences—particularly the exciting, unusual, frightening, novel, emotional, and dangerous events that comprise "real police work" and are therefore most likely to connect with core elements of the police self—is one of the bases for the special sense of identification and connection between long-term partners.

Beyond the fact that they experience the same spectrum of powerful formative images and events, partners also depend upon one another for ongoing emotional support and for their physical safety in objectively dangerous situations. Quite literally, cops often entrust their very lives to their partner's care and rely on the implicit belief that the partner will provide backup without hesitation in dangerous situations even if it requires putting himself at equal or greater risk. The potential of objectively dangerous situations to intensify affiliations and stimulate loyalty is evident throughout the literature of combat psychology, and in the police context it can be glimpsed in an anecdote related by Robert Leuci.[12] A rookie at the time, Leuci (quoted in Kania, 1988) was working with an admired veteran officer and trying to break up a knife fight when one combatant turned on him.

> My partner pushed me aside. "You move toward my partner again, and I'll kill you." And all of a sudden I got this feeling. He didn't say "You move toward me," but he said, "You move toward my partner." Whether he would have killed this guy or not, had the guy come at him, I don't know. But he would have killed him if the guy came at me. When hearing that, in that sort of context, you have this feeling of something very, very special about working with someone when your life may be in danger. So I was with a guy who was fifteen years my senior and a wonderful policeman. The first time he went in to get dinner, and came out with a sandwich I asked, "Did you pay for it?" He answered, "No, it's okay." It was in fact okay coming from him. It was okay. This man would not do anything wrong; he would not do anything criminal certainly, and what was so terrible about this?

The sense of reciprocity and loyalty these situations create underlies one of the police culture's strongest and most universal tenets: a good cop always puts his partner's safety first and does not under any circumstances or in any way betray a partner by putting him at unnecessary risk. A corollary to this code, followed more in rhetoric and ideal than in actual practice, is the demand that one never become separated from a partner. This code is frequently violated in practice quite simply because the exigencies of a particular situation may demand that the two separate or may somehow preclude their remaining together.

During and after the extreme and emotionally compelling situations partners face together, the most intimate and personal details of the self may be revealed: does the cop have the physical courage and emotional fortitude to handle whatever comes his way? Will each partner unfailingly support the other, or will one act primarily in his own self-interest? Is the cop prone to overreaction or particularly susceptible to certain patterns of response? In formative-symbolic terms, can one be relied upon to fulfill culturally and situationally appropriate schemas for enactment without becoming immobilized? One's partner is generally the only person who really knows these intimate truths and the only one who sees them tested repeatedly. Quite a few collaborators—sergeants, homicide detectives, and police survivors—as well as other cops I've known articulated a staunch belief that their precise and detailed knowledge of a steady partner's personality, professional strengths and weaknesses, and behavioral tendencies permit them to predict his behavior in difficult situations with almost perfect accuracy, and to adapt their own behavior accordingly. They said that in difficult situations the two thought and acted virtually as one entity, and that their unspoken connection and communication at such times was almost telepathic.

Quite apart from the extreme and dangerous situations they face together, partners also reveal a great deal of themselves during the hours they spend together handling more mundane police tasks or awaiting the next assignment. Because the relationship begins with a sense of personal and professional respect or friendship that is further solidified in the intense crucible of police experience, partners feel comfortable sharing personal details they might never confide in others. Radio car conversations often revolve around issues and problems in the personal sphere, intimate confidences and personal secrets are inevitably exchanged, and cops often turn to their trusted partner for various forms of advice and reassurance. One police survivor described how he and his murdered partner would often discuss personal issues, and each knew all the other's most intimate secrets.

All the things I knew, after he died, about his wife and family. People would talk sometimes and I'd say, "Yeah, I knew that." I knew all his secrets. But most of the time I'm not saying anything because what I know stays between us, my partner and me. And that's where it stays even now.

Many partners spend a great deal of time together off-duty, attending holiday or family gatherings at each others' homes, vacationing together or participating in sports or other leisure activities. Because they spend so much time together under such unique circumstances, partners typically know a great deal about each other and often develop tremendous respect and esteem for one another. To paraphrase one officer, a partner is a special person because even though he knows absolutely everything there is to know about you, he still likes and respects you.

Given the depth of their friendship, the historical experiences they've shared and the fact that their professional identities are so closely intertwined, the death or serious injury of a steady partner can be one of the most profoundly personal survivor experiences a cop can have. Because the cop's personal and professional identity is so closely bound to that of his partner, such an event truly represents one of the most profound kinds of encounter a cop can have with his own mortality. When these incidents occur, the manifestations of survivor psychology are particularly pronounced, even if the cop is personally uninjured or is not actually physically present to witness his partner's death. Indeed, the fact that he was not there at his partner's moment of greatest need can raise a host of guilty constellations related to separation, disintegration, abandonment, and a sense of personal and professional betrayal.

At the same time, a cop who acts heroically to protect his partner in a mortal combat event—especially if he risks his own life to do so—has rather little to feel guilty about, and the other themes of survivor psychology he may experience are mediated by the powerful status conferred upon him by the organization and the police culture. Tales of cops who save a partner's life are the stuff of cultural legend, and although they may have a profound and intimate immersion in death by virtue of having killed another human being, their survivor experience is markedly different from those who witness a cop's death. As we will see, a host of organizational and cultural immortality systems become available to them to help prevent, mediate, and repair the damage done to their self-image.

This brief explication of the broad impact a police officer's line-of-duty death or severe injury has upon his partner and immediate coworkers sets the stage for our examination of the extreme features of survivor psychology experienced by police survivors.

Psychic Numbing

Because police survivors' physical and psychic contact with death is so much closer than that of other officers we consider, and because the death images they experience can so fundamentally challenge their sense of immortality in so many ways, they are apt to experience a far more debilitating kind of numbing and considerably more formative impairment. We recall from earlier discussions that the quality of numbing and amount of formative impairment survivors experience during and after a death immersion is generally proportional to the realistic threat potential involved: notwithstanding the importance of subjective variables that mediate the experience, the greater the objective threat to the individual's biological survival, the greater the numbing and impairment that results. We also recall that numbing is a functional and protective psychic mechanism that tends to ensure the individual's biological survival by diminishing the affective elements of traumatic experience that could easily distract, overwhelm, or immobilize him, at the same time permitting cognition to remain relatively intact. Although some immediate and perhaps some residual formative impairment accompanies the numbing, for the most part the survivor can cognitively assess the threatening event and respond to it. He can, in other words, take in traumatic images, separate out their potentially immobilizing emotional components, adequately process them in a cognitive way, and generally fulfill schemas for enactment that tend to ensure his biological survival.

The cops whose task environments and survivor experiences we explored in previous chapters all experienced some degree of numbing and some formative impairment, but their death encounters posed little or no realistic threat to the officer's actual continued biological existence. The images involved may have raised difficult issues or concerns about the cop's mortality, and some subtle elements of real or perceived danger may have infiltrated his thoughts, but because the situations were not objectively likely to result in the officer's actual death the numbing tended toward the constructive dimension of partial professional numbing. We also posited that in many cases the basic tendency toward partial professional numbing is developed at routine death events taking place early in one's police career and refined through subsequent death exposures, leading to the capacity to selectively invoke partial professional numbing at other emotionally difficult events. Recalling Marmar's (1997) observation, we can see how previous dissociative experiences during less objectively traumatic events facilitate the onset of more profound numbing in the face of profoundly threatening psychic trauma.

Because many police survivors *are* involved in mortal combat situations that readily present a potentially overwhelming flood of emotional images, and because they *do* face objectively real threats to their biological existence, their numbing is considerably more profound and tends toward the debilitating pole of psychic closing-off. They experience substantially more formative impairment, significantly greater separation of cognition and emotion, and often some degree of physical and/or psychic immobility. Their loss of the formative capacity for ongoing symbolization is usually temporary and is most pronounced at and around the time the death encounter takes place, but with some exceptions a generalized numbing and a tendency toward chronic despair comes to characterize their subsequent lifestyles and life experiences. This tendency toward chronic despair, as well as the police survivors' tendency to see their lives as having two distinct phases—a time of vitality that existed before their death immersion and a world of emptiness afterward—was reflected in the words of an officer whose partner was murdered:

> For some reason, since this happened things just haven't been going well for me. Things just haven't been right. You just wish you could go back to the way things were before. You find comfort in religion and family and stuff but the main thing is you just wish you could go back to the way it was. People say, "Get back on the horse and ride. Just accept it." You want to let it go, but I just can't. I just wish I could go back. And it's the loneliness. The loneliness, the loneliness. You try to control it but you can't. That loneliness. You miss him like you'd miss a spouse. You try to move on but there's always that thought: "I wish we could go back. Then it would be okay." . . . It's hard now because it seems like everywhere I go it's

just not working out. I'm doing what I've got to do and maybe it's just a dark cloud. Why? Why should I be going through this? They tell me it's part of the trauma. You're never the same.

Extreme Forms of Numbing: Psychic Closing-Off

In some exceptional cases, again depending in part upon the quality and quantity of objectively threatening images presented in the event and in part upon the individual's previous subjective experiences, the police survivor may undergo the extreme kind of numbing Lifton calls "psychic closing-off"—his cognitive and emotional processes almost entirely shut down and he becomes virtually immobilized in both an emotional and a physical sense. Instances in which an officer completely "freezes" and fails to respond to the threatening event as it takes place are, fortunately, quite rare: in the vast majority of cases the officer is able to at least partially execute the schemas for enactment he has developed through various formal and informal modalities of police training and has further refined by reflecting upon various "what-if" scenarios. As we might imagine, it is quite difficult to excavate and explore the experiences of officers who become completely immobilized, since few might be expected to physically survive such an objectively realistic threat, but even when an officer manages to survive there are also strong cultural and official proscriptions against discussing these events.

Still, despite their extreme rarity and the degree of delicacy required in discussing them, it would be intellectually dishonest to maintain that these incidents have never occurred. They are part of the overall police experience with death, and they deserve some mention. None of the police survivors I interviewed completely froze during their death encounter, so we cannot explore the phenomenon through first-person narrative, but by conflating features of several shared collegial versions that circulate in the NYPD we can generally discern how the themes of survivor psychology play out for officers who experience the immobility of extreme psychic closing-off. We must approach these versions with extra caution, though, and must concede that they invariably take on rancorous and possibly apocryphal cultural overlays in their retelling. In fairness to surviving officers who may be the subject of these tales, we should also bear in mind that psychic closing-off represents one pole of a broad continuum of natural and protective human responses to extreme events that lie well outside the realm of "ordinary" human experience. Given a sufficiently threatening and extraordinary event, any individual might experience this profound immobilization.

We recognize that an officer who fails to achieve some degree of enactment— who fails to do something in the face of a life-threatening mortal combat event— but nevertheless manages to survive has committed a cardinal violation of the police culture's ethos: for all intents and purposes he has acted the coward, and his transgression is all the more abhorrent for having survived. The gravity of this transgression is also magnified if it takes place in conjunction with the taboo of putting one's partner at risk by abandoning him or failing to completely back him up. Especially if another officer died or was injured as the result of his inaction, the immobilized cop's survival is perceived by other cops as illegitimate, shameful, and purchased at the cost of individual and cultural betrayal. The survivor may experience substantial guilt that may be repeatedly reactivated when other cops shun him or remind him of the incident in various subtle or overt ways.[13] The survivor certainly constructs a personal version of the event, perhaps reconstructing it in a way that protects and reinforces core elements of the self, but he is not likely to be given much opportunity to share his version. His narrative—the one that perhaps contains the greatest quantity of objective truth—does not inform the cultural narrative to any great extent, and regardless of previous or subsequent acts of bravery he will continue to bear the stigma of cowardice throughout his career. If another officer also survives the same event, that cop may be reticent to denounce his partner—although according to cultural definitions he has been grossly betrayed and endangered by a partner who failed to fully back him up, any articulation of blame would in itself be a betrayal and a violation (albeit a lesser one) of the same cultural norms.

At the same time, some other officers may at some level of awareness recognize that the immobility was an entirely natural reaction to an extreme and horrific experience ("there but for the grace of God . . . ") and, notwithstanding peer pressures to isolate and ostracize, be somewhat sympathetic or solicitous toward him. Their well-meaning articulations of concern can, of course, ultimately reinforce the survivor's isolation by reanimating constellations of rational or irrational guilt, shame, and suspicion of counterfeit nurturance.

Given the implications of cowardice in our larger culture and the public-relations dilemmas such events can pose, the agency is unlikely to play up these events in the media and would almost certainly not publicly castigate the survivor. Official narrations of the event such as the unusual occurrence report would likely be crafted with exceptional care, and their distribution would be carefully controlled on a "need-to-know" basis. The agency might strategically postpone the release of all relevant information to the media on the grounds the matter remains under investigation, delaying the release of information until some point when media attention has flagged and public attention is captured by some other event. Absent timely official pronouncements, the collegial narrative is informed by perceptions and innuendoes as well as by incomplete and often inaccurate news accounts rather than by objective factual analysis. The agency may in fact respond to an incipient public-relations crisis by formally honoring the survivor—especially if another cop is killed, the pressure to produce a symbol of bravery may be great—but attempts to manufacture a hero in this way are perceived as illegitimate and deceitful and will engender great resentment among cynical cops who believe they know the "real story."

The officer who freezes in the face of extreme threat but survives the encounter is even more intensely victimized and devitalized than other police survivors. He is deeply affected by each of the themes and features of survivor psychology, and he becomes trapped in the death equivalent states of separation, stasis, and disintegration that come to infiltrate his overall existence because the police culture continually denies him effective means to experience an immortalizing sense of connection, movement, and integrity that would be available to a less immobilized cop.

At the other end of the psychic numbing spectrum are those cops who experience little rather debilitating numbing, immobility, or impairment, and thus can easily assess the threat and respond by fulfilling schemas for enactment during a gunfight. They typically experience some degree of psychic numbing in terms of perceptual anomalies and often a transitory narrowing of consciousness that permits them to focus sharply on the event and the threat, but because the cognitive process is relatively unimpaired they are not unduly immobilized and can respond effectively. Experience and training kick in and the cop acts to neutralize the threat or take other situationally appropriate action. These officers are generally so focused on the moment that they are not consciously aware of their own numbed state, and it is only afterward, when the threat is neutralized and they recall or reconstruct the event, that they recognize the functional perceptual anomalies that facilitated their survival.

In sharp contrast to those who become immobilized, these cops can adequately fulfill appropriate schemas for enactment and, as a result, they are generally regarded and treated as heroes. They are embraced and lauded by the agency and the culture, and this provides them with an important sense of connection. They are often rewarded with accolades, medals, and career advancement that impart a sense of movement, and their newfound hero status and peer approbation as a "good cop" who can "handle whatever comes his way" affirm the cop's integrity by expressing a consonance between his reputation and his self-image. The unfortunate thing for these cops is that the rewards of having survived by fulfilling appropriate schemas for enactment are purchased at a fairly high price: the cop must struggle with the knowledge that he has killed another human being.

Formative Impairment and Perceptual Anomalies

The acute numbing and formative breakdown police survivors experience around the time of their death encounter accounts for the various perceptual anomalies and sensory alterations they frequently report. These relatively temporary dissociative phenomena—which Marmar (1997) and his associates (Marmar, Weiss, Metzler, and Delucchi, 1996; Marmar et al., 1994) refer to as "peritaumatic dissociation," and which Reiser and Geiger (1984) and Artwohl and Christensen (1997) describe as occurring frequently among cops involved in highly traumatic situations—can affect several sensory modalities and generally involve a shift toward an altered state of consciousness that imparts an aura of unreality to the situation. David Klinger's (2001) recent research empirically measured the frequency of these perceptual impairments among a sample of 80 cops involved in a total of 133 shooting incidents, and he determined that nearly all (95 percent) experienced some form of perceptual distortion before, during, or immediately after the deadly encounter. The most common perceptual distortion was diminished sound (82 percent), although many (20 percent) also reported that some sounds were exceptionally loud. Slightly more than half reported a narrowing of focus along the lines of tunnel vision, more than half experienced a sense of heightened visual acuity, more than half perceived the event as if in slow motion, and about one-quarter experienced it as if in fast motion. Klinger (2001) found great variability in the specific rates and types of perceptual distortion reported in previous studies of police deadly force encounters (Campbell, 1992; Solomon and Horn, 1986; Nielsen, 1981; Artwohl and Christensen, 1997), but the important and consistent finding to emerge from this cluster of research is that substantial formative impairment is very likely to take place proximate to a mortal combat situation.[14]

While none of the police survivors I interviewed experienced the extreme forms of psychic closing-off that entirely immobilized them in a physical way, all reported some degree of numbing proximate to and after their death encounter. All were able to physically respond to the situations they faced, but all experienced some blunting of emotion. In their numbed state, the police survivor's impaired formative process does not permit him to adequately process and integrate the flood of threatening imagery, and we will see how these fragmentary and often troubling images often become part of the death imprint.

Manifestations of Numbing

For those who survive a gunfight, and to somewhat lesser extent for those who witness the death of another cop, the most salient and most functional manifestation of numbing is the transitory narrowing of consciousness they often experience at the time of the event. Police survivors of mortal combat events who collaborated in this research all described, in one way or another, a heightened clarity of perceptual focus during the event, but not all experienced it with the same degree of intensity or the same accompanying features of perceptual anomaly. This heightened clarity is often, but not always, accompanied by the perception that time has slowed down, and, along with the fact that none of the police survivors experienced immediate emotions as the deadly encounter took place, these features illuminate their numbed temporary separation of cognition and affect.

> Everything really slows down. My hearing went, everything was like when you have cotton in your ears. You don't really hear the way you're supposed to hear. It was a hushed, muffled sound. Your vision, you have no peripheral vision at all. You're focused in on the gun and the body, on what's absolutely critical. I could feel my heart was pounding. And I remember—you're going to think I'm crazy—hearing in my mind "Step to the left, punch the gun out." Exactly the words they say at the [firearms training] range. I heard it 50 times there, and that's what I did.

Police survivors recalled a host of specific images and some fairly complex cognitive assessments and rational judgments during this time, although to some extent their narratives also reflected a dissociated aura of unreality in the whole experience.

> You feel like you're planted there and it's an effort to move. Everything is in slow motion, very deliberate, but I had ample time to do everything because time slowed down. In my mind I was able to count slowly to four before squeezing off a round but [my partner later] told me I ran up,

pulled my gun out of the holster and just fired. It was instantaneous for [my partner] but for me, I was able to look at the situation, ask myself should I [join in the physical struggle] or should I shoot. And I said I can't [join in] because if I do [the situation would be more dangerous for my partner]. And I had this entire conversation with myself. . . . As he turned with the gun, in my mind I counted to four, slowly, one, two, three, four. And I said to myself, "Well, here goes," and I fired a round and it sounded like a little puff, not like a gunshot. Quieter than when you're at the range and wearing ear protectors. And I looked, as if I could see where the bullet was going. I was able to stand there and have all this going on in my mind and count slowly to four, but [my partner] said it was [snaps his fingers] instantaneous.

This cop went on to say that he subsequently experienced a comparable sensation of slowed-down time when his car flipped and rolled over in an automobile accident—the event "seemed to take forever. You see everything and know exactly what's happening."

Another cop noted that after he was shot he felt disembodied—the perspective or point of view from which he recalls the scene was not that of a man lying slumped against a wall, but rather from a point on the wall opposite to him. It seemed, in other words, as if he was watching himself and the scene from a disembodied position several feet from where he lay. Regardless of his vantage point, he retains the image of himself covered in blood and lying in a pool of blood—an image that reflected the actuality of the scene.

I'm 95 percent out of the scene by this point. I'm like on another planet. I'm contemplating my own death now. I actually had those conscious thoughts. "How could I do this to my mother," and "It's not so bad to die, it's almost pleasant." What I believe was happening was I lost a lot of blood and went into shock. I did actually go into shock.

Some portion of this officer's numbed condition may in fact be attributable to the physical symptoms of shock and loss of blood, but he also experienced the same kind of slowing of time and other perceptual anomalies uninjured officers experienced. He distinctly recalls the excruciatingly slow-motion image of his gun's hammer coming back and falling on the cylinder as he returned fire, for example, and he recalls considering how many rounds of department-issue ammunition—which he considered underpowered—it would take to neutralize his opponent. He wondered if he could, in fact, fire a sufficient number of rounds to neutralize his adversary before lapsing into unconsciousness. Although he watched his assailant fire at him repeatedly he was so focused on the assailant's actions he was not consciously aware of where or even whether the subsequent bullets struck him, and he learned the full extent of his gunshot injuries only when he was stabilized at the hospital. He took in and cognitively processed the image of the assailant firing at him at point-blank range, and the horror of that image stays with him now, but at the time his emotions were so suppressed or disconnected from cognition it was experienced without any conscious awareness of fear or terror. The conscious realization of his fear and terror followed a few moments later.

We recognize, of course, that time did not actually slow to allow police survivors to actually take in, process, assess, and make rational judgments about all these images, but rather that their cognitive processes, unencumbered by emotional distraction, went into a kind of adaptive overdrive that facilitated their biological survival: they absorbed and processed the images at a highly accelerated rate. Despite their numbed emotional state, they were able to assess and respond to the situation and fulfill the schemas for enactment they developed in training. Although all the death encounters took place in a matter of a few seconds, I observed that the police survivors whose encounters took somewhat longer to unfold and who were therefore confronted with more images over the course of the encounter seemed more likely to perceive time as slowing down. We should also recognize that "somewhat longer," as used here, is a relative term: like many or most police mortal combat situations, all the collaborators' deadly encounters lasted from about 5 to 15 seconds from the point of threat recognition to the point at which the assailant was killed or neutralized. Despite this exceedingly brief time frame, police survivors provided up to 5 full minutes of highly detailed and uninterrupted narrative to describe the event and the images actually presented to them in a matter of a few seconds.

Numbing and Cognitive Focus

One collaborator described his transitory narrowing of consciousness and constriction of perception as a "focus," and the level of abstraction expressed in his description reflects the fact that he was speaking of his perceptual experience both at the time of the deadly encounter as well as in other situations involving physical or psychic threat that took place before and after that event. The "focus" was particularly intense during the deadly encounter, but this psychological process was by no means unknown to him.

> I'd describe it as your attention is so focused on a situation, on one point, that you tend to take everything else around you for granted. So in other words, it's a focus where I see all the fine details that I know from experience most people don't. Or they can't. They stand there, and I'm always a step ahead of everyone else. My gun is always out first, you know, I always see the gun in the car first. There is like a focus of great intensity . . . You see every detail. It's like moving a little faster than everyone around you, and everyone around you is moving a little slower. You see the guy reaching for his waistband but you already saw that before he started. It's uncanny. You already have him covered. For example, I did a car stop once, and there was something about the car that just triggered the focus. My partner goes to the driver's side and I went to the passenger's side. Something about the car was wrong, and going up to the car I was so focused I could see him kicking something under the seat and it was a gun. They had just shot up a club down the block. It's something that you feel, and you go into like an overdrive. Experience kicks in and you go into such a fine tuned focus that you don't think about the *Patrol Guide*, you don't

think about anything but the situation. You're the good guy and he's the bad guy. Training, I guess, is what kicks in at that point. . . . It's like you're moving faster than everyone so you see things with more clarity, but some things get blocked. Like you don't hear the radio any more. They can be yelling for you on the radio, you're not going to hear it.

This collaborator went on to volunteer that he first experienced this "focus" at his first DOA, where he was left alone at the scene of an obese person's death to complete the paperwork and notifications. The partially decomposed body was lying on the floor beneath the apartment's only telephone, and in order to reach the wall phone and make the notifications the officer had to literally straddle the decaying corpse. This proximity to a decomposing corpse and the powerful visual and olfactory images involved were emotionally quite difficult for him, but he steeled himself and forced his mind to "block out" the image—to "put it in another place in my mind and deal with it later." He had also described another difficult DOA early on in his career in which he had to pick up and put evidence tags on multiple body parts strewn along a roadway after an accident. Even more than the first DOA, he said, forcing himself to perform those tasks and to confront those disintegrative images helped him to develop the "focus" he now conjured, in a functional and adaptive way, at dangerous or emotionally difficult events. Moreover, he expressed the firm conviction that the ability to call forth this focus—almost at will—to separate out the emotional component of an experience, to depersonalize it, and to go into the cognitive "over-drive" he described—made him a better, safer and more effective cop.

I think that the experience becomes heightened in time. There was a time when I would do a car stop, for example, and I would not appreciate the full danger of the situation. In other words, the more you see and the more you do, the more you realize the dangers, and you stop trusting people. You treat people nicely, but things come into sharper focus at that point. Certain guards go up and it's almost something physical. Certain guards go up and you become more focused. In a car stop, with the level of focus, you still know exactly where your partner is and you still know where you are, but your attention is into this car and into this man's movements. So I think, talking about it now, that there are different levels of intensity. In the extreme situations, everything else gets blocked out except *that*. When I say it had to do with my first experience, I think it's because my first experience was just that—trying to block out. It was the beginning of a sense that I refined as time went by. And at this point I'm very, very good at what I do. And I know it, my partner knows it, my bosses know it. It's something you refine over time, and something you make better. And you know, in the majority of cases, 98 percent of the cases where I experience that focus, I find it difficult afterwards to recall what the guy looked like. I don't see the face. I recall everything else, but I don't see the face. But it's like a natural high. Afterwards you're pumping.

The collaborator's inability to recall the faces of individuals during these periods of intense focus reflects both the general tendency toward depersonalization and the overall impairment of formative processes that accompanies psychic numbing. The numbed survivor, deprived of this capacity to integrate and make complete sense of the traumatic incident, is left with fragmentary images that can be extremely powerful in evoking other memories and feeling-states associated with the death immersion. We consider these and other traumatic images associated with the death event in the following section, where we take up the theme of the death imprint.

The Death Imprint

In our previous discussions of survivor psychology we saw that the death imprint is a durable and intrusive image that continues to reactivate other images associated with the horror of the death encounter as well as residual feelings of guilt, and it may also reactivate earlier images and constellations of separation, stasis, and disintegration. We saw the difficulty some survivors face as they attempt to master the image through some kind of appropriate enactment or to reconstruct it in a way that will let them once again experience a sense of vitality by breaking free of these death-equivalent constellations and guilty feelings. Because the police survivor's death immersion is so profound and because the death imprint can be so durable and so easily conjured, though, it is practically impossible to fully integrate the image or to find sufficient appropriate enactment for it. The survivor remains forever in the imprint's thrall.

We saw that because the survivor is unable to escape this powerful image he feels forever changed and forever tainted by his death encounter, and that his tainted sense of being possessed by death is reinforced when others associate him with death and treat him differently because of it. We also noted that the imprint image imparts an acute sensitivity to death that may take the form of either a heightened sense of vulnerability toward death or reinforced feelings of invincibility. Some of the collaborators whose experiences we consider in this chapter were left feeling extremely vulnerable to death, to death equivalents, and to death imagery, while others seemed strengthened by their death immersion. Those who fell in the former category had substantial difficulty in resuming an active police career; they no longer possess that magical sense of invulnerability that is so important to operational police officers. Their self-confidence was profoundly shaken, if not shattered. One collaborator, for example, wistfully described the self-confidence and vitalizing sense of purpose he felt before his severe injuries, noting that in conjunction with his imposing physical presence he felt capable of handling any eventuality. A great deal of that confidence died, he said, when he was shot and almost killed. He recovered well enough physically, but the experience left him an emotionally changed man. Other police survivors, though, emerged from their struggle with a stronger and more powerful sense of both their individual and professional self. Some police survivors expressed a belief that their profound and highly personalized death encounter—and more specifically, the death taint they bear—ultimately made them a better cop.

As we observed among collaborators in the task environments explored in earlier chapters, some survivors achieve a partial but always imperfect sense of mastery over death by subsuming their death taint within their professional identity. The death taint that sets them apart from ordinary society is one of the bases for the professional identity that connects them with similarly tainted cops. They embrace and reify the taint, using it as a vehicle to reformulate their identity and achieve satisfying forms of connection, movement, and integrity. In a similar way, some police survivors experience an immortalizing sense of invulnerability to death by fully embracing their death taint and incorporating it as part of a heroic identity. Like the classical heroes of myth, these police survivors have ventured into death's realm, grappled with and overcome it, and emerged from the struggle with a special and sacral knowledge. In proclaiming them heroes, we take a great deal of the sting from their death taint: there is always some ambivalence toward heroes, but for the most part we regard them with respect and awe rather than revulsion. We are attracted to heroes, not repulsed by them. To the extent their death taint is contagious, we cautiously seek to get close to it and perhaps become mildly infected. As we will see in this section, the extent and quality of heroic recognition afforded a police survivor mediates in important ways the kind of death taint he feels and others perceive in him.

Different Manifestations of the Death Imprint

All of the police survivor collaborators I interviewed were deeply affected by one or more death imprint images retained from their experience, and in one way or another all the imprint images captured the particular horror of their situation in a subjectively meaningful way. We recall the officer, quoted above, who consciously believed he would die as he saw himself slumped against a wall covered in blood, and we can easily recognize why that horrible and highly personalized disintegrative image—experienced contemporaneous with the conscious expectation that he would die—would be so difficult to master or integrate. This officer was grievously wounded, and so it seems appropriate that this death imprint image is one that powerfully encapsulates the prospect of his own mortality. The death imprint images of collaborators who killed an adversary but were themselves uninjured, on the other hand, were images of the adversary rather than of themselves. Officers who witness the death of a partner or another cop tend to retain death imprint images involving the dead officer.

A collaborator whose partner was murdered noted there were three specific images he retained from the event. The first image was auditory—the electrifying scream of a female crime victim calling for the police. The officer, a highly experienced and tenured street cop, described how the sound galvanized him and immediately evoked the very specific memory of a scream in a training film he had seen in the police academy many years before. He does not specifically recall the subject of the film, other than that the female victim was being stabbed to death and that the police arrived too late to prevent her murder. There was something about that scream that always vaguely bothered and stayed with him through the years, but none of the other screams he'd ever heard evoked that specific memory or haunted him in the same way. The auditory image contained an immediate schema for enactment that was consistent with the police identity: he ran toward the sound. In doing so, however, he briefly outpaced the other officers with him. The image remains particularly troubling, he said, not only because he was puzzled that it revived a specific unintegrated memory from so long ago, but because it continually reminded him of the guilt he felt at having left his partner. Perhaps if he hadn't responded in that way, he thought, the situation might have unfolded differently and his partner might have lived. In this particular case, the officer's guilt was almost certainly irrational, and he knew it: the fact that he ran toward the sound of screaming had absolutely no bearing upon an entirely separate chain of events that subsequently led to his partner's death. Symbolically, though, it subsumed many images tied to guilt, separation, stasis, and personal and professional integrity—issues and themes that the circumstances of this death encounter made especially compelling for him.

The second image this collaborator retained was the absolute horror of seeing his partner's body lying in a pool of blood. Again, the image contained an immediate schema for enactment: he and other cops picked the partner up and ran to an ambulance that had arrived on the scene. Interestingly, in his numbed state the collaborator knew the wounded officer's identity, called him by name, and spoke to him in the ambulance, but he has been told by other cops that after he arrived at the hospital he kept asking them who had been shot and if they knew where his partner was. We can easily understand how the horrible image of seeing one's partner so badly wounded would have a lasting impact.

Finally, this collaborator recalls the image of his partner in the ambulance on the way to the hospital, and of paramedics ripping his uniform off to treat his wounds. Again, in his numbed state the gravity of the situation did not entirely sink in ("I said, 'What the fuck are you doing? He's going to need that uniform again'"). The collaborator helped pull off his partner's boots, and he retains the image of how white his partner's ankles were. "His ankles were really, really white. I kept looking at them, and I was talking to him and his eyes rolled back and that's when I knew it was bad." The relatively benign screen image of his partner's ankles rather than the more alarming image of his eyes rolling back certainly encapsulates the dreadful recognition of the seriousness of injuries, but also functions to shield this officer from the full impact of that moment and of an even more traumatic image.

Collaborators who killed an adversary typically described a death imprint image involving their assailant, often at the moment of his death or immediately thereafter. A collaborator who engaged in a prolonged hand-to-hand struggle before shooting his opponent retains an image of the adversary turning and bringing a gun to bear on him, as well as another image of the man still reaching toward him at the moment of death. Another recalled his mortally wounded adversary's futile but nevertheless horrifying struggle to once again raise and fire his gun at the cop. In the darkness of the scene he could barely see his wounded opponent raising his hand, and he could not discern whether it held a gun. Conscious thoughts—"Where is the gun? Wait for the gun! Wait for the gun!"—ran through his mind that he could not morally fire again until he was absolutely certain the hand held a gun and that it was pointed at him. The instant it took for the hand to emerge from the shadows seemed an eternity. The two were little more than arm's length apart, so his adversary's collapse before firing spared the officer the trauma of essentially administering a coup de grâce.

To escape the death imprint image and the guilt and/or death-equivalent constellations it may conjure, survivors struggle to transform it by finding alternative forms of appropriate and life-affirming enactment. Some continually dwell on the event and the images, trying to reconstruct the event in a way that reduces rational guilt and trying to integrate and make it more comprehensible. Many try to justify or rationalize their actions, offering detailed explanations why their actions were appropriate and the event was unavoidable, even when they are intellectually convinced their actions were reasonable under the circumstances and even when no one asks them to justify their actions.

The struggle to transform the death imprint image is also tied to the struggle to integrate the death taint and forge a new identity, and some police survivors are more successful than others in integrating tainted elements of identity. Generally speaking, the police survivor collaborators who were recognized as heroes by the agency and by their peers after killing an adversary in a "clean shooting"— a clearly justified shooting that does not result in accusations of excessive force, a protracted legal process that casts aspersions on the officer's conduct or character, or scandalous media coverage—fared better than others in terms of bearing their taint.

Heroism and the Death Taint

Bona fide heroes enjoy a very special status within the police culture that can function to diminish many of the death taint's pejorative elements. They are recognized and admired as legitimate heroes because they exemplify various values cherished in the police culture—they performed their duties bravely, they were resolute in the face of compelling danger, they remained faithful to and protective of their partners, and they vanquished evil—and because they exemplify these core values all cops can vicariously participate in their exploits. They have also triumphed in an arena—the gunfight or mortal combat situation—that all cops regard with simultaneous dread and attraction. These cops have truly "been there" as participants in police work's ultimate experience, they acquitted themselves well, and they lived to tell of it.

Various tangible and intangible benefits accrue to these heroes, and many or all of the benefits have immortalizing qualities that help transform the death taint into a personal and professional attribute. At an organizational level, the hero is typically awarded a medal that symbolizes his membership in a very exclusive group of survivor cops, and the department often gives its heroes enhanced opportunities for coveted assignments and career advancement. The hero gets to meet dignitaries and ranking officers he would ordinarily never encounter, and they articulate their respect and admiration for the cop.

Many more positive things happened in connection with this than negative things. Number one, knowing that I could do my job no matter what came up. There was also the support I was able to give other cops in other situations—you know, like the mentoring aspect. Shortly thereafter I got into Anti-Crime, and eventually I wound up going to [another highly desirable assignment]. I received [a litany of various awards from the police union, a newspaper, police fraternal groups, and community groups] and one of those hanging medals at Medal Day.[15]

I met people at all these functions, and that plus the different assignments expanded my horizons by exposing me to a larger understanding of the Job. I don't want to say that it made my career because I was always out there making my collars and ready to mix it up if need be and I already had a good reputation, but people only looked at me in a more positive light afterwards. I got a lot of mileage out of it because I rose to the occasion. . . . [While in uniform] I always wore my [breast] bar and got a bit of mileage out of it. People recognized what it means. It was clear I was no empty suit, and I do have credibility. And I'm able to use it to help other cops, to give them advice and guidance.

Even before the cop is officially recognized as a hero, his coworkers begin to treat him differently and in many subtle and overt ways they demonstrate their esteem and respect for him. Given the overall importance of danger in the police culture and the value the culture places on being able to handle danger, we can see how surviving and even thriving in these most dangerous encounters establishes an indisputable track record of reliability that leads to high status. One hero collaborator, who had fairly limited tenure at the time of his shooting, noted that senior cops in the precinct who previously had little to do with him suddenly treated him like a celebrity. He was invited to join them for drinks after work, for example, and their respect was evident in the fact that when one of their steady partners took a day off he was invited to fill in or "take the seat." Their respect, he said, was rooted in the knowledge that this young cop could handle himself—the facts and circumstances of the incident and his role in the shooting solidified his reputation as a "good cop" and immediately gained him the kind of acceptance and peer respect young cops crave. The incident effectively ended his tenure as a rookie and elevated his status tremendously. Another cop described the heady feeling of attending a racket[16] where cops from other commands whom he did not know recognized and addressed him by name. Other collaborators who were recognized as heroes described similar experiences within their commands, and all felt a gratifying sense of connection to other cops.

They had all sorts of nicknames for me, like "One-Shot Stopping," or "The Red Light Killer," "Stop 'Em and Drop 'Em [first name]." But that's the cop humor coming out and it was affectionate. They're saying, "We respect him because he did what he had to do. He's one of us, one of the guys." So I'm a cop's cop now. I can handle all the big things. I had been a very active cop and I liked the Job and making collars, so I wouldn't say it *made* my reputation, but everyone recognized it. It was like a barometer that everyone judged me with.

As pointed out above, full access to these immortality systems is usually afforded to cops involved in "clean" shootings in which no officer is killed or severely injured, and the sense of movement, connection, and integrity they provide goes a long way toward transforming the death taint into a positive attribute of the professional self. However, a very different set of circumstances may unfold when another cop is killed or badly injured or when the agency and/or the culture withholds approbation and recognition. As we will see when we take up the theme of death guilt, the death or injury of another cop introduces special elements of guilt to the death taint.

Death Taint and Death Guilt

A collaborator involved in a shooting that was eventually (but not immediately) deemed "clean" had an entirely different kind of experience, and he described how the adversarial process affected his self-esteem, his personal and professional identities, and his subsequent behaviors as a cop. He was never formally accused or charged with any wrongdoing or even a procedural violation, but due perhaps to political concerns the police department delayed releasing its official finding for several months. The officer, a very active and enforcement-oriented cop who was convinced all along that his act was legally and (more importantly to him) morally appropriate, was neither officially recognized nor formally disciplined or admonished. He was in a kind of limbo, effectively denied the means to transform his taint into a professional virtue or to fully experience a vitalizing sense of connection, movement, and integrity. Largely because of the prolonged investigation that followed the incident, members of his command still refer in a half-joking way to the "dark cloud" that follows him.

> Afterwards I thought, maybe I should have just let the whole thing go. Because after all you have to go through, afterwards I thought is it really worth it to get involved? You know something, afterwards I was reluctant to make collars. I would make collars but I'd look for the easy collars. I just don't want to go through that again—the grand jury, the shooting investigation—because I feel that for the flick of a finger I could lose my life, my job. The stigma that would be attached to me. You cannot work with your partner, they'll break you up. A way of life that you're very comfortable with is taken away just because you're doing your job.

One police survivor noted that after his partner was murdered other cops with whom he previously enjoyed a close relationship began to avoid or act coolly toward him at work and at social events. Sensitive to their actions and keenly aware of his death taint, he confronted one cop, and his narrative clearly reflects the cycle of taint and guilt, the need for nurturance, and the sense of despair that comes to permeate many police survivors' existence.

> There'll always be blame. There'll always be blame. The biggest thing is when you see people. The biggest thing to hurt, and it still hurts to this

day, is when you see people you worked with and they're sort of avoiding you. You run into them or you go somewhere for a drink and after they have a couple in them they wander over and, "Hey, how's it going?" And you ask them, "What's up? Every time I see you you're avoiding me." One guy asked me to go in the back, and we got out in the back and he just starts crying. Tears. Crying, crying, crying. He says "[Name], the reason I'm avoiding you is that every time I see you I think of [your partner]. And I can't come to terms with the fact he's dead." And I go, "So what the hell about me?" And he says, "I'm sorry, it's just that every time I see you I think of [your partner], and I just can't deal with it." And down the road you realize there's a lot of people feel the same way. When they see me they think of [my partner] and they get upset so they figure let them avoid [me]. How the hell do you think that makes me feel? There is nothing, nothing you can do about it. It hurts you more because you need the comfort from other people and they get uncomfortable around you. They're not doing it on purpose, it's just a reaction but it's upsetting. It makes me angry, but you just have to learn to accept it.

Dreams and the Imprint Image

Because the death imprint image can never be entirely mastered, it often becomes manifest in the dreams and nightmares many police survivors suffer. Interestingly, none of the hero survivors who managed to partially transform the imprint image and incorporate their taint as part of a viable and vitalizing new identity reported being greatly troubled by nightmares. They may have had intermittent dreams about their deadly encounter shortly after it took place, but their dreams were not particularly horrific and they did not become a recurring feature of their survivor experience. One hero survivor of a "clean" shooting, in fact, adamantly denied ever dreaming about the event or losing any sleep over it. The shooting was a "him or me" situation, and he said he felt absolutely no guilt in relation to it.

The police survivors who most clearly felt a pejorative and guilty death taint, whose imprint image was least reconstructed, and who experienced the most objectively profound encounters with their own mortality reported recurring nightmares and substantial continued sleep disruptions. They reexperienced their death immersion in their dreams, and in line with the struggle to reconstruct the imprint image often rewrote the event with a different and more favorable outcome. Moreover, their dream imagery often reflected their waking fantasies: a cop who witnessed the death of another cop and fantasized the cop was still alive often had similar dreams. Another collaborator was deeply troubled by nightmares about his encounter, but eventually the nightmares took on highly symbolized guilty overlays of unmerited blame and recrimination. He was also prone to these recurring dreams after such routine death encounters as handling a DOA.

I have the same dream over and over. Disjointedly, perhaps. Call it a nightmare if you like. You actually see the life expunged, you imagine the spirit leaving the body and it stands there looking at you and hating you for what you did even though I didn't do that. It hates you and you imagine its family hates you because you've changed someone's life, its wife's life or father or mother, the children. You ask, "Do I have the right to do this?"

Conclusion: The Death Imprint

None of the police survivor collaborators I interviewed were entirely unaffected by the death imprint, and depending upon the circumstances and magnitude of their death immersion some remain deeply in its thrall. The death imprint image or images can never be entirely mastered, and so for some these fragmentary images remain a frequent and haunting reminder of their experience and the devitalization it engendered. Similarly, all the police survivor collaborators were affected by a death taint, but those who were recognized as heroes for having fulfilled culturally valued schemas for enactment had much greater success transforming the taint into a vehicle for experiencing a vitalizing sense of connection, movement, and integrity. To a large extent, this sense of vitality helped repair their damaged identity and offset their immediate and continued devitalization. As we'll see in the following section, situations and circumstances that resurrect the death imprint or illuminate the death taint are readily capable of conjuring feelings of survivor guilt.

Death Guilt

On several occasions we've alluded to the fact that the irrational forms of guilt the survivor experiences simply for having survived while another died—that is, an amorphous guilt related to the notion of survival priority—can be magnified and reinforced when the survivor has some rational reason to believe that his actions or inactions may have contributed in some way to the death of another person. The rookies, sergeants, CSU technicians and homicide detectives whose experiences we've examined did not evidence a great deal of rational guilt; they might feel some amorphous guilt at having joked about or minimized a person's death, for example, but for the most part have no conscious and rational basis for imagining their own complicity in the death. They are generally called to the scene of a stranger's death after the death occurs, and the various process by which they make meaning of the death and determine its proximate and ultimate causes provides a kind of rational reassurance that they hold no personal responsibility for it. Their survivor guilt is usually just that: the vague sense of guilty unease that arises simply because they continue to live while another has died.

This is clearly not the case for police survivors who, by definition, participated in the death and have reason to identify with the victim—either a murdered cop or an adversary they killed—in a substantially more meaningful way. The formidable death event these collaborators experienced was either their own near-death encounter, the death of a close friend, or a death they actually caused. If the death is that of a friend or partner and the police survivor was physically present at the scene, he can easily become plagued with doubts about the actions he took or failed to take to prevent it. Regardless of the factual circumstances, he may feel an irrational and amorphous guilt conjured by the police subculture's taboos against abandoning a partner even if that abandonment is purely symbolic. If he was not physically present, he may be plagued with lingering guilt because of something he might have done if only he *had* been there. We recall the survivor's generalized "touchiness" around issues and images that reactivate his sense of guilt or impairment, and we can see how oblique or direct references other cops make to the death can raise and reinforce patterns of guilt. The same can be said when the cop actually caused the death of another person or when he is nearly killed.

One collaborator who survived a shooting noted his own sensitivity to comments other cops made about the event and the tactical decisions he and his partner made. His comments also reflect the sense of connection and empathy police survivors feel for other cops murdered or seriously injured in the line of duty.

> Months later, people would walk up and say, "Why did you [pursue a particular tactical option]?" Yeah, well tactically maybe it's not the best thing to do but you weren't there. That's why I'll never Monday-morning-quarterback another cop. Like people used to say maybe Byrne fucked up. I say "Hey, you weren't there, you don't know. And if he did, so what?"

This angry theme—"You weren't there. How can you know? Who are you to judge me?"—resonates through death-immersed police survivor collaborators' narratives and lives. Police survivors are hypersensitive to remarks that could be construed as impugning or minimizing the legitimacy of their survivor credentials, since these comments reinforce the inescapable death taint they feel and animate the guilty constellations that lie so close to the surface of their consciousness. One police survivor described his rage when another cop saw him wearing an "In Memory Of" T-shirt at a police racket and asked if he knew the murdered cop. The survivor quietly replied that the dead cop had been his partner and the officer, who had been drinking, made a casual remark to the effect of "Wow. That must suck. Were you there?" To the survivor, the offhand nature of the comment minimized his partner's sacrifice as well as his own, and the question about his presence evoked such guilty feelings that he lashed out at the offending officer ("Of course I was there, he was my partner and I was with him. I did not abandon him. I was faithful to the canons of our culture"). In retrospect, the survivor acknowledged he knew the remark was not intended to minimize his or his partner's sacrifice, but he could not contain his outburst. Survivors can easily explode in anger when offhand comments animate their guilty constellations, or when others who weren't there make judgments they are not (in the police survivor's estimation) entitled to make. A collaborator assigned to a highly desirable detail after the death of his partner—a detail he characterized as populated largely by cops "on a contract" rather than by cops who earned the position legitimately through experience and hard work—had this to say:

> The thing that bothered me in [that detail] was when narrow-minded supervisors, narrow-minded detectives, and narrow-minded cops would

say "Hey, it's a terrible thing you lost your partner but look at so-and-so. He took a bullet in the leg." Well, what's your point? What you're telling me is that I watched my partner die and watched him bleed and watched his body turn white and his eyes roll and blood come out of his mouth and when they took his pants I watched his underwear covered with blood. I saw the guy die. My best friend die. He turned to talk to me and he couldn't talk. I watched him go out of the picture and I had his blood on my hands and on my face that I didn't even know. And when we got to [the hospital] and they told me he was dead I blacked out and fainted on the floor. And when I got up again I saw his blood on my face and my hands and I passed out again. They injected me with some jungle juice that made my blood pressure so high they wanted to admit me. I went through the whole wake and the whole funeral, the whole mess, and because he took a bullet in the leg there's a difference there? How dare you. How *dare* you compare me to anyone else because you think you know? Who the fuck are you? What do you know? Who the fuck are *you* to judge *me?* You know. Yeah, you *know.* That pissed me the hell off, when people would say, "I heard what happened to you and it's pretty tragic but life goes on. Look at Joe So-and-so, he was shot." Yeah, okay, what are you trying to tell me? What are you trying to tell me?

This resounding theme—"You weren't there. Who are you to judge me?"— reflects the survivor's belief that only a person who has so profoundly touched and been touched by death can truly make sense of their experience, and in this regard it also reflects their sense of survivor exclusivity and reinforces their ties to other police survivors. They feel that only other survivors—particularly other cops who are survivors—can really understand them and their experience, and because they believe that other cop survivors will be sensitive and nonjudgmental they refrain from judging them. This belief system binds survivor cops together without fear of judgment or guilt, and so there is a great affinity between police survivors, whether or not they are personally acquainted. Police survivors feel and subtly express a sense of connection to each other, but they also identify with cops murdered in the line of duty. This became evident in the way collaborators evidenced a marked tendency to physically and temporally locate their own death encounters in relation to other survivors' events: "This was about 3 months after [officer] was killed and about 4 blocks from where [another officer] got killed in [year]." Some collaborators also compared the facts of their own death encounter to incidents resulting in another cop's demise, and it was clear that they knew the details of these and other deadly incidents. Finally, several collaborators departed briefly from their narratives to interject an anecdote connecting themselves, sometimes in a tenuous way, to a murdered cop.

Police survivors' sensitivity to the needs of other survivors is not limited only to other police officers, and several collaborators commented that they felt a special connection to certain crime victims or even to individuals they never knew. One, for example, noted that he remained haunted by a story he read in the newspaper about a child who died a tragic death. The circumstances of the child's death were quite unlike the circumstances of his own death immersion, however.

To this day I can't get out of my head the terror that kid felt. I associate with it because I know that terror. That was just after I was shot and I think I associate it with my shooting because I had a very long time to consider my own death when I got shot. And because it was a little kid and it was so avoidable. I'm a father. Even now when a cop gets shot, certainly when a cop gets killed but even more when a cop gets shot, it just breaks my heart. Eddie Byrne, for example, I associate with my own shooting. He was a friend . . .

Guilt and Integrity

To some extent police survivors are reticent to discuss their experiences and reveal their feelings to others, especially to those who have little insight into police work and police culture or those who they feel may not appreciate the depth and power of their experience. They are generally distrustful of the media, for example, and do not believe their stories will be accurately related. One police survivor noted he declined an offer to appear on a nationally broadcast daytime television show to talk about his experiences. His refusal to participate was based in a distrust of the media, a fear that they would sensationalize and cheapen the sacrifice he and others made, and an inability to exercise adequate control over the show's content. He also rejected requests for interviews from several prominent national news magazines. Survivors want and need to talk and to bear witness, and at some level they want the kind of public recognition that may help alleviate some of their guilt, transform their taint, and restore a sense of vitality to their lives, but they are also very cautious about the venue and the audience.

Suspicion of counterfeit nurturance makes police survivors exceptionally wary of being compromised or of gaining attention for the wrong reasons. In order to maintain their personal and professional integrity (and in some cases to remain faithful to their dead partner by upholding his integrity), the actions they undertake must not be for their own aggrandizement. To do otherwise would be inauthentic, and so we see the tendency to understate the heroic nature of their own bravery and exploits. None of the police survivor collaborators indulged in even minor braggadocio, but on the contrary they seemed very concerned with accurately narrating their experience with full acknowledgement of their virtues as well as their venality. Police survivors subtly expressed concerns that I would render their accounts in a fair, honest, and accurate way, often going into great detail to be sure I understood a particular point. Their concern was not so much that I would fail to portray them in a positive or heroic light, but on the contrary that I would fail to render their narrative with the integrity and truth it deserved.

Police survivors' touchiness about the event that has so fundamentally transformed their identity subsumes a special sensitivity toward statements that mischaracterize the event or that could be construed as diminishing the importance of salient facts. Erroneous statements rankle because they reinforce the survivor's guilt and may be interpreted as impugning or subtly implicating his important sense of integrity and dignity, compelling the cop to continually resurrect and recount his experience in order to defend his fragile self-image. That the survivor feels compelled to defend his actions, integrity, and dignity is a secondary victimization. Police survivors' insistence that all the facts and circumstances be related completely and accurately was not in service of burnishing their own reputation or self-image or reducing their death guilt: on several occasions police survivors volunteered details of the event or elements of their own behavior that were somewhat embarrassing to them. That they raised these issues without prompting and of their own volition underscores their concerns for factual accuracy—an accuracy that helps them to manage and diminish rational survivor guilt—and their need to capture and express a sense of integrity. It also speaks to their integrity needs: if they are to be judged, let the judgment rest upon a full and truthful accounting of the facts, not speculation and innuendo. Finally, it speaks to their sensitivity about being judged without full consideration of all the salient facts—"You weren't there"—and their discomfort around the disparity between their own experience of a life-altering event and the less accurate collegial and official versions.

Police survivors' reticence to publicly discuss the details of their death immersion is at least partially due to an inability to fully integrate it, as well as the difficulty of articulating the complex emotions they feel in a way that will not be misconstrued or taken out of context. Their reluctance also involves the survivor's basic struggle with guilt—they avoid situations where guilt-evoking questions might be asked—as well as a basic need to recapture and assert integrity. Particularly in the immediate aftermath of their deadly encounter, a time when issues of personal and professional integrity may be compelling, police survivors become concerned with the factual veracity of media accounts.

> One of the worst things for me was reading the newspapers for the next few days because there were so many inaccuracies. They were rife with inaccuracies about where it happened, what happened, how it happened. So after a while I stopped looking at the papers. You want to look to see what's happening and what they're saying about you, but on the other hand you don't want to read it. I'm reading it and thinking, "Did it happen this way?" No, it didn't happen that way. I was there and it didn't happen that way. You start to second-guess yourself after reading it in the papers.

Another collaborator expressed anger and frustration over media distortions of the nature of his injuries and was upset these inaccuracies infiltrated the cultural narrative, since they diminished the scope and nature of his personal sacrifice:

> He punched the gun out at me and fired and the first one hit me in the [names body part]. And to this day I resent totally when people call it a graze wound. Because you know how bullshit makes the world go round in this Job? Well the initial reports on *Live at Five* and the other news shows, they had to rush to get the story on the air and the initial reports said the

cop's wounds weren't severe. That wasn't even fucking close. It was a through and through entry and exit wound. I needed all kinds of surgery, I had multiple concussions and contusions. I had transfusions. There was all blood all over. With [this kind of] injury you bleed more.

Another officer commented about how upset he became when media reports misstated some relatively minor facts when he killed an armed adversary. He acknowledged that the distortions or misstatements were almost immaterial to the overall narrative of the event and that the stories portrayed him as a hero—he could quote the various tabloids' front page headlines from memory—but these collateral errors of fact nevertheless troubled him. Once again, this speaks to the survivor's need to have others understand the factual circumstances, and in a larger sense it illuminates concerns that their personal narrative can differ—at times significantly—from collegial and official versions of the event. Yet another collaborator, whose partner was murdered, described with great emotion how troubling it was when initial news stories contained factual inaccuracies about the event and when, in later renditions during the trial, news summaries elided details he felt were especially important. In particular, the elided details painted a more compelling picture of the defendant's guilt.

Questions and Guilt

Questions that conjure guilt exacerbate the police survivor's touchiness and make him difficult to deal with, ultimately leading to a vicious cycle that interferes with his need to develop and maintain satisfying relationships. One collaborator, for example, described becoming fairly close to certain members of his murdered partner's family, but in their own quest to comprehend the event they continually questioned him about his own and other cops' actions and inactions. The implication he derived was that they believed he could have done more to prevent the death. Although their inquiries aggravated his amorphous and irrational sense of survivor guilt—he was rationally convinced his and others' actions were entirely proper and tactically sound—his feelings of commitment to his partner and, by extension, to his partner's loved ones made him continue participating in the dialogues. He tried as well as he could to explain the circumstances, but in their own ignorance of police procedures and tactics (or perhaps in their overriding need to affix blame) the relatives seemed unable or unwilling to understand. Underscoring his sensitivity to guilt and issues of integrity, he felt particularly betrayed when he learned they attempted to verify his account with other cops. Eventually the guilty feelings aroused by these conversations became untenable, and the relationship virtually ended. The point here is not simply that police survivors are sensitive to questions that raise guilty issues or that the death of a cop with whom they identify closely can lead to a heightened sense of connection and a willingness to act compassionately toward other survivors even when that compassion hurts, but that the particular features and manifestations of one individual's survivorship can easily antagonize or aggravate features of another's survivorship.

At the same time, this officer's relationship with his murdered partner's spouse deepened as a result of their shared loss, and this is largely attributable to the spouse's unquestioned belief that he did all that was humanly possible on behalf of his partner. The spouse never intimated any doubt about his culpability, and in fact frequently expressed an appreciation for all the partners meant to one another, essentially absolving him as a potential source of guilt. Having been married to a cop for many years, the spouse was also somewhat more knowledgeable about police procedures and the realities of police work than other relatives were, and having known the partner for many years was also more accepting of the idea that he would never do anything to let his partner down. He tearfully related that when his murdered partner's spouse was informed of the death, the spouse's first question was about his own safety, and so guilt and recrimination were never part of their relationship. On the other hand, the relatives' quest to make meaning of the event aggravated the survivor's residual death guilt as well as other touchy constellations related to separation, stasis, and lack of integrity. Underlying this dynamic, from the officer's point of view, is the same guilt-tinged theme: "You weren't there. Who are you to judge me?"

Guilt and Commitment

The connection and commitment police survivors feel for a murdered cop's spouse or for other survivors can be partially rooted in guilt and in a sense of shared grief, but the connection can also be vitalizing—it can give the police survivor the sense that he is "doing the right thing" by contributing to the spouse's welfare and quality of life. The connection may help ease or atone for residual guilt emanating from feelings of separation from the partner, it shows integrity and fidelity to one's partner, and it can be a way of symbolically carrying on the partner's life mission or life activities. Given these guilty roots, though, the relationship also continually evokes images and reminders of the death immersion. Embracing the relationship in this way can become exhausting in terms of the emotional and physical energy involved as well as the continued contact with guilt-inducing images and experiences, and in conjunction with the police survivor's overall touchiness it can ultimately lead to difficulties in the officer's other relationships. In light of survivor competition for attention and nurturance among a surviving spouse and other relatives, the police survivor can easily get caught in the middle. As we've seen, because all parties have the need to make sense of the death in their own way, they may continually ask questions (honestly or in anger) that reactivate the partner's guilt.

Several collaborators, including some with a great deal of experience counseling troubled cops, observed that some partners, close friends, and members of a murdered cop's command initially demonstrate great compassion and commitment to his spouse, children, family, and others touched by the tragedy. In time, though, the inherent burden of sustaining these difficult relationships becomes untenable, and all parties may need to sever connections associated with the death. Each police survivor struggles to find his own way to deal with the death, and each struggles to find appropriate (but, in the final analysis, always insufficient) enactment. Both the type of enactment they seek and the way they seek it differs from person to person. Partners and the cops closest to the dead cop never seem to completely lose contact, but it can degenerate to the point that contact is infrequent. The cops involved in these incidents tend to remain closer since they are united by their shared experience of danger as well as by the proximity of their work and continual encounters, but it can be an uneasy relationship.

"Clean" Shootings and Guilt

Guilt, especially rational guilt, is considerably less pronounced among cops who kill armed adversaries in a so-called clean shooting—one in which the officer is deemed to have acted properly in defense of his own or another's life. Cops who survive these types of mortal combat have less reason to feel rational guilt since the situation often involves a "kill or be killed" scenario, and a common refrain in these officers narratives was "It was a matter of him or me. He, not I, created the situation and this was the outcome. I did not cause this."

> Initially, when you know someone's dead, it's like, "Wow. I killed somebody. I *killed* somebody." Then I immediately snapped into "Well, look, this wasn't my choice. It was *his* choice." It was his choice because he could have stopped. I had no other choice. If I didn't do what I did he would have certainly injured or killed one or both of us. I did what I had to do to protect my partner and myself. I was kind of matter-of-fact about it at the time. I snapped into a mode of "Look, I did what I had to do," and I didn't have any problem with it.

All of the police survivors were performing their jobs and acting in conformity with their social role and professional identity when circumstances conspired to thrust them into a situation they would have truly preferred to avoid. They did not actively seek out an encounter that could result in a death, and in many cases the police survivor's guilt is also reduced by the knowledge that he exercised great restraint or took extraordinary steps *not* to harm or kill his adversary. In every case, though, the cop was a reluctant participant, and by virtue of the fact that they survived the deadly encounter they acted appropriately and therefore have little implicit basis for rational forms of guilt.

Guilt is further reduced because for the most part cops who kill an adversary have previous images and constellations with which to make sense of their experience. All cops have imagined themselves in some sort of mortal combat encounter, and all have participated in training designed to prepare them to use deadly force in defense of their own or another person's life. Although their images and constellations may not specifically match the situation that actually occurred, the imagined situations and training provide schemas for enactment at the same time they impart sufficient meaning to help make some immediate and long-term sense of what happened. Peer approbation and reassurance that they "did the right thing," as well as positive media accounts, a thorough investigation, and an official determination that the event was a "clean shooting," go a long way toward reducing rational guilt. The accolades that ensue when an officer is recognized for heroism may not preclude others from asking them questions, but because the questions are presented in an entirely different context and expressed in an entirely different tone they do not conjure or implicate guilty images in the same way.

The collaborators who killed an armed adversary in a "clean shooting" and were recognized as genuine heroes who performed properly, in fact, had almost no rational guilt about having killed. This is not to say they did not betray a sadness for the fact that they took another life or did not wish that the event never transpired, but circumstances placed them in an untenable "it's him or me" situation, and they had little guilt about the choice they made.

> I felt bad about having to kill somebody, anybody, but not him in particular. Any human being, because life is so valuable. I didn't feel bad for him as an individual, I felt bad for having to take a life. It wasn't personal, it was the fact that I killed a human being. I felt bad for having been put into a situation where I had to take a life but I didn't personalize it. . . . I can't really say I felt bad for him. No one goes to work with the idea that they're going to kill someone, and I don't relish what I had to do. It's not something you look forward to. You hope you can avoid it but he made the choice and I gave him every opportunity to stop what he was doing. . . . I think now, if it were the same situation, there wouldn't be any hesitation at all. In retrospect, having lived through it, there wouldn't be any hesitation. If the situation is that clear, someone is pointing a gun screaming "I'm going to kill you," there's no reason to hesitate because his intentions are quite clear.

This collaborator felt little guilt or affinity for the man he killed but did identify with and feel sorrow for the individual's family and loved ones. These feelings were aroused when another cop made an unkind reference to the dead man's mother.

> And at that moment I felt bad, really bad, not about killing him but about him dying. I thought, "What a way for his mother to receive him. She probably had hopes he would do better, and maybe she thought he was [doing better]." Everyone loves their son and I felt bad for her because she's receiving him back dead. I felt bad for his mother, but I really can't say I felt bad for him.

Guilt and the Legal Process

One powerful and evocative depiction of the trauma, the guilt, and the innumerable indignities a cop can suffer when his partner is murdered is Joseph Wambaugh's (1973) *The Onion Field*. Briefly, it recounts how two LAPD officers, Karl Hettinger and Ian Campbell, were disarmed and kidnapped by two felons who removed them to a desolate onion field near Bakersfield, California, and murdered Campbell. Hettinger, who survived by running away from the killers, was essentially branded a coward by the LAPD and ordered to address roll calls at every precinct to explain himself to his peers. Moreover, the LAPD promulgated the so-called Hettinger Memorandum (Patrol Bureau Memorandum Number 11) forbidding officers from surrendering their weapons under any circumstances. Hettinger's guilt at having survived while his partner died was solidified and magnified by the agency's response and by the reactions of other officers, and the prolonged series of trials, appeals, and retrials for Campbell's killers stimulated additional guilt as defense attorneys attempted to shift responsibility for Campbell's death to tactical decisions he and Hettinger made. The protracted legal proceedings also denied Hettinger any sense of closure, and he was unable to get on with his life. He was eventually arrested for shoplifting—an act Wambaugh (1973) characterizes as a symbolic bid to be caught and punished—and fired from the LAPD, but he eventually won a psychological disability pension.[17]

In its extremity, Hettinger's experience highlights the dimension, magnitude, and etiology of the guilty feelings many police survivors experience, but it also illuminates how the legal process following many mortal combat situations exacerbates their guilt and prolongs their suffering. Several collaborators thus experienced great trepidation at the prospect and the reality of testifying about the event.

As part of the research process I attended the trial of an individual ultimately convicted of murdering a police officer and heard the testimony of virtually every police witness. I was also able to informally discuss the murder with many of the witnesses after they testified, and I saw how the process reanimated various themes of survivor psychology, especially amorphous feelings of survivor guilt. Witnesses almost universally articulated rage at the fact that the defense attempted to impugn their proficiency, their tactics, and the veracity of their testimony, implying they were conspiring to cover up their share of the responsibility for a fellow officer's death. This defense tactic, along with the fact that they had to relive and give detailed testimony about the event they witnessed, resulted in powerful emotions. Indeed, every police witness—with the important exception of the dispassionate crime scene unit technicians—showed profound emotions and grief on the witness stand. Because the dead cop's partner broke down in uncontrollable sobbing and tears on several occasions (when he described finding his partner's body, when he had to handle and identify his partner's uniform and shield, and at several other compelling points), he required a number of recesses to regain his composure.

I had several conversations with this officer before the trial began and after it concluded, and prior to it he voiced great trepidation that the process would rekindle the deep emotions, including guilt, he struggled with. He nevertheless anxiously looked forward to putting himself through the ordeal for two related reasons: he sought to bring his partner's killer to justice and vindicate his self-blame by formally fixing responsibility, and he sought some means to put the terrible event behind him. Subsequent conversations revealed that to some extent the conviction addressed the former, but overall the trial did not bring the closure and peace he sought.

The criminal process also affects police survivors who kill an adversary, albeit somewhat differently. Collaborators who killed an adversary in a clean shooting had little difficulty testifying before a grand jury, but these hearings were somewhat pro forma affairs whose outcomes were readily predictable. Their reputations and judgments were not assailed and the nature and tone of the prosecutor's questions did not conjure or imply any guilty responsibility—a grand jury case is presented by a prosecutor, and there are no antagonistic defense attorneys present. This is not to say cops have a cavalier attitude toward the investigations and/or the criminal process. The survivor of a "clean" shooting had this to say:

> They sat me down and read me my [Miranda] rights. That really hit home. It was like a wake-up call. I was just, "Wow. This is for real." After that, any time I read someone their rights I never did it the same way because I know what it feels like to be read your rights when there's a criminal investigation.

A collaborator who was not immediately cleared of wrongdoing had a very different view of the legal process, to the extent that he expressed a tempered reluctance to ever again become involved in dangerous situations that might lead to his use of deadly force. Particularly important to him was the impact the legal hearings had on his self-concept and his sense of integrity.

> I don't want to have to go to the grand jury again and hear different sides of the story. To hear people pick at my conscience. To make me feel, to say that all I wanted to do was go there and kill somebody. Like as if I got up that day and said, "Hey, I've got to go find someone to kill." I don't want to be made to feel like I have blood on my hands. To go home and wash your hands like Pontius Pilate, to shower until the hot water runs out. To feel like you'll never feel clean again.

Police survivors always struggle to incorporate and carry around their guilty knowledge and some struggle with the self-concept as a killer of men. One collaborator, displaying an uncommon degree of introspection and an admittedly unusual philosophical bent, described how radically different a person he had become as the result of his participation in the death of another person. His initial conception of himself as someone dedicated to always being the protector and helper of others was transformed to an identity he saw in part as a "killer of man." He clearly struggled with that identity and sought to maintain the earlier and healthier self-concept, fearing that he would again be called upon to take action that would reinforce the latter.

> In this Job we are dedicated to valuing human life, and we do, but there are also times when there is a life you must take. It is a conflict that plays in our minds. It certainly plays in my mind. And I prefer to value life because if I don't, if I walk away from conscience, then why don't you just go all the way? Where do you stop? The Job gives us the choice of the best or the worst we can be and we have to balance that choice every day. You have to fight to find another option [to killing] because if you don't you will become everything you stand against. If I let myself play God then I'm no better than the guy who's killing people for fun.

You come to realize it's like the saying in Indian philosophy: "I am Shiva the destroyer, death, the shatterer of worlds, the deadly tiger that stalks." That's what you can become and I don't want to be that. I don't want to be Shiva, who is the god of death. But you come to feel death is your companion and is following you because you have observed death. You made death possible. You don't want to be the instrument of death. That's not what I came to the Job for. I came to make things better. I came for life, and to protect the weak, but not at the expense of being the tool of death.

Conclusion: Death Guilt

In examining the patterns of guilt among police survivors, we see distinct differences in the type and quality of guilt survivors feel, and these differences tend to equate with the actuality of the circumstances involved in the death encounter. Cops who are severely injured or who witness the death of a partner or another cop are far more consumed with guilt and far more cognizant of their death taint than cops who are recognized as heroes for having killed someone in a "clean" shooting. This makes a great deal of sense because cops who survive a "clean" shooting generally have less reason for rational guilt—it was often a clear case of "him or me"—and greater access to the powerful immortalizing subparadigms of movement, connection, and integrity the culture and organization provide. Access to these subparadigms help buffer the survivor's death taint and death guilt and permit him to begin repairing his damaged self-concept. We will see this dichotomy operating again as we turn our attention to the theme of suspicion of counterfeit nurturance.

Suspicion of Counterfeit Nurturance

Because they continually dwell on the events that so thoroughly devitalized and impaired them, because the images with which they contend are so readily susceptible to reactivation, and because these reactivated images can conjure such powerful emotional responses, survivors who have been deeply immersed in death and deeply affected by guilt find death taint and other features of survivor psychology can be quite difficult to take. Survivors, especially those who suffer the greatest impairment, are noticeably touchy about issues associated with their traumatic immersion, and they are often moody, morose, and prone to explosive anger at their situation as well as at others' reactions to them. Because they are so devitalized, survivors may wittingly or unwittingly make great demands on those around them, and their special needs for emotional and/or physical support can be very difficult to fulfill. Survivors often have great difficulty developing and sustaining the kind of nurturing relationships they need to overcome impairment and manage their tainted identity, and their intensity often alienates those around them.

On one hand police survivors appreciate the exalted status and the often deferential treatment they receive from other members of the culture—and to some extent from civilians who are awed when they learn of the survivor's experience—and a great deal of this cultural esteem is based in a genuine respect for their having journeyed to the most extreme perimeters of police experience. They are respected for having participated in the ultimate experience of "real police work"—the kind of experience every cop imagines and at the same time fears. The ambiguity with which others regard them derives from the taint they carry, which is complex because it symbolizes both the most honored and the most terrible experiences in which an officer can become involved. Like the classic hero of myth, the police survivor has actually or symbolically journeyed into the realm of death and returned bearing a special and sacral knowledge that changes him in ways that set him apart from others.

Earlier, we identified the irresolvable conflict or catch-22 the death immersion creates. At the same time the survivor needs and seeks out specific forms of emotional and perhaps physical support to repair his damaged identity and to reexperience a sense of vitality, at some level he often resents the support he receives and the individuals who provide it precisely because the nurturance he craves reinforces his death taint and reminds him of his devitalization. The need for sustenance and for nurturing relationships can be compelling, but even the survivor's recognition of those needs undermines his self-confidence and damages his self-esteem. The survivor finds himself trapped in a complex struggle between dependence and independence.

Nurturance and Self-Regard

The erosion of confidence and self-esteem can be difficult for any survivor to manage as he attempts to reformulate a new identity that incorporates his death taint and accounts for his emotional and/or physical needs at the same time it permits him to reexperience a sense of vitality, but the erosion can be especially problematic when the survivor is a cop. As we've seen, the cop's sense of confidence and competence—the very things that help define him as a good cop—are a key element in his ability to confront and adequately respond to dangerous situations. Absent this level of confidence and sense of professional competence, the cop may be plagued with self-doubts that in turn inhibit him from acting decisively. He may become, in police parlance, "shaky." The synergistic spirals of undermined confidence, diminished self-esteem and heightened sensitivity to death taint may take additional turns when others recognize his shakiness and respond to him differently.

In any case, the devitalized and shaky survivor's reduced capacity to confront and respond effectively to dangerous situations strikes at the very core of his "good cop" identity, as does the recognition that he may become a liability to other cops at critical moments. He may no longer be, or as importantly, no longer be *seen* as the predictably dependable cop he once was. Other cops, attuned to his special needs as well as his shakiness, respond differently to him. Some may subtly attempt to shoulder a larger share of dangerous burdens, while others more concerned with their own safety and effectiveness may avoid working with him altogether. The hypersensitive police survivor inevitably picks up on these signals, reinforcing his tainted identity and illuminating his humiliating struggle to overcome devitalization and dependence.

Quite apart from these dangerous professional situations, well-meaning cops may sincerely inquire about his emotional state. At one level the reassurance that other cops know and care about his difficulties is gratifying, and genuine expressions of concern from peers who have some insight and understanding of what he must be facing paves the way for a satisfying and vitalizing sense of connection to other cops and to the culture. Depending upon the way these concerns are articulated and the context in which they are delivered, they can either bolster or derail the police survivor's attempts to reformulate a viable identity. They can either partially satisfy his need for a renewed sense of connection, progress, and integrity or they can point up and antagonize his devitalization and tainted identity.

Similarly, the agency's formal response to the police survivor and his special needs has a great deal to do with the satisfaction of those needs and, ultimately, his success in reformulating a new identity. The survivor who is formally recognized as a hero whose sacrifice is cherished and respected, who is given the opportunity for career advancement or a detail assignment that utilizes his skills and abilities, and who is generally afforded special consideration for his special needs is better able to repair his damaged sense of self. These important and vitalizing immortality systems help blunt some of the rougher edges of survivor experience.

The formal agency response, however well-intentioned and delivered, is scarcely a panacea. For one thing, it is the nature of complex bureaucratic organizations to develop generic "one-size-fits-all" programs and policies, and this approach is simply not suitable for every survivor's subjective needs. Moreover, several problems identified earlier in this chapter as applicable to precinct personnel in the aftermath of a police death or serious injury are also applicable to the individual police survivor. The fact that department executives and city officials show up at a wounded officer's bedside can do a great deal for his self-esteem, but depending upon a variety of factors including the specific message of support they articulate, they can also generate resentment—"Where were you before?"— and suspicion—"Are you going to exploit my tragedy for political gain?" A related issue is that these officials may assure the officer of their continued support, but are not in fact there for him when he needs help at a later date. The organizational memory, especially in terms of the personal commitments its executives make on its behalf, tends to be short. The police survivor who is initially reassured that the agency will do its best to address his needs and to support him in his struggles can easily lapse into cynical resentment and a deep sense of betrayal if the sustenance promised him is not ultimately delivered.

Nurturance and Disciplinary Actions

The issue of expectations and promises of nurturance is a delicate one, since police survivors may be as resentful of nurturance offered as of nurturance denied. Survivors can be very touchy about the way minor disciplinary problems are resolved, for example, regardless of whether they perceive they were afforded or denied special treatment. Several police survivors spoke to this issue, and although the circumstances and outcomes of their disciplinary problems were quite different, one officer's treatment when a supervisor reprimanded him for a minor administrative omission captures this paradox.

The officer appeared for one of our interviews in a somewhat agitated state, and in response to my inquiry he said his boss had given him a hard time over a minor administrative transgression. Specifically, he was outraged because the boss concluded by saying, in essence, "Look, I know you've been through a lot so I'm only giving you a warning on this." As the survivor saw it, the supervisor should have either ignored the offense—a reasonable approach, in his view, given its nature and his overall conscientiousness—or dealt with it formally or informally without referring to his profound death immersion. The cop felt it was entirely unnecessary and offensive to allude to his death encounter since, in his interpretation of the exchange, it implied some parity between the depth of his trauma and personal sacrifice and the quality of the "favor" being done for him. He claimed not to want any special treatment, but nevertheless felt entitled to it and to a degree of respect he felt was lacking in the supervisor's attitude. Underscoring the survivor's vulnerability to repeated reactivations of sensitive images and experiences, it was only toward the end of this conversation that I learned the exchange between the officer and his supervisor had taken place about a month earlier. Another image or event that occurred shortly before our meeting apparently triggered this upsetting memory.

Another police survivor—one recognized as a hero—said that his status and reputation often kept him out of trouble because his bosses respected him and gave him the benefit of the doubt when minor disciplinary issues arose. An important difference, though, is that his bosses never referred to his experience or implied they were letting him off easy because of it. If they had, his reaction might have been quite different. In both of these cases we can see that the survivor's struggle around disciplinary issues is linked to his larger struggle around issues of integrity and authenticity.

Parenthetically, we might also note that some police survivors may be more likely to be involved in disciplinary matters than other cops simply because their demands for sustenance and special treatment often put them in conflict with supervisors and peers. The survivor's compelling need to reassert his integrity can also result in an unwillingness to compromise on matters of personal or professional principle, and along with demands for everything he believes is his due, the survivor can easily run afoul of supervisors and other cops.

Personal Relationships

Relationships with family, friends, and casual acquaintances outside the professional sphere can sometimes provide necessary nurturance, but expressions of concern and offers of help can also lead to conflict over identity and dependency issues. The police survivor's difficulty here is often that those outside the world of policing do not truly understand the quality or dimension of his needs. The matter-of-fact tone of condolences offered by an acquaintance who does not appreciate the depth of a steady partner relationship, for example, can engender great resentment as well as a sense of isolation. From the survivor's perspective, the condolences may seem to minimize his suffering and loss and underscore his sense that no one truly understands him and his traumatic experience. A strong subtextual theme in many police survivors' narratives was that "people outside the Job just don't understand me and my needs." We noted earlier that many cops do not discuss their professional experiences with spouses and family members, but I was surprised when several collaborators said they had never fully shared the facts of their death immersion with their spouse. They certainly told their spouses that the event had occurred, but did not share all the details or, in many cases, their innermost feelings with them. To whatever extent they previously withheld information or shielded spouses and family members from the knowledge of police work's realities and dangers, their silence may prove to work against their need for understanding and appropriate comfort.

Some police survivors, notably those who survived a deadly force encounter by killing an adversary, find that other cops are seemingly attracted to them, to their hero status, and to the sacral knowledge and power they hold over death. Like those who have lost a partner and/or been severely injured themselves, they are regarded with awe and respect, but it is an awe and respect of a somewhat different quality. By surviving the encounter and killing a dangerous assailant, they are confirmed as "good cops" who can handle the ultimate in danger, violence, and trouble in the most extreme situations. Others gravitate to them in part so that they can vicariously participate in their heroic experience.

Because they see so many compassionate expressions as counterfeit, or at least suspect the motives of those who want to share in their experience without having actually earned or experienced it themselves, police survivors are particularly sensitive to issues of integrity. This emphasis on integrity, also a response to the constellations of disintegration and guilt they feel, takes on a particular prominence in their lives and lifestyles. One reason they demand so much of those participating in memorials, survivor missions, and other activities aimed at honoring or immortalizing dead or injured cops is that they insist on honesty and integrity. Their own survivor mission demands that they maintain a sense of personal integrity, that they maintain fidelity to the cultural ideals of good police work (that is, being a good cop), and that they demonstrate loyalty and integrity in what they say about other cops (especially if a partner was killed).

The Quest to Make Meaning

Throughout this chapter we've seen how the police survivor's extreme immersion in death imagery devitalizes and impairs him, effectively shattering his self-image and his world. The profound death encounter alters the type and quality of his relationships with others, it burdens him with an indelible death imprint that is continually reactivated and impossible to fully master, it imposes physical and/or emotional needs that require special forms of sustenance, and it leaves him feeling numbed to experiences that would ordinarily vitalize and animate him. He may be consumed with guilt and rage, tainted by others' fears of death's contagion, suspicious of those around him, caught up in conflicts over dependence and independence, and generally estranged from the comfortable and ordered existence he once knew. Incongruity, detachment, and absurdity characterize police survivors' existence. To overcome their debilitation, police survivors struggle to reformulate a viable identity that accounts for their death immersion but nevertheless permits them to transcend it, and that restores some semblance of rational and moral order to their lives. Part of this struggle involves an attempt to extract significance and meaning from a devastating situation.

In their ultimately futile attempt to master the death immersion and restore rational and moral order to their lives, survivors continually struggle to make rational and moral sense of the death event and of their subsequent lives. To recreate such a world, survivors seek to understand why the event took place and how it so devastated them, and they seek redress against those who perpetrated the wrongs against them and others. In their quest to integrate and make coherent meaning of their experience through the formative process, survivors ultimately seek the means to once again feel fully alive. As we've seen, some police survivors—notably those who are least immersed in death imagery and who are provided with access to cultural and organizational immortality systems that facilitate some immediate repair of their damaged identity—are better able than others to reconstruct their self-image and make sense of their world.

In terms of making rational sense of their experience, their world, and themselves, survivors may continually dwell on the death event and may struggle to rewrite it in a more comprehensible way. They may, in fact, fantasize that the event never occurred or that it had a different outcome ("You try to move on, but there's always that thought: 'I wish we could go back. Then it would be OK'"). Depending upon the degree of their death immersion and the potency of their subjective survivor psychology, some police survivors never seem to be capable of moving beyond the immersion in an emotional way, while other less-immersed survivors find some capacity to integrate and reformulate the experience and ultimately to put a great deal of it behind them. In the broadest sense, the survivor's quest to make meaning of his reality involves a quest to reformulate a sense of self he and others can easily comprehend.

The quest to make meaning has several dimensions. Survivors often become consumed with a compelling urge for justice: to restore a sense of moral order, they seek to have those truly responsible for their devitalization and for the absurdity of their existence acknowledge their culpability and receive punishment for their acts. Because so much of police work and so much of the police identity is concerned with the pursuit of justice and other moral issues, the need for justice may be especially powerful among police survivors. The urge for justice, however, can sometimes lead to a scapegoating formulation in which the police survivor narrowly focuses blame upon the person he perceives as responsible for his death immersion and, ultimately, all his troubles. The quest to make meaning is also expressed in the survivor's will to bear witness to his own experience, to the experience of other survivors, and especially to the lives of those who died in the event he managed to survive. The will to bear witness can be transformed into a survivor mission—an ongoing project or crusade that permits the survivor to experience meaning, vitality, and a sense of commitment and connection as he pursues the restoration of a morally ordered world.

The Urge for Justice

Given the concerns for justice that are present in police work and in the police identity, the urge to seek justice has particular resonance among police survivors. Experienced cops have well-developed ideas, images, and constellations of justice that provide them with effective schemas for enactment, so it is relatively easy for police survivors to fulfill those schemas and experience the sense of vitality such enactment provides. The police survivor who pursues justice for himself, for other survivors, and for the dead can reconnect with each of the life-affirming subparadigms. There is a certain personal and professional integrity or consonance between philosophical ideal and actual behavior in bringing the perpetrator to justice, the process of pursuing justice through the court system can provide a sense of movement toward a worthy goal, and the involvement of others in the process provides an important sense of connection with other people united in a common and valuable purpose.

As we observed in the experience of the officer described above who faced the trial of his partner's accused murderer with great trepidation, the pursuit of justice through the judicial system can often be painful because it reactivates so many traumatic images and guilty constellations. In his need to make sense of the death and to vitiate his own guilt by publicly fixing responsibility for it, however, the officer felt compelled to put himself through the ordeal. To some extent the trial, and especially the difficult chore of testifying to the facts and circumstances of his partner's death and his own emotional state, provided a forum for him to explain and justify himself to the public, to the media, and to his peers. His role as witness rather than defendant confirmed, in a symbolic and practical way, that he was not on trial—he was not to be judged—for playing any part in the death.

Consistent with their professional identity, police survivors are often consumed with a compelling need to bring those responsible for their victimization to justice, and to large extent they attempt to satisfy the need by bearing witness to the event. Especially in the police context, bearing witness can take at least two forms: police survivors bear witness in a formal sense when they testify in criminal court against the people they hold responsible for the event, and they also bear witness by creating memorials and pursuing survivor missions.

Scapegoating

In the extreme, the urge to seek justice can lead to a scapegoating formulation in which the survivor seems to lose perspective on the crime committed against him, and he focuses all blame exclusively on the person or people he perceives as responsible for his victimization. Survivors possessed of this formulation tend to lack objectivity insofar as they lay *all* blame for *every* real or imagined injustice done to them or others upon the selected target of their rage, while others manage a more reasoned and rational approach that allots guilt more equitably. The urge to lay blame can also be more generalized and amorphous, and so we see some police survivors apportion blame more equitably and rationally. One collaborator focused a great deal of anger on the person instrumentally responsible for his victimization but reserved an amorphous but nevertheless powerful rage for the police department and for certain officials he felt betrayed him after the fact by failing to deliver the promised sustenance he was due. In his estimation, this was a highly immoral betrayal, since he paid dearly to fulfill his responsibilities but the agency violated the expected reciprocity norms and ignored his special needs. His quest for personal justice was somewhat satisfied when the person responsible for the criminal act was convicted and imprisoned, but his rage against the agency had not abated. His personal crusade to force the agency to accept responsibility for abusing him and to atone for its transgressions has become a matter of principle, and he pursues this mission almost entirely without regard for the career consequences.

Other traces of the tendency toward scapegoating can be glimpsed in the case of the officer cited above who was angered when media accounts elided details that pointed more forcefully toward the guilt of his partner's accused murderer. To him, it was important not only that others knew he was not morally or factually responsible for his partner's death, but that they knew all the facts about the horribly immoral crime so they could share in his vehement rage toward the murderer.

The Survivor Mission

At various points in this chapter and elsewhere in this book we've pointed out ways the police agency, the police culture, and individual police survivors pursue activities that symbolically immortalize slain cops. These expressions of the urge to immortalize the cop by keeping his memory alive include erecting memorial plaques and inscribing his name on various walls of honor, wearing "In Memory Of" T-shirts and breast bars, and dedicating police boats, streets, schools, parks, and playgrounds in his name. Permanent memorials enshrining the slain cop's name ensure that he receives the kind of honors reserved for a special few, and to some extent they may symbolically connect with one or more modes of expressing symbolic immortality. Parks and playgrounds, for example, symbolically connect the cop with eternal nature and with locations we associate with youth and vitality, and the renaming of schools provides some connection with the immortalizing notion of positively affecting the development of future generations. Breast bars and T-shirts demonstrate the individual's personal connection with the dead cop and permit him to symbolically represent his own survivorship, and retiring the officer's shield also has special significance. These and other memorials are created partly in service of restoring some moral order to the world: in a morally ordered universe, the ultimate sacrifice these heroes made would be celebrated at the same time they are treated with somber respect, and they would always be remembered. Each of these expressions, however, is directed primarily toward memorializing the cop's death rather than celebrating his life.

Other immortalizing expressions are more life affirming insofar as they are geared toward carrying the officer's legacy forward through good works, especially those that actually or symbolically connect with his interests in life, extract lessons from the circumstances of his death, or define and amplify his relationships with other cops. Thus we see the creation of charitable foundations that support injured or traumatized cops, scholarships that may be earmarked for the children of other cops, political activities to support various kinds of legislation, and other forms of communal activity that bring people together for the dual purpose of effecting positive social change and creating a legacy for a life cut short. These activities often take on special symbolic features with particular meaning for the dead cop and/or the survivors: the dollar amount given in one memorial scholarship, for example, equals the dead officer's shield number. Finally, we can see that "fun runs," golf outings, and other sporting events honor the slain officer at the same time they promote vitalizing physical activity and group participation.

What each of these endeavors has in common is the potential for uniting groups of people, especially cops, in vitalizing activities that permit access to a mode of symbolic immortality at the same time they honor the officer's memory and legacy. Paradoxically, they operate to restore rational order to the world by permitting survivors to imagine or briefly fantasize that he is still present among them. Especially for those police survivors who dedicate substantial time and effort to organizing and carrying out these events and activities, they comprise a kind of survivor mission that expresses integrity, connection, and movement.

Individual police survivors can also be possessed of personal and private survivor missions that tend to reflect their subjective needs, vulnerabilities, and particular forms of devitalization. Perhaps especially in the case of cops whose partners or close friends were killed in the line of duty, survivor missions that carry on life projects the dead cop left unfinished permit them to confirm their fidelity to the culture and the demands it imposes upon partners. An example of a survivor's mission to symbolically take up and complete a dead officer's professional mission can be seen in the case of one cop whose story was related by another collaborator. After the cop's brother was murdered in the line of duty, he requested that his brother's shield be assigned to him, and he requested a transfer to his brother's precinct, sector, and squad.

These missions to carry on life projects often involve the tremendous sense of commitment many police survivors have to the dead cop's spouse, children, and family. To help carry on the dead cop's life work, for example, cops may take on a special protective or nurturing role on behalf of their partner's children, taking them along on family outings or becoming deeply involved in the children's education and development. A collaborator who assumed such a role said he did so because his partner's children had been that officer's most important priority in life, and he felt a special responsibility to care for them in his partner's absence. His partner would certainly do the same for his kids, and to do otherwise would be a symbolic betrayal and abandonment of his partner in his time of greatest need. The same dynamic applied to his supportive outreach to his partner's spouse, who was also included in family activities and with whom he communicated, often briefly but without fail, on practically a daily basis. These efforts and activities, he said, were rooted in the eternal and irrevocable bond of police partnership: "This is just what you do for a partner, and he will always be my partner."

More Inclusive Survivor Missions

Some death-immersed cops try to reify their experience and translate the death imprint image into appropriate actions that atone for the guilt they feel, especially actions involving a commitment to other dead or injured cops, and their sense of commitment and identification ultimately expands outward to embrace all other police survivors. They may, for example, make special efforts to attend police funerals and memorials for other slain cops, but as one collaborator with a great deal of experience counseling traumatized and injured cops pointed out, attending funerals often brings their own event back to them. Nevertheless, he said, despite the emotional pain they endure, they feel compelled to attend. We can understand how their emotional distress adds a special kind of self-sacrifice and integrity to this form of witnessing. Others get involved with charitable activities and groups geared toward memorializing fallen cops, helping out cops in need, or supporting other survivors. All the police survivors evinced some kind of strengthened connection to the police culture and all participated in some sort of activities aimed at helping other cops. These connections and behaviors usually included a great concern for officer safety, permitting them to carry out their mission and to bear witness to their own death immersion while experiencing an immortalizing sense that they have a positive influence on the future of other cops.

Again, although the profound death imprint image can never be truly mastered through enactment, some survivors feel compelled to seek and carry out survivor missions that benefit other cops, but they are often frustrated that despite their best efforts and best intentions they can never do quite enough in service of troubled cops and their physical and emotional safety. In particular, they want to bear witness to their own suffering and to carry the dark message that every cop should be prepared for the possibility of a similar fate.

> Is there anyone who goes out there and talks to cops? Is there anyone to go out there and talk to cops who are partners or just cops in general and tell them? People don't want to believe it can happen to them but I'm telling you right now it *can*. People say, "You were partners for [many] years?" "Yeah." "And you watched him die?" "Yeah." "Oh, shit. I can't talk about this. I'm sorry." "Hey, no problem." People don't want to get into it, they don't want to think about it. It *can* happen. *I'm* telling you it can happen.

One collaborator noted that although he became a member of an organization of cops devoted to supporting other traumatized cops, he ultimately drifted away because he found it too depressing to be continually exposed to cops who had been very badly injured, who suffered a catastrophic illness, or who experienced other traumatic life events. Although the officer remained supportive of the group's aims, believed its members were well intentioned, and was grateful for the support it had given him in his time of greatest need, he found the intimate discussions of other cops' problems too difficult to handle. This officer also had his own well-founded and very specific survivor mission, a mission that did not easily fit within the group's broad mandate to help cops experiencing a broad range of trauma-related problems. Some police survivors become so caught up in their own mission and have such a compelling need to fulfill it that they cannot easily deal with the distractions of others' missions.

There are, however, limits to the kind of emotional trauma survivors can bear, and some activities conjure especially painful memories. One collaborator noted that although he never failed to visit memorials honoring his partner or other cops killed in the line of duty, he could not bring himself to visit the National Law Enforcement Officers' Memorial in Washington, D.C., or its annual event to honor cops killed in the line of duty. Several cops brought him rubbings of his partner's name as it appeared on the memorial wall, but he and his partner had vacationed together in Washington with their spouses and those happy memories made the prospect of visiting the city again too painful.

Quiet Missions

Partners and close friends of a murdered cop often take a high-profile leadership role in organizing the mission, but almost all of those affected by the death engage in some sort of altruistic or immortalizing activities. They often go about these activities quietly and may not seek to attract attention to themselves or their good deeds. The parents of one officer killed in the line of duty, for example, told of visiting their son's grave site and finding flowers and various mementos with special symbolic connection to their son's life that indicated many others had visited the grave. They were touched by these gestures and sought, through various means, to determine which of their son's friends and colleagues had visited in order to thank them. The visits eased concerns that their son would not be remembered.

Over the years I've heard of or witnessed many instances in which cops performed quiet, even anonymous acts of kindness that benefited a slain officer's family or preserved his memory in some way. Interestingly, many of the officers performing these acts did not know the dead officer well: their acts represent a larger and more encompassing connection to the circumstances of the death or to a sense of cultural connection. One patrol officer I knew, for example, would often park his patrol car at a particular location between calls for service. When asked why he frequently chose that particular location to sit or to drink coffee, he explained, with the slight embarrassment many cops exhibit when they are caught in the act of a benevolent gesture, that the family of a cop murdered in the line of duty lived on the street and he just wanted to make sure that their block was particularly safe. Importantly, he always parked so that the marked patrol car could not be seen from the dead officer's home, since he was sensitive to the idea that the image of the patrol car might conjure troubling memories for the family. That he never personally knew the murdered officer did not deter him from acting as a kind of unseen guardian angel watching over the officer's home and family.

Meaning, Connection, and Religious Faith

As they struggle to find meaning and extract value and vitality from the death, survivors often seek symbols and images that capture and express the deceased officer's essential goodness and altruism or that offer a special kind of personal connection to him. There is certainly always a tendency to reconstruct our memories of a deceased loved one and cast them in a more positive light, and this tendency goes hand in hand with an unwillingness to tolerate criticisms of him, but in the case of a murdered cop there may be more of these images available to connect with existing forms and constellations. As we observed earlier, members of police families (especially children) view police work in an idealized light—they are convinced of the inherent goodness and nobility of police officers and police work and they believe the police are a powerful moral force acting in the best interests of society. Their implicit loyalty and commitment to the police culture and its ideal values are reinforced when official and cultural expressions of support sustain them and when they participate in police immortality rites and ceremonies. In many cases their affinity for cops and for the police culture deepens, and in experiencing this connection they also experience a sense of immortality for themselves and their loved one.

Police survivors and family members not only actively seek these immortalizing symbols and images, but they also tend to invest them with highly personalized special meanings and to find significant connections between seemingly disparate events and images. Police survivors and family members often take refuge in the comforts of religious faith—several noted their death immersion led to a deeper and more fulfilling religious or spiritual life, and many of the images and symbols they embraced have religious significance. Several police survivors, for example, noted they experienced a kind of spiritual rebirth after almost being killed. A collaborator who said he'd always been moderately religious began attending Mass and taking the sacrament of Communion on a daily basis. When he was unable to attend services, he often stopped at a church for a few minutes of silent prayer and quiet reflection that left him feeling more centered, and he and his spouse frequently went to a local beach for a period of contemplation and meditation. Sunday Mass became a family event, and while he said he was "certainly not a holy roller," he found great comfort and a sense of transcendent connection to his faith, to his family, and to others in religious experience. Consonant with the doctrines of his faith and because his own near death made him sensitive to the potential for unexpected death, he believed it was important to remain in a state of grace.

Several collaborator narratives evidenced a connection between religious faith and eternal nature, and immortalizing images in nature often took on special significance. A family member of an officer killed in the line of duty, for example, recalled being in his backyard a few days after the death, sobbing as he looked at newspaper clippings. He became aware of a small rabbit sitting quietly at his feet— a symbol of new life, he said—and took it as a sign his loved one was in a better place. The rabbit has returned to the yard again and again, and each time he sees it as an affirmation of the connection with the dead officer. On another occasion shortly after the death he saw a particular symbol—one he associates with the officer but that also has some religious significance as well as a tangential association with policing—in the configuration of a cloud, and he went on to describe how this image has reappeared in various forms at significant events.

> Are they coincidences? I don't think so. I see them as God's indicators. They are my connections and proof that life does not end. It continues, but in different ways. I know that God cares.

This family member's attempt to reclaim meaning and significance from death mirrored the kind of attempts many other collaborators made to find something positive to take away from their profound death immersion, and all ultimately managed to do so. A common theme among all police survivor collaborators was that through their immersion and struggle with death—an immersion and struggle that deprived them of the capacity to fully enjoy life—they came to a greater appreciation of the value of life. As we've seen, some come to find a kind of transcendent peace and achieve a worldview that underscores the importance of affirming rather than destroying life. As one collaborator put it:

> Something like this makes you appreciate how fragile and valuable human life is—yours or another person's. And how easy it is to die or to take a human life. That's something you already know, but something like this makes it concrete and real. It teaches you what is really important in life.

Another collaborator expressed it this way:

> Yes, I would say something good came out of this. It prepared me better for my career and my life, in that I know I never want to get involved in anything like this again. Everything I do now is geared toward finding an alternative. Not just because the department says to find an alternative, but because I never want to go through this again. As a cop, you must remain committed to life.

Conclusion

The police survivors whose experiences we've explored in this chapter survived some of the most horrific kinds of death experiences cops can encounter, and these experiences resulted in the most penetrating manifestations of survivor psychology we've seen. Their experiences changed their personal and professional identities in profound ways, and they continually struggle to manage these identities. Some police survivors fare better than others, and those who have immediate access to powerful immortality systems are rather quickly able to begin reformulating a new identity that allows them to once again experience some vitality. No matter how well some survivors do, though, they are never quite the same person they were before. They are, to far greater extent than any of the other survivors we've seen, forever tied to the horror of the death imprint and forever caught up in devitalizing and interlocking cycles of guilt, taint, formative impairment, and damaged identity.

Police survivors struggle with a myriad of issues, some of which are entirely subjective and some of which are particular to the specific facts and circumstances of their death immersion, but these lasting struggles illuminate how powerfully they are affected by each of the five themes of survivor psychology. As we've examined these themes, we've seen how closely intertwined and synergistic they are, and how difficult it is to explore one theme without recognizing how it affects and is affected by other themes.

It would be a disservice to these men and women not to acknowledge again that they bear their tainted identities, their guilt, their devitalization, and the horrors of their experience with tremendous integrity. They struggle against the rage, the guilt, and the taint they feel, not only because these features of survivorship impair their own capacity to fully experience the vibrancy and vitality life once offered them, but also because their death immersion ultimately makes them more sensitive to the plight of others and more committed to activities they can undertake on behalf of others. Although many feel they have been horribly wronged by their experience and by the actions and reactions of others, they struggle against bitterness and despondency, and they fight to maintain an optimistic view of themselves, their world, and of others who inhabit it. They remain deeply committed to the altruism and the idealism that first drew them into policing—the constellations and values that lie at the core of their police identity and at the core of police culture—and in some cases their death immersion has reinforced these constellations to make them more humane and caring cops. If I were able to relate to the reader all the facts and details of their struggles and of the events that so transformed them, their narratives would be all the more compelling. In one sense these details might have permitted me to be a more authentic witness on their behalf, but my commitment to the survivors and my respect for their integrity and privacy would not permit it.

There is great pathos in their narratives, but none of the collaborators was in any way pathetic. They are men and women of good impulse who have been thrust into extreme situations that few human beings ever confront, and despite a fearful knowledge that they might one day have to confront these situations they did not shrink away. They are, in every sense of the word, heroic men and women who continue to live heroic lives.

There is rather little to add at this point, and further exposition or analysis would serve only to make their very human experiences more abstract and intellectualized. Perhaps the best summary of the police survivor's experience and the challenges they face is reflected in the words of one collaborator. Although his remarks specifically concerned the experience of spouses and children of officers murdered in the line of duty and the police department's response to them, the words seem equally descriptive of police survivors in general.

The hierarchy feels they do the best they can. You know, there are scholarships for the children, there are events and children's parties they get invited to. They feel the widows are remembered, there are memorial services. They feel these individuals are not forgotten. What the hierarchy may not be aware of is the children who are acting out, who are in therapy, who have nightmares, who are teased in the schoolyard—"Oh, you don't have a daddy." What the Department doesn't get is how their individual lives are impacted every single day. When they go to the supermarket and walk down the corridor and cry when they see their husband's favorite food on the shelf. It all comes back months later. How they can't sleep at night. How they are tremendously lonely. And it's great to have a support network, it's great to be able to call another widow on the phone at 1:00 in the morning, but it's just not enough. Those are the things the Department just doesn't realize. That holding four or five events during the year for this person just doesn't meet that person's needs. These are desperately wounded souls, and there is nothing, nothing you can ever do to restore them.

9.

Reflections
and Observations

We began our explorations of the psychological impact of exposure to death in contemporary urban policing by observing that although exposure to death is a powerful variable in human psychology, and although police officers frequently encounter death in many forms and in all sorts of situations and conditions, we know rather little about the particular kinds of impact such exposures have upon individual officers or their occupational culture. Our prospective exploration was an intellectual journey in which we would undertake to learn more about this terra incognita—the psychological nexus of death and policing—in order to develop a more complete, detailed, and comprehensive knowledge of it. We undertook this exploration not merely to expand the field of knowledge, but to come away with a more sweeping grasp of an important but often ignored human dimension of policing, and hopefully to gain practical insights into police psychology and behavior. We did not anticipate that this project would ultimately answer every question or illuminate every aspect of this complex subject, and in fact we recognized that the research might well raise more questions than it answered. This research certainly does not represent the final word on exposure to death in policing, but our intellectual journey has taken us a long way toward a fuller understanding of the consequential issues we investigated.

It is the nature and part of the attraction of exploratory research—especially exploratory research to which one feels a strong sense of personal and professional commitment—that we never know when we begin precisely where the project will take us physically, emotionally, or intellectually. We go, in essence, where the theory and data lead us, and we exploit the unanticipated potentials of the moment as they arise. As evidenced by the length, depth, and breadth of this research, the complexity of the paradigm and perspective it involved, and the compelling nature of the issues it explored, this was an intensive and ambitious project. One should never embark on such a difficult intellectual journey without a sincere commitment to it, and one should be aware that it requires a tremendous investment of time and intellectual effort. One should also be aware that he may be profoundly touched and even changed by the experiences of the people he meets on the journey, and this seems particularly true when he is a cop who comes in intimate contact with the lives and experiences of other cops.

Academics are quite properly concerned with maintaining an objective view of their subject, but all too often our concerns for objectivity interpose a psychological and emotional distance from the human issues with which we must also be concerned. In undertaking an uncertain intellectual journey of this kind and in dealing so closely with these human beings and human issues, one is also bound to struggle with objectivity and commitment. Researcher and collaborator are drawn more closely together when they mutually explore the kind of intimate personal experiences that are the substance of this work, and the connection that develops can make it difficult to remain detached from one's topic. In a project as concerned with significant human issues as this research is, complete detachment is not only a practical impossibility, but also inadvisable. The researcher always brings his personal experiences, biases, and intellectual strengths and weaknesses to the project, so claims to complete objectivity are disingenuous. In the extreme, complete objective detachment raises the risky prospect of depriving the study of its essential humanity and also denies the humanity of the researcher.

Early on in our explorations we discussed the stance Lifton (1986, p. 14) calls "advocacy and detachment," and it would be wrong and inauthentic of me not to address this issue or to leave the reader with the impression that I did not become emotionally engaged with and sympathetic toward many of my collaborators. Although it was often a struggle to maintain the advocacy and detachment stance, I believe I was largely successful in mastering that struggle, and my acknowledged advocacy for these survivors who shared their lives and experiences with me did not cloud my objectivity or immoderately infiltrate my analysis. Because I knew from the beginning that this would be an issue of concern, I remained aware of its risks throughout the research process and did my best to maintain fidelity to the principles of objectivity without ignoring my own humanity. There are always elements of uncertainty and ambitious risk in research that ventures into uncharted intellectual territory, but for several additional reasons this research project was particularly ambitious and particularly risky.

First, this research is concerned with human issues that are of profound psychological, philosophical, and ethical consequence, at the same time they are issues many would prefer to ignore. There is always some resistance to discussing or even reflecting upon our own death—our death encounters always remind us of our own mortality—but even when we get beyond this obstacle to embrace and conceptualize the intricate issues involved, we often find it difficult to articulate our thoughts, feelings, and insights in a meaningful and revealing way. This set of problems operates for the interviewer as well as for the collaborator, but it is the researcher's responsibility to bear witness to the collaborators' experience in a meaningful and honest way. I did not know at the outset what quantity or quality of data I would collect, nor whether the data would support or refute my intuitive assumptions about the phenomena under study or about the feasibility of the paradigm to adequately explain whatever findings I actually obtained.

This project was also ambitious in its complexity and its objectives, since we looked at the common experiential themes that emerge from police death encounters and examined these themes at three levels of analysis. In essence, we attempted to explore and explicate, in a logically structured way, phenomena that defy precise measurement, classification, and structure. We looked at the impact police death encounters have upon the individual officer, upon their occupational culture, and upon the police organization as a whole. To better grasp how death encounters subjectively affect cops, we needed to understand who these cops were and how they got to be that way, we needed to understand the values and belief systems that animate and support their culture, and we needed to understand something about the specific kinds of work they do in relation to death events. Grasping how these three forces or factors—the individual cop, his culture, and his task environment—intersect at a given death event and interact to mediate his experience of that event was difficult enough, but from the writer's point of view the need to adequately describe and do justice to each without becoming mired in minutia or exposition that would lead us too far astray from our primary subject made the endeavor even more difficult.

Finally, the project was ambitious and complex because it sought to analyze, explain, and make meaning of police and police work by applying Robert Jay Lifton's formative-symbolic paradigm and because it sought to analyze, explain, and make meaning of police death encounters by applying Lifton's psychology of survival perspective. This required a thorough reconceptualization of police psychology, socialization, and culture, since neither the formative-symbolic paradigm nor the psychology of survival had ever been previously applied in a large-scale study of policing. As a result, there was no extant literature written from the formative-symbolic viewpoint to directly support many of my observations and conclusions about police officers or police work. To a large extent, this research took an entirely new and untested approach to understanding police and police work, requiring that we reexamine many of the observations others have made and recast them in language and conceptual forms that aligned with our approach.

Early on in this book we outlined some basic principles about human responses to death and reactions to death encounters, drawing many of our observations from a fairly eclectic body of literature dealing with various death work occupations. We refined these observations by pointing out some similarities and differences between these occupations and the kind of death exposures they entail and the realities of contemporary urban policing. The many points of correspondence and divergence we found illuminated the fact that police officers encounter death under somewhat different circumstances than other death workers, and in turn our observations identified several facets of policing that required further exploration and amplification so that the impact of these similarities and differences could be better understood. We therefore took a number of excursions along our intellectual journey, exploring and expanding upon these facets before returning to our primary subject matter.

These similarities and differences, along with the absence of an extensive and coherent body of literature dealing specifically with police death encounters, also hinted at the kind of research plan we would need to excavate data about police experiences with death. We saw, for example, that a great deal of the research on police death encounters consists of quantitative research into police shootings and police murders that offers few insights into cops' subjective experience of these or other death encounters. More specifically, the literature pointed to the fact that we would have to obtain our primary data directly from police officers—to "get inside their heads" to truly understand their experience—using a depth interview method supported by other forms of direct and indirect observation.

Rather than focusing entirely on the subjective experience of individual officers, we adopted a shared themes approach that allowed us to operate at a certain level of abstraction and to discern larger and more universal patterns of psychological response among officers who experienced somewhat similar death events. The shared themes approach nevertheless allowed us to maintain a humane and person-focused orientation and to hear the voices of collaborators whose narratives expressed these themes in especially representative, powerful or evocative ways. The formative-symbolic paradigm provided us with a sufficiently broad and adaptable structure to analyze, examine, and explain police behavior in general, and the psychology of survival allowed us to focus more narrowly on the specific psychological themes or patterns of psychological response that result from death encounters.

At this point there seems little to be gained from attempting to thoroughly recapitulate or summarize all the findings, observations, and conclusions we might wring out of the preceding chapters, just as there is little to be gained from additional analysis of the data. This book contains a tremendous amount of complex data that is often expressed subtly in the collaborators' narrative voices, and in trying to succinctly restate it we run the risk of eliding important nuances and observations. Similarly, additional analysis poses the distinct risk of an overly academic approach that would ultimately impoverish the research and undermine its value by raising essentially human expressions to an unsuitable level of psychologized abstraction. We might not hear the collaborators' voices.

We simultaneously pursued a variety of goals and objectives in this research; in order to close out our inquiry with conclusions, we can conceptually group these goals and objectives into three major areas or categories. First, we sought to explore the psychological impact of police death encounters by determining how various objective, subjective, and situational factors influence the event's traumatic potential and ultimately affect officers. Second, we sought to apply the formative-symbolic paradigm and the psychology of survival to this research, and to assess their viability and explanatory power for our areas of concern. Finally, we sought to identify areas that might prove fruitful for future research and to extract some pertinent observations that could help address some of the problems and psychological issues that result from police death encounters.

In our initial review of the literature of death work occupations and the psychology of death, we observed that the traumatic potential of a given death event can be aggravated or mitigated by various factors. These include the individual's previous experiences with death and his subjective vulnerability to death trauma, his interaction with others at the scene, the specific tasks and behaviors in which he engages, the duration of the exposure, the gruesomeness of the death and the condition of the corpse, his physical proximity to the corpse, and the extent to which he identifies or has a relationship with the deceased. We also discovered that death events in which the individual plays an instrumental role in causing the death are especially traumatic.

We saw how previous death encounters, especially professional encounters, shape the experience of cops in each task environment. The rookie collaborators, for example, had no earlier professional death encounters, and so they lacked adequate images, forms, and constellations with which to integrate and make sense of an encounter. Their related lack of adequate schemas for enactment further exacerbated their discomfort and unease at the death scene. Rookies also lacked earlier professional opportunities to develop and refine their capacity for partial professional numbing, making their first encounter all the more traumatic.

Collaborators in the other task environments, though, had substantial prior professional dealings with death, sufficient images and constellations that helped them integrate and make sense of their encounters, and adequate schemas for enactment to fulfill organizational roles as well as their personally and culturally mandated urge to *do something*. Because earlier encounters helped develop their capacity for partial professional numbing, their death encounters usually resulted in less psychic trauma.

Subjective vulnerabilities to death imagery are, by their nature, less amenable to broad generalizations, but we certainly met collaborators whose personal vulnerabilities made certain deaths more difficult. We recall here the veteran homicide detective reduced to tears—more than 10 years after the incident—while discussing the death of a child under circumstances that paralleled his own son's near death.

The cop's interactions with others at the death scene certainly affect his experience, and we saw the influence of different patterns of typical interaction with other cops and with the deceased's family and friends. Rookies, who have the potential for a great deal of interaction with family and friends, often try to avoid this interaction by busying themselves with paperwork. Because they want to be "good cops" and generally have a service orientation, some rookies force themselves to deal with family and friends as compassionately as their limited repertoire of experiences and constellations will allow. Tenured cops are generally more comfortable interacting in this way, and the emotional costs that accrue may be offset by the sense of personal and professional integrity, movement, and connection they receive from compassionate response as well as by reinforcing of their "good cop" identity. Crime scene unit technicians, on the other hand, are continuously confronting grotesque and violent death and they have neither a tolerance nor a professional need for interactions with people other than cops—especially emotionally distraught people. Their professional identity is tied up in objective detachment and technical proficiency, and the nature of their work allows them to entirely avoid interactions and the complicating emotional connections that might result.

In terms of specific tasks and behaviors shaping the death encounter experience, we have seen that the duties the task environment prescribes can either attenuate or exacerbate psychic threat. Examples are the handling of human remains and the inventorying of personal effects, tasks typically delegated to the rookie and supervised by the patrol sergeant, and we saw that officers in both categories specifically cited the handling of personal effects as a psychologically difficult job that enhanced their sense of identification with the deceased. This task resulted in an uneasy feeling that they were in some way violating the deceased's privacy by snooping around in his most private papers and possessions. They see it as a superfluous administrative duty of uncertain necessity, but for homicide detectives and crime scene unit technicians it is an integral part of the investigative process that helps define their professional self and achieve their professional goals. It poses less psychic threat for them in part because it connects with and reinforces their professional identity, in part because partial professional numbing and prior experiences with the task have inured them to much of its trauma, and in part because it helps them make meaning of the death and pursue justice. Handling human remains or a deceased person's possessions may stimulate guilty constellations of separation, stasis, and disintegration among rookies and patrol sergeants, but the same activities provide a sense of professional connection, movement, and integrity for homicide detectives and crime scene unit technicians. For crime scene unit technicians, in fact, the capacity for dispassionate examination of even the most grotesque human remains to discover evidence is an intrinsic element of their work and their professional identity.

The death encounter's traumatic potential is magnified when it involves exposure to grotesque, violent, or particularly disintegrative images, and so we saw that the physical condition of the corpse influences the cop's overall experience. A recent benign death—a "fresh DOA," for example—generally involves less traumatic imagery than one involving a decomposing corpse. These "ripe DOAs" assault the cop's senses with a host of visual, olfactory, and perhaps tactile images, and his visceral reaction can be amplified when his exposure is prolonged. We saw that rookies required to "sit" on a decomposing body for extended periods often become physically ill and/or psychologically immobilized, and we saw that experienced cops in other task environments equip themselves with cigars and other means to mask the stench of putrefaction, and sometimes with books or other means of intellectual stimulation. Death imprints often involve grotesque or disintegrative imagery, and the numbing these exposures naturally evoke can be more profound when the officer has to physically handle gruesome remains. Thus we saw that because all but the most inured cops—notably, crime scene unit technicians—have a distinct aversion to handling remains, cultural conventions have evolved to dictate that unless a compelling professional reason to the contrary exists, such tasks are delegated to the rookie. In turn, the process of overcoming reluctance to have physical contact with a corpse—especially a decomposing corpse or detached body parts—represents a rite of passage within the larger "first DOA" rite of passage, ultimately helping rookies develop the capacity for partial professional numbing. In particular, we recall the collaborator who felt a physical sense of dissociated numbing overcome him as he forced himself to straddle a decomposing corpse and on another occasion forced himself to pick up and tag body parts strewn along a highway. We also recall the transit division sergeant who, following his traumatic experiences dealing with disintegrative death as a patrol cop, exercised his supervisory discretion not to enter the proximity of "space cases" and "men under."

A cop's psychic trauma is often amplified when he has some sense of connection to the deceased or when some basis exists for a close connection. We saw some evidence that cops are particularly troubled when they share personal characteristics with the deceased, including similarities in age, race, sex, and social condition, or when they relate to the circumstances of the death in especially powerful ways. Here we recall the young cop who was stirred to special action by the near death of a young woman—the kind of girl he "would have dated"—with whom he shared many points of identification.

These and many other factors or situational variables may be present or absent at a particular death scene, and to a large extent the officer's task environment dictates the quality and quantity of his exposure to them. The same factors may be present at mortal combat death scenes, and because these situations involve infinitely greater personal involvement and psychic threat—they are truly encounters with one's own mortality rather than casual encounters with the deaths of strangers—their overall impact is likely to be magnified tremendously.

The Formative-Symbolic Paradigm and the Psychology of Survival

We sought to apply the formative-symbolic paradigm and the psychology of survival perspective in this research and to assess their viability and explanatory power for the specific area of police death encounters as well as for a broader conceptualization of police psychology and police behavior at the cultural and organizational levels. In all respects, the formative-symbolic paradigm and the psychology of survival proved to be exceptionally powerful analytical tools that gave structure to our explorations and meaning to our data.

The formative-symbolic paradigm illuminated a host of individual police behaviors, organizational activities, and cultural rites, rituals, and belief systems that can impart a vitalizing sense of symbolic immortality: they permit cops to participate, symbolically or actually, in an endeavor of historic significance that is greater, more important, and more enduring than the individual. We also saw the five modes of accessing and expressing the quest for a sense of immortality in these behaviors, activities, rites, and rituals, and we saw how each mode provides cops with a sense of connection, movement, and integrity. Further, the paradigm allowed us to analyze policing in a way that adds depth and texture to observations others have made.

Other observers have commented that there is often a family tradition in policing, for example, but by viewing it as part of the quest for symbolic immortality we can better appreciate its power and appeal. The family tradition expresses the biological mode of symbolic immortality by connecting one's own history to the history of policing and it expresses a kind of integrity or consonance between one's own activities, aspirations, beliefs, and lifestyle and those of one's biological forebears. The family tradition also involves a sense of movement by permitting participants to feel they are continuing the work and fulfilling the legacy of their predecessors, or that their own work and legacy is being carried on into the future. Biosocial variations on this theme include the importance and strength of relationships between police mentors and protégés, and we saw how the sense of biohistorical continuity ultimately expands to encompass the idea of being part of a durable and eternal police culture. Hence cops subtly distinguish between "the Job," a construct with overtones that imply personal and professional fidelity to a set of eternal values, truths and belief systems, and the more ephemeral "Department"—a construct laden with some suspicion and perhaps some cynicism regarding its integrity and durability.

We saw how expressive symbols like the police officer's shield permit ties to the past and future at the same time as they represent participation in a powerful romantic tradition involving honorable, chivalric, and self-sacrificing values. The symbolism of the shield can be invested with special meaning when it is subsumed within the family tradition, but even when cops have no access to the family tradition the continuity of the shield and its passing from officer to officer unites the individual self with the people and the activities of the past and future, permitting the cop to feel a special symbolic connection to the eternal flow and continuity of the policing enterprise.

Another particularly meaningful mode of expressing symbolic immortality is that of creative works, which involves the urge to affect the lives of others—especially their future lives—in positive ways. Again, this mode underlies mentorship relationships and the formal and informal transmission of cultural values, myths, and police "tricks of the trade," as well as what we called the "urge to do justice." To greater or lesser extent police aspirants and police recruits possess this urge to achieve a sense that one makes a significant and lasting contribution to society, and images that accrue through police experience can either add substance and dimension to these rudimentary and inchoate constellations or erode them. The urge to do justice also shows the specific manifestations and forms of expression a universal mode of symbolic immortality can take when it is shaped and influenced by powerful cultural and organizational precepts and values.

The symbols and immortality systems that express the quest for symbolic immortality take on special significance in terms of police death encounters, and we saw how these symbols and images are used to assert connection, continuity, integrity, and vitality in memorializing murdered cops and other police heroes. The fact that police survivors of extreme death immersions who were afforded access to powerful immortality systems fared better, in terms of immediately re-pairing their damaged identities, than cops who were denied access to the same systems underscores the systems' tremendous capacity to impart a healthy sense of vitality and to maintain the viability of the self in the aftermath of powerful psychic trauma.

The biological/biosocial mode and the urge toward creative works are cer-tainly powerful within the contemporary urban police context, but they are by no means the only ones uncovered in our explorations. We discovered aspects and features of all five modes, and each expressed the essential elements of connec-tion, movement, and integrity in ways that were especially appropriate to police officers. Many of the police behaviors, activities, and belief systems these modes encompass were casually observed by others, but the formative-symbolic para-digm allowed us to explain them in an entirely new and especially informative way.

The formative-symbolic paradigm also allowed us to explore the process of police socialization and the development of a police identity, as well as to extract important new insights and meanings from them. The paradigm's emphasis on creating increasingly complex and meaningful images, forms, and constellations within the formative process—a process that is inherently vitalizing and there-fore especially salient in light of the cop's sense of social estrangement—allowed us to see the importance of different kinds of police experience in forging an indi-vidual identity, a police identity, and a cultural identity. Here again, other research-ers have stressed the importance of police experience in identity development and some have even noted how police officers place extraordinary emphasis on sub-jective experience as the primary determiner of truth, but I am aware of no other psychological analysis that describes a specific cognitive/emotional process by which these subjective images and experiences integrate with earlier forms to cre-ate increasingly complex constellations that give meaning and vitality to individual and group experience. The formative-symbolic paradigm also shows us that im-ages, forms, and constellations have inherent schemas for enactment that are often rooted in training and socialization processes, and these schemas helped us under-stand how and why police respond to a given event in a particular way.

Finally, the formative-symbolic paradigm gave us insight into the way police develop a professional identity that can appear very different from the persona they adopt outside the work environment. From our early review of the death work literature, for example, we posited that cops with the least developed role identity and the poorest sense of agency would experience greater distress in their death encounters. The rookie collaborators' narratives certainly bear this out, but per-haps more significantly we refined these concepts to bring them into line with the formative-symbolic paradigm. We saw how the "sense of agency" develops once sufficient images are acquired to create constellations with viable schemas for enactment and once the young cop feels sufficiently confident to actualize them, and we reworked the concept of role identity by observing how these images ulti-mately lead to the emergence of a kind of dual identity we called the "police self" and the "personal self."

The "police self" is the inclusive sum of all the images experienced in officers' occupational lives as well as some elements of images, forms, and constellations imported from outside their working world. Core elements of the "personal self" are the basis for the "police self," but although the personal identity certainly preexists the police identity, it also inevitably takes on and incorporates some images, forms, and constellations the cop experiences at work. The socialized cop—certainly the "good cop"—is a very different person than he was as a police aspirant or a police recruit. There is substantial overlap and substantial give-and-take between these two identities, since some images inhabit and infiltrate both spheres, and throughout this intellectual journey we saw how cops struggle to manage their identities.

On the one hand we saw cops struggle to compartmentalize their working experiences and isolate traumatic images so they would not intrude in their personal lives—these include the cops who rarely if ever inform their families and significant others about their hard and cynical working life, the violence and inhumanity they witness, or the deaths they encounter—but at the same time many of these cops struggle to bring the most humane and caring elements of their personal self to bear at work. We also saw myriad examples of cops struggling not to let their personal feelings, beliefs, attitudes, and urges adversely affect or implicate their work.

To some extent cops erect these semipermeable psychic firewalls between their dual selves in service of protecting their loved ones from the ugliness they witness and that ultimately comes to inhabit their professional self, but it is also psychologically necessary for them to have a kind of psychic refuge from their hard and cynical working world. The cop who can adeptly move between these two selves and two worlds can access rewarding images that connect with and animate many more and many different aspects or dimensions of his personality. He can, in other words, be a more complete, more fulfilled, and more authentic human being.

In the extreme, this duality of self could conceivably lead to what Lifton calls "doubling," a concept developed in his studies of Nazi doctors to explain their capacity to engage in atrocious medical experiments and death camp selections at virtually the same time they practiced the kind of "good medicine" we often associate with caring medical professionals. Although we did not encounter evidence of doubling among the collaborators and therefore did not discuss the phenomenon here, it remains an area for future research that may help to explain some forms of police corruption and criminal misconduct. A great deal of anecdotal evidence suggests that some officers—some "good cops," in fact—are also capable of appalling acts of corruption and brutality.

We also reconceptualized the notion of professional efficacy, recasting it in formative-symbolic terms as the meanings associated with the police-self constellation of a "good cop." Part of the "good cop" constellation, of course, involves the urge to *do something* to effectively prevent or repair a problematic situation, and we saw how this urge often intersects with the urge to do justice. Here again, we saw the value of the formative-symbolic paradigm in explaining police psychology, since experienced officers who developed sufficient images, forms, and constellations (with attendant schemas for enactment) around death events were much better able to utilize these schemas to perform their duties in a way that conformed to the demands of their personal and professional identities. As "good cops," they were capable of flexible responses that allowed them to do justice (in the police idiom, to "do the right thing") and also met the demands of both their personal and professional selves. They could, in other words, fulfill schemas for enactment that satisfied the personal urge for a humane and caring response at the same time as they realized professional demands to remedy the situation in conformity with organizational objectives, often through behaviors the culture transmits and defines as appropriate.

Experienced cops with a well-developed and healthy sense of both selves are generally able to move back and forth between these personas with some ease, calling forth the images, forms, constellations, meanings, and schemas for enactment required of the "good cop," but there is always a certain tension between these two facets of personality and it becomes manifest in the cop's struggle to manage the two. As evidenced by the rookies' struggle to remain aloof and to maintain an austere professional demeanor despite personal inclinations to import humane elements of their personal selves into a situation, cops are better able to manage this struggle when they develop a well-defined and robust sense of self in both spheres.

Throughout this research we saw a general pattern for the emergence and development of these two senses of self. To summarize that pattern, we saw that police recruits enter the agency with some preconceived notions or images of police work and a kind of amorphous vision or image of the kind of cop they hope to become, but they lack a true sense of themselves as police officers. The images, forms, and constellations experienced and developed in training and in early experience gradually coalesce to add substance and dimension to their incipient police identity. The urge to develop and assert the professional self is impelled in part by the young officer's generally anomic experience: his existing "civilian" sense of self is at odds with the new social role he has taken up. Because he has not yet developed a comfortable identity that fits with his own or others' expectations, he attempts to shed older and less valuable elements of his civilian self that do not, in his estimation, conform to the identity he seeks. He may consciously or unconsciously adopt behaviors and express attitudes he perceives as "coplike," and this explains in part the hardened and impervious demeanor he adopts at DOAs and other early career events that call for sympathetic interaction.

In time, and through the accumulation of police experience, the young officer incorporates images that support and nurture his police identity and eventually that identity begins to evolve in its own right. This is perhaps the most critical and, in terms of the police organization's role in personnel development, the most ignored phase of identity formation. As they become comfortable in their new identity, and as that identity takes on greater depth and dimension, many young cops see that the "good cops" they emulate can move fluidly between personas, and they begin to follow suit. As young officers develop the capacity to manage images and selectively permit them to connect with either the professional or personal self—a capacity supported in part by their increased capacity to invoke partial professional numbing—they find that some images and experiences derived at work can enrich their personal sense of self, and that the importation of some personal images and experiences can make them a better and more effective cops. In time, the two selves develop in tandem, sharing many of the same images, forms, constellations, and experiences while excluding others. Other young officers fall prey to the influence of cynical role models—whom they may misperceive as "good cops" worthy of emulation—and to images and experiences that do not provide sufficient access to a sense of movement, connection, and integrity.

The formative-symbolic interpretation of the process of "becoming a cop" sheds new light on police socialization and the development of a police identity. Like other interpretations, it recognizes the importance of early police experiences in determining the quality and direction of the police career, but it also cogently and coherently explains the interplay of social and psychological processes in police identity development.

The Psychology of Survival

The gist of our exploration was the police officer's psychological response to professional death encounters, and so we devoted considerable attention to discussing the psychology of survival and its five constituent themes. We will not attempt to summarize or recapitulate every facet and nuance of survivor psychology elicited from collaborators' narratives, but rather we will make some general observations about the psychology of survival's value in understanding cops, their world, and especially their death encounters.

Numbing

One of the first observations we can make concerns the significance of numbing, especially partial professional numbing, as a self-protective phenomenon and process. The capacity to selectively invoke partial professional numbing is a useful attribute that shields an officer from psychic threat by making him less open to his own emotional feelings and responses and less receptive to the emotional feelings and responses of others. Too much emotional involvement in the difficult events he witnesses could easily prove debilitating and, in the longer term, hasten burnout and cynicism. Partial professional numbing also lets him focus cognitively on the task at hand, an especially valuable capacity in light of the many dangerous situations he encounters. On other occasions, we saw that by opening themselves to certain emotional experiences, cops can experience vitality and reinforce elements of their personal and/or professional identity, so the capacity for *selective* invocation of partial professional numbing is an essential part of identity management.

More profound and often involuntary forms of numbing can accompany severe psychic threats, and this diminution of feeling and emotion also serves a protective function: by essentially separating affect from cognition, at the same time leaving cognition largely intact and viable, the cop forestalls potential psychic immobilization. He can cognitively focus on the physical and/or emotional threat, analyze it with some dispassion, and mobilize appropriate schemas to neutralize or escape the threat. Numbing thus facilitates his biological survival.

Every collaborator in every category reported some numbing at their first DOA, and several were quite explicit in asserting the value they found in it: in particular we recall the insightful police survivor who credited his first DOA experience with helping him develop the "focus" that made him so effective a cop in dangerous situations. Partial professional numbing was perhaps most pronounced among crime scene unit technicians, for whom it acted as a kind of perceptual filter: it allows them to filter out the emotional elements of very gruesome and potentially disturbing images. They do not see the remains of a human life, they see "a very interesting piece of evidence."

Partial professional numbing is also a valuable asset for the homicide detective who separates his personal and professional feelings from cognition while interviewing and interrogating, but the extreme forms of numbing police survivors typically experience can easily become chronic features of their lifestyles. Chronic numbing can easily overtake the police survivor and function to prevent him from moving beyond his death immersion by locking him in to the death-equivalent states of stasis, disconnection, and disintegration. As we repeatedly observed in the experience of the various categories of officers, there is a continuum of numbing that ranges from beneficial forms of partial professional numbing that can protect the self by enhancing cognitive performance to extreme forms that involve immobility and psychic closing-off. These extreme forms, which are more characteristic of the profound death immersions police survivors experience, enervate the self and chronically impair the formative process that would otherwise permit an animating sense of vitality.

The Death Imprint Image

Cops in each nominal category were affected by haunting death imprint images, but we saw some distinct differences in the type and quality of those images depending upon the cops' task environments and the objective potency of the threatening images they encountered. Every collaborator in every category could recall specific images associated with their first DOA, for example, regardless of the circumstances of that death. Images of benign and grotesque first DOA deaths were recalled with seemingly equal ease, although collaborators in all categories were generally able to offer more detailed and coherent descriptions of benign death scenes: as a function of the more extensive numbing cops experience at grotesque deaths, the images they retain from those encounters are typically more fragmented and incomplete. As a group, rookie collaborators also had greater difficulty offering coherent narratives with complete descriptions of the images involved, and this occurred precisely because they had significantly less time to integrate and make sense of these images than tenured cops in other task environments. Subsequent exposures gave tenured cops images and constellations with which to retrospectively integrate and make sense of their early professional death encounters, and so despite the passage of time their first DOA narratives were far more cohesive.

In sharp contrast, police survivors offered detailed, comprehensive, and coherent descriptions of the imprint images involved in their profound death immersion, but their overall narratives were often quite fragmented. A tendency toward fairly loose associations between particular images and events and the highly disintegrative nature of the overall experience made police survivors' narratives somewhat jumpy, but they had spent a great deal of time dwelling on the powerful death images that so debilitated and devitalized them, and they had spent considerable time and effort attempting to integrate and make sense of them.

For other collaborator groups, the imprint images retained were of unusually grotesque deaths, events to which they had an unusual subjective vulnerability, or otherwise atypical deaths that did not easily integrate with their personal and professional constellations. Thus we recall the veteran homicide detective haunted by the grotesque and especially disintegrative imprint image of a child partially consumed by a polar bear, and we recall the tremendous accuracy of the visual image he retained after more than 15 years. Integrating the death was especially difficult because there was no real investigation to be done—although the death had many elements of absurdity, its cause was immediately apparent and was not criminal in nature—and there was no real enactment to be had through a pursuit of justice. We also saw that crime scene unit technicians, who had the greatest facility for partial professional numbing and for whom a detached response to grotesque death was a valued attribute of professional identity, seemed least haunted by death imprints, despite the tremendous number of death scenes they visit.

Death Guilt

To greater or lesser extent, all the collaborators evidenced some quantity of survivor guilt, and once again the dimensions and specific manifestations of guilt varied according to their task environments and the degree of psychic threat their encounters involved. Members of the four task environments dealt primarily with the deaths of others and they had little or no reason to imagine their own complicity or responsibility for the deaths they witnessed, so their death guilt was of an amorphous and irrational type. Police survivors, especially those who participated in an event where another cop or a partner died, had more extraordinary manifestations of guilt and were especially susceptible to rational forms of death guilt.

Most of the time cops in the four task environments did not actually witness the death itself, but rather were called to the scene some time after it occurred. Given this lapse of time, it is difficult to rationally imagine one's responsibility for the death. For homicide detective and crime scene unit technicians, the meaning making involved in the investigative process reassures them that another person is responsible. Guilt was an extremely potent manifestation among police survivors, since so many other themes and features of survivor psychology animate and/ or exacerbate the rational and irrational forms they feel. We saw the important influence of the police agency and the legal system in determining the kind of guilt some survivors feel: those quickly cleared of wrongdoing by the department and by a grand jury feel vindicated and have less rational or irrational guilt than police survivors for whom the process drags on without clear resolution. These authorities essentially certify that the cop's actions were justified. Whether they kill an assailant or not, police survivors who witness the death of another cop have far greater potential to feel rational and irrational guilt. Their tendency for self-blame and self-doubt—was there anything more they could have done to save another cop's life?—can be magnified by a host of events or by the questions others ask.

Suspicion of Counterfeit Nurturance

We did not see very many overt manifestations of suspicion of counterfeit nurturance among rookies, patrol sergeants, crime scene unit technicians, or homicide detectives, and this was attributable primarily to the simple fact that few forms or expressions of nurturance are offered them. With few exceptions, tenured cops did not inquire about rookies' feelings or the emotional difficulties they faced in dealing with their first death encounter, and when inquiries were forthcoming they were almost always directed toward the rookie's comfort with the procedural tasks and responsibilities required of him. Indeed, several patrol sergeants who supervised rookies articulated a belief that overcoming emotional difficulties was an important and functional part of the job that toughened the young officer, and that it was not within the scope of their own responsibilities to coddle young cops. They'd had similar experiences themselves and ultimately profited from the experience, so no special forms of nurturance or expressions of concern were necessary. They recognized the first death encounter was a rite of passage, but absent an extreme traumatic impact they generally saw no compelling reason to interfere or to lessen its subjective impact.

With the exception of police survivors, tenured cops in each of the task environments experienced most death encounters as fairly routine and ordinary events that did not merit special consideration of their own or others' emotions. When fellow officers recognized that a particular death encounter was especially difficult for another cop, they were reluctant—embarrassed, almost—to illuminate the cop's distress by confronting the issue. We recall, for example, the sergeant who unsuccessfully attempted to resuscitate a baby and his memory of cops who stood around uncomfortably, aware of his distress but unable or unwilling to offer words or gestures of comfort. In actuality there are few words or gestures that can truly remedy such distress, but the cultural emphasis on a stoic, detached, and austere demeanor also precluded nurturing expressions. There were no culturally acceptable forms of comfort to offer. We saw that when comforting words were forthcoming in exceptional cases, they were almost always offered in private by a trusted partner, and almost always in an understated way. These subtle forms of nurturance, in other words, were always offered and taken as sincere and genuine expressions of caring regard by and for a trusted friend, and so they did not unduly or publicly illuminate the cop's debilitation or undermine his personal or professional self-esteem. They were seen as authentic, not counterfeit.

Police survivors who witnessed the death of another cop were a different story, though. Their death immersion and their impairment were so extreme and their need for comfort was so great that even the most genuine expressions of solace could animate constellations of guilty devitalization and suspicious resentment. Resentment and suspicion could arise virtually regardless of the relationship with the person offering the nurturance or the setting in which it took place, but certain relationships and certain settings could be especially aggravating. These police survivors have a compelling need for special sustenance, but in whatever form it takes, their overall touchiness ultimately makes expressions of comfort risky for the person offering them.

Police survivors who were lauded as heroes did not exhibit particularly powerful needs for continued sustenance since individual, cultural, and organizational acknowledgments of their heroism acted to prevent radical impairment and to quickly repair—even strengthen—their self-image. Inquires as to their state of mind and physical well-being were presented in an entirely different way—they were couched within larger congratulatory expressions—and the attitude of respect others displayed did not conjure guilt or implicate police survivors' impairment, nor did they present much additional psychic threat.

The Struggle for Meaning

Officers in each of our categories and task environments struggled to integrate and make meaning of their death encounters at a proximate and ultimate level, and the particular forces and factors operating upon them in each category shaped their quest in powerful ways. Rookies, who had few constellations of death's meaning in the professional context and who were not responsible for reaching many substantive conclusions about the cause or reason for the death, had great difficulty in extracting any proximate meaning and almost no success in finding ultimate meaning in it. Their primary concern was in developing adequate professional constellations of death that could impart some immediate subjective understanding of their experience and help them make sense of their own immediate physical and emotional discomfort around death. At that early point in their careers, finding proximate meaning for their own experience was a more compelling need than coming to grips with the philosophical and metaphysical issues involved.

The patrol sergeant's task environment, on the other hand, involved some demands to make objective sense of the death and to use this understanding to make and act upon various judgment calls: did the facts and circumstances indicate the death was a homicide, suicide, or of a suspicious nature, thereby calling for some further action on his part? For the most part patrol sergeants did not spend a great deal of time at death scenes, but they did have to view the scene and ask the cops, witnesses, and/or family members various questions. They also had to cognitively assess this information in order to conduct a brief preliminary investigation. This task requirement was, in essence, a formal agency demand to make limited meaning of some aspects of the death. Sergeants did not evince great concern for the philosophical or metaphysical issues death raises, but even though they were more inured to death they were to some extent possessed of a personal and professional philosophical outlook on death that rookies generally lacked.

The task environments of homicide detectives and crime scene unit technicians involved implicit demands for a meaning-making process and they evidenced tremendous professional concern for understanding the death. Their concern was not merely to grasp the proximate cause of the death, but to develop a more complete understanding of the events that preceded and perhaps followed it. In their investigative role, the construction of larger meanings is a primary task responsibility. Their approaches to the meaning-making process differed somewhat— crime scene technicians were concerned with what the physical evidence could tell them and homicide detectives gained their information about motives and behaviors through human interactions—but both groups used facts and informed conjecture to construct a particular type of meaning. Homicide detectives and crime scene unit technicians also had well-developed and rather complex preexisting constellations they used to help them make sense of the situation, and although they ultimately developed quite different philosophical outlooks on death they were somewhat more concerned with these issues than either rookies or patrol sergeants.

Police survivors sought, often desperately, to make proximate and ultimate meaning of their experience. Because theirs were infinitely more personal encounters with their own mortality that could potentially alter the contours of self in profound ways, the need to understand the "how and why" of their experience took on special salience. Importantly, we saw that the police survivors who justifiably killed someone in the line of duty typically fared better in this regard than those who witnessed the death of another cop or were themselves severely injured in the line of duty. They had existing constellations that could immediately impart some meaning to the event, and they had previously imagined themselves in analogous mortal combat situations. To some extent they knew what to expect from the situation they confronted, and these constellations facilitated their understanding of it at a proximate level. The reactions of other cops, of the culture and of the organization also imparted some immediate meaning to their experience, characterizing them and their behaviors as heroic and creditable. Because they generally suffered less impairment and because the death event often strengthened their sense of professional self, their need to repair the self through the meaning-making process was less compelling.

Cops who witnessed the death of another cop or were severely wounded had more difficulty understanding these events, which were more complex both in terms of their own psychological involvement and in terms of the actual events that transpired. They struggled to make sense of the event in part to integrate the images in restructured professional and personal self-concepts, and for the most part they did not have existing well-developed constellations that could give adequate meaning to the kind of event they survived. The struggle for meaning, and specifically the tendency to reformulate the event in a less psychically threatening way, was also part of their struggle to resolve guilt and to overcome the death imprint image. The struggle to render their absurd death encounter sensible and to determine proximate and ultimate responsibility for it also explains their tendency toward scapegoating and their concern that the person or persons truly responsible for their impairment are publicly recognized and punished accordingly.

The profoundness of their encounter also raised a host of philosophical issues, including issues of personal and professional integrity. They were, to far greater extent than any other collaborators, concerned with the ultimate truths that could be distilled from their extreme immersion in death. Although in time most extract some ultimate philosophical and metaphysical insights from the event—insights that provided a degree of emotional comfort and typically resulted in placing great emphasis on their own integrity and on the sanctity and value of human life—they never quite achieve a reassuring understanding of why they survived the event or how their immersion so profoundly changed them.

A Concluding Note

As we conclude our exploration of the impact of exposure to death in contemporary urban policing, it is appropriate and necessary to point out that this research holds some important potential implications for police agency policy and for police management. Given the overwhelmingly qualitative nature of this study and the limitations we've identified, it is also appropriate and necessary to acknowledge some caveats regarding the strengths and the limitations of our data and the conclusions that flow from them.

This research was, and is, an exploratory study of a fairly narrow—albeit critical—area of police experience. It was never intended to establish immutable principles, conclusions, or recommendations that would be entirely applicable across the landscape of the American policing enterprise. We were concerned with urban policing, and we focused almost entirely upon the NYPD, the nation's largest police agency. That agency has a rich and vibrant culture, and we glimpsed how the organizational culture, along with the procedural requirements and prescribed duties that are the substance of the task environment, mediates officers' experiences. It would be wrong to assert, imply, or assume that the specific results obtained in one agency are automatically and perfectly generalizable to cops in every large American police department, however. Every agency has its own unique elements of occupational culture that distinguish it from others, and the specific tasks and duties their officers perform can also be expected to differ from those in the NYPD.

We should also recognize that the internal and external social dynamics in smaller urban and nonurban police agencies, as well as the procedures that guide their officers' duties and activities, differ substantially from those in larger urban departments. In a small rural agency, for example, officers might encounter death with greater or lesser frequency than in New York City, but they are probably much more likely to have a preexisting relationship with the deceased simply because they tend to be more integrated into the smaller community in which they often reside. These and a multitude of other factors that include the incidence of violent deaths and the lack of specialization that characterizes many small agencies—in a small agency, for example, forensic and investigative responsibilities may be separately undertaken by a county or state law enforcement agency—make it more difficult to generalize our specific findings to them. These officers certainly deal with death, but certainly not precisely the same way as urban police officers in large agencies. The specific features of these death encounters in other police contexts and their impact upon the psychology of survival's outcomes require further study.

Nevertheless, the shared themes approach gave us a fairly broad brush with which to depict NYPD cops' experiences, and it allows us some latitude in generalizing our findings. There are sufficient similarities between large urban police departments to permit us to make broad comparisons and to apply our conclusions confidently, but in a general way, to other urban police environments. Our observations about the extremely close relationship between long-term partners and that relationship's influence in culture and survivor psychology, for example, may not apply as forcefully within urban agencies where solo patrol predominates. Other agencies may also have slightly different immortality systems—the symbolism of the shield, for example, may not apply in precisely the same way—but we can intuitively suppose that some other immortalizing systems exist to perform essentially similar functions.

Most important, police agencies should utilize the lessons of this research to develop policies and procedures that are more sensitive to the needs of cops and more cognizant of the personal and professional struggles that result from their death encounters, without necessarily interfering in those struggles. The agency can do a lot more to support its good cops and to ensure that all its members maximize their own potential to be good cops, and that support begins with sensitivity and compassion for the issues cops face rather than with standardized and formal written policies or procedures.

I am thinking here of the patrol sergeant we met who recognized the death encounter's potential as a learning experience and took an uncommon initiative to influence the experience so that rookies felt a sense of personal and professional connection, movement, and integrity. He conscientiously assumed the responsibility to informally structure rookies' death encounters to maximize their personal and professional growth, in large measure because his own powerful death experiences illuminated the need for flexible humane response. He did not relieve them of their responsibilities, but rather went to great lengths to ensure they properly performed their duties while conducting themselves in a caring, professional, and humane way. The rookies and tenured cops he influenced felt some immediate sense of connection, movement, and integrity during their death encounters. Because he was a good cop possessed of the urge to positively influence the lives of those around him, and because he had great insight into his own experiences around death, he was more concerned with being a good human being than with fulfilling the procedural demands imposed by the organization. This approach and this type of behavior should be the norm, rather than the exception.

If this sensitivity and this sensibility were recognized and reinforced by an executive cadre that understood and exploited the formative-symbolic paradigm's potential as a motivational and management tool, greater sensitivity toward cops' death encounters might eventually infiltrate the culture and become standard practice. This approach would be all the more effective because it would be achieved without resorting to the kind of standardized "one-size-fits-all" formal policy directives that often stifle flexibility and inhibit compassion. A host of agency practices can be improved, encouraged, or discouraged through heightened awareness of death's impact and heightened appreciation of the psychology of survival's formidable influence in police officers' personal and professional lives.

I will conclude our exploration with a call for greater sensitivity—at all levels of policing—toward the plight of the police officers who survived profound and personally consequential death immersions. We've seen that some of these police survivors are quite properly recognized and publicly applauded for the tremendous personal and professional sacrifices they willingly made on behalf of others, and we've seen that they tend to emerge from their death immersions with fewer and less profound psychic consequences. Others, by virtue of the extreme features of their death immersion, which may be exacerbated by individual, cultural, and organizational failures to support and nurture them, have an eminently more difficult ordeal from which they never truly recover. Here my collaborator's words resonate: "These are wounded souls, and there is nothing, nothing you can ever do to restore them."

We do not end on a note of resigned futility, though. These are men and women of heroic stature, and their real heroism is not for the mere fact of having survived a deadly encounter. In many respects these officers resemble the classic heroes of myth, but their heroism and their experience also differ from that of the classic hero in important ways. Like the classic hero, they have endured an extreme ordeal, symbolically entered the underworld of profound death immersion, and returned to our world of "ordinary" experience bearing a special knowledge and a special message from which all of us can learn. Unlike many police heroes, though, the mythic hero's return to our world is almost always heralded and his message is almost always received and acted upon. The classic hero is vindicated, his tale is communicated with reverence and awe, and the depth of his sacrifice is understood and cherished by those who hear of it. Dire consequences await those who fail to heed and act upon the classic hero's message. The classic hero is restored and empowered by his ordeal and by his return to the rational world of the living.

For far too many police heroes—those who are heralded and those who are not—the return to our world of order, rationality, and meaning is never complete. Because they can never fully escape the extremity and the power of their death immersion, police survivors remain perpetually in its thrall. Although they struggle to restore order and meaning to their world, they find that their death experience has rendered that world unalterably absurd. Police survivors' real heroism lies not in merely having survived a death encounter or having endured a few moments of absolute horror, but in their eternal Sisyphean struggle against the overpowering weight of the death and the absurdity they carry with them.

Police survivors' real heroism, which is too often unrecognized, lies in their courageous and lifelong struggle to integrate their extreme death immersion experience within a cohesive and comfortable sense of self, and in their continuing struggle to extract meaning, vitality, and hope from a terribly shattered existence. Their heroism and courage—more a moral courage than a physical courage—impose on the cops, on police culture, and on the police organization a burden of reciprocation and esteem that must be expressed in caring, perceptive, flexible, and humane compassion for them and for their struggle. We can hope for no less from the organization, we can expect no less from the culture, and we can demand no less from good cops.

Epilogue

September 11, 2001

The call came in a few minutes before nine on an excruciatingly beautiful late summer morning. One of the striking images everyone seems to retain from that day is its tremendous natural beauty—the exceptionally clear blue sky, the warm air, the unlimited visibility, the low humidity. It was the kind of halcyon day that, in a different context perhaps, people would not hesitate to describe as one that makes you glad to be alive, and therein lay the irony of it: especially when set against the tremendous destruction and massive death that would soon follow and change everything, in truth it ultimately was still a day to be happy that you're alive. I later reflected on this ironic fact when I recalled how the first bomb fell on Hiroshima on the same kind of pristine and gentle summer morning, how the narratives of so many of those survivors, the *hibakusha*, contained descriptions of a clear, beautiful morning that offered no warning of events to come.

We were still having coffee, talking about where we'd go for lunch or some such nonsense. My partner Dennis took the call, and he spoke quietly into the phone for a few minutes. A month or so later, I would learn that the call came from our other partner Pete, who was stuck in traffic on the FDR Drive.

"Turn on the TV—a plane hit the Trade Center."

We had an old TV in the office—one of those small black and white units old-timers like Dennis and Paul used to sneak into their radio cars and plug into the cigarette lighter on the midnight tour. Even with strips of foil hanging from the antenna the image on the screen was all static and snow, but at least we could hear the audio. We sat silently, hunched over the set, fiddling with dials as the sound of multiple sirens came up from the street—certainly not an unfamiliar sound to us, but one that, at the time, was both sobering and eerily chilling. The sounds of sirens were so familiar, in fact, that neither of us had really noticed them until the call came in.

Dennis and I were both thinking, both hoping, the same thing: some guy in a Cessna had had a heart attack and hit the tower. A B-25 hit the Empire State Building in 1945 during a storm, and it had sustained only minor damage. That building still stands, but today would prove to be different than any other day, any other time, as all of the familiar assumptions that ordinarily shaped our thoughts and guided our behavior would be challenged, many of them dashed. The old images and constellations would soon lose much of their capacity to inform us, to provide adequate direction and meaning, to furnish adequate schemas for enactment. The day was clear and cloudless, and the sky was the most amazing deep blue. It just had to be an accident. Some guy in a Cessna had had a heart attack, plain and simple. The alternative, a deep and horrible thought that nagged unspoken between us, was just too terrible. It was, after all, the Trade Center, and residual memories and images from 1993 still lingered. That day was wet and cold and nasty, so unlike this day.

When the reporter said it was a large plane, an airliner, we looked at each other. There were still no words between us, just more and more sirens in the background. "It had to be an accident, and the report is either wrong or exaggerated," I thought. The disembodied, staticky voice from the television then announced another report—a second plane had hit the South Tower. Dennis and I stared at each other for a long moment. It was true; we could no longer pretend that this was not happening.

"Let's do it. Everyone into the bag, hats and bats."[1]

We headed the hundred or so feet down the hall to the chief's office, but none of the big bosses were in yet. The reality—perhaps more accurately, the unreality—of it all took hold in that instant as we walked down the hall, and I remember having a terrible realization. I think I grasped the magnitude of this historic event and the impact it would certainly have, but at that point the true and full dimension of it all was beyond anyone's actual comprehension. It was certainly beyond my comprehension, but the old images and modes of behavior still held sway. No one had yet given authority to the fact that this was a terrorist attack, and we certainly had no idea of its extent or ultimate consequences, but a profound and overpowering consciousness overtook me then—from this point in time the world will never be the same. The thing we feared and had kept at a distance was upon us; it was no longer an intellectual abstraction. Just how different it would be was at that time well beyond my capacity to imagine, but like so many others I would come to see that day and the days and weeks that followed as the pivotal divide between a relatively comfortable and familiar existence and the very different psychological and social world we each inhabit today. None of us, I think, will ever see the world in quite the same way.

We were under attack from an unseen and as-yet unknown enemy—the most dangerous and fearful kind of enemy—and as cops, we would certainly become targets. We still had absolutely no hard information about the enemy, his identity, his strength, or his tactics, and in fact there was still a very remote chance we may be entirely wrong in assuming we're under attack. Especially in the absence of hard cognitive intelligence, we had to make doubtful assumptions and act upon incomplete reports at the same time we were trying to avoid excessive or irrational responses.

A series of images from a past incident flashed through my mind as I went down the hall, and their seeming irrelevance to the present context briefly puzzled me. The images were so puzzling, in fact, that they remained with me, unintegrated, returning intermittently for some time before they began to make sense. One night, years ago, my partners and I came under fire from someone in a huge, unruly crowd outside a nightclub on a midtown street, and we could neither distinguish the shooter nor safely return fire. The impulse was to shoot back, but there was no target and therefore no possibility of enactment. We had no effective cover or concealment, so we stood there in the open street with guns in our hands trying to find a target in the darkness as the shots went off around us. The bad guy ultimately got away.

That series of unintegrated images—some of which remain ambiguous even to this day—recurred over and over again in the weeks and months following the attack. Eventually I recognized what conjured that particular bit of imagery: the fear, impotence, defenselessness, unfocused rage, and concern for my partners, myself, and the innocent civilians we protected were almost identical to what I felt while walking down that hall. The sense of fear was real and in a way quite palpable and close to consciousness, but at the same time, it had a strangely disembodied quality. I was aware that these emotions were at play, yet was oddly disconnected from and unaffected by them. Far from being an immobilizing force, on both occasions fear had stimulated, animated, and energized me in a transcendent way, propelling me toward a more centered and focused consciousness.

As I walked down the hall, I could literally feel the numbing overtake me, and the situation was even more surreal in that I knew, cognitively, that my emotions were becoming submerged and separated. I recognized this physically and mentally exhilarating process, both from having studied it and from having experienced it before, and I exulted in it; I knew it would serve me well, that I could essentially invoke and control it and work it to my advantage. I felt bulletproof: invincible, focused, and strong.

We knew nothing about the enemy yet, but I had to assume this was only the first wave in a coordinated series of attacks. I've read a great deal about terrorism and terrorist methods, about counterterrorist strategies, and about the theories and principles of asymmetric warfare. The enemy—domestic or international—was unknown, but we had to assume we were under attack. "Are there more planes? Car or truck bombs? Grenade or rocket attacks?" I asked myself. A proven terrorist strategy is the secondary attack, and the scenario seemed very real to me; lure all the emergency responders to the scene and then take them out with a second attack. Immobilize us, cripple our capacity to respond.

I didn't know it then, but the idea of an imminent secondary attack or series of attacks would operate for me and for others, adding an overshadowing sense of foreboding, apprehension, and urgency to everything we did in the days and weeks to come. There would be no such thing as relaxing—hypervigilance would prevail, and everything we did, everyone we contacted would be scrutinized. Whoever was responsible, it was clear this would not be over soon. People—civilians and even cops—would be panicking, acting irrationally on the basis of rumor and bad information, and that posed a special danger to all of us. Calm people down, maintain a commanding presence—these were things I could do.

The cop impulse to get down to the Trade Center, to help, to *do something*, was compelling. I had an urgent fantasy of commandeering a cab or a bus to get to the site; subways would be useless and I didn't want to wait for department transport. "Run toward the trouble and deal with it like a cop." Schemas developed over a lifetime are compelling. That was my role, my responsibility, my identity, and I had the sobering and very clear conscious realization that however long this took, I would be called upon to use every shred of experience, skill, and knowledge acquired over twenty years of police work. That thought had a powerful impact; it galvanized me. This was a test—not an academic test or make-up exam, no second chance or partial credit—of everything I was or had thought I was. I fully comprehended that to a far greater extent than anything else in my professional or personal life, this was the real deal. There was a conscious and oddly exhilarating recognition that everything I'd seen and done and experienced and learned in twenty years of being a cop had been in unknowing preparation for this moment. "Do I have the stuff I think I have? Am I the good cop I think I am?" The challenge was so formidable; the stakes were so high. This was all about survival, about avoiding biological extinction and psychological breakdown. This was the moment I had trained for my entire life, and I consciously perceived and engaged and embraced it as a sublime opportunity to assess my personal and professional limits and capabilities.

I knew that some people must be dying down at the Trade Center—although, perhaps two minutes after hearing that planes have struck the buildings, there was still no indication of the massive death that would take place—and I wanted desperately to get there to aid in the rescue. But wrapped up in all of that was the urge to put myself to the test. I had been away from street policing for too long, and I wanted to embrace this challenge to face danger and death. I *needed* to embrace this trial, to face danger and death. I needed to answer some questions for myself: "Do I have the stuff? Am I authentic?"

This whole interconnected complex of abstractions, along with their implications and permutations—there were many other numbed and disconnected thoughts and speculations as well, but these are the ones I remembered months later—literally took place and were registered and processed in the space of the three or four actual seconds it took me to walk down the hall. Looking back, they seemed fragmented and disconnected, but in my state of seemingly absolute and undistracted intellectual clarity, they made utterly perfect sense. These abstractions became concrete rather than abstract as I moved toward a deepening state of numbing, and they meshed together in a seamless and holistic way. These thoughts and all their permutations would stay with me and operate, continually and fluidly moving between the background and foreground of consciousness, over the weeks and months that followed. So, too, would the impression that the tremendous quantity of bizarre images and cognitive data I was processing had perfect clarity and made perfect sense at the instant they were being processed. Even moments later, though, when I tried to retrospectively retrieve them, analyze them, to consider them in light of new images and information, they often seemed fragmented, incomplete, and unrelated.

A few cops—those who weren't teaching—and a few civilian employees had heard the news of the attack by this point, and they gathered in confused knots in the chief's outer office and in the hall. There was apparently no one present in the Police Academy above the rank of lieutenant, and Dennis—a lieutenant with 28 years on the Job—took command. He fell into the role naturally as we began trying to impose some semblance of order on the chaos that prevailed as word spread throughout the building.

There were a hundred things to do. Training and experience kicked in, facilitated by more-than-partial professional numbing. Orders were given: "Call Recruit Operations. Have them notify every instructor to roster up their recruits. We need a count on how many people we have available: recruits, cops, and sergeants. Break out the reserve helmets, sticks, and vests—how many do we have? Have Police Science break out the radios. Turn on the TV—what does CNN have on this? Get more TVs in here, and turn on the all-news radio stations. We'll need batteries, bullhorns, all the equipment we have—find it and break it out. There are 75 detectives in the CIC course—send them back to their commands. What other In-Service courses are up? Roster up all the uniformed personnel. Call Operations and let them know we're on board and ready to go. We'll get them the availability numbers as soon as they're in. Make sure the Outdoor Range has been notified, and lock it down; it is the main arsenal and ammunition depot and a target if there's a second-wave attack coming. It will also be a mobilization point for off-duties coming in from upstate. Call Driver Training, too, and get a count on available people and vehicles. All training is down—roster them up and hold everyone but CIC."

My first concerns were for safety and security. The Police Academy is the second largest police facility in the city; we would have been a high-value target if a second-wave attack had occurred. The building itself encompasses almost an entire city block, fronting on East 20th and East 21st streets, and faces Cabrini Hospital's Emergency Room entrance directly across the street. In addition to the Academy itself, the 21st Street side of the building houses the 13th Precinct, the Emergency Services Unit base for Lower Manhattan, the Manhattan South Patrol Borough Headquarters, the Detective Borough Manhattan South Headquarters, as well as a number of specialized investigative unit offices. The Academy had, at that time, about 750 recruits on the day tour, another 750 coming in for the four-to-twelve tour, and a couple of hundred instructors, supervisors, staff, and administrative personnel—all in all, there were about 1,200 people present in the building. On the rooftop Muster Deck[2] is painted a huge NYPD logo. It took only a second to grasp that we were a *very* high-value target.

"What about car or truck bombs? Seal off the block—make sure there is no vehicle or pedestrian traffic on 20th or 21st Streets. Call the security desk out front, make sure they know what's up and have them secure the intersections and divert traffic. Get some cops down there to help."

I called the range in the basement and got Sergeant Jimmy Boyle. His brother, a firefighter, would die that day. "Jimmy, break out the sniper rifles and MP-5s, put your guys on the roof forthwith. If you have radios and binoculars, take them. I'll be up. We're at war, man."

I headed into the vacant office of the Director of Training. Jim O'Keefe, a good man, left two weeks ago to take a position as a college professor, and his spot hadn't been filled yet. His cousin, a firefighter, would be dead in about an hour. I grabbed a couple of cops and started setting up a command post. "Go down to the Boro and get maps of Lower Manhattan. Big maps and small maps. Start photocopying them—especially the First Precinct—a couple of hundred copies. There's a radio scanner in the library—go get it, bring it here and lock it in on the First Division and citywide frequencies. Get me some easels and flip charts."

I got Operations on the phone and told them what we had. I also gave them the phone numbers for the command post. It had not been easy to get through—the phone system was bad enough under ordinary circumstances, but on September 11, it was entirely overloaded. I had tried to call my wife, who was a hundred miles away and hopefully safe at our country house, but the department is cheap and most department phones have a block that does not allow for long distance calls outside the city. Of all the days to have forgotten my cell phone—it was sitting on my desk at home. I borrowed a cell phone but couldn't get a signal—there was no service.

Calls started coming in. "Lieutenant so-and-so is on the way; Driver Training has cars and vans available in Brooklyn; Operations wants the chief to call in when he shows up." Some idiot, oblivious to the fact that the Trade Center had been attacked, wanted to know if we were having a retirement racket for Jim O'Keefe.

When I finally got an open line that would call outside the city, the circuits were busy; I still couldn't get through to my wife. The cheap bastards who don't even trust their own cops locked out the phones, but they had made sure they had private lines for themselves. Now, I was having to use the private lines to deal with the emergency. I would keep trying, unsuccessfully, to get through to my wife for the next four hours, to let her know I was OK.

"Evacuate the top two floors and get all the civilians down to the cafeteria. Have the recruits muster by company in the gym. Make sure all the cops and sergeants have hats and bats. Has Police Science gotten the radios yet? Make sure the rooftop is secured—call out to let them know you're coming before you walk onto the roof. Get some more TVs in here and hook them up to the cable news shows." I felt like I was on a highly energized, sharply focused autopilot, aware of everything and integrating everything, but calm and somehow untouched by it.

The Pentagon had been attacked. Someone informed me that the news was reporting that five more airliners were unaccounted for.

One of the big bosses finally showed up, half in a panic, giving orders. He wanted the recruits out of the building forthwith, lined up shoulder-to-shoulder along the FDR Drive and blocking the ramps. I told him, sharply and publicly, that no one was leaving the building until we had them rostered—until we knew who they were, where they were going, who they were with, and how we could find them and bring them back safely. "We are rostering the recruits right now, but until that is finished no one can leave." The exchange didn't earn me any points, and I would pay for it later—I was a sergeant and he was a big boss. Ordinarily, what I had just said to him would have been considered insubordination and I was usually much more diplomatic, but I really didn't care at this point—none of the ordinary rules applied now. They wouldn't apply for quite a while, and that knowledge was liberating. I did what made sense to me. In this new reality, expertise, experience, and coolheadedness were important, and right then I felt entirely justified in violating petty rules on a wholesale basis. I was completely convinced I could handle whatever I was called upon to do because I felt absolutely calm and composed, logical and rational, physically and mentally invigorated, exhilarated, even cheerful.

Since the phone call came in, I had been entirely focused, with scarcely a bit of emotion, just focusing on what needed to be done and what was the most expedient way to do it. With only minor variations in the intensity of the numbing, I would stay that way—calm, focused, exhilarated, and almost entirely without emotion—for the next two days and nights.

My psychological world at that time was one of pure cognition and intellect, and I was living entirely in the moment, focused and engaged to an extent I had never before experienced, certainly not for this length of time. Despite all the activities which were taking place around me, I was completely aware of it all and nothing distracted me. Crisis and chaos, albeit crises and chaos of an entirely different order, were not novelties to me, and there was a crystalline clarity in my powers of perception. My cognition and memory had never felt sharper.

Ordinarily, I'm not good at recalling phone numbers—if I don't call the number frequently, I have to look it up. I needed to call the Outdoor Range, Operations, and the security booth, but then I simply picked up the phone and punched numbers and the person or unit answered. It was as if I were on autopilot or operating like a machine; I was able to easily retrieve deeply embedded scraps of information quickly. Somehow, I knew the bulletproof vests were being held for distribution to recruits in a particular storage room on the 5th floor, and I knew that Dave Richmond had the key.

I was able to completely engage in a conversation and mentally tick off a list of things to do while I simultaneously keyed into—and integrated—information from other conversations taking place across the room. I was entirely confident—more confident than I had ever been—I would thrive in this crisis, no matter what it entailed. There was no inhibiting sense of fear, no anger—they would come later—just a state of pure and invigorating cognition.

I experienced—and in a strangely detached way, consciously *knew* I was experiencing—the kind of pure state some collaborators describe in gunfight narratives. I had certainly experienced objectively similar but much more ephemeral and much less intense states during chases, "gun runs,"[3] and other police experiences in the past, but this differed substantially in terms of its quality, its depth, and its duration. It was simultaneously deep, enveloping, intoxicating, and ultimately transcendent. Although the intensity would fluctuate somewhat, this focus and clarity would stay with me despite the distractions and fatigue of the coming weeks and months. I knew that people—including cops—were dying in my city less than two miles away, yet I had never felt such passionate vitality. I also knew, intellectually, that I should probably feel somewhat guilty about feeling so alive and invigorated at a time like this, but I also knew precisely why I felt so intensely animated and elated in the midst of this tragedy. The intellectual knowledge that my numbed reaction was entirely natural essentially forestalled any sense of rational or irrational guilt around this particular issue.

One of the oddest things—something that would occur again and again over the weeks and months to follow—was that I was acutely aware of what was taking place psychologically within myself as well as in those around me. I *knew* that I had reached the peak of partial professional numbing; I could see that others were numbed and emotionless—some were on the verge of immobilization and I had to keep them going.

This unique insight and knowledge added to the aura of unreality surrounding the whole situation, though. I was operating simultaneously on multiple levels of consciousness, able to extract a singular kind of meaning from the images and experiences all the various situations afforded. I came to have the sense that although thousands of cops were participating in this collective experience, because I had studied these phenomena so intensely for so many years, I was perhaps the only person interpreting events in this particular way. The rookies, sergeants, detectives, CSU technicians, and survivors I interviewed gave me the gift of insight, of knowledge, and the conviction to put my whole-hearted trust in that insight and knowledge. If most cops had made survivor psychology work for them, I could certainly make it work for me. I recognized the emerging features of my own survivor psychology—most notably the numbing—and I recognized the power and truth of the psychoformative paradigm, just as I recognized how bizarre it was to be operating simultaneously at so many levels of awareness. I trusted in it and let it carry me through.

I knew that utilizing survivor psychology would be part of the test and the challenge—could I put my knowledge to practice, using it in a therapeutic way to benefit other cops? Would I be able to learn more and assess the paradigm's viability and manifestations under extreme conditions? I was ethically bound—as a cop and as a moral human being—to use my knowledge to get others through this crisis intact or perhaps even more resilient than they were before. But above all, this was an opportunity to be the best "good cop" I could be, a test of whether or not I had the right stuff. Did I have the integrity and the authenticity the challenge required?

Of course, all of this took much longer to read and write than it did to experience and comprehend. With the seeming expansion and contraction of time, awareness of all this took hold of me in the space of seconds and remained operating in the background while I focused entirely on hundreds of necessary tasks.

At this point, it was about twenty after nine and TVs had been brought in from classrooms. The Pentagon had been attacked and reporters began asking questions such as, "Will attacks on the White House or Capitol be next? Are there additional targets in New York? How many planes have been hijacked?" I remembered that someone had said five more planes were unaccounted for. What were the scenarios? If they—whoever they were—wanted to take out the city's protective infrastructure, the police department could be next. Second-wave attacks on police and emergency services facilities were definitely, a possibility, but what form would they take? The strategies we needed to survive, to anticipate and respond effectively to the scenarios, came from more abstract and unpracticed constellations than from previous experience.

The TV stations were showing the burning towers as people were beginning to leap from the upper floors. Bodies plummeted a thousand feet to the ground. "What conditions, what kind of horror is taking place on those floors if leaping to certain death is preferable to remaining? What horrors do they experience as they fall? Can those few extra seconds of life before certain death be worth the horror?"

I couldn't stay here and watch this; I had to get there to help.

Although I felt frustrated and immobilized at the Academy, there were still things to be done before I could—before I had to—actualize my impulse to race toward the trouble.

At some point, I got to the locker room and changed into uniform. Other than for a couple of brief ceremonies or police funerals, I hadn't worn a uniform in about ten years. Although the uniform fit, the combat boots I had in my locker were so old and desiccated they would cut my feet to shreds in a couple of hours. It would be two days before I could get another pair, but the pain became an abstract thing. I would need boots, not shoes, if I was going to be of any value in the rescue, and that was the important thing right now—to help. Over the coming weeks, I would change my bloody socks for clean ones several times a day. Even though I still can't wear them, I kept my old boots—they're still in my closet.

I went up to the roof to make sure the snipers were in place and that they knew what to do. There was no air traffic over the city, and we could see the plume of smoke rising from the Trade Center about thirty blocks away. One of the cops asked me what to do if he saw a plane approaching low, and I really didn't know what to tell him; he would not be able to take it down, even if we did know whether it was hijacked or not. But supposing that he could take it down, it would just crash and take different lives. We were impotent against these weapons, and that impotence to neutralize a potential threat strikes deeply at our core sense of self-as-cop. The impulse to *do something* is powerful, but it cannot be actualized. I told him not to shoot at planes, to watch the street for cars or trucks bursting through the barrier cars that were now in place, and to watch the nearby rooftops and buildings for possible snipers. There were other, taller buildings nearby, certainly within range of shoulder-fired missiles or rocket propelled grenades. Was I getting paranoid? In the absence of information to the contrary we had to anticipate and prepare for every eventuality at the same time we restrain the nearly overwhelming impulses that resulted from faulty or partial images.

I think this interaction occurred after I changed into uniform, but there are so many fragmented images of that day that are out of sequence and I was up and down to the roof to check the snipers and haul them bottled water so many times that day I cannot be sure. There was no air traffic in that pristine blue sky, except for a lone jet fighter streaking by at what seemed to be only slightly higher than the surrounding buildings. It was gone in a flash. I was speaking with one of the cops, and we just stopped and looked at each other for a moment. "Christ," he said, "did you ever think you'd see that over the city of New York?" It was only the beginning of things we never thought we'd see.

I was back at the command post when, a few minutes after ten, someone informed me that one of the towers fell. As rumors were going to be a big part of this thing, they had to be squashed or people would start acting on bad information. "Bullshit," I said. "I was on the roof two minutes ago and the towers were up. A B-25 hit the Empire State Building in 1945 and it's still there." In the back of my mind, I wondered about the Trade Center's construction, and from somewhere I retrieved an embedded memory that the Empire State Building was made of poured reinforced concrete. It took only a year to build. I had been in the Trade Center scores of times, and it had insubstantial curtain wall construction. I had seen the six-story crater a truck bomb made in the basement garage during the 1993 bombing.

"Look," he said, and I turned to confront the televised image of the collapsed tower still enveloped in a rising cloud. I recall thinking, without emotion, that thousands must now be dead and injured. "How many people work in the Trade Center towers? Maybe fifty thousand? How many were evacuated? How many cops and firefighters and civilians were still inside?" I had to get down there and do what it was my nature and my training to do. Again, I attempted to call my wife to reassure her that I was OK, that I hadn't yet gone to the scene, but I still wasn't able to get a line outside the city. For several hours, there would be practically no cell phone signals.

Two days later I met an old acquaintance, a highly experienced detective from a specialty squad. He responded to the Trade Center that morning, helped evacuate people, and was ordered to redeploy elsewhere just a few minutes before the first tower fell. Like so many others, he did not realize just how much structural damage had been done to the building and had no idea it was about to fall. Standing outside, he managed to get a cell phone signal to call home and leave a voice mail message for his wife. "Honey," he had said, "you know what I do for a living and you know I went in there, but I'm out now and I'm safe and I'm standing on the sidewalk. Just know that I'm OK and I'll call you later. I love you." His wife came home a few minutes later, still oblivious to the attack. She listened to the voice mail, which made no sense to her until she turned on the television just in time to see the second tower collapse. The detective was unable to contact his wife for a day, and for that entire day she believed him dead. He still hadn't been home when I saw him.

The gym was a chaotic scene, with some cops, bosses, recruits in formation, and others milling around. The big bosses had started to arrive, and the chaos increased as they began to display their leadership credentials. One moved around with a bullhorn directing groups to form up, making inane announcements and issuing inane orders while others worked quietly to establish a sense of order and organize a response. No one from the Academy would be going to the Trade Center site; I planned to get out of there and go before someone grabbed me for traffic detail. I grabbed a couple of citywide radios—one for the guys on the roof so that they could communicate, and one I would keep with me for the next month. The radio is a lifeline that provides information and an important sense of connection.

"Get the radio to the snipers on the roof. Check the 7th and 8th floors again, make sure they're evacuated." Back in the command post, information trickled in slowly, primarily from the array of TV sets. Training and procedures kicked in again, and at some point I started an Incident Command Log, trying to recall the specific procedures to be followed in opening the log. Only a few entries were made before I recognized the absurdity of it and abandoned the project. The second tower had collapsed now, and I was still miles away; I reassured myself that once things settled down a bit, I would get down there to help. I was a cop and I didn't feel like I was fulfilling my responsibilities. There were so many questions racing through my head. "Are the attacks confined to the city? Are more attacks on the way, and if so what form will they take? The phone lines are still down; is my wife safe? Does she know that I'm safe?"

It would be the middle of that afternoon before my wife and I made contact. She had also been trying without success to reach me and finally started dialing other numbers within the Police Academy exchange. She got through to a cadet who informed her I was still alive and hadn't left the building. The cadet found me and relayed the message that she knew I was OK. At least I knew she was safe and she knew that I was OK. I sat down and kept calling until I reached her. We would only actually be together once during the next month—she remained at our country house and I stayed at our apartment in the suburbs on those occasions when I could get home. After a couple of days, we worked out a schedule—we would speak by cell phone at exactly 2:10 A.M. for about ten minutes. Our conversations were as disjointed and fragmented as our respective experiences, but the contact and the human connection was the important thing. She understood what I was doing and why. When we were eventually able to be together, we became even closer than we had been before.

Once the recruits were deployed, the gym was converted to a triage center for the emergency room across the street, and Dennis was in charge—"Who has special skills and training we will need?" My secretary, Marie Garcia, was trained as an EMT when she was in the military, so I asked her to report to Dennis in the gym. Others with advanced first aid or medical training were also ordered to report to Dennis. Later he would tell me about laying down gym mats, piling bandages, and medical supplies that arrived from who-knows-where to create about a hundred triage stations on the gym floor, followed by the interminable wait for casualties to arrive. They had organized and prepared and waited, but no one came. One of the most horrible and most resisted realizations of that day was the fact that there were no survivors of which to speak. This was against everything our experiences led us to expect—even in an event of this magnitude, there *had to be* casualties. How bad was it down there, and why were we still here? Where are the injured, the survivors? It didn't make sense; I knew city officials had mobilized hospitals and called in medical personnel as far as a hundred miles away, but there weren't any casualties coming into an emergency room thirty blocks away. Even in an event this incomprehensible and unimagined, the imagery we possessed still held out some hope and everyone still expected survivors. The assumption was that there would be "hundreds dead, thousands injured," but none of the old assumptions or expectations would avail today. Expectant doctors and nurses milled around outside the emergency room, smoking cigarettes and looking down the street, straining to hear the sirens of ambulances approaching from downtown, but all the sirens passed us by, heading downtown.

Eventually word reached Dennis—there were no survivors to carry into the gym today; he was to prepare a temporary morgue. Ultimately, there were no bodies for the temporary morgue, but the fruitless cycle of activity and waiting and eventual realization recommenced, once again compounding the trauma. None of the expectations were valid, and none of the old assumptions worked any more. Would anything ever be the same?

Early that afternoon, while Dennis was still trying to get his morgue operational, I walked down to the corner to check security. A civilian standing at one of the barricades asked to speak with me—his son, a student at Stuyvesant High School—two blocks or so from the Trade Center—was missing. He went to try and find his son, but police would not let him into the area. All they would tell him was that his son had been removed to the Police Academy. Those were the words the cops used—"removed to the Police Academy." They gave him no more information. The man was obviously upset and fearful, and from his sweated and disheveled appearance, it looked like he had been running all over the area looking for help. My first thought was that his son was dead, his body on the way to Dennis's morgue. "Oh, God, the man doesn't know his son's been sent to the morgue." I thought that in the middle of all this I'd have to tell him his son is dead.

I wrote down his son's name and went to find out what I could. It took a little while, but I found out that apparently no Stuyvesant High School students were killed or seriously injured. His son was not being treated at Cabrini Hospital. The students were simply released from school and told to go north, away from the Trade Center. The kid was probably roaming around, perhaps trying to get home. I went back to tell the gentleman that his son was not at the Academy and grabbed two bottles of water on the way. There must have been something about my affect or the way I handed him the bottle, but for just an instant the look in his eyes was one of pure and unrestrained grief—he thought I was about to tell him his son was dead. "No, no," I explained. "Your son's not here, not at the hospital. He was released from school and no students were injured." I directed the man as best I could, took his number, reassured him I would call if his son came to the Police Academy, and sent him on his way. Later I would feel a little guilty about that, and much more guilty about the way I had handled the situation with the water bottle. The bottom line was that there *were* objectively more important things to do, and even if I didn't handle it as well as I would have liked to, I tried to do what I could for him.

Through all this, and although I felt almost no emotion, I was still focused and composed, even cheerful about the whole thing. Times like this called for leadership, and I fully believed I could provide that. I was aware, on a cognitive level, that this was a test of my mettle, of everything I believed myself to be. "Focus on the cops; you are responsible for their safety and welfare," I told myself. "Smile and call them by name. Ask them if they had called home. Does your family know you're safe? Call them now, and if you can't get through leave a message with a friend or neighbor that you're OK. Let them know you'll be here a while, and you won't be home for dinner." Remaining calm and confident to set an example was all part of being a good cop. The cops and recruits had enough to worry about— they needed to be reassured they were in good hands. I focused on the cops, especially on the recruits. They had been in the Academy less than two months and had absolutely no police experience, no images, forms, constellations, or schemas for enactment to get them through this. It was up to me and my partners and other senior cops to provide these kids with the leadership and the confidence they needed. One thing they did have, as vague and amorphous and inchoate as it may be, was the impulse to *do something*, and I realized I knew how to make it work for them and for me—I would provide them with the images, forms, and constellations of meaning that would permit them to interpret this new reality of isolation and fragmented disintegration. That would make them feel they were moving toward being good cops. With less than two months in the Academy, they really hadn't begun their socialization toward being cops in any meaningful way, and the "good cop" image or construct hadn't taken on any substantial meaning for them yet. Nevertheless, I was confident it could be developed—there were certainly enough images available, and the key would lie in how they interpreted and made meaning of them. I could lead them through the experience and help them interpret it in a positive and life-affirming way. Part of my mission became to help as many recruits as I could to become good cops.

Over the next few weeks, my partner Lieutenant Paul Kennedy and I would be responsible for about two hundred recruits, cops, and sergeants deployed in and around what everyone would call Ground Zero—the secure and exclusive area around the site of the wreckage where the world's attention was focused but where only police, fire, and emergency workers were permitted. Our feelings of exclusiveness were reinforced as we sailed through checkpoints unchallenged. No one else was permitted in this special place.

The term "Ground Zero" was laden with meaning, with connotations of devastation and holocaust, but at some point along the way, Paul, I, and the others began referring to it simply as "The Pile" or "The Zero." Our detail was called the "Un-zoned Posts," and it consisted of ten or fifteen disparate work details spread all over Lower Manhattan and Ground Zero. We were lucky insofar as other Academy supervisors were given more static traffic zones—Canal Street from river to river, for example—but we were able to move about the area freely in a radio car or four-wheel-drive vehicle. We were mobile where most others were generally not. We took the responsibility for the recruits' safety seriously—their physical safety as well as psychological well-being—and recognized the situation as a salient opportunity for training recruits and developing cops. We took the opportunity as much for ourselves as for them; we could make a difference in their lives and careers. Some of our police experiences would live on in them.

We moved about, continually talking to the kids, treating them with the respect we would treat real cops; the ordinary Police Academy Mickey-Mouse disciplinary nonsense had no place here. We would load up the trunk of the car with water and food and distribute it to the kids, but we made it a kind of game—"Officer, you can have some water if you can name three of the six items the Patrol Guide specifies must be secured in the trunk of a supervisor's RMP." Or, "Give me the definition of Burglary Second Degree and you can have a donut." No one was denied water or food—the point was to poke fun at the situation and perhaps to engage in a bit of mutual self-mockery, as well as to get them focused that they *were* doing police work. They *were* being cops.

Some of the recruits were deployed along the Zero's secure perimeter, and because none of them had ever walked a post before, we spent a great deal of time explaining the mechanics of effective post management, passing along "real cop" tips of the trade. Few had any concept of getting their memo book "scratched" by a supervisor, so we taught them the "real cop" ritual of it.[4] We tried to get them to pretend, in a way, that this was ordinary police work and that their assignment was no different than if they had been assigned to walk this post as a precinct cop. We asked them questions about another police term—"post conditions"—which we, of course, had to explain to them.

"Where is the nearest payphone or fire callbox? Where is the nearest subway station, what trains stop there, and what are the hours of operation for the token booth? If it was late at night and you had to use a restroom, where would you find one? Where is the nearest hospital, and what is the fastest route there?"

We gave them questions they would be forced to ponder and discuss among themselves, returning later for answers and to award "prizes" of additional water and snacks. We got them to start paying attention, in other words, to the everyday duties and routines "real cops" would use. We got them to start practicing the jargon and the rituals that connected cops to one another, to feel as if they were moving toward something ultimately desirable, rather than feeling like they were immobilized and stuck at the perimeter of an historic event in which they were only marginally participating. We continually reinforced that no matter the difficulty they faced today, this experience would benefit them because it would make them better cops, and one day they would have the opportunity and the responsibility to pass on their experience, to carry on the tradition of which they were now a part, to a young recruit.

It helped that Paul was such an old-timer. With 34 years in the Job, a ladder of hash marks denoting his years of service running up his sleeve, and a rack of medals above his shield, he was the very image of police experience. The fact that he kept on going despite obvious exhaustion was an inspiration to younger cops.

Paul and I would make this our practice over the next weeks, continually praising the recruits for the great job they were doing and gently correcting them when they made errors. We got the older cops and sergeants involved, building them up and focusing them on themes of movement and connection and integrity by continually reminding them of their role and responsibility to train and pass on their wisdom and experience to the new generation. We got everyone's mind involved, off the tragedy, got them moving with a sense of agency and purpose. We took the recruits aside and told them, in seeming confidence, how fortunate they were to be working with a particular officer or supervisor who really knew his stuff. "Pick his brain, ask him questions," we'd say. "He'll help you and teach you and make you a better cop, but you have to ask. Don't pass up this opportunity to work with a great cop like him." This focus on the recruits and cops became part of my mission in the weeks following the attacks.

Few recruits other than the ones we supervised were getting to the Zero. Most found themselves on traffic details uptown. Paul and I were able to get ours to the Pile, and others cautiously approached us at morning musters to ask that they be taken along with our detail. They knew it was a breach in protocol for a recruit to approach a boss with such a request, and they were a bit embarrassed about their urge to get to the Pile. Some hastened to clarify that they were not looking to sightsee, they just really wanted to be there, to make a difference. We accommodated as many as we could, and some of the kids were truly outstanding.

One afternoon, we needed extra bodies for the Un-Zone, so I went back to the Academy to pick up some recruits who had been held in reserve and were going off duty in about two hours. I went into the room and said I needed volunteers for a detail that would quite possibly take quite a while, but most of the kids volunteered. Some even jostled their way to the front of the room to get picked first. They knew nothing about the detail and had no idea how late they would stay, but they volunteered nevertheless. I picked the number of recruits we needed and couldn't resist addressing the volunteers, telling them loudly in the earshot of the others how the actions we take in times of crisis distinguish the kind of cops we are. Perhaps I did the others a disservice, and perhaps they had legitimate reasons for not volunteering, but I told the volunteers how honestly proud I was of them. I don't think they quite knew what to say, but I knew it meant a lot to them.

A little before eleven o'clock on the morning of the 11th, I saw a recruit in the hall with a tray of sandwiches for the chief's staff—they looked like the Riker's Island cheese sandwiches we used to feed prisoners being transported between jail and court. I had no idea where they came from, but it was time for a lesson. I took a sandwich and told the recruit to eat one as well. Since he was a recruit, he was a little reluctant to take a sandwich obviously meant for the chief's staff. There was a lesson here, though, I told him. "I'm not really hungry, but I'm going to eat this sandwich because I have no idea when I'll have the opportunity to eat another. Here's an ironclad rule of police work that will serve you well in your future—when you have the opportunity but not necessarily the need, take the opportunity because if you pass it up then, when you have the need, you will most definitely not have the opportunity. That goes for food, for water, and for personals."[5] The kid laughed and ate his sandwich, having understood my lesson. He had also learned, as good cops do, that there are times when it is entirely appropriate to break the rules.

On Thursday evening—two nights later—I realized I hadn't eaten anything since that cheese sandwich. I had drunk water but had no urge to eat and no awareness of hunger. I still wasn't hungry, but I ate then anyway.

The first information about casualties started coming in, and it was estimated that thousands, perhaps tens of thousands, were dead. Hundreds of cops and firefighters were unaccounted for. Seven World Trade Center was also down, as well as the mayor's emergency operations command center—the $15 million "Rudy Bunker"—on the 26th floor of that high-rise. The emergency operations center was built there a couple of years ago amid great public and media criticism—both the exorbitant costs and the wisdom of putting the city's primary command and control center in a building that was even then recognized as a potential target fueled a minor scandal at the time. The mayor and all the emergency operations people were forced to relocate to the Academy, which was to become the new citywide operations center. Now they realized the threat, and the fact that we would be the new emergency center was to remain a secret—because the mayor, the governor, and all the big shots would be coming here—as it seemed a virtual certainty that if subsequent attacks occurred we would be a primary target. Whoever the people were who planned the attack, they were not stupid—they must have recognized that taking out our command and control capability would immobilize the city and cripple its response.

Someone told me that most of the Police Department's commanders were wiped out when the towers fell; the rumor was already circulating that the First Deputy Commissioner, the Chief of Department, and a slew of other chiefs were missing and presumed dead in the rubble. Importantly, in terms of plausibility as well as symbolism, the rumor had it that they were gathered in the mayor's operations center when it fell, not actively participating in the real-cop work of rescue operations. This became part of the narrative—they were in the office, not on the street.

In the absence of accurate information, "facts" were frequently misinterpreted and rumors remained rampant for the next few weeks. Bizarre and frightful rumors were especially prevalent in the first few days, and as new images infiltrated and embellished the narratives they became even more fantastic in the retelling. Although many were eventually clarified and dispelled, at this point they had all the weight and reality of fact since there was practically no other source of information other than what cops told you. Cops acted upon the bits of information as if they were verified facts, compounding the chaos and making the overall experience that much more unreal. At a proximate level, cops gave credence to those rumors precisely because they fit the fragmented, bizarre, and death-immersed themes and imagery they were currently confronting. At a more ultimate level, they were given plausibility because their symbolism resonated so well within the street-cop culture.

Bosses, too, fell back on the constellations and schemas for enactment they had forged over the course of their careers. On the afternoon of the 11th, I had gone down the street to check security. The mayor, the governor, a host of commissioners, and public officials of every stripe were in the building, and we were therefore a target. The street was clogged with the officials' cars, essentially abandoned when they arrived, and there would be no way to evacuate the building if something happened. Everyone would be trapped. On the next block over was a huge, empty schoolyard—maybe half a city block in size—but its gates were chained. There was a young captain standing on the corner, directing others directing traffic, so I told him he should have someone open the schoolyard and get the cars off the Academy block. The captain replied in all seriousness that he couldn't do that without the permission of a school official, and I was dumbstruck.

I went around the corner to the Emergency Services Unit base and got an Emergency Services Unit cop with a Sawz-All. We then cut down a stanchion and the locks off the gate. "You sure about this, Sarge?" he asked. I pointed to my shield and nameplate. "It's H. E. N. R. Y." He grinned back. "That's all I need, Boss," and with that, we got a dozen recruits to pick up a car blocking the curb and moved it into the schoolyard. The entrance was cleared, and the parking problem was solved despite the immobility of rule-bound bosses.

There was also a kind of synergy operating to create and disseminate factually inaccurate rumors, and this was intensified by the interplay of extensive numbing, the partial breakdown of symbolization that accompanied it, and the state of physical and mental hyperarousal we all felt. Eventually, the effects of physical and mental fatigue would enter into the equation as well. In this process, the attempt to integrate and make sense of so many subjectively unfamiliar and objectively incomplete or fragmented images—a symbolizing process which was difficult enough under less threatening conditions—was complicated by innumerable distractions and by the dissociative effect of pronounced numbing. Under these difficult conditions, survivors were particularly susceptible to the kind of familiar symbols and images that seemed to make the most sense and therefore integrated more easily—images that fit well with preexisting images and constellations and therefore readily imparted some type of meaning to the situation and restored a comforting feeling of reality and actuality to their experience. The meanings they derived from these narratives, however, remained incomplete and could not fully satisfy the compelling urge to make meaning of the experience.

Cops continually repeated their own and others' narratives as part of the quest to find immediate and ultimate meaning, and this "talking through" of experiences would continue for some months as they tried out various combinations of images—images derived from their own experience or imported from the narratives of others—in an effort to construct a more objective and comprehensive meaning in the events. Cops revisited, revised, and repeated their own narratives in conversations with others, and they listened avidly to the narratives of other cops in an effort to find images that fit the empty spaces in their own construction, images that would help them understand what had happened. These accounts, however, were fundamentally disjointed and highly subjective in nature. They did not integrate easily. Although they were laden with culturally meaningful symbols and resonating images, the narratives of others did little to satisfy the powerful urge to make meaning.

For months, one feature of the police survivor's need to understand what had happened to his psychological and physical world would be the tendency to dwell on the experience and repeat his experiences to others. At first, it seemed as if almost everyone, including cops and rescue workers as well as civilians whose knowledge and understanding of the Trade Center events were based less on personal exposure than upon media accounts, would be receptive to hearing these narratives and sharing their own experiences. Indeed, many civilians would approach and actively engage cops in conversation in hopes of satisfying their own urge to make meaning. And when cops got together it seems the Trade Center was implicit in every topic of conversation. Generally speaking, though, members of the public would lose their appetite for Trade Center stories before the cops, firefighters, and other on-scene rescue workers did; the resulting sense that one's experience had no real meaning to the vast majority of people reinforced this group's survivor identity—this group's members felt that no one understood them or their experiences except for another member, another cop who was there. In short, the situation arose that no one seemed to want to listen anymore to these survivor stories except for another cop or firefighter who was there. When the public's need to move on and put the Trade Center experience behind them outstripped our need to talk about that experience, we felt as if we became an irritation or annoyance.

But the public also irritated and annoyed us—what else was there to talk about but the Zero, the Pile? In sharp contrast to the unprecedented levels of high esteem with which the public seemed to hold us as well as the unparalleled outpouring of individual and collective public support that occurred in the immediate aftermath of the event—touchingly genuine sentiments that nurtured and supported us in a way I can scarcely explain—cops found themselves becoming increasingly estranged from civilians. Not only had our experience made us different, but others began to regard us differently as well. We bore a death taint that at first attracted others to us before it eventually repelled them, and expressions of resentment toward a fickle public began to emerge within the ranks of cops and firefighters. Before that happened, though, we reveled in a magical outpouring of individual and community love and appreciation whose extent cops had never before experienced.

Although every cop and firefighter reveled in the intoxicating public adulation and the sense of connection it provided, Paul and I recognized early on that it would not last, and we told the recruits that they should enjoy the attention but should not expect it to continue. We were not merely being cynical here, although to some degree a cynicism born of our police experience undoubtedly operated to shape our perspective. It was objectively unreasonable to expect that the public would maintain this type of thoughtful kindness for long, especially since relations with the public had been strained before September 11. While we did not fully consider or intellectualize the dynamic at the time, at some level of awareness cops seemed to understand that this outpouring of public affection and appreciation was rooted in the public's transitory elation at having survived, in their ephemeral recognition that cops, firefighters, and other rescue workers were in some respect responsible for their survival. The manifestations of this public adulation were at times truly intoxicating, and these added to the unreality of the situation. Crowds of people lined the West Street approach to Ground Zero, cheering and holding banners expressing their appreciation and gratitude. As they waved and cheered, we recognized the extraordinary strangeness and peculiar elation of waving back like heroes at a parade. Other groups set up impromptu stations on the street that offered bottled water and food, and trays of homemade comfort food and cases of drink streamed into police facilities from grateful civilians and businesses. People offered their thanks and tried in their own ways to nurture and sustain our efforts.

The sense of appreciation seemed universal, transcending all levels and strata of society. One day, early on, we had a small security detail deployed outside Kofi Annan's residence on Sutton Place—the very high rent district where studio apartments can sell in excess of a million dollars—and an attractive, well-coifed mature woman, whose picture one might see in the society pages of the *Times*, approached me with a plastic tub of cookies. She addressed me as "Captain," making it obvious that she didn't usually have much to do with cops, and asked if it would be alright if she gave the cookies she baked to my officers. She didn't say "the cookies I had my maid bake" or "the cookies I bought from some fancy bakery." She really didn't seem the baking type, but she baked the cookies as a way of saying thanks—of expressing her genuine gratitude to people I'm certain she rarely gave a second look or a passing thought.

Another day, or perhaps it was the same day, a group of teenage African-American kids, who had undoubtedly dealt more frequently and intimately but very differently with cops than the well-coifed woman, approached me with high-fives on the Lower East Side. "Yo, Sarge. Thanks, man," they said in the interaction which was as strained and unusual for them as it is for me. Yet, their gratitude seemed genuine.

A week following the attacks, I drove home one evening on the Long Island Expressway. A small crowd stood on an overpass, clapping and holding up a bedsheet banner: "We Love NYPD, FDNY, EMS Heroes." It overwhelmed me, and I got choked up, as I still do when I pass that overpass.

Still, rumors continued, spreading alarm and false information. On the night of the 11th, for example, I was told that the entire Manhattan South Task Force and the entire day tour from the First Precinct were wiped out when the first tower fell. The rumor had it that they were standing in formation on the sidewalk outside the tower as it burned, waiting for their bosses to formulate a plan. The image of cops standing in ranks evoked images of police funerals. The rumor fit the grotesque and extraordinary themes and imagery of that day as well as the more familiar themes and imagery that resonate in police culture—the tale certainly reflected death-equivalent images of stasis, separation, and disintegration, as well as images of massive death—not just the deaths of numerous individuals, but more specifically and more horrifically the complete annihilation of an entire command *a la* Fort Zinderneuf. Implicit in the narrative was a profound hostility directed at the bosses allegedly responsible for the supposed deaths—the bosses having failed in a primary responsibility toward their officers.

Early on in the crisis, the traditional theme of ill will between street cops and management cops became magnified to an unprecedented level of enmity as leadership structures effectively disintegrated. A prevalent theme those days was that ranking bosses were absent or immobilized—they stood around planning and dawdling while street cops and civilians were in danger—and numerous stories circulated that many cops had essentially mutinied against their bosses. One cop told me of an Inspector chasing a mob of unheeding street cops down the street as they headed toward the Trade Center. "Come back here. I said come back here. Stop, I'm telling you to stop," he had cried, but the street cops knew what needed to be done, and they had the integrity to do it regardless of orders to the contrary. Regardless of rank and threats to their own personal safety, these real cops saw the need to do something, and they did what they could to actualize their schemas for enactment.

This collective sense among street cops that management cops were counterfeit and that they alone were authentic would be reinforced several months later when, a few days before leaving office, the police commissioner awarded Medals of Valor to a handful of ranking chiefs for their actions at the Trade Center. Whether or not the medals were legitimately earned is almost immaterial as the timing of the awards ceremony, the secrecy surrounding it, and the fact that so many other cops who had actually distinguished themselves for conspicuous bravery had not yet been officially or adequately recognized (nor, perhaps, would they ever be) conferred an aura of illegitimacy and cronyism in the commissioner's actions and reinforced cultural notions that the big bosses were venal and entirely self-serving. Adding to the perception that something sneaky and underhanded was afoot was the fact that the medals were awarded in a private ceremony in the commissioner's office and were not published in Department Orders. Within the ranks of real cops, but perhaps particularly among those officers who legitimately earned their medals for heroism and who continue to struggle with all the repercussions and consequences of their profound death encounters, this incident reinforced the collective cultural view that the real cops were on their own and that the management cops were inauthentic poseurs.

One of the most frightening rumors circulated was that shortly after the planes hit the towers a high-ranking city official charged with emergency management responsibilities grabbed a police radio and ordered Police Department helicopters to crash into any aircraft approaching Lower Manhattan—in essence, to engage in a suicide attack in the line of duty. The idea was absurd on its face—the possibility that an errant aircraft might drift over Manhattan was real, and there was no way to ensure that a plane, even one containing terrorists, would crash in an area that would not take thousands of additional lives. The official in that rumor was identified by name, making the rumor credible. Rumors also circulated that the same official had a nervous breakdown and was forcibly removed to a psychiatric hospital but that this information had to be suppressed so as not to alarm the public. Such a rumor made me wonder what other lies were we being fed.

No one had the whole picture, so everyone sought more information to make sense of what was going on. The rumor about the deaths of the brass eventually proved to be unfounded—it was not the NYPD's chiefs who died, but the Fire Department's First Deputy Commissioner and Chief of Department. The facts had been distorted, given the weight of reality. They also fit right into the emerging and very unsettling perception that no one was actually in charge, that we street cops could no longer depend upon the entities and assumptions that, under ordinary circumstances, have always defined and directed our actions. The rumors echoed my anomic perception that the rules no longer applied.

In conjunction with the powerful images of disintegration and the drastic breakdown of symbolization that so frequently took place throughout the crisis, cops had no preexisting schemas for enactment to adequately prepare them for dealing with crises of this type or magnitude. Collectively and individually, these factors exacerbated the overall psychological impact of the crisis by further isolating cops and by promoting individual action rather than teamwork. A resounding and recurring theme among virtually everyone I spoke with at the time—cops and firefighters as well as civilians—was that the loss of the Trade Center and all the death and devastation accompanying it had been beyond virtually everyone's imagination or beyond even their capacity to imagine. There was no imagery to prepare anyone for what they faced, and therefore no viable and comprehensive schemas for enactment which might inform or shape collective activities. Especially at the earliest stages of the event, cops responded as individuals to individual problems they encountered, and there was little or no organized coordination among the responders. Subsequent inquiries and investigations certainly revealed how little coordination there was at the organizational and interorganizational levels. Cops and firefighters had separate command posts at the Trade Center, and because they used different radio frequencies, no capacity to communicate. NYPD Aviation Unit cops issued a warning to evacuate the rescuers as the buildings started to crumble, but the warning could not reach the FDNY personnel.

The overall effect isolated individual cops from the groups and social supports that are so important during and after death encounters. That disconnected sense of isolation inevitably exacerbated cops' psychic trauma. In many respects, units of cops stopped functioning as teams as the line of command broke down at the scene of the disaster, forcing cops to openly defy their bosses.

The rumors continued for days and weeks, and in at least one respect, they mirrored reality—there *was* a significant breakdown in command and leadership to the extent that there was apparently no effective effort on the part of executives to dispel rumors and foster focused collective activity by keeping cops informed of developments. If there was such an effort, it didn't work.

Throughout the crisis, despite the fact that Paul and I were responsible each day for the activities and safety of more than 200 recruits, cops, and sergeants, we received only one short briefing on the current condition of terrorist threats; although the briefing was ostensibly motivated by an executive's concern for officer safety, the information provided to us in that briefing was both incomplete and factually incorrect. Paul had actually gleaned more information about the subject of the briefing—the theft of a utility truck that terrorists might use to pass through security checkpoints—from his own field inquiries than from the information provided by the intelligence officer.

Cognizant of the need to facilitate communication and security, Paul prepared a list of important phone numbers, locations, and items of information which he updated daily for distribution to all our cops and supervisors. Intuitively, he knew that it was therapeutic and necessary for cops to be connected and informed—so if someone asked them for the location of the temporary morgue or the contact information for the temporary headquarters, for example, and they didn't know, their feelings of their lack of agency would only be heightened and reinforced.

On the afternoon of the 11th, someone told me that the Fire Department's chaplain, Father Mychal Judge, had died giving Last Rights to a dying firefighter. The informant pronounced the name "Mickel," but I very calmly and rationally—I still felt no emotion—explained that despite the unusual spelling his name is pronounced "Michael." I had known Mike Judge for 25 years and still have tremendous respect for the man. In another time and place, Mike Judge was assistant to the president of a college I attended before becoming a cop. His life was an authentic example of the Franciscan tradition he stood for. He had confidence in me and gave me a chance when others were reluctant to do so, which made a big difference in my life.

My temporal ordering of events remains confused even after all this time—but at some point I saw the now-famous photo of Father Mike being carried from the cloud of smoke and debris. The image is like a modern-day Pieta as a dying priest in flowing robes was carried from the swirling debris cloud by two firefighters, a uniformed police lieutenant, and two civilians from the Office of Emergency Management. They laid him on the altar of Saint Peter's Church. He died a good death, I thought at the time, a priest's death. He died in a state of grace, administering a sacrament to one of the firefighters who were his special ministry. For Mike Judge, the man I knew, there could be no better death.

I recognize the lieutenant in the photo as another acquaintance—one of those people in large organizations who you frequently encounter and say hello to without knowing their names. Months later I'd learn that he is the son of a friend—a retired cop who was a friend and contemporary of my own father—and that the lieutenant and I had played together as children. The ties that bind cops together may often be obscure, but they are real in their impact.

That day I would also learn that Glenn Pettit from the Academy's Video Unit was missing and presumed dead. He and I spoke that very morning in the hallway outside my office, but I could not recall his face until I went downstairs to his office to look at a photo of him. I photocopied the image and distributed it to cops, recruits, and hospitals in the hope that he was simply injured and unable to contact anyone. For months I'd be unable to recall Glenn's face without referring to a photo, as if all my memories of him were erased.

At that time I was too distant, too focused on the cognitive to feel any emotion about Father Mike's death, just as I was too distant to recall the familiar image of Glenn's face. The degree of numbing I experienced varied a bit over the next few days. There were times I was aware of some emotion, but the emotions had a somewhat disembodied quality, and I didn't truly *feel* or act upon them. As evidenced by my lasting inability to fully locate all those events in time, to some extent I'm still plagued by the results of those dissociative effects, especially the inability to integrate and attribute meaning to certain images and experiences.

Three days later, when I was finally able to get home long enough to pick up my car and cell phone before returning to work, I made my way to the Long Island Rail Road and sat on the almost-empty late-night train, dirty and exhausted, next to an Irish tourist. The woman, recognizing that I was a cop, asked all sorts of questions about the attacks and about the area that had already become known as Ground Zero. A couple of others on the train were obviously straining to listen in, at once attracted and repelled as my death taint still captivated others.

"Were you there when it happened?," she asked.

"No, I was at the Academy."

"You've been to Ground Zero, though? What is it like?"

"It's horrible. Too much to describe. It looks nothing like anything I've ever seen."

"Did you lose any friends?"

"Well, yes. We still don't know how many cops and firemen are dead, but Mike Judge is dead. Glenn Pettit and Mike Judge are dead." I said, feeling the realization sink in. The knowledge of Mike Judge's death, like the knowledge of all the other deaths—the known and the unknown—had been with me for three days, but I never truly *felt* the impact of those deaths. I knew in a cognitive way that Mike Judge was dead, that Glenn Pettit was probably dead, that Moira Smith and Bobby Fazio and all the others were dead. For all I knew, a great many other friends were dead. When I pronounced the words, though, all the emotions of the past three days crashed in on me and I began to sob. I couldn't control it, and I just sat there on a nearly-empty train sobbing and shaking and crying with my head in my hands. It wasn't just the death of an acquaintance and a man that I deeply respected or the deaths of cops I knew and worked with over the years, it was the fact that I wasn't there to help. It was the entire experience of being immersed in death for three days without feeling any of the appropriate emotions, and once the dam broke all the emotions seemed to overtake me at once. It wasn't an emotion tied to a particular thing or a particular image that flooded in, but rather a pure and unfocused feeling-state so complex and so convoluted it defies description.

People began to move away quietly; perhaps they were embarrassed or perhaps they just wished to give me solitude and space, and I looked up to see the conductor whispering to a passenger in the vestibule and pointing sadly to the spectacle of the shaking, sobbing cop. I sat alone crying in the empty car for nearly forty-five minutes.

It had little to do with the death of Mike Judge, per se, although to this day I cannot look at that photo of him without choking up. For a long time I would have to fight back tears when I saw that image, and this particular passage was not written without tears. I had never had that kind of reaction to the death of an acquaintance before. That photo became, for me, a kind of screen image that had come to encapsulate and represent all the horror, fear, pain, and death of the entire Trade Center experience. It remains a visually compelling image with multiple and simultaneously overlapping elements of death, struggle, religious meaning, good and evil, strength and weakness, detachment and connection, as well as despair and heroic action. I suppose the fact that I know several of those depicted in it imparts a special meaning for me, and despite those meanings, both objective and personal, that image conjures, they are to a large extent still unintegrated meanings—I have struggled and will continue to struggle to make sense of them. I keep that photo in my desk and am often drawn to it.

Despite the fact that so many of the images from that time are fragmented and incomplete, many or most involve a host of associations that evoke other seemingly unrelated images and feelings. This is due in part to the dissociation other cops and I experienced, and in part to the fact there was so little information available to us those first few days. Most of the cops involved in the rescue and recovery activities at the Zero had no opportunity to read newspapers or access other media accounts that might have given us a bigger picture, a more comprehensive idea of what was taking place outside our immediate sphere, and Police Department managers and executives seemed to have either little interest or little ability to inform cops and dispel rumors. Especially during the first few days, we existed primarily in our own narrow and constricted psychological worlds.

This is not to say there was no sense of connection to others—on the contrary there was a tremendous sense of philosophical connection to the rescue and recovery effort and a more intimate and personalized sense of connection to others in the Job. I truly felt a part of something larger and more important than any individual. Some of the most honest and intimate exchanges I had ever had with any cops took place in those days, and the honesty and integrity of it all was real and purifying as there was no time or place for pretense or reserve. With so many profound images of connection and integrity, I experienced a sense of pride in my partners and the cops I saw and worked with as well as pride in myself for being a cop.

The images from that day and the weeks that followed remain, occasionally evoked by an association. Some are integrated and others not. There is the image of a uniformed cop, his casted arm in a sling, directing traffic at Chambers and West. Of Lauren Foster, who worked for me, refusing to report sick after a severe asthma attack. Of my partner Paul Kennedy, who had never called in sick during 34 years on the Job, arguing with the Inspector and refusing to take an inside job after paramedics found his blood pressure to be dangerously high. In five months he would need bypass surgery and would be surveyed off the Job, but until then he would not step aside from his duty for his own health and safety.

There are subtler images which exist as well—the frightened faces of recruits nevertheless desperate of fulfill the impulse to be a cop. They are the young cops in the making who, given the opportunity to sit out the last two hours of their tour in the relative comfort of the Academy, nevertheless volunteer for an assignment whose duties and duration they have not been told. The faces of those same kids, stammering and demurring when I ask why they volunteered, and embarrassed but bursting with pride in front of their peers when I tell them why. I tell them it is because their character leaves them no choice in the matter, that they are good cops who will one day be great cops, and good cops just have to do what it is their nature to do. There is the image of a good friend I saw being treated in the emergency room, hunched over with an oxygen mask on his face, and his adamant demand to discontinue treatment, to get his gun and shield, and go back to the carnage downtown.

There is the memory of standing on Canal Street east of the Bowery, a few days into the crisis, when Canal Street was the northern perimeter of the frozen zone. Three gentlemen, two Hispanics and one Caribbean-American, approach and explain they are ministers from congregations in the Bronx who are there to pray for cops and firefighters. "Was there anyone in particular I'd like them to pray for?" they ask. I tell them about Mike Judge and Glenn Pettit. I tell them of some cops I know who are having a particularly rough time. One of the Hispanics has to translate my English into Spanish for the Caribbean-American. Another asks if they can pray for me, and I say sure. Though I'm not a particularly religious man and whatever their faith is certainly isn't mine, my impulse is to accept their prayers gratefully. I misunderstood them, though. They meant they would pray for me *now*. The three put their hands on my shoulder, and we bow our heads and stand in the gutter on one of New York City's busiest and most congested streets as they pray for me in Spanish for what must have been three or four full minutes. I haven't felt such a special spiritual connection in years, if ever. I still have no idea what they said. But it was a powerful spiritual experience that had nothing to do with words and everything to do with connection. The image of the cop and the preachers must have been compelling because a wonderful thing happened—everything got quiet as people and traffic stopped. Everyone gave us that moment, and I think everyone shared in it as well. There was no movement, no horns, no noise at the checkpoint. It was magical.

There is also the image of the little girl who approached Paul and me as we sat in our radio car in front of a firehouse on the perimeter of Ground Zero, restless and enervated, watching the crowds of the curious. A small, impassive face with blue eyes and blond hair appeared at the open car window. We startle as a little girl of perhaps five years of age, accompanied by her parents and a toddler and pulling a little red wagon, thrusts a plastic sandwich bag containing three or four homemade cookies into the car without a word. She has one bag for me and one for Paul. Attached to each bag is a child's crayon drawing, maybe five inches by seven inches, of two towers and an American flag, with scraps of red, white, and blue paper stapled to it. The words are in a child's stilted print, as if copied with the coaching of an adult, "Thanks!" it reads. "You are heroes." Wordlessly, she blows us a kiss and disappears down the block pulling her red wagon with its bags of homemade chocolate chip cookies. Paul and I just look at each other and then at the tiny collage. Both of us kept that shred of paper, and mine sits now framed in my office. It is the only souvenir I kept from that time, and it means much more to me than I can explain.

I want to make it clear that I am not a hero, and in writing this there is no false modesty. After all my interviews with collaborators, after all of the true heroes I met through the years and saw during the Trade Center crisis, I know what real heroism is. I cannot count myself among them. I was witness to their integrity, and to include myself within their ranks would be to minimize their struggles and to betray the hard-won integrity that defines them. Though the term hero is such a seductive label, it does not apply to me and I reject almost anyone's attempt to fix it on me. I did nothing extraordinary and nothing that required any special strength of character; Paul, Dennis, Pete, and I, along with thousands of other cops, did what it was or has become our nature to do. We can be proud of our response and of the way we acquitted ourselves, but we have not earned the right to be called heroes. I reject the label of hero from anyone but that little girl. If she needs a hero, then I owe it to her to be her hero.

Within the few days following the attack, it seemed as if everyone had been overtaken by an extraordinary physical and mental fatigue—a fatigue that was extraordinary not only for its depth and dimension but also because it belied a concomitant energizing focus on our mission and, especially during the early days, on issues of safety and danger. That energizing focus precluded any rest or relaxation, even if events had provided the opportunity for rest. Everyone I spoke with was bone tired, and despite the mental and physical exhaustion, most say they had great difficulty sleeping for the few hours we had off between tours.

At about 11:30 on the night of the 11th, Paul, Dennis, Pete, and I learn that our next tour of duty will begin at 3:00 A.M. By midnight, we were sprawled on cots and desk chairs in the office, but we were all too energized to sleep. Everyone was wired, and none of us had a chance to doze off for more than 45 minutes. By 3 o'clock we were up again, showered, dressed, and on deck. For the next four nights none of us would get more than two hours of what passed for sleep, and for the next three weeks there would be only one day in which I got more than four hours of fitful sleep. Someone defined it as "the sleep that yields no rest," and the term stuck with me. It was an exhausted sleep riddled with bizarre, disjointed, and sometimes troubling dreams. Everyone was dragging—dead tired, yet wide awake. It seemed especially difficult for the recruits, many of whom slept on cots in the gym that has been converted once again to a huge dormitory and feeding station. The room bustled with activity around the clock and was no place to sleep.

We were told we would be working twelve-hour tours for the duration of the crisis, but the formally prescribed and self-determined responsibilities of lieutenants and some sergeants (including myself) required that we work fourteen- or sixteen-hour tours. All of the details in the Un-Zone were designated for face-to-face relief, which meant that no one could leave their post until the entire relieving detail had arrived on the post and was completely deployed. Given the logistical difficulties of rostering, deploying, and transporting more than a thousand recruits, cops, and supervisors from the Academy, this process added several hours to every tour, and we were forced to stay until every cop and supervisor had returned to the Academy and had been accounted for.

Everyone seemed to experience a compelling urge to reconnect with the reassuring familiarity of home and family life, but circumstances dictated that many would be unable to do so. Even those who lived within the city felt ambivalent about going home, even for periods of brief duration—they were at once compelled by the natural inclination to touch base with their families and constrained by the professional urge to do more—to be cops. Some cops volunteered to go back to Ground Zero for the few hours they had off to sift through the rubble as part of the backbreaking "bucket brigade," in which they would search for survivors but, in actuality, would recover little more than body parts. They willingly subjected themselves to this labor and to the fragmented and toxic images it entailed.

After a week or so a recruit informed me his wife had had a baby that he had not yet seen or held for more than a few minutes. I offered to try to get him some time off to be with them, but he replied, with simultaneous reluctance and embarrassment, that he would be OK, that he did not really need the time off. I completely understood—in an intellectual sense, perhaps better than he did—his struggle between fulfilling the responsibilities of his identity as a husband and father and those of his emerging identity as a cop. He has all the makings of a damn good cop, and I have great admiration and respect for the man.

A week or so following the collapse, a Red Cross worker asked me to speak with a young cop who had not yet been home. He had been in contact with his wife who was at home in the suburbs with their children, and she would not accept the fact that he could not come home. His wife, petrified that he would be killed, wanted him to quit, if necessary, and come home to his family. I placed him and his wife in cell phone contact with my wife. The long-time spouse of a cop, she understood the dynamics only too well, and she reached out to the young cop's wife. There was little more that I could do for them, though, in that situation, which was painful for me.

Two weeks following the attack the bosses told us everyone had to take a day off. They told us they were concerned for our health and safety, that we would start falling apart if we didn't take a day's rest. The prospect of a day off to reconnect with my wife, to be in the familiar surroundings of home, and perhaps to get a few hours of real sleep had an exceptionally powerful draw, but I was nevertheless conflicted. I had been fantasizing about going home, but like many others, I felt guilty at the thought of leaving the city to tend to my own needs in such a time as that. What if something happened while I was away? What if I was needed and wasn't able to get back? If something went down, I wanted to be in the middle of it; I didn't want to be stuck and unable to help the next time around. I briefly considered volunteering for the bucket brigade on my day off, but the appeal of going home for even a few hours was overwhelming. It would be a much-needed chance to recharge, to try and experience the world as I knew it before it changed so radically. Over the previous two weeks the absurdity of my existence had come to seem real and almost normal, and that worried me. I wanted to be assured that there was, in fact, another world out there, something familiar to return to after this thing was over. I would go to the beach and connect with nature, I thought—the weather had remained warm and beautiful. Most important, I would get to touch and talk with Lydia, whom I had missed terribly and who needed to be with me as much as I needed to be with her.

I pack the trunk of my car with everything I would need if another crisis erupted—a spare uniform, boots, a blanket, a raid jacket, a cell phone, extra batteries for the police radio, and a "Go bag" which contained extra food, bottled water, and all the essentials I would need if I had to hurry back to the city. I kept the police radio on and with me for the entire time I was off, even though it wouldn't receive transmissions that far from the city. The car stayed packed that way until June.

The bosses were solicitous—they kept saying the ordered day off was for our health and safety, so a lot of cops looked forward to it. Some of us suspicious old dogs knew the real score, though; according to federal labor law, if we work more than fifteen days without a day off, we had to be paid overtime for every hour we work and not just for the hours beyond the regular forty-hour week. We weren't doing this for the overtime—if we were it would be blood money—but those counterfeit bosses tried to spin the story that the day off was for our benefit and not for their budget.

I took the "day off" and drove the hundred miles out to the country in search of familiarity and normalcy. A month before, we had been invited to a fundraising event scheduled for that evening, and because I wanted to break away from the Trade Center—to pretend things were as they had been before—my wife and I decided to go to it. We would pretend that nothing was different. I stopped at home to shower and put on a suit before heading to the event with my wife. The affair was elegant, and there were a lot of vaguely familiar faces. But the air of normalcy and familiarity I had hoped for was somehow missing. It didn't seem altogether real, it didn't quite ring true, but beyond the fact that people have red, white, and blue ribbons pinned to their lapels, I couldn't identify what was different. I became edgy and distracted. I sat with my wife and a few friends, uninterested in trying to connect with anyone else, but everyone seemed to be staring at me surreptitiously. Ordinarily, I keep a low profile and very few people in my community knew I was a cop. I knew enough to make a conscious resolve to try and control the urge to talk about the Zero. They looked at me then as if they knew I had been there. How did they know? What did they think?

I went up to the buffet table where the chef, a nice young man, asked me how I'd like my tuna medallions prepared. I wanted to strike out at him. For the past two weeks, I had been subsisting on Power Bars and eating in Red Cross tents. None of us—none of my partners and none of the people I had shared these powerful and intimate experiences with—had slept more than four hours in one stretch, and in many ways our existence had been more animal than human. We were physically and emotionally exhausted, we had been immersed in death and destruction on a scale that was previously incomprehensible to us, but that eventually came to seem real. In essence we had been existing in a bizarre physical and psychological war zone for the past two weeks. Feelings of extreme, unfocused, and almost overwhelming rage overtook me as I stood before the chef. "How would I like my fucking tuna medallions prepared?" I thought. "Don't you know? Don't all of you know what's fucking going on? How can you continue to live your fucking lives as if nothing is different?" I felt angry, superior, proud of myself, of my partners, and of the recruits who had acquitted themselves so well through the horrors and grotesqueness of the past two weeks. These people at this banquet had no idea how fragile their precious safe existence was, and that made me furious. We were the only ones who knew, the cops and firefighters and rescue workers at the Zero. How dare they stare at me! How dare they go about their lives pretending that nothing was different. Didn't they know that Mike Judge, Glenn Pettit, Moira Smith, Bobby Fazio, John Perry, and all the other cops, along with more than 300 firefighters, had sacrificed themselves trying to preserve the normalcy they so casually went about living?

I was angry at them, but I was also furious with myself, because I knew I also wanted to embrace the pretense that everything was fine and ordinary. That was why I came here—to escape into a familiar reality I was comfortable with. I found the familiar reality, but it was not at all comfortable.

I was also angry and unsettled because I wondered whether there would ever be the kind of ordinary reality we all knew before, whether the experiences had changed me to the point that I would ever really fit in outside the Zero, which was where I really wanted to be right then. Over the two weeks before this night, the Zero had become my familiar and ordinary reality.

The brief rage passed quickly. I sat down to have my tuna medallions, seared on the outside and rare in the middle. These were good people, and they deserved to have their illusions of safety. It was a nice affair, and eventually we got ready to leave. At the door an older man whom I didn't know stopped me, shook my hand, and simply said, "Thank you." I choked up, and not just because of the genuine sentiment he expressed—he was the only one who said anything to me directly all night—but because he made me feel so proud to be a cop, because these good folks should not have to deal with the things I had to. His thanks defined me.

The next day, I tried to go about my normal day-off routine. I went for a haircut, but I started talking about the Zero, and it made someone so uncomfortable that he had to leave. I saw tears in his eyes as he walked out. I ran into an acquaintance who looked haunted. Again I couldn't stop talking about what had happened, and I chased her away as well. I drove down to the empty beach and took a walk. It was warm and clear, and the water was cold and rough; there was no one else on the beach. I left my shirt, wallet, shield, and gun in a pile and waded out waist-deep in the cold water to scream at the sky.

After a few days, the manifestations of sleep deprivation and stress became apparent: in conjunction with the continuing and residual effects of numbing and all the mental weariness that came from the ongoing intellectual struggle to make sense of so many broken and unfamiliar images, it became increasingly difficult to formulate cogent thoughts, much less communicate them. It became something of an ongoing joke—no one seemed able to complete a sentence without getting off track or forgetting what they wanted to say. I noticed that cops' thought and speech patterns changed to resemble those of schizophrenics or functional psychotics; they became tangential as associations loosened. Word salads emerged, and although individual phrases within a sentence made sense, they seemed to be out of order, and no one was able to get to the point. This was not to say that cops actually became psychotic or schizophrenic, merely that the similarity in speech patterns reflected the broken or shattered character of their respective psychological universes.

Some cops had a particularly hard time of it. On the night of the 11th, Sergeant Mary Young, who was a POPPA peer counselor,[6] told me there were injured cops in Cabrini's ER, but no one from the department's Psych Services had gone there to help them. We went over to help, to listen, and after a while some Psych Services shrinks finally showed up. They stayed for a while but then left just as suddenly as they had arrived. Mary and I remained to talk with an old timer—a detective from a busy squad—who was hooked up to a heart monitor. "I'm okay," he said. "Go see about my partner." His partner, also hooked up to a monitor, said the same thing: "Take care of my partner. Make sure he's okay." Both of these detectives had watched the bodies fall and had heard, up close, the sound they made when they hit the sidewalk after a one-thousand-foot plummet. One detective had counted the falling bodies, but he stopped at 20 when he saw one split in half as it hit the steel beams of the atrium. "I can't stop seeing them. I see them when my eyes are open, and I see them when my eyes are closed. I can't stop seeing them. And the sound they make . . . " Intuitively, I tried to get them to talk about what they saw and did, to integrate and process images as best they could, but their narratives remained broken and their responses to questions seemed unconnected.

Across the ER, I was shocked to see a friend, a young cop I had known for his entire time on the Job. He and his partner had been treated and were trying to get released. He was as intense, as formal, and as serious as I had ever seen him. "Sarge, you've got to help us. They took our guns and shields, our leather and uniforms. You've got to get them back for us." Since no one knew then what kind of poisons or biological agents might be in the air downtown, everyone coming in for treatment was being decontaminated—their uniforms and gear were taken away before they were sprayed down with a fire hose and issued hospital greens or sweat suits. They needed their gear because they wanted to go back out, and there was no negotiating this. They were going back, in sweat suits if they had to, but they were going back and they wanted their shields and guns. I understood it was the mentality of being a good cop, so I got them their guns and shields for them. They walked out without another word and went back to the carnage.

There were only a handful of cops in the ER, which was quieter than what you would expect on a normal night. There was a young cop, only six months on the Job, in what I would call a near-catatonic state. His knee was broken. Mary and I talked with him for nearly an hour and received only monosyllabic responses from him. His affect was entirely passive except for his fingers, which ripped frantically at a piece of hospital gauze. A Psych Services shrink was with us. The young cop was on his way to court and had come out of the subway just as the plane hit. Someone said he kept going into the building and carrying people out, that he fought another cop who tried to stop him from going back in as the tower was collapsing and debris was crashing to the sidewalk around them. His mother came to the hospital, so Mary and I left him with her and the shrink, and when we came back a little while later, all of them were gone. More than a month later, I would learn that his paperwork had "somehow fallen through the cracks" and that he had received no follow-up care from department doctors or shrinks. He sat home, alone, for more than a month. We never did get anything but monosyllables from him.

Another friend, a boss, was brought in. One of his cops was missing and would be listed as such until his remains were recovered. We talked for a while, and he told me how he had wandered the streets in search of this cop, making the rounds of the hospitals. He told me over and over again of searching for his missing cop as I got him to talk, to integrate the images. A month or so later, when we talked again, he would have no recollection of meeting or speaking with me at the hospital.

There are still so many images of those days that remain. The heat of the Pile was so intense it would melt the soles of your boots. You could feel the heat as you approached from a block away, and there was also the dust and smoke, a taste of metal in your mouth that no amount of water could wash away. In February 2002,

I visited my ophthalmologist for treatment of burning eyes; he said I still had microscopic glass particles—"cementuous debris"—lodged in the pores between my eyelashes. The muffled sound of cops and firefighters as they talked through respirators. Tables filled beyond capacity as they were piled high with flashlights, respirators, work gloves, goggles and hardhats we were supposed to wear on the Pile.

There is the indescribable sight of the Pile itself, especially in the first few days when there were no recognizable human artifacts in the debris, just twisted metal. Paul and I scrutinized the debris of the Pile to try to find something we could recognize—a shred of carpet, the leg of a desk chair, a pencil—but there was nothing. Someone pointed out that there weren't even any toilets or sinks in the Pile because the intense heat had completely melted even the porcelain fixtures. What were we breathing?

Looking south at where the towers once stood a block away, squinting into the sun and blocking its rays with my hand, I realized that for the past thirty years no direct ray of sunlight had struck the earth in the place where I was currently standing. I worked a few blocks away at headquarters and remembered walking and shopping there at lunchtime, when the streets teemed with people. There were lunchtime concerts, a fountain in the plaza between the towers. I remember having buffet lunches in the atrium restaurant or at Windows on the World with my good friend Hamura, the Tokyo Police liaison with the NYPD. I knew these streets intimately, but now I was disoriented. I saw a firefighter in full bunker gear lying sprawled on the sidewalk, and when we knelt to touch him he awoke with a start. "Are you OK, brother?" "I'm OK." Without another word he got up and headed back to the Pile.

There was a chain link fence along West Street, and in every cavity there was a single piece of paper blown in by the force of the explosion, looking as if some deranged child had neatly filled each one. Paul and I stopped once and pulled out a page; it was from an insurance policy which described coverage for hurricanes, earthquakes, and storms. Acts of war apparently weren't covered. Everything was covered with a fine gray dust, inches deep in some places. People had written on the dusted windows: "Firefighter So-and-So—Engine X—where are you?" "Fuck who did this. We will not forget." "God Bless All." "God Bless America." Entire fire engines were crushed, some compacted to no more than four or five feet high.

Then the flags appeared and became ubiquitous on buildings, uniforms, and vehicles. We wrapped ourselves in the flag and what it stands for. God Bless America. We would not forget.

Tombstones in the churchyard of St. Paul's Chapel, located directly across the street from where the towers once stood, were miraculously spared but were covered in inches of dust and paper. Signers of the Declaration of Independence were buried here. I interviewed a collaborator on a bench in that cemetery; he chose the place because he felt comfortable there. The smell of death was everywhere on the Pile, but in some places, the stench became especially powerful, indicating proximity to a group of bodies. There is no way to avoid breathing it in, and it becomes part of us. I met an old friend assigned to the canine unit, who told me her dog was quickly retrained to sniff out cadavers. The odor of death was so pervasive that the dogs couldn't handle it; they got confused. There was a small playground set aside for the dogs and handlers off West Street in which they could rest, but her dog had been working very hard and was very depressed.

Most horrifically, there were the fallen bodies or body parts blown out of the towers by the impact, on rooftops several blocks away. The skin had shredded right off the body with that kind of impact, so that the body was often nothing more than the slab of flesh the skin once covered. Cops who found those bodies and body parts spent a lot of time debating which particular body parts they had found.

The fact that cameras were officially banned from Ground Zero did not deter many cops from bringing small disposable or digital cameras onto the site. They were compelled by the urge to capture and memorialize the images, to document and connect themselves to the monumental historic event of which they were a part. Several cops would later tell me they were repeatedly drawn back to the photographic images they took—images they were more likely to share with other cops than with family or friends.

The urge to continually revisit those photos was part and parcel of the difficult meaning-making process many cops faced during and after the event. For several months after things settled down, for example, I was consumed nearly to the point of obsession with the need to read everything I could about September 11, and other cops told me they were similarly consumed. The natural and universal urge to understand what happened to bring about such profound changes in one's world was compounded by the fact that so many cops had little or no access to the news media for information. We simply had no time to watch television, listen to the radio, or read newspapers and therefore experienced huge gaps in our knowledge of what occurred. Much of the information we did receive—rumors, for example—proved to be erroneous. When things began to quiet down and media sources again became available, we consumed them voraciously in an effort to construct forms and constellations that would give meaning to our world and to our experiences at both the proximate and ultimate levels.

My own urge to make meaning and to obtain images and information that would fill in the gaps was heightened by the fact that, within a few days of the 11th, I essentially lost the capacity to read. I could certainly recognize words, phrases, and sentences and obtain meaning from them individually, but in conjunction with sleep deprivation, I was no longer able to concentrate or focus my attention long enough to process these images in a way that would allow me to retain their meaning. By the third sentence of a newspaper article, for example, I would entirely forget the subject of the article or what information the previous sentences contained. As a result of this incapacity to process written words as well as the inaccessibility of information sources, I had huge gaps in my knowledge of the terrorist attacks. It would later prove quite ironic and embarrassing when conversations and interactions made it clear that I was entirely ignorant of important facts and information that were well known to members of the general public. For months afterward, I would spend inordinate amounts of time on the Internet, scrutinizing and downloading images, articles, and reports, trying to make sense of them and trying to reconstruct the experience in the larger and somewhat more objective context most people understand it.

Many months after September 11th, my Internet explorations led me to a Web site that contained audio files of the police and fire department radio transmissions of that morning. I listened to those frantic and broken transmissions in real time on the morning of September 11th, but in my numbed state, I focused entirely on cognitively understanding what was taking place and experienced almost no emotion. Listening for a second time was a completely different experience, partly because I heard things I hadn't heard the first time and partly because they were infused with all the meanings and emotions constructed and accrued over the ensuing months. I heard a female voice calling a 10–13—"officer needs assistance"—a call I hadn't heard or processed the first time—and now know that it's Moira Smith's last transmission. The dispatcher tried to raise her, but there is no response. Cops trapped in the rubble call for help in other transmissions, but they could not provide a location for would-be rescuers. I was thirty blocks away and unable to help. After the collapse, cops called out for their partners by name. I was alone in my house when I listened to those audio files and I didn't even try not to cry.

Even in the rare quiet moments of the day, fragmentary and sometimes disquieting images infiltrate my thoughts. Some, like the fleeting smell of death and transient visual images of the Pile, are clearly related to the Trade Center and I understand where they come from and why they intrude. Because I understand their etiology within the context of survivor psychology, I can deal with them in an intellectual way, and they do not unduly distress me. On the contrary, I pay attention to these images and, in focusing on them, actively try to extract their proximate and ultimate meanings. Other transitory thoughts and images are invariably as disjointed and incomplete, but because they evoke a sense of connection or movement or integration they are not at all disturbing. Some are even pleasantly reassuring and life-affirming, and I try to use them to enhance my understanding of survivor psychology and my own experience. Other thoughts and images, however, appear to have no immediate connection to the events I'm experiencing, and they are bothersome because they defy my attempts to integrate them or understand their source. In the following spring, for example, I was in a Home Depot store when I suddenly felt edgy and hyper, until I realized I was in the aisle with the work gloves, hard hats, flashlights, and respirators—the gear we wore on the Pile.

There was, for example, a melody, or rather a series of snippets or pieces of a gentle and peaceful melody that I knew were connected, that ran through my thoughts at odd moments during those days. It was a somewhat familiar yet haunting melody, and my sense was that at one time I knew it well, but it slipped away to elude me every time I attempted to grasp or identify the tune or the lyrics that should accompany it. It seemed the more I tried to take hold of it, the more elusive and transitory it became. The intrusive melody became bothersome and annoying precisely because I was not able to fully take hold of the image or fathom its meaning, and identifying it becomes an intellectual preoccupation of sorts. One afternoon as Paul and I sat in a radio car outside a firehouse, the melody came together and I recognized it.

The tune is an old and fairly obscure song I hadn't heard in perhaps ten or fifteen years, but one that I once knew well. It is a song by David Bromberg called

"Kaatskill Serenade," and the song is about Washington Irving's fictional Rip Van Winkle. Moments after identifying the song and "listening" to the lyrics it all comes together—Rip Van Winkle is the ultimate literary symbol of the psychohistorical dislocation we were all feeling.

In the story, Rip Van Winkle is radically dislocated in time and place, awakening one day to find that he inhabits an unfamiliar world in which his friends are dead, his familiar places have changed, and even his dog no longer recognizes him. Practically nothing is as it was before he slept and there is no hope of reclaiming the comfort of his earlier psychological world. I "listen" to the tune as it plays in my head and the lyrics resonate.

> Where are the men that I used to sport with,
> And what has become of my beautiful town?
> Wolf my old friend, even you don't know me.
> This must be the end, my house has fallen down.
>
> My land was rich but I wouldn't work it.
> I guess I made a shrew of my wife.
> My duty clear, I could always find some way to shirk it.
> I dreamed away the best years of my life.
>
> It seems like only this morning I went up into the mountain,
> No word of warning just her usual curse.
> I hated the house with her nagging and shouting
> But to be in this strange world is a thousand times worse.
>
> Where are the men that I used to sport with,
> And what has become of my beautiful town?
> Wolf my old friend, even you don't know me.
> This must be the end, my house has fallen down.
>
> He called me by name, he bought me that cheaply.
> He called me by name, I didn't know what to think.
> I joined their loud game and oh, I drank deeply.
> But no one had ever asked me to drink.
>
> And you know that stolen liquor, it was sweeter than whiskey
> And many times quicker just to put me to sleep.
> But drinking with strangers can be very risky.
> A sleep that was long, it was twenty years deep.
>
> Where are the men that I used to sport with,
> And what has become of my beautiful town?
> Wolf my old friend, even you don't know me.
> This must be the end, my house has fallen down.

There is so much to tell about those days and the weeks and months that followed. In early October 2001, we stepped down to regular duties at the Academy and tried to begin again the work of manufacturing cops. New curriculum had to be developed for recruits and in-service training to address the newly recognized realities of terrorism. Everything was different since so many relationships had been redefined. The transition was not seamless.

We tried to resume our ordinary lives, but at the same time we were unwilling and unable to put it all behind us; we clung to the experiences, struggled to understand them and ourselves, and attempted to make ourselves better cops for having had them. There was a renewed sense of pride in being a cop and a spirit of collegiality. At the same time there was also an aura of uncertainty and a vague fear that overshadowed everything we did. Our personal and professional identities had changed, and that took some getting used to. Security remained high throughout the department as cops and supervisors were frequently detailed to continue the work at Ground Zero. I enjoyed going back there and did so at every opportunity, since it helped me recapture that seductive sense of urgency and importance. Tempers remained short, and although conflicts frequently would arise, there was also a will, born of a renewed sense of commitment and connection to each other and to the values we had rediscovered, to easily forgive or overlook the conflicts. Life went on, albeit differently.

Things will continue to change. Paul, Dennis, Pete and I all retired within the year, as did literally hundreds of others with whom we shared the terrible struggles and the sublime joys of September. We are proud of what we did, and we feel fortunate and grateful for the opportunity the tragedy offered us to recapture the sense of purpose and integrity that so often erodes over the course of a police career. The struggle was more difficult and more painful than anything we had previously experienced or anything we could have imagined. While we still deal with a host of unresolved residual images that continue to haunt us, it was altogether worth it to feel like a cop again. Everyone, it seems, finished their career on a high note, with a tremendous sense of purpose, meaning, pride, and connection that had long eluded us. Paul, Dennis, Pete and I were tight friends to begin with, but the experiences we shared further tightened our bonds and deepened our personal and professional respect and admiration for one another. We still get together for lunch from time to time, and I think we always will. We may no longer be officially part of the department, but we remain, more than ever, part of the Job.

Notes

1. In his earlier work, Lifton calls his theoretical model for understanding human behavior the "psychoformative paradigm." In later work that fleshed out and expanded upon his conceptual framework, he uses the terms *formative-symbolic perspective* and *continuity-of-life model* to describe the paradigm. The terms are essentially synonymous and are used interchangeably throughout this book.

Chapter 1

1. Generally speaking, coroners are elected officials who, unlike medical examiners, do not necessarily have a medical credential or a background in pathology.

2. It is important here to emphasize the important differences between posttraumatic stress disorder, a clinically defined pathological disorder, and the adaptive human responses that are the subject of our inquiries. While many similarities and points of correspondence may admittedly exist between police officers' extreme encounters with death and the traumatic experiences that may give rise to PTSD among combat veterans and others, and notwithstanding the fact that some police officers may ultimately develop the clinical symptoms of posttraumatic stress disorder, these two constructs are conceptually and operationally distinguishable. It must be recognized that exposure to death, per se, is neither a necessary or sufficient cause of PTSD—the diagnostic criteria do not demand that a death encounter occur, and one may in fact experience multiple, extreme, and personally consequential encounters with death and never develop the relatively durable clinical symptoms of posttraumatic stress disorder as the result of work-related trauma. In marked contrast, the death encounter is a necessary and constituent element of Lifton's psychology of survival perspective.

3. *Graves registration* is a military term for the tasks and duties involved in recovering, identifying, and processing the bodies of combat fatalities.

4. Alcohol has a prominent place in the informal rites and rituals of policing's subculture, since drinking is a legal and (to large extent) socially acceptable means of numbing

oneself to emotional traumata. With particular reference to residual death trauma, groups of police officers often engage in excessive alcohol consumption following police funerals. Indeed, excessive alcohol consumption was a defining issue in the minor NYPD scandal following the 1995 Police Memorial Day ceremony in Washington, DC: following a solemn ceremony commemorating the line-of-duty deaths of officers from across the nation, officers from a host of agencies gathered at a nearby location where alcohol was freely served. Local news media aired lurid stories and images of drunken officers (including NYPD officers commemorating the recent line-of-duty deaths of two members of the agency) cavorting at the postceremony party. The official NYPD report on the incident simplistically blamed their behavior on the effects of alcohol. Internal affairs personnel are now routinely assigned to supervise police funerals and the annual Washington event in an effort to prevent drinking.

5. Police Service Areas (PSAs) and Transit Districts are the functional equivalent of precincts within the department's Housing and Transit Bureaus. Housing Bureau officers patrol the city's public housing developments, and Transit Bureau officers patrol the city's rapid transit system. It should also be noted that some small proportion of these patrol personnel are assigned to nonenforcement or administrative duties such as arrest processing, property officer, or integrity control officer duties.

6. As used here and throughout this book, *DOA* refers to "dead on arrival," a euphemism used in the NYPD and elsewhere to refer to a dead human body.

7. Because age and sex breakouts are not available for the National Safety Council's accidental death data, Southwick's conclusions about accidental death risks are based on a comparison of police to all American workers.

8. The NYPD compiles an annual statistical report (the "SOP-9" report) of officer-involved shootings and alters its annual firearms qualification training to reflect historical trends the report identifies. If, for example, the distance between officers and their assailants was less than 6 feet in approximately half the shooting incidents of the previous year, officers will fire about half their qualification rounds at less than 6 feet from their target. Similarly, the tactical situations presented in the lecture/demonstration component of the annual firearms qualification cycle are typically based on actual events of the preceding year or on identified historic trends. If the number of accidental discharges increased in the previous year, the training cycle is likely to address this safety issue.

Chapter 2

1. Among the groups Lifton studied were survivors of the Hiroshima atomic bombing (1967a, 1970), survivors of natural disasters (Lifton and Olsen, 1976), and Vietnam War veterans (1973). The perspective was also developed and refined in studies of Nazi doctors and the medicalization of killing (1986), the psychology of genocide (1986, 1990), the threat of nuclear extinction (1982, 1987, 1990), and the dynamics of cults and the process of "thought reform" (1963).

2. Freud's insistence that fear of death is compensatory and secondary to the fear of castration is inaccurate, Lifton (1979) asserts, and is the result of two confusions. First, Lifton challenges Freud's claim that death has no representation in the unconscious (and therefore cannot be a primary experience or a primary motivation for behavior) through the notion of death's *inchoate image,* as described below. Lifton also points out that although the fear of death and the fear of castration (i.e., fear of the loss of masculine vitality) are often related, man is often willing to risk death on behalf of a larger vision—either a vision one wishes to affirm or a fear or doubt (including doubts about masculinity) one wishes to combat. In both cases the larger motivating image is one of vitality and life. Accordingly,

castration anxiety and fears about masculinity should be subsumed by a larger symbolic structure of death and continuity, and not the reverse (1979, pp. 47–49).

3. An extremely simplified example can be found in the case of a child who burns his hand on a hot pot. Every parent has warned his child not to touch objects on a stove ("No! Hot!"), creating in the child an incipient and undeveloped image that in itself holds relatively little meaning. When the child nevertheless touches the hot pot, the sensory stimuli he receives in the form of an immediate tactile image ("Ouch! Pain!") connect with and activate the existing image; the existing image becomes more sophisticated and complex, and both the immediate and preexisting image take on meaning: the child now better understands the meaning of "hot," his understanding of "no" becomes more sophisticated, and he comes to associate "no" with "hot" and "pain." On the next occasion the child experiences the image of a pot on the stove, he will (hopefully) connect that image to his now more elaborate psychic image ("No! Hot!" and "Ouch! Pain!") and follow through on the anticipatory interpretation or schema for action it provides—he will avoid touching the pot. In time, images from additional experiences will activate and connect with the image of the hot stove and its association with pain, adding even more sophistication and complexity as well as a more comprehensive anticipation of the environment. Thus the image will move further toward form and, as the process continues, ultimately become a constellation. At some point, the simple image of "hot stove" becomes part of a much larger and more highly symbolized constellation of "dangerous and potentially painful things that should be avoided."

4. Lifton also makes clear the distinction between the term *psychic numbing* and the Freudian concept of *repression,* a term that suggests the act of forgetting experiences and ideas by actively excluding them from consciousness and relegating them to the realm of unconscious. As part of the Freudian model, repression refers to the organism's compensatory effort to cope with the instinctual forces that dominate emotional life. In the formative-symbolic paradigm, psychic numbing does not equate with the repression of instinctual impulses and does not so much encapsulate and banish formed memories to the realm of the unconscious as it impairs the formative process by which images are created and integrated. Psychic numbing is an adaptive form of desensitization that involves the blocking or absence of inner forms or imagery that can connect with such experience in the first place (Lifton, 1974b, p. 273; 1976b, pp. 26–27). Lifton's model also sees psychic numbing as a reversible form of symbolic death, undertaken defensively in order to avoid a permanent physical or psychological death. In the case of acute psychic trauma, the undertaking is entirely involuntary.

5. This observation was borne out in Kardiner and Spiegel's (1947) study of soldiers traumatized in battle and the subsequent traumatic neuroses they suffered and is also supported by a host of research in the area of posttraumatic stress disorder. Hilton (1997), for example, describes a case in which a flood of traumatic images that had been dormant for more than 50 years was triggered when a veteran watched media images of World War II combat.

6. We can see elements of the survivor mission in the host of constructive legal and political projects undertaken by survivors on behalf of crime victims: the so-called Megan's Law and Kendra's Law come to mind as projects initiated by survivors as a testament to their own suffering and as a memorial to the victim. We can also see a remarkable survivor mission in the political career of Representative Carolyn McCarthy, a Long Island nurse and housewife whose husband was murdered and son critically injured in the December 1995 Long Island Railroad massacre. Her resulting advocacy of gun control led to a political career as one of Congress's staunchest advocates for gun control and victims' rights.

7. The phrase "back to command, no meal" illustrates this point. The term derives from a superior officer's discretionary ability to give officers working outside their usual command (at parades, demonstrations, or other details) an early dismissal from duty ("an early blow") or to require them to return to patrol duty at their command while forfeiting their meal period. Depending upon the context in which it is used, this simple phrase can refer concretely to such a dismissal, to the actions of a "by-the-book" supervisor, to an event that spoils an otherwise pleasant aspect of duty, or to management's overall disregard for the welfare of officers.

Similarly, an allusion to the ubiquitous "Detective McCann"—as in "the case was referred to Detective McCann"—refers not to a particular person but to a type of police-citizen interaction. At one time, when a detective determined that the likelihood of solving a case was minimal but the complainant continued to pester him about it, it was a common practice to inform the complainant that the case had been assigned to Detective McCann. Every cop knew that a person calling for Detective McCann (the name derives from a trash can) was to be informed that he was in court, working another tour, or on vacation; in time, the complainant would lose interest and stop calling. In a more general sense, the name of this illustrious investigator is invoked to refer to any case or assignment in which a citizen is "stroked." Police jargon is replete with such nuanced aphorisms.

8. Because "management cops" are more removed from the kind of situations that are likely to involve death encounters, and because virtually all data were obtained from those in an operational sphere, unless otherwise noted all references to the police subculture should be construed as pertaining primarily to the "street cop" culture.

9. At the time this portion of the research was conducted, the police academy operated on a 7-day basis and recruits were assigned to the same rotating "scooter chart" duty schedule many patrol officers work. In the "scooter chart" cycle, officers work 5 day-shift tours (called "day tours") followed by 2 days off, then 5 evening-shift tours (called "4 to 12s") with 3 days off.

Chapter 3

1. Niederhoffer's basic research was conducted as part of his 1962 doctoral dissertation, in which he developed a police cynicism scale and administered it to New York City Police officers in various assignments and at various career stages. The remarkable consistency of his results in successive replications in so many agencies speaks to the durability of the fundamental conflicts shaping the cynical attitude among police.

2. The tactical considerations cops learn on the job also become habituated and intrude upon their personal off-duty lives. Experienced cops will often peer through a store window before entering, lest they be taken unawares by a "dangerous" or criminal situation unfolding inside. Other manifestations include standing to the side when knocking on a door (someone may shoot them through the door) and insisting on a seat that allows them to watch those entering and leaving a bar or restaurant. These and other ritualistic off-duty behaviors can be (and often are) a source of annoyance and concern for friends and family members, and the infiltration of attitudes and behaviors that are appropriate and necessary in the professional environment into the personal sphere is emblematic of a blurring of the boundaries separating the personal and professional identities.

3. The extent to which Bittner's (1980, p. 7) description infiltrates the police psyche can be seen in the images and symbols some units or precincts adopt. In particular, we can see how their position "on the perimeters of order and justice" and their battles to "deter the forces of darkness and chaos" are reflected in what we might call the "fortress mentality." The embattled 41st Precinct in the Bronx gained notoriety as "Fort Apache" in a book written by its former captain that was subsequently made into a controversial film of the same

name. Other precincts have adopted, with a modicum of self-mockery, such enduring yet illustrative names as "Fort Despair," "The Alamo," and "Fort Surrender." Most germane to our exploration of death imagery, though, is Brooklyn's 73rd Precinct, known as "Fort Z." While many officers today believe the name alludes in some way to being "at the end of the line," old-timers know the precinct was originally dubbed "Fort Zinderneuf"—a reference to the doomed fort in the Foreign Legion film *Beau Geste,* in which the major themes are brotherly loyalty, honor, sacrifice, and treachery. Movie buffs will recall how the desert garrison, essentially written off as expendable by superiors and commanded by a brutal and sadistic sergeant, was separated from relief forces and attacked by an overwhelming surrounding force. The film's climactic image is particularly powerful and evocative of the police officer's sense of integrity and connection in the face of separation, stasis, and disintegration, as well as his sense of irony and cynicism: a relief column arrives to find the "infidels" have given up their attack on the indomitable outpost, and as they enter the fort they find the entire command dead but still propped at the parapets. Even in death, there is integrity: the heroic troops have repelled the forces of chaos and fulfilled their duty.

4. A "buff" is a citizen with a great interest and some knowledge about police work. For the most part, buffs have a strong positive regard for cops, they often sprinkle their speech with police jargon, and in almost a fawning way they have a seemingly insatiable appetite for police "war stories" and other "inside information." While their inquiries may confer some status upon the rookie, experienced cops generally regard them as pests and dismiss them as "wannabes," largely because they've never had direct police experience. They want to be "part of the club," but they haven't paid their dues. Buffs also seem particularly fascinated with the elements of power, danger, and authority in police work.

5. Department regulations (*Patrol Guide* procedure 105–01) require officers to wear all authorized breast bars or the corresponding medals at all times while in uniform. These medals include the Medal of Honor, which is awarded (often posthumously) to "a member who intelligently and in the line of police duty distinguished himself/herself by the performance of an act of gallantry and valor at imminent personal hazard to life with knowledge of the risk, above and beyond the call of duty." The Combat Cross is awarded "for the successful performance of an act of extraordinary heroism while engaged in personal combat with an armed adversary at imminent personal hazard to life in the intelligent performance of duty." The Medal of Valor is awarded "for an act of outstanding personal bravery intelligently performed in line of duty at imminent personal hazard to life under circumstances evincing a disregard of personal consequences." The Purple Shield is "awarded to members of the service who have suffered extremely serious physical injury or death, permanent disfigurement, protracted or permanent impairment of health, or protracted or permanent impairment of any bodily organ function" in the line of duty (*Patrol Guide* 120–34). As a practical matter, with few exceptions the recipients of the three top medals have killed an adversary in the line of duty, and many or most recipients suffered significant physical injuries in the encounter.

6. Officers do not typically present an objective view of policing when (and if) they discuss their work with children and spouses: they generally do their best to downplay the physical and emotional dangers, and they generally emphasize the prosocial aspects of their work. Further, the adventures they share tend to be of the humorous rather than the dangerous kind, or they serve as cautionary tales. The attitudes, beliefs, and perceptions an officer's family members take on may not be entirely realistic or accurate.

7. Again, within the NYPD culture these terms take on various shades of meaning depending upon the context in which they are used. One can refer, in a general yet inclusive sense, to a third party as one's brother or sister officer (as in "My brother and sister officers do a fine job under difficult circumstances"), but to refer to a particular individual in terms

of a sibling (as in, "Oh, Charlie? He's my brother") or to address another officer as a brother (as in "How are you, my brother?") connotes a special warmth and affinity for that particular individual.

8. We can better understand how the police officer's basic struggle to achieve good and vanquish evil—a common theme in policing—plays into the idea of symbolic immortality and the quest to achieve a sense of vitality if we unpack these concepts a bit and recognize their respective associations with the subparadigms of movement versus stasis, integrity versus disintegration, and connection versus separation. They reflect the polarity of good and evil to the extent that the life-affirming images and forms of movement, integrity, and connection are typically associated with the concept of good, and to the extent that images of stasis, disintegration, and separation are associated with evil. The police officer's struggle around images, forms, and constellations associated with death—a struggle he undertakes on a personal psychological level as well as on behalf of others—is part and parcel of the more easily conceptualized and more easily expressed quest to advance the good and overcome evil.

9. When an NYPD officer is killed in the line of duty, his shield is officially retired and will not be reissued except in exceptional circumstances. For example, the shield might be reissued upon request to a family member. I am aware of several cases in which the shield of an officer killed in the line of duty was requested by and reissued to a murdered officer's brother or child.

10. An officer related an anecdote in which the son of a retired officer requested his father's shield and learned it had been reissued to a rookie officer. His father went to the rookie officer's precinct and personally asked that he return the shield so that his son could carry on the family tradition, but the young officer refused. The narrator, hinting that the young officer had earned an enemy and would eventually suffer some sanction as the result of his refusal, offered that perhaps the young officer didn't understand why the tradition of the shield was important because "he was Chinese and a rookie." Certainly only an "outsider" rookie—a "foreigner" who was not fully integrated into the police culture—would fail to comprehend the importance of the tradition.

11. Many officers develop a potent emotional attachment to their shield, and time and again I have heard the reminiscences of retired officers who struggled with a loss of identity upon surrendering it. A recurring motif is that of a civilian employee at the department's shield desk somehow mishandling the shield, essentially interrupting or refusing to participate in the officer's personal ritual of separation, or otherwise treating the shield's surrender in a perfunctory manner. That this ritual of separation has great personal significance is also illustrated in the way some use it as a metaphor for the agency's failure to properly value the personal commitment and devotion of its personnel, as in "when you leave they throw your shield in a box and forget you."

12. In the Roman Catholic faith, Saint Michael the Archangel, general of the heavenly hosts that drove Satan from heaven at the beginning of time, is designated the patron saint of knights and police officers. Revelation (12:7–9) says he will again lead the angels and slay the dragon (Satan) at the end of time. According to the Catholic Encyclopedia Online, Michael has several offices: to fight against Satan, to rescue the souls of the faithful from the powers of evil (especially at the hour of death), to be champion of Christians and Jews, and to call men's souls to heavenly judgment. In art he is "represented as an angelic warrior, fully armed with helmet, sword and shield (often the shield bears the Latin inscription Quis ut Deus [Who is like God]), standing over the dragon, whom [sic] he sometimes pierces with a lance. He also holds a pair of scales with which he weighs the souls of the departed . . . or the Book of Life, to show he takes part in the judgement" (Catholic Encyclopedia Online, 2001a). The NYPD's fraternal organization for members of the Protestant

faiths is the Saint George Association. Saint George, a martyr and warrior-saint, is similarly depicted in art as a dragon-slayer. According to apocryphal legend, the errant knight came upon a dragon about to devour the King of Libya's daughter and, although urged to save himself, bravely fought and transfixed the dragon with his lance. Eschewing the king's reward, George bade the people to convert and the king to have pity on the poor before he rode off. Medieval Crusaders and the English Order of the Garter adopted him as their patron (Catholic Encyclopedia Online, 2001b).

13. As a general statement, the tendency to purchase and wear these items of apparel seems especially pronounced among rookies and less tenured officers, and we can infer at least two reasons for this. First, the rookie's identity struggle involves, in part, the outward presentation of his evolving self, and these items tangibly display his social role. Second, tenured cops who are more comfortable with their role and identity are concomitantly more aware that these items make them the potential target of a "symbolic assailant" or a bona fide criminal. In contrast to rookies, they tend to conceal their occupation as a form of protection.

14. Niederhoffer (1967) cited police department surveys of police academy recruits circa 1962 as evidence for this position, noting also that the vast majority of recruits came from a working-class or lower-class background. He argues elsewhere that recruits are nevertheless possessed of a fairly high degree of idealism. Niederhoffer seems to have accepted the recruits' self-reports at face value, but it could also be argued that the surveys were colored to the extent that working-class and lower-class masculine culture does not facilitate or reward disclosure of idealistic attitudes or altruistic tendencies.

15. In describing his first day at the police academy, unabashed idealist and retired NYPD lieutenant David Durk relates a telling anecdote about an icebreaking exercise in which all the recruits in his class were asked to explain their reasons for joining the agency. The first several recruits described job security, pay, and benefits as the primary factors, but after Durk gave an impassioned speech about the capacity of the police to make a difference in peoples' lives, the remaining recruits also spoke of the altruism and concern for social welfare that motivated them (Lardner, 1996, p. 156). Interestingly, in line with our observations about chivalry and knighthood, Durk's biography is entitled *Crusader.*

16. Two first-grade detectives I interviewed, for example, said they became police officers simply because of the pay and benefits, but both stated strongly that once they experienced police work they were "hooked." "Within 1 year," one said, "I knew this is the job for me." Their enthusiasm and commitment are evidenced by the exalted rank they achieved as well as their unusual tenure in the agency: one detective served 38 years before reaching mandatory retirement age, and the other retired on a line-of-duty disability after 32 years.

Chapter 4

1. The rookie's confusion about the type of assignment reflects a common rookie experience. Several officers described receiving a "difficulty breathing" or "unconscious aided" call and responding rapidly with the expectation of rendering medical aid to a sick person, only to be surprised when they found a dead body. Tenured officers tended to describe this in a self-mocking way that poked fun at their own youthful aggressiveness and lack of sophistication: the assignment cannot be dispatched as a DOA until the person is officially pronounced dead. One tenured collaborator recalled becoming irritated when his senior partner did not interrupt his morning coffee-and-doughnuts ritual and rush off to render medical assistance on an "elderly unconscious" call until it was explained that such early morning calls invariably involve a person who died in their sleep or, in police argot, "woke up dead."

2. Telephone switchboard, or the precinct's main telephone line. An ME is a medical examiner.

3. If an individual (particularly an elderly or chronically ill person) who dies of apparently natural causes was treated by a physician within the past 30 days, and if the private physician is willing to attest to the cause of death and sign the death certificate, the medical examiner's office will often release the body to a funeral director without further investigation or autopsy. This expedient trick of the trade can significantly decrease the amount of time an officer is required to spend at the death scene.

4. We have noted that rookies seek to combine compassion with administrative competence because they correctly perceive this capacity to be part of the effective cop's repertoire, and that they may be disturbed by the insensitivity of senior officers. As we will see, insensitive expressions and macabre humor are part of many police death encounters, and indeed many cops will engage in such behavior either to shock the rookie or to deal with their own death anxiety. An important nuance is that this insensitive behavior is quite acceptable among police so long as it is "backstage" behavior that is not open to public view—in other words, so long as it does not implicate the public image of police.

5. With time and additional experience the rookie will pick up an informal typology of police terminology that explicitly depersonalizes, trivializes, and objectifies the dead. These terms generally become more colorful and trivializing as the grotesqueness of the corpse increases. An ordinary recent death might be called a DOA or a "stiff," but a partially decomposed corpse is a "ripe DOA," a "dry floater," or in extreme cases a "two-canner"—a reference to the practice of scorching coffee grounds (two cans, in severe cases) to dispel the odor of putrefaction. A body recovered from the water is a "floater," and a body mangled in a vehicle accident is often called a "road pizza." For a more detailed exploration of this typology, see Henry (1995).

6. The temporary expiration of a federal age discrimination exemption for police agencies briefly opened a window of opportunity for NYPD applicants over the age of 30.

7. It is interesting to note the similarities between this officer's experience and that of the officer who recalled the image of the woman clawing at her drapes. Both encounters involved disintegrative deaths involving elements of separation and stasis; both death imprint images involved features of grotesqueness and humiliation. These were the only two collaborators who mentioned questioning their reasons for joining the police department. The fact that their doubts were raised so proximate to their confrontation with the death image speaks to the image's potency.

8. Later, a morgue attendant observed his distress and produced a bottle of Brut cologne with which he could swab his nostrils. Though cognizant of his anxiety, the morgue attendants nevertheless began joking about the death in a way that intensified his distress.

9. The rookie listened to these calls when other officers played them earlier, and this glimpse into the deceased's private life added another element of identification to the situation. He related how the morgue attendants later upset him by joking about the messages as part of the display they put on for his benefit. When the attendants entered the bedroom they played the messages again and spoke to the corpse, saying, "Hey, you've got some messages! Don't forget to call Sally, because she's got a friend who wants to meet you."

10. That he provided an unknown civilian with his home phone number is unusual, and would be all the more unusual if he had more police experience. In line with the "symbolic assailant" construct and a general suspiciousness of civilians, officers quickly learn not to reveal too much about themselves or their private lives to strangers. The vast majority of tenured police officers I know have unlisted telephone numbers, and many cops take pains to conceal or expunge personal information from publicly available sources. This is often attributed to the need to protect oneself and one's family from harassment and danger, but also serves to erect a kind of protective firewall between the professional and personal self.

11. He noted the swollen corpse was too large to fit in a standard body bag and eventually had to be placed in a special crate and removed by emergency service unit officers.

12. *The American Heritage Dictionary* (3rd ed.) defines *skell* as a slang term for "a homeless person who lives as a derelict," and the related term *skellum* (derived from Scots) as a rascal or rogue, but it has broader and even more derogatory application in the NYPD officer's lexicon. It is a generic disparaging term used by NYPD officers to describe a shiftless, insignificant, obnoxious, or inferior person, encompassing vagrants, lowlifes, social parasites, or any other individual who is morally and/or physically repugnant. The term—actually a constellation of generalized images, forms, and meanings—is broadly applied and inherently dehumanizing. Interestingly, some officers have told me (apparently incorrectly) that the term derives from Latin and means a person who does not deserve to live. In a somewhat different context, see Lifton (1986, pp. 85–89) concerning the links between the concept of "life unworthy of life" and medicalized killing in Auschwitz and the genocidal mentality in general.

13. None of the rookie officers I interviewed happened to experience the death of a child as his first DOA.

14. Generally speaking, the first unit to arrive at the scene of an incident takes charge and is held responsible for the way it is handled. This convention generally holds true regardless of what unit is officially assigned to the job.

15. The officer's use of the term *limbo* conjures some interesting associations in the meaning it holds for members of the Roman Catholic faith. As a matter of church doctrine, Catholic children are taught in the catechism that the souls of unbaptized infants are excluded from heaven on account of their "original sin," but a merciful God does not condemn them to hell or purgatory because they are without personal sin. Instead, their souls go to limbo (the *limbus infantium or puerorum*), a place where they will eternally remain as infants, knowing neither communion with God and the saints or connection with damned souls. In terms of the continuity-of-life model, limbo is a place or state of ultimate death equivalence: stasis, separation, and disintegration prevail and where there is no hope of movement, connection, or integrity. Especially in terms of death-equivalence, the Catholic Encyclopedia (www.newadvent.org/ cathen/09256a.htm) provides an interesting exposition of Catholic doctrine and theological speculation on limbo.

16. The capacity of places to conjure associations with past death encounters is quite common. Although none of the other collaborators directly referred to this phenomenon, I have had similar personal experiences and other officers with whom I've worked frequently pointed out locations where significant death encounters took place. In a slightly different but related occupational context, death-immersed emergency medical technician Frank Pierce, the protagonist in Joe Connelly's bildungsroman *Bringing Out the Dead,* frequently makes reference to the "ghosts" that inhabit his psychic world. He sees the "ghosts" of those he has failed to revive everywhere, and he identifies buildings and locations in terms of the deaths that occurred there. Some of these ghosts—especially the innocent Rose—stalk him silently but evaporate when he tries to make a connection with them. They are "spirits born unfinished, homicides, suicides, overdoses, and all the other victims, innocent or not, still grasping at lives so abruptly taken away. Rose's ghost was only the last and most visible of so many who seemed to have come back solely to accuse me—of living and knowing, of being present at their deaths, as if I had witnessed an obscene humiliation for which they could never forgive" (p. 45).

17. A number of tenured cops admitted, some with a tone of mild embarrassment, that they often say a silent prayer for the deceased and his family. I've known other cops who carried the Act of Contrition inside the clear plastic pocket that lines their uniform cap. It

is a matter of Roman Catholic doctrine that if a person makes a sincere profession of the act (or, by proxy, if another person makes the profession on his behalf before the immortal soul leaves the body), his sins are absolved and he can enter heaven in a state of grace. I once asked a gruff old veteran, in a teasing way, why he carried the prayer in his hat. "Why do you think?" he growled, turning the hat over. Perhaps embarrassed at being "caught out" in his seemingly uncharacteristic charity, he remained brusque with me for the remainder of our tour.

18. The psychological importance of sports or other forms of play extends beyond their simple capacity to temporarily divert attention: these life-affirming activities offer connections to others and access to several modes of symbolic immortality. In addition to providing an immediate sense of physical vitality, vigorous sports or intense play can stimulate a transcendent state or impart an ecstatic quality to one's experience, elevating the player from the ordinary plane of profane existence. Especially when seen as part of a dialectical pattern involving death or death equivalents, they represent connection, movement, integrity, and creative self-expression in the face of separation, stasis, and disintegration, and they can "jump-start" the creative process in the aftermath of psychic numbing. Sports and play can also have a spiritual component insofar as they involve the individual in an inclusive enterprise that extends beyond the self.

Chapter 5

1. The New York City Administrative Code requires that the residence of a person who lived alone must be secured and valuable property including wills, insurance policies, and important personal papers must be inventoried and removed to the precinct, where they are vouchered for safekeeping until the public administrator at surrogate's court designates an executor for the estate. The premises are sealed after removal of the remains. If the deceased lived with family or friends, these steps are not required.

2. The sergeant's comment on integrity issues refers to the department's cognizance of the potential for stealing property from the corpse or the premises, and these concerns underlie the agency's formal procedural demands that the search be conducted in the presence of a supervisor. This integrity issue is apparently not confined to the NYPD (see, for example, George 2000; "Rotting Corpses," 1996; New South Wales Independent Commission against Corruption, 1997).

3. "Scratch" is NYPD argot describing a supervisor's review and endorsement of the entries in an officer's activity log memo book. The supervisor makes a brief entry in the memo book and signs it to document his own presence at the scene as well as to attest to the accuracy of the officer's entries and the appropriateness of the officer's actions.

4. Lardner and Reppetto (2000, p. 62) note that this term entered NYPD argot in the 1870s, and they say it derives from the song "Shoo, Fly, Don't Bother Me," which was popular at that time. While few cops would be expected to know its exact derivation, the fact that it remains in use after more than a century illuminates the durability of the police subculture's idioms as well as the subculture's emphasis on maintaining links to the historic past.

5. Although we did not specifically discuss this issue during the sergeants' interviews, other supervisors and tenured cops have frequently commented that the traditional practice of cops making the boss's life easier by performing some of his required duties at the scene of any incident is not as common as it once was. There is no need within the scope of this research to empirically measure the quality of the expectation or the extent of its actual practice, but this theme is quite prevalent in the police culture. The sentiment is often expressed, in one form or another, that "young cops these days are not as committed/smart/ sharp/tough/insightful/skilled/knowledgeable/respectful of authority as they were in my day." Those who voice this sentiment will nevertheless admit they overheard tenured cops

expressing the same thoughts when *they* were rookies. Regardless of its validity, this enduring chestnut is important because it represents a kind of death anxiety organized around the culture itself—it encapsulates old-timers' fears about the perceived disintegration of their culture, the demise of traditions that connect its members, and the culture's ability to viably continue into the future.

6. The sergeant's reference is to the potential corruption hazard and possible allegations of "steering" as well as to the kind of personal involvement entailed in such a request. Neither is a "good thing."

7. Officers I've known over the years—officers who served before and during the 1970 Knapp Commission investigations into police corruption—have said that the practice of referring customers to particular funeral homes was not uncommon at that time, and cops would receive a gratuity for each "steer" that resulted in business.

8. An episode ("Subway") in the television series *Homicide: Life on the Street* portrayed a "space case" in an unusually powerful, sensitive, and realistic way, capturing many of the subtle conflicts and psychological issues officers face at such scenes.

9. The officer's hasty clarification of his aversion to suicide should be viewed in light of three factors. First, the general principles of denial appear to operate in many discussions of suicide, and police discussions are no exception. Second, the social stigma that applies to suicide and suicidal ideation is somewhat magnified in police culture since it is often seen as the "coward's way out." Finally, many officers are ambivalent about the police department's policies toward suicide and depression: while they support the idea that officers should seek help for these issues, they see the agency's reactive policies as stigmatizing and draconian, and probably few would voluntarily disclose their own depression or suicidal ideation unless they reach critical proportion. Indeed, the high rate of suicide and attempted suicide among cops suggests that many resist seeking help even when a true suicidal crisis occurs. In essence, when a cop reveals his suicidal ideation the agency's policy is to take away his guns and place him on modified assignment (desk duty) status pending a psychiatric evaluation—a strategy designed to remove the officer from stressful situations and to deprive him of the means with which to kill himself. But the gun is almost as central to the cop's identity as his shield, and its removal both stigmatizes the officer in the eyes of his peers and deprives him of an important symbol of his police identity. Even if the psychiatric evaluation determines the officer is not suicidal, he may spend several months on desk duty (in police department parlance, "on the rubber-gun squad") before he is returned to full duty. Rather than confiding their problems to the department, a great many officers seek the confidential assistance of a union-sponsored members assistance program peer support network. The number of officers seeking assistance under the terms of this program could not be determined, but intuition and experience lead to the conclusion the number is substantial.

10. An NYPD pamphlet on suicide prevention ("Getting Help") identifies the "warning signs of stress and/or depression: drastic changes in eating habits; difficulty sleeping and/or nightmares; forgetfulness; hyperactive, either physically or mentally; irritability; avoiding contact with friends or family; excessive weight gain or loss; preoccupied or easily distracted; looks sad or cries for no apparent reason; declined interest in activities that used to give the person pleasure." Note that with the possible exception of weight gain or loss, each of the "warning signs of suicide" are behavioral characteristics often exhibited by survivors.

11. In Connelly's novel *Bringing Out the Dead,* dissociated paramedic Frank Pierce scans the family photographs lining a cardiac victim's bedroom wall and bureau as he administers CPR, and in his reverie constructs an imaginary narrative of the man's entire life story. That reverie and resulting sense of identification and commitment to the man and his family magnify Pierce's immersion in death and facilitate his eventual disintegration.

12. When a death occurs in a public place—on the street or in a subway car, for example—a police supervisor can request that emergency medical service ambulance personnel immediately remove the corpse without waiting for the medical examiner if the remains are an "affront to public dignity." There is also a somewhat obscure and rarely invoked rule that EMS must remove the body to a hospital if anyone formally contests the attendant's pronouncement of death. Experienced cops or sergeants may jokingly "break the balls" of an EMS technician by threatening to assert that the victim (often a decomposing corpse) may still be alive.

13. The limited training the army provided him prior to this assignment emphasized that he might be placed in physical danger: prominent among the "war stories" that comprised the majority of his training was one relating how a survivor's assistance officer had been taken hostage at gunpoint by family members who demanded to know more information about the circumstances of their son's death. While none of my collaborators were ever physically assaulted making a death notification, most were aware of the potential for violence and one described how the mother of a young man "went EDP" (emotionally disturbed person) at the scene and had to be hospitalized. Eth, Barton, and Pinoos (1987) found this fear of physical assault during death notifications was highly prevalent among the Los Angeles Police homicide detectives they interviewed. While the actuarial likelihood of being assaulted during a death notification is an empirical question that lies beyond the scope of this study, we might refer again to Garner and Clemmer's (1986) observation that the chaos and uncertainty of family disputes—conditions that are often not unlike those at the chaotic scene of a death notification—contributes to cops' perception that these assignments are objectively among the most dangerous.

14. His lasting commitment was evident in the fact that in 1984, 12 years after completing military service, he visited the Vietnam War Memorial in Washington and looked up the names of "his" soldiers on the wall. He then contacted their families to let them know they were not forgotten.

15. The preparation of an Unusual Occurrence Report must be understood in the context of what is unusual in a given precinct. Several sergeants who had been transferred between high-crime and low-crime precincts commented that an event requiring the report in one precinct (for example, a shooting incident with relatively minor injuries) would not necessarily result in a report in another, higher-crime precinct. In other words, what is informally defined as a major crime of violence in one work environment is considered commonplace or unworthy of special mention in another. In practical psychological terms, this implies that some victims are deemed less worthy of police attention than others.

16. Like rookies, sergeants could rarely recall the names of specific DOAs. Among rookies, the failure to recall names resulted from their extreme numbing and perhaps some active exclusion of detailed personal information that might lead to enhanced identification. This exclusion from conscious thought and indifference to personal information may play out to some degree among sergeants, but we should also recognize how difficult it would be to recall the names of so many DOAs, especially when one's exposure to them is so brief and impersonal.

17. In the early 1990s, for example, New York City experienced a highly publicized spate of deaths of young children who were struck by stray bullets fired in shoot-outs between drug dealers. Given the randomness of the deaths and the perceived innocence of the children, some of whom were shot in their homes or beds by bullets that entered a window after being fired from a distance, the tragedy of the deaths captured the public's attention as well as the attention of police. At that time a new term entered the NYPD vernacular: a child or other innocent victim of a stray bullet is known as a "mushroom." While the ety-

mology of the term is obscure, it is believed to refer in part to the fact that, like mushrooms, these victims "pop up" unexpectedly in dark places.

Chapter 6

1. The number of teams responding to a specific crime scene and the length of time they remain there depend upon the characteristics of the crime and the difficulty of processing the scene. A CSU detective described a difficult and highly publicized rape-murder in Central Park—a large, unsecured outdoor crime scene in a public place—that resulted in the dispatch of multiple teams working around the clock for a period of 2 weeks. Obviously the corpse did not remain at the scene for this period, and the images they encountered were probably quite benign, but the anecdote illustrates that in difficult cases CSU technicians can easily be exposed to death imagery for a protracted period.

2. A "CUPPI" or "cause undetermined pending police investigation" is a death in which the medical examiner cannot immediately determine cause based solely on forensic evidence. CUPPIs typically require additional investigation into the victim's background and the events leading up to the death.

3. The NYPD *Patrol Guide*'s (NYPD, 2001) Section 116–05 mandates that the crime scene unit be notified and requested to respond to all homicides, forcible rapes, robberies, or hijackings with injury caused by a firearm, aggravated assaults with a dangerous instrument where the victim is likely to die, burglaries involving forced safes, circumvented alarms, or cases referred to the burglary squads, and "any crime in which the services of the Crime Scene Unit will assist in the investigation." As a practical matter, CSU members tend to resent being sent to "minor" crimes that fall in the latter catchall category. On one occasion I witnessed, a ranking officer requested response on a politically sensitive case involving a fairly minor crime, and the CSU supervisor demanded that authorization come from the forensic investigation division's commanding officer, a full inspector. The technicians ultimately dispatched on the run were very resentful that their time and expertise, in their view better utilized on "real" crimes like homicides and rapes, was wasted on a minor offense.

4. As previously noted, Fiefel (1969) argued that death anxiety influences medical doctors' choice of specialization—specifically, that some choices may be motivated by a counterphobic reaction to death anxiety. I did not specifically test whether this hypothesis applied to some CSU members, although it should be noted that several CSU technicians were licensed morticians or embalmers prior to joining the unit. Whether some have an affinity for death is uncertain, but certainly none engaged in behaviors demonstrating a clear aversion to dealing with it.

5. In 1994 police unions were successful in lobbying for New York state legislation requiring the NYPD and other large municipal agencies to promote police officers to the rank of detective after they have served 18 months in designated investigative units. An assignment to CSU puts police officers on the fast track to promotion.

6. In the department's argot, a "hook" or a "rabbi" (the more dated term) is a powerful sponsor who uses his influence to orchestrate assignment to a detail, to arrange for some other perquisite, or to somehow intercede favorably on one's behalf. The specific arrangement or deal is called a "contract." Although these informal arrangements and relationships are an entrenched part of the NYPD's history and culture, and although they are often spoken of with pejorative overtones—the implication being that someone gained an unfair advantage in an assignment or received some benefit not generally available to another through nepotism or raw internal politics—to some extent we see old-boy networks operating in all modern bureaucratic organizations. Moreover, they are not always an entirely bad thing. In many cases, "hooks" are motivated to give a qualified candidate a special push

toward a position that benefits the agency as well as the individual by furthering his career development. A hook's influence can, in this way, work to counter the stagnating bureaucratic processes as well as the subculture's potentially excessive emphasis on tenure as the primary basis for advancement. As we saw with some sergeants, this kind of relationship can resemble that of mentor and protégé. As such, these positive relationships can often work to the agency's ultimate advantage at the same time they have immortalizing qualities that connect both parties to a greater and more noble ideal or tradition.

7. In the past several years, an emphasis on more efficient investigations and more strategic deployment of personnel resources led to organizational restructuring and the formation of boroughwide evidence collection teams to replace the precinct-level latent print teams. Evidence collection team members receive additional and somewhat more specialized training than precinct "print men," but perform essentially the same duties at the scenes of minor crimes falling within the purview of the patrol bureau.

8. CSU technicians' compelling interests in these subjects are made even more apparent by the fact that they usually purchase these books and journals at their own considerable expense. Upon inquiry, I learned that the department's budget for such materials is absurdly small. I was acquainted with several of the texts I saw and knew that the publisher's price for each approached $100.

9. While I frequently use the term *expert* to characterize the skills and competencies of CSU members, it should be pointed out that the term also has a specific legal meaning with some applicability to our explorations of the CSU technician's work and sense of self. In order to testify in court as an "expert witness," an individual must be certified as one by the court. The first few times a technician (or any other prospective expert giving forensic testimony of some sort) testifies, the prosecutor will typically elicit fairly detailed testimony about his education, training, and experience, ultimately petitioning the court to accept the testimony as evidence of his expert status for the purposes of the trial. Eventually the "court-certified" technician can cite this credential and the approximate number of times his expert status has been recognized, minimizing the need to continually review his credentials in depth. Notwithstanding certification as an expert, prosecutors typically review credentials to impress the jury with the quality of testimony they are about to hear, and defense attorneys typically make at least a half-hearted attempt to diminish his expertise. In some cases, an egregious error in judgment or conclusions can result in decertification.

10. Criminal investigators often speak of the unwritten "24-hour rule"—the idea that for every 24-hour period elapsing from the time of the homicide the likelihood of solution by arrest decreases by half. This old chestnut has face validity insofar as solvability can be expected to decline when witnesses are not located or when perpetrators flee, develop an alibi, or "lawyer-up" (retain an attorney who advises them not to cooperate with or speak to the police). Police agencies tend to devote more resources at the early stages of an investigation, and the majority of homicide arrests take place within a few days of the crime. In the present context, the rule means that detectives need reliable information quickly in order to create a viable theory of the crime and to immediately focus on possible suspects.

11. Given the possibility that HIV infections or other blood-borne pathogens could be transmitted through open wounds, the CSU technicians I spoke with were quite reticent to probe wounds (see, for example, Kennedy, Homant, and Emery, 1990). All wore latex gloves while examining corpses. Several technicians mentioned that this reticence was not always the case, and they described how some old-timers in the unit had absolutely no aversion to probing puncture wounds. In my own experience, I distinctly recall witnessing CSU detectives at a homicide inserting fingers into a corpse to estimate the depth of a stab wound.

12. It is not at all uncommon for a defense attorney to try to coax a testifying officer into venturing an opinion in an area outside his expertise and then attack his overall credibility or the opinions of bona fide experts testifying in the case. In my own experience, defense attorneys have attempted to lure me into making definitive "expert" statements about ballistics, firearms, and fingerprint evidence—areas in which I have minimal formal training—as a means of confusing the jury with testimony that conflicts with that offered by the prosecution's real experts.

13. "The Squad" can refer specifically to members of a precinct detective squad or, as in this case, be more generally applied to include criminal investigators from such specialized units as the homicide or special victims squads.

14. This is to ensure that none of the bullet wounds were missed in their examination. Perhaps contrary to public perception, bullet entry wounds and stab wounds do not always leave gaping holes in flesh but in some circumstances create a tiny puncture that seems to seal up with little or no external bleeding. Additionally, if clothing holes do not align perfectly with wounds, it may indicate the clothing was bunched up or in disarray, and this can provide clues as to what the victim was doing at the time he was shot or stabbed.

Chapter 7

1. See, for example, Niederhoffer's (1967) general discussion of detectives and patrol officers' attitudes toward them.

2. In the argot of the NYPD, "the bag" is the uniform. Being "out of the bag" in almost any plainclothes assignment confers a special status in part because of its identification with detective work, but also because it removes the overt stigma of identification with police work and allows one to shed the outward appearance of the police identity. The relative anonymity of plainclothes work is also appealing to the extent it allows one to avoid involvement with the public and with the petty problems they often bring to the uniformed cop's attention.

3. "Catching" a case refers to being the assigned lead detective responsible for bringing the investigation to conclusion.

4. Here it is useful to point out the semantic and practical differences between an assignment to a precinct detective squad and a homicide squad. In addition to 76 precinct detective squads (one per patrol precinct), the detective bureau has a variety of "specialty squads" with shared or exclusive jurisdiction over specified major offenses, and these currently include six geographically based borough homicide squads. In the early and mid-1970s (when some collaborators began investigating murders), homicide squad detectives caught all the murders and precinct squads investigated more mundane crimes. Following a detective bureau reorganization, precinct squad detectives began catching homicides but homicide squad detectives respond to render ongoing assistance to the catching detective. In precinct squads with high murder rates, one or more highly experienced detectives are designated as "homicide specialists" and, in addition to reinvestigating cold homicide cases, they either catch or team up with the catching detective. In essence, homicide specialists provide the in-house expertise and assistance that homicide squad members might ordinarily provide. Homicide squad detectives still respond to all murders within their geographic compass and typically render some form of investigative assistance, but they rarely have the ultimate responsibility to bring the case to closure. We will discuss these exceptions below.

5. As is the case with many other policies, this typical or formal career path applies in most, but certainly not all, instances. It is possible to earn direct transfer to a "white shield" assignment in the squad, although it is not common.

6. A homicide squad supervisor (who was not a collaborator, per se) related some of the difficulties and conflicts involved when high-ranking patrol bureau supervisors show up and attempt to traipse through a homicide scene. One strategy to deter them was to insist that a comprehensive official log of all people entering the scene be maintained—the "big bosses," fearful that they might be called upon to testify in the case or to explain the need for their presence, would remain outside the crime scene area.

7. This refers to the provisions of the NYPD's retirement system, in which officers can retire with an annual pension amounting to half their salary after completing 20 years of service. Additional pension increments are earned for each year of service beyond 20. Although many officers avail themselves of this opportunity, detectives as a group have traditionally remained on the active rolls well beyond their date of pension eligibility. Again, this speaks to the higher status, increased salary, generally better working conditions, and other advantages to being a detective relative to other assignments in the NYPD.

8. Contrary to public perception, serial murders and pattern murders are rare. When patterns are identified, the cases are typically consolidated and a task force consisting of the catching detectives and homicide squad detectives is formed.

9. "Dinosaur" is another piece of argot that may paradoxically have complimentary or pejorative connotations depending on its context. An old-timer who refers to himself as a dinosaur implicitly acknowledges that his attitudes and beliefs lack currency but are nevertheless emblematic of his membership in a small, exclusive, and highly experienced group that ascribes to a different and much stronger cultural code. It is an act of hubris for an officer with less than, say, 20 years' experience to call himself a dinosaur, but quite a few old detectives and patrol cops who are comfortable with a bit of self-mockery wear small lapel pins bearing the image of a Tyrannosaurus Rex. In a different context, the term can be used as an epithet to derisively imply that another cop is a slow, dimwitted, and cumbersome anachronism whose time has passed.

10. Show-ups are a kind of on-scene corporeal identification process in which eyewitnesses confirm that the person in custody is the person they saw engage in a specific behavior. The show-up, the legitimacy of which is governed by various statutes and a fairly complex body of case law, establishes the bedrock of probable cause underlying the custodial detention and the interrogation that follows. A lineup will subsequently be conducted to verify the eyewitness identification. Absent a lawful show-up, probable cause for the custodial interrogation and all the evidence that flows from it may be excluded at trial. The important point here is that the detective begins building a viable prosecution virtually from the moment he arrives at the scene, requiring him not only to focus attention on the immediate images but also to concomitantly consider how they will influence the final outcome of the investigation as a whole. Because this requires him to integrate cognitive knowledge with immediate images to make important judgments, and because it requires him to follow the viable schemas for enactment the resulting forms and constellations prescribe, he cannot afford any gross formative impairment. In particular, he cannot afford to become immobilized by powerful personal feelings about the victim or the suspect.

11. Detectives are careful to distinguish between the terms *interview* and *interrogation,* which have particular legal meanings and connotations. Without putting too fine a legal point on it, specific legal rights attach at the moment the detective considers the subject a suspect in the case and determines the individual is not at liberty to leave. When the detective decides the suspect is in custody and not free to leave, Miranda rights become applicable and must be read to him, and the interview becomes an interrogation.

12. In this sense, there is an inherent similarity between the tasks, objectives, and methods of the homicide investigator and the qualitative field researcher. Both "go where the

evidence takes them" and neither has, at the outset, an entirely clear picture of what conclusions and observations will emerge at the conclusion of his inquiries.

13. A "white-shield investigator" or "white-shield detective" is an official in the rank of police officer who is assigned to investigate duties but has not yet earned his coveted "gold shield" that denotes promotion to the detective rank.

14. A fine but important distinction should be made here. As one homicide squad supervisor pointed out, the detective should never point out inconsistencies during an initial interview with a *witness* or accuse him of equivocating; the idea is to give the witness the latitude to commit himself to a particular fact pattern that can later be revisited after additional information is obtained. In sharp contrast, a convention of tactical interviewing demands that a detective conducting the custodial interrogation of a *suspect* immediately "call him" on any lies or factual misrepresentations in order to maintain and augment the power dimension and the psychological pressures placed on him.

15. Appellate courts have not significantly eroded the admissibility of evidence obtained from witnesses or suspects through deception. There is a fairly complex and continually evolving body of case law governing the use of deception that detectives must know, integrate, and apply during the interview as they make judgments about the appropriate limits of misleading witnesses and suspects.

16. There is a conventional wisdom among detectives, confirmed through statistics on successful case closures and convictions, that most homicide victims are murdered by a person known to them. The FBI's *Uniform Crime Report* data, for example, consistently reveal that among the murders and nonnegligent homicides in which a relationship between the victim and offender is known, almost 20% were committed by an immediate family member, about half were committed by other family members, around 15% were committed by friends, neighbors, or coworkers, and slightly less than 20% were committed by strangers (Sourcebook of Criminal Justice Statistics, 2001).

17. In practice, this dynamic operates in sharp contrast to many media depictions of homicide investigation. In films and television shows, homicide detectives are often depicted making a personal commitment to a surviving family member by promising to solve the case. While this dramatic device advances the plot, develops characters, and sets the stage for the dogged detective's ultimate triumph, in reality few detectives are willing to make this costly commitment.

18. This snippet of dialogue must be understood in the larger context of our interview. The detective did, in fact, develop a commitment to particular cases and particular victims— a murdered police officer and a murdered child—and during our interview we discussed these cases separately. His remarks here specifically concern the range of "ordinary" homicides he investigated.

19. He subsequently noted the prayer was Reinhold Neibuhr's "Serenity Prayer," often recited by members of Alcoholics Anonymous: "God, grant me the serenity to accept the things I cannot change, the courage to change the things I can, and the wisdom to know the difference."

20. That is, he was relieved of all other investigative responsibilities for 6 weeks to concentrate solely on this case. Detectives are rarely taken "off the chart" for more than a week to pursue a homicide investigation.

21. He is referring here to the special sense of affection, respect, and devotion often shared between police partners. The connection between partners is rooted not only in the fact that they spend a great deal of time together—more time, for example, than one typically spends with a spouse—but in the deeply personal secrets they share and the kind of intimate knowledge they have of one another by virtue of having both participated in the same dangerous or emotionally difficult experiences. Within the crucible of "real" police expe-

rience, one learns a great deal about a partner's true character. As one officer put it, "your partner is the only person who really knows everything about you, and despite all that, he still likes you."

Chapter 8

1. Similar national declines in the level of violence directed against law enforcement officers have occurred. The FBI tracks murders and assaults against law enforcement officers nationwide in its annual *Law Enforcement Officers Killed and Assaulted* report, and the report for calendar year 2000 reveals 42 law enforcement officers were feloniously slain in 39 line-of-duty incidents in 1999—the lowest recorded figure in more than 35 years—and 63 others were accidentally killed in the performance of their duties. Twenty-five officers were slain with handguns (5 of these with their own weapon), 11 with rifles, 5 with shotguns, and 1 was killed with a vehicle. The 2001 report disclosed that 140 law enforcement officers were killed in the line of duty, but this total includes 37 Port Authority of New York and New Jersey Police Department officers, 23 NYPD officers, and 11 other law enforcement officers killed in the September 11 terrorist attacks. Sixty law enforcement officers were murdered with firearms in 2001 (45 with handguns, 11 with rifles, and 4 with shotguns), 7 were killed with vehicles, 1 with a blunt force weapon, and 1 was killed with physical force. We should also consider the fact that there are approximately 700,000 law enforcement officers employed in various capacities throughout the United States.

2. For example, the official Unusual Occurrence Report narrative (or '49) prepared by a ranking officer will recapitulate, often in excruciating detail, the factually verifiable circumstances of the death and the results of the initial on-scene investigation. Every officer at the scene and every department official notified will be listed. The shield and tax ID numbers, the patrol car numbers and sector of assignment, a full description of the clothing worn by officers and perpetrators, the dates of appointment or promotion and the tour of duty performed by every officer involved will be recounted. Even such seemingly obscure facts as the serial number of the deceased officer's flashlight may be recorded. Conspicuously absent from the narrative, which is typically written in the rather stilted bureaucratized style of so many police reports, are any subjective inferences or statements about the traumatic elements affecting any officer. The purpose of the Unusual is to memorialize factual information, and so emotions and other subjective experience are essentially beside the point.

3. While there is certainly no direct evidence suggesting Byrne actually dozed off or acted imprudently, cops may reasonably reflect on this possibility in attempting to make sense of the event. We should also point out that strong subcultural proscriptions operate against suggesting or insinuating that an officer might be in any way responsible for his own death, so even if cops privately suspect that Byrne dozed off they are reluctant to articulate their suspicion to those outside their subculture.

4. NYPD cops were not and are not altogether unfamiliar with the notion of being randomly targeted for symbolic murder, since the Black Liberation Army waged a terrorist assassination campaign in New York in the late 1960s and early 1970s that claimed the lives of six officers. Their names—Piagentini and Jones, Foster and Laurie, Glover and Reddy— and some details of their deaths remain part of the lore despite the elapsed years, but that ambush campaign was carried on almost three decades ago by political terrorists operating under the guise of a "war," not by organized crime figures. The memory of these crimes has to some degree faded because these murders took place before many young cops were born, and relatively few old-timers who were part of the agency during that era and privy to the details of the murders remain in the agency to keep this part of the cultural lore alive. Finally, Byrne's death was made all the more incomprehensible because it violated a fun-

damental cultural expectation that members of organized crime—drug dealers included—do not order the execution of cops (see, for example, Roberts [1988]).

5. The names of more than 14,000 law enforcement officers killed in the line of duty are inscribed, in random order, on the walls of the National Law Enforcement Memorial in Washington, D.C. Visitors consult a large directory to determine a particular name's location on the walls. On a recent visit to the memorial I was struck by the fact that a large check mark—the only one in the entire directory—had been inked next to one name: Edward Byrne.

6. Political concerns can be glimpsed in the way the brief posthumous citations contained in the department's annual Medal Day program booklets generally reflect current political rhetoric and public discourse about crime and justice issues. The officer's death is reconstructed in a narrative that serves, in an especially powerful way, to exemplify the evils of current public and political discourse. It is a matter not of the death becoming a catalyst for public policy change or of raising an issue to public consciousness, but of tailoring the narrative to advance or conform to preexisting political agendas. Again reflecting the relatively ephemeral concerns of "the Department" as opposed to "the Job," the event is officially interpreted and communicated in terms of the prevailing constellations of political meaning.

7. The salience and importance of the locker is made clearer by the fact that although it is department property, it is one of the few places where a cop has some privacy rights. Lockers can be searched only for cause, and separate male and female locker rooms exist for police officers, sergeants, and lieutenants. Other than during a cursory inspection of the locker room each tour by the desk officer—who almost always knocks before entering—it is a strict convention that supervisors never enter the police officers' locker room, nor do police officers ever enter a supervisors' locker room. What is stored in the locker and what goes on between cops in the locker room, in other words, is generally not subject to official or unofficial scrutiny. Because the locker symbolically or actually contains one's most intimate and secret things, the combination is generally shared only with one's trusted partner.

8. The officer showed me the watch, which he wears every day. He also noted that other cops asked him for personal items from the locker as mementos of their fallen comrade, but although he understood their requests he refused because he felt his partner would have wanted everything to go to his spouse. The watch is, of course, a highly personal and evocative symbol of continuity that links past, present, and future.

9. One cop (not a collaborator, per se) related to me that more than 20 years earlier he had helped arrange a desirable assignment for a friend (in police parlance, he "put in a contract" for him). After a few days in the new assignment, the officer was murdered, and the cop still feels an amorphous and largely irrational guilt that his act of friendship somehow contributed to his friend's murder. Even after 20 years he was deeply affected by this guilt.

10. I distinguish here, as the police culture does, between "steady partners" and partners who work together occasionally. Cops can and do refer to other officers they have occasionally worked with as "partners," but "steady partners" are cops who choose to work together on a permanent basis.

11. In addition to the time partners spend together, the depth and quality of their connection can cause difficulties in the personal sphere. It is not at all uncommon for spouses and significant others to experience some jealousy and resentment when they perceive the relationship between the partners as healthier, more intimate, more trusting, and more viable than the one they share with the cop.

12. Leuci, a former corrupt NYPD narcotics detective, was the protagonist of Robert Daley's (1978) *Prince of the City* and the Sidney Lumet film of the same name.

13. In one collegial version, an officer reputedly froze, gun in hand, while another cop struggled with two assailants. One assailant wrested the other cop's gun from its holster and shot him with it, and the other assailant reportedly took the gun from the immobilized officer's hand and fled with it. When the uninjured cop was transferred to another command, cops showed up at roll call with their guns lashed to their holsters and continually engaged in other forms of torment that pointed up the officer's alleged cowardice. The reputation stuck, and subtle snubs and gibes continued over the course of the immobilized officer's career.

14. We should exercise caution in generalizing these statistical data directly to the experience of NYPD officers, especially because the researchers used different instruments and methods to gather data from officers in various law enforcement environments and assignments. Klinger (2001), for example, candidly admits his sample included a disproportionate number of special weapons and tactics (SWAT) team members as well as deputy sheriffs working in rural and suburban agencies in four states. These data are cited for illustrative purposes, and no attempt was made in this research project to empirically measure the number or percentage of overall shooting incidents in which NYPD officers experienced perceptual distortions.

15. The officer's modest mention of "one of those hanging medals" refers euphemistically to one of the agency's top commendations for bravery above and beyond the call of duty. Although the survivors who have won these medals wear them proudly, they never flaunt them in an immodest way.

16. Rackets are organized and often quite raucous parties, including retirement or promotion affairs or fundraisers, attended almost exclusively by cops.

17. For a more thorough analysis of this case from a formative perspective, including the elements of survivor psychology it entails, see Henry (1995).

Epilogue

1. "The bag" is the NYPD's informal jargon for "uniform," and "hats and bats" refers to riot helmets and nightsticks. In a larger context, the term refers to a violent and chaotic situation in which cops are under attack.

2. The Muster Deck is a large open area used to assemble and inspect recruits during pre-tour musters.

3. A "gun run" is an incident or call involving an armed perpetrator, typically one who is firing shots or menacing someone.

4. A "scratch" is the NYPD term for a supervisor's notation and signature in an officer's memo book signifying that the officer was inspected on post. As explained to the recruits, the informal ritual involves the supervisor's approaching the officer in such a way that the officer is not caught off guard and knows the RMP or marked department vehicle contains a supervisor and his driver rather than a pair of officers. A decent boss—one who is not looking to hurt the cop or catch him "off base"—will typically put his arm out the window to display chevrons or the white shirt lieutenants wear and/or put a supervisor's hat on the dashboard so that the gold braid is visible. The boss may also gesture with his hand as if writing to indicate his intention and to distinguish the approach from an on-post visit that will not require presentation of the memo book. This forewarning gives the street cop a few moments to get his act or story together, to ditch a cigarette butt, etc. As a form of reciprocation, the officer approaches the car, gives the boss a sharp salute or "highball," and presents his memo book open to the last entry. The supervisor may ask if the officer "needs a line" if all entries are apparently not complete and, after reviewing the day's entries, signs the book to indicate that the officer has been duly inspected. This subtle ritual and the jar-

gon that goes along with it is never formally explained to recruits as part of the formal Academy curricula, but it is something they will either learn quickly or be greatly embarrassed when assigned to a precinct. The recruits, anxious to accumulate and practice "real cop" behaviors, quickly began explaining the ritual of the scratch to other recruits and some actually began approaching us on patrol to demonstrate their new-found skill. They were trying on their new identities and wanted us to know that they were moving toward "real cop" status.

5. A "personal" is an NYPD euphemism for "personal necessity," or a break to use toilet facilities. It is stipulated in the Patrol Guide that an officer is entitled to leave assigned patrol duties for "personal necessity" for a period of no longer than twenty minutes twice on each tour of duty.

6. POPPA is the acronym for the Police Organization Providing Peer Assistance, a group of about 200 volunteer Peer Support Officers trained in crisis intervention and counseling. POPPA, formerly known as the Members Assistance Program, maintains a 24-hour hotline cops can call for assistance from peer support officers. Insofar as the organization has no official ties to the NYPD, maintains confidentiality, and utilizes cops to help and support other cops, it enjoys a positive reputation among officers.

Bibliography

Alpert, G. P., & Fridell, L. A. (1992). *Police vehicles and firearms*. Prospect Heights, IL: Waveland Press.

Alvarez, L. (1996, October 24). A blue line in Queens pays tribute to a comrade. *New York Times*, p. B3.

American Psychological Association (APA). (1982). *Ethical principles in the conduct of research with human participants*. Washington, DC: American Psychological Association.

Anderson, D. C. (1992, August 28). Editorial notebook: Why T.N.T. fizzled. *New York Times*, p. A24.

Aries, P. (1974). *Western attitudes toward death: From the middle ages to the present* (P. M. Ranum, Trans.). Baltimore, MD: Johns Hopkins University Press.

Aries, P. (1975a). Forbidden death. In E. Shneidman (Ed.), *Death: Current perspectives*. Palo Alto, CA: Mayfield.

Aries, P. (1975b). The reversal of death: Changes in attitudes toward death in Western societies. In D. E. Stannard (Ed.), *Death in America* (pp. 134–58). Philadelphia: University of Pennsylvania Press.

Artwohl, A., & Christensen, L. W. (1997). *Deadly force encounters: What cops need to know to mentally and physically prepare for and survive a gunfight*. Boulder, CO: Paladin Press.

Babbie, E. (1992). *The practice of social research* (6th ed.). Belmont, CA: Wadsworth.

Bahn, C. (1984). Police socialization in the eighties: Strains in the forging of an occupational identity. *Journal of Police Science and Administration, 12*, 390–394.

Baker, M. (1985). *Cops: Their lives in their own words*. New York: Simon and Schuster.

Balch, R. W. (1972). The police personality: Fact or fiction? *Journal of Criminal Law, Criminology, and Police Science, 63*, 106–119.

Bartone, P. T., Ursano, R. J., Wright, K., & Ingraham, L. K. (1989). The impact of a military air disaster on the health of assistance workers: A prospective study. *Journal of Nervous and Mental Disease, 199*, 317–328.

Bayley, D. H., & Bittner, E. (1984). Learning the skills of policing. In R. C. Dunham & G. P. Alpert (Eds.). (1993). *Critical issues in policing: Contemporary readings* (2nd ed.) (pp. 106–

129). Prospect Heights, IL: Waveland Press. (Reprinted from *Law and Contemporary Problems, 47,* 35–59.)

Bayley, D., & Garofalo, J. (1989). The management of violence by police patrol officers. *Criminology, 17*(1), 1–26.

Beaming with pride. (1998). *Spring 3100, 61*(2), p. 32.

Becker, E. (1973). *The denial of death.* New York: Free Press.

Becker, E. (1975). *Escape from evil.* New York: Free Press.

Bennett, R. R. (1984). Becoming blue: A longitudinal study of police recruit occupational socialization. *Journal of Police Science and Administration, 12*(1), 47–58.

Binder, A., & Scharf, P. (1980). The violent police-citizen encounter. *Annals of the American Academy of Political and Social Science, 452,* 111–121.

Bittner, E. (1974). Florence Nightingale in pursuit of Willie Sutton: A theory of the police. In J. Jacobs (Ed.). *The Potential for Reform of the Criminal Justice System* (pp. 17–41). Thousand Oaks, CA: Sage.

Bittner, E. (1980). *The functions of the police in modern society.* Cambridge, MA: Olegschlager, Gunn, and Hain.

Black, D. J. (1980). *Manners and customs of the police.* New York: Academic Press.

Bolkosky, Sydney M. (1987). Interviewing victims who survived: Listening for the silences that strike. *Annals of Scholarship, 4*(2), 33–52.

Bonifacio, P. (1991). *The psychological effects of police work: A psychodynamic approach.* New York: Plenum.

Bosk, C. L. (1979). *Forgive and remember: Managing medical failure.* Chicago: University of Chicago Press.

Bourke, J. (1999). *An intimate history of killing: Face to face killing in 20th-century warfare.* New York: Basic Books.

Boyd, Gerald M. (1988, April 14). Execution backed in drug slayings. *New York Times,* p. D27.

Breslau, N., & Davis, G. C. (1987). Posttraumatic stress disorder: The etiologic specificity of wartime stressors. *American Journal of Psychiatry, 144,* 578–583.

Brinberg, D., & McGrath, J. (1985). *Validity and the research process.* Newbury Park, CA: Sage.

Brown, M. (1981). *Working the street: Police discretion and the dilemmas of reform.* New York: Russell Sage.

Brown, N. O. (1959). *Life against death: The psychoanalytical meaning of history.* Middletown, CT: Wesleyan University Press.

Burbeck, E., & Furnham, A. (1985). Police officer selection: A critical review of the literature. *Journal of Police Science and Administration, 12*(1), 58–69.

Campbell, J. H. (1992). *A comparative analysis of the effects of post-shooting trauma on the special agents of the Federal Bureau of Investigation.* Unpublished doctoral dissertation, Michigan State University, Ann Arbor.

Cassell, E. J. (1973). Being and becoming dead. In Arien Mack (Ed.), *Death in American experience.* New York: Shocken.

Catholic Encyclopedia Online. (2001a). *St. Michael the Archangel.* Available from http://www.newadvent.org/cathen/10275b.htm.

Catholic Encyclopedia Online. (2001b). *St. George.* Available from http://www.newadvent.org/cathen/06543a.htm.

Cervantes, R. (1984). Psychological stress of body handling, part II and part III: Debriefing of Dover AFB personnel following the Gander tragedy and the body handling experience at Dover AFB. In R. Ursano & C. Fullerton (Eds.). *Exposure to death, disasters, and bodies*. Bethesda, MD: F. Edward Hebert School of Medicine, Uniformed Services University of the Health Sciences (DCIT: A203163).

Chandler, E. V., & Jones, C. S. (1979). Cynicism: An inevitability of police work. *Journal of Police Science and Administration, 7*(1), 65–68.

Charmaz, K. (1975). The coroner's strategies of announcing death. *Urban Life, 4,* 296–316.

Charmaz, K. (1980). *The social reality of death: Death in contemporary America.* New York: Random House.

Clark, R. E., & Labeff, E. E. (1982). Death telling: managing the delivery of bad news. *Journal of Health and Social Behavior, 23,* 366–380.

Clarke, C., & Zak, M. J. (1999). Fatalities to law enforcement officers and firefighters, 1992–1997. In *Compensation and Working Conditions* (pp. 3–7).

Connelly, J. (1998). *Bringing out the dead.* New York: Alfred A. Knopf.

Coombs, R. H., & Powers, P. S. (1976). Socialization for death: The physician's role. In L. Lofland (Ed.). *Toward a sociology of death and dying* (pp. 15–36). Beverly Hills, CA: Sage.

Count, E. W. (1995). *Cop talk: True detective stories from the NYPD.* New York: Pocket Books.

Crank, J. P. (1998). *Understanding police culture.* Cincinnati, OH: Anderson.

Cullen, F. T., Link, B. G., Travis, L. F., & Lemming, T. (1983). Paradox in policing: A note on the perception of danger. *Journal of Police Science and Administration, 11*(4), 457–462.

Daley, R. (1978). *Prince of the city.* Boston: Houghton Mifflin.

Deal, T. E., and Kennedy, A. A. (1982). *Corporate cultures: The rites and rituals of corporate life.* New York: Addison-Wesley.

Death Notification Guidelines Committee. (1992). *"In person, in time"—Recommended procedures for death notification.* Des Moines, IA: Iowa Department of Justice.

Denzin, N. K., & Lincoln, Y. S. (Eds.). (1994). *Handbook of qualitative research.* Thousand Oaks, CA: Sage.

Dickinson, G. E., Lancaster, C. J., Winfield, I. C., Reece, E. F., & Colthorpe, C. (1997). Detached concern and death anxiety of first-year medical students: Before and after the gross anatomy course. *Clinical Anatomy, 10,* 201–207.

DiMaio, D. J. and DiMaio, V. J. (1993). *Forensic pathology.* Boca Raton, FL: CRC Press.

DiMaio, V. J. M. (1993). *Gunshot wounds: Practical aspects of firearms, ballistics, and forensic techniques.* Boca Raton, FL: CRC Press.

Dunlap, D. W. (1989, May 20). System lashed as police honor 5 slain on duty. *New York Times,* p. 31.

Eth, S., Barton, D. A., & Pinoos, R. (1987). Death notification. *Bulletin of the American Academy of Psychiatry and Law, 15*(3), 275–281.

Federal Bureau of Investigation. (1970–1999). *Uniform crime reports: Law enforcement officers killed and assaulted* (annual report). Washington, DC: U.S. Department of Justice.

Federal Bureau of Investigation. (2001, March 15). Law enforcement officers killed and assaulted, 1999 (press release). Washington, DC: FBI National Press Office. Available from http://www.fbi.gov/pressrel/pressrel01/leoka031501.htm.

Feifel, H. (1969). Death—relevant variable in psychology. In R. May (Ed.), *Existential psychology* (2nd ed.) (pp. 58–71). New York: Random House.

Feifel, H. (Ed.). (1959). *The meaning of death.* New York: McGraw-Hill.

Firestone, D. (1994, December 7). Saying a painful farewell to a "hero for our times": 10,000 attend funeral for a slain officer. *New York Times,* p. B3.

Fisher, R. P., & McCauley, M. R. (1995). Information retrieval: Interviewing witnesses. In

N. Brewer and C. Wilson (Eds.). *Psychology and policing* (pp. 81–100). Hillsdale, NJ: Lawrence Erlbaum Associates.

Fletcher, C. (1990). *What cops know.* New York: Pocket Books.

Fontana, A., & Frey, J. H. (1994). Interviewing: The art of science. In N. K. Denzin & Y. S. Lincoln (Eds.), *Handbook of qualitative research* (pp. 361–376). Thousand Oaks, CA: Sage.

Freud, S. (1961). Thoughts for the times on war and death. In J. Strachey (Ed. and Trans.). *Standard edition of the complete psychological works of Sigmund Freud* (vol. 14). London: Hogarth Press. Original work published 1923.

Fridell, L., & Pate, A. (1993). Death on patrol: Killings of American law enforcement officers. In R. C. Dunham & G. P. Alpert (Eds.), *Critical issues in policing: Contemporary readings* (2nd ed.) (pp. 568–597). Prospect Heights, IL: Waveland Press.

Fridell, L. A., & Pate, A. M. (1992, November). Death on patrol: Killings of American law enforcement officers. Paper presented at the Annual Meeting of the American Society of Criminology, New Orleans, LA.

Fried, J. (1988a, February 27). Officer guarding drug witness is slain. *New York Times,* p. A1.

Fried, J. (1988b, October 14). Officer's killing "a message to police." *New York Times,* p. B3.

Fried, J. (1989a, February 22). Byrne's slaying called "symbolic message." *New York Times,* p. B3.

Fried, J. (1989b, March 2). Witnesses recall talk about killing an officer. *New York Times,* p. B3.

Fried, J. (1990, May 22). Site of officer's slaying will be a center of hope. *New York Times,* p. B3.

Friedman, P. (1967). Suicide among police: A study of ninety-three suicides among New York policemen, 1934–1940. In E. S. Shneidman (Ed.), *Essays in self-destruction* (pp. 414–449). New York: Jason Aronson.

Fullerton, C. S., McCarroll, J. E., Ursano, R. J., & Wright, K. M. (1992). Psychological responses of rescue workers: Fire fighters and trauma. *American Journal of Orthopsychiatry, 112,* 371–378.

Fyfe, J. J. (1980). Always prepared: police off-duty guns. *Annals of the American Academy of Political and Social Science, 452,* 72–81.

Fyfe, J. J. (1981). *Police use of deadly force.* Washington, DC: Police Foundation.

Fyfe, J. J. (1982). Blind justice: Police shootings in Memphis. *Journal of Criminal Law and Criminology, 73,* 702–722.

Fyfe, J. J. (1988). Police use of deadly force: Research and reform. *Justice Quarterly, 5,* 165–205.

Gallers, J., Foy, D. W., & Donohue, C. P. (1988). Posttraumatic stress disorder in Vietnam combat veterans: Effects of traumatic violence exposure and military adjustment. *Journal of Traumatic Stress, 1,* 672–678.

Garfinkel, H. (1956). Conditions of successful degradation ceremonies. In R. A. Farrell & V. L. Swigert (Eds.). (1978). *Social deviance* (2nd ed.) (pp. 135–42). New York: J. B. Lippincott. (Reprinted from *American Sociological Review, 61,* 420–424.)

Garner, J., & Clemmer, E. (1986). Danger to police in domestic disturbances—a new look. *Research in Brief* series, National Institute of Justice.

Gaska, C. W. (1980). *The rate of suicide, potential for suicide, and recommendations for prevention among retired police officers.* Unpublished doctoral dissertation, Wayne State University, Ohio.

Geberth, V. J. (1993). *Practical homicide investigation: Tactics, procedures, and forensic techniques* (2nd ed.). Boca Raton, FL: CRC Press.

Geiselman, R. E., & Fisher, R. P. (1988). The cognitive interview: An innovative technique for questioning witnesses of crime. *Journal of Police and Criminal Psychology, 4*(2), 2–5.

Gelb, B. (1975). *On the track of murder: Behind the scenes with a homicide commando squad.* New York: William Morrow.

Geller, W. A., & Scott, M. (1992). *Deadly force: What we know—A practitioner's desk reference to police-involved shootings.* Washington, DC: Police Executive Research Forum.

George, T. (2000, April 25). Morgue worker nabbed in theft from corpse. *New York Daily News*, p. 7.

Goffman, E. (1961). *Asylums: Essays on the social situation of mental patients and other inmates.* Garden City, NY: Doubleday Anchor.

Goldstein, H. (1977). *Policing a free society.* Cambridge, MA: MIT Press.

Gorer, G. (1955). The pornography of death. *Encounter, 5*, 49–52.

Gourevitch, P. (2000, February 14). A cold case: Suddenly, a New York cop remembered a long-ago murder. *The New Yorker*, 43–60.

Grady, D. A., Woolfolk R. L., & Budney, A. J. (1990). Dimensions of war zone stress: An empirical analysis. *Journal of Nervous and Mental Disease, 177*, 347–350.

Green, B. L., Lindy, J. D., Grace, M. G., & Gleser, G. C. (1990). Multiple diagnosis in post-traumatic stress disorder: The role of war stressors. *Journal of Nervous and Mental Disease, 177*, 329–335.

Grossman, D. (1996). *On killing: The psychological cost of learning to kill in war and society.* Boston: Little, Brown.

Haberman, C. (2000, June 13). On subway, the horror of the "12–9." *New York Times*, p. B1.

Hall, M. (1982). Law enforcement officers and death notification: A plea for relevant education. *Journal of Police Science and Administration, 10*(2), 189–193.

Hampson, R. (1994, August 21). Determined detective gathers clues, makes arrest in 13-year-old murder; New York police officer refused to give up on the case, in which a doctor was shot for the $5 in his wallet. *Los Angeles Times*, p. A8.

Harruff, R. C., Llewellyn, A. L., Clark, M. A., & Hawley, D. A. (1994). Firearms suicides during confrontations with police. *Journal of Forensic Sciences, 39*, 402–411.

Heiman, M. F. (1975). The police suicide. *Journal of Police Science and Administration, 3*(3), 267–273.

Helm, A., & Mazur, D. (1989). Death notification: Legal and ethical issues. *Dimensions of Critical Care Nursing, 6*, 382–385.

Hendin, D. (1973). *Death as a fact of life.* New York: W. W. Norton.

Hendricks, J. E. (1984). Death notification: The theory and practice of informing the survivors. *Journal of Police Science and Administration, 12*(1), 109–116.

Henry, V. E. (1995). The police officer as survivor: Death confrontations and the police subculture. *Behavioral Science and Law, 11*(1), 93–112.

Hershiser, M. R., & Quarantelli, E. L. (1976). The handling of the dead in a disaster. *Omega, 7*(3), 195–203.

Hess, J. E. (1997). *Interviewing and interrogation for law enforcement.* Cincinnati, OH: Anderson Publishing.

Hess, J. E., & Gladis, S. D. (1987). Benevolent interrogation. *FBI Law Enforcement Bulletin, 56*(7), 20–23.

Hilton, C. (1997). Media triggers of post-traumatic stress disorder 50 years after the Second World War. *International Journal of Geriatric Psychiatry, 12*, 862–867.

Horwich, P. G. (Ed.). (1993). *World changes: Thomas Kuhn and the nature of science.* Cambridge, MA: MIT Press.

Hutson, H. R., Anglin, D., Yarbrough, J., Hardaway, K., Russell, M., Strote, J. Canter, M., & Blum, B. (1998). Suicide by cop. *Annals of Emergency Medicine, 32*, 665–669.

Inbau, F. E., Reid, J. E., & Buckley, J. P. (1985). *Criminal interrogation and confessions* (3rd ed.), Baltimore, MD: Williams & Wilkins.

James, G. (1988, March 11). Officer's father thanks public for outpouring. *New York Times,* p. B3.

James, G. (1992, December 24). The endless quest for a daughter's killer. A Queens detective's mission: To find answers for a grieving mother. *New York Times,* p. B1.

Johnson, R. (1989). *Death work: A study of the modern execution process.* Pacific Grove, CA: Brooks/Cole.

Jones, D. R. (1985). Secondary disaster victims: The emotional effects of recovering and identifying human remains. *American Journal of Psychiatry, 142,* 303–307.

Jung, C. G. (1933). *Modern man in search of a soul* (W. S. Dell & C. F. Baynes, Trans.). New York: Harcourt, Brace, & World.

Kania, R. E. (1988). Should we tell the police to say "yes" to gratuities? *Criminal Justice Ethics, 2,* 37–49.

Kappeler, V. E., Sluder, R., & Alpert, G. P. (1994). *Forces of deviance: Understanding the dark side of policing.* Prospect Heights, IL: Waveland Press.

Kardiner, A., & Spiegel, H. (1947). *War stress and neurotic illness.* New York: Paul B. Hoebner.

Kasper, A. M. (1959). The doctor and death. In H. Feifel (Ed.). *The meaning of death* (pp. 259–270). New York: McGraw-Hill.

Kennedy, D. B., Homant, R. J., & Emery, G. L. (1990). AIDS concerns among crime scene investigators. *Journal of Police Science and Administration, 17*(1), 12–19.

Kirk, J., & Miller, M. L. (1986). *Reliability and validity in qualitative research.* Newbury Park, CA: Sage.

Klinger, D. (2001). Police response to officer-involved shootings. Advanced draft of a report submitted to the National Institute of Justice, Office of Justice Programs (award number 97–IJ-CX-0029).

Klockars, C. B. (Ed.). (1983). *Thinking about police: Contemporary readings.* New York: McGrawHill.

Kuhn, T. S. (1962). *The structure of scientific revolutions.* Chicago: University of Chicago Press. Original work published 1962.

Kutscher, A. H. (1973). Anticipatory grief, death, and bereavement: A continuum. In E. Wyschogrod (Ed.), *The phenomenon of death: Faces of mortality* (pp. 40–54). New York: Harper & Row.

Lardner, J. (1996). *Crusader: The hell-raising police career of detective David Durk.* New York: Random House.

Lardner, J., & Reppetto, T. (2000). *NYPD: A city and its police.* New York: Henry Holt.

Laufer, R. S., Frey-Wouters, E., & Gallops, M. S. (1985). Dimensions of posttraumatic stress disorder among Vietnam veterans. *Journal of Nervous and Mental Disease, 173,* 538–545.

Laufer, R. S., Gallops M. E., & Frey-Wouters, E. (1984). War stress and trauma: The Vietnam veteran experience. *Journal of Health and Social Behavior, 25,* 65–85.

Leash, R. M. (1994). *Death notification: A practical guide to the process.* Hinesburg, VT: Upper Access.

Lester, D. (1992). Suicide in police officers: A survey of nations. *Police Studies, 15*(3), 142–147.

Lester, D. (1993). A study of police suicide in New York City, 1934–1939. *Psychological Reports, 73*(2), 1395–1398.

Lesy, M. (1987). *The forbidden zone.* New York: Farrar, Straus and Giroux.

Lifton, R. J. (1963). *Thought reform and the psychology of totalism: A study of brainwashing in China.* New York: W. W. Norton.

Lifton, R. J. (1967a). *Death in life: Survivors of Hiroshima.* New York: Basic Books.

Lifton, R. J. (1967b). *Revolutionary immortality: Mao Tse Tung and the Chinese cultural revolution.* New York: W. W. Norton.

Lifton, R. J. (1969). *Boundaries: Psychological man in revolution.* New York: Touchstone.

Lifton, R. J. (1970). *History and human survival.* New York: Random House.

Lifton, R. J. (1973). *Home from the war: Vietnam veterans: Neither victims nor executioners.* New York: Basic Books.

Lifton, R. J. (1974a). On death and the continuity of life: A "new" paradigm. *History of Childhood Quarterly: The Journal of Psychohistory, 1,* 681–696.

Lifton, R. J. (1974b). The sense of immortality: On death and the continuity of life. In R. J. Lifton & E. Olson (Eds.). *Explorations in psychohistory: The Wellfleet papers* (pp. 271–287). New York: Simon & Schuster.

Lifton, R. J. (1976a). Advocacy and corruption in the healing professions. In N. L. Goldman & D. R. Segal (Eds.), *The social psychology of military service.* Beverly Hills, CA: Sage.

Lifton, R. J. (1976b). *The life of the self: Toward a new psychology.* New York: Touchstone.

Lifton, R. J. (1980). The concept of the survivor. In J. E. Dimsdale (Ed.), *Survivors, victims, and perpetrators: Essays on the Nazi holocaust* (pp. 113–126). New York: Hemisphere.

Lifton, R. J. (1983). *The broken connection: On death and the continuity of life.* New York: Basic Books. Original work published 1979.

Lifton, R. J. (1986). *The Nazi doctors: Medical killing and the psychology of genocide.* New York: Basic Books.

Lifton, R. J. (1987). *The future of immortality.* New York: Basic Books.

Lifton, R. J., & Olson, E. (1976). The human meaning of total disaster: The Buffalo Creek experience. *Psychiatry, 39,* 1–18.

Lotz, R., & Regoli, R. M. (1977). Police cynicism and professionalism. *Human Relations, 30*(2), 175–186.

Lyall, S. (1988a, February 27). Lone officers aren't unusual, authorities say. *New York Times,* p. A34.

Lyall, S. (1988b, March 1). 10,000 at slain officer's mass display resolve. *New York Times,* p. A1.

Machell, D. F. (1993). Combat post-traumatic stress disorder, alcoholism, and the police officer. *Journal of Alcohol and Drug Education, 38*(2), 23–32.

Manning, P. K. (1978). The police: Mandate, strategies, and appearances. In P. K. Manning & J. van Maanen (Eds.). *Policing: A view from the street* (pp. 7–31). Santa Monica, CA: Goodyear.

Manning, P. K. (1997). *Police work: The social organization of policing* (2nd ed.). Prospect Heights, IL: Waveland Press.

Marmar, C. (1997). Trauma and dissociation. *PTSD Research Quarterly, 8*(2), 1–6.

Marmar, C. R., Weiss, D. S., Metzler, T. J., & Delucchi, K. (1996). Characteristics of emergency services personnel related to peritraumatic dissociation during critical incident exposure. *American Journal of Psychiatry, 153*(7), 94–102.

Marmar, C. R., Weiss, D. S., Schlenger, W. E., Fairbank, J. A., Jordan, K., Kulka, R. A., & Hough, R. L. (1994). Peritraumatic dissociation and post-traumatic stress in male Vietnam theater veterans. *American Journal of Psychiatry, 151,* 902–907.

McAllester, M., & Plevin, L. (1994, December 4). 400 officers and family at cop's wake. *Newsday,* p. A6.

McCracken, G. (1988). *The long interview.* Newbury Park, CA: Sage.

McKenna, T., & Harrington, W. (1996). *Manhattan north homicide: The true story of one of New York's best homicide cops.* New York: St. Martin's.

Murder of rookie officer inspires anti-drug drives. (1992, May 3). *New York Times,* p. 50.

Murrell, M. E., Lester, D., & Andarcuri, A. F. (1978). Is the police personality unique to police officers? *Psychological Reports, 43.*

Nelson, Z., & Smith, W. (1970). The law enforcement profession: A high incidence of suicide. *Omega, 1,* 295–298.

New South Wales Independent Commission against Corruption (1997). *Report on the investigation into the Glebe morgue.* Sydney: Independent Commission against Corruption.

New York City Police Department. (1970–2000). *Firearms discharge and assault report* (annual report). New York: New York City Police Department.

New York City Police Department. (2003). *Patrol guide.* New York: New York City Police Department.

Niederhoffer, A. (1967). *Behind the shield: The police in urban society.* Garden City, NY: Doubleday.

Niederhoffer, A., & Niederhoffer, E. (1978). *The police family: From station house to ranch house.* Lexington, MS: Lexington Books.

Nielsen, E. (1981). *Salt Lake City Police deadly force policy shooting and post-shooting reactions.* Salt Lake City, UT: Salt Lake City Police Department.

Officer guarding witness slain. (1988, February 26). *Los Angeles Times,* p. 1.

Pate, A. M., & Fridell, L. A. (1993). *Police use of force: Official reports, citizen complaints, and legal consequences.* Washington, DC: Police Foundation.

Pierson, D. S. (1999). Natural killers: Turning the tide of battle. *Military Review, 79*(3), 59–65.

Pinnizotto, A. J., Davis, E. F., and Miller, C. E. (1997). *In the line of fire: A study of selected felonious assaults on law enforcement officers.* Washington, DC: National Institute of Justice/Federal Bureau of Investigation.

Pogrebin, M., & Poole, E. (1988). Humor in the briefing room: A study of the strategic uses of humor among police. *Journal of Contemporary Ethnography, 17,* 183–210.

Punch, M. (1993). *The politics and ethics of fieldwork.* Newbury Park, CA: Sage.

Punch, M. (1994). Politics and ethics in qualitative research. In N. K. Denzin & Y. S. Lincoln (Eds.), *Handbook of qualitative research* (pp. 83–97). Thousand Oaks, CA: Sage.

Putnam, F. W. (1989). Pierre Janet and modern views of dissociation. *Journal of Traumatic Stress, 2,* 413–429.

Quinnett, P. (1998). QPR for police suicide prevention. *FBI Law Enforcement Bulletin, 67*(7), 19–24.

Rachlin, H. (1991). *The making of a cop.* New York: Pocket Books.

Rachlin, H. (1994a). Police officer deaths: Funerals. *Law and Order, 42*(9), 137–143.

Rachlin, H. (1994b). Police officer deaths: Memorials. *Law and Order, 42*(9), 166–169.

Rachlin, H. (1994c). Police officer deaths: The bagpipe. *Law and Order, 42*(9), 171–172.

Rachlin, H. (1995). *The making of a detective.* New York: W. W. Norton.

Rank, O. (1950). *Will therapy.* New York: Alfred Knopf.

Rank, O. (1958). *Beyond psychology.* New York: Dover.

Raphael, B., Singh, B., Bradbury, L., & Lambert, F. (1983). Who helps the helpers? The effects of disaster on the rescue workers. *Omega, 14,* 9–20.

Raub, R. A. (1988). Death of police officers after retirement. *American Journal of Police, 7*(1), 91–102.

Regoli, B., Crank, J. P., & Rivera, G. F. (1990). The construction and implementation of an alternative measure of police cynicism. *Criminal Justice and Behavior, 17*(4), 395–409.

Regoli, R. M. (1976). An empirical assessment of Niederhoffer's police cynicism scale. *Journal of Criminal Justice, 4,* 231–241.

Regoli, R. M., Poole, E. D., & Hewitt, J. D. (1979). Exploring the empirical relationship between police cynicism and work alienation. *Journal of Police Science and Administration, 7,* 336–339.

Reiser, M., & Geiger, K. P. (1984). Police officer as victim. *Professional psychology, 15*(3), 315–323.

Reuss-Ianni, E. (1983). *Two cultures of policing: Street cops and management cops.* New Brunswick, NJ: Transaction.

Roberts, S. (1988, March 7). Crack dealers rewriting rules among criminals. *New York Times,* p. B1.

Roberts, S. (1994, March 20). Police funeral: Sorrowful rite and potent symbol. *New York Times,* p. 35.

Robinson, M. (1981). Informing the family of sudden death. *American Family Physician, 23,* 115–118.

Rotting corpses best to rob from, inquiry is told. (1996, June 18). *Queensland Courier-Mail,* p. 11.

Scharf, P., & Binder, A. (1983). *The badge and the bullet: Police use of deadly force.* New York: Praeger.

Sewell, J. D. (1994). The stress of homicide investigations. *Death Studies, 18*(6), 565–582.

Simon, D. (1991). *Homicide: A year on the killing streets.* Boston: Houghton-Mifflin.

Singer, M. S., Singer, A. E., & Burns, D. (1984). Police cynicism in New Zealand: A comparison between police officers and recruits. *Police Studies, 7*(2), 77–83.

Skolnick, J., & Fyfe, J. (1993). *Above the law: Police and the excessive use of force.* New York: Free Press.

Skolnick, J. H. (1966). *Justice without trial: Law enforcement in democratic society.* New York: John Wiley.

Skolnick, J. H. (1994). *Justice without trial: Law enforcement in democratic society* (3rd ed.). New York: Macmillan.

Skolnick, J. H., & Leo, R. A. (1992). The ethics of deceptive interrogation. *Criminal Justice Ethics, 11*(1), 3–12.

Smith, A. B., Locke, B., & Fenster, A. (1970). Authoritarianism in police who are college graduates and non-college police. *Journal of Criminal Law, Criminology, and Police Science, 61,* 313–315.

Smith, S. S., and Shuy, R. W. (2002). Forensic psycholinguistics. *FBI Law Enforcement Bulletin 71*(4), 16–22.

Solomon, R. M., & Horn, J. H. (1986). Post-shooting traumatic reactions: A pilot study. In J. T. Reese & H. A. Goldstein (Eds.). *Psychological services for law enforcement officers* (pp. 383–393). Washington, DC: Government Printing Office.

Solomon, Z. (1989). Psychological sequelae of war: A 3-year prospective study of Israeli combat stress reaction casualties. *Journal of Nervous and Mental Disease, 177,* 342–346.

Sourcebook of Criminal Justice Statistics Online. (2001). *Table 3.139: Murders and non-negligent manslaughter known to the police by victim-offender relationship and circumstances of the offense, United States, 1999.* Albany, NY: State University of New York at Albany. Available from http://www.albany.edu/sourcebook/1995/pdf/section3.pdf.

Southwick, L. (1998). An economic analysis of murder and accident risks for police in the United States. *Applied Economics, 30,* 593–606.

Strozier, C. B., & Flynn, M. (1992). Lifton's method. *Psychohistory Review, 20*(2), 131–145.

Sudetic, C. (1995, April 25). Legendary detective wages war on word "unsolved." *New York Times,* p. B3.

Swanton, B. (1980). Social isolation of police: Structural determinants and remedies. *Police Studies, 2*(3), 14–21.

Symonds, M. (1970). Emotional hazards of police work. *American Journal of Psychoanalysis, 30*(2), 155–160.

Thompson, J., & Solomon, M. (1991). Body recovery teams at disasters: Trauma or challenge? *Anxiety Research, 4*(3), 235–244.

Thousands mourn slain NY policeman. (1988, March 1). *Los Angeles Times,* p. 2.

Tucker, P., Pfefferbaum, B., Doughty, D., Jordan, F. B., Jones, D. E., & Nixon, S. J. (2002). Body handlers after terrorism in Oklahoma City: Predictors of posttraumatic stress and other symptoms. *American Journal of Orthopsychiatry, 72*(4), 469–475.

Ursano, R. J., & Fullerton, C. (Eds.). (1984). *Exposure to death, disasters, and bodies.* Bethesda, MD: F. Edward Hebert School of Medicine, Uniformed Services University of the Health Sciences (DCIT: A203163).

Ursano, R. J., Fullerton, C. S., Oates, G. L., Ventis, W. L., Friedman, H., Shean, G. L., Wright, K. W., & McCarroll, J. E. (1995). Gruesomeness, emotional attachment, and personal threat: Dimensions of the anticipated stress of body recovery. *Journal of Traumatic Stress, 8*(2), 343–349.

Ursano, R. J., & McCarroll, J. E. (1990). The nature of a traumatic stressor: Handling dead bodies. *Journal of Nervous and Mental Disease, 177,* 396–398.

van der Kolk, B., & Fisher, R. (1995). Dissociation and the fragmentary nature of traumatic memories. *Journal of Traumatic Stress, 8,* 505–525.

van der Kolk, B. A., & van der Hart, O. (1989). Pierre Janet and the breakdown of adaptation in psychological trauma. *American Journal of Psychiatry, 146,* 1530–1540.

van Maanen, J. (1973). Observations on the making of policemen. *Human Organizations, 32,* 407–418.

van Maanen, J. (1975). Police socialization: A longitudinal examination of job attitudes in an urban police department. *Administrative Science Quarterly, 20*(6), 257–268.

van Maanen, J. (1978a). Kinsmen in repose: Occupational perspectives of patrolmen. In P. K. Manning & J. van Maanen (Eds.). *Policing: A view from the street* (pp. 115–128). Santa Monica, CA: Goodyear.

van Maanen, J. (1978b). The asshole. In P. K. Manning & van Maanen, J. (Eds.). *Policing: A view from the street* (pp. 231–238). Santa Monica, CA: Goodyear.

van Maanen, J. (1980). Beyond account: The personal impact of police shootings. *Annals of the American Academy of Political and Social Science, 452,* 145–156.

van Maanen, J. (1985). Making rank: Becoming an American police sergeant. *Urban Life, 13,* 155–176.

van Maanen, J., & Manning, P. K. (1978). *Policing: A view from the street.* New York: Random House.

Vasquez, I. J. (1985). Police homicides by misidentity. *FBI Law Enforcement Bulletin, 54*(3), 22–25.

Vessel, D. (1998). Conducting successful interrogations. *FBI Law Enforcement Bulletin, 67*(10), 1–6.

Violanti, J. M. (1996). The impact of cohesive groups in the trauma recovery context: Police spouse survivors and duty-related death. *Journal of Traumatic Stress, 9*(2), 379–386.

Violanti, J. M., Vena, J. E., & Marshall, J. R. (1996). Suicide, homicides, and accidental death: A comparative risk assessment of police officers and municipal workers. *American Journal of Industrial Medicine, 30*(1), 99–104.

Wagner, M., & Brzeczek, R. J. (1983). Alcoholism and suicide: A fatal connection. *FBI Law Enforcement Bulletin, 52*(8), 8–15.

Wambaugh, J. (1972). *The blue knight.* Boston: Little, Brown.

Wambaugh, J. (1973). *The onion field.* New York: Dell.

Wambaugh, J. (1975). *The choirboys*. New York: Dell.

Webb, E. J., Campbell, D. T., Schwartz, R. D., & Sechrest, L. (1966). *Unobtrusive measures: Nonreactive research in the social sciences*. Chicago: Rand-McNally.

Wenz, F. V. (1979). Death anxiety among police officers. *Journal of Police Science and Administration, 7*, 230–235.

Westley, W. (1953). Violence and the police. *American Journal of Sociology, 49*, 34–41.

Westley, W. (1956). Secrecy and the police. *Social Forces, 34*, 254–257.

Westley, W. (1970). *Violence and the police: A sociological study of law, customs, and morality*. Cambridge, MA: MIT Press.

Westley, W. A. (1951). *The police: A sociological study of law, customs, and morality*. Unpublished doctoral dissertation, University of Chicago, Illinois.

Wilt, G. M., & Bannon, J. D. (1976). Cynicism or realism: A critique of Niederhoffer's research into police attitudes. *Journal of Police Science and Administration, 4*(1), 38–45.

Witness says revenge led to officer's killing. (1989, December 5). *New York Times*, p. B13.

Yarmey, A. D. (1992). *Understanding police and police work: Psychosocial issues*. New York: New York University Press.

Yehuda, R., Southwick, S. M., & Giller, E. (1992). Exposure to atrocities and severity of chronic posttraumatic stress disorder in Vietnam combat veterans. *American Journal of Psychiatry, 149*, 333–337.

Index

accidental death risk, 32–33, 358n7
acknowledging death, 15, 196–97
Act of Contrition, 365–66n17
adaptive responses, 19–21, 28, 45, 357n2
adversary deaths, 276–77, 281, 283–84
advocacy, 74–76, 303
afterlife, 47, 51
aggressive humor, 196–98
Alamo, The, 360–61n3
alcohol consumption, 22, 357–58n4
Alcoholics Anonymous, 373n19
alcoholism, 21–22, 235
altruism, 52, 89–90, 98–99, 363nn14,15
ambiguity in social relationships, 87–94
Annan, Kofi, 339
anticipatory grief, 28
antidrug campaigns, 246–47, 248
Apache, Fort, 360–61n3
aphorisms, 74, 360n7. *See also* jargon, police
Aries, P., 7
Artwohl, A., 264
atrocities, 22
audio files, 354
auditory images, 270–71
Auschwitz concentration camp, 365n12
automobile accidents, 266
avoidance, 20–21

"the bag," 323, 376n1
Baker, M., 204

"ball breaking," 196–98
Bartone, P. T., 19
Bayley, D. H., 102
bearing witness, 70, 198, 256, 279, 292, 296
Beau Geste (film), 360–61n3
Becker, Ernest, 7
biological immortality, 51, 95–98, 246, 309–10, 362nn9–11
Bittner, Egon, 9, 87–88, 91, 97–98, 102, 203, 360–61n3
Black Liberation Army, 374–75n4
Blue Knight, The (Wambaugh), 97
Blue Knights motorcycle club, 97
body armor, 33
body handling, 23–24, 352–53
Bonifacio, P., 87, 91
Bosk, C. L., 16–18
Boyle, Jimmy, 326
breast bars, 36–37, 92, 361n5
Bringing Out the Dead (Connelly), 367n11
Bromberg, David, 354
Brown, N. O., 7
"buff stuff," 91–92, 361n4
bullet wounds, 187, 191, 371n14
Bush, George H. W., 247
Byrne, Edward, 245–49, 277, 374–75nn3–5

Campbell, Ian, 284–85
canine units, 352–53
cannibalism, 197

castration, 48, 358–59n2
catching detectives, 204, 209, 253, 371n3, 372n8
cautionary tales
in family relationships, 93–94, 361n6
mortal combat events as, 31–32, 35, 245, 247
centering, 56–57
Central Park rape-murder, 369n1
charitable trusts, 70
Charmaz, K., 15, 18, 27, 28, 196
children, death of, 23
crime scene technicians and, 199
homicide detectives and, 223, 225–28, 233, 373n18
patrol sergeants and, 161–62, 368–69n17
police survivors and, 278–79
rookie officers and, 135–39, 365nn13–16
chivalry, images and metaphors of, 95, 97, 362–63nn12,13,15
"choir practice," 22
Christensen, L. W., 264
Christian tradition, 51
chronic despair, 261
classic hero, 288, 321
"clean" shootings, 274, 275, 283–86
Clemmer, E., 33, 368n13
closure, 285
code phrases, 74, 360n7. See also jargon, police
cognitive focus, 267–69
collaboration, 78
collegiality, 217, 229
collegial versions of deadly force encounters, 31–32, 244–49
police survivors and, 255–56, 263, 280
Combat Cross, 361n5
combat stress reactions, 18–23
compassion. See humane interactions
confessions, 232, 234
confidentiality, 83
connection vs. separation, 55
death imprint and, 123, 126–27, 196, 270, 274
psychic closing-off and, 263–64
psychic numbing and, 192–94
September 11 terrorist attacks and, 345
survivor missions and, 235, 255–57, 298–99
symbolic immortality and, 95–96, 362n8
Connelly, J., 367n11
contagion anxiety, 67
continuity-of-life model. See formative-symbolic paradigm
coroners, 18, 357n1
courtroom testimony, 186–88, 193, 198–99, 285, 370–71nn9,12

crack epidemic, 245
Crank, J. P., 93–94
creative mode of symbolic immortality, 52, 70, 95, 99, 309–10, 366n18
crime scene technicians, 41, 178–201, 369nn1–3
death guilt and, 194–96
death imprint and, 196–98
psychic numbing and, 192–94
quest to make meaning and, 198–200
task environment of, 73, 181–92:
organization of work, 189–92; scientific training and orientation, 183–89, 370nn8–11; selection and experience, 182–83, 369–70nn4–6
Crusader (Durk), 363n15
Cullen, F. T., 32
cults, 358n1
CUPPI ("cause undetermined pending police investigation"), 179, 369n2
cynicism, 89–90, 98, 263, 339, 360n1

Dahmer, Jeffrey, 197
Daley, Robert, 375n12
danger, 30–37, 358n7
perception of, 32–34, 37
deadly force encounters. See mortal combat situations
death anxiety, 366–67n5
Freud on, 48
in medical profession, 16–18, 369n4
in rescue workers, 23
in rookie officers, 28
death encounters
crime scene technicians and, 306–7
death guilt and, 131–39, 276–87
death imprint and, 63, 122–30, 269–76
homicide detectives and, 218, 235
patrol sergeants and, 148–77, 320
police survivors and, 239–301
psychic numbing and, 62–63, 109–22, 260–69
quest to make meaning and, 68–71, 139–44, 291–94
research on, 7–10, 304–8
rookie officers and, 108–47, 168–69, 306:
humane interaction, 116–19, 364n4; identification with victims, 119–20; presence of others, 116, 363–64nn1–3; "sitting on the body," 114–16
routinization of, 148–77
survivor missions and, 294–99
suspicion of counterfeit nurturance and, 67, 130–31, 287–91
death equivalents, 54–55
death fear, 7–8

death guilt, 25, 45, 65, 315–16
  crime scene technicians and, 194–96
  death taint and, 274–75
  homicide detectives and, 228–30
  patrol sergeants and, 160, 164, 171–75, 368–69nn16,17
  police survivors and, 276–87: "clean" shootings, 283–84; commitment, 282–83; death taint, 271–72, 274–75; legal process and, 284–87; psychic closing-off, 262–63; questions, 281–82
  rookie officers and, 126–27, 131–39, 364n11: attachment to victims, 134–39, 365nn13–16; limiting identification with victims, 133–34
death immersion, 240–42, 321
death imprint, 45, 63–65, 314–15
  crime scene technicians and, 196–98
  homicide detectives and, 224–28
  patrol sergeants and, 159–67
  police survivors and, 269–76
  rookie officers and, 122–30: death guilt, 126–27, 364n11; gruesomeness, 123–24, 364nn7,8; identification with victims, 124–26, 364nn9,10; lasting impact, 129–30; subjective differences, 127–29
death notifications, 170–71, 236, 368n13
death taint
  crime scene technicians and, 182, 193, 195, 197
  death guilt and, 274–75
  heroism and, 272–74, 376nn15,16
  homicide detectives and, 203, 230–31
  police survivors and, 255, 270, 272–75, 339, 376nn15,16
"death wish," 68
death-work occupations, 8–9, 15–28
  medical/medico-legal professions, 15–18
  military combat personnel, 18–23
  police, 26–28
  rescue workers, 23–25
decentering, 56–57
deceptive tactics, 219–20, 232, 373n15
degradation ceremony, 155
denial, 7–8, 47–48
Dennis, 322–23, 326, 332–33, 346–47, 356
"the Department," 105–6, 375n6
depersonalization strategies, 24, 134
desensitization hypothesis, 23, 28
Despair, Fort, 360–61n3
detached concern, 16–17
detachment, 74–76, 303
detective mystique, 203
Diagnostic and Statistical Manual of Mental Disorders, III, 19
Dickinson, G. E., 16–18, 23

"difficulty breathing," 116, 363n1
"dinosaur," 210, 372n9
disciplinary actions, 155–56, 289–90
discretionary decision making, 102
disembodiment, 266
disintegration, 54, 55–56
  death imprint and, 123, 126, 196, 225–27, 364n7
  "the Job" and, 106
  line-of-duty deaths and, 245–46
  psychic closing-off and, 263
  quest to make meaning and, 198–99
  September 11 terrorist attacks and, 340, 342
  survivor missions and, 235
  symbolic immortality and, 95, 362n8
dissociation, 58–60, 265, 343–45, 359n5
distancing strategies
  crime scene technicians and, 181–92
  gallows humor as, 25, 173–75, 364nn4,5
DOA (dead on arrival), 26, 28, 307–8, 358n6, 363n1, 364n5
domestic dispute calls, 33
"doubling," 311
Dragnet (television series), 61
dreams, 275–76
drug dealers, 245–46, 374–75n4
"dupe," 97
Durk, David, 363n15

ecstatic states, 53, 96, 366n18
elite status
  of crime scene technicians, 182–83, 369n5
  of homicide detectives, 203–5
  of police survivors, 255
emergency calls, 174, 175
Empire State Building, 323
endowments, 70
Eth, S., 368n13
ethical considerations, 82–83
European Romanticism, 52
evidence collections teams, 182, 370n7
experiential transcendence, 53, 96–97
expert witnesses, 186–88, 193, 198–99, 370–71nn9,12

families of victims, 235–38
  homicide detectives and, 220–23, 225, 373nn16–18
  rookie officers and, 116–20, 122
"family album" photos (CSU), 180–81, 184, 188–89, 228
family relationships, 92–94, 361n6. See also biological immortality
  crime scene technicians and, 193–94
  homicide detectives and, 223–24

partners and, 259, 275n11
police survivors and, 247, 250, 281–82, 295–301
September 11 terrorist attacks and, 347–49
fast-motion effect, 264
Fazio, Bobby, 344, 349
fear of death, 7–8
Feifel, H., 7, 16, 369n4
field observations, 5–7
fingerprint details, 182, 370n7
firearms qualification training, 34–35, 358n8
Fire Department of the City of New York (FDNY), 342–43
firefighters, 25, 326–27, 339, 342–43, 352
flashbacks, 64–65
flaunting death, 15, 28, 196–97
Fletcher, C., 173
Flynn, M., 80
Fontana, A., 75–76
forensic experts. See crime scene technicians
formative impairment, 264–66, 376n14
formative-symbolic paradigm, 45–71, 304, 308–13, 320, 357n1, 359n4
fortress mentality, 91, 360–61n3
Foster, Lauren, 345
"four-to-four," 22
Freud, Sigmund, 7, 47–49, 358–59nn2,4
Frey, J. H., 75–76
friends, relationships with, 92–94
"fugazy," 97
Fullerton, C. S., 24–25
funeral arrangements, 116, 158–59, 364n3
funerals, police, 35–37, 73, 247, 248, 278, 296
Fyfe, J. J., 33

gallows humor, 15, 25, 173–75, 195–96, 364nn4,5
Garcia, Marie, 332
Garner, J., 33, 368n13
Geiger, K. P., 60, 264
genocide, 358n1, 365n12
George, Saint, 362–63n12
Goffman, Erving, 100
"gold shield" rank, 206
Goldstein, Herman, 204–5
"good cops," 105–6, 311–13
patrol sergeants and, 154
police survivors and, 264, 273, 288
rookie officers and, 306
September 11 terrorist attacks and, 329, 345
good vs. evil, 95, 362n8
Gorer, G., 7
grace, 51
Grady, D. A., 22

grand juries, 286
graves registration, 21, 357n3
Green, B. L., 21–22
gross anatomy course, 16–18
grotesque deaths
crime scene technicians and, 41, 179–80
death imprint and: patrol sergeants, 159–61, 166–67; rookie officers, 123–24, 307–8, 364nn7,8
homicide detectives and, 218, 225
military combat personnel and, 21–22
rescue workers and, 23–25
grounding, 56–57
Ground Zero, 334–36, 339, 344–56
guilt. See death guilt
gun control, 359n6
"gun runs," 328, 376n3

Hall of Heroes, 164, 247, 249
Hamura, 352
"Happy Land" nightclub arson-murder, 179
"hats and bats," 323, 376n1
hearing impairment, 264, 265
Hendin, Herbert, 16, 18
hero-founders, 51
heroism
death imprint and, 270, 272–74, 376nn15,16
immortality systems and, 96, 164, 321
medals for, 36, 92, 247, 264, 361n5
official versions of, 31, 248
September 11 terrorist attacks and, 346–47
suspicion of counterfeit nurturance and, 288
Hettinger, Karl, 284–85
hibakusha, 322
hiding death, 15, 196–97
Hilton, C., 359n5
Hiroshima atomic bombing, 358n1
HIV infections, 370n11
homicide detectives, 40–41, 202–38
crime scene technicians and, 187, 370n10
death guilt and, 228–30
death imprint and, 224–28
interactions with others, 29
line-of-duty deaths and, 253
personal relationships and, 91
psychic numbing and, 218–24
quest to make meaning and, 231–38
survivor missions and, 70, 232, 235–38, 373–74nn20,21
suspicion of counterfeit nurturance and, 230–31
task environment of, 205–18: death imagery, 210–13; experience and status, 206–10, 237, 371–72nn4–9, 373n20;

interactive skills, 213–15; organizational factors, 215–18
Homicide: Life on the Street (television series), 367n8
homicide specialists, 208–9
"hook," 182, 369–70n6
Housing Bureau Police Service Areas, 26–27, 358n5
humane interactions
　homicide detectives and, 218–19
　patrol sergeants and, 157–58, 367n6
　rookie officers and, 116–19, 143–44, 364n4
human remains, 23–24, 352–53
Human Subjects Research Committee (CUNY), 83
hypervigilance, 90, 360n2

idealism, 89, 98–99, 363nn14,15
identification with victims, 25
　homicide detectives and, 220–23, 225–27, 373nn17–21
　patrol sergeants and, 158–59, 161–64, 166–67
　rookie officers and, 145–47: death guilt, 133–34; death imprint, 124–26, 364nn9,10; psychic numbing, 119–20
immortality, sense of, 47–48, 50–53
　death imprint and, 63
　mortal combat situations and, 241
　police survivors and, 255–57
　psychic closing-off and, 263
　survivor hubris and, 231
immortality systems, 95–98, 309–10
　heroism and, 273–74
　line-of-duty deaths and, 164, 245, 246, 260
　mentoring and, 167
inchoate imagery, 54, 358–59n2
individual subjective version of deadly force encounters, 31–32, 244–45
integrity vs. disintegration, 55–56
　death guilt and, 279–81
　death imprint and, 123, 196–97, 270, 271, 274
　"the Job" and, 106
　psychic closing-off and, 263–64
　psychic numbing and, 192–93, 219
　quest to make meaning and, 198–99
　September 11 terrorist attacks and, 345
　survivor missions and, 235, 257
　symbolic immortality and, 95, 212–13, 362n8
interactive skills, 213–15, 372–73n12
interrogations, 212, 232–35, 372n11
interviewing, 5–6, 76–83
　mutual exploration in, 76–78
　protocol, 79–80, 83
　sample frame and technique, 80–82, 360n9
　technique, 78–79

interviews, police, 212, 219, 221, 232–35, 372n11, 373nn14,15
intrusion, 20–21
investigator as instrument, 73–74
invulnerability, 251, 269–70
Irving, Washington, 355
Israeli combat veterans, 20–21, 25

Janet, Pierre, 58–59
Japanese Shinto tradition, 51, 52
jargon, police, 74, 95, 104–5, 360n7, 364n5, 376–77nn4,5
Jewish survivors, 67
"the Job," 105–6, 257, 345, 351, 356, 375n6
"jocular aggression," 196–98
Joe Friday (*Dragnet* character), 61
joking about death. *See* gallows humor
Judge, Mychal, 343–44, 346, 349
Jung, C. G., 48–49
justice
　crime scene technicians and, 193
　homicide detectives and, 212–13, 217, 219, 225, 235–36
　police survivors and, 292–93
　rookie officers and, 141–44

"Kaatskill Serenade" (Bromberg), 355
kami, 51–52
Kardiner, A., 251, 359n5
Kendra's Law, 359n6
Kennedy, Paul, 334–36, 339, 342, 345, 346, 352, 356
Klinger, David, 264–65, 376n14
Klockars, C. B., 10
Knapp Commission, 367n7
knighthood, images and metaphors of, 95, 97, 362–63nn12,13,15
Kuhn, Thomas, 46
Kutscher, A. H., 28

Lardner, J., 366n4
latent print teams, 182, 370n7
Laufer, R. S., 22
Law Enforcement Officers Killed and Assaulted (FBI), 374n1
legal process
　courtroom testimony in, 186–88, 193, 198–99, 285, 370–71nn9,12
　death guilt and, 284–87
　expert witnesses and, 186–88, 193, 198–99, 370–71nn9,12
Leuci, Robert, 258, 375n12
Lifton, Robert Jay, 22, 45–84, 359n4
　strategies of inquiry, 71–84
　theoretical perspective, 45–71, 75, 303, 304, 308–13

"limbo," 138, 365n15
line-of-duty deaths, 239–301, 374nn1,2
    collegial and official reactions to, 244–52,
      374–75nn3–6
    competition for survivor status and, 255–
      57
    death guilt and, 276–78
    death imprint and, 163–64, 270–72
    handling personal effects and, 252–53
    images and associations of, 253–54
    partners and, 257–62
    psychic numbing and, 261–62
line-of-duty funerals, 35–37, 73, 247, 248, 278,
    296
lockers, 252, 375n7
Long Island Railroad massacre, 359n6
Lumet, Sidney, 375n12

macabre humor, 25, 173–75, 364nn4,5
MacDonald, Steven, 244
Machell, D. F., 22
management cop culture, 75, 340–41, 345,
    360n8
manufacturing distance, 74
"man under," 27, 160
Marmar, Charles, 59–60, 264
masculine identity, 20–21, 358–59n2
McCann, Detective (fictitious character),
    360n7
McCarroll, J. E., 120
McCarthy, Carolyn, 359n6
McCracken, G., 73–74, 76, 83
meaning, quest for. See quest to make
    meaning
Medal Day ceremonies, 31, 247, 273
Medal of Honor, 361n5
Medal of Valor, 341, 361n5
medals, 92, 247, 272–73, 341, 361n5, 376n15
media, 263, 279, 280–81, 329–30
medical examiners (MEs), 18, 116, 357n1, 363–
    64nn2,3
medicalization of killing, 311, 358n1, 365n12
medical/medico-legal professions, 8, 15–18,
    369n4
Megan's Law, 359n6
memorial foundations, 70, 295
mentoring, 167–68, 182, 208, 320, 369–
    70n6
methodological strategies. See research
    process
Michael, Saint (Archangel), 362–63n12
military combat personnel, 8, 18–23, 251
minimizing death, 15, 196–97
Miranda rights, 286, 372n11
morgue attendants, 364nn8,9

mortal combat situations, 31–32, 240–44,
    374nn1,2
    death guilt and, 283–84
    heroism and, 272–74
    medals for, 92, 361n5
    psychic numbing and, 260–69
mortality, sense of, 53–54, 115, 240
mourning bands, 36
movement vs. stasis, 56
    death imprint and, 123, 196, 270, 274
    psychic closing-off and, 263
    psychic numbing and, 192–93
    survivor missions and, 235, 257
    symbolic immortality and, 95, 362n8
murder rates, 32–33
Muster Deck, 326, 376n2
mythological hero, 288, 321

National Law Enforcement Memorial
    (Washington, DC), 297, 375n5
natural disaster survivors, 358n1
nature as mode of symbolic immortality, 52–
    53
Nazi doctors, 311, 358n1
Neibuhr, Reinhold, 373n19
New York City Administrative Code, 26,
    366nn1,2
New York Police Department (NYPD)
    author as member of, 76
    cynicism and, 360n1
    death encounters and, 26–28, 358n5
    family relationships in, 93
    homicide detectives in, 204, 371n2
    mortal combat situations in, 242–44
    pensions, 208, 372n7
    police shields and, 96–98, 362nn9–11
    as sample frame, 80–81, 319–20
    September 11 terrorist attacks and, 322–56
    tactical training in, 34–35, 358n8
Niederhoffer, Arthur, 10, 36, 89–90, 98, 203–
    4, 360n1, 363n14
Niederhoffer, E., 10
nightmares, 275–76
nuclear extinction threat, 358n1

objectivity, 7, 17, 32, 72, 303
occupational cultures, 10–12, 24–25
odors, 24, 124–26, 268, 364n8
off-duty behaviors, 90, 360n2
official versions of deadly force encounters,
    31, 244–49, 374n2, 375nn5,6
    police survivors and, 280
    psychic closing-off and, 263
"off the chart," 207, 237, 373n20
O'Keefe, Jim, 327

old-boy networks, 182, 369–70n6
Onion Field, The (Wambaugh), 65, 284–85, 376n17
"out of the bag," 203–4, 371n2

paradigms, 46–47. *See also* formative-symbolic paradigm
partial professional numbing, 17, 57–58, 60
    crime scene technicians and, 180–81, 183, 192
    homicide detectives and, 213, 218, 220–21
    patrol sergeants and, 152, 153, 156–59, 162, 171, 176
    rookie officers and, 109, 117, 120–22
    September 11 terrorist attacks and, 324–25, 329, 343
participant observation activities, 73
partners
    families of victims and, 237, 373–74n21
    police survivors and, 242, 251, 257–60, 375nn10,11: competition for survivor status, 255–57; death guilt, 276–78, 281–83; death imprint, 270–72, 274–75; psychic numbing, 261–63, 265–66
    September 11 terrorist attacks and, 323–24, 334, 350–51, 356
Patrol Guide (NYPD), 39, 151, 206, 369n3
patrol sergeants, 40, 148–77
    death guilt and, 171–75, 368–69nn16,17
    death imprint and, 159–67
    psychic numbing and, 156–59, 367n6
    quest to make meaning and, 167–71
    survivor mission and, 167–71, 368nn13,14
    suspicion of counterfeit nurturance and, 175–76
    task environment of, 151–56, 172: subcultural dimensions, 153–56; "typical" DOA, 151–53
patron saints, 362–63n12
pattern murders, 209, 372n8
pensions, 208, 372n7
Pentagon terrorist attacks, 327, 329
perceptual anomalies, 59–61, 264–66, 376n14
peritraumatic dissociation, 59–60, 264
Perry, John, 349
personal effects, handling of, 164–66, 252–53, 307, 366nn1–3, 375nn7,8
personal relationships, 90–94, 290–91, 360n2. *See also* family relationships
"personals," 336, 377n5
Pete, 346–47, 356
Pettit, Glenn, 343–44, 346, 349
the Pile. *See* Ground Zero
plainclothes assignments, 371n2
Pobregin, M., 196

police academy, 81, 99–101, 326–37, 347, 355–56, 360n9
police corruption, 159, 367nn6,7
police culture, 10–12, 193
    aggressive humor in, 196–97
    alcohol in, 22, 357–58n4
    altruism in, 52
    cautionary tales in, 31–32
    crime scene technicians and, 73, 181–92, 193
    family relationships and, 93–94, 361n6
    funerals in, 35–37, 73
    heroism and, 273–74
    immortality systems in, 95–98, 212–13, 247, 361–62n7
    jargon in, 74, 95, 104–6, 360n7, 361–62n7
    mortal combat situations and, 240
    patrol sergeants and, 153–56, 172, 366–67nn4,5, 368n15
    police survivors and, 255, 296, 298
    psychic closing-off and, 262–64, 376n13
    street cop vs. management cop, 75, 360n8
police identity
    crime scene technicians and, 193, 196–97
    development of, 85–107, 310–13
    homicide detectives and, 212
    partners and, 257–60
    patrol sergeants and, 157, 163
    police survivors and, 240, 270, 288–89
    rookie officers and, 101–4
Police Memorial Day (Washington DC), 357–58n4
Police Service Areas (PSAs), 26–27, 358n5
police shields
    biological immortality and, 96–98, 309, 362nn9–11
    homicide detectives and, 206, 218, 373n13
    survivor missions and, 36, 247, 294–95
police solidarity, 90, 95
police suicides, 162–64, 367nn9,10
police survivors, 10, 42, 239–301
    competition for survivor status and, 255–57
    death guilt and, 254, 274–75, 276–87, 375n9
    death imprint and, 269–76
    handling personal effects, 252–53
    images and associations, 253–54
    partners and, 257–60
    psychic numbing and, 260–69
    quest to make meaning and, 291–94
    reactions to line-of-duty deaths, 244–52
    sensitivity toward, 320–21
    September 11 terrorist attacks and, 338–39
    survivor missions and, 70, 294–99
    suspicion of counterfeit nurturance and, 263, 279, 287–91

political events, 247–49, 375n6
political projects, 70, 359n6
political terrorists, 374–75n4
Poole, E., 196
POPPA (Police Organization Providing Peer
    Assistance), 350, 377n6
posttraumatic stress disorder (PTSD), 18–23,
    59, 357n2, 359n5
prayer, 143, 236, 346, 365–66n17, 373n19
precinct life, 101–7, 363n16
Prince of the City (Daley), 375n12
professional development, 192–93
professional identity. *See* police identity
Prospect Park Zoo (Brooklyn), 227
proxemics, 234
psychiatric disorders, 19
psychic closing-off, 57–58, 61, 262–64, 376n13
psychic numbing, 45, 57–63, 313–14, 359n4
    crime scene technicians and, 192–94
    dissociation and, 58–60
    homicide detectives and, 218–24
    patrol sergeants and, 156–59, 367n6
    perception of, 59–61
    police survivors and, 260–69: cognitive
        focus, 267–69; formative impairment
        and perceptual anomalies, 264–65,
        376n14; manifestations of numbing,
        265–67; psychic closing-off, 262–64,
        376n13
    psychology of survival and, 61–63
    rookie officers and, 109–22: controlling of
        environment, 121–22; forced numbing,
        120–21; humane interaction, 116–19,
        364n4; identification with victims, 119–
        20, 364n5; presence of others, 116, 363–
        64nn1–3; "sitting on the body," 114–16;
        Solomon on, 20–21
psychoanalytic paradigm, 47–48, 358–59n2
psychoformative paradigm. *See* formative-
    symbolic paradigm
psychological processes, 85–107
    altruism and idealism and, 98–99
    conflict and ambiguity and, 87–94
    immortality systems and, 95–98
    police academy and, 99–101
    precinct life and, 101–7, 363n16
psychology of survival, 45–71, 304, 308–13, 358n1
public ambivalence, 87–91
Punch, M., 83
Purple Shield, 361n5

quest to make meaning, 45, 68–71, 317–19
    crime scene technicians and, 198–200
    homicide detectives and, 231–38

patrol sergeants and, 167–71
police survivors and, 291–94: scapegoating,
    293–94; survivor missions, 294–99; urge
    to do justice, 293
rookie officers and, 139–47: integrating
    competence and compassion, 144; urge
    to do justice, 141–44

"rabbi," 182, 369–70n6
Rachlin, H., 173
rackets, 273, 277, 327, 376n16
Rank, Otto, 48–49
Raphael, B., 24–25
reciprocity, 154, 366–67n5
recruits, police, 335–36, 339, 345, 347
Red Cross, 332
Reiser, M., 60, 264
religious faith, 298–99, 346
Reppetto, T., 366n4
repression, 48, 359n4
rescue workers, 8, 23–25, 120, 339
research process, 71–83
    on death encounters, 7–10, 303–8
    expectations for, 42–43
    strengths and limitations of, 319–21
retirement, 55, 356
Reuss-Ianni, Elizabeth, 75, 248
Richmond, Dave, 328
Rip Van Winkle, 355
role models, 101–2
role-play scenarios, 34, 171
Roman Catholic faith, 362–63n12, 365–
    66nn15,17
rookie officers, 39–40, 364n6
    cautionary tales and, 31–32
    death encounters of, 27–28, 108–47: death
        guilt, 131–39, 174–75; death imprint, 122–
        30, 364nn7–9; psychic numbing, 109–22,
        268; quest to make meaning, 139–44,
        168–69; suspicion of counterfeit
        nurturance, 124, 130–31
    line-of-duty deaths and, 245–49
    police academy and, 100–101
    precinct life and, 101–7, 154–55
    socialization process and, 87, 91
routinization of death, 15, 27–28
    patrol sergeants and, 148–77: death guilt,
        171–75, 368–69nn16,17; death imprint
        and, 159–67; psychic numbing, 156–59;
        quest to make meaning, 167–71;
        subcultural dimensions, 153–56; survivor
        mission, 167–71, 368nn13,14; suspicion of
        counterfeit nurturance, 175–76; "typical"
        DOA, 151–53

"Rudy Bunker," 337
rumors, 337, 340–42, 345

Saint George Association, 362–63n12
Saint Peter's Church, 343
sample frame and technique, 80–81, 360n9
scapegoating, 69–70, 198–200, 293–94
"scratch," 152, 335, 366n3, 376–77n4
screen images, 64–65
secondary victims, 220–23, 235–38, 373nn17,18
sensitivity, 320–21
sensory images, 24, 49–50, 54, 268, 270–71,
    359n3
separation, 54–55
    death imprint and, 123, 126, 196, 225–27,
        271, 364n7
    line-of-duty deaths and, 245–46
    psychic closing-off and, 263
    September 11 terrorist attacks and, 340
    survivor missions and, 235
    symbolic immortality and, 95, 362n8
September 11 terrorist attacks, 6–7, 322–56
"Serenity Prayer," 373n19
serial murders, 372n8
shared themes approach, 4–6, 78
shields. See police shields
Shiva, 287
"shoofly," 154, 366n4
show-ups, 212, 372n10
Sisyphean struggle, 321
"sitting on the body," 114–16, 151, 154–55, 174–
    75
"skell," 134, 365n12
Skolnick, Jerome, 30, 34, 88–89, 90, 242
slow-motion effect, 60, 264, 265–67
Smith, Moira, 344, 349, 354
snipers, police, 330–32
snowball sampling, 80–81
socialization processes, 85–107, 310
    altruism and idealism and, 98–99
    conflict and ambiguity and, 87–94
    immortality systems and, 95–98
    police academy and, 99–101
    precinct life and, 101–7, 363n16
Solomon, Z., 19–21, 25
SOP-9 report, 243, 358n8
Southwick, L., 32–33, 358n7
"space case," 27, 160–61, 367n8
Spiegel, H., 251, 359n5
spiritual quests, 51
sports, 146, 366n18
"the Squad," 190, 206, 371n13
stab wounds, 187, 370n11, 371n14
"stand-up guy," 154

stasis, 54, 56
    death imprint and, 123, 126, 196, 225–27,
        271, 364n7
    line-of-duty deaths and, 245–46
    psychic closing-off and, 263
    September 11 terrorist attacks and, 340
    survivor missions and, 235
    symbolic immortality and, 95, 362n8
status symbols, 36, 92
"steering," 159, 367nn6,7
stoicism, 89, 118, 154, 175–76, 230
St. Paul's Chapel, 352
strategies of inquiry. See research process
street cop vs. management cop, 75, 340–42,
    345, 360n8
Strozier, C. B., 80
struggle for meaning. See quest to make
    meaning
"suicide by cop," 241
suicide ideation, 162, 367nn9,10
suicides, 166–67. See also police suicides
Surrender, Fort, 360–61n3
survival psychology. See psychology of
    survival
survivor exclusiveness, 68
survivor hubris, 67–68, 231
survivor missions, 70, 359n6
    homicide detectives and, 232, 235–37, 373–
        74nn20,21
    patrol sergeants and, 167–71, 368nn13,14
    police survivors and, 247, 255–57, 294–99
    rookie officers and, 131, 134
"survivor paranoia," 67
survivor priority, 229
survivors, 4, 29. See also police survivors
    death guilt and, 65, 131–39
    death imprint and, 63–65
    psychic numbing and, 58, 61–63
    quest to make meaning and, 68–71, 359n6
    suspicion of counterfeit nurturance and,
        66–67
survivor status, 255–57
suspicion of counterfeit nurturance, 45, 66–
    68, 316–17
    homicide detectives and, 230–31
    patrol sergeants and, 175–76
    police survivors and, 263, 279, 287–91:
        disciplinary actions, 289–90; personal
        relationships, 290–91; self-regard, 288–89
    rookie officers and, 124, 130–31
SWAT (special weapons and tactics) teams,
    376n14
symbolic assailant construct, 30, 34, 90,
    364n10

symbolic heroes, 248
symbolic immortality, 51–53, 95–98, 308–10,
   362nn8,9
   homicide detectives and, 208, 212–13
   "the Job" and, 106
   police survivors and, 295
   sports and, 366n18
symbolic murders, 246, 374–75n4

tactical training, 33, 34–35, 358n8
task environments
   of crime scene technicians, 181–92, 306–7
   of homicide detectives, 205–18, 307
   of patrol sergeants, 151–56, 172, 307
telephone switchboard (TS), 116, 363n2
television shows, 91, 373n17
10–13 emergency call, 174, 175
terrorist attacks, 6–7, 322–56
testifying in court, 186–88, 193, 198–99, 285,
   370–71nn9,12
theological mode of symbolic immortality,
   51–52, 95
"thought reform," 358n1
TNT (tactical narcotics team), 247
"total institution," 100
transcendence, 51, 53, 96–97, 213, 366n18
Transit Districts, 26–27, 358n5
triangulation, 72
triggering images, 253–54
tunnel vision, 60, 264, 265
"20 and out," 208, 372n7
"24–hour rule," 214, 370n10

"unconscious aided" call, 153, 363n1
Uniform Crime Report (FBI), 373n16
Unusual Occurrence Report, 172, 368n15,
   374n2
Ursano, R. J., 23, 120
U.S. Department of Justice, 247

van Maanen, John, 31–32, 35, 98, 99, 157, 241, 244
victim consciousness, 67
victims' rights, 359n6
Vietnam War veterans, 21–22, 67, 170, 358n1,
   368nn13,14
violence, 30–37, 358n7
vitality, struggle for, 54–55
vouchered property, 252

wakes, 36, 73, 248
Wambaugh, Joseph, 65, 97, 284–85, 376n17
war stories, police, 31–32, 35, 91, 167, 220, 361n4
Webb, E. J., 72, 76
Wenz, F. V., 26, 28
Westley, W., 88
"white-shield investigators," 206, 218, 373n13
witnesses. *See* courtroom testimony; expert
   witnesses
World Trade Center attacks, 6–7, 322–56

Yarmey, A. D., 29
Young, Mary, 350

the Zero. *See* Ground Zero
Zinderneuf, Fort, 340, 360–61n3